Rights

The International Library of Essays in Law and Legal Theory

Second Series

Series Editor: Tom D. Campbell

Titles in the Series:

Freedom of Speech, Volumes I and II
Larry Alexander

Privacy
Eric M. Barendt

Comparative Legal Cultures
John Bell

Contract Law, Volumes I and II
Brian Bix

Corporate Law
William W. Bratton

Law and Democracy
Tom D. Campbell

Legal Positivism
Tom D. Campbell

Administrative Law
Peter Cane

International Trade Law
Ronald A. Cass and Michael S. Knoll

Sociological Perspectives on Law, Volumes I and II
Roger Cotterrell

Intellectual Property
Peter Drahos

Family, State and Law, Volumes I and II
Michael D. Freeman

Natural Law
Robert P. George

Commercial Law
Clayton P. Gillette

Competition Law
Rosa Greaves

Chinese Law and Legal Theory
Perry Keller

International Law, Volumes I and II
Martti Koskenniemi and David Kennedy

Constitutional Law
Ian D. Loveland

Interpretation of Law
D. Neil MacCormick and Fernando Atria

Human Rights
Robert McCorquodale

Anti-Discrimination Law
Christopher McCrudden

Medical Law and Ethics
Sheila McLean

Mediation
Carrie Menkel-Meadow

Environmental Law
Peter S. Menell

Criminal Law
Thomas Morawetz

Law and Language
Thomas Morawetz

Law and Anthropology
Martha Mundy

Gender and Justice
Ngaire Naffine

Law and Economics
Eric A. Posner

Japanese Law
J. Mark Ramseyer

Justice
Wojciech Sadurski

The Rule of Law
Frederick Schauer

Regulation
Colin Scott

Restitution
Lionel D. Smith

Company Law
David Sugarman

Freedom of Information
Robert G. Vaughn

Tort Law
Ernest J. Weinrib

Rights
Robin West

Welfare Law
Lucy A. Williams

Rights

Edited by

Robin West

Georgetown University Law Center, USA

Ashgate

DARTMOUTH

Aldershot • Burlington USA • Singapore • Sydney

Published by
Dartmouth Publishing Company
Ashgate Publishing Limited
Gower House
Croft Road
Aldershot
Hants GU11 3HR
England

Ashgate Publishing Company
131 Main Street
Burlington, VT 05401-5600 USA

Ashgate website: http://www.ashgate.com

British Library Cataloguing in Publication Data
Rights. – (International library of essays in law and legal theory. Second series)
1. Human rights – Philosophy 2. Human rights – Law and legislation 3. Human rights – Social aspects
I. West, Robin, 1954–
323'.01

Library of Congress Cataloging-in-Publication Data
Rights / edited by Robin West.
p. cm. — (International library of essays in law and legal theory. Second series)
Includes bibliographical references.
ISBN 0-7546-2030-1
1. Civil rights—Philosophy. I. West, Robin, 1954– II. Series.

K3240 .R54 2000
323'.01—dc21 00-036310

ISBN 0 7546 2030 1

Printed by Cromwell Press, Trowbridge, Wiltshire.

Contents

Acknowledgements

The editor and publishers wish to thank the following for permission to use copyright material.

Duke Law Journal for the essay: Steven J. Heyman (1991), 'The First Duty of Government: Protection, Liberty and the Fourteenth Amendment', *Duke Law Journal*, **41**, pp. 507–71. Copyright © 1991 Duke Law Journal, Duke University School of Law.

Ronald Dworkin (1992), 'Unenumerated Rights: Whether and How *Roe* Should be Overruled', *University of Chicago Law Review*, **59**, pp. 381–432. Copyright © 1992 Ronald Dworkin.

Harvard Journal of Law & Public Policy for the essay: Akhil Reed Amar (1990), 'Forty Acres and a Mule: A Republican Theory of Minimal Entitlements', *Harvard Journal of Law & Public Policy*, **13**, pp. 37–43.

Harvard Law Review for the essay: Robin L. West and Alan M. Dershowitz (1999), 'The Case of the Speluncean Explorers: Revisited', *Harvard Law Review*, **112**, pp. 1891–913. Copyright © 1999 Harvard Law Review Association.

Harvard Law School Publication Center for the essays: Patricia J. Williams (1987), 'Alchemical Notes: Reconstructing Ideals from Deconstructed Rights', *Harvard Civil Rights–Civil Liberties Law Review*, **22**, pp. 401–33. Copyright © 1987 President and Fellows of Harvard College; Lisa Heinzerling (2000), 'The Rights of Statistical People', *Harvard Environmental Law Review*, **24**, pp. 189–207. Copyright © 2000 President and Fellows of Harvard College; David Luban (1999), 'The Warren Court and the Concept of a Right', *Harvard Civil Rights–Civil Liberties Law Review*, **34**, pp. 7–37. Copyright © 1999 President and Fellows of Harvard College; Morton J. Horwitz (1988), 'Rights', *Harvard Civil Rights–Civil Liberties Law Review*, **23**, pp. 393–406. Copyright © 1988 President and Fellows of Harvard College.

Indiana University Press for the essay: Eva Feder Kittay (1995), 'Taking Dependency Seriously: The Family and Medical Leave Act Considered in Light of the Social Organization of Dependency Work and Gender Equality', *Hypatia*, **10**, pp. 8–29. Copyright © 1995 Eva Feder Kittay.

The Michigan Law Review Association for the essay: Susan Bandes (1990), 'The Negative Constitution: A Critique', *Michigan Law Review*, **88**, pp. 2271–347. Copyright © 1990 Michigan Law Review Association.

Joseph Raz (1995), 'Rights and Politics', *Indiana Law Journal*, **71**, pp. 27–44. Copyright © 1995 Joseph Raz.

Texas Law Review for the essay: Peter Gabel (1984), 'The Phenomenology of Rights-Consciousness and the Pact of the Withdrawn Selves', *Texas Law Review*, **62**, pp. 1563–99.

University of California Press for the essay: Michael J. Sandel (1989), 'Moral Argument and Liberal Toleration: Abortion and Homosexuality', *California Law Review*, **77**, pp. 521–38. Copyright © 1989 Michael J. Sandel.

University of Chicago Press for the essay: Will Kymlicka (1989), 'Liberal Individualism and Liberal Neutrality', *Ethics*, **99**, pp. 883–905. Copyright © 1989 University of Chicago.

Wisconsin Women's Law Journal for the essay: Elizabeth B. Clark (1987), 'Religion, Rights, and Difference in the Early Women's Rights Movement', *Wisconsin Women's Law Journal*, **3**, pp. 29–57.

Every effort has been made to trace all the copyright holders, but if any have been inadvertently overlooked the publishers will be pleased to make the necessary arrangement at the first opportunity.

Preface to the Second Series

The first series of the International Library of Essays in Law and Legal Theory has established itself as a major research resource with fifty-eight volumes of the most significant theoretical essays in contemporary legal studies. Each volume contains essays of central theoretical importance in its subject area and the series as a whole makes available an extensive range of valuable material of considerable interest to those involved in research, teaching and the study of law.

The rapid growth of theoretically interesting scholarly work in law has created a demand for a second series which includes more recent publications of note and earlier essays to which renewed attention is being given. It also affords the opportunity to extend the areas of law covered in the first series.

The new series follows the successful pattern of reproducing entire essays with the original page numbers as an aid to comprehensive research and accurate referencing. Editors have selected not only the most influential essays but also those which they consider to be of greatest continuing importance. The objective of the second series is to enlarge the scope of the library, include significant recent work and reflect a variety of editorial perspectives.

Each volume is edited by an expert in the specific area who makes the selection on the basis of the quality, influence and significance of the essays, taking care to include essays which are not readily available. Each volume contains a substantial introduction explaining the context and significance of the essays selected.

I am most grateful for the care which volume editors have taken in carrying out the complex task of selecting and presenting essays which meet the exacting criteria set for the series.

TOM CAMPBELL
Series Editor
The Faculty of Law
The Australian National University

Introduction: Revitalizing Rights

Rights, according to modern liberal theorists, are based on some aspect of our human nature, and both morally and legally limit what a liberal state might do to us.[1] We are, for example, according to virtually all liberal theorists, by nature, autonomous and rational individuals, equally deserving of dignity and respect, and we therefore have rights to free speech, thought and worship, meaning that the state may not, through law, dictate our thoughts, ideas, spiritual values or individually held visions of the good. Because we are essentially rational creatures, we must be free to determine such visions of the good and spiritual values for ourselves (Dworkin, 1996). We are, to take a very different example asserted by some liberal theorists, the sorts of creature who are made secure against the natural elements, against the aggression of others, and even against the possibility of state tyranny by our ownership of private possessions, and we therefore have a *right* to property: our property cannot be taken from us by the state without compensation and process, even should the state decide to do so for the very best of reasons (Epstein, 1985, 1984). We are also, according to a now well-established line of liberal thought, much enhanced by the enjoyment of a sphere of privacy and intimacy and we therefore have a right not to have our privacy intruded upon by the state without compelling state justification (Richards, 1986). Because our lives are enhanced by privacy, we have a right against states that seek to invade it. To take one final example, according to some liberal rights theories, we are naturally such that we will benefit from a good, consensually struck bargain – we are natural bargainers – and we therefore have a right not to have our free markets unnecessarily overregulated. Finally, although liberals differ on what precisely we are, they agree that *all* of us, universally, share the essential core – if any of us are, then all of us – not just some of us – are sufficiently rational to formulate our own conceptions of the good, made secure through ownership of property, benefit from unregulated trade, and are enriched through the enjoyment of a sphere of privacy and intimacy (Dworkin, 1978, p. 199). We are all of these things by virtue of our *humanity*, not by virtue of caste, class, skin colour, gender, religious affiliation or ethnicity. We therefore have a right not to be subjected to laws that invidiously and irrationally discriminate against some of us, or deprive some of us of these rights, for the benefit of others. We have, in short, a right to enjoy our rights – our rights to property, privacy, free thought and speech or contract – equally.

We have these rights – rights to free speech, rights to the free exercise of our religion, rights to privacy, rights to property and rights to the equal protection of the law – according to liberal theory, for moral reasons. The state should not act in such a way as to interfere with our privacy, property, contract, speech, thought or religion, and it should not do so because of who and what we are: we are creatures whose lives are best lived in, and whose potential is most enhanced by, a state that respects these freedoms. The *justification* for rights, and for the particular rights we have, is, in other words, distinctively moral. The *consequence* of having a right, however, is legal and political. That we have a right entails that the state may not, legally, interfere with us in those prescribed ways. That we have a right, by definition, means that the state is legally prohibited from acting in a certain way; should the state do so, it will have done something illegal, as well as immoral. A right, to use a common metaphor, is a bridge between the moral and the legal: that we have a right means both that the state should not act against us in a particular way, and that, if it does so, it is acting illegally. Liberal rights are the means by which our natural liberty and equality become not just attributes of our nature, but also the wellspring of political and legal entitlements. They are the means by which, to put it differently, our natural capacities become our political liberties.

Of course, for a liberal right, so understood, to be anything but nonsense on stilts, there must be some mechanism by which rights can be authoritatively identified and then enforced against recalcitrant states. One possible way to do so is through a hierarchy of ascending law, with the highest law codifying our rights, and then somehow controlling and constraining lower law produced by the state. Thus, a liberal state's domestic law might be bound by international law, which in turn could consist, in part, of a catalogue of human rights which no state may violate. Should a state do so, it would be acting illegally: it would be in violation of international law. A second possibility is that a liberal state could establish an independent branch – courts, for example – which could then, through common law adjudication, acknowledge, recognize and enforce rights against errant legislative enactments. In this way courts could recognize and articulate an evolving 'natural law', which in turn could consist of rights loosely grounded in an idealized conception of what and who we are. Historically, a number of liberal states have adopted one or the other or both of these mechanisms for the enforcement of liberal rights.

A third possible way for a liberal state to acknowledge and enforce rights, which combines the hierarchic feature of the international approach and the judicial role of the common law approach, is through the adoption, interpretation and enforcement of a Constitution. Thus, a nation or state's Constitution might enumerate certain rights (or might be read as enumerating certain rights) which the liberal state may not legally invade, and courts might then be charged with the duty of enforcing those rights against the state's or the nation's law-making bodies. This third possible vehicle for the enforcement of liberal rights – through constitutionalism – has received its greatest elaboration in the United States. In the United States, and now in a number of other liberal democracies adopting the US model, liberal rights are widely understood to be enumerated in the national Constitution and then enforced against states that infringe upon them by independent courts, which possess the power to strike the offending state enactments as void. In this Introduction, I will sometimes refer to this model as the liberal–constitutional understanding of rights.

Rights generally, and the liberal–constitutional understanding of rights in particular, have been the subject of intense debate, and in a number of disciplines, during the 200 years since the revolutions they rhetorically inspired. In political theory, conservative theorists of the state, following Edmund Burke, have argued that rights effectively destroy the bonds of community, hierarchy and tradition, and all in the name of a falsely abstracted, over-rational, ideal conception of the individual (Burke, 1790). In jurisprudence, positivist critics, following Jeremy Bentham, have argued that rights obscure the political origin of law, thus frustrating or muting clearheaded criticism, and hence reform, of existing law: by obscuring the line between the 'is' and the 'ought', rights unduly complicate the task of holding acts of power to the light of reason (Bentham, 1995). In constitutional theory, democratic majoritarians and moral sceptics have joined forces to argue that rights do nothing but stymie the will of majorities and their duly elected representatives (Bork, 1990, pp. 187–241), while 'originalists' add that, unless clearly grounded in the intent of a constitution's drafters, rights violate fundamental principles of the rule of law (ibid., pp. 161–86). In recent decades some economists trained in law (and some lawyers interested in, or trained in, economics) have criticized rights on the basis of their manifest inefficiencies: by definition rights virtually 'trump' utilitarian goals such as efficiency or utility, and if utility or efficiency is the lodestar of value and justice, then rights must either be limited to those that are wealth-maximizing or they are themselves unjust (Posner, 1983a; Dworkin, 1980a; 1980b).[2] None of these debates – what might be called the 'classic rights debates' – shows any signs of abating. The modem economic critique of rights continues to have a substantial effect on the contours of rights scholarship, and the older, even ancient debates – primarily over the philosophical coherence and political legitimacy of rights – are as alive today as they were 200 years ago.

In the last 25 years, however, a quite distinctive line of criticism of the liberal constitutional rights tradition has developed, primarily in the legal academies of the United States, England, Canada and Australia. The authors of this more modern criticism of rights, sometimes called the 'rights critique', argue, in essence, that rights, rights discourse and, very generally, the liberal rights tradition, have failed us, not so much as a matter of jurisprudential coherence, or as a matter of fidelity to history or tradition, or as a matter of democratic integrity – as argued by rights' classic detractors – but, rather, they have failed us as a matter of moral, or utopian, *aspiration*. Overall and in the long run liberal rights have just not been a very good thing. Even when fully recognized by a liberal state – indeed, especially when so recognized – they have not been, to quote one of the critique's primary architects, a victory for the party of humanity (Tushnet, 1984). They have not improved the quality of either individual or community life in those liberal states which recognize them. Rather, rights, when recognized, have inspired at best a false hope and have ideologically served to obscure, rather than illuminate, the contours of a truly moral ideal state. Accordingly, not only rights themselves, but also faith in rights – 'rights-consciousness', 'rights discourse' or, as it is sometimes called, 'rights-talk' – according to the 'rights critics', have not been vehicles for justice. Rights have constituted obstacles – and in a time of global corporatism, they threaten to be ever-growing obstacles – to the creation or maintenance of humanistic, egalitarian, diverse, environmentally healthy and just communities.

The 'rights critique', its label notwithstanding, is not one critique at all but rather, a cluster (or family) of moral criticisms of the idea and history of liberal rights. Nor is it the only critique of rights currently on the philosophical landscape; as noted above, the jurisprudential, political and constitutional debates that liberal rights have engendered over the last 200 years are still very much unresolved. Nevertheless, it is fair to say that the myriad criticisms that are loosely embraced by the umbrella term 'rights critique' of the last 25 years had a distinctive impact on the direction of rights scholarship in the latter part of the twentieth century, particularly in the legal academy where it was born, that sets it apart from these more longstanding debates. First, the rights critique introduced a major and unexamined question into rights scholarship – the aspirational or moral value of rights discourse itself. But, second, the rights critics have often urged, on moral and political grounds, an abandonment rather than a reformation of 'rights-talk', and their guidance has seemingly proven persuasive, at least to some. Rights and rights-talk *have* indeed been abandoned, rather than reformed, by at least some of the very scholars most inclined to take to heart the liberal, progressive or universalist ideals of equality, fraternity and liberty that animate the rights tradition. For both reasons, the rights critique is an idea – or set of ideas – that has mattered.

The essays in this volume are an exploration of the aspirational strengths and weaknesses of a liberal–constitutional rights culture, many of them either pivotal contributions to the rights critique of the 1970s and 1980s, responses to it or explorations of alternative directions that liberal rights discourse might take in light of it. The essays are divided into four Parts. The essays in Part I by David Luban and Ronald Dworkin introduce the constitutional liberal rights tradition, and then defend it against a recurrent and traditional objection: that unless tied to an explicit constitutional provision, the recognition of a liberal right by a court of law is an essentially lawless act.

All the essays except one in Part II of this volume spell out some of the moral, political or aspirational objections to liberal conceptions of rights that have emerged over the last 30 years. The final essay in that section, 'Rights and Politics' by Joseph Raz identifies two philosophical fallacies in what he characterizes as the standard understanding of liberal constitutional rights: their reliance on universalist, transcendent premises and their individualist character. Although Raz himself does not draw out the connection, if his argument is persuasive, both philosophical fallacies might underlie at least some of the moral or aspirational shortcomings of rights decried by the rights critics.

The essays in Part III, as well as the remainder of this Introduction, defend rights against some of the strands of the rights critique explored in Part II. These essays all suggest, in different ways, that liberal rights don't necessarily display the moral or political shortcomings cited by their critics. Finally, the brief exchange between West and Dershowitz in Part IV debates the moral role of rights in mediating the relations of citizens and states, in the context of a fictional prosecution for an alleged murder, first propounded by Lon Fuller 50 years ago. The first fictional opinion, by West, briefly defends the continuing centrality of rights to a moral conception of the rule of law. The last, and decidedly more sceptical word, is given to Professor Dershowitz.

In the remaining three sections of this Introduction, I assess the cost of the critique itself. I conclude that we should refashion, not abandon, the liberal rights traditions, if we wish to articulate, much less move closer, towards defensible conceptions of the good society.

The Rights Critique

Liberal rights fail, according to the rights critics, in a number of ways, as the essays in Part II of this volume attest, but two particular criticisms are perhaps the most salient, or at least the most recurrent. The first and perhaps most important objection lodged against liberal rights by their critics is basically political. Rights, as liberals insist, limit the power of states to meddle in private spheres of life. However, precisely by virtue of doing so – and whatever the value of doing so – they also thereby create entitlements to the exercise of unchecked power, within those private spheres, by private individuals or entities on others. Within those spheres of insularity, private power is then often used in ways that subordinate or oppress. Put somewhat differently, and, as argued in this volume by Morton Horwitz (Chapter 3) and Mary Becker (Chapter 4), and elsewhere with tremendous force by, among others, Mark Tushnet (1984, pp. 1386–88), Alan Freeman (1978; 1988) and Reva Siegal (1996), individual (or corporate) rights to the non-interference of the state create economic, racial and sexual spheres of private entitlement and private privilege within which the powerful can exploit the powerless, with no fear of state redress. Within those private spheres such actions are within the ambit of 'individual rights': the state may not intervene. Rights create, in effect, a privilege to exploit others.

Thus, the right to free speech, to take an example, does assure the individual a degree of freedom from state censorship. But, on the other hand, it also assures that those who suffer the consequences of hateful utterances hurled by the rights-empowered will have no hope of redress (Shiffrin, 1994): the right to free speech immobilizes the state from acting. The right to contract, to take another example, assures the individual that a liberal state will not paternalistically alter his or its freely struck bargains. Yet, this freedom of contract also assures that those who suffer the consequences of economic oppression will have little relief from the state: again, contractual freedom stays the state's hand. The 'right of privacy', similarly, implies that the state will not unduly meddle in an individual's intimate affairs but, for the victim of domestic violence, what it means (or has meant) is that the violence inflicted upon her will go unchecked, and that her abuser's power, furthermore, will be imbued with constitutional majesty (Siegel, 1996, pp. 2153–70). The 'right to equal protection', to take a final example, requires that states refrain from legislating on the basis of race or other impermissible characteristics. It also, however, assures that those subjected to multiple and subtle forms of private racial discrimination will have a difficult obstacle to overcome, if seeking relief from the state: the state is precluded, by virtue of the individual right to be free of racially explicit legislation, from acting affirmatively so as to address private racism, just as it is precluded by virtue of the same right from malign forms of discrimination. In all these spheres, rights limit the power of states, and in all these spheres, rights perpetuate social injustice by doing so.

Furthermore, according to their critics, liberal rights promote injustice in this way not because they are susceptible to misuse by machiavellian political actors but, rather, by *structural design*: rights are overwhelmingly, in many liberal states – and virtually by definition in the United States – *negative*. It is, of course, because we have rights *against* the state (and only against the state), rather than rights *to* some particular sort of state action or state intervention, that rights protect the individual against an overreaching state in the manner celebrated by rights advocates. But it is also because of rights' negativity that they necessarily insulate private hierarchies and thereby empower the strong to subordinate the weak. If the state cannot intervene on the side of the weak because of rights possessed by both, the stronger party will be made all the stronger by virtue of even the weaker party's possession of rights, to say nothing of the stronger's. A negative right disempowers the state from pernicious, intermeddling, paternalistic or malign intervention into the private affairs of individual citizens, but by virtue of so doing it also disempowers the state from intervening in the private sphere for the democratically progressive purpose of redistributing power within it. It equalizes the citizen vis-à-vis an overreaching, paternalistic state but, by staying the paternalist' s intervening hand, it subordinates that citizen to his stronger brother.

Thus it is by virtue of the fact that my right to free speech is a *negative* right against the state that it implies the disempowerment of the victim of hate speech. If that right were, instead, a positive right to speak, or a positive right to literacy, or to education, or to information, instead of a right to be free of state intervention into private speech markets, it would be an open question whether or not the right was most endangered by censorial state actors or censorial private actors, and whether the state should act or refrain from acting so as to protect that right.

Similarly, it is by virtue of the fact that the right to privacy is a *negative* right against state meddling that it implies the disempowerment of the victim of domestic assault. If it were, instead, cast as a positive entitlement to the enjoyment of some sphere of privacy, it would similarly be an open question whether or not the right was more endangered by the private, assaultive, intrusive conduct of abusive partners, or by the intervention of public actors, and accordingly whether the state should act or refrain from acting so as to protect it. It is by virtue of the fact that rights of contract and property are viewed as *negative* rights against state intervention that they operate as protectors of free markets, and hence of private material inequality. If they were understood as rights to the enjoyment of some minimal material quality of life, then again it would be open to debate whether the right is best protected by state inaction or state guarantees of jobs, welfare or income that limit rather than insulate labour markets. Finally, it is by virtue of the fact that the right to equal protection is cast as a *negative* right against a certain sort of state irrationality that it has become such a powerful weapon against those who would use the state to rectify the imbalances created by private forms of racism. Were it understood, instead, as a positive right to be free of certain manifestations of racism, it would be an open question whether or not that right is most endangered by private or state action, and whether it is best protected by colour-blind or race-conscious legislation. The rights critics' political case against the liberal rights tradition, in other words, concerns primarily that tradition's insistence that rights by definition *limit*, rather than inform or guide, state action.

Rights, then, whatever good they do, have this negative political externality: they create private spheres of privilege within which the exploitation or subordination of the weak by the strong goes unchecked by the state. Those spheres, and even the subordination that occurs within them, are then cloaked with the mantle of constitutional and moral righteousness. The very utopian universalism of rights and rights-consciousness instills in the privileged the false and panglossian belief that all is morally well and fair with the world, even in the face of glaring and unjustified material inequality, because whatever may be the case with respect to material well-being, the rights that protect those material possessions are universally bestowed (Kairys, 1998, pp. 285–311; Tushnet, 1984, pp. 1386–88). The poor's rights to their meagre belongings are, after all, no less robust than the rights of the wealthy. Even more damaging, however, rights instill in the relatively underprivileged the false sense that their own lack of material well-being is justified by – or at any rate morally offset by – the rights they possess: I may not have much but, by right, you cannot deprive me of what I do have. Protection of the rights of the wealthy to their wealth, I may come to believe, is simply the price paid for the protection of my rights to my belongings against the invasive interests of those who have even less – and so on down the ladder. And they instill in all of us, privileged and underprivileged, the false belief that the rights protected by liberalism are grounded in our nature and hence immutable to change. We come to believe, wrongly, that not only is our inherited world of rights and that to which we by right are entitled a just one, but that it is a necessary and unchangeable one as well. Thus, rights, according to the rights critics, don't just protect, they also disguise private realms of abuse, violence and oppression that are sites of injustice, and they protect it against the very democratic interventions that might redistribute the power within them, or at least ameliorate the more extreme harms occasioned by them. Rights – virtually by definition – permit the strong to subordinate the weak in private and without intervention by the state, and then celebrate that subordination as the exercise of rights. They first politically protect, and then they ideologically valorize, private subordination and exploitation of the weak by the strong, and all under the umbrella of constitutional authority.

The second failing of the liberal rights tradition, very generally, according to the critics, is *existential*: it goes to how we construct our self-identity. As argued in this volume by communitarians as politically diverse as Michael Sandel (Chapter 8; also 1996; 1997), Peter Gabel (Chapter 5) and MaryAnn Glendon (Chapter 6; also 1991), rights and rights-consciousness render us unduly, and inhumanely, *atomized*. In liberal societies that take rights seriously, individuals are first wrongly described as, but then tragically become, isolated from each other in individualized rights-spun cocoons, increasingly incapable of even approaching each other, much less achieving any meaningful moral or political empathetic connections with fellow citizens. Rights erode, rather than enhance, our feelings of obligations toward our neighbours, co-citizens, and arguably even our intimates and family members. We come to view ourselves, and then increasingly come to be, possessors of individual rights against each other and the state, but with no responsibilities, duties or even commonalities toward or with our larger communities. By overprotecting our individual contractual and property entitlements, and doing so in the name of our nature, they leave us identified with our holdings, rather than each other. As a result, we each become dangerously and tragically unmoored from the communities that could more truly nurture our lives.

This existential cost of rights, like the political cost, is also a function of rights' essential core, rather than a function of their distortion. Rights theorists, according to their critics, have wrongly but emphatically embraced a fundamentally false conception of human nature. We are, each of us, according to rights' architects, self-sufficient, idiosyncratic, autonomous, free-thinking, rational, insular and atomistic. We each have a fundamental 'right to be left alone', for example, because we each want to be left alone, and thrive when left alone. We revel in our idiosyncratic individualism, unencumbered by responsibility, connection, duty, culture or society. This perceived insularity, or atomism, sometimes has tragic costs. First, it is logically tied to rights' negativity: the individual assumed by liberalism is largely unaffected and even unharmed by relative and unequal distributions of private power, because he is more fundamentally unaffected by community itself. He enjoys the freedom negative rights bestow and is simply untouched by their political and existential costs. But, second, that same understanding of individual nature is also tied to liberalism's signature insistence on state neutrality towards competing conceptions of the good life: because we each, individually and idiosyncratically, author our own understanding of the good, the state (or collective) is obviously incapacitated from doing so on our behalf. The resulting insistence on state neutrality towards competing conceptions of the good, as argued in this volume by Sandel (Chapter 8), Chai Feldblum (Chapter 9) and Charles Taylor (Chapter 10), and elsewhere and at greater length by Leon Trakman (1997), renders liberalism, as a politics, peculiarly moot on issues regarding the nature of the good. The result is not only alienated individuals, but also a sterile and unsatisfying reluctance on the part of liberal states to endorse some conceptions of the good – such as a commitment to multiculturalism, preservation of traditions, or the value of marriage as a way of life – over others, even where such a commitment seems clearly in the national interest. This neutrality, itself largely a function of the excessively atomistic view of human nature that drives it, is itself a serious moral failing.

But that understanding of our nature – that understanding of the nature of individual life – according to the rights critics, not only has serious costs, it is also simply not a true one. We are not insular atoms, sufficient unto ourselves, wanting nothing but to be left alone. Rather, for substantial parts of our lives, we are dependent on the caregiving of others for our very survival, and throughout our lives, we remain interdependent social beings. These basic social and biological facts of life, furthermore, inform not just our self-understanding, but our moral sense as well: we have moral obligations to the weak and to those dependent on us, and we know we have those moral obligations, because we know we have been, and will be, weak and dependent ourselves. We sympathize with others in crisis or in need, and we depend on their sympathetic response when we are in need ourselves. We build community because we are communal creatures who depend on it. It is, therefore, not surprising that the liberal world, justified by a false understanding of who we are, is so apparently morally barren. It is at war with our moral intuitions about the way in which we ought to live, because it is at war with the true conception of our nature that informs our moral sense.

Thus, it is by virtue of liberalism's commitment to a falsely individualistic and falsely insular conception of human nature that the individual possesses relentlessly negative rights of property, privacy and contract, and it is by virtue of those rights that the individual has the dubious and amoral freedom to both keep his wallet in his pocket and avert his gaze and conscience from the panhandler on the street. The understanding of our nature is false and hence the moral freedom posited upon it seems morally false as well. Similarly, it is by virtue of his asserted nature, and then by virtue of his rights justified by that nature, that the liberal individual need not feel or act on civic, moral or religious duties of charity or fraternity. Again, the understanding of our nature is false, so the circle of obligation and responsibility constructed by reference to it is unduly circumscribed. By virtue of his profit-seeking and self-sufficient nature, an employer, whether corporate or individual, has property, privacy and contract rights, which permit him to ignore or deny knowledge of any community of human interest between his employees in his hire and himself. But we are not only profit-seeking entities, and we are not by nature self-sufficient, so the corporate entities and individual rights that we have constructed in the wake of that false depiction seem unsurprisingly amoral. By reference to a false conception of her insularity, liberalism has constructed a right to privacy, from which it follows that a pregnant woman need not acknowledge the gravity of her moral duties towards the human life growing within her. But she is not so insular, and she *is* burdened by moral obligations – the error lies in assuming them away. By virtue of their wrongly assumed and acausal atomism, and the absolute property rights to which it leads, a gun manufacturer need not acknowledge the risk that his firearm poses to others, a polluter need not acknowledge the harms he occasions, nor the tobacco manufacturer the disease wrought by his product and profits. But, again, the acausality is mistaken, we are far more connected to each other than liberalism wants to concede and, consequently, the moral conclusion is unwarranted as well. Very generally, it is by virtue of their insulating negative rights that both individuals and corporations in liberal societies need not acknowledge their debts owed to others, their responsibilities towards them, the chains of causation that unite them, or the common fate in store for them. But it is by reference to the individual's presumed nature that those rights are in turn justified. That conception of our nature is false, and the moral conclusions to which it leads are wrong. The human nature presupposed by the autonomous holder of negative rights, in short, is atomized and individuated to the point of social pathology – but falsely so. That nature is not ours. The panoply of rights constructed upon it may be liberal, but they are profoundly inhuman.

The rights critics, to summarize these threads, are haunted by the spectre of a rights dystopia. In a world defined by rights, we have rights to keep the state out of our lives, but no obligations to help each other. Children are taught the morality of individual rights, and mature into adults who abandon or neglect civic bonds – untutored, as they are, in the moral language of responsibility. Religious fundamentalists use the power of their protected rhetoric underscored by their right to religious freedom to homeschool their children in the lessons of contempt for those who do not share their faith. Patriarchs enjoy rights of familial privacy, and family members have no legitimate expectation that the state will protect them against his abuse. Every individual or corporate employer has the right to profit from the labour of his brother, but no one has the responsibility – and eventually, no one has even the inclination – to share, or reduce, his brother's burden. Every individual has the right to be left alone and takes full advantage of it, and neighbourhoods, communities, states, even families, and civic life in general wither on the vine as a consequence. This does not sound like a world anyone would want or choose to live in. It is, however, increasingly, the world that liberalism has wrought. Rights, according to their critics, are at the very heart of it.

A Critique of the Rights Critique

Why, though, if it is, on the one hand, the negativity of rights and, on the other, a false conception of our human nature that underlie the diseased culture which the rights tradition has created, have the rights critics faulted the idea of a liberal right *itself*? There may be nothing intrinsic in the nature of a right that requires either its negativity, or that it be forever conjoined with a false description of our nature. If so, then the rights critics' conclusion – that we should abandon, rather than reform, rights – is overbroad, even if their substantive premises – that the negativity of rights protects injustice, and that their understanding of human nature is largely false – are warranted. Some of the critics – notably, both Mark Tushnet and Peter Gabel – have made clear their belief that the critique of rights rests on contingent features of national identity, not intrinsic features of liberal rights culture. But these qualifications have apparently gone unheeded, and for the most part have not led to efforts to reform rights-talk in a way that retains its value. As a consequence, those of us at all persuaded by the rights critique may have thrown the baby out with the bathwater. Let me address, first, rights' purported negativity, and then the overdrawn atomistic conception of our nature.

First, with regard to rights and negativity, there is nothing about a right that logically *requires* that it be understood as a constraint on state action, forbidding interference with individual spheres of privacy or liberty, rather than as a state obligation, entitling the individual to some form of state intervention. The notion of a positive right may be disfavoured in contemporary liberal discourse, but it is by no means oxymoronic. Ronald Dworkin, in his seminal, mid-1970s writings on liberal constitutional rights, did indeed focus overwhelmingly on the rights that follow from the moral constraints on liberal states (Dworkin, 1978, pp. vi–xv, 184–205). But he suggested no reason to define rights in such a way, nor does anything in the remainder of his powerful jurisprudential treatment of rights depend on it. A right could as readily be defined as including *both* the individual entitlement that follows from the moral obligations of liberal states, as well as the entitlements that follow from constraints upon them: rights could be defined as the individual entitlements that follow from what states are morally required to do *and* what liberal states are morally prohibited from doing (ibid., pp. 193–4). Doing so would seemingly be consistent, rather than inconsistent, with the robust moral imperative that, according to Dworkin, underlies liberalism – that every individual must be accorded equal dignity, equal concern and equal respect. To accord all individuals dignity, concern and respect sometimes requires the state to refrain from acting, and sometimes to act. Further, rights have, as Elizabeth Clark (Chapter 15), Susan Bandes (Chapter 18) and Akhil Amar (Chapter 16) all suggest, at different times and for different subcultures in American history, been widely understood as positive rather than negative in character. It would also be consistent with usage in the rest of the world – any number of liberal states, as Mary Ann Glendon notes in Chapter 6, recognize positive rights. They do not noticably sacrifice their liberality by doing so.

Furthermore, it is worth noting that the recognition that rights might sometimes be positive entitlements to state action, as well as negative entitlements to be free of it, is *truer* to the liberal classics that animate the liberal tradition, than is the increasingly perverse insistence of both liberal constitutionalists and their critics, on rights' essential negativity. For example, Thomas Hobbes, notoriously no friend of rights, regarded the utterly positive *obligation* of the state to protect individuals against private violence as central to the social contract, and the individual's right to that protection as virtually the only right which he carries with him from nature into civil society. That bargain – the individual's relinquishment of the use of self-help, in exchange for the state's obligation to protect him from violence and his right to that protection – was, for Hobbes, the heart of the state's very existence: the Leviathan's protection of the individual against the private violence of others is the *quid pro quo* for the individual's relinquishment of his right to self-help available to him in the state of nature (Hobbes, 1651, pp. 120–21, 153–54). The state's obligation to protect the citizen against private violence, as well as the citizen's continuing right to receive it, in Hobbes' view, was foundational and inalienable.

What follows from such a firm and clear state obligation, in the modern language of rights, is that an individual has a right to the state's protection against violence or aggression from other private parties – indeed, this may be, as Steven Heyman argues in Chapter 17 of this volume, the 'first duty of government'. The right to that protection, in turn, is clearly positive in character: if the state is obligated to protect the citizen against private violence, then the individual has a *right* to it, and it is a right, in turn, not to inaction but, rather, to the state's affirmative intervention into what would otherwise be a natural, private, and life-shortening state of war. The state is required to do something – to protect the individual – not just refrain from doing something. If this very positive right to protection against violence is central, rather than peripheral, to the liberal social contract, then the distinctively modern claim that liberal rights are essentially negative – whether insisted by rights proponents, rights critics, or Supreme Court justices – is mistaken, and even perverse. The core, foundational right to which the liberal state owes its existence is indisputably positive in character.

There is even less reason to think that rights, in order to be rights, must be obsessively directed towards, and justified by, reference to a false conception of individual nature which reduces to not much more than an adolescent anti-authoritarian narcissism in misleadingly adult-like garb. Rights, in the liberal tradition, are indeed justified by, and emanate from, some conception of our human nature, but there is nothing in the rights tradition *per se* that obligates it to honour a *false* conception of our nature. Indeed, although classical liberals undoubtedly highlighted our autonomy and our individuality, the centrality of the 'right to be left alone' to the rights tradition, and the neurotic understanding of our nature on which such a right rests, is a late nineteenth- and early twentieth-century invention. Such a view is central to liberalism, or to liberal states, only to the extent that the state, the Constitution or the tradition that defines rights designate it as such. Rights could as readily be grounded in a view of our nature that both respects our individuality and also gives full recognition to our social, rather than sociopathic, nature: our extended periods of biological dependence on caregivers, the resulting dependence of those caregivers on the support of others, our obligations to our communities and neighbourhoods, our civic and charitable duties to others, and our responsibilities to engage in civic life.

A liberal state might, for example, recognize the rights of caregivers to care for dependents without jeopardizing their own or their dependents' safety or well-being. Such a right would go a long way towards aligning the idea of rights with a conception of our nature that acknowledges both our natural dependencies and our social responsibilities toward others, rather than a conception of our nature that insists falsely and dangerously on our self-sufficiency. Although we presently do not, we could recognize, through rights, the value and vulnerabilities of relational living – both in family and community – just as we could recognize, through rights, the need to attend to the vulnerabilities of individuals within those relations. We could recognize, through rights, not only our natural desire, and need, to be left alone, but also our natural desire, and need, to bestow love on our children and aging parents without threatening ours or their well-being, as Eva Kittay (Chapter 19) suggests. To take another example, we could recognize as well, through rights, as Lisa Heinzerling argues in Chapter 20, our ties and commitments to future generations or far-flung populations as well. We could recognize, through rights, as William Forbath (1999) has argued at length, our natural needs for meaningful engagement with the world of work, and hence accord a right to meaningful work at a living wage, rather than our right to individually strike our own contractual terms for alienating our labour. We could cast the rights net widely, bestowing, as Patricia Williams would have it, rights on rocks, stones, animals and fish, with correlative obligations on all of us to tend to them (see Chapter 12). We could surely grant rights to the enjoyment of traditional cultures or differentiating ethnic identities, as Will Kymlicka, Charles Taylor and Leon Trakman all urge. Liberal rights, in short, could as readily be morally grounded in a full, decent and true conception of our social nature, as they are presently grounded in a truncated and atomized one. There is nothing in the nature of a right that commits a rights regime to a falsely atomized or insulated conception of the human nature that requires them.

The Costs of the Rights Critique

Some of the rights critics, of course, have argued for precisely the reformulation that I am suggesting above. Nevertheless, most rights critics, and certainly those who first and most influentially coined the phrase, have urged an abandonment, not a reformulation, of rights and rights discourse. Rights, according to the most far-reaching critics, are almost invariably negative and inevitably tied to a falsely insular conception of individual nature. For both reasons, while they may from time to time guarantee a measure of individual freedom, they also – and inexorably – benefit the privileged, give false hope and a false sense of security to the subordinated, teach complicity in one's own disempowerment, and hold out the possibility of small progressive steps forwards only towards the end of coopting their beneficiaries, and ultimately securing large steps back. There is nothing to gain and quite a bit to lose, then, by even envisioning a progressive or positive alternative rights agenda, much less striving to put one in place. The idea that we might profit from a reformulation of rights as positive and honouring our social rather than asocial nature is worse than a harmless utopian chimera; it is a dangerous delusion. If put in practice, it promises at most a pointless diversion of resources. At worst, it promises continuing liberal complicity in the work of injustice.

This is not a groundless worry; there is plenty in our recent and not so recent history that explains the rights critics' most extreme forms of rights scepticism. The last great American rights revolution – the civil rights movements of the 1950s and 1960s – became the shell of the reactionary anti-affirmative action movement of the 1980s and 1990s. The reproductive rights movement of the mid- and late-twentieth century has similarly become nothing but a bare commodificationist right to purchase an abortion, rather than a positive entitlement to exercise meaningful autonomy or choice in one's reproductive life. Negative rights of free speech – fervently sought by dissidents as a way of protecting the interests and liberties of persecuted pacifists, anarchists and communists at the mid-century – have become, at the beginning of the twenty-first century, the vehicle by which advertisers manipulate public desire with impunity, and corporate wealth maintains its headlock on the levers of political decision-making. As this volume goes to press, the peculiarly American so-called 'right to bear arms', intended to protect the rights of colonial citizens against a centralized, distant, military force, has become instead the means by which citizens terrorize each other, reducing the state to such cartoonish minimalism that the right threatens to return us all to the very Hobbesian state of nature from which *The Leviathan* promised deliverance. The rights critics have, in essence, urged us to internalize the moral of these examples and innoculate ourselves against future delusions: this is the way of all rights movements, hopes, and ambitions. There is no articulable right that will not eventually – probably sooner than later – become the vehicle for reactionary politics. The entrenchment of the status quo achieved by such a discourse is never worth whatever momentary gain might be had through an expansion of rights.

There are, however, costs in abandoning rights instead of joining the debate regarding their substance. The first concerns our moral aspirations and the relative power or impoverishment of the rhetoric with which we articulate them. When we disown rights, we distance ourselves from a tradition that has unquestionably been unduly attentive to individualistic needs for property, contract and privacy and insufficiently attentive to needs for non-subordinationist policies and communitarian practices. But we also distance ourselves from a discourse that, whatever its historic shortcomings, has enabled us to attend to what we might universally share, and to focus on the utopian aspirations we might universally hold, and then to strive to bring that vision to earth. It is a language that has permitted – indeed, required – us to think in terms of what we morally ought to do and be, before dictating, as law-makers, judges or citizens, what we will or won't do and be. It has been a language that instructs the state to limit, in the name of justice, what it might do. It has been a language that explicitly teaches that occasionally, at least, it is right and just to trump social benefits for the sake of the dignity of even one individual, and to simply absorb whatsoever social costs might be incurred by doing so. There are not all that many ways by which critics, citizens or even legislators can make the simple point that moral judgement rather than *real politik* ought guide the business of politics. It is not so clear that the abandonment, rather than reform, of one such language – whatever its flaws – will prove to be a benefit for the party of humanity.

The second cost of abandoning rights-consciousness is borne by the state of our normative doctrinal scholarship. Should we heed the critics' call to abandon rights talk, the development, through scholarship, of various and alternative directions that legal doctrine could take will bear the mark of that abandonment as well. To a considerable degree, we can already trace the effects of that retreat. We still lack a credible jurisprudence of welfare rights, for example, and we lack it partly because those who might have otherwise been inclined to produce it have been convinced not only of the futility of the project, but also of its counterproductivity. We lack a credible jurisprudence of education rights, and it is at least possible that we lack it, in part, because of that same scepticism. We lack a jurisprudence of dignitary rights, and labour rights, and environmental rights, and we lack them partly because those who might produce the scholarship have become convinced that rights and rights-talk cannot be productively turned to collective, communitarian or progressive political ends. Obviously, other factors have also played a role – most importantly, the turn among left-wing scholars to an explicitly anti-normative sceptical postmodernism fuelled the late twentieth century retreat, at least in the legal academy, from visionary, utopian scholarship. Nevertheless, the explicit disavowel of rights is both a part of that story, as well as reflective of it.

Third, there is a direct political cost in abandoning, rather than reforming, rights as well: the abandonment of rights discourse by those critical of rights' negativity or of its excessive individualism virtually ensures that the rights critique will be a self-fulfilling prophecy. When we forego the task of creating a positive rights jurisprudence, we also forego the opportunity to assert a credible counterweight, *within* rights discourse, to the assertion of negative rights which do indeed protect and legitimate injustice, and in precisely the ways urged by the critics. With no credible counterweight, when a negative right of the sort the rights critics lament *is* asserted, it is typically met, in a rights impoverished discourse, not with a positive right that might counter it, but instead with a claimed 'policy' to be weighed against it. But rights, as both their proponents and critics know, trump policy; that is their function. If we had what we currently don't have – a developed jurisprudence of positive rights, group rights and relational rights – a negative, individualist right might alternatively, or additionally, be met with the claim that it conflicts with a positive one, in courts of law and in courts of public opinion. Conflicting rights do not trump each other; rather, conflicting rights must be read in such a way as to reduce the conflict. We have been dissuaded, in part by the rights critique, from developing the jurisprudence that might support precisely the arguments that could conceivably counter the rights which the rights critics rightly decry.

Let me illustrate with one example. In a recent Texas case, a federal district court judge held that a man's constitutional right to bear arms was unconstitutionally abridged by a federal law which forbade domestic violence offenders from owning firearms.[3] The court accordingly struck the law as unconstitutional. In that case, the state attempted, unsuccessfully, to meet the defendant's claimed assertion of the negative right to bear arms by arguing, first, that the Second Amendment right on which the defendant rested his case does not exist[4] and, second, that if it does, it should be balanced or weighed against, or limited by a policy favouring public safety.[5] But policy arguments rarely win against asserted rights. They're not supposed to. The very logic of a right – that it must be protected even in the face of sound policies that conflict with it – virtually assures as much. Rights, again, by definition, trump policy. It is inherent in rights that they do so.

Alternatively, if we had a robust and developed understanding of positive rights, the negative right to bear arms in the Texas case could conceivably have been met not just with a claimed policy favouring disarmament of violent domestic abusers, but with a *right*: even if the right to bear arms exists, it must be understood in such a way as not to conflict with our more fundamental positive right to a liberal state that protects us against private violence. Such a right, had it been asserted, could not simply be trumped by a conflicting right. The court would have been forced to reconcile, in a principled way, the right to bear arms with the civil right to be protected by the state against private violence. How the court would have achieved that reconciliation is an open question; the claim that the negative right to bear arms would have to be limited so as to accommodate the positive right to be protected against a known threat of violence from an identified offender with a history of abuse, may or may not have proven persuasive. It probably would not have proven persuasive to the judge who wrote the majority opinion, although it may have captured the legal imagination of a judge writing in dissent. My point here, however, is that the rights critique dissuades us from the need to build the case for the constitutional rejoinder. That alone is a cost.

It is not difficult to imagine other examples. Property owners and, increasingly, courts, argue that environmental regulations that impact upon the value of privately held property unconstitutionally restrict the property owners' various negative rights of property. Such a claim, one might think, ought ideally to be met with a robust argument that we have a positive right to a state that protects our wilderness, air, water and public health. Instead, it is typically met by a plea that the property owner's multiple and conceded negative rights to own property free of state regulation ought to be balanced against environmental policy. But, again, in a rights versus policy debate, it will probably be the right that trumps. For environmentalism, the consequence of abandoning the attempt to construct a positive jurisprudence of environmental rights is clearly not good. In a similar vein, the claim that a landlord's contract and property rights are infringed by laws requiring him to rent to couples regardless of sexual orientation is met only by the hope that the court will, in its discretion, come to view such non-discrimination laws as protecting compelling state interests, rather than by a strongly asserted positive right to shelter, unburdened by litmus tests of moral propriety. The claim that a propagandist's hate speech is unconstitutionally infringed by a speech regulation, or that broadcasters' news coverage is unconstitutionally infringed by broadcast regulations, is met by asserted policies in freedom from harm or fairness, rather than with the claim that liberalism ought properly to honour not only our negative rights to be free of censorship but also our positive rights to a political dialogue unpolluted by hate or profit. In short, without a tradition of positive rights on which to draw, we meet constitutional claims of negative speech rights, property rights, contract rights and gun rights with exhortations of policy – exhortations which sometimes are, but more often are not, heard. However, the fact that these cases are all posed, and understood, as asserted rights on the one hand and policies on the other, does not bode well for the regulatory state. Rights, by definition, trump policy. Negative rights, unchecked by positive rights that might counter them, threaten to reduce that regulatory state to vanishing point. Such a reduction would hardly be a victory for the party of humanity.

Finally, the failure to articulate a positive rights jurisprudence has encumbered the articulation of a meaningful counterweight not only within rights discourse, but also to the balancing of costs and benefits that increasingly dominates ordinary, or non-rights-based, legal analysis. The result is that legal analysis, across the map, is now driven *in toto* either by the logic of negative rights or, in the absence of rights, by an economic calculus that funnels all values into monetary equivalents, assigning some to the cost and some to the benefit side of the ledger, balancing the one against the other and then according victory to whichever comes out on top. The failure to enrich the rights tradition with a positive rights jurisprudence and a defensible conception of our social nature, has thus greased the wheels of the ascendency of an economic method of legal analysis that relentlessly asserts the comparability, fungibility and commensurability of all values, their translation into dollar terms, and the ease of trading one off against the other – the cost of health balanced against lost profits, the value of future life measured against current dollars, the cost of suffering against the cost of prevention, the monetary benefits of speech against the cost of permitting it, the cost of sexual harrassment against the benefits of non-intervention. This cost-benefit analysis has, by now, widely recognized and well-known pitfalls: it relies on real or shadow market values that are themselves reflective of little but the forces of profit; it ferociously solidifies and legitimates the status quo by steadfastly ignoring the effects of given distributions on felt entitlements; it discriminates between us by valuing our lives differently on the basis of our projected or actual incomes; it creates a wealth-based mentality that measures all, including goodness, truth and justice, by reference to profit. But for all its problems, for all its well-known absurdities, cost-benefit analysis now dominates legal analysis. It does so primarily because of the absence of credible normative alternatives.

Here again, this is a loss felt not only in theory but in doctrine as well. As Lisa Heinzerling demonstrates in Chapter 20, the costs of environmental protection to individuals and corporations, for example, are now routinely balanced against the benefits to individuals, where the benefits of health and well-being are then measured by projected incomes, and then discounted by various factors, such as the non-proximity of the lives in question to us, in terms of either time or distance. Rather than present a rights-based challenge to this entire normative apparatus, advocates of environmental regulation instead, typically, debate the amounts, challenge the discount rates or question various economic assumptions behind the economic models. What we do not hear, even from environmentalists, is a principled moral and legal argument, based on rights, that we are entitled to some degree of state-protected environmental health *regardless of cost*. Accident victims and their advocates similarly tally their costs in lottery-styled torts cases, rather than assert a right to health care to which we are entitled, as a matter of right and, again, *regardless of cost*. Sexually harrassed workers or their advocates debate the subtleties of the value of an harrassment-free environment as implied by their employment contracts, rather than assert a right to dignified labour, *regardless of cost*. Our legal system, as well as our discourse, have been thoroughly transformed by a cost-benefit econometric, and without a rights discourse to offset, trump or challenge it, there is little relief in sight. By eschewing rights and rights-talk, we have, arguably, engendered a more efficient state. But it is not at all clear that we have accordingly created a more just or humane community.

Rights Revitalized: Towards a Jurisprudence of Positive and Relational Rights

What might be worth considering, in light of the real and potential costs of the rights critique, is the possibility of revitalizing the rights tradition, rather than abandoning it altogether, and doing so by correcting those of its problematic features that prompted the critique. What might a positive rights jurisprudence be, and what might a liberal state look like, if it recognized both negative and positive rights grounded in our universality? What might that tradition come to be, if it rested on a conception of our nature equally attentive to our interdependence, our dependency and our communitarian inclinations, as it is presently attentive to our idiosyncratic individualism?

As the essays in Parts III and IV of this volume attest, there would be (at least) two fundamental differences between such a liberal rights regime and the understanding of rights that prompted the rights critique and has come to dominate liberal legal systems. First, a liberal state unspooked by the spectre of positive rights might explicitly recognize the natural reality behind the metaphoric social contract: our nature is such that the state must monopolize the tools and instruments of violence, if our lives are to be relatively secure. The state therefore has an obligation – a first duty – to protect its citizens against private violence and aggression. Such a state would be forced to reckon with the citizen's correlative positive right to be so protected. A state that fails to provide such protection, then, violates the individual's right, as well as the state's 'first duty' (Heyman, Chapter 17). For example, a state that failed to criminalize or failed to enforce existing laws that criminalize domestic violence, marital rape, or violence against lesbians and gay men, or people of colour, would violate those citizens' right to protection – and equal protection – of the law. These would be clear, unequivocal violations. Less blatant, and even unintentional or neglectful failures to protect citizens from violence, however, might also violate such a right; a failure, for example, to enact adequate gun control legislation so as to ensure the safety of schoolchildren or urban residents might constitute a failure to provide for the protection of the safety of citizens, and hence violate their rights to protection of the law. A consistent pattern of punishing violence against a group of citizens more leniently than the same crimes committed against another less favoured group might also constitute such a violation, as Randall Kennedy (1988), has argued.

But, second, a recognized, robust, centralized and positive right to protection might evidence the existence of, and justification for, additional, penumbral positive rights, in the manner first recognized by the Warren Court, and explored here in greater detail by David Luban (Chapter 1). What might be the penumbral rights implied by the recognition of a positive right to protection against private violence? If we have a positive right to protection against private violence, and if we have it because of our natural vulnerability to the violent propensities of others, then we might also want to recognize that we have a positive right to the state's protection against other sorts of natural calamities. We might, for example, have a positive welfare right to be protected against natural disaster, misfortune, or even disfavour, if the consequences of that disfavour are brutal (Michelman, 1969). Equally, if we recognize a positive right to protection against the violence of others, we might also reason that such a right implies the existence of penumbral rights to be broadly protected against extreme forms of private aggression, whether or not that aggression takes the form of physical violence. We may, then, have a positive right to be protected against the harmful effects of a polluted environment, or an unregulated and dangerous product, or exploitative employers. Again, whether or not such a right exists would depend, partly, on whether the claim could be sustained that our nature – idealized or actual – for some reason demands as much, and whether sufficient textual authority could be found for them in the Constitution. But the case for them should not be burdened by their positivity. Welfare rights, labour rights, environmental rights and dignitary rights, in other words, should not be disfavoured, simply because they impose obligations on, rather than constraints against, a state.

Relatedly, were a liberal state to recognize positive rights, then our better established negative rights to state inaction – the right to speak, the right to own a gun, the right to privacy, the right to religious freedom, all free of state interference – would have to be recast, wherever they abut a positive right that requires some form of positive state action. If a right to own firearms is weighed against a public interest in safety, the public interest might well lose, simply by virtue of the nature of the weights: a right versus a policy is weighted in favour of the right. If the right to own a firearm is weighed against a right to the protection of the state against violence, however, the question is entirely different: neither trumps the other; the two must be reconciled in a principled manner. Similarly, a familial right to privacy will trump a state's intrusive insistence, in the name of public policy, to insure the safety of those within it – or so it has in the past (Siegel, 1996). It is not so clear, however, that it could trump a competing right to protection against intrusive violence. The right to contract or an employer's property rights will trump a public interest in a pacific workplace, but it is not so clear that it would trump a competing right to dignified, meaningful and adequately paid labour (Forbath, 1999). Competing rights must be adjudicated in a principled fashion. Again, neither clearly trumps the other.

The second salient difference, should a positive rights tradition strive for a truer conception of our nature, would be in the content of the rights viewed as deserving protection. We do not, contrary to Hobbesian myth, spring upon this earth mushroom-style, as fully formed, autonomous adults. Rather, we enjoy or suffer an extended period of absolute dependency on our mothers or other caregivers. As adults, most of us enjoy or suffer (or both) an even longer period during which we bestow care on infants and children dependent on us, and eventually on aging parents in similar need. We are not just interdependent creatures, we are also, for substantial periods, fully dependent on others, and others are, for substantial periods, fully dependent on us. As a consequence, when we are infants and children, and likewise when we are sick or aged, we desperately need not the rights of autonomy and independence so central to classical liberalism, but a regime that protects us in our dependent state, and protects those on whom we are dependent as well. When we are caregivers, we desperately need not rights that falsely presuppose our autonomy and independence, but rights that frankly acknowledge our relational reality: when infants, children, or aging parents are dependent on us, we are dependent on others for support and sustenance.[6] A rights tradition that forthrightly acknowledged the natural reality of our inescapable dependence on each other – to say nothing of our social nature – would give pride of place to what might be called relational rights that protect the care bestowed in dependency relationships. Those who give care over extended periods of time need material security – whether provided by an employer's maternity policy, a shared family wage from an employed partner, or community assistance through the state. One cannot see to the needs of an infant and produce an income at the same time. Falsely assuming that we can, is, ultimately, just as disastrous and self-destructive as falsely assuming that grown men and women will naturally and peacefully cohabit in the state of nature. An utterly artificial, socially constructed, civil leviathan has proven necessary to protect us against the second false illusion – the illusion of our own invulnerability and natural sociability. A similarly artificial, socially constructed, civil network of support must be constructed to provide us protection against the first – the illusion of our natural independence. A right to care, grounded in our nature and protective of the caregiver's security, safety and material well-being when she relinquishes her independence so as to care for the needs of dependent others, should be a part of that social construction.

A rights tradition freed of the taboo against positivity, and forthright in its recognition of our dependent nature, would go a long way towards responding to the moral indictment of rights propounded by the rights critique of the 1970s, 1980s and 1990s. First, if unencumbered by the false constraint of negativity, positive rights could be fashioned so as to protect us from each other, just as our negative rights protect us from the state, and could thereby further, rather than hinder, the attempt to address private forms of oppression. Positive rights to protection against private violence are the most obvious example. Additional positive rights might readily be implied, as there are surely other means, in addition to violence, by which private parties oppress each other. A right to non-subordination, as developed by Catherine MacKinnon (1991) and Ruth Colker (1986) can be readily derived from the right to equal protection and the state's obligation to provide it. Nowadays, private parties that subordinate sexual or racial subgroups are at least as much of a threat to individual well-being as states that do so, and a state's obligation to provide equal protection of the law might be read as implying a right – protected by the state – to be free of such subordination. Rights to dignified labour and a living wage might similarly be implied from a state's obligation to protect against private aggression. If so, then the liberal rights tradition could be employed to address and limit the damage wrought by private sovereignties of wealth, race and gender that hinder the full development of individuals in liberal societies, rather than relentlessly protect them.

Even if successful, of course, this reconstruction of rights from negative to positive and from atomistic to holistic does not establish that any of these rights actually *exist*: the right – whether to non-subordination, to care, to dignified labour, to a living wage, to welfare – must also be found in the language, logic or history of a state or a nation's Constitution. Constitutions may or may not explicitly provide for positive rights, and Constitutions that do not do so may or may not be read so as to implicitly endorse them. There is, of course, a great deal of constitutional law, authority and scholarship in constitutional democracies debating the interpretive limits and possibilities of particular constitutional provisions. Much of that debate, furthermore, centres on the possibility of locating positive rights within a document that seemingly provides for negative rights only.

Nevertheless, one obstacle to the recognition of positive rights stems not from constitutional law at all but rather from constitutional, legal, political and moral theory – namely, the widely held conviction that the notion of a postive right is somehow oxymoronic, that rights *by definition* constrain states from certain acts, rather than requiring certain acts of them. But this is a definitional distinction that ought to be laid to rest. Rights, justified by reference to our nature, direct as well as constrain states; they show what states must do to provide for civic liberty, equality and well-being, as well as what states must not do (see also Sunstein and Holmes, 1999). The liberal tradition, generously read, requires states to protect our individualistic capacity for free thought and our desire to master our own fate, and it requires states to do so, largely, by refraining from paternalistic intrusion. It also, however, generously read, requires the state to protect our capacity for self-rule free of the subordinating effects of the oppression of others, and it requires it to do so by perfecting our rights to its protection (Berlin, 1969, pp. 131–34). Such a right is distinctively positive, and if it is at the heart of liberalism, then the widely held belief that liberalism can at most embrace a negative understanding of rights is deeply mistaken.

Second, if committed to a full and true conception of our nature, rather than a truncated one, liberal rights could be aligned with the work of fashioning a social fabric that protects us in our cross-generational web of dependencies, rather than one that blithely ignores them. Caring for those who are dependent on us is at least as central to our human identity as our capacity for free thought, or our propensity to bargain through contracts, or the security we gain through our possessions. The nature and quality of the care we bestow on those who are dependent on us marks our species and, as a set of practices, generates an ethical way of being in the world that is at least as integral both to a well-led individual life and the well-being of our communities, as our individualized capacity for autonomous conviction or independent action (Gilligan, 1982). A liberalism that embraced at its core a right to give care without incurring unjustified vulnerability – a liberalism that would marry, so to speak, a recognition of the importance of care to the well-being of the species with the robustness of the liberal rights tradition – would, by so doing, thereby acknowledge a relational and communitarian world substantially different from the over-atomized individualistic hell decried by liberalism's critics. Furthermore, a right to care could conceivably generate not only penumbral rights and responsibilities but also penumbral visions and conceptions of the good. Conceptions of the good might then contain, at their core, precisely the duties and responsibilities owed to elders, neighbours and communities that communitarian and existential critics of the rights tradition now find so lacking in liberalism. Such a world would surely be more explicitly communitarian than the libertarian world of eccentrics and narcissists that our liberal traditions currently foster. Such a world might also be more liberal, however. Care, nurture and a decent upbringing are essential to a healthy adult individuality. A liberal society defined in part by its recognition of rights to care, and a liberal culture that took the care to embellish its assumptions, would enrich, not undermine, the egalitarianism and individualism of citizens that the liberal rights tradition, to its credit, has always sought to foster.

Most important, if we revitalize rights, rather than abandon them, we won't risk losing either the utopian universalism, or the critical edge, that rights have long lent to our political and legal practices. How we conceive of our rights informs our practices, which in turn inform our ideals, which in turn influence how we think of our rights. The language of rights connects politics with the hope that law both can and should structure a decent social world. How we conceive of such a world is clearly a political question and, in a conservative and libertarian time, the language of rights will reflect those politics – the rights we have or recognize will always reflect the dominant political discourse, and our dominant political discourse now is both conservative and libertarian. But it does not follow that rights have a necessary connection to those or any other set of political ideals; even less does it mean that those who envision a different political ideal than the reigning one should abandon them. Rights, whatever their content, are premised on the grandly egalitarian assumption that we have a shared nature, from which universal norms follow. If we give up on rights, we have given up on one way of envisioning our fate in a way that honours our shared humanity.

There are, of course, many ways to think of, and envision, our ideals, and it is true that we can articulate our visions, and urge political action on behalf of them, in language that makes no reference to our rights. It is not the case that, without rights-talk, we are automatically reduced to the *real politik* of costs, benefits, preferences, markets and sites of power and influence. There are other ways – alternatives to both rights and efficiency – to think about what we ought to be and what we ought to do. Nevertheless, rights are, and have been, one way of asserting claims about what ought to be and what we ought to do with respect to our states and our laws, on behalf of all humanity (Hartog, 1988). When we turn our backs on rights, we relinquish one way of insisting that moral judgement, moral choice and moral vision – and not just interests, preferences, votes, power and money – guide political and legal action. We turn our backs on a path – not the only path, but a path – for transforming universalistic utopian ideals into political realities.

Notes

1 See generally Dworkin (1978). A serious regard for rights, Dworkin argues, rests on 'the vague but powerful idea of human dignity, . . . [which] supposes that there are ways of treating a man that are inconsistent with recognizing him as a full member of the human community, and holds that such treatment is profoundly unjust' (p. 198). H.L.A. Hart and others have noted that Dworkin does not specify a sufficiently thick view of human nature to sustain a strong case for any particular set of rights, thus distinguishing him from classical liberal rights theorists such as J.S. Mill. See Hart (1983). Nevertheless, Dworkin's defence of the idea of rights itself rests directly on an appeal to a conception of human life, which he himself labels 'Kantian', and from which the basic rights to equal concern and respect are directly derived. For further examples of rights arguments that rely, to varying degrees, on specified accounts of human nature, see, for example, Tribe (1988); Grey (1980); and Richards (1979).
2 For an exchange between Dworkin and Posner on the relation of wealth and rights, see Posner (1983b) and Dworkin's reply (Dworkin, 1983, pp. 295–98).
3 *United States* v. *Emerson*, 46 F. Supp.2d 598, 610–11 (ND Tex. 1999).
4 Ibid., at 600.
5 Ibid., at 609–10.
6 For a sustained argument to this effect, see Kittay (1998).

References

Bentham, Jeremy (1791), *Anarchical Fallacies: Being an Examination of the Declaration of Rights Issued During the French Revolution*, reprinted in *The Works of Jeremy Bentham, Vol. II, Published under the Superintendence of his Executor, John Bowing*, Bristol: Thoemmes Press, 1995.

Berlin, Isaiah (1969), *Four Essays on Liberty*, New York: Oxford University Press.

Bork, Robert (1990), *The Tempting of America*, New York: Free Press.

Burke, Edmund (1790), *Reflections on the Revolution in France*, (1987), Buffalo, NY: Prometheus Books.

Colker, Ruth (1986), 'Anti-Subordination Above All: Sex, Race, and Equal Protection', *New York University Law Review*, **61**, p. 1003.

Dworkin, Ronald (1978), *Taking Rights Seriously*, Cambridge, Mass: Harvard University Press.

Dworkin, Ronald (1980a), 'Is Wealth a Value?', *Journal of Legal Studies*, **9**, p. 191.

Dworkin, Ronald (1980b), 'Why Efficiency?', *Hofstra Law Review*, **8**, p. 563.

Dworkin, Ronald (1983), 'Reply by Ronald Dworkin', in Marshall Cohen (ed.) (1984), *Ronald Dworkin and Contemporary Jurisprudence*, Totowa, N.J.: Rowman & Allanheld, pp. 295–98.

Dworkin, Ronald (1996), 'Why Must Speech be Free?', in *Freedom's Law*, Cambridge, Mass.: Harvard University Press, pp. 200–205.

Epstein, Richard (1984), 'Toward a Revitalization of the Contract Clause', *University of Chicago Law Review*, **51**, p. 703.

Epstein, Richard (1985), *Takings: Private Property and the Power of Eminent Domain*, Cambridge, Mass.: Harvard University Press.

Forbath, William (1999), 'Caste, Class, and Equal Citizenship', *Michigan Law Review*, **98**, p. 1.

Freeman, Alan David (1978), 'Legitimizing Racial Discrimination Through Antidiscrimination Law', *Minnesota Law Review*, **62**, pp. 1049, 1072.

Freeman, Alan D. (1988), 'Racism, Rights and the Quest for Equality of Opportunity: A Critical Legal Essay', *Harvard Civil Rights–Civil Liberties Law Review*, **23**, pp. 295, 331.

Gilligan, Carol (1982), *In a Different Voice*, Cambridge, Mass.: Harvard University Press.

Glendon, Mary A. (1991), *Rights Talk*, New York: Free Press.
Grey, Thomas C. (1980), 'Eros, Civilization and the Burger Court', *Law and Contemporary Problems*, **43**, p. 80.
Hart, H.L.A. (1983), 'Between Utility and Rights', in Marshall Cohen (ed.) (1984), *Ronald Dworkin and Contemporary Jurisprudence*, Totowa, N.J.: Rowman & Allanheld.
Hartog, Hendrik (1988), 'The Constitution and the Rights That Belong to Us All', *Journal of American History*, **74**, p. 1017.
Hobbes, Thomas (1651), *The Leviathan*, (1991), Richard Tuck (ed.), New York: Cambridge University Press.
Kairys, David (1998), *The Politics of Law: A Progressive Critique*, (3rd edn), New York: Basic Books.
Kennedy, Randall (1988), '*McClesky* v. *Kemp*: Race, Capital Punishment, and the Supreme Court', *Harvard Law Review*, **101**, pp. 1388, 1421–29.
Kittay, Eva F. (1998), *Love's Labor*, New York: Routledge.
MacKinnon, Catharine A. (1991), 'Reflections on Sex Equality Under Law', *Yale Law Journal*, **100**, p. 1281.
Michelman, Frank (1969), 'On Protecting the Poor Through the Fourteenth Amendment', *Harvard Law Review*, **83**, p. 7.
Posner, Richard A. (1983a), *The Economics of Justice*, (1981), Cambridge, Mass.: Harvard University Press.
Posner, Richard A. (1983b), 'Dworkin's Critique of Wealth Maximization', in Marshall Cohen (ed.) (1984), *Ronald Dworkin and Contemporary Jurisprudence*, Totowa, N.J.: Rowman & Allanheld, p. 238.
Richards, David (1979), 'Sexual Autonomy and the Constitutional Right to Privacy: A Case Study in Human Rights and the Unwritten Constitution', *Hastings Law Journal*, **30**, p. 957.
Richards, David (1986), 'Constitutional Privacy and Homosexual Love', *New York University Review of Law and Social Change*, **14**, p. 895.
Sandel, Michael J. (1989), 'Moral Argument and Liberal Toleration: Abortion and Homosexuality', *California Law Review*, **77**, pp. 521, 523–25.
Sandel, Michael J. (1996), *Democracy's Discontent: America in Search of a Public Philosophy*, Cambridge, Mass.: Belknap Press of Harvard University Press.
Shiffrin, Steven H. (1994), 'Racist Speech, Outsider Jurisprudence, and the Meaning of America', *Cornell Law Review*, **43**, pp. 83–86.
Siegel, Reva B. (1996), 'The Rule of Love? Wife Beating as Prerogative and Privacy', *Yale Law Journal*, **105**, p. 2117.
Sunstein, Cass and Holmes, Steve (1999), *The Cost of Rights*, New York: W.W. Norton.
Trakman, Leon (1997), 'Native Cultures in a Rights Empire Ending the Dominion', *Buffalo Law Review*, **45**, p. 189.
Tribe, Lawrence (1988), *American Constitutional Law*, (2nd edn), Mineola, N.Y.: Foundation Press.
Tushnet, Mark V. (1984), 'An Essay on Rights', *Texas Law Review*, **62**, pp. 1363, 1364.

Part I
The Liberal Rights Tradition

[1]

The Warren Court and the Concept of a Right

*David Luban**

The Warren Court is dead. None of its Justices remain on the bench—indeed, only Justice White survives—and the recent history of the Supreme Court has been in large part a history of repudiating controversial Warren Court doctrines. Public opinion likewise repudiates Warren-style judicial activism, and constitutional scholarship—which as recently as the mid-1980s consisted in considerable measure of theoretical defenses for Warren Court-inspired methods of interpreting the Bill of Rights—has grown increasingly skeptical of expansive interpretive strategies. It is quite possible that future constitutional historians will regard the Warren era as an aberration. The Warren Court, after all, was not just the most liberal Supreme Court in American history, but arguably the *only* liberal Supreme Court in American history.

Is there any reason, beyond a nostalgia that is by no means universally shared, to continue discussing the Warren Court? It seems that nearly everyone now agrees that judicial activism is pernicious and judicial restraint desirable. And everyone seems to believe that this opinion, if true, requires one to discard the Warren Court's jurisprudence. I will argue that these conclusions are mistaken, for the hackneyed contrast between activism and restraint misses the true significance of the Warren Court, the real reason that its jurisprudence merits continued discussion. That significance lies not in the Warren Court's transformation of the judicial role, but in its transformation of the concept of a legal right.

The problem with focusing on judicial role is this: "Judicial activism" and "judicial restraint" originated as obscure lawyers' terms for concepts that had a fairly precise meaning, or rather, a handful of fairly precise meanings. To Holmes's law partner and Brandeis's teacher James Bradley Thayer, who wrote the first major article on the subject, the doc-

---

* Frederick Haas Professor of Law and Philosophy, Georgetown University Law Center. B.A., University of Chicago, 1970; Ph.D., Yale University, 1974. This Article was originally delivered as a public lecture at the annual Bertram Morris Colloquium at the University of Colorado. I subsequently presented the paper to the philosophy department at the University of Maryland at Baltimore County, to legal theory workshops at George Washington University and the University of Maryland, and as a Phi Beta Kappa lecture at the State University of New York at Albany. I am grateful to my hosts at these institutions, to members of my audiences for their astute comments on the talk, and to Tim Brennan, Judith Lichtenberg, Douglas MacLean, Peter Quint, Jim Nickel, Mark Tushnet, David Wasserman, and Robin West for suggestions on an earlier draft. I am especially grateful to Jonathan Bennett, whose penetrating questions caused me to recast my argument in a way that avoids what I now regard as a major error, and to Akhil Amar for conversations about the exclusionary rule.

trine of restraint meant simply that judges should defer to legislatures in close constitutional cases. Judges should invalidate legislation only when it is not merely unconstitutional but *obviously* unconstitutional.[1] Holmes, Brandeis, and Frankfurter adopted the substance of Thayer's understanding.[2] To later jurists, such as Herbert Wechsler, judicial restraint meant refraining from constitutional judgments unless they can be grounded in neutral principle.[3] To Alexander Bickel, as perhaps to Brandeis and Frankfurter, restraint meant avoiding constitutional decisions that the country was not yet ready to deal with politically.[4] For all these jurists, judicial restraint was one of the cardinal virtues in a judge.[5]

This latter assessment changed with the Warren Court, the quintessentially "activist" Court. The Warren Court made the vigorous and aggressive defense of civil rights and liberties a principal judicial virtue; it was the only Court that ever seemed heroic. In the course of this transformation, the Warren Court became identified not with a theory of jurisprudence but with a group of controversial decisions. These began with the segregation cases, then the free-speech-for-Communists cases. There followed the "rights of criminals" decisions, which generated the pernicious myth that the courts habitually turn criminals loose on mere technicalities; then the school prayer decisions, which in the eyes of critics drove God from the schools; and the contraception decisions, which paved the way to the Burger Court's protection of abortion in *Roe v. Wade*.[6]

In short, the Warren Court's history reads like a compendium of the social issues that have divided liberals from conservatives for thirty years. This fact was skillfully exploited by politicians who made the demand for judicial restraint a political issue. Of course, the politicization of this issue goes back at least to Franklin D. Roosevelt's effort to pack the Supreme Court with "restrained" justices who would uphold New Deal legislation. Moreover, national debate about judicial activism has been virtually continuous since *Brown v. Board of Education*[7] was decided in 1954. But the issue seems to have entered national *electoral* politics for the first time in President Richard Nixon's 1972 re-election campaign. Nixon's advisors recommended that he use his power of judi-

---

[1] *See* James Bradley Thayer, *The Origin and Scope of the American Doctrine of Constitutional Law*, 7 HARV. L. REV. 129 (1893).

[2] *See* Wallace Mendelson, *The Influence of James B. Thayer upon the Work of Holmes, Brandeis, and Frankfurter*, 31 VAND. L. REV. 71 (1978).

[3] *See* Herbert Wechsler, *Toward Neutral Principles of Constitutional Law*, 73 HARV. L. REV. 1 (1959).

[4] *See* ALEXANDER BICKEL, THE LEAST DANGEROUS BRANCH 111–98 (2d ed. 1986).

[5] Yet I do not believe that a coherent argument exists on behalf of judicial restraint as developed by Thayer and his successors. *See* David Luban, *Justice Holmes and the Metaphysics of Judicial Restraint*, 44 DUKE L.J. 449, 456–61 (1994).

[6] 410 U.S. 113 (1973).

[7] 347 U.S. 483 (1954).

cial appointments to divide Southern from Northern Democrats. A memorandum to the President from Patrick Buchanan, then one of Nixon's chief political advisors, argued that nominating a "Southern Strict Constructionist will force Democratic Northern Liberals and major candidates to anger either the South with a veto vote or the blacks and the labor movement and the northern liberals."[8] Nixon put this strategy to effective use in the 1972 campaign.

The Warren Court's opponents won the rhetorical battle that ensued, for nowadays even liberal jurists shrink from the label "activist." As a result, "judicial activism" has become, in the hands of the politicians, little more than a euphemism for judicial protection and promotion of reverse discrimination, crime on the streets, atheism, and sexual permissiveness while "judicial restraint" has become a rallying cry for conservative opposition to these so-called policies. Any more precise juridical or philosophical meaning has been drained from the terms.

My own focus is quite different from these political issues. If, as Oliver Wendell Holmes wrote, great cases make bad law, it is likewise true that great political controversies make bad jurisprudence, and for much the same reason "great cases are called great," according to Holmes, "not by reason of their real importance in shaping the law of the future, but because of some accident of immediate overwhelming interest which appeals to the feelings and distorts the judgment."[9] In my view, the lasting achievement of the Warren Court lies neither in the legacy of decisions it left us (which have suffered and continue to suffer erosion at the hands of subsequent Courts), nor in its supposed expansion of the judicial role. It lies instead in a seemingly abstract issue of jurisprudence—the nature of a legal right. The Warren Court proceeded from a sophisticated understanding of what rights are, based on an analysis of how they must be secured. My aim is to explain and defend that understanding. If I am right, to abandon the Warren legacy is to misunderstand the very idea of legal rights.

This Article is by no means a survey of Warren Court jurisprudence. My aim is analytic, not synthetic. Instead of collecting cases to prove points, my method is to choose a small handful of decisions for philosophical elaboration—decisions that display what I take to be most characteristic of the Warren Court understanding of rights. Indeed, I focus largely on just two cases, *Mapp v. Ohio*[10] and *Griswold v. Connecticut*.[11] Even in those cases, I isolate a single strand of the argument, drawing out implications and assumptions that are implicit in the opinions them-

[8] Memorandum from Patrick Buchanan to President Richard Nixon, *quoted in* JONATHAN SCHELL, THE TIME OF ILLUSION 184 (1975).

[9] Northern Sec. Co. v. United States, 193 U.S. 197, 364 (1904) (Holmes, J., dissenting).

[10] 367 U.S. 643 (1961).

[11] 381 U.S. 479 (1965).

selves. I do not attempt to prove that the concept of rights I extract from these cases is representative of the Warren Court's jurisprudence in its full range. For one thing, there is a fallacy involved in speaking of the Warren Court as a unitary body—as, in Kenneth Shepsle's terminology, an "it" rather than a "they."[12] The Warren Court justices held different theories, and the opinions I will be discussing have different authors. Some justices would undoubtedly have disagreed with the conception of rights I am defending here, and they too wrote Warren Court opinions. My justification for speaking of the Warren Court's theory of rights is that despite the tensions on that Court and its decisions that do not fit the pattern I describe, I believe that there is nevertheless a distinctive theory of legal rights that makes sense of many of the Warren Court's most characteristic cases. Here, the aim is philosophical rather than historical: it is to extract, elaborate, and defend a conception of legal rights that one can fairly associate with the Warren Court. My reason for elaborating it, however, is not that I associate it with the Warren Court. My reason for elaborating it is that I believe it to be true.[13]

Interpreters of the Warren Court focus on different cases as paradigms of what the Court was about. For those who admire the Warren Court as a champion of human rights, *Brown v. Board of Education*[14] is the paradigm decision. For John Hart Ely, who understands the work of the Warren Court as the policing of the democratic process against its infirmities, the reapportionment cases concentrate the essence of the Court's activities.[15] For critics of the Court's invention of new rights, such as Robert Bork, Justice Douglas's strange rhetoric in *Griswold v. Connecticut* of "penumbral" rights "emanating" from constitutional provisions and then fusing to create new constitutional rights reveals the essential dishonesty of judicial activism.[16] In the final section of this Article, I too will concentrate on *Griswold*, the paradigm right-to-privacy case, but I begin my argument with two of the Warren Court's most controversial criminal procedure cases, *Mapp* and *Miranda v. Arizona*.[17]

---

[12] *See* Kenneth A. Shepsle, *Congress Is a "They," Not an "It": Legislative Intent as Oxymoron*, 12 INT'L. REV. L. & ECON. 239 (1992).

[13] It should be obvious from these remarks that I disagree with scholars who reject the entire concept of rights, notably writers in the Critical Legal Studies movement. In my view, to call something a right is to assert that it is a value of such great importance that it deserves especially stringent legal protection. If critics mean something different by the notion of rights, they will have to find some other word to denote a value of such great importance that it deserves rigorous legal protection. Otherwise, they must argue that *no* values are that important. The first alternative is a pointless semantic substitution; the second is a deeply implausible political belief. *See* DAVID LUBAN, LEGAL MODERNISM 76–78 (1994).

[14] 347 U.S. 483 (1954).

[15] *See* JOHN HART ELY, DEMOCRACY AND DISTRUST 120–24 (1980). The reapportionment cases are *Baker v. Carr*, 369 U.S. 186 (1962), and *Reynolds v. Sims*, 377 U.S. 533 (1964).

[16] *See* ROBERT H. BORK, THE TEMPTING OF AMERICA 95–100 (1990).

[17] 384 U.S. 436 (1966).

Mapp imposed the exclusionary rule on states,[18] while *Miranda* required arresting officers to inform suspects of their constitutional right to remain silent, and to have an attorney. In both cases, the Court devised novel remedies to prevent police from violating defendants' rights. As I now argue, the Warren Court approached the concept of a right by rethinking the nature of a remedy.

I.

The literature on rights is enormous, and philosophers have offered various definitions of a right. On all accounts, however, a right is a value of particular importance, and the protection of rights is a central aim of public institutions. Indeed, to acknowledge a value as a right is just to assert that it warrants especially stringent protection. Our rights are those background expectations we can count on, and thus, they must be not merely *protected* but *secured*. For this reason, the question of what it takes to secure rights is a central question facing any political and legal theory that includes the concept of rights in its vocabulary. On one common understanding of the question, rights are protected *reactively*: an individual whose rights have been infringed may seek satisfaction of some sort, either compensation or punishment of the infringer, after the violation has occurred.

Reactive remedies are defined by two characteristics. First, they are imposed after the wrongdoing they remedy. Second, they are imposed directly against the wrongdoer, in the sense that the wrongdoer must pay compensation, suffer punishment, or both. Let us call these two characteristics the "Ex Post Feature" and the "Directness Feature" of the remedy.

We may call a remedy that lacks the Ex Post Feature an "ex ante remedy," while one that lacks the Directness Feature is an "indirect" remedy. It is clear that a remedy can be ex ante without being indirect. For instance, an injunction imposing a prior restraint on dangerous conduct is ex ante but direct. Less obviously, a remedy may be indirect without being ex ante. For example, proposed statutes permitting suits against gun manufacturers and vendors whose wares have been used in wrongdoings are not ex ante, since the lawsuits will be filed in response to, rather than in anticipation of, gun-related injuries. Yet they are indirect, inasmuch as they aim to control harmful conduct by gun-users by sanctioning parties other than the gun-users themselves. Finally, some remedies are both indirect and ex ante. A court order to a legislature to budget funds for a new prison in order to remedy Eighth Amendment violations is ex ante, because it aims to prevent future violations rather than compensating or punishing past ones. At the same time, it is indirect, because

[18] *See* 367 U.S. at 659.

it does not directly regulate the conduct of individuals such as prison administrators and guards who commit the violations.[19]

I begin my argument by observing that *Miranda* and *Mapp* illustrate (respectively) the ex ante and indirect remedial strategies. *Miranda* requires a novel set of police behaviors, *Miranda* warnings, prior to questioning a criminal suspect, in order to forestall constitutional violations in that questioning. Consequently, *Miranda* warnings amount to an ex ante remedy for such violations. By requiring *Miranda* warnings, the possibility of coerced confessions, the third degree, and grueling interrogations without an attorney is reduced *in advance.* Without such advance protection, the victim of police overreaching is given over to the tender mercies of the tort system or the police disciplinary system for redress.

By contrast, *Mapp*'s exclusionary rule provides an indirect remedy for Fourth Amendment violations in that it imposes neither punishment nor the requirement of compensation from police, but rather aims to control police conduct by indirectly changing their structure of incentives. (The remedy is not ex ante, of course, because the suppression of evidence occurs after the violation.) Prior to *Mapp*, an individual's right to be free from illegal searches by police was protected only reactively. The victim of an illegal search could seek monetary damages or internal police disciplinary action; however, the illegally seized evidence could still be used at trial. To those who share the reactive conception of rights protection, the exclusionary rule seems irrational. In Cardozo's memorable objection to the rule, "The criminal is to go free because the constable has blundered."[20] In the critics' view, punishing the violation by undermining the police's purpose in conducting an illegal search confuses issues that should be held distinct. Sue the constable, but don't coddle the crook.

Justice Clark's draft opinion in *Mapp* emphasized the inefficacy of reactive remedies in this context as "worthless and futile."[21] "How can we expect to defend 'the indefeasible right of personal security' by telling him who suffers its invasion to seek damages for 'the breaking of doors?'" Clark asked, adding that "aroused public opinion and internal police discipline" are "equally without the deterrent value."[22] The exclu-

---

[19] Of course, remedies can have both ex ante and ex post aspects. An ex post remedy such as punishment aims, at least partly, at special or general deterrence. Indeed, insofar as it aims at general deterrence, it also combines direct and indirect strategies: it directly punishes one person, and thereby indirectly deters others. Thus, the distinctions between ex ante and ex post remedies, and direct and indirect remedies, are matters of degree rather than kind. Even when both aspects of the distinctions are present, however, one or the other usually predominates.

[20] People v. Defore, 150 N.E. 585, 587 (N.Y. 1926).

[21] *Quoted in* BERNARD SCHWARTZ, SUPER CHIEF: EARL WARREN AND HIS SUPREME COURT—A JUDICIAL BIOGRAPHY 394 (1983).

[22] *Id.*

sionary rule, by contrast, protects rights indirectly, not reactively, by removing the incentive for the unlawful search.

In my view, the most important feature of the Warren Court's approach to rights is its appreciation that standard, reactive remedies for rights violations are often inadequate (for reasons that I discuss below). For that reason, the Court turned again and again to what I shall term *activist* remedies, a generic term including both ex ante and indirect remedies.

It should be clear that I am using the term "activist" in this context quite deliberately. One of my principal contentions in this Article is that the Warren Court's judicial activism should best be understood as a heightened predilection for ex ante and indirect remedies in preference to reactive remedies. It is for this reason that I earlier described the contrast between judicial activism and judicial restraint as hackneyed: the more significant contrast, I believe, is not between activism and restraint but between activism and reactivism. The activism/restraint schema distinguishes between interpretive strategies; the question it implies is, "Should judges appeal to their own moral values in interpreting general constitutional language, or rest content with inferences from framers' intent, American tradition, plain language and structure, or other impersonally available legal sources?" Alternatively, the activism/restraint schema may distinguish between loosely and tightly constrained conceptions of the judicial role. On this reading the implicit question is not interpretive but moral: "Should judges ever depart from merely interpreting the law in order to achieve justice or advance national well-being?" By contrast, the activism/reactivism schema distinguishes remedial strategies, and its implicit question is neither interpretive nor moral. It asks, "Should judges secure rights through ex ante and indirect remedies or only through reactive remedies centered on ex post punishment of, or compensation by, rights violators?"

It may seem that defining activism in terms of remedial strategies is simply an exercise in conclusory labeling that illicitly ducks the interpretive and moral questions in the preceding paragraph. But the identification of activism with a set of remedial strategies does not duck the interpretive and moral questions—it answers them, and that is why it is more than a play on words. The pursuit of activist remedial strategies requires activist rather than restrained interpretive strategies, as well as an activist rather than restrained conception of the judicial role. Let us see why.

Unlike reactive remedies, both ex ante and indirect remedies aim to secure rights by granting additional rights (for example, to *Miranda* warnings, or to exclude evidence) that at first glance appear to go beyond the scope of the violation they aim to cure. As we shall see in greater detail below, this difference is why a predilection for activist remedies requires activist interpretive strategies, at least to the extent that these lead judges to find unanticipated rights implicit in legal entitlements that make no mention of them. Indeed, it is precisely this feature of activist remedies that generates the accusation that the Warren Court engaged in the wholesale manufacture of rights without foundation in law.

Moreover, the use of indirect remedies, as opposed to the rote imposition of punishment or compensation, requires greater judicial ingenuity, inventiveness, and improvisation in order to rearrange incentives to discourage rights violations. The judge must determine, based on the particularities of the issue, which additional rights should be recognized in order most effectively to nip threatened primary rights violations in the bud. It is this heightened engagement of judicial discretion in granting ex ante and indirect remedial rights that leads to the suspicion of a judiciary that has become a law unto itself, answerable only to judicial conscience and unchained from doctrinal moorings. Hence comes the accusation of an inflated conception of the judicial role on the part of activist judges.

Shortly, I will argue that this accusation, like the accusation that the Warren Court engaged in promiscuous rights manufacture, merely begs the question of how broad the judicial role and the roster of rights are. However, even before going into that argument, let me indicate in a preliminary way why activist protections of rights have at least as good intuitive credentials as their more familiar reactive counterparts.

This point may be seen most easily by reflecting on *Mapp*. The conventional wisdom of law has always held that the purpose of a remedy is to make the victim whole—to restore, insofar as it is possible to do so, the state of affairs that would have obtained had the victim's rights not been violated. Plainly, if there had been no illegal search, the police would not have obtained the evidence—that, at any rate, is what a court must presume. This basic fact shows that the exclusionary rule, which eliminates the improperly obtained evidence, is the genuine make-whole remedy. Punishing the transgressor or obtaining the payment of damages is merely a second- or third-best surrogate. It is equally clear that if an ex ante remedy succeeds, the infringement of rights will not take place, and that this too is the genuine make-whole remedy. Reactive remedies, by contrast, provide only surrogates for making the victim whole. In the case of punishment, reactive remedies give the victim the satisfaction of knowing that her pain has been met by the pain inflicted on her injurer. In the case of compensation, reactive remedies award the victim a monetary substitute for a loss that may not be monetizable. Obviously, in some instances reactive remedies are the best we can do. However, the burden is plainly on the reactivist to show why we should settle for surrogate make-whole remedies when we can have the real thing. The activist's challenge may be stated in the simplest of slogans: "Accept no substitutes!"

Akhil Amar has objected that this argument proves far too much.[23] It proves, for example, that if the government confiscates a ton of marijuana as the result of an illegal search, it would have to make the defendant whole by returning the marijuana. If the government recovers stolen property in an illegal search, it must return the property to the thief, not the victim. And, if the police cut legal corners to find a kidnap victim, must they really turn around, cover their eyes, and count to twenty to allow the kidnapper to enjoy the status quo ante? Plainly not. Why adopt a remedy that benefits only wrongdoers—a rule such as the exclusionary rule or the hypothetical rule of returning the marijuana—merely because it is the only way to restore whatever status quo would have existed had the constitutional right not been infringed?

But I deny that the exclusionary rule is really indistinguishable from the rule of marijuana return. Giving a ton of marijuana to marijuana distributors is itself a wrongful and, indeed, a criminal act. Abetting a theft or kidnapping are also wrongful and criminal acts, whereas excluding improperly seized evidence is not. Even in cases where excluding marijuana or stolen goods from evidence leads to acquittal, the distributor and thief do not and should not get the contraband back. This is because even if the police have no right to the evidence, the distributor and thief have no right to the marijuana or stolen goods, so there is no reason to make them whole in the sense of restoring them to the unlawful status quo ante.

Amar's parallel argument in the exclusionary rule case would have to proceed as follows: the criminal has no right to evade conviction for his crime, so there is no reason to make him whole in the sense of restoring him to the unlawful status quo ante in which he escapes criminal liability. Thus, there is no reason for the exclusionary rule, which would restore him to an unlawful status quo ante by helping him evade conviction. The analogy breaks down, however, because the status quo ante in which the guilty defendant gets away with his crime is not unlawful. The crime itself is unlawful, but there is no additional crime in getting away with it. If a factually guilty defendant lawfully talks the prosecutor out of indicting him, or the jury out of convicting him, he has not committed a further crime.

The difference between the examples is this: No one has a right to retain illegal drugs, stolen goods, or kidnapped people, but we each have a right to retain our presumptive not-guilty status until the state convicts us through lawful processes. If the state resorts to unlawful processes by seizing evidence improperly, the make-whole remedy is to remove the advantage it achieved by breaking the law. That is what the exclusionary rule aims to do.

---

[23] *See* Akhil Reed Amar, *Fourth Amendment First Principles*, 107 HARV. L. REV. 757, 795 (1994).

This argument provides a backward-looking defense of the exclusionary rule, by justifying the rule as the appropriate way to right a wrong, to make an injured person whole. However, from the Warren Court's point of view, an equally important (or perhaps more important) justification of activism is forward-looking. Well-crafted activist protections of rights create ripple effects leading to further and better protections: they treat the disease, not merely relieve its symptoms. As Judge Richard Neely observed, before the Warren Court criminal procedure cases, police departments (particularly in rural areas) often consisted of poorly trained, poorly screened goons. In Neely's words:

> In the early 1960s, the average criminal defendant was treated like a piece of meat on its way to dressing and processing . . . .
>
> Men were routinely picked up off the street without a warrant, brought down to the police station, left to set on hard benches without access to water, food, or sometimes even a clean restroom for hours at a time before "questioning," which frequently involved humiliating insults and a good bit of slapping around. In many cases, the police had nothing more to direct them to their particular suspect than a prior criminal record, the "suspicious behavior" of the arrested person, or personal animosity. The entire "questioning" process went on without any regard for the person's need to be at his job, his school, his wife's side in the hospital, or anywhere else. The convenience of the authorities organized the lives of those without power who came to the authorities' attention. And who was available to give redress? The political process, where most aspirants for office run on a "crack down on crime" platform? The local judge, who would need to dress down the local sheriff or police chief in the morning before they all went out for lunch together? The executive authority, whose very henchmen all these rights violators were? Not very likely.[24]

After the criminal procedure cases, municipalities suddenly discovered that the badly trained officers in the police departments of the mid-1960s were bringing cases that would be thrown out of court. The prospect of criminals walking out the door because "the constable had blundered" by jamming his nightstick into the suspect's kidneys brought about considerable political problems for prosecutors and police chiefs. As Neely puts it, "Oddly enough, jury damage suits, constitutional mandates, the elective political process, and general notions about unmerited suffering and consideration for one's fellowman could not clean up the

[24] RICHARD NEELY, HOW COURTS GOVERN AMERICA 154–55 (1981).

system, but the fear of unemployment managed very neatly."[25] There is little doubt that the investigative abuses Neely describes in the passage quoted above have become less frequent, and that police departments have become better trained, better educated, more professional organizations that no longer investigate crimes merely by rounding up the usual suspects. This, in turn, means that rights are better secured *before*, rather than after, their violation.

Let us generalize from this example. The Warren Court insisted that to enjoy meaningful protection, and thus to count as rights at all, primary constitutional rights must often be hedged with derivative, prophylactic rights designed to forestall infringements before they happen. This is an activist approach to rights protection. The reactive approach, by contrast, does not find derivative rights implicit in the constitutional guarantee of rights; it rests content with compensating or punishing infringements of primary rights after they have occurred.

Neely may be overly optimistic about how clean the system has become. In fact, some observers believe that the "due process revolution" has only forced police to become more subtle in their constitutional violations.[26] It is also obvious, in the wake of the 1997 torture of Abner Louima by New York City police, the Rodney King beating, and the Los Angeles riots that resulted from it—as well as thousands of less well-publicized instances of police brutality—that police departments still include a substantial number of officers who have nothing but contempt for procedural niceties and even for basic human rights. Far from undercutting Neely's observations about the efficacy of the Warren Court's activist approach in criminal procedure cases, however, contemporary police brutality cases demonstrate only that the Warren Court's successors declined to take its approach far enough, by extending it from the context of investigation to those of arrest and ordinary patrolling. In *Rizzo v. Goode*,[27] victims of police brutality sought an injunction forcing the Philadelphia Police Department to set up internal procedures to deal with complaints of brutality. Justice Rehnquist, writing for the Court,

[25] *Id.* at 157–58.

[26] For example, David Wasserman writes,

> [W]e have observed the double-edged character of appellate review, in exposing error but refining its concealment. The due process revolution . . . has led to more professional and restrained police conduct but also encouraged police perjury, as in the notorious "dropsy" cases; it has reduced the frequency of prosecutorial misconduct, but it also increased its subtlety. These examples suggest the dialectic of appellate review: trial-level actors are subjected to stricter or more searching review; they learn, sometimes with appellate coaching, how to insulate their conduct from this heightened scrutiny . . . .

DAVID T. WASSERMAN, A SWORD FOR THE CONVICTED: REPRESENTING INDIGENT DEFENDANTS ON APPEAL 245 (1990).

[27] 423 U.S. 362 (1976).

held that the plaintiffs did not have a sufficient personal stake in the outcome of the case to satisfy the case or controversy requirement.[28] Justice Rehnquist, evidently, held to a purely reactive conception of legal rights, and the Court declined to impose an ex ante remedy by requiring the Philadelphia police to take precautions against future brutality. Even more to the point of the Rodney King case was *City of Los Angeles v. Lyons*.[29] Adolph Lyons, a twenty-four-year-old black man, was initially stopped by Los Angeles police officers because of a burned-out tail light on his car. Thereafter, he was searched, beaten on the head, and choked to unconsciousness.[30] In the subsequent legal action, Lyons requested not only damages, a reactive remedy, but also an injunction forbidding the police from using chokeholds in the future against suspects who are not threatening violence, an ex ante remedy. The Court agreed that Lyons could sue for damages, but denied him standing in seeking an injunction.[31] Had the Court adopted an ex ante rather than a reactive conception of rights protection, both these cases might have been decided differently, with practical consequences for the prevention of police brutality about which one can only speculate.[32]

II.

Not every rights violation requires additional rights fashioned to forestall similar violations in the future. In many cases reactive remedies will suffice. Activist protection is required principally when the rights violation is a part of an institutionalized pattern of violations. Let me introduce a concept from Henry Shue's analysis of rights—the concept of a "standard threat."[33] The ordinary working of institutions often creates typical, persistent, and chronic threats to our rights. The example of a poorly trained and poorly disciplined police force illustrates this point, as does the example of Jim Crow institutions. When poorly trained police brutally interrogate a suspect, or when segregationist institutions violate the rights of blacks, these are clearly not isolated incidents. They are not the handiwork of a single rogue or maverick official. They entail the pre-

---

[28] *See id.* at 371–77.

[29] 461 U.S. 95 (1983).

[30] *See id.* at 98.

[31] *See id.* at 96.

[32] If citizens confronted by police brutality could obtain injunctions requiring the police to forego abusive or dangerous practices like the chokehold, it is quite possible that those practices might be halted much more quickly than they are now; lives would very likely be saved. Of course, it is also possible that judges would deny the injunctions in all but the most egregious cases and that the police might take denials as a green light to engage in even more brutality. Judicial denials of injunctions might also evolve into liability-screening legal doctrines. Activist judges need a healthy respect for the law of unintended consequences.

[33] *See* HENRY SHUE, BASIC RIGHTS: SUBSISTENCE, AFFLUENCE, AND U.S. FOREIGN POLICY 29–34 (1980).

dictable effect of an institutional cause—a standard threat. In my view, it is principally in cases of standard threats that we have a derivative constitutional right to have the threat dissolved.

We have a right to activist protection only against standard threats, because the world produces too many non-standard threats to protect against them all. To anticipate and guard against all these would require an omnipresent, omnipotent, omni-intrusive, and very expensive government that abandoned all its activities except one: anticipating improbable rights-threatening scenarios that must be warded off. It makes more sense, I think, to leave the unusual rights violations to a purely reactive remedy system. Only the standard threats need to be guarded against in advance. Thus, both activist and reactive rights protections have a proper place in a system of rights.

It is important to see that the two strategies differ markedly in their implications about what our rights are. The activist strategy insists that each primary constitutional right implicitly includes a protective belt, or buffer zone (to use Robert Bork's term),[34] of derivative rights to have standard threats to the primary right curtailed. (In *Griswold*, Justice Douglas uses the term "peripheral rights" to describe the rights lying in the buffer zone.)[35] The reactive strategy, by contrast, simply denies that primary rights entail additional, secondary rights such as the right to *Miranda* warnings or the right to exclude illegally seized evidence. By denying additional rights, it leaves only the right to ex post satisfaction—punishment or compensation—from the rights violator. Thus, an activist strategy of rights protection will recognize more rights than a reactive strategy.

It should now be clear why it begs the question to accuse judges who employ activist strategies of fabricating rights. Against this accusation, we must insist that, as a point of general jurisprudence, a stance favoring activist remedies to standard threats is essential to ensuring that rights are not mere words on paper. We should infer from this that implicit in any legal right are the derivative, prophylactic rights required to protect it. Finally, we may conclude that anyone who denies the bona fides of these derivative rights has simply misinterpreted the concept of a right.[36]

---

[34] *See* BORK, *supra* note 16, at 97.

[35] 381 U.S. 479, 483 (1965).

[36] The idea that the choice of remedial strategies is not merely a contingent afterthought in a theory of rights, but rather that remedies specify both the content and the meaning of rights, is developed and defended in Jules L. Coleman & Jody Kraus, *Rethinking the Theory of Legal Rights*, 95 YALE L.J. 1335, 1342 (1986). Coleman and Kraus follow the Calabresi-Melamed classification scheme for remedial strategies, distinguishing liability rules, property rules, and inalienability rules. *See* Guido Calabresi & Douglas Melamed, *Property Rules, Liability Rules, and Inalienability: One View of the Cathedral*, 85 HARV. L. REV. 1089, 1105–15 (1972). This classification scheme does not map neatly onto the reactive/ex ante/indirect scheme developed here, although a liability rule, which protects rights by permitting a party to obtain compensation from the right-infringer, is plainly a reactive remedy. Coleman and Kraus recognize one of the central features that I

Opponents of activism will deny the premise that rights by their nature demand prophylactic protection from potential infringements. That, they suggest, amounts to a presumption that officials will violate the Constitution if ever given the chance. Instead, reactivists insist, we should presume—pending decisive evidence to the contrary—that officials will respect constitutional rights. To think that every constitutional right also includes the right to have officials deterred from violating it is simply silly.

This difference in perspective highlights an important feature of the activist theory of rights. The theory sometimes requires the restructuring and reform of institutions, frequently governmental institutions, that pose standard threats to constitutional rights.[37] But that entails a willingness to entertain suspicions about social institutions and about government. One must be willing to scrutinize powerful institutions in order to see if a rights violation was merely an isolated incident or, on the contrary, the consequence of the institution's standard operating procedure. Thus, built into the activist outlook is an anti-authoritarian tilt coupled with a penchant for entertaining social and structural explanations of rights violations. Reactivists, by contrast, localize the analysis of responsibility to the single incident that triggered the case. They implicitly attribute rights violations to the misconduct of maverick officials rather than to the sociological structure of the whole system. Similarly, reactivists typically insist as a point of method on granting public authority the benefit of the doubt.[38] Reactivists self-consciously begin with the presumption that public authority is in the main rightly exercised. Thus, advocates of the activist theory typically adopt a skeptical stance toward authority—"Question Authority," in the words of the bumper sticker. Reactivists

attribute to the Warren Court's jurisprudence: "The very idea of a 'liability rule entitlement,' that is, of a right secured by a liability rule, is inconceivable." Coleman & Kraus, *supra*, at 1339. If one adds the idea that a constitutional right is to be not merely protected but secured, then this point implies that the Warren Court's is the only conceivable notion of constitutional rights.

[37] My distinction between activist and reactive strategies of rights protection is related to Owen Fiss's distinction between structural reform litigation and dispute-resolving litigation. *See* Owen Fiss, *Two Models of Adjudication*, *in* How Does the Constitution Secure Rights? 36 (Robert A. Goldwin & William A. Schambra eds., 1985); Owen Fiss, *The Social and Political Foundations of Adjudication*, 6 Law & Hum. Behav. 121 (1982); Owen Fiss, *Foreword: The Forms of Justice*, 93 Harv. L. Rev. 1 (1979). Indeed, my argument draws inspiration from Fiss's analysis of structural reform litigation.

[38] To take one well-known example, then-Judge Warren Burger wrote in *Bush v. United States*, 375 F.2d 602, 604 (D.C. Cir. 1967): "[I]t would be a dismal reflection on society to say that when the guardians of its security are called to testify in court under oath, their testimony must be viewed with suspicion." On such reasoning, a New York court rejected a proposal offered jointly by the defense and the New York County District Attorney that when the police alleged that a defendant had "dropped" a packet of drugs, the burden of proof that the evidence is admissible should shift to the state. *See* People v. Berrios, 270 N.E.2d 709 (1971). Yet the "dropsy" cases in which police aiming to evade search and seizure requirements falsely testified that drugs had been abandoned were frequent and notorious—so frequent and notorious that the District Attorney was willing to stipulate to the gravity of the problem.

typically adopt a deferential stance—"Honor Authority," as the counter-sticker has it.

It is, I believe, this double tendency of the Warren Court's activist account of rights—toward anti-authoritarianism and toward structural explanations—that attracts the wrath of conservative theorists, just as the particular results the Court achieved attract the wrath of conservative politicians. If my argument is correct, however, these features of Warren Court jurisprudence should be accepted as implications of a superior understanding of the nature of rights, rather than dismissed as a mere left-wing crotchet.

Of course, many critics of Warren-style activism base their objections on institutional rather than jurisprudential grounds. They argue along the following lines: "Suppose you are correct that primary rights implicitly include derivative rights to have violations of the primary rights forestalled, including derivative rights to institutional reform. Even if that belief is true—indeed, *especially* if it is true—courts are unsuited to determine which derivative rights and institutional reforms will best protect primary rights. That is a quintessentially legislative task, and it is best left to Congress, to state and local governments, or to the institutions of civil society and the market."

The primary point of this objection is that creative social engineering is hardly the judiciary's forte, because judges are neither elected nor trained to the task. It would be far better if other institutions took on the task of reform. This would reinforce the important point that upholding rights is the responsibility of all governmental institutions and ultimately of all citizens.

But if other institutions were spontaneous defenders of rights, we could dispense with courts altogether. It is a little much to expect the very same institutions of government, civil society, and market that *constitute* standard threats to eliminate them. Misbehaving police officials do not usually dismiss themselves, and racist zoning boards seldom resign in protest over their own policies. Other agencies get along by going along. In the context of reactive remedies, it's obvious why we need courts to protect rights. The only reason it is less obvious when the issue is choosing a regime of prophylactic rights or institutional reforms is that these look like policy initiatives. In one sense they are policy initiatives, but the whole point of my argument has been that they are also entailments of legal rights—and that makes them the proper business of courts. The institutional competence objection tacitly assumes a sharp distinction between policymaking and rights enforcement; but that assumption begs the very question at issue, namely whether in the face of standard threats rights-enforcement requires policymaking. Even if courts are normally at a comparative disadvantage to other institutions when it comes to policymaking, they are at a comparative advantage when the other institutions themselves are the problem.

III.

So far, I have distinguished two strategies of rights enforcement, the reactive and the activist. In addition, I have intimated that the Warren Court adopted an activist understanding of rights, and that this accounts for many of the so-called "new rights" established by the Warren Court. These include not only the rights of the accused, but others as well: restructuring of institutions to abolish race segregation "root and branch"; the judicial takeover of prisons and mental hospitals that abuse and torment their inmates; the rigid separation of church and state that the Warren Court believed essential to prevent believers from pressuring religious minorities to pray to an alien god—all of these may best be understood as activist protections of constitutional rights.

Finally, I have claimed that the activist approach to standard threats better corresponds with the concept of rights as values deserving especially stringent protection. In saying this, I have assumed that rights can be protected better ex ante or indirectly than reactively, but I have not yet argued that this is so. I do so now, initially presenting the argument in bare bones form and then filling in the gaps.

A familiar maxim of bureaucratic life has it that it's always easier to get forgiveness than permission.[39] I shall call this maxim the "Principle of the Fait Accompli." A fait accompli is harder to undo than to prevent. From this principle, weighty consequences flow. It's always easier to get forgiveness than permission. Therefore, it's always harder to get after-the-fact recompense for official misbehavior than before-the-fact protection from it. Accordingly, reactive rights protection is inherently less reliable than ex ante rights protection that nips the infringement in the bud or indirect rights protection that removes the incentive for rights violation. Q.E.D.

"Q.E.D." supposes that the Principle of the Fait Accompli is true. It is true, I believe, for three overlapping reasons.

First, permission can be denied privately or secretly, and therefore, denying officials permission to misbehave may be virtually costless to their superiors. But after-the-fact discipline of misbehaving officials generally occurs in response to a public complaint and, consequently, requires publicly visible action. That makes it disagreeable and costly. It creates scandal and bad publicity. It raises questions about why the misbehaving

[39] I first heard the principle put this way at a conference on nuclear weapons about fifteen years ago, when a military representative made an off-the-cuff remark that if he were in command of NATO forces during a Warsaw Pact assault, he would fire his nuclear weapons regardless of his orders. He explained, "It's always easier to get forgiveness than permission." The principle is an ancient one. Kant refers to the Roman slogan *fac et excusa*, roughly meaning "act first, make excuses later," as a time-honored maxim of political conventional wisdom. *See* IMMANUEL KANT, *Perpetual Peace*, *in* KANT'S POLITICAL WRITINGS 93, 120 (Hans Reiss ed. & H.B. Nisbet trans., Cambridge Univ. Press 2d ed. 1991) (1795).

official was not better supervised. It generates resentment on the part of the disciplined official, because he has been humiliated. It elicits sympathetic resentment from his co-workers. Moreover, if the official is valuable to the organization, it may be risky to chastize him in public. All of these factors explain why the temptation for a police chief to forgive and forget transgressions by overzealous officers—to stonewall, to deny everything, and to ride out the storm—is enormous. It's easier to get forgiveness than permission, because punishing rather than forgiving is costly, while denying permission is relatively costless.

Second, it is often hard to get reactive satisfaction for rights violations, because the violation has itself put the victim in a worse position to pursue a claim. If a mugger takes all of my money, I cannot call the police on a pay-phone. If a vindictive caseworker throws me off public assistance, I may not have the resources to pursue reinstatement. If I am convicted of a felony based on illegal police procedure, I will have to pursue satisfaction from the confines of a prison cell—knowing that in any future hearing it will be the word of police officers against the word of a convict.

Third, in line with the previous point, the rights violator may benefit from the violation so that he is less likely to be caught and punished for his wrongdoing. The elected official whose organization has fraudulently denied registration to minority voters can now use his power and patronage to squash the investigation and sanitize the files. Similarly, the police control the physical evidence of their own misbehavior. Moreover, they are now public heroes for cracking the hard cases, making it more politically inexpedient to discipline them than before the newspapers ballyhooed their crime-busting exploits.

Taken together, these three reasons allow us to generalize Justice Clark's skepticism about reactive remedies for rights violations. Because it is too likely that offending officials will get forgiveness, we cannot count on reactive remedies. That is why the Warren Court aimed to deny them permission.

It is important to understand what this argument does and does not say. The Principle of the Fait Accompli asserts that it is easier for officials to deny permission to wrongdoers than to redress their wrongs after the fact. The Principle does *not* assert that getting institutions to deny permission is easier than compelling them to offer redress. Just the opposite is most likely true. Compelling institutions to deny permission requires activist judicial strategies, such as institutional reform or incentive restructuring. Officials are more likely to resist these activist remedies than a series of lawsuits for compensation, which they find less disruptive of business-as-usual and which they know they will often win for the reasons I have just discussed. To put this distinction another way, the Principle of the Fait Accompli implies that an activist remedy is more likely to stop rights violations than a reactive remedy, but it does not imply that an effective activist remedy is easier to fashion. If anything, the Principle suggests that effective activist remedies will be harder to force on recalcitrant wrongdoers than reactive remedies, precisely because they pose bigger threats to the unconstitutional status quo. The Principle of the Fait Accompli explains both why activist remedies are harder for courts to devise and more effective when they succeed.

Now, the Principle of the Fait Accompli is a reasonably good rule of thumb, but I do not mean to claim more than that. I do not insist that reactive remedies are invariably worse than their activist counterparts, and in cases where an effective reactive remedy can be devised, a court may well prefer it to an activist one. The exclusionary rule is one example of an activist remedy that might bear reconsideration. In the article I cited earlier,[40] Professor Amar advocates abandoning the exclusionary rule in favor of tort remedies against police who unconstitutionally seize evidence. In line with my arguments for the Principle of the Fait Accompli, I remain frankly skeptical that juries will award tort damages against the police to convicted felons, even in the unlikely case that the felons are in a position to pursue them. But other reactive alternatives might work better.

For example, when a defendant raises a Fourth Amendment objection to evidence, police could be required to post a hefty bond consisting of projected compensatory and punitive damages for the alleged constitutional violation. If a court finds that the evidence was indeed improperly seized, the state would forfeit the bond, immediately and automatically. The award could go partly to the defendant, partly to his attorney in order to give attorneys an incentive for pursuing Fourth Amendment claims, and partly to a compensation fund for crime victims. A self-executing tort remedy like this could provide a deterrent equivalent to the exclusionary rule, without the justice-defeating effects that rightly disturb opponents of the exclusionary rule. Prosecutors casting a worried eye on their budgets would probably not even attempt to introduce improperly seized evidence, so that in practice the proposed remedy might turn out to be functionally equivalent to the exclusionary rule. If convicting the criminal is important, however, the state could bite the bullet by electing to introduce the evidence and forfeit the bond.

But don't hold your breath. No legislature will ever enact this alternative proposal, and no contemporary court will have the temerity to order it. For that reason, the activist exclusionary rule should remain intact as the best feasible alternative. Remember that the preference for activist remedies derives from an empirical, political judgment of what it takes to secure rights against standard threats. As I have argued, the proposition that rights must be secured by an effective remedy is an entailment of the very concept of a right, but what kind of remedy best secures our rights is

---

[40] *See* Amar, *supra* note 23.

not an issue for the armchair. It is a question about the art of the possible, not the art of the hypothetical. So long as we live in a second-best world (or worse), the bare fact that effective reactive alternatives to activist remedies may be imagined is beside the point, because imaginary remedies do not secure rights against standard threats that are all too real.

IV.

One way of understanding the activist account is that any right that is a pragmatically necessary condition for the protection of a constitutional right is itself a constitutional right. But this goes too far. As Richard Mohr has pointed out, such an argument seems to establish an enforceable constitutional right to "breakfast and kidney machines,"[41] since these are certainly necessary to the enjoyment of constitutional rights by those who need them. It sounds very implausible that the concept of rights protection implies legally enforceable welfare rights as a corollary to the Bill of Rights.

As a matter of fact, a powerful argument can be made on behalf of constitutionalized welfare rights. It *has* been made by Frank Michelman in a distinguished series of articles at the end of the Warren Court era.[42] In a philosophical rather than constitutional vein, Henry Shue has offered a powerful argument of this form in his theory of international human rights. Shue defines basic rights as those rights necessary to enjoy other rights and argues persuasively that welfare rights are just as basic in this sense as are rights to personal security.[43] In its broad outlines, I agree with this argument.

Yet, I also agree that courts and the Supreme Court would vastly overstep their authority if they tried to enforce constitutional welfare rights on an activist theory of rights protection. The theory I have been outlining insists on activist protections only against standard threats to our rights that can be attributed to badly structured institutions. Is poverty, the lack of the means to buy breakfasts and kidney machines, a standard threat in this sense? It is, provided that we can locate its origin in structurally flawed institutions. Doing so is not hard—on the contrary, it is easy. But that is itself the problem. For every one of our truly deep-seated social woes, such as poverty, social scientists offer us a welter of

---

[41] Richard D. Mohr, *Mr. Justice Douglas at Sodom: Gays and Privacy*, 18 COLUM. HUM. RTS. L. REV. 43, 59 (1986-87).

[42] *See* Frank I. Michelman, *In Pursuit of Constitutional Welfare Rights: One View of Rawls' Theory of Justice*, 121 U. PA. L. REV. 962 (1973); Frank I. Michelman, *The Supreme Court, 1968 Term—Foreword: On Protecting the Poor Through the Fourteenth Amendment*, 83 HARV. L. REV. 7 (1969); Frank I. Michelman, *Welfare Rights in a Constitutional Democracy*, 1979 WASH. U. L.Q. 659 (1979); Frank I. Michelman, *The Supreme Court and Litigation Access Fees: The Right to Protect One's Rights* (pts. 1 & 2), 1973 DUKE L.J. 1153, 1974 DUKE L.J. 527.

[43] *See* SHUE, *supra* note 33, at 13, 34.

competing structural and theoretical explanations. Is the cause of a social phenomenon located in concrete past events—*l'histoire eventuelle*—as many historical chroniclers suppose? Or in class structure, as Marx proposes? Or in technology, as Lynn White ingeniously argues when he attributes the rise of feudal society to the invention of the stirrup?[44] Or in geography, as Montesquieu and Fernand Braudel both suggest?[45] Or, on the contrary, is the whole notion of social causality pluralistic and indeterminate, as writers as diverse as Braudel, Alasdair MacIntyre, and Michel Foucault argue?[46] These questions do not admit of simple answers—or perhaps even complex answers. The more grandiose the effect, the more question-begging the theoretical apparatus needed to locate its cause with any degree of confidence.

This fact, I suggest, is a good or even decisive reason why a court of law ought to steer clear of venturing a diagnosis and cure of poverty—even if it is an activist court that is eager to seek out structural explanations of rights violations. Is the "standard threat" of poverty the product of capitalism, as Marxists believe? Perhaps so, but it seems wrongheaded to base a legal remedy on a theory with as many plausible competitors, not to mention alternative formulations, as Marx's. Even contemporary Marxist economists still disagree about whether and how the foundations of the theory can be put into defensible form.

We ought to range rights violations along a continuum. At one end will be those that involve quite small-scale and common sense structural explanations; on the other, those that require the grandest speculations to explain. The former include such items as illegal searches, explained by the way the police department is run. The latter include phenomena such as poverty and homelessness. Activist courts can venture confident judgments about which standard threats must be forestalled in the former cases, but must steer clear of the latter.[47]

---

[44] *See* LYNN WHITE, JR., MEDIEVAL TECHNOLOGY AND SOCIAL CHANGE 1–39 (1962).

[45] *See generally* 1 FERNAND BRAUDEL, THE MEDITERRANEAN AND THE MEDITERRANEAN WORLD IN THE AGE OF PHILIP II (Siân Reynolds trans., Harper Colophon Books 1972); 1 BARON DE MONTESQUIEU, THE SPIRIT OF THE LAWS, bks. 14–18, at 221–91 (Thomas Nugent trans., 1949) (tracing the nature of laws to the climate and soil of a nation).

[46] *See generally* FERNAND BRAUDEL, AFTERTHOUGHTS ON MATERIAL CIVILIZATION AND CAPITALISM (Patricia M. Ranum trans. 1979); ALASDAIR MACINTYRE, AFTER VIRTUE: A STUDY IN MORAL THEORY (2d ed. 1984); MICHEL FOUCAULT, THE ARCHAEOLOGY OF KNOWLEDGE (A. Smith trans., 1972).

[47] Of course, people can disagree about the causation even of very small-scale matters, such as illegal searches. Some people may blame the police for caring more about arrests than constitutional rights; others may blame unclarity in the Fourth Amendment jurisprudence, which makes it impossible for police officers to know what they can and cannot do. No doubt a court considering an interventionist remedy should first consider hearing evidence on contested factual issues. There remains a world of difference, however, between hearing evidence about why the police conduct illegal searches and why poverty persists. The former seems perfectly plausible, while the latter would be ludicrous. So the continuum is not a slippery slope that threatens to devour all remedial efforts.

In the same way, it seems simply bizarre to think that a court could order the abolition of the capitalist system, even if the judge was confident that Marx's explanation of poverty is right. So just as courts should attempt to ward off standard threats only when their institutional source can be diagnosed with some confidence, they should likewise do so only when the source is one that they can plausibly do something about. (This perhaps explains why so many Warren-era structural reform cases focused on restructuring governmental institutions: they are the easiest to reform, for federal courts simply have more leverage over these than over non-governmental structures.) Finally, it is essential to note that truly deep-seated social restructuring to safeguard the rights of some may require intrusions that violate the rights of others. That is scarcely an argument against sweeping social change, but it *is* an argument against justifying sweeping social change solely by reference to a theory of rights. The protection of rights may itself constrain courts in their reformative efforts, if these efforts are to be justified on the rights-based grounds that I am suggesting motivated the Warren Court.

V.

So far, I have tried to locate the Warren Court's penchant for finding so-called "new rights" in its preference for ex ante and indirect remedial strategies over reactive strategies as a means for securing rights against standard threats. This activist understanding implies that primary constitutional rights create derivative or secondary rights needed to forestall standard institutional threats to them. However, this is not the only way the Warren Court expanded rights, for it recognized rights that are not derivative in this sense from textual rights. Most notably, the Court in *Griswold v. Connecticut*[48] found a general constitutional right to privacy. In *Griswold*, the Court struck down a Connecticut statute forbidding the sale and use of contraceptives, holding that the statute violated a right to privacy implicit in the First, Third, Fourth, Fifth, and Ninth Amendments.[49] Yet none of these amendments mentions privacy, and none of them has anything to do with contraception, cohabitation, or copulation. As Justice Black remarked acidly in conference, "The right of association . . . is for me a right of assembly and the right of the husband and wife to assemble in bed is a new right of assembly for me."[50] The key passage in Justice Douglas's *Griswold* opinion is this:

> [S]pecific guarantees in the Bill of Rights have penumbras, formed by emanations from those guarantees that help give

[48] 381 U.S. 479 (1965).
[49] *Id.*
[50] SCHWARTZ, *supra* note 21, at 577.

> them life and substance . . . . Various guarantees create zones of privacy . . . . The present case . . . concerns a relationship lying within the zone of privacy created by several fundamental constitutional guarantees.[51]

This passage, with its penumbras and emanations, is a strange one, and I can attest from personal experience that it attracts a great deal of ridicule in law school faculty lounges. I shall attempt to explain this passage and then to defend it, connecting it in the process with our previous discussion of the activist protection of rights.

I begin with an important and incisive criticism of Douglas's emanation theory by Robert Bork:

> Douglas began by pointing out that "specific guarantees in the Bill of Rights have penumbras, formed by emanations from those guarantees that help give them life and substance." There is nothing exceptional about that thought, other than the language of penumbras and emanations. Courts often give protection to a constitutional freedom by creating a buffer zone, by prohibiting a government from doing something not in itself forbidden but likely to lead to an invasion of a right specified in the Constitution . . . .
>
> Douglas named the buffer zone or "penumbra" of the first amendment a protection of "privacy" . . . Douglas then asserted that other amendments create "zones of privacy." These were the first, third . . . , fourth . . . , and fifth . . . .
>
> None of the amendments cited, and none of their buffer or penumbral zones, covered the case before the Court . . . . Justice Douglas bypassed that seemingly insuperable difficulty by simply asserting that the various separate "zones of privacy" created by each separate provision of the Bill of Rights somehow created a general but wholly undefined "right of privacy" that is independent of and lies outside any right or "zone of privacy" to be found in the Constitution. Douglas did not explain how . . . the Court could . . . invent a general right of privacy that the Framers had, inexplicably, left out.[52]

Three points stand out in Judge Bork's analysis. First, he analyzes Douglas's "penumbral rights" as buffer zones "prohibiting a government from doing something not in itself forbidden but likely to lead to an inva-

---

[51] 381 U.S. at 484–85.
[52] Bork, *supra* note 16, at 97–98.

sion of a right specified in the Constitution."[53] That is, Bork understands penumbral rights to be *exactly* the derivative, secondary rights implied by an activist theory of rights protection. *Miranda* warnings and the exclusionary rule of *Mapp* are penumbral rights.

Second, Bork has no objection at all to the idea of penumbral rights; although he finds Dòuglas's terminology "exceptional," he accepts the theory itself. Bork is an activist.[54]

Third, however, is Bork's actual criticism of Douglas. What Bork objects to is not penumbral rights, nor even penumbral rights creating zones of privacy—though he doubts that privacy is the real issue. What he objects to is the idea that the specific privacy rights emanating from various amendments can somehow fuse and create a general, self-standing privacy right—one that exists on an equal footing with the explicit guarantees of the Bill of Rights and that is capable of independent growth and development. He puts the objection most clearly in an earlier version of the argument I have just quoted:

> Justice Douglas . . . performed a miracle of transubstantiation. He called the first amendment's penumbra a protection of "privacy" and then asserted that other amendments create "zones of privacy." . . . One more leap was required. Justice Douglas asserted that these various "zones of privacy" created an independent right of privacy, a right not lying within the penumbra of any specific amendment. He did not disclose, however, how a series of specified rights combined to create a new and unspecified right.[55]

Bork's analysis of *Griswold* has the advantage of great lucidity. On his view, the Warren Court reached the right of privacy in two steps. First, it inferred penumbral rights from explicit constitutional guarantees, using the method expounded in the first section of this paper. Second, it fused various penumbral rights of privacy into a kind of super-right of privacy. According to Bork's analysis, the first step is sound, but the second is not. That is why Justice Douglas's argument fails.

Bork never actually argues that the second step is unsound. To see more clearly why specific privacy rights cannot be fused into a general right of privacy, it will help to examine a similarly unsound argument from a wholly different area of law, the law of testimonial privileges. The common law recognized five chief privileges: the privilege against self-incrimination, the attorney-client privilege, the physician-patient privi-

---

[53] *Id.* at 97.

[54] Indeed, penumbral analysis carries no built-in bias toward left-of-center values. *See* Glenn H. Reynolds, *Penumbral Reasoning on the Right*, 140 U. PA. L. REV. 1333 (1992).

[55] Robert Bork, *Neutral Principles and Some First Amendment Problems*, 47 IND. L.J. 1, 8–9 (1971).

lege, the clergy-communicant privilege, and the spousal privilege. All of these except the right against self-incrimination are in reality double privileges. For example, the attorney-client privilege grants attorneys the right to refuse to testify about their clients, but it also grants clients the right to compel their attorneys not to testify about them even if the attorneys want to do so. The other three privileges are similarly two-sided.

The law governing these privileges is complex, and the privileges are riddled with exceptions and exceptions to these exceptions. None of that will be my concern in this Article. Here I am concerned only with the underlying motivation of these privileges and with whatever light it may cast on Justice Douglas's derivation of the right of privacy.

Let us leave the privilege against self-incrimination to one side and consider only the four interpersonal privileges. Each of these is justified most commonly by an instrumental argument having to do with chilling effects. Without the privileges, so the argument goes, communication between attorney and client, physician and patient, clergyman and communicant, and husband and wife would be chilled by the fear that the other party to the communication could be compelled to reveal guilty secrets in a court of law. The law grants the privileges because it officially recognizes the intrinsic importance of these four relationships and the goods realized by free communication within them.

Two points are particularly relevant to our present inquiry. First, when the privileges are justified by the standard instrumental argument about chilling effects, we see that each privilege is a penumbral right. Because I have a right to confer with legal counsel I need ex ante protection, via the attorney-client privilege, against the chilling of that right; and similarly with the other privileges.

Second, not only are these testimonial privileges, they are penumbral rights of privacy. The derivation of the five testimonial privileges thus corresponds to the first step in Douglas's derivation of the right of privacy, at least as Bork reconstructs it. This characterization allows us to comprehend the devastating power of Bork's criticism of the second step. For the corresponding second step in the law of testimonial privilege would drop the limitation to five specified relationships and discover something like *a general testimonial privilege* lurking in the penumbras. And what is a general testimonial privilege? The closest I can come is this: it is a general presumption that no one may be compelled to offer testimony about anyone else, combined with a general presumption that any litigant may prevent testimony against him. A general testimonial privilege would simply bring adjudication as we know it to an end. Thus, what we have here is a *reductio ad absurdum* of the two-step procedure for deriving self-standing rights from overlapping penumbral rights. If Bork is correct that this was Justice Douglas's procedure, we should accept his critique and acknowledge that the right of privacy was nothing more than the Warren Court's constitutional concoction.

It is my view that Bork's analysis of *Griswold* is, for all its lucidity, dead wrong. The key passage in Douglas's opinion—the theory of penumbras and emanations—does not employ the two-step procedure. Rather, it employs a very different procedure—one that is richer, more philosophical, far more ancient, *and much more radical* than the emanation and fusion of penumbral rights.

To see what is wrong with Bork's two-step reading of *Griswold*, we must begin not with the second, "fusion" step, but with the first. In the first step, specific zones of privacy are constructed on the periphery of primary constitutional rights in order to protect the primary rights in an activist manner. The primary rights Douglas names include rights contained in the First, Third, Fourth, and Fifth Amendments. For simplicity, or perhaps perversity, I will focus on the Third Amendment, which reads, "No Soldier shall, in time of peace be quartered in any house, without the consent of the Owner, nor in time of war, but in a manner to be prescribed by law."[56] The example is simple, because there has been only one domestic federal case ever on the Third Amendment and no Supreme Court case.[57] Thus, we don't have to distract ourselves with alternative construals of the Third Amendment.

The right of privacy, then, is supposed to be an indirect protection of our Third Amendment right to exclude soldiers from our homes. But how? A right to privacy does not exclude soldiers from our homes any more effectively than does the Third Amendment itself. In fact, the relationship makes sense only the other way around. Though the right to privacy does not help protect our Third Amendment rights, the Third Amendment can help protect the relevant right to privacy, namely privacy in our own home. A platoon of soldiers billeted in the basement would dampen not only freewheeling political talk around the dinner table, but also the noisy nocturnal activities that *Griswold* indirectly contemplates. By forbidding the government from installing infantry in the house, the Third Amendment wards off what might otherwise become a standard threat to privacy.

The Third Amendment thus belongs to the penumbra of the right of privacy, not the other way around. The Fourth Amendment right against illegal searches and the Fifth Amendment right against forced self-incrimination are similarly penumbral rights—activist protections of our privacy against standard governmental threats.

At this point, let us return to the key sentence in *Griswold*: "[S]pecific guarantees in the Bill of Rights have penumbras, formed by emanations from those guarantees that help give them life and substance."[58]

[56] U.S. Const. amend. III.

[57] *See* Engblom v. Carey, 677 F.2d 957 (2d Cir. 1982); *see also* Ramirez de Arellano v. Weinberger, 724 F.2d 143 (D.C. Cir. 1983).

[58] 381 U.S. at 484–85.

Bork reads the sentence as though it contains a comma after the second occurrence of "guarantees"; in that case, "those guarantees" refers to the specific guarantees in the Bill of Rights which have penumbras. On this reading, the sentence means:

> Specific guarantees in the Bill of Rights create penumbras that help give the specific guarantees life and substance.

This construal simply restates the activist theory of rights. But, as Richard Mohr has pointed out in a penetrating analysis of Douglas's penumbra metaphor, the wording and punctuation of Douglas's sentence point to a different reading. Let me repeat Douglas's sentence with appropriate emphasis: "[S]pecific guarantees in the Bill of Rights have penumbras, formed by emanations from *those guarantees that help give them life and substance*." Mohr argues that it should be understood as follows: "Specific guarantees have penumbras which are formed by emanations from those *general* guarantees that help give the specific guarantees life and substance. The right to privacy is just such a general guarantee."[59] Mohr goes on to explicate the "penumbra" metaphor:

> Penumbras—areas of half light and half shadow—are not caused by the areas of full light which they abut. Rather the light of penumbras and the light of areas of full illumination have *the same source* . . . . The specific explicit guarantees of the Constitution are areas of full illumination. The right to marital contraception and the like are areas of half light and half shadow, and what the state may bar or require is an area of total shadow. Privacy understood as a general right is the source of light producing *both* explicit *and* implicit protections of the Constitution . . . . [C]ritics . . . have misconstrued his careful metaphor.[60]

I think this is largely correct. In a moment, I will want to vary Mohr's reading of the metaphor, but before doing so let us notice a peculiar implication of these arguments. On Mohr's reading of *Griswold*, Douglas's key sentence refers to general constitutional guarantees that are nowhere mentioned in the Constitution, but whose existence must be posited to give the specific guarantees life and substance. We have seen how an activist theory of rights protection can derive nontextual rights as penumbras of the specific guarantees. However, the general guarantees we are

---

[59] Mohr, *supra* note 41, at 62.

[60] *Id.* at 62–63. For another attempt to puzzle out the metaphor, see Burr Henly, *"Penumbra": The Roots of a Legal Metaphor*, 15 HASTINGS CONST. L.Q. 81, 96–100 (1987). *See also* Steven L. Winter, *Transcendental Nonsense, Metaphoric Reasoning, and the Cognitive Stakes for Law*, 137 U. PA. L. REV. 1105, 1172 n.212 (1989).

speaking of now are not penumbral rights; rather, they are the light sources that create the penumbras.

The same result follows from my discussion of the Third Amendment, according to which the Third Amendment must be understood as a penumbra of the right of privacy, not the other way around.[61] That is, the Third Amendment belongs to the penumbra of a right that isn't in the document at all. Mohr, Douglas, and I seem to regard textual rights as mere corollaries of an invisible and unwritten right. What can this mean?

To answer this question, I want to venture a slightly different reading of the penumbra metaphor. Every shadow has a penumbra, but the word is most commonly used when we talk about one particular shadow—the shadow cast by the moon on the earth in a solar eclipse. If this is indeed the imagery Douglas meant to invoke, the general right of privacy is not just any source of illumination. It is the Sun itself. The penumbra of a solar eclipse has the important property that those people who are in it—unlike those in the umbra, the full shadow—can see the Sun.[62] The Third Amendment in its penumbral aspect provides a vantage point from which we can see the Sun—the right of privacy that is protected by forbidding the quartering of soldiers.

Figure 1

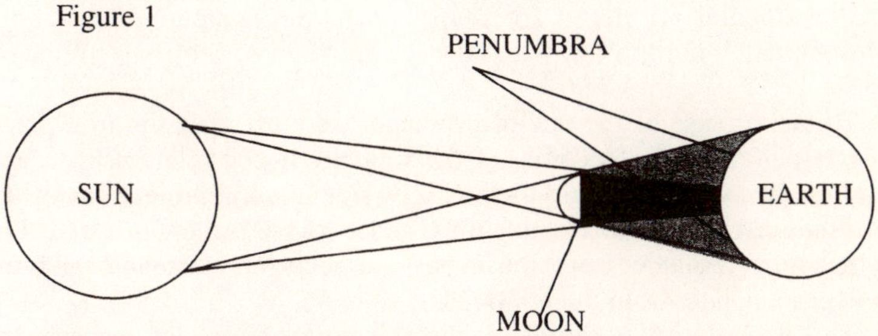

To see what this metaphoric talk of vantage points might mean, let us return for a moment to testimonial privileges, which are best thought of as activist or penumbral protections of our right to enjoy confidential relationships with our attorneys, our doctors, our clergymen, and our spouses. The natural question that occurs to us is "why just these?" The physician-patient privilege has been extended to psychologists and coun-

[61] Douglas's language in *Griswold* confirms this reading. He states, "The Third Amendment in its prohibition against the quartering of soldiers 'in any house' in time of peace without the consent of the owner is another facet of that privacy." 381 U.S. at 484. Douglas states that the Third Amendment is a facet of the right to privacy—the same right to privacy, as the context makes clear, that the First, Fourth, and Fifth Amendments also manifest. Douglas does *not* state that the right to privacy is a facet of the Third Amendment or a right on the periphery of the Third Amendment (the way that the right of association lies on the periphery of the First Amendment). *See* 381 U.S. at 483.

[62] *See infra*, Figure 1.

selors; the spousal privilege has been extended in three states to a parent-child privilege; and several jurisdictions have established accountant-client privileges. Why not extend the privilege to financial planners, insurance salesmen, who often receive sensitive financial information from their customers, grandparents, unmarried lovers, or best friends? What principle limits the privilege to certain people and relationships?[63]

To answer these and similar questions, one needs some sense of what makes the four original relationships especially important. I suggest that these four relationships correspond to four fundamental aspects of human social personality. I am, firstly, a physical body subject to all the infirmities and corruptions of the flesh; hence, the right to speak confidentially with my doctors. Secondly, I am a social and loving being who may find a life's companion to share that love—a love that demands openness; hence, the spousal privilege. Thirdly, I am a moral and spiritual being, with a soul to tend and a burden of guilt that must be given voice; hence, the clergy-communicant privilege. Fourthly, I am a citizen, a juridical person living in a network of public rights and relationships that are fragile, shifting, and hard to understand; hence, the attorney-client privilege. By recognizing and sanctifying the physical self, the social and loving self, the moral and spiritual self, and the juridical self, these testimonial privileges are shaped to fit the contours of an entire philosophical anthropology—an answer to Kant's question "What is man?"

To make sense of the law of privilege, we must view the four privileges as penumbral protections of the four privileged relationships; and these, in turn, we best regard as themselves penumbral protections of the four fundamental aspects of human existence I have just enumerated. The relationships emanate from these basic aspects of existence, and the privileges emanate from the relationships.

This way of putting things, a scholastic might have said, corresponds to the "order of being." In the "order of knowing," however, we reason in reverse. We begin, therefore, with the positive law as we find it—in this case the particular testimonial privileges. The standard chilling effect argument directs our attention to the relationships that the privileges are there to protect, and reflecting on those relationships leads in turn to the human goods that make them so special.

This analysis allows us to understand what it means to regard a piece of positive law as a vantage point from which to glimpse a more general principle that gives it life and substance. It means that the positive law forms the starting point for a dialectical inquiry into the principles that underlie it. To apply this dialectical mode of analysis to the Third Amendment, we first ask what is so burdensome about quartering soldiers in

---

[63] *See* Sanford Levinson, *Testimonial Privileges and the Preferences of Friendship*, 1984 DUKE L.J. 631.

one's home. This question directs us to what is valuable about a home. One plausible answer is that a home is a protection of the life that goes on within it, fostering it by shielding it from the outside world.[64] In this way our vision is directed to the importance of private activities in leading a decent life.

We are led dialectically up the ladder of being from the positive law to the basic values it protects. We are turned from the shadows to gaze at the Sun from which our rights emanate. By this time, it should be obvious what set of allusions I find in Douglas's metaphor, for he is calling to mind one of the basic images in Western philosophy and religion. It is, of course, the analogy of the Sun in Plato's *Republic*, where Socrates likens the Good to the Sun.[65] He provides an elaborate set of metaphors—the Sun, the divided line,[66] the myth of the Cave[67]—to explain that any properly conducted inquiry leads us up the ladder of generality from particular instances or images to general principles. Finally, it leads us to the Good itself, just as the cave-dweller turns his gaze from shadows to the things that cast them and then steps out of the Cave into the light of the Sun. This light is too bright to apprehend directly, but it makes all other seeing possible.

I do not know whether Douglas consciously and specifically intended a Platonic allusion. But Plato's image is a familiar figure in Western letters, readily available to the imagination even of those who have never studied the *Republic*. The Platonic metaphor is a natural one for anyone who, like Douglas, has enjoyed the benefit of a traditional education in the humanities.[68]

---

[64] "The home derives its pre-eminence as the seat of family life. And the integrity of that life is something so fundamental that it has been found to draw to its protection the principles of more than one explicitly granted Constitutional right." Poe v. Ullman, 367 U.S. 497, 551–52 (1961) (Harlan, J., dissenting). On the analysis I am presenting here, Harlan's argument should be turned around: the integrity of family life is so fundamental that explicitly granted Constitutional rights (such as the Third Amendment) draw their underlying principle to its protection.

[65] *See* PLATO, THE REPUBLIC 508b–c. (In view of the large number of editions and translations of the *Republic*, I do not cite any edition in particular, but rather use the standard Platonic reference system.)

[66] *See id.* at 509c–511e.

[67] *See id.* at 514a–517c.

[68] Henly, *supra* note 60, comes close to this analysis of the penumbra metaphor, but in the end fails to appreciate the metaphor's full significance. He notices the solar imagery in the penumbra, but objects that in that case Douglas should have spoken of a corona rather than a penumbra. *Id.* at 97–98, 98 n.109. This misses the point: the corona is part of the Sun's atmosphere; the penumbra is part of the surface of the Earth. A bit later, Henly treats the metaphor more or less as Mohr does, *see id.* at 99 fig.4, but expresses puzzlement at the light source, which he suggests may be the police power or the majority will. *See id.* at 99. My reading puts together these two pieces of the puzzle, interpreting them in the light of the Platonic allusion.

For that matter, the "emanation" metaphor is also Platonic in origin. Plotinus, the most important neo-Platonist in antiquity, describes the whole of existence as an "emanation" that "may be compared to the brilliant light encircling the sun." PLOTINUS, THE ENNEADS 374 (4th ed. 1969, S. MacKenna trans.). Plotinus's followers developed elaborate and in-

What I am suggesting, then, is this. *Griswold* does not use a two-step method to construct the right of privacy, with one step deriving penumbral rights and the next step fusing them, as Bork suggests. *Griswold*'s method is instead a Platonic mirror-image of the activist derivation of penumbral rights. Instead of deriving rights penumbral to the Third Amendment, Douglas regards the Third Amendment as itself the penumbra of some principle that allows us to understand what it is doing in the Constitution. Presumably, critics such as Bork would agree that the framers included rights in the Bill of Rights because they perceived certain standard threats that must be warded off—threats such as forced self-incrimination, illegal searches, or the quartering of soldiers. Douglas asks what values these threats endanger. Just as Plato insists that we view tangible objects as mere images of the invisible mathematical laws that explain them, the Warren Court insisted that we view positive law, including constitutional rights, as an image of the underlying values positive law seeks to protect. Ronald Dworkin's jurisprudence is a faithful representation of this half of the Warren Court's approach to rights.[69]

It is instructive to compare this approach with Justice Harlan's concurring opinion in *Griswold*. Harlan sees no need to begin with the specific rights in the Bill of Rights in order to discover through dialectial inquiry which general rights enjoy constitutional protection. Instead, he states,

> the proper constitutional inquiry in this case is whether this Connecticut statute infringes the Due Process Clause of the Fourteenth Amendment because the enactment violates basic values "implicit in the concept of ordered liberty." . . . While the relevant inquiry may be aided by resort to one or more of the provisions of the Bill of Rights, it is not dependent on them or any of their radiations. The Due Process Clause of the Fourteenth Amendment stands, in my opinion, on its own bottom.[70]

Harlan's approach is much more vulnerable than Douglas's to the accusation that it invites judges to project their own social philosophies onto the Constitution. An inquiry like Douglas's is constrained by the requirement that general rights must plausibly explain specific rights by tying them to values important enough to belong in a constitution. Harlan's inquiry is constrained only by the requirement that general rights must be

---

comprehensible emanation-theories, but lost their sectarian battles with the early Christians. However, St. Augustine incorporated Platonic and neo-Platonic doctrine into the mainstream of Western Christianity; and the imagery of all existence emanating from God is a familiar one in Christian mysticism.

[69] *See generally* RONALD DWORKIN, LAW'S EMPIRE (1986); RONALD DWORKIN, TAKING RIGHTS SERIOUSLY (1978).

[70] 381 U.S. 479, 500 (1965) (Harlan, J., concurring). The phrase "implicit in the concept of ordered liberty" comes from *Palko v. Connecticut*, 302 U.S. 319, 325 (1937).

implicit in the concept of ordered liberty. Harlan's constraint is not entirely empty, but whatever content it has derives from an analysis of the concept of ordered liberty—in other words, from an elaborated social philosophy unmoored in the specific values protected elsewhere in the Constitution.

This isn't to say that Douglas's procedure provides a formula for cranking out incontestable answers to constitutional questions. Fundamental disagreements are possible over what values specific rights protect and what threats they protect against. Is the value underlying the Free Speech Clause personal expression, political debate, or market liberty? Is the Bill of Rights a guarantee of federal protection against standard threats posed by state governments, as liberals believe, or a limitation on the standard threat of a tyrannical federal government in order to allow the states to legislate more freely, as conservatives prefer to think? Douglas's procedure alone cannot answer these questions. (Nor does it tell us whether they should be answered by original intent, textualism, or living constitutionalism). But it can and does show us what questions need to be answered and why answering them may lead from textually specific rights to general rights mentioned nowhere in the text.

Putting Douglas's Platonic way of viewing legal rights together with the activist approach I discussed earlier, we can at last appreciate the full magnitude of the Warren Court's contribution to the theory of rights, particularly constitutional rights. The Warren Court began with specific textual rights and then proceeded to elaborate them simultaneously in opposite directions. First, the Court reasoned from these rights "down the line" to the penumbral rights that must be recognized and explicitly stated in order to secure the textual rights from standard institutional threats. Second, the Court reasoned from the textual rights "up the line" to the general values that these rights protect. In this way, the Warren Court gave meaning to the notion of a right as the moral and legal embodiment of a value that stands in need of stringent protection. The Court's activism secured the protection, and its Platonism measured the value.

[2]

Unenumerated Rights: Whether and How *Roe* Should be Overruled

Ronald Dworkin†

Judge Posner and I have been asked to debate the subject of unenumerated rights. I am at a disadvantage, because I think that the distinction between enumerated and unenumerated constitutional rights, a distinction presupposed by our assignment, is bogus. I shall explain why, but it would be unfair to end my contribution to the expected debate with that explanation. The topic "unenumerated rights" on a conference menu leads the audience to expect some discussion of abortion, the most violently debated constitutional issue of our era. So I shall try to explain how that constitutional issue should be resolved once the distinction between enumerated and unenumerated rights is safely shut up with other legal concepts dishonorably discharged for bad philosophy.

I. The Real Bill of Rights

We are celebrating the Bill of Rights, which we take to include the Civil War Amendments. I begin by asking you, in your imagination, to *read* that part of the Constitution. Some parts of the

---

† Professor of Law, New York University, and Professor of Jurisprudence and Fellow of University College, Oxford University. This Article is based on a much expanded version of remarks at *The Bill of Rights in the Welfare State: A Bicentennial Symposium*, held at The University of Chicago Law School on October 25-26, 1991. I would like to thank Arnand Agneshwar, Alice Hofheimer, Sharon Perley, and Richard Posner for very helpful information, comments and advice, and also to thank the Filomen D'Agostino and Max E. Greenberg Research Fund of New York University Law School.

Bill of Rights are very concrete, like the Third Amendment's prohibition against quartering troops in peacetime. Others are of medium abstraction, like the First Amendment's guarantees of freedom of speech, press, and religion. But key clauses are drafted in the most abstract possible terms of political morality. The Fourteenth Amendment, for example, commands "equal" protection of the laws, and also commands that neither life nor liberty nor property be taken without "due" process of law. That language might, in some contexts, seem wholly concerned with procedure—in no way restricting the laws government might enact and enforce, but only stipulating how it must enact and enforce whatever laws it does adopt. Legal history has rejected that narrow interpretation, however, and once we understand the constitutional provisions to be substantive as well as procedural, their scope is breathtaking. For then the Bill of Rights orders nothing less than that government treat everyone subject to its dominion with equal concern and respect, and that it not infringe their most basic freedoms, those liberties essential, as one prominent jurist put it, to the very idea of "ordered liberty."[1]

II. The Natural Reading of the Bill of Rights

On its most natural reading, then, the Bill of Rights sets out a network of principles, some extremely concrete, others more abstract, and some of near limitless abstraction. Taken together, these principles define a political ideal: they construct the constitutional skeleton of a society of citizens both equal and free. Notice three features of that striking architecture. First, this system of principle is comprehensive, because it commands both equal concern and basic liberty. In our political culture these are the two major sources of claims of individual right. It therefore seems unlikely that anyone who believes that free and equal citizens would be guaranteed a particular individual right will not also think that our Constitution already contains that right, unless constitutional history has decisively rejected it. That is an important fact about constitutional adjudication and argument, to which I shall return.

Second, since liberty and equality overlap in large part, each of the two major abstract articles of the Bill of Rights is *itself* comprehensive in that same way. Particular constitutional rights that follow from the best interpretation of the Equal Protection Clause, for example, will very likely also follow from the best interpreta-

[1] Justice Cardozo in *Palko v Connecticut*, 302 US 319, 325 (1937).

tion of the Due Process Clause. So (as Justice Stevens reminded us in the address which opened this conference)[2] the Supreme Court had no difficulty in finding that, although the Equal Protection Clause does not apply to the District of Columbia, racial school segregation in the District was nevertheless unconstitutional under the Due Process Clause of the Fifth Amendment, which does apply to it. Indeed, it is very likely that, even if there had been no First Amendment, American courts would long ago have found the freedoms of speech, press, and religion in the Fifth and Fourteenth Amendments' guarantees of basic liberty.

Third, the Bill of Rights therefore seems to give judges almost incredible power. Our legal culture insists that judges—and finally the justices of the Supreme Court—have the last word about the proper interpretation of the Constitution. Since the great clauses command simply that government show equal concern and respect for the basic liberties—without specifying in further detail what that means and requires—it falls to judges to declare what equal concern really does require and what the basic liberties really are. But that means that judges must answer intractable, controversial, and profound questions of political morality that philosophers, statesmen, and citizens have debated for many centuries, with no prospect of agreement. It means that the rest of us must accept the deliverances of a majority of the justices, whose insight into these great issues is not spectacularly special. That seems unfair, even frightening. Many people think that judges with that kind of power will impose liberal convictions on less-liberal majorities. But they are equally likely to impose conservative convictions on less-conservative majorities, as the Supreme Court did in *Lochner*, and is now doing again in, for example, its affirmative action decisions. The resentment most people feel about unelected judges having that kind of power is bipartisan.

III. Constitutional Revisionism

In any case, many academic constitutional theorists have for a long time thought that their main job is to demonstrate to themselves, the legal profession, and the public at large that the Constitution does not mean what it says—that it does not, properly understood, actually assign that extraordinary and apparently unfair power to judges. The revisionist strategy is a simple one. It denies

---

[2] Justice John Paul Stevens, *The Bill of Rights: A Century of Progress*, 59 U Chi L Rev 13, 20 (1992).

that the Bill of Rights has the structure I said was its natural interpretation. It aims to picture it differently, not as defining the skeleton of an overall conception of justice, but as only an antique list of the particular demands that a relatively few people long ago happened to think important. It hopes to turn the Bill of Rights from a constitutional charter into a document with the texture and tone of an insurance policy or a standard form commercial lease.

In one way this collective revisionist effort has been remarkably successful. It has achieved the Orwellian triumph, the political huckster's dream, of painting its opponents with its own shames and vices. It has persuaded almost everyone that turning the Constitution into an out-of-date list is really *protecting* that document, and that those who stubbornly read the Constitution to mean what it says are the actual inventors and usurpers. Even judges who accept the broad responsibility the Constitution imposes on them still adopt the misleading names their revisionist opponents assign them. They call themselves "activists," or "noninterpretivists," or champions of "unenumerated rights," who wish to go "outside" the "four corners" of the Constitution to decide cases on a "natural law" basis.

In that important political way, the massive effort to revise and narrow the Bill of Rights has been successful. But in every substantive way, it has failed—not because it has constructed coherent alternative interpretations with unattractive consequences, but because it has failed to construct any coherent alternative interpretations at all.

Part of the revisionist effort has not even attempted an alternative *interpretation*. I refer to what I call the "external" revisionist strategy, which does not propose an account of what the Constitution itself actually means, but rewrites it to make it more congenial to what the revisionists consider the best theory of democracy. In its rewritten version, the Constitution leaves as much power to government as is possible, consistent with genuine majority rule and with what the text of the Constitution uncontroversially forbids. Learned Hand held a version of this theory,[3] and John Hart Ely has provided its most elaborate form.[4] The external revisionist strategy plainly begs the question. "Democracy" is itself the name of an abstraction: there are many different conceptions of democracy, and political philosophers debate which is the most

---

[3] See, for example, Learned Hand, *The Bill of Rights* (Harvard, 1958).

[4] See John Hart Ely, *Democracy and Distrust: A Theory of Judicial Review* (Harvard, 1980).

attractive. The American conception of democracy is whatever form of government the Constitution, according to the best interpretation of that document, establishes. So it begs the question to hold that the Constitution should be amended to bring it closer to some supposedly purer form of democracy.[5]

For the most part, however, the revisionists have indeed tried to disguise their revisionism as only "better" interpretations of the actual Constitution. They argue that the natural interpretation I described—that the Constitution guarantees the rights required by the best conceptions of the political ideals of equal concern and basic liberty—is not in fact the most accurate interpretation. They say that that natural interpretation neglects some crucial *semantic* fact, some property of language or communication or linguistic interpretation which, once we grasp it, shows us that the abstract language of the great clauses does not mean what it seems to mean. Constitutional scholars have ransacked the cupboard of linguistic philosophy to find semantic constraints of that character and power. They found in that cupboard, for example, the important idea that what philosophers call the "speaker's meaning" of an utterance may differ from the meaning an audience would likely assign the utterance if it were ignorant of any special information about the speaker.

Some constitutional lawyers try to transform that point into a so-called "framers' intention" theory of constitutional interpretation. They argue that the great constitutional clauses should be understood, not to declare abstract moral requirements, as they do if read acontextually, but in the supposedly different and much less expansive sense which some presumed set of "framers" supposedly "intended."

That suggestion is self-destructive, however, as Robert Bork's unsuccessful attempt to defend it (largely by abandoning it) in his recent book shows.[6] We must take care to make a distinction on which the philosophical idea of speaker's meaning crucially depends: the distinction between what someone means to say and what he hopes or expects or believes will be the consequence for the law of his saying it. Many of the framers undoubtedly had dif-

[5] See Ronald Dworkin, *A Matter of Principle* ch 2 (Harvard, 1985); Ronald Dworkin, *Law's Empire* ch 10 (Harvard, 1986); and Ronald Dworkin, *Equality, Democracy and the Constitution: We the People in Court*, 28 Alberta L Rev 324 (1990).

[6] See Robert H. Bork, *The Tempting of America: The Political Seduction of the Law* (Free Press, 1990) (especially chapters 7, 8, and 13). See also Ronald Dworkin, *Bork's Jurisprudence*, 57 U Chi L Rev 657, 663-74 (1990), for my review of Bork's book.

ferent beliefs from mine about what equality or due process requires, just as my beliefs about that differ from yours. They thought that their abstract commands about equality and due process had different legal implications for concrete cases from the implications you or I think those abstract commands have. But it does not follow that they meant to *say* anything different from what you or I would mean to say if we used the same words they did. We would normally use those words to say, not that government is forbidden to act contrary to the speakers' own conceptions of equality and justice, but that it is forbidden to act contrary to the soundest conception of those virtues. All the evidence (and common sense) suggests that that is what they meant to say as well: they meant to use abstract words in their normal abstract sense. If so, then strict attention to speakers' meaning only reinforces the broad judicial responsibility that the revisionists hope to curtail.

IV. Enumerated and Unenumerated Rights

The distinction I am supposed to be discussing, between enumerated and unenumerated rights, is only another misunderstood semantic device. Constitutional lawyers use "unenumerated rights" as a collective name for a particular set of recognized or controversial constitutional rights, including the right of travel; the right of association; and the right to privacy from which the right to an abortion, if there is such a right, derives. They regard this classification as marking an important structural distinction, as the terms "enumerated" and "unenumerated" obviously suggest. If the Bill of Rights only enumerates *some* of the rights necessary to a society of equal concern and basic liberty, and leaves other such rights unmentioned, then judges arguably have only the power to enforce the rights actually enumerated.

Some lawyers accept the distinction, but deny the inference about judicial power. They say that judges *do* have the power to enforce unenumerated rights, and claim that the Court has often done so in the past. But lawyers who argue in this way have conceded a very great deal to their opponents who deny that judges should have this kind of power. Their opponents are then able to say that judges have no *authority* to add to the enumerated. If we allow judges to roam at will beyond the "four corners" of the Constitution, they add, we abandon all hope of limiting judicial power. That is the argument made by Justice White in *Bowers v Hardwick*, for example, to explain why the Court should not recognize a right of homosexual sodomy.[7] He said that judge-made constitutional law was particularly suspect when it had "little or no cognizable roots in the language or design of the Constitution";[8] and he presumably had in mind the putative right of abortion, as well as that of homosexual sodomy.

So the distinction between enumerated and unenumerated rights is widely understood to pose an important constitutional issue: the question whether and when courts have authority to enforce rights not actually enumerated in the Constitution as genuine constitutional rights. I find the question unintelligible, however, as I said at the outset, because the presumed distinction makes no sense. The distinction between what is on some list and what is not is of course genuine and often very important. An ordinance might declare, for example, that it is forbidden to take guns, knives, or explosives in hand luggage on an airplane. Suppose airport officials interpreted that ordinance to exclude canisters of tear gas as well, on the ground that the general structure of the ordinance, and the obvious intention behind it, prohibits all weapons that might be taken aboard and used in hijacks or terrorism. We would be right to say that gas was not on the list of what was banned, and that it is a legitimate question whether officials are entitled to add "unenumerated" weapons to the list. But the distinction between officials excluding pistols, switch-blades and hand-grenades on the one hand, and tear gas on the other, depends upon a semantic assumption: that tear gas falls within what philosophers call the *reference* of neither "guns" nor "knives" nor "explosives."

No comparable assumption can explain the supposed distinction between enumerated and unenumerated constitutional rights. The Bill of Rights, as I said, consists of broad and abstract principles of political morality, which together encompass, in exceptionally abstract form, all the dimensions of political morality that in our political culture can ground an individual constitutional right. The key issue in applying these abstract principles to particular political controversies is not one of reference but of *interpretation*, which is very different.

Consider the following three constitutional arguments, each of which is very controversial. The first argues that the Equal Protection Clause creates a right of equal concern and respect, from which it follows that women have a right against gender-based discriminations unless such discriminations are required by important

[7] 478 US 186 (1986).

[8] Id at 193-94.

state interests. The second argues that the First Amendment grants a right of symbolic protest, from which it follows that individuals have a right to burn the American flag. The third argues that the Due Process Clause protects the basic freedoms central to the very concept of "ordered liberty," including the right of privacy, from which it follows that women have a constitutional right to abortion. By convention, the first two are arguments (good or bad) for enumerated rights: each claims that some right—the right against gender discrimination or the right to burn the flag—is an instance of some more general right set out, in suitably abstract form, in the text of the Constitution. The third argument, on the other hand, is thought to be different and more suspect, because it is thought to be an argument for an unenumerated right. The right it claims—the right to an abortion—is thought to bear a more tenuous or distant relationship to the language of the Constitution. It is said to be at best implied by, rather than stated in, that language.

But the distinction cannot be sustained. Each of the three arguments is interpretive in a way that excludes the kind of semantic constraints the distinction assumes. No one thinks that it follows just from the meaning of the words "freedom of speech" either that people are free to burn flags, or that they are not. No one thinks it follows just from the meaning of the words "equal protection" that laws excluding women from certain jobs are unconstitutional, or that they are not. In neither case does the result follow from the meanings of words in the way it follows from the meaning of "gun" that it refers to pistols but not to canisters of gas. Nor are the three arguments different in how they are interpretive. Each conclusion (if sound) follows, not from some historical hope or belief or intention of a "framer," but because the political principle that supports that conclusion best accounts for the general structure and history of constitutional law. Someone who thinks that this manner of constitutional argument is inappropriate—who thinks, for example, that framers' expectations should play a more decisive role than this view of constitutional argument allows—will have that reservation about all three arguments, not distinctly about the third. If he thinks that the third argument is wrong, because he abhors, for example, the idea of substantive due process, then he will reject it, but because it is wrong, not because the right it claims would be an unenumerated one.

In his reply to my remarks, Judge Posner constructs a Socratic dialogue in which the straight man is brought to see that "speech" in the First Amendment includes flag burning, though Posner concedes that the argument might have gone the other way.[9] He does not construct a parallel dialogue in which another dupe is made to agree that gender is a suspect category under the Equal Protection Clause, though it is easy to see how that second dialogue might go. And it would be equally easy to construct a third dialogue ending with a straight man's startled recognition that abortion is, after all, a basic liberty protected by the Due Process Clause. Posner does suggest that this argument might take us "further" from the text. But the metaphor of distance is wholly opaque in this context: it means or suggests nothing. Posner cannot mean, for example, that a right to abortion is further away from the Constitution's language than a right against gender-discrimination is, in the sense that "tear gas" is further from the meaning of "gun" than "pistol" is. "Pistol" is closer because "gun" refers to a pistol and does not refer to tear gas. But since neither a right to abortion nor a right against gender-discrimination follow from the meanings of textual words, neither can be closer to or further from the text than the other in that sense.

It is sometimes said that the Constitution does not "mention" a right of travel, or of association, or of privacy, as if that fact explained why these rights are usefully classified as unenumerated. But the Constitution does not "mention" flag burning or gender discrimination either. The right to burn a flag and the right against gender-discrimination are supported by the best interpretation of a more general or abstract right that is "mentioned." It is true that the phrase "right to privacy" is itself more abstract than the phrase "right to burn a flag as protest," and that the former phrase therefore figures more in the conversation and writing of constitutional scholars than the latter. But these facts reflect accidents (or highly contingent features) of usage. Scholars have found it useful to develop a name of middling abstraction—the right of privacy—to describe a stage in the derivation of particular concrete rights from the even more abstract rights named in the constitutional text. But it hardly follows that those concrete rights—including the right to abortion—are more remote from their textual beginnings than are concrete rights—such as the right to burn a flag—that are derived by arguments that do not employ names for rights of middling abstraction. Constitutional lawyers might well have adopted the middling terms "right of symbolic protest" or "right of gender equality" in the way they have

---

[9] Richard A. Posner, *Legal Reasoning From the Top Down and From the Bottom Up: The Question of Unenumerated Constitutional Rights*, 59 U Chi L Rev 433, 437-38 (1992).

adopted "right of privacy." It is hardly a deep fact of constitutional structure that they have not.

I must be clear. I am not arguing that the Supreme Court should enforce unenumerated as well as enumerated constitutional rights, any more than I meant to argue, in my remarks about speaker's meaning, that the Court is right to ignore or modify what the framers said. I mean that the distinction between enumerated and unenumerated rights, as it is commonly used in constitutional theory, makes no sense, because it confuses reference with interpretation.

I should say—to complete this exercise in provocation—that I take much the same view of a variety of other distinctions popular among constitutional lawyers, including those Posner discusses in his reply. He distinguishes between what he calls a "top-down" and a "bottom-up" method of legal reasoning, and also between a "clause-by-clause" and a "holistic" approach. He apparently regards the second of these distinctions as more important than the first. Though he says he agrees with me that "there isn't much to bottom-up reasoning,"[10] he thinks that I am wrong to criticize Bork's "clause-by-clause" approach,[11] and also that I would do better to make my own arguments about abortion more explicitly "holistic."[12]

Neither of the two distinctions makes any sense, however. We cannot understand a particular precedent, for example, except by construing that decision as part of a more general enterprise, and any such constructive interpretation must, as I argued at length in *Law's Empire*, engage the kind of theoretical hypothesis characteristic of what Posner calls top-down reasoning.[13] So bottom-up reasoning is automatically top-down reasoning as well. The same point also erodes the distinction between clause-by-clause and holistic constitutional interpretation. Legal interpretation is *inherently* holistic, even when the apparent target of interpretation is a

---

[10] Id at 435.

[11] Id at 439-40. Posner objects to my claim that Bork has no coherent constitutional philosophy, that Bork has theories of particular clauses, but not of the Constitution as a whole. But Bork does not, as Posner says he does, distrust general theory. On the contrary, Bork claims a perfectly general, comprehensive, constitutional theory. He claims that all of the Constitution, not just particular clauses, are exhausted by the intentions of the Framers, and he argues for that global theory by appealing to a single, global theory of democracy and a single, global account of what law, by its very nature, is like. Bork does not have a coherent constitutional philosophy, as I argued in *Bork's Jurisprudence*, 57 U Chi L Rev 657 (cited in note 6). But that is not because he does not claim one.

[12] Posner, 59 U Chi L Rev at 444-45 (cited in note 9).

[13] Dworkin, *Law's Empire* (cited in note 5). See particularly id at 65-68.

single sentence or even a single clause rather than a document. Any interpreter must accept interpretive constraints—assumptions about what makes one interpretation better than another—and any plausible set of constraints includes a requirement of coherence. An interpretation of the Bill of Rights which claims that a moral principle embedded in one clause is actually rejected by another is an example not of pragmatist flexibility, but of hypocrisy.

V. Law's Integrity

Where do we stand? The most natural interpretation of the Bill of Rights seems, as I said, to give judges great and frightening power. It is understandable that constitutional lawyers and teachers should strive to tame the Bill of Rights, to read it in a less frightening way, to change it from a systematic abstract conception of justice to a list of discrete clauses related to one another through pedigree rather than principle. These efforts fail, however, and are bound to fail, because the text and history of the Bill of Rights will not accept that transformation. They are bound to fail, moreover, in a paradoxical and disastrous way. Because the semantic distinctions on which the efforts are based have no sense as they are used, they are powerless themselves to define any particular set of constitutional rights. As the recent history of the Court amply demonstrates, a judge who claims to rely on speaker's meaning, "enumeration," or a preference for clause-by-clause interpretation must actually choose which constitutional rights to enforce on grounds that have nothing to do with these semantic devices, but which are hidden from view by his appeal to them. The search for limits on judicial power ends by allowing judges the undisciplined power of the arbitrary.

Posner's reply acknowledges that fact, with typical candor. He says that the semantic devices beloved of conservative lawyers "could end up with a document that gave answers only to questions that no one was asking any longer,"[14] and that judges who say they are constrained by those useless devices will necessarily decide according to their own "personal values,"[15]—according, he says, to what makes them "puke."[16] His own personal values en-

---

[14] Posner, 59 U Chi L Rev at 446 (cited in note 9).

[15] Id at 449.

[16] Id at 447. Posner takes this phrase—which gives new meaning to the old realist thesis that the law is only what the judge had for breakfast—from Holmes. I should say that though I understand Posner's hagiographic admiration for that jurist, I do not share it. Holmes wrote like a dream. His personal conversion from the view that the First Amend-

dorse "stretching" the Due Process Clause to yield *Griswold*, and, if I read correctly between the lines, *Roe v Wade* as well. But he knows that other judges have stronger stomachs about society dictating sexual morality: their puke tests will flunk affirmative action programs instead.[17] The idea that the Constitution cannot mean what it says ends in the unwelcome conclusion that it means nothing at all.

What is to be done? We can finally, after the 200 years we celebrate in this symposium, grow up and begin to take our actual Constitution seriously, as those many nations now hoping to imitate us have already done. We can accept that our Constitution commands, as a matter of fundamental law, that our judges do their best collectively to construct, re-inspect and revise, generation by generation, the skeleton of liberal equal concern that the great clauses, in their majestic abstraction, demand. We will then abandon the pointless search for mechanical or semantic constraints, and seek genuine constraints in the only place where they can actually be found: in good argument. We will accept that honest lawyers and judges and scholars will inevitably disagree, sometimes profoundly, about what equal concern requires, and about which rights are central and which only peripheral to liberty.

We will then acknowledge, in the political process of nomination and confirmation of federal judges, what is already evident to anyone who looks: that constitutional adjudicators cannot be neutral about these great questions, and that the Senate must decline to confirm nominees whose convictions are too idiosyncratic, or who refuse honestly to disclose what their convictions are. The second stage of the Thomas confirmation hearings was, as most people now agree, physically revolting. But the first stage was intellectually revolting, because candidate and senators conspired to pretend that philosophy had nothing to do with judging, that a nominee who said he had abandoned convictions the way a runner sheds clothing was fit for the office he sought.[18]

---

ment must be limited to a Blackstonian condemnation of prior restraint to the radically different view that it must be understood as a much more abstract and general principle, was an epochal event in American constitutional history. But most of his gorgeous epigrams were the vivid skins of only very lazy thoughts, and his philosophical pretensions, almost entirely in service of an unsophisticated, deeply cynical form of skepticism, were embarrassing—as I believe the metaphysical observations Posner includes in his own new collection of Holmes's writings demonstrate. See Richard A. Posner, *Introduction*, in Richard A. Posner, ed. *The Essential Holmes* xvii-xx (Chicago, 1992).

[17] I discuss Posner's own recommendations in note 22.

[18] Ronald Dworkin, *Justice for Clarence Thomas*, NY Rev Books 41 (Nov 7, 1991).

The constitutional process of nomination and confirmation is an important part of the system of checks through which the actual Constitution disciplines the striking judicial power it declares. The main engines of discipline are intellectual rather than political, however, and the academic branch of the profession has a responsibility to protect that intellectual discipline, which is now threatened from several directions. Of course, we cannot find a formula which will guarantee that judges will all reach the same answer in complex or novel or crucial constitutional cases. No formula can protect us from a *Lochner*, which Posner tells us stinks, or from a *Bowers*. The stench of those cases does not lie in any jurisdictional vice or judicial overreaching. After a near century of treating *Lochner* as a whipping-boy, no one has produced a sound mechanical test that it fails. The vice of bad decisions is bad argument and bad conviction; all we can do about those bad decisions is to point out how and where the arguments are bad. Nor should we waste any more time on the silly indulgence of American legal academic life: the philosophically juvenile claim that, since no such formula exists, no one conception of constitutional equality and liberty is any better than another, and adjudication is only power or visceral response.[19] We must insist, instead, on a principle of genuine power: the idea, instinct in the concept of law itself, that whatever their views of justice and fairness, judges must also accept an independent and superior constraint of *integrity*.[20]

Integrity in law has several dimensions. First, it insists that judicial decision be a matter of principle, not compromise or strategy or political accommodation. That apparent banality is often ignored: The Supreme Court's present position on the politically sensitive issue of affirmative action, for example, cannot be justified on any coherent set of principles, however conservative or unappealing.[21] Second, integrity holds vertically: a judge who claims a particular right of liberty as fundamental must show that his claim is consistent with the bulk of precedent, and with the

---

[19] See Ronald Dworkin, *Pragmatism, Right Answers and True Banality*, in Michael Brint, ed, *Pragmatism and Law* (forthcoming 1992). See Posner, 59 U Chi L Rev at 447 (cited in note 9).

[20] I discuss integrity at considerable length in *Law's Empire* at ch 7 (cited in note 5).

[21] I believe that Professor Fried unwittingly demonstrated this incoherence in defending the position in his recent book. See Charles Fried, *Order and Law: Arguing the Reagan Revolution—A Firsthand Account* (Simon & Schuster, 1991), and my review of this book in Ronald Dworkin, *The Reagan Revolution and the Supreme Court*, NY Rev Books 23 (Jul 18, 1991). See also Fried's letter to the editor and my letter in reply, in NY Rev Books 65 (Aug 15, 1991).

main structures of our constitutional arrangement. Third, integrity holds horizontally: a judge who adopts a principle must give full weight to that principle in other cases he decides or endorses.

Of course, not even the most scrupulous attention to integrity, by all our judges in all our courts, will produce uniform judicial decisions, or guarantee decisions you approve of, or protect you from those you hate. Nothing can do that. The point of integrity is principle, not uniformity: We are governed not by a list but by an ideal, and controversy is therefore at the heart of our story. We are envied for our constitutional adventure, and increasingly imitated, throughout the democratic world: in Delhi and Strasbourg and Ottawa, even, perhaps, in the Palace of Westminster, and perhaps tomorrow or the day after, in Moscow and Johannesburg. In all those places people seem ready to accept the risk and high promise of government by ideal, a form of government we created in the document we celebrate. We have never fully trusted that form of government. But unless we abandon it altogether, which we will not do, we should stop pretending that it is not the form of government we have. The energy of our best academic lawyers would be better spent in making, testing, and evaluating different conceptions of liberal equality, to see which conception best fits our own history and practice. They should try to guide and constrain our judges by criticism, argument, and example. That is the only way to honor our great constitutional creation, to help it prosper.[22]

---

[22] Posner describes my account of integrity-based constitutional reasoning as "holistic" and "top-down." He says it is "too ambitious, too risky, too contentious." Posner, 59 U Chi L Rev at 446 (cited in note 9). He says that when judges are called upon to interpret the great abstract moral clauses of the Constitution they should react as their "conscience" demands: they should cite the abstract moral language of these clauses to strike down only what they instinctively find "terribly unjust." Id at 447. He would not require a judge to provide much, if anything, by way of a principled explanation of how or why he believes a law unjust, or to aim at consistency of principle even himself, from one day to the next, let alone with decisions other judges have made on other days. His views, as always, are striking and powerful. But how can he think that advice less "risky," or less likely to produce "contentious" decisions, than the more familiar advice that judges should at least do their best, as their time and talent allows, to discipline their initial reactions by accepting those responsibilities?

Is Posner right, at least, that his proposals are less "ambitious" because less "holistic?" He says judges should declare statutes unconstitutional, on moral grounds, only when there is a "compelling practical case" for doing so. Id at 447. The word "practical" is a familiar obscuring device in pragmatist philosophy: it is meant somehow to suggest, with no further argument, that moral decisions can be based not on "reason" but on more hard-headed sounding "experience" in the shape of obvious social needs. But Posner's extended discussion of *Griswold* shows that Connecticut's ban on contraceptives was not impractical but unjust. That will be true in almost every case in which a Posnerian judge's "can't helps" are in play: his decision will engage his moral convictions, not his practical good sense. Posner

VI. Abortion: What is the Argument About?

In the discussion of abortion that I promised, I shall try to illustrate the role that integrity should play in legal argument. I begin by briefly summarizing claims about the constitutional status of that issue that I have argued elsewhere,[23] and will argue in much more detail in a book about abortion and euthanasia now in manuscript.[24] A woman, I assume, has a constitutionally protected right to control the use of her own body. (I shall later consider the constitutional source of that right.) Therefore a pregnant woman has a right to an abortion unless her state's government has some legitimate and important reason for prohibiting it. Many people think governments do have such a reason, and would have no difficulty in saying what it is.

A state must make abortion a crime, they say, in order to protect human life. That is indeed what many state officials have said, in preambles to regulatory statutes, in legal briefs and in political rhetoric. That is, moreover, what the Supreme Court justices who dissented in *Roe v Wade*, or who later announced their view that it is wrong, say a state's reason for forbidding abortion is. And even justices and lawyers who support that decision say something similar. In his opinion for the Court in *Roe v Wade*, Blackmun recognized that a state had an interest in protecting what he called "fetal life."[25] He said that a state's interest in protecting life did not

---

insists, however, that his moral convictions are discrete "instincts," not the product of some comprehensive theory of the entire Constitution. But the distinction is mysterious in this context, because any judge's opinions about whether a ban on contraception is profoundly unjust, or maximum-hours legislation deeply unfair, or affirmative action an insult to the very idea of equal citizenship, will reflect and be drawn from much more general opinions and attitudes that will also fix his reactions to other legislation he tests "viscerally" against other clauses, at least if he is acting in moral good faith on any of these occasions. If any judge's immediate reaction really was one off—if it really was just a response to one set of facts with no implications for others—it would not be a response of *conscience* at all, but only a whim or a tic.

So Posner's contrast between clause-by-clause and holistic adjudication seems wildly overdrawn. He uses the reason-passion vocabulary of eighteenth-century philosophical psychology. But he has in mind, not an epistemological distinction between different mental faculties judges might use, but a contrast between two views of judicial responsibility. He rejects integrity, which insists that judges do the best they can to exhibit a principled basis for their decisions, in favor of a different standard that encourages them to keep that basis dark. I do not claim, in the discussion of abortion that follows, that integrity produces only one plausible view, or that it can end controversy. But I shall claim, at several points, that integrity rules out some accommodations that politics or weariness or even laziness might recommend, accommodations I fear Posner's unbuttoned license would guarantee.

[23] See Ronald Dworkin, *The Great Abortion Case*, NY Rev Books 49 (Jun 29, 1989).

[24] This book, to be published by Alfred Knopf in 1993, is not yet titled.

[25] 410 US 113, 163 (1973).

give it a compelling reason for prohibiting abortion until the third trimester, but he conceded that it did have that interest throughout pregnancy.[26] The premise on which so many people rely is, however, dangerously ambiguous, because there are two very different aims or purposes a state might have, each of which might be described as protecting human life. A good part of the confusion that surrounds both the legal and the moral argument about abortion is the result of ignoring that ambiguity. Consider the difference between two kinds of reasons a government might have for prohibiting murder within its territory. First, government has a responsibility to protect the rights and interests of its citizens, and chief among these, for most people, is an interest in staying alive and a right not to be killed. I shall call this a derivative reason for prohibiting murder, because it presupposes and derives from individual rights and interests. Government sometimes claims, second, a very different kind of reason for prohibiting murder. It sometimes claims a responsibility not just to protect the interests and rights of its citizens, but to protect human life as an objective or intrinsic good, a value in itself, quite apart from its value to the person whose life it is or to anyone else. I shall call this responsibility a detached one, because it is independent of, rather than a derivative of, particular people's rights and interests.

If government does have a detached responsibility to protect the objective, intrinsic value of life, then its laws against murder serve both its derivative and detached responsibility at once. They protect the rights and interests of particular victims, and they also recognize and respect the intrinsic value of human life. In some cases, however, the two supposed responsibilities might conflict: when someone wishes to kill himself because he is in terrible pain that doctors cannot relieve, for example, or when relatives wish to terminate the mechanical life support of someone who is permanently unconscious. In such cases, suicide or terminating life support might be in the best interests of the person whose life ends, as he or his relatives think it is. These acts nevertheless seem wrong to many people, because they think that any deliberate killing, or ever allowing someone to die who might be kept alive longer, is an insult to the intrinsic value of human life. It makes a great difference, in such cases, whether a government's legitimate reasons for protecting human life are limited to its derivative concern, or whether they include a detached concern as well. If the latter, then

[26] Id at 162-64.

government is entitled to forbid people from ending their lives, even when they rightly think they would be better off dead.

We have identified two different claims a state that proposes to forbid abortion in order to protect human life might be making: a derivative claim and a detached claim. The derivative claim presupposes that a fetus already has rights and interests. The detached claim does not, though it does presuppose that the intrinsic value of human life is already at stake in a fetus's life. You will notice that I did not describe either of these claims as claims about when human life begins, or about whether a fetus is a "person," because those runic phrases perpetuate rather than dissolve the ambiguity I described.

Though scientists disagree about exactly when the life of any animal begins, it seems undeniable that in the ordinary case a fetus is a single living creature by the time it has become implanted in a womb, and that it is human in the sense that it is a member of the animal species *homo sapiens*. It is, in that sense, a human organism whose life has begun. It does not follow that it also has rights and interests of the kind that government might have a derivative responsibility to protect. Nor that it already embodies the intrinsic value of a human life that a government might claim a detached responsibility to guard. But when people say that a fetus is already a living human being, they often mean to make either or both of these further claims.

"Person" is an even more ambiguous term. We sometimes use it just as a description (in which use it is more or less synonymous with human being) and sometimes as a term of moral classification, to suggest that the creatures so described have a special moral standing or importance that marks them out from other species. So someone who said that a just-conceived fetus is already a person might simply mean that it is a member of the human—rather than some other animal—species. Or he might mean, not just that a fetus is alive and human, but that it already has that special kind of moral importance. But even the latter claim is ambiguous in the way I described. It might mean that a fetus is already a creature with the interests and moral rights we take persons, as distinct from other creatures, to have. Or it might mean that a fetus is already a creature whose life has the intrinsic moral significance the life of any person has. So the clarity of the public debate is not improved by the prominence of the questions "Is a fetus a person?" or "When does human life begin?" We do better to avoid that language so far as we can. I suggest that we consider, instead, whether states can justify anti-abortion legislation on one of the two grounds—derivative or detached—that I described.

Most people think that the great constitutional debate about abortion in America is obviously and entirely about a state's derivative grounds. They think the argument is about whether a fetus is a person in the sense in which that means having a right to life. That is why one side claims, and the other denies, that abortion is murder. (Some might add that the detached ground I described is too mysterious or metaphysical even to make sense, let alone to provide a plausible ground for anti-abortion legislation.) Not just the political argument, but the legal and academic discussion as well, seems to assume that view of the controversy. Lawyers and philosophers discuss whether a fetus is a person with rights. They speculate about whether abortion is morally permissible even if a fetus does have a right to life. But they almost all assume that if it does not, then there is no moral objection even to consider.

In the following two sections I shall assess the constitutional argument understood in that familiar and popular way. I shall interpret the claim that states have a responsibility to protect life to mean that they have a derivative responsibility to protect the right to life of a fetus. I shall argue, however, that if we do understand the dispute that way, then the constitutional argument is a relatively simple one. On that basis, *Roe* was not only correct but obviously correct, and its many critics are obviously wrong. I conclude that the constitutional debate about abortion is actually *not* about whether a fetus has rights and interests. It must be understood, if at all, as about the different claim I just conceded some people may find mysterious: that a state can legitimately claim a detached responsibility to protect the intrinsic value of human life.

VII. Is a Fetus a Constitutional Person?

The national Constitution defines what we might call the constitutional population. It stipulates who has constitutional rights that government must respect and enforce, and therefore whose rights government must take into account in curtailing or limiting the scope of other people's constitutional rights in cases of conflict. States would of course have a derivative reason for forbidding abortion if the Constitution designated a fetus as a constitutional person, that is, as a creature with constitutional rights competitive with those of a pregnant woman. Our analysis must therefore begin with a crucial threshold question. Is a fetus a constitutional person? In *Roe v Wade*, the Supreme Court answered that question in the only way it could: in the negative. If a fetus is a constitutional person, then states not only *may* forbid abortion but, at least in some circumstances, *must* do so. No justice or prominent politician has even advanced that claim.

It is true, as a number of legal scholars have pointed out, that the law does not generally require people to make any sacrifice at all to save the life of another person who needs their aid. A person ordinarily has no legal duty to save a stranger from drowning even if he can do so at no risk to himself and with minimal effort.[27] But abortion normally requires a physical attack on a fetus, not just a failure to come to its aid. And in any case parents are invariably made an exception to the general doctrine. Parents have a legal duty to care for their children; if a fetus is a person from conception, a state would discriminate between infants and fetuses without any justification if it allowed abortion but did not permit killing infants or abandoning them in circumstances when they would inevitably die.[28] The physical and emotional and economic burdens of pregnancy are intense, but so are the parallel burdens of parenthood.

We may safely assume, then, that the national Constitution does not declare a fetus to be a constitutional person whose rights may be competitive with the constitutional rights of a pregnant woman. Does this leave a state free to decide that a fetus shall have that status within its borders? If so, then *Roe v Wade* could safely be reversed without the politically impossible implication that states were required to prohibit abortion. The Supreme Court could then say that while some states have chosen to declare fe-

---

[27] These scholars argue that for that reason anti-abortion laws are unconstitutional even if a fetus is considered a person, and they would certainly reject my much stronger claim that in that event many laws permitting abortion would be unconstitutional. The legal arguments rely on a famous and influential article about the morality of abortion by Judith Jarvis Thompson: *A Defense of Abortion*, 1 Phil & Pub Aff 47 (1971). The legal arguments applying Thompson's views to constitutional law are best and most persuasively presented in Donald H. Regan, *Rewriting* Roe v. Wade, 77 Mich L Rev 1569 (1979). Thompson does not argue that every pregnant woman has a right to an abortion, even if a fetus is a person, but only that some do, and she recognizes that a woman who voluntarily risks pregnancy may not have such a right. In any case, her arguments assume that a pregnant woman has no more moral obligations to a fetus she is carrying, even if that fetus is a person with rights and therefore her son or daughter, than anyone has to a stranger—to a famous violinist a woman might find herself connected to for nine months because he needs the use of her kidneys for that period in order to live, for example.

[28] In the article cited in the preceding note, Regan questions the analogy between abortion and infanticide on the ground that parents have the option of arranging an adoption for their child. Regan, 77 Mich L Rev at 1597 (cited in note 27). But that is not inevitably true: minority infants, in particular, may not be able to find adoptive homes, and their parents are not permitted to kill them, or abandon them in circumstances that will inevitably lead to their death, whenever they can in fact make no alternative arrangement.

tuses persons within their jurisdiction, other states need not make the same decision.

There is no doubt that a state can protect the life of a fetus in a variety of ways. A state can make it murder for a third-party intentionally to kill a fetus, as Illinois has done, for example, or "feticide" for anyone willfully to kill a quickened fetus by an injury that would be murder if it resulted in the death of the mother, as Georgia has. These laws violate no constitutional rights, because no one has a constitutional right to injure with impunity.[29] Laws designed to protect fetuses may be drafted in language declaring or suggesting that a fetus is a person, or that human life begins at conception. The Illinois abortion statute begins, for example, by declaring that a fetus is a person from the moment of conception.[30] There can be no constitutional objection to such language, so long as the law does not purport to curtail constitutional rights. The Illinois statute makes plain, for example, that it does not intend to challenge or modify *Roe v Wade* so long as that decision remains in force.[31]

So qualified, a declaration that a fetus is a person raises no more constitutional difficulties than states raise when they declare, as every state has, that corporations are legal persons and enjoy many of the rights real people do, including the right to own property and the right to sue. States declare that corporations are persons as a shorthand way of describing a complex network of rights and duties that it would be impossible to describe in any other way, not as a means of curtailing or diminishing constitutional rights that real people would otherwise have.

The suggestion that states are free to declare a fetus a person, and thereby justify outlawing abortion, is a very different matter, however. That suggestion assumes that a state can curtail some persons' constitutional rights by adding new persons to the constitutional population. The constitutional rights of one citizen are of course very much affected by who or what else also has constitutional rights, because the rights of others may compete or conflict with his. So any power to increase the constitutional population by

---

[29] It is a separate question whether a state would violate the Eighth Amendment if it punished feticide with the death penalty. Though Illinois does use the death penalty, the statute making the killing of a fetus murder rules out that penalty for that crime. Homicide of an Unborn Child, Ill Rev Stat ch 38, ¶ 9-1.2(d) (1989).

[30] Abortion Law of 1975, id at ch 38, ¶ 81-21(1).

[31] Id.

unilateral decision would be, in effect, a power to decrease rights the national Constitution grants to others.

If a state could not only create corporations as legal persons, but endow each of those corporations with a vote, it could impair the constitutional right of ordinary people to vote, because the corporations' votes would dilute theirs. If a state could declare trees to be persons with a constitutional right to life, it could prohibit publishing newspapers or books in spite of the First Amendment's guarantee of free speech, which could not be understood as a license to kill. If a state could declare the higher apes to be persons whose rights were competitive with the constitutional rights of others, it could prohibit its citizens from taking life-saving medicines first tested on those animals. Once we understand that the suggestion we are considering has that implication, we must reject it. If a fetus is not part of the constitutional population, under the national constitutional arrangement, then states have no power to overrule that national arrangement by themselves declaring that fetuses have rights competitive with the constitutional rights of pregnant women.

I am uncertain how far Posner disagrees with that conclusion. He says that states can indeed create new persons. But he adds that it remains an open question how far they can treat these new persons' interests as if they were the interests of real people. This leaves mysterious what he thinks creating a new person amounts to. Perhaps he means only to agree with me that though a state can create persons for a variety of purposes, it cannot thereby acquire a power to abridge constitutional rights that it would not otherwise have had.

That position would be consistent with the examples he offers. He says, for example, that states can create property and liberty in ways that affect people's procedural rights under the Due Process Clause.[32] These are not, however, powers to decrease constitutional rights by adding competing rights-holders to the constitutional scheme. They are powers to create new rights under state law that, once created, satisfy standing conditions for constitutional protection without decreasing the constitutional rights of others. He also says that states can decide whether "death means brain death" or "a stopped heart"[33] and that it follows that they can "decide when life begins."[34] A state can certainly decide when life begins and

[32] Posner, 59 U Chi L Rev at 444 (cited in note 9).
[33] Id.
[34] Id.

ends for any number of reasons, as I said a moment ago. It can fix the moment of death for purposes of the law of inheritance, for example, just as it can declare that life begins before birth in order to allow people to inherit through a fetus. But it cannot change constitutional rights by its decisions about when life begins or death happens. It cannot escape its constitutional responsibilities to death-row prisoners by declaring them already dead, or improve its congressional representation by declaring deceased citizens still alive for that purpose. I cannot think of any significant constitutional rights that would be curtailed by treating someone as dead when his brain was dead, however. So none of Posner's examples suggest that he really accepts the position I reject.

Nor, I dare say, do many of even the strongest opponents of *Roe v Wade* really accept it, because it is inconsistent with other views they hold. Chief Justice Rehnquist, who dissented in that case, had "little doubt" that a state could not constitutionally forbid an abortion that was necessary to save a pregnant woman's life.[35] Of course, if a state could declare a fetus a constitutional person, it could prohibit abortion even when the pregnancy threatens the mother's life, just as it normally forbids killing one innocent person to save the life of another.

VIII. Do Fetuses Have Interests?

Consider this argument, however. "Even if a fetus is not a constitutional person, and states have no power to make it one, a state can nevertheless legislate to protect a fetus's interests, just as it can legislate to protect the interests of dogs, who are not constitutional persons either." States can protect the interests of non-persons. But it is extremely doubtful whether a state can appeal to such interests to justify a significant abridgement of an important constitutional right, such as a pregnant woman's right to control her own body. It can do that only in deference to the rights of other constitutional persons, or for some other "compelling" reason.

But it is important to see that this argument fails for another reason as well: a fetus has no interests before the third trimester. Not everything that can be destroyed has an interest in not being destroyed. Smashing a beautiful sculpture would be a terrible insult to the intrinsic value that great works of art embody, and also very much against the interests of people who take pleasure in see-

[35] 410 US at 173 (Rehnquist dissenting).

ing or studying it. But a sculpture has no interests of its own; a savage act of vandalism is not unfair to *it*. Nor is it enough, for something to have interests, that it be alive and in the process of developing into something more mature. It is not against the interests of a baby carrot that it be picked early and brought to table as a delicacy. Nor even that it is something that will naturally develop into something different or more marvelous. A butterfly is much more beautiful than a caterpillar; but it is not better for the caterpillar to become one. Nor is it enough, for something to have interests, even that it is something *en route* to becoming a human being. Imagine that, just as Dr. Frankenstein reached for the lever that would bring life to the assemblage of body parts on the table before him, someone appalled at the experiment smashed the apparatus. That act, whatever we think of it, would not have been harmful to the assemblage, or against its interests, or unfair to it.

These examples suggest that nothing has interests unless it has or has had some form of consciousness—some mental as well as physical life.[36] Creatures that can feel pain of course have an interest in avoiding it. It is very much against the interests of animals to subject them to pain, in trapping them or experimenting on them, for example. Causing a fetus pain would be against its interests too. But a fetus cannot feel pain until late in pregnancy, because its brain is not sufficiently developed before then. Even conservative scientists deny that a fetal brain is sufficiently developed to feel pain until approximately the twenty-sixth week.[37]

---

[36] Catholic doctrine, it is true, now holds that a fetus is endowed with an eternal soul at conception, and has interests for that reason. (Earlier in its history the Church held that God ensouled a fetus at some point after conception: at forty days for a male and eighty for a female, and that abortion before that point, though wrong because it violated the intrinsic value of God's creation, was not murder. Laurence H. Tribe, *Abortion: The Clash of Absolutes* 31 (Norton, 1990).) That argument offers a counter-example to my claim that nothing can have interests without a brain, though not to my more general claim that nothing can have interests without some form of consciousness, because I assume that a soul, which can suffer, is itself a special form of consciousness. If someone accepts this argument, then he does have a reason for insisting that a fetus (or more accurately the soul it contains) has an interest in continuing to live. But states are not entitled to act on reasons of theological dogma.

[37] See Clifford Grobstein, *Science and the Unborn: Choosing Human Futures* 130 (Basic, 1988):

> To provide a safe margin against intrusion into possible primitive sentience, the cortical maturation beginning at about thirty weeks is a reasonable landmark until more precise information becomes available.
>
> Therefore, since we should use extreme caution in respecting and protecting possible sentience, a provisional boundary at about twenty-six weeks should provide safety against reasonable concerns. This time is coincident with the present definition of viability . . . .

Of course many things that are against people's interests cause them no physical pain. Someone acts against my interests when he chooses someone else for a job I want, or sues me, or smashes into my car, or writes a bad review of my work, or brings out a better mousetrap and prices it lower than mine, even when these things cause me no physical pain, and, indeed, even when I am unaware that they have happened. In these cases my interests are in play not because of my capacity to feel pain but because of a different and more complex set of capacities: to enjoy or fail to enjoy, to form affections and emotions, to hope and expect, to suffer disappointment and frustration. I do not know when these capacities begin to develop, in primitive or trace or shadowy form, in animals including humans. Infants may have them in at least primitive form, and therefore so may late-stage fetuses, whose brains have been fully formed. But of course such capacities are not possible before sentience, and therefore, on conservative estimates, not before the twenty-sixth week.

We must beware the familiar but fallacious argument that abortion must be against the interests of a fetus, because it would have been against the interests of almost anyone now alive to have been aborted. Once a creature develops interests, then it becomes true, in retrospect, that certain events would have been against those interests if they had happened in the past. It obviously does not follow that these events were therefore against interests someone had *when* they happened. Suppose we assume that it was good for me that my father was not sent on a long business trip the night before my parents conceived me, rather than, as in fact happened, two days later. It does not follow that it would have been bad for anyone, in the same way, had he left on the earlier date. There never would have been anyone for whom it could have been bad.

Of course, when a fetus is aborted, there is something for whom someone might think this bad, a candidate, as it were. But the fetus's existence makes no difference to the logical point. If the fact that I would not now exist had my father left early does not entail that there was some creature for whom it would have been bad if he had, as it plainly does not, then the fact that I would not exist if I had been aborted doesn't entail that either. Whether abortion is against the interests of a fetus must depend on whether the fetus itself has interests, not on whether interests will develop if no abortion takes place.

This distinction may help explain what some observers have found puzzling. Many people who believe that abortion is morally permissible nevertheless think it wrong for pregnant women to smoke or drink or otherwise to behave in ways injurious to a child they intend to bear. Critics say that this combination of views is contradictory: since killing something is worse than injuring it, it cannot be wrong to smoke and yet not wrong to abort. But if a woman smokes during pregnancy, someone will later exist whose interests will have been seriously damaged by her behavior. If she aborts, no one will exist against whose interests that will ever have been.

IX. The Real Issue in *Roe v Wade*

An important conclusion follows from my argument so far: If the only issue at stake in the constitutional debate was whether states could treat a fetus as a person whose rights are competitive with those of a pregnant woman, then *Roe v Wade* would plainly be right. But that is not the only issue at stake, and (though this is widely misunderstood) that is not even the central issue in the underlying national debate about the *morality* of abortion. Most people, it is true, say that both the moral and the legal debate turns on some question about the moral personality, or rights, or interests of a fetus. They say that it turns, for example, on whether a fetus is a metaphysical or moral person, or whether a fetus has interests of its own, or how its interests should rank in importance with those of a pregnant woman, or some other question of that sort. In fact, however, most people's actual views about the morality of abortion in different circumstances make no sense if we try to understand these views as flowing from a set of consistent answers they give to questions about fetal personhood or rights or interests.

Most people think, for example, that abortion is always morally problematic, and must never be undertaken except for very good reason, but that it is nevertheless sometimes justified. Some think it justified only to save the life of the mother. Other overlapping but non-identical groups think it justified in other circumstances as well: to protect the mother from non-life threatening physical impairment, for example, or in cases of rape and incest, or in cases of serious fetal deformity. Some people who think abortion always morally problematic also think it justified when childbirth would severely cripple a mother's chances for a successful life herself. Many people also think that a pregnant woman should be free to decide about abortion for herself, even when she chooses abortion in circumstances in which they believe it morally impermissible. None of these complex positions flows from a consistent answer to the question whether a fetus is a moral person, or how its interests compare in importance to other people's interests.

Most people's views about abortion can only be understood as responses to a very different set of issues. They assume that human life is *intrinsically* valuable, and worthy of a kind of awe, just because it is human life. They think that once a human life begins, it is a very bad thing—a kind of sacrilege—that it end prematurely, particularly through someone's deliberate act. That assumption does not presuppose that the creature whose life is in question is a person with rights or interests, because it does not suppose that death is bad *for* the creature whose life ends. On the contrary, the assumption explains why some people think suicide morally wrong even in circumstances in which they believe suicide would be best for the person who dies. Most people take a parallel view about the destruction of other things they treat as sacrosanct, which plainly involve no moral personhood: works of art, for example, and particular animal species. Our attitude toward the destruction of human life has the same structure, though it is, understandably, much more intense.

Though most people accept that human life is sacrosanct, and must be respected as such, the American community is divided about what that respect actually requires in the kinds of circumstances I just described: rape, incest, fetal deformity, and cases in which motherhood would have a serious and detrimental impact on the potential mother's own life. Some Americans think that respect for life forbids abortion in some or all of these circumstances; others think that respect for life recommends and even requires abortion in some or all of them.[38] As I argue in the forthcoming book I mentioned, these differences reflect profound differences in people's views about the relative importance of divine, natural and human contributions to the overall intrinsic value of a human life. They also reflect, as Kristin Luker has argued, different convictions about the appropriate lives for women to lead in our society.[39] The public is deeply divided about these matters. It is divided, however, not into two bitterly opposed groups—one of which affirms and the other of which denies that a fetus is a person—but in a much more complex way, because judgments about whether abortion dishonors or respects the intrinsic value of life in different circumstances involve a large variety of separate issues.

---

[38] *McRae v Califano*, 491 F Supp 630, 727-28 (E D NY), rev'd as *Harris v McRae*, 448 US 297 (1980).

[39] Kristin Luker, *Abortion and the Politics of Motherhood* ch 8 (California, 1984).

So what I take to be the uncontroversial propositions that a fetus is not a constitutional person, and that a state may not enlarge the category of constitutional persons, do not, after all, entail that *Roe v Wade* was right. Neither paintings nor animal species nor future human beings are constitutional persons. But no one doubts that government can treat art and culture as having intrinsic value, or that government can and should act to protect the environment, endangered animal species, and the quality of life of future generations of people. The majority in a community can levy taxes that will be used to support museums. It can forbid people to destroy their own buildings if it deems these to be of historical or architectural value. It can prohibit building or manufacturing that threatens endangered species or that will injure future generations. Why should a majority not have the power to enforce a much more passionate conviction—that abortion is a desecration of the inherent value that attaches to every human life?

So the most difficult constitutional issue in the abortion controversy is whether states can legitimately claim a detached interest in protecting the intrinsic value, or sanctity, of human life. Does our Constitution allow states to decide not only what rights and interests people have and how these should be enforced and protected, but also whether human life is inherently valuable, why it is so, and how that inherent value should be respected? We cannot dispose of that question in the quick way some liberals might prefer: we cannot say that an individual woman's decision whether or not to have an abortion affects only herself (or only herself and the fetus's father) and that it is therefore none of the community's business which decision she makes. Individual decisions inevitably affect shared collective values. Part of the sense of the sacred is a sense of taboo, a shared sense of horror at desecration, and it is surely harder to maintain a sense of taboo about abortion in a community in which others not only reject the taboo but violate it openly, especially if they receive official financial or moral support. It is plainly more difficult for a parent to raise his or her children to share the conviction that abortion is always a desecration in such a community than in one in which abortion is branded a crime.

The constitutional question I describe therefore lies at the intersection of two sometimes competing traditions, both of which are part of America's political heritage. The first is the tradition of religious and personal freedom. The second is a tradition that assigns government responsibility for guarding the public moral space in which all must live. A good part of constitutional law consists in reconciling these two ideas. What is the appropriate balance in the case of abortion?

X. Government's Legitimate Concerns

One idea deployed in both the majority and dissenting opinions in *Roe* might have seemed mysterious: that a state has an interest in "protecting human life." I have now assigned a particular sense to that idea. A community has an interest in protecting the sanctity of life—in protecting the community's sense that human life in any form has enormous intrinsic value—by requiring its members to acknowledge that intrinsic value in their individual decisions. But that statement is ambiguous. It might describe either of two goals, and the distinction between them is extremely important. The first is the goal of responsibility. A state might aim that its citizens treat decisions about abortion as matters of moral importance, that they recognize that fundamental intrinsic values are at stake in their decision, and that they decide reflectively, not out of immediate convenience but out of examined conviction. The second is the goal of conformity. A state might aim that all its citizens obey rules and practices that the majority believes best capture and respect the sanctity of life, that they abort only in circumstances, if any, in which the majority thinks abortion is appropriate or at least permissible.

These goals of responsibility and conformity are not only different; they are antagonistic. If we aim at responsibility, we must leave citizens free, in the end, to decide as they think right, because that is what moral responsibility entails. If, on the other hand, we aim at conformity, we deny citizens that decision. We demand that they act in a way that might be contrary to their own moral convictions, and we discourage rather than encourage them to develop their own sense of when and why life is sacred.

The traditional assumption that states have a derivative interest in preventing abortion, which I have rejected, submerges the distinction between the two goals. If a fetus is a person, then of course the state's dominant goal must be to protect that person, just as it protects all other people. The state must therefore subordinate any interest it has in developing its citizens' sense of moral responsibility to its interest that they reach, or at least act on, a particular moral conclusion: that killing people is wrong.

But when we shift the state's interest, as we have, to its interest in protecting a particular intrinsic value, then the contrast and opposition between the two goals moves into the foreground. The sanctity of life is, as I said, a highly contestable value. What it requires in particular cases is controversial: when a fetus is deformed, for example, or when having a child would seriously depress a woman's chance to make something valuable of her own life. Does a state protect a contestable value best by encouraging people to accept the value *as* contestable, with the understanding that they are responsible for deciding for themselves what it means? Or does the state protect that value best by itself deciding, through the political process, which interpretation is the right one, and then forcing everyone to conform? The goal of responsibility justifies the first choice; the goal of conformity the second. A state cannot pursue both goals at the same time.

I can think of no reason, grounded in a plausible conception of either equal concern or basic liberty, why government should not aim that its citizens treat decisions about human life and death as matters of serious moral importance. The benefits of such a policy are evident and pervasive. So in my view the Constitution allows states to pursue the goal of responsibility; but only in ways that respect the distinction between that goal and the antagonistic goal of wholly or partly coercing a final decision. May a state require a woman contemplating abortion to wait twenty-four hours before the operation? May it require that she receive information explaining the gravity of a decision to abort? May it require a pregnant teen-age woman to consult with her parents, or with some other adult? Or a married woman to inform her husband if she can locate him? Must the government provide funds for abortion if, and on the same terms as, it provides funds for the costs of childbirth for those too poor to bear those costs themselves? Constitutional lawyers have tended to discuss these issues as if they were all governed by *Roe*, as they would be if the only pertinent issue were whether a fetus is a person. If that were the only issue, and if *Roe* is right that a fetus is not a constitutional person, then on what ground could a state require women contemplating abortion to wait, or to discuss the question with an adult? On what ground could Congress aid women who wanted to bear their fetuses but not those who wanted to abort?

Much of the media discussion about how far the Supreme Court has amended *Roe* in its recent decisions presupposes that questions about responsibility and questions about conformity are tied together in that way. That explains why the Court's decision in *Webster*[40] was widely viewed as in itself altering *Roe*,[41] why the New York Times said that the Third Circuit's recent *Casey* decision upholding a comprehensive Pennsylvania regulatory statute assumed that *Roe* would soon be overturned,[42] and why so many commentators expect the Supreme Court, which has agreed to review the Third Circuit decision, to use that opportunity further to narrow *Roe* or perhaps to overrule it altogether, even though the Court requested parties only to brief issues the Third Circuit had actually addressed.[43]

Many of these commentators say that *Roe* gave women a fundamental right to abortion, which states need a compelling reason to curtail, and that *Webster* undermined *Roe*, and *Casey* will undermine it further, by allowing states to curtail the right without such a reason. But when we understand *Roe* as I suggest, this analysis becomes too crude. The fundamental right *Roe* upheld is a right against conformity. It is a right that states not prohibit abortion before the third trimester, either directly or through undue burdens on a woman's choice to abort. *Roe* itself did not grant a right, fundamental or otherwise, that states not encourage responsibility in the decision a woman makes or that states not display a collective view of which decision is most appropriate.

It is a further question, certainly, whether a particular regulation—say, a mandatory waiting period or mandatory notification or consultation—makes abortion much more expensive or dangerous or difficult to secure, and so does unduly burden the right against conformity.[44] And of course I agree that it would be naive to read the Court's recent decisions as carrying no threat to *Roe* at all. The past statements of at least four justices, and the likely views of the two newest appointees, are threatening indeed. But we do no favor to the crucial right *Roe* recognized by insisting that

[40] *Webster v Reproductive Health Services*, 492 US 490 (1989).

[41] Professor Tribe, for example, says that "[i]f constitutional law is as constitutional law does, then after *Webster*, *Roe* is not what it once was." Tribe, *Abortion* at 24 (cited in note 36).

[42] See Michael de Courcy Hinds, *Appeals Court Upholds Limits For Abortions*, NY Times A1 (Oct 22, 1991), discussing *Planned Parenthood v Casey*, 947 F2d 682 (3d Cir 1991), cert granted in part by 60 USLW 3388 (1992), and in part by 60 USLW 3446 (1992). In fact the majority opinion in *Casey* assumed the distinction between responsibility and conformity I defend in the text, and interpreted Justice O'Connor's "undue burden" test in *Webster*, 492 US at 529-31 (O'Connor concurring), to presuppose that distinction as well.

[43] See, for example, Sheryl McCarthy, *Climactic Battle Is at Hand*, Newsday 5 (Jan 22, 1992); *Washington Brief*, Natl L J 5 (Feb 3, 1992).

[44] In *Casey*, the Third Circuit, claiming to follow Justice O'Connor, proposed that the pertinent test should be whether the regulation imposed an "undue burden" on a woman's right to have an abortion if after reflection she wished one. 947 F2d at 695-97, 706-07.

every decision pro-life groups applaud is automatically another nail in *Roe*'s coffin.

The real question decided in *Roe*, and the heart of the national debate, is the question of conformity. I said that government sometimes acts properly when it coerces people in order to protect values the majority endorses: when it collects taxes to support art, or when it requires businessmen to spend money to avoid endangering a species, for example. Why (I asked) can the state not forbid abortion on the same ground: that the majority of its citizens thinks that aborting a fetus, except when the mother's own life is at stake, is an intolerable insult to the inherent value of human life?

XI. Conformity and Coercion

I begin my reply to that question by noticing three central and connected reasons why prohibiting abortion is a very different matter from conservation or aesthetic zoning or protecting endangered species. First, the impact on particular people—pregnant women—is far greater. A woman who is forced by her community to bear a child she does not want is no longer in charge of her own body. It has been taken over for purposes she does not share. That is a partial enslavement, a deprivation of liberty vastly more serious than any disadvantage citizens must bear to protect cultural treasures or to save troubled species. The partial enslavement of a forced pregnancy is, moreover, only the beginning of the price a woman denied an abortion pays. Bearing a child destroys many women's lives, because they will no longer be able to work or study or live as they believe they should, or because they will be unable to support that child. Adoption, even when available, may not reduce the injury. Many women would find it nearly intolerable to turn their child over to others to raise and love. Of course, these different kinds of injury are intensified if the pregnancy began in rape or incest, or if a child is born with grave physical or mental handicaps. Many women regard these as not simply undesirable but terrible consequences, and would do almost anything to avoid them. We must never forget that a great many abortions took place, before *Roe v Wade*, in states that prohibited abortion. These were illegal abortions, and many of them were very dangerous. If a woman desperate for an abortion defies the criminal law, she may risk her life. If she bows to it, her life might be destroyed, and her self-respect compromised.

Second, it is a matter of deep disagreement within our culture, as I said, what someone who is anxious to respect the intrinsic value of human life should therefore do about abortion. There is no parallel disagreement in the case of the other values I mentioned. No one could plausibly claim that respect for future generations sometimes means leaving the planet uninhabitable for them or that respect for animal species sometimes means allowing their extinction. When the law requires people to make sacrifices for those values, it requires them, at most, to sacrifice for something that they do not believe to be important, but that the rest of the community does. They are not forced to act in ways that they think are not only disadvantageous to them but ethically wrong.[45] A woman who must bear a child whose life will be stunted by deformity, or a child who is doomed to an impoverished childhood and an inadequate education, or a child whose existence will cripple the woman's own life, is not merely forced to make sacrifices for values she does not share. She is forced to act not just in the absence of, but in defiance of, her own beliefs about what respect for human life means and requires.

Third, our convictions about how and why human life has intrinsic importance, from which we draw our views about abortion, are much more fundamental to our overall moral personality than the other convictions about inherent value I mentioned. They are decisive in forming our opinions about all life-and-death matters, including not only abortion but also suicide, euthanasia, the death penalty and conscientious objection to war. Their power is even greater than this suggests, moreover, because our opinions about how and why our *own* lives have intrinsic value crucially influence every major choice we make about how we should live.[46] Very few people's opinions about architectural conservation or endangered species are even nearly so foundational to the rest of their moral personality, even nearly so interwoven with the other major structural convictions of their lives.

These interconnections are most evident in the lives of people who are religious in a traditional way. The connection between their faith and their opinions about abortion is not contingent but constitutive: their convictions about abortion are shadows of more general foundational convictions about why human life itself is im-

[45] Of course, government sometimes forces people to do what they think wrong—to pay taxes that will be used to fight a war they think immoral, for example. But in such cases government justifies coercion by appealing to the rights and interests of other people, not to an intrinsic value those who are coerced believe requires the opposite decision.

[46] See Ronald Dworkin, *Foundations of a Liberal Equality*, in 11 *The Tanner Lectures on Human Values* 1 (Utah, 1990).

portant, convictions at work in all aspects of their lives. A particular religion, like Catholicism, could not comprehensively change its views about abortion without becoming a significantly different faith, organized around a significantly different sense of the ground and consequences of the sacrosanct character of human life. People who are not religious in the conventional way also have general, instinctive convictions about whether, why and how any human life—their own, for example—has intrinsic value. No one can lead even a mildly reflective life without expressing such convictions. These convictions surface, for almost everyone, at exactly the same critical moments in life—in decisions about reproduction and death and war. Someone who is an atheist, because he does not believe in a personal god, nevertheless has convictions or at least instincts about the value of human life in an infinite and cold universe, and these convictions are just as pervasive, just as foundational to moral personality, as the convictions of a Catholic or a Moslem. They are convictions that have, in the words of a famous Supreme Court opinion, "a place in the life of its possessor parallel to that filled by the orthodox belief in God . . . ."[47]

For that reason we may describe people's beliefs about the inherent value of human life, beliefs deployed in their opinions about abortion, as *essentially* religious beliefs. I shall later try to defend that claim as a matter of constitutional interpretation: I shall argue that such beliefs should be deemed religious within the meaning of the First Amendment. My present point is not legal but philosophical, however. Many people, it is true, think that no belief is religious in character unless it presupposes a personal god. But many established religions—some forms of Buddhism and Hinduism, for example—include no commitment to such a supreme being. Once we set aside the idea that every religious belief presupposes a god, it is doubtful that we can discover any defining feature that all but only religious beliefs have. We must decide whether to classify a belief as religious in a less rigid way: by asking whether it is similar in content to plainly religious beliefs.[48] On that test, the belief that the value of human life transcends its value for the creature whose life it is—that human life is objectively valuable from the point of view, as it were, of the universe—is plainly a religious belief, even when it is held by people

[47] *United States v Seeger*, 380 US 163, 166 (1965).

[48] Kent Greenawalt, *Religion as a Concept in Constitutional Law*, 72 Cal L Rev 753 (1984); George Freeman III, *The Misguided Search for the Constitutional Definition of "Religion"*, 71 Georgetown L J 1519 (1983).

who do not believe in a personal deity. It is, in fact, the most fundamental purpose of traditional religions to make exactly that claim to its faithful, and to embody it in some vision or narrative that makes the belief seem intelligible and persuasive.

Religion in that way responds to the most terrifying feature of human life: that we have lives to lead, and death to face, with no evident reason to think that our living, still less how we live, makes any genuine difference at all. The existential question whether human life has any intrinsic or objective importance has been raised in many ways. People ask about the "meaning" or "point" of life, for example. However it is put, the question is foundational. It cannot be answered by pointing out that if people live in a particular recommended way—observing a particular moral code, for example, or following a particular theory of justice—this will make them, individually or collectively, safer or more prosperous, or that it will help them fulfill or realize their human nature, as understood in some particular way. The existential question is deeper, because it asks why any of that matters.

In that way beliefs about the intrinsic importance of human life are distinguished from more secular convictions about morality, fairness and justice. The latter declare how competing interests of particular people should be served or adjusted or compromised. They rarely reflect any distinctive view about why human interests have objective intrinsic importance, or even whether they do.[49] That explains why people with very different views about the meaning or point of human life can agree about justice, and why people with much the same views about that religious issue can disagree about justice dramatically. Of course many people believe that fairness and justice are important only because they think that it is objectively important how a human life goes.[50] But their particular views about what justice requires are not, for that reason, themselves views about why or in what way that is true.

Religions attempt to answer the deeper existential question by connecting individual human lives to a transcendent objective value. They declare that all human lives (or, for more parochial

[49] John Rawls, for example, distinguishes his own and other theories of justice from what he calls comprehensive religious or ethical schemes; political theories of justice, he says, presuppose no opinion about what is objectively important. In particular, they presuppose no opinion about if or why or in what way it is intrinsically important that human life continue or prosper, though of course political theories of justice are compatible with a great variety of such opinions. See John Rawls, *Justice as Fairness, Political not Metaphysical*, 14 Phil & Pub Aff 223 (1985).

[50] See Dworkin, *Foundations of a Liberal Equality* (cited in note 46).

religions, the lives of believers) have objective importance through some source of value outside human subjective experience: the love of a creator or a redeemer, for example, or nature believed to give objective normative importance to what it creates, or a natural order understood in some other but equally transcendental way. People who think that abortion is morally problematic, even though a fetus has no interests of its own, all accept that human life is intrinsically, objectively valuable. Some think that human life is intrinsically important because it is created by a god, others because human life is the triumph of nature's genius, and others because human life's complexity and promise is in itself awe-inspiring. Some people in each of these groups believe that because human life has intrinsic importance abortion is always, or almost always, wrong. Others in each group have reached a contrary conclusion: that abortion is sometimes necessary in order truly to respect life's inherent value.[51] In each case the belief affirms the essentially religious idea that the importance of human life transcends subjective experience.

XII. The Right of Procreative Autonomy

These three ways in which abortion is special, even among issues that involve claims about inherent value, suggest an interpretation of the much-discussed constitutional right of privacy. That constitutional right limits a state's power to invade personal liberty when the state acts, not to protect rights or interests of other people, but to safeguard an intrinsic value. A state may not curtail liberty, in order to protect an intrinsic value, (1) when the decisions it forbids are matters of personal commitment on essentially religious issues, (2) when the community is divided about what the best understanding of the value in question requires, and (3) when the decision has very great and disparate impact on the person whose decision is displaced.[52]

I should say again (though by now you will be tired of the point) that the principle of privacy I just defined would not guarantee a right to abortion if a fetus were a constitutional person

---

[51] *McRae*, 491 F Supp at 690-702. I develop this point at length in the forthcoming book I mentioned earlier.

[52] I do not mean that no stronger constitutional right of personal autonomy can be defended as flowing from the best interpretation of the Constitution as a whole. Indeed I think a significantly stronger right can be. But I shall not defend any principle broader than the more limited one just described, because that principle is strong enough to ground a right of privacy understood to include a right to procreative autonomy.

from the moment of conception. The principle is limited to circumstances in which the state claims authority to protect some inherent value, not the rights and interests of another person. But once we accept that a fetus is not a constitutional person, and shift the ground of constitutional inquiry to the different question of whether a state may forbid abortion in order to respect the inherent value of human life, then the principle of privacy plainly does apply.

It applies because ethical decisions about procreation meet the tests the principle provides. That is why procreative decisions have been collected, through the common law method of adjudication, into a distinct principle we might call the principle of procreative autonomy. That principle, understood as an application of the more general principle of privacy, provides the best available justification for the Court's decisions about contraception, for example. In the first of these cases—*Griswold v Connecticut*[53]—the Justices who made up the majority provided a variety of justifications for their decision. Justice Harlan said that laws forbidding married couples to use contraceptives violated the Constitution because they could only be enforced by police searching marital bedrooms, a practice that struck him as repulsive to the concept of ordered liberty.[54]

This justification was inadequate even for the decision in *Griswold*—a prohibition on the purchase or sale of contraceptives could be enforced without searching marital bedrooms, just as a prohibition on the sale of drugs to or the use of drugs by married couples can be enforced without such a search. And it was plainly inadequate for the later decisions in the series. In one of these, Justice Brennan, speaking for the Court, offered a different and more general explanation. "If the right of privacy means anything," he said, "it is the right of the *individual*, married or not, to be free from government intrusion into matters so fundamentally affecting a person as the decision whether to bear or beget a child."[55]

I take the principle of procreative autonomy to be an elaboration of Brennan's suggestion. It explains the sense in which individual procreative decisions are, as he said, fundamental. Many decisions, including economic decisions, for example, have serious

[53] 381 US 479 (1965).

[54] Id at 500 (Harlan concurring) (referring to his dissent in *Poe v Ullman*, 367 US 497, 539-45 (1961)).

[55] *Eisenstadt v Baird*, 405 US 438, 453 (1972) (emphasis in original).

and disparate impact. Procreative decisions are fundamental in a different way, because the moral issues on which a procreative decision hinges are religious in the broad sense I defined. They are issues touching the ultimate point and value of human life itself. The state's power to prohibit contraception could plausibly be defended only by assuming a general power to dictate to all citizens what respect for the inherent value of human life requires: that it requires, for example, that people not make love except with the intention to procreate.

The Supreme Court, in denying the specific power to make contraception criminal, presupposed the more general principle of procreative autonomy I am defending. That is important, because almost no one believes that the contraception decisions should now be overruled. It is true that Bork had challenged *Griswold* and the later decisions in speeches and articles before his nomination.[56] But during his hearings, he hinted that *Griswold* might be defended on other grounds.[57]

The law's integrity demands, as I said, that principles necessary to support an authoritative set of decisions must be accepted in other contexts as well. It might seem an appealing political compromise to apply the principle of procreative autonomy to contraception, which almost no one now thinks the states can forbid, but not to apply it to abortion, which powerful conservative constituencies violently oppose. But the point of integrity—the point of law itself—is exactly to rule out political compromises of that kind. We must be one nation of principle: our Constitution must represent conviction, not the tactical strategies of justices anxious to satisfy as many political constituencies as possible.

Integrity does not, of course, require that justices respect principles embedded in past decisions that they and others regard as *mistakes*. It permits the Court to declare, as it has several times in the past, that a particular decision or string of decisions was in error, because the principles underlying those decisions are inconsistent with more fundamental principles embedded in the Constitution's structure and history. The Court cannot declare everything in the past a mistake: that would destroy integrity under the pretext of serving it. It must exercise its power to disregard past

---

[56] See, for example, Robert H. Bork, *Neutral Principles and Some First Amendment Problems*, 47 Ind L J 1, 7-10 (1971).

[57] Nomination of Robert H. Bork to be Associate Justice of the Supreme Court of the United States, Hearings Before the Senate Committee on the Judiciary, 100th Cong, 1st Sess 250 (Sep 16, 1987). See Ethan Bonner, *Battle for Justice* 221-22, 260 (Norton, 1989).

decisions modestly. But it must also exercise that power in good faith. It cannot ignore principles underlying past decisions it purports to approve, decisions it would ratify if asked to do so, decisions almost no one, not even rabid critics of the Court's past performance, now disapproves or regards as mistakes. The contraception cases fall into that category, and it would be both dangerous and offensive for the Court cynically to ignore the principles presupposed in those cases in any decision it now reaches about abortion.

So integrity demands general recognition of the principle of procreative autonomy, and therefore of the right of women to decide for themselves not only whether to conceive but whether to bear a child. If you remain in doubt, then consider the possibility that in some state a majority of voters will come to think that it shows *disrespect* for the sanctity of life to continue a pregnancy in some circumstances—in cases of fetal deformity, for example. If a majority has the power to impose its own views about the sanctity of life on everyone, then the state could *require* someone to abort, even if that were against her own religious or ethical convictions, at least if abortion had become physically as convenient and safe as, for example, the vaccinations and inoculations states are now recognized as having the power to require.

Of course, if a fetus were a person with a right to live, it would not follow from the fact that one state had the right to forbid abortion that another would have the right to require it. But that does follow once we recognize that the constitutional question at stake in the abortion controversy is whether a state can impose a canonical interpretation of the inherent value of life on everyone. Of course it would be intolerable for a state to require an abortion to prevent the birth of a deformed child. No one doubts, I think, that that requirement would be unconstitutional. But the reason why—because it denies a pregnant woman's right to decide for herself what the sanctity of life requires her to do about her own pregnancy—applies with exactly equal force in the other direction. A state just as seriously insults the dignity of a pregnant woman when it forces her to the opposite choice, and the fact that the choice is approved by a majority is no better justification in the one case than in the other.

XIII. Textual Homes

My argument so far has not appealed to any particular constitutional provision. But, as I said, the general structure of the Bill of Rights is such that any moral right as fundamental as the right of procreative autonomy is very likely to have a safe home in the Constitution's text. Indeed, we should expect to see a principle of that foundational character protected not just by one but by several constitutional provisions, because these must necessarily overlap in the way I also described.

The right of procreative autonomy follows from any competent interpretation of the Due Process Clause and of the Supreme Court's past decisions applying that clause. I have already indicated, in my discussion of the contraception cases, my grounds for that claim. I shall now argue, however, for a different and further textual basis for that right. The First Amendment prohibits government from establishing any religion, and it guarantees all citizens the free exercise of their own religion. The Fourteenth Amendment, which incorporates the First Amendment, imposes the same prohibition and the same responsibility on the states. These provisions guarantee the right of procreative autonomy. I do not mean that the First Amendment defense of that right is stronger than the Due Process Clause defense. On the contrary, the First Amendment defense is more complex and less demonstrable as a matter of precedent. I take it up because it is, as I shall try to show, a natural defense, because it illuminates an important dimension of the national debate about abortion, and because the argument for it illustrates both the power and the constraining force of the ideal of legal integrity.

Locating the abortion controversy in the First Amendment would seem natural to most people, who instinctively perceive that the abortion controversy is at bottom essentially a religious one. Some of you may fear, however, that I am trying to revive an old argument now rejected even by some of those who once subscribed to it. This argument holds that since the morality of abortion is a matter of controversy among religious groups, since it is declared immoral and sinful by some orthodox religions—conspicuously the Catholic Church—but permissible by others, the old idea of separation of church and state means that government must leave the subject of abortion alone. That would indeed be a very bad argument if states were permitted to treat a fetus as a person with rights and interests competitive with the rights of a pregnant woman. For the most important responsibility of government is to identify the differing and sometimes competing rights and interests of the people for whom it is responsible, and to decide how these rights may best be accommodated and these interests best served. Government has no reason to abdicate that responsibility just because (or when) organized religion also takes an interest in those matters. Religious bodies and groups were among the strongest campaigners against slavery, and they have for centuries sought social justice, the eradication of suffering and disease, and a vast variety of other humanitarian goals. If the distinction between church and state barred government from also taking up those goals, the doctrine would paralyze government altogether.

But we are now assuming that the issue whether a fetus is a person with rights and interests of its own has already been decided, by secular government, in the only way that issue can be decided under our constitutional system. Now we are considering a different constitutional issue: whether states may nevertheless prohibit abortion in order to endorse a controversial view about what respect for the intrinsic value of human life requires. That is not an issue about who has rights, or how people's competing interests should be balanced and protected. If states are forbidden to prohibit conduct on the ground that it insults the intrinsic value of human life, they are not therefore disabled from pursuing their normal responsibilities. On the contrary, it is one of government's most fundamental duties, recognized throughout Western democracies since the eighteenth century, to insure that people have a right to live their lives in accordance with their own convictions about essentially religious issues. So the reasons for rejecting the bad argument I described are not arguments against my suggestion that the First Amendment forbids states to force people to conform to an official view about what the sanctity of human life requires.

We must now consider arguments for that suggestion. It is controversial how the Establishment and Free Exercise Clauses should be interpreted, and the Supreme Court's rulings on these clauses are somewhat unclear.[58] I cannot offer an extended consideration of those rulings here, and my immediate purpose is not to compose a full and detailed legal argument for the First Amendment defense, but rather to indicate the main structural lines of that defense. Any satisfactory interpretation of the Religion Clauses of the amendment must cover two issues. First, it must fill out the phrase "free exercise of religion" by explaining which features make a particular belief a religious conviction rather than a non-religious moral principle or a personal preference. Second, it must interpret "establishment" by explaining the difference between secular and religious aims of government.

[58] See Greenawalt, 72 Cal L Rev 753 (cited in note 48); Freeman, 71 Georgetown L J 1519 (cited in note 48).

Difficult cases arise when government restricts or penalizes conduct required by genuinely religious convictions, but for the secular purpose of serving and protecting other people's interests.[59] Such cases require courts to decide how far the right of free exercise prevents government from adopting policies it believes would increase the general secular welfare of the community. It is a very different matter, however, when government's only purpose is to support one side of an argument about an essentially religious issue. Legislation for that purpose which substantially impaired anyone's religious freedom would violate both of the First Amendment's Religion Clauses at once.

Of course, if a fetus were a constitutional person, with interests government is obliged and entitled to protect, then legislation outlawing abortion would fall into the first of these categories even if convictions permitting or requiring abortion are genuinely religious in character. Such legislation would plainly be constitutional: rights of free exercise would not extend to the killing of a fetus any more than they extend to human sacrifice in religious ritual. But a fetus is not a constitutional person. If people's convictions about what the inherent value of human life requires are religious convictions, therefore, any government demand for conformity would be an attempt to impose a collective religion, and the case would fall into the second category.

What makes a belief a religious one for purposes of the First Amendment? The great majority of eighteenth-century statesmen who wrote and ratified the Constitution may have assumed that every religious conviction presupposes a personal god. But, as the Supreme Court apparently decided in *United States v Seeger*, that restriction is not now acceptable as part of a constitutional definition of religion, in part because not all the major religions represented in this country presuppose such a being.[60] Once the idea of

---

[59] We can regard the Supreme Court's decision in *Smith v Employment Division*, 494 US 872 (1990), as an example of that kind of case, whether or not we agree with the decision.

[60] 380 US 163. The Court in that case construed a statute rather then the Constitution. But since the Court's decision contradicted the evident statutory purpose, commentators have assumed that the Court meant to imply that the statute was constitutional only if so construed.

In a recent book, which I received while this Article was in galleys, Professor Peter Wenz argues for a ground of distinction between religious and secular opinions that is different from the two possible distinctions I mention here (which he calls "epistemological"). He accepts the traditional view, that the argument over abortion is about whether a fetus is a person, but insists that the question whether an early fetus is a person is a religious one because it cannot be decided "entirely" on the basis of "methods of argumentation that are

religion is divorced from that requirement, however, courts face a difficulty in distinguishing between religious and other kinds of conviction. There are two possibilities: a conviction can be deemed religious because of its content—because it speaks to concerns identified as distinctly religious—or because it has very great subjective importance to the person who holds it, as orthodox religious convictions do for devout believers. In *Seeger*, the Court suggested that a scruple is religious if it has "a place in the life of its possessor parallel to that filled by the orthodox belief in God of one who clearly qualifies for the exemption."[61] That statement, taken by itself, is ambiguous. It might mean that a conviction is religious if it answers the same questions that orthodox religion answers for a believer, which is a test of content, or that it is religious if it is embraced as fervently as orthodox religion is embraced by a devout believer, which is a test of subjective importance.

The opinion as a whole is indecisive about which of these two meanings, or which combination of them, the Court intended, and the ambiguity has damaged the development of constitutional law in this area. In any case, however, a subjective importance test is plainly inadequate, by itself, to distinguish religious from other forms of conviction, or indeed from intensely felt preferences. Even people who are religious in the orthodox way often count plainly non-religious affiliations, like patriotism, as equally or even more important. Some test of content is at least necessary, and may be sufficient.

I argued, earlier, that a belief in the objective and intrinsic importance of human life has a distinctly religious content. Convictions that endorse that objective importance play the same role, in providing an objective underpinning for concerns about human rights and interests, as orthodox religious beliefs provide for those who accept them. Several of the theologians the Court cited in *Seeger* made the same claim. The Court called the following statement from the Schema of a recent Ecumenical Council, for example, "a most significant declaration on religion": "Men expect from the various religions answers to the riddles of the human condi-

integral to our way of life." Peter Wenz, *Abortion Rights as Religious Freedom* 131 (Temple, 1992). I agree with the conclusion he reaches: that the abortion debate is primarily a religious one governed by the First Amendment. But his test is not acceptable, because government must make and impose decisions on a wide variety or moral issues about which people disagree profoundly, and which cannot be decided on empirical grounds or by appeal to any convictions shared by everyone or by methods that are in any other way "integral" to any collective way of life.

[61] Id at 165-66.

tion: What is man? What is the meaning and purpose of our lives?"[62]

I can think of no plausible account of the content a belief must have, in order to be religious in character, that would rule out convictions about why and how human life has intrinsic objective importance, except the abandoned test that requires a religious belief to presuppose a god. It is, of course, essential that any test of religious content allow a distinction between religious beliefs, on the one hand, and non-religious political or moral convictions, on the other. I have already suggested, however, how the belief that human life has intrinsic objective importance, and other beliefs that interpret and follow directly from that belief, differ from most people's opinions about political fairness or the just distribution of economic or other resources.[63]

We can see the distinction at work in the Supreme Court's disposition of the conscientious objector cases. In *Seeger*, the Court presumed that the Constitution would not allow exempting men whose opposition to all war was based on theistic religion but not men whose similar opposition was grounded in a non-theistic belief. In *Gillette*, on the other hand, the Court upheld Congress's refusal to grant exemption to men whose opposition to war was selective, even to those whose convictions condemning a particular war were supported by their religion.[64] Though the Court offered various practical grounds for the distinction, these were unpersuasive. The distinction can in fact be justified—if it can be justified at all—only by supposing that though a flat opposition to all war is based on a conviction that human life as such is sacred—which is a distinctly religious conviction—selective opposition is at least normally based on considerations of justice or policy, which justify killing in some cases but not others, and which are not themselves religious in content even when they are endorsed by a religious group. As the Court said,

> A virtually limitless variety of beliefs are subsumable under the rubric, "objection to a particular war." All the factors that might go into nonconscientious dissent from policy, also might appear as the concrete basis of an objection that has roots in conscience and religion as well. Indeed, over the realm of pos-

---

[62] See *Draft Declaration on the Church's Relations with Non-Christians*, in Council Daybook 282 (Vatican II, 3d Sess, 1965), quoted and cited in *Seeger*, 380 US at 181-82 & n 4.

[63] See text accompanying notes 49-51.

[64] *Gillette v United States*, 401 US 437.

> sible situations, opposition to a particular war may more likely be political and nonconscientious, than otherwise.[65]

So the popular sense that the abortion issue is fundamentally a religious one, and some lawyers' sense that it therefore lies outside the proper limits of state action, is at bottom sound, though for reasons somewhat more complex than is often supposed. It rests on a natural—indeed irresistible—understanding of the First Amendment: that a state has no business prescribing what people should think about the ultimate point and value of human life, about why life has intrinsic importance, and about how that value is respected or dishonored in different circumstances. In his reply, Posner objects that if my view of the scope of the Free Exercise Clause were correct, government could not forbid "an aesthete to alter the exterior of his landmark house."[66] But he has misunderstood my view: he apparently thinks that I use a test of subjective importance to identify religious convictions. He points out, as a *reductio ad absurdum* of my argument, that "economic freedom *is* a religion" to a variety of libertarians,[67] suggesting that taxation, which libertarians find particularly offensive, would on my argument violate their religious freedom.

I argued, however, that convictions about the intrinsic value of human life are religious on a test of content, not subjective importance. A law forbidding people to tear down Georgian houses does not raise essentially religious issues, no matter how much some people would prefer to build post-modern pastiches instead, because that law does not presuppose any particular conception of why and how human life is sacred, or take a position on any other matter historically religious in character.[68] It is even plainer that my argument would not justify exempting Milton Friedman from tax on grounds of his free-market faith. Government collects taxes in order to serve a variety of secular interests of its citizens, not to declare or support a particular view about any essentially religious

---

[65] Id at 455 (footnotes omitted). The Court also endorsed, as on a careful view supporting the distinction between universal and selective opposition, the government's claim that opposition to a particular war necessarily involves judgment that is "political and particular" and "based on the same political, sociological, and economic factors that the government necessarily considered" in deciding whether to wage war. Id at 458 (citing government's brief).

[66] Posner, 59 U Chi L Rev at 444 (cited in note 9).

[67] Id at 443.

[68] Such laws do raise other issues about intrinsic value, and in some extremely unusual circumstances might violate a more powerful form of the principle of privacy than the weak form I described and defended.

matter. It is, of course, true that some people resist paying taxes for reasons that do implicate their convictions about the intrinsic value of human life. Some people refuse to pay taxes to finance war on that basis, for example. In such cases compulsory taxation does plausibly impair the free exercise of religion. But the problem falls into the first of the two categories I distinguished, and the appropriate balancing sustains the tax, given the limited character of the infringement of free exercise and the importance of uniform taxation.

I conclude that the right to procreative autonomy, from which a right of choice about abortion flows, is well grounded in the First Amendment.[69] But it would be remarkable, as I said, if so basic a right did not figure in the best interpretation of constitutional liberty and equality as well. It would be remarkable, that is, if lawyers who accepted the right did not think it fundamental to the concept of ordered liberty, and so protected by the Due Process Clause, or part of what government's equal concern for all citizens requires, and so protected by the Equal Protection Clause. Posner is amused that different scholars who endorse a right of procreative autonomy have offered a variety of textual homes for it: he says that in my account, *Roe v Wade* "is the Wandering Jew of constitutional law."[70] But of course, as he would agree, it is hardly an embarrassment for that right that lawyers have disagreed about which clause to emphasize in their arguments for it. Some constitutional lawyers have an odd taste for constitutional neatness: they want rights mapped uniquely onto clauses with no overlap, as if redundancy were a constitutional vice. Once we understand, however, that the Bill of Rights is not a list of discrete remedies drawn up by a parsimonious draftsman, but a commitment to an ideal of just government, that taste makes no more sense than the claim that freedom of religion is not also liberty, or that the protection of freedom for everyone has nothing to do with equality.

---

[69] I should mention a complexity. I have been arguing that many women's decisions about abortion reflect convictions, which may well be inarticulate, about whether abortion or childbirth would best respect what they believe intrinsically valuable about human life. That is not necessarily true of all women who want abortions, however, and the free exercise claim might therefore not be available, as a matter of principle, for everyone. But states could not devise appropriate and practicable tests for discriminating among women in that way, and in any case prohibition would be the establishment of an essentially religious position, even in cases when it worked to outlaw abortion for someone whose grounds were not religious in any sense.

[70] Posner, 59 U Chi L Rev at 441 (cited in note 9).

XIV. Dignity and Concern

I pause for a brief summary. We must abandon the traditional way of understanding the constitutional argument about abortion. It is not an argument about whether a fetus is a person. It is rather a dispute about whether and how far government may enforce an official view about the right understanding of the sanctity of human life. I described a constitutional right—the right of procreational autonomy—which denies government that power. I suggested that this right is firmly embedded in our constitutional history. It is the best available justification of the "privacy" cases, including the contraception cases. Those cases are conventionally understood as residing, by way of textual home, in the Due Process Clause of the Fourteenth Amendment. I argued that they might also rest on the Religion Clauses of the First Amendment.

Posner suggests that my argument is more powerful construed holistically, that is, as an argument about what the Constitution as a whole requires. I do not, as I said, see a difference between clause-by-clause and holistic interpretations of the Bill of Rights. But I nevertheless accept the spirit of his suggestion—that it is important to notice the place the right I have been describing holds not only in the structure of the Constitution, but in our political culture more generally. Cardinal in that culture is a belief in individual human dignity: that people have the moral right—and the moral responsibility—to confront for themselves, answering to their own conscience and conviction, the most fundamental questions touching the meaning and value of their own lives. That assumption was the engine of emancipation and of racial equality, for example. The most powerful arguments against slavery before the Civil War, and for equal protection after it, were framed in the language of dignity: the cruelest aspect of slavery, for the abolitionists, both religious and secular, was its failure to recognize a slave's right to decide issues of value for himself or herself. Indeed the most basic premise of our entire constitutional system—that our government shall be republican rather than despotic—embodies a commitment to that conception of dignity.

So the principle of procreative autonomy, in the broad sense, is a principle that any remotely plausible explanation of our entire political culture would have to recognize. It is also a principle we would want our Constitution to contain even if we were starting on a clean slate, free to make any constitution we wanted. I want to guard against an interpretation of my argument that I would disown, however. It does not suppose that people either are or should be indifferent, either as individuals or as members of a political community, to the decisions their friends or neighbors or fellow citizens or fellow human beings make about abortion. On the contrary it recognizes several reasons why they should not be indifferent. As I have already noticed, individual choices together create a moral environment that inevitably influences what others can do. So a person's concern for his own life, and for that of his children and friends, gives him a reason for worrying about how even strangers treat the inherent value of human life. Our concern that people lead good lives is not naturally limited, moreover, nor should it be, to concern for our own lives and those of our family. We want others, even strangers, not to lead what we regard as a blighted life, ruined by a terrible act of desecration.

But the most powerful reason we have for wanting others to respect the intrinsic value of human life, in the way we think that value demands, is not our concern for our own or other people's interests at all, but just our concern for the value itself. If people did *not* think it transcendently important that human lives not be wasted by abortion, then they would not have the kind of commitment my argument assumes people do have. So of course Americans who think that almost all abortion is immoral must take a passionate interest in the issue: liberals who count such people as deranged busybodies are insensitive as well as wrong. Nevertheless, we must insist on religious tolerance in this area, as in other issues about which people once cared just as passionately and in the same way, and once thought sufficiently important to wage not just sit-ins but wars. Tolerance is a cost we must pay for our adventure in liberty. We are committed, by our Constitution, to live in a community in which no group is deemed clever or spiritual or numerous enough to decide essentially religious matters for everyone else. If we have genuine concern for the lives others lead, moreover, we will also accept that no life is a good one lived against the grain of conviction, that it does not aid someone else's life but spoils it to force values upon him he cannot accept but can only bow before out of fear or prudence.

XV. *Roe* Reconsidered

We must now take a fresh look at *Roe v Wade*. *Roe* did three things. First, it re-affirmed a pregnant woman's constitutional right of procreative autonomy, and declared that states do not have the power simply to forbid abortion on any terms they wish. Second, it recognized that states nevertheless do have a legitimate interest in regulating abortion. Third, it constructed a detailed regime for balancing that right and that interest: it declared, roughly, that states could not forbid abortion for any reason in the first trimester of pregnancy, that they could regulate abortion in the second trimester only out of concern for the health of the mother, and, finally, that they could outlaw abortion altogether after fetal viability, that is, after approximately the beginning of the third trimester. We must inspect those three decisions against the background of our argument so far.

Our argument confirms the first decision. The crucial issue in the constitutional abortion controversy is not whether a fetus is a person—*Roe* was plainly right in holding that a fetus is not a person within the meaning of the Constitution—but whether states have a legitimate power to dictate how their members must respect the inherent value of life. Since any competent interpretation of the Constitution must recognize a principle of procreative autonomy, states do not have the power simply to forbid abortion altogether.

Roe was also right on the second score. States do have a legitimate interest in regulating the abortion decision. It was mysterious, in *Roe* and other decisions, what that interest was. Our account identifies it as a legitimate interest in maintaining a moral environment in which decisions about life and death, including the abortion decision, are taken seriously, treated as matters of moral gravity.

It remains to consider whether *Roe* was right on the third score. Does the trimester scheme it announced allow states to pursue their legitimate interests while adequately protecting a pregnant woman's right of autonomy? That trimester scheme has been criticized as arbitrary and overly rigid, even by some lawyers who are sympathetic to the narrowest decision in *Roe*: that the Texas statute was unconstitutional. Why is the point of viability the crucial point? We might put that question in two ways. We might ask why viability should mark the earliest time at which a state is entitled to prohibit abortion. If it can prohibit abortion then, why not earlier, as a majority of citizens in some states apparently wish? Or we might ask why viability should mark the end of a woman's right to protection. If a state cannot prohibit abortion before viability, then why may it prohibit it after that point? Both questions challenge the point of viability as arbitrary though from different directions. I shall first pursue the second form of the question. What happens at viability to make the right I have been describing—the right of procreative autonomy—less powerful or effective?

Two answers to that question might figure in any defense of the *Roe v Wade* scheme. First, at about the point of viability, but not much before, fetal brain development may be sufficient to allow pain.[71] So at the point of viability, but not much before, a fetus can sensibly be said to have interests of its own. That does not mean, I must emphasize, that a state is permitted to declare a fetus a person at that point. The question who is a constitutional person, with independent constitutional rights in competition with the rights of others, must be decided nationally, as I argued. But a state may nevertheless act to protect the interests even of creatures—animals, for example—who are not constitutional persons, so long as it respects constitutional rights in doing so. So at the point of viability, the state may claim a legitimate derivative interest that is independent of its detached interest in enforcing its collective conception of the sanctity of life.

Second, choosing the point of viability gives a pregnant woman, in most cases, ample opportunity to reflect upon and decide whether she believes it best and right to continue her pregnancy or to terminate it. Very few abortions are performed during the third trimester—only about .01 percent[72]—and even fewer if we exclude emergency abortions necessary to save a mother's life, which almost no one wants to prohibit even near the end of pregnancy. It is true that a very few women—most of whom are very young women—are unaware of their pregnancy until it is nearly complete. But in almost all cases, a woman knows she is pregnant in good time to make a reflective decision before viability. That suggests that a state does not violate most women's right to choose by insisting on a decision before that point, and it also suggests an important reason why a state might properly so insist.

It is an almost universal conviction that abortion becomes progressively morally more problematic as a fetus develops towards the shape of infanthood, as the difference between pregnancy and infancy becomes more a matter of location than development. That widespread conviction seems odd so long as we suppose that whether abortion is wrong depends only on whether a fetus is a person from the moment of conception. But the belief is compelling once we realize that abortion is wrong, when it is, because it

[71] See Grobstein, *Science and the Unborn* at 54-55 (cited in note 37).

[72] *Facts in Brief: Abortion in the United States* (Alan Guttmacher Institute, 1991). See also Stanley K. Henshaw, *Characteristics of U.S. Women Having Abortions, 1982-83,* in Stanley K. Henshaw and Jennifer Van Vort, eds, *Abortion Services in the United States: Each State and Metropolitan Area, 1984-85* 23 (Alan Guttmacher Institute, 1988).

insults the sanctity of human life. The insult to that value is greater when the life destroyed is further advanced, when, as it were, the creative investment in that life is greater. Women who have a genuine opportunity to decide on abortion early in pregnancy, when the impact is much less, but who actually decide only near the end, may well be indifferent to the moral and social meaning of their act. Society has a right, if its members so decide, to protect its culture from that kind of indifference, so long as the means it chooses do not infringe the right of pregnant women to a reflective choice.

Taken together, these two answers provide, I believe, a persuasive explanation of why government is entitled to prohibit abortion, subject to certain exceptions, after the sixth month of pregnancy. But do they provide an answer to the question asked from the other direction? Why may government not prohibit abortion earlier? The first answer would not justify any much earlier date, because, as I said, the central nervous system is not sufficiently developed much before the end of twenty-six weeks of pregnancy to admit of pain.[73] But must that be decisive? The second answer does not depend on attributing interests to a fetus, and, by itself, seems an adequate justification of state power to prohibit abortion after a sufficiently long period. Would women not have a sufficient opportunity to exercise their right of autonomy if they were forbidden abortion after just five months? Four? Three?

Blackmun chose a point in pregnancy that he thought plainly late enough to give women a fair chance to exercise their right, in normal circumstances, and that was salient for two other reasons, each captured in the overall explanation I gave. As I said, viability seems, on the best developmental evidence, the earliest point at which a fetus might be thought to have interests of its own, and the point at which the natural development of a fetus is so far continued that deliberately waiting until after that point seems contemptuous of the inherent value of life. These three factors together indicate viability as the most appropriate point after which a state could properly assert its interests in protecting a fetus's interests, and in responsibility. Blackmun's decision should not be overruled. So important a decision should not be overruled, after nearly twenty years, unless it is clearly wrong, and his was not clearly wrong. On the contrary, the arguments for choosing viability as the key date remain impressive.

---

[73] See note 37.

But it is important to acknowledge that a different test, bringing the cut-off date forward by some period, would have been acceptable if it had afforded women enough time to exercise their right to terminate an unwanted pregnancy. Of course, the earlier the cut-off time, the more important it would be to provide realistic exceptions for reasons the mother could not reasonably have discovered earlier. Suppose that the Court had substituted for the fixed scheme of *Roe*, not another fixed scheme, but rather a constitutional standard drafted in terms of overall reasonableness, which the federal courts would enforce case-by-case. Such a standard might have provided, in effect, that any prohibition would be unconstitutional if it did not provide women a reasonable time to decide upon an abortion after discovering that they were pregnant, or after discovering medical information indicating defects in the fetus or an increased risk to the mother of pregnancy, or other facts pertinent to the impact of childbirth on their lives.

In the end, as Blackmun no doubt anticipated, the Court would have had to adopt more rigid standards that selected at least a *prima facie* point in pregnancy before which prohibition would be presumptively unconstitutional. But the Court might have developed those standards gradually, perhaps deciding, in the first instance, that any statute that forbade second-term abortions would be subject to strict scrutiny to see whether it contained the exceptions necessary to protect a woman's right to a reflective choice. That approach still would have struck down the Texas law in *Roe*. It would also strike down the equally strict laws that some states and Guam have recently adopted, each hoping to provide the lawsuit that will end *Roe*.

Would it make much practical difference if the Supreme Court now substituted such a case-by-case test for *Roe*'s rigid structure? A case-by-case test might not, in fact, much reduce legal abortion. In 1987, only ten percent of abortions took place in the second trimester,[74] and many of these were on medical or other grounds that would still be permitted in any legislation acceptable under the more flexible test I have described. If a more flexible test were adopted, publicity might bring home to more women the impor-

[74] The U.S. Bureau of the Census reports that ten percent of the 1,559,100 abortions performed in 1987 occurred at thirteen or more weeks gestational age. U.S. Department of Commerce, Economics and Statistics Administration, Bureau of the Census, *The Statistical Abstract of the United States* 71 (111th ed 1991). Since about .01% of all abortions are performed after twenty-four weeks, see note 72 and accompanying text, it can be inferred that about 9.99% of the abortions performed in 1987 occurred in the second trimester.

tance of deciding and acting early. Medical developments in the technology of abortion might soon increase the percentage of very early abortions anyway. For instance, the abortion pill being developed in France, RU 486, which permits a safe abortion at home early in pregnancy, will allow pregnant women a more private method of abortion, if they decide and act in a timely way.[75] Of course, no statute that banned that pill would be constitutional, even under the more flexible standard.

I believe, as I said, that *Roe v Wade* should not be substantially changed. The line it draws is salient and effectively serves the legitimate state purpose of promoting a responsible attitude toward the intrinsic value of human life. But the most important line, as I said, is the line between that legitimate goal and the illegitimate goal of coercion. It will be disappointing, but not intolerable, if *Roe* is amended in some such way as I have been discussing. But it would be intolerable if *Roe* is wholly reversed, if the constitutional right of procreative autonomy is denied altogether. Some of you already think that recent appointments to the Court, and recent decisions by it, signal a dark age for the American constitutional adventure, that this symposium should have been convened as a wake, not as a celebration. I hope that your bleak judgment is premature. But it will be confirmed, spectacularly, if the Supreme Court declares that American citizens have no right to follow their own reflective convictions in the most personal, conscience-driven and religious decisions many of them will ever make.

---

[75] The RU 486 pill may in any case defuse the public controversy by reducing the need for abortion clinics that act as magnets for protesters, as in Wichita.

Part II
Rights Critiques

[3]

RIGHTS

*Morton J. Horwitz**

In a recent issue of this journal,[1] some minority group scholars sharply challenged the various criticisms of rights theories put forth by scholars associated with the Critical Legal Studies movement. In addition, the recent Bork nomination hearings focused attention on the important role that the discourse of rights has come to play in American legal and political culture. This comment is an attempt to define the controversy and to suggest the ways in which theories of rights have both helped and hurt the struggle for a more just society.

Since the late 1930's, the concept of rights has served overwhelmingly to create a legal and political culture that has legitimated the protection of civil liberties for political,[2] religious[3] and racial[4] minorities and, much more recently, has provided an emancipatory set of ideas or entitlements for cultural minor-

---

* Charles Warren Professor of American Legal History, Harvard Law School.

[1] Minority Critiques of the Critical Legal Studies Movement, 22 Harv. C.R.-C.L. L. Rev. 297–447 (1987).

[2] *See, e.g.*, Communist Party of Indiana v. Whitcomb, 414 U.S. 441 (1974) (invalidating a statutory loyalty oath required as a condition of access to the state ballot); Williams v. Rhodes, 393 U.S. 23 (1968) (overturning Ohio statutes which would have barred George Wallace and his American Independent Party from appearing on the 1968 presidential ballot).

[3] *See, e.g.*, Wisconsin v. Yoder, 406 U.S. 205 (1972) (holding that the state must modify its compulsory education requirements to accommodate the tenets of the Amish religion); Sherbert v. Verner, 374 U.S. 398 (1963) (holding that the state must alter its unemployment compensation requirements to accommodate those who observe a Saturday sabbath); West Virginia State Bd. of Educ. v. Barnette, 319 U.S. 624 (1943) (holding that children of Jehovah's Witnesses could not be required to salute the flag at school).

[4] *See, e.g.*, Brown v. Board of Educ., 347 U.S. 483 (1954) (holding that black children have the right to equal educational opportunities in non-segregated schools); Regents of the Univ. of California v. Bakke, 438 U.S. 265 (1978) (holding that university admissions programs may consider race as a factor in the selection process).

ities,[5] women[6] and homosexuals.[7] Similarly, the marginal and the scorned—the criminally accused,[8] prisoners,[9] aliens,[10] indigents,[11] welfare recipients[12] and illegitimate children[13]—have employed the language of rights in successful legal challenges.

---

[5] *See, e.g.*, Kelley v. Johnson, 425 U.S. 238, 252 (1976) (Marshall, J., dissenting from the Court's decision upholding a police department regulation of officers' hair styles); Village of Belle Terre v. Boraas, 416 U.S. 1, 12 (1974) (Marshall, J., dissenting from the Court's decision upholding a zoning ordinance prohibiting groups of three or more persons unrelated by blood from sharing the same household).

[6] *See, e.g.*, Roberts v. United States Jaycees, 468 U.S. 609 (1984) (upholding a Minnesota anti-discrimination statute which prohibited the Jaycees from barring women); Califano v. Goldfarb, 430 U.S. 199 (1977) (holding that a Social Security Act provision treating widows and widowers differently violated the equal protection clause of the fourteenth amendment); Frontiero v. Richardson, 411 U.S. 677 (1973) (invalidating a federal statute imposing a greater burden upon female members of the armed services for claiming spouses as "dependents" in order to increase quarters allowances and gain medical and dental benefits for their spouse).

[7] *See, e.g.*, Watkins v. United States Army, 837 F.2d 1428 (9th Cir. 1988) (holding that an army regulation barring homosexuals from military service violated the equal protection clause). *But see* Bowers v. Hardwick, 478 U.S. 186 (1986) (Blackmun, J., dissenting from the Court's decision which held that Georgia's sodomy statute did not violate the fundamental rights of homosexuals).

[8] *See, e.g.*, Miranda v. Arizona, 384 U.S. 436 (1966) (holding that statements obtained from defendants during interrogation without full warning of constitutional rights were inadmissible because admission would violate defendants' fifth amendment privilege against self-incrimination); Gideon v. Wainwright, 372 U.S. 335 (1963) (holding that all criminal defendants have the right to assistance of counsel and that an indigent defendant has the right to appointed counsel).

[9] *See, e.g.*, Wolff v. McDonnell, 418 U.S. 539 (1974) (holding that a disciplinary proceeding against an inmate must satisfy some due process requirements); Gagnon v. Scarpelli, 411 U.S. 778 (1973) (holding that revocation of probation without a hearing violates due process); Morrissey v. Brewer, 408 U.S. 471 (1972) (holding that minimal due process requirements for parole revocation include a preliminary hearing and a revocation hearing).

[10] *See, e.g.*, Sugarman v. Dougall, 413 U.S. 634 (1973) (holding that states may not bar aliens from holding court service position); *In re* Griffiths, 413 U.S. 717 (1973) (holding that states may not prevent resident aliens from practicing law); Graham v. Richardson, 403 U.S. 365 (1971) (holding that states cannot deny welfare benefits to aliens).

[11] *See, e.g.*, Griffin v. Illinois, 351 U.S. 12 (1956) (holding that states must provide indigent criminal appellants with a free transcript of trial proceedings); Edwards v. California, 314 U.S. 160 (1941) (striking down law making it criminal to bring a nonresident indigent into the state).

[12] *See, e.g.*, Goldberg v. Kelly, 397 U.S. 254 (1969) (holding that a welfare recipient must be given an "evidentiary hearing" before her benefits may be terminated since receiving welfare payments is a right protected by the Constitution against arbitrary withdrawal). *See generally* C. Reich, *The New Property*, 73 Yale L.J. 733 (1964) (arguing that new forms of government-created property should be protected by constitutional safeguards).

[13] *See, e.g.*, Trimble v. Gordon, 430 U.S. 762 (1977) (invalidating total exclusion of illegitimate children inheriting from their fathers); Levy v. Louisiana, 391 U.S. 68 (1968) (striking down Louisiana's refusal to allow unacknowledged illegitimate children to have a wrongful death action for their mother's death).

And, as we have all just recently been made aware,[14] the right to privacy is an important and accepted part of American constitutional culture.[15] Our modern, broad conceptions of rights have transformed our legal culture for the better, often providing legitimacy and entitlement to the weak and the powerless far beyond what their actual political power could have produced.

Why should anyone committed to an emancipatory conception of law have the slightest hesitancy in applauding these developments? The answer lies in our constitutional history.

If we think back just fifty years ago to the moment of triumph of a New Deal majority on the Supreme Court,[16] we can see that the discourse of rights just recently began to aid the weak and the powerless. In the early 1900's, Progressive legal opinion was overwhelmingly hostile to rights discourse.[17] Few sophisticated legal thinkers in that era regarded natural rights as anything more than an intellectual illusion developed in an era of laissez-faire capitalism.[18] Its central idea of a radically individualistic set of Lockean pre-political entitlements, progressive legal thinkers believed, was antithetical to any notion of communitarian values and was developed from the time of the American Revolution to protect private property against a more equitable distribution of wealth.[19]

---

[14] I am referring here to the centrality of Griswold v. Connecticut, 381 U.S. 479 (1965), in the recent confirmation hearings for Judge Bork. *Griswold* struck down a law which forbade the use of contraceptives as violative of the notions of privacy surrounding the marital relationship.

[15] *See, e.g.*, Roe v. Wade, 410 U.S. 113 (1973) (holding that the right to decide whether to end a pregnancy is fundamental); Eisenstadt v. Baird, 405 U.S. 438 (1972) (invalidating a regulation making it more difficult for unmarried as opposed to married couples to obtain contraceptives).

[16] The Court's 5-4 decision in West Coast Hotel Co. v. Parrish, 300 U.S. 379 (1937), which upheld a state minimum wage law for women, marked a philosophical shift toward greater deference to legislative intervention in economic affairs.

[17] *See* E. Corwin, The "Higher Law" Background of American Constitutional Law (1955) (originally published in 42 Harv. L. Rev. 149 (1928) and 42 Harv. L. Rev. 365 (1929)); C. Haines, The Revival of Natural Law Concepts (1958) (originally written in 1929); B. Wright, American Interpretations of Natural Law: A Study in the History of Political Thought (1931). *Cf.* Cohen, *Property and Sovereignty*, 13 Cornell L.Q. 8 (1927) (applying a natural rights theory to assert that it is just for the state to limit or take private property without compensation for the benefit of the public).

[18] *See* Corwin, *supra* note 17; Haines, *supra* note 17; Wright, *supra* note 17.

[19] *See* S. Fine, Laissez Faire and the General Welfare State: A Study of Conflict in American Thought, 1865–1901 (1956); C. Jacobs, Law Writers and the Courts (1954); A. Paul, Conservative Crisis and the Rule of Law: Attitudes of Bar and Bench, 1887–1895 (1960); B. Twiss, Lawyers and the Constitution: How Laissez Faire Came to the Supreme Court (1942).

The New Deal triumph emerged after a generation of Progressive assaults on the very idea of rights, particularly on the constitutionally based conception of freedom of contract annunciated in *Lochner v. New York*.[20] Attacks by social reformers on the very concept of rights was a familiar pattern by the 1900's. In England, Bentham's scathing denunciation of rights discourse in the year 1776[21] had set the stage for the identification of social reforms with parliamentary supremacy and the identification of rights with reaction.[22] In all of Europe as well, from the time of the French Revolution, the party of reform identified its cause with popular sovereignty while identifying all "higher law" arguments either with a discredited Catholic natural law philosophy or with efforts to endow the remnants of privilege left over from the Old Order with an undeserved fundamentality.[23]

Until 1937, natural rights constitutionalism overwhelmingly meant the protection of private property.[24] The *Dred Scott Case*[25] itself was written as a vindication of private property rights. It was not until Justice Stone's famous *Carolene Products* footnote[26] in 1938 that the constitutional era in which rights discourse could be used as a tool for the oppressed began to emerge.[27] History thus shows us that rights are a double-edged

---

[20] 198 U.S. 45 (1905) ("There is no reasonable ground for interfering with the liberty of persons or the right of free contract, by determining the hours of labor, in the occupation of a baker." *Id.* at 57.).

[21] J. Bentham, A Fragment on Government (1776). For a discussion of Bentham's influence on other thinkers, see E. Halevy, The Growth of Philosophic Radicalism (1928).

[22] *See* J.W. Gough, Fundamental Law in English Constitutional History (1955); F. Neumann, The Democratic and the Authoritarian State (1957).

[23] *See* M. Cappelletti, Judicial Review in the Contemporary World (1971). Capelletti also notes that the widespread acceptance of rights occurred in Europe immediately following World War II, perhaps as a reaction to Nazism. *Id.* at vii–viii. An example of a country which followed this trend is Germany, where there was a shift from the Weimar Constitution, which contained no "bill of rights," to the 1949 Constitution of the German Federal Republic, containing the German Basic Law and emphasizing individual rights.

[24] *See generally supra* note 19.

[25] Dred Scott v. Sandford, 60 U.S. 393 (1857) (holding that "the negro might justly and lawfully be reduced to slavery for [the white man's] benefit." *Id.* at 407).

[26] United States v. Carolene Products Co., 304 U.S. 144, 153 n.4 (1938) ("[P]rejudice against discrete and insular minorities may be a special condition, which tends seriously to curtail the operation of those political processes ordinarily to be relied upon to protect minorities, and which may call for a correspondingly more searching judicial inquiry.").

[27] Holmes sowed the seeds in his "free speech" dissent in Abrams v. United States, 250 U.S. 616 (1919). *See infra* note 28.

sword, and for most of our constitutional history, in fact, a single-edged sword. The development and application of the Holmes freedom of speech doctrine[28] provides a useful illustration of the continuing double-edged sword quality of rights discourse.

While the Holmes position on freedom of speech was finally accepted by a Supreme Court majority after World War II,[29] it rarely provided significant protection in practice until the late 1960's. Particularly during the McCarthy Era, free speech doctrine was usually honored only in the breach.[30] The modern strict scrutiny era of free speech doctrine really began less than twenty years ago in *Brandenburg v. Ohio*[31] and the double-edged

---

[28] In his dissent in *Abrams*, Holmes wrote: "[W]e should be eternally vigilant against attempts to check the expression of opinions that we loathe . . . , unless they so imminently threaten immediate interference with the lawful and pressing purposes of the law that an immediate check is required to save the country." 250 U.S. at 630.

[29] In his concurring opinion in Kovacs v. Cooper, 336 U.S. 77 (1949) (upholding an ordinance barring sound trucks from broadcasting in a loud and raucous manner), Justice Frankfurter asserted that "[t]he ideas now governing the constitutional protection of freedom of speech derive essentially from the opinions of Mr. Justice Holmes. . . . Mr. Justice Holmes was far more ready to find legislative invasion where free inquiry was involved than in the debatable area of economics." *Id.* at 95. Yet, even while invoking Holmes, Frankfurter was critical of the Court's speaking of "[t]he preferred position of freedom of speech," *id.* at 88, deeming it "a mischievous phrase, if it carries the thought, which it may subtly imply, that any law touching communication is infected with presumptive invalidity," *id.* at 90.

[30] *See, e.g.*, Barenblatt v. United States, 360 U.S. 109 (1959) (holding the House Committee on Un-American Activities did not violate first amendment by compelling testimony about past or present membership in Communist Party); Uphaus v. Wyman, 360 U.S. 72 (1959) (holding Attorney General of New Hampshire's investigation of subversives could compel director of summer camp to produce lists of camp's guests). The end of the Court's collaboration with McCarthyism only slowly emerged between Yates v. United States, 354 U.S. 298 (1957) (holding the Smith Act does not prohibit advocacy and teaching of forcible overthrow of government as an abstract principle, divorced from any effort to instigate action to that end), Scales v. United States, 367 U.S. 203 (1961) (holding the membership clause of Smith Act, making membership in an organization which advocates forcible overthrow of government a felony, did not violate the first amendment rights of a member of Communist Party) and Alberton v. Subversive Activities Control Bd., 382 U.S. 70 (1965) (holding Communist Party members could invoke fifth amendment privilege when ordered to submit membership lists). The Court's infamous decisions in *Barenblatt* and *Uphaus*, both of which upheld legislative interrogations of "subversives," were only finally put to rest in Gibson v. Florida Legislative Investigation Comm., 372 U.S. 539 (1963), which held that the state must convincingly show both a substantial relation between the information sought and an overriding and compelling state interest to compel the testimony of an individual who claims a legislative investigation intrudes upon his first amendment association rights, and DeGregory v. Attorney Gen. of New Hampshire, 383 U.S. 825 (1966), which held that the state interest was too remote to override a first amendment right of an individual called to testify before Attorney General of New Hampshire.

[31] 395 U.S. 444 (1969) (holding statute criminalizing advocacy and assembly with

398 Harvard Civil Rights-Civil Liberties Law Review [Vol. 23

nature of rights emerged immediately within the modern doctrine itself. The extension of the "money is speech" idea of *Buckley v. Valeo*[32] to *First National Bank of Boston v. Bellotti*[33] underlines the continuing ability of rights discourse to preserve the privileges of the rich and the powerful. In *Bellotti*, state regulation of corporate influence over election campaigns was held to be an infringement of the first amendment rights of free speech.

Another example of the way rights discourse is still used to protect the interests of the powerful is found in the recent revival of the just compensation clause. Beginning this past term, the law and economic ideologues at the University of Chicago[34] appear to have convinced the Court to revive the Lochnerian just compensation clause so that virtually any governmental regulation is capable of being regarded as a "taking."[35] In the "Chicago" view, a progressive income tax should be unconstitutional[36] and all other redistributive social programs are considered "takings."[37] This notion of rights survives from

---

others to advocate crime, violence or unlawful methods of terrorism facially unconstitutional under first and fourteenth amendments).

[32] 424 U.S. 1 (1976) (holding unconstitutional a Congressional statute limiting campaign expenditures of presidential candidates as violating first amendment rights to political expression).

[33] 435 U.S. 765 (1978).

[34] *See* R. Epstein, Takings: Private Property and the Power of Eminent Domain, at ch. 5 (1985); Easterbrook, *The Supreme Court, 1983 Term—Foreword: The Court and the Economic System*, 98 Harv. L. Rev. 4 (1984).

[35] *See* Nollan v. California Coastal Comm., 107 S. Ct. 3141 (1987) (holding that grant of permission to rebuild house could not be conditioned on property owners' grant to public of easement across beachfront property without paying compensation); First English Evangelical Church of Glendale v. County of Los Angeles, 107 S. Ct. 2378 (1987) (holding that land use regulation which denies a land owner even temporary use of his land is a taking requiring just compensation). *Cf.* Keystone Bituminous Coal Ass'n v. DeBenedictis, 107 S. Ct. 1232 (1987) (holding that Pennsylvania Subsidence Act which regulated the taking of coal which would lead to subsidence of surface was not an unconstitutional taking because it did not make the mining of certain coal commercially impracticable).

[36] Epstein, *supra* note 34, at 295–303. Epstein argues that the sixteenth amendment allows unequal apportionment of income tax burden between the states, but not between individuals. *Id.* at 296 n.42.

[37] For example, Epstein considers minimum wage laws and maximum hours laws to be takings from the employer. *Id.* at 280. Indeed, as Epstein admits, "[i]t will be said that my position invalidates much of the twentieth-century legislation, and so it does." *Id.* at 281. For a critique of Epstein, arguing that his theory fails on its own terms, see Note, *Richard Epstein on the Foundations of Takings Jurisprudence*, 99 Harv. L. Rev. 791 (1986).

the good old-fashioned Lochnerian conception of rights[38] and is very different from the notion of rights that we associate with the protection of the politically weak and oppressed.

Part of the explanation for the endurance of this double-edged quality of rights discourse is that rights conceptions emerged in a 17th- and 18th-century intellectual environment in which the religious basis for natural law was rapidly crumbling.[39] The disintegration of religious-based natural law and the simultaneous emergence of a positivist distinction between objective facts and subjective values set the intellectual background for the emergence of social contract and Kantian theories of rights.[40] One of the most important tendencies of liberal rights theories is that they achieve universality (and thus "objectivity") by sacrificing substantive content. The most famous example of the kind of abstract formality that typically characterizes liberal rights theory[41] is Kant's contentless categorical imperative.[42]

The liberal legal theory of rights has attempted to mediate between substantive values ("subjectivism") and forms of legal positivism that seek to obtain "objectivity" by denying any moral content to law.[43] The result has been an ungrounded conception of rights that allows anyone to propose his or her favorite right. Thus, it seems to be part of the indeterminate nature of rights discourse that it can be deployed with equal logic to protect the existing structure of privilege as well as to challenge and delegitimate that structure.[44]

In addition to the problem posed by the historically double-edged quality of rights, there are at least three other aspects of the discourse of rights which foreshadow undesirable long-term consequences.

First, natural rights conceptions were conceived in radical individualism and continue to express an individualistic per-

---

[38] *See* Sunstein, *Lochner's Legacy*, 87 Colum. L. Rev. 873 (1987).

[39] *See* Gough, *supra* note 22; A.P. D'Entreves, Natural Law: An Introduction to Legal Philosophy (1970).

[40] See I. Shapiro, The Evolution of Rights in Liberal Theory (1986).

[41] *See* A. MacIntyre, After Virtue (1981).

[42] Translated, Kant's categorical imperative is: "Act only on that maxim through which you can at the same time will that it should become a universal law." The Moral Law—Kant's Groundwork of the Metaphysic of Morals 29 (H.J. Paton trans. 1948).

[43] *See* R. Unger, Knowledge and Politics (1976).

[44] *See* Kennedy, *Critical Labor Law Theory: A Comment*, 4 Indus. Rel. L.J. 503 (1981).

spective on social relations.[45] Natural rights philosophy is rooted historically in an adversarial vision of human interactions and a negative idea of human freedom as the absence of external restraint.[46] Its libertarian premises lead to a minimalist "night-watchman" state and to denunciation of social duties or legislation protecting the socially weak as "paternalistic" or as redistributive.[47] It is a frequent observation that the revolutionary spin of the natural rights philosophy of the Declaration of Independence was reshaped into a conservative pro-property doctrine after the American Revolution, especially in order to relegitimate slavery.[48]

Even the modern emancipatory conception of rights has been laden with individualistic premises. For example, it is often observed that a "specific intent" requirement[49] for proving discrimination expresses a private law "fault" model of the violation of individual rights, rather than an understanding of discrimination as societal and systematic.[50] In this way, the vindication of rights is set in an exclusively legal and individual-specific framework, drawing energy and imagination away from structural change. Indeed, framing issues of social justice in terms of individual rights has the additional effect of denying equal legitimacy to claims that the overall social distribution of wealth and power is unjust.[51]

There is also the specific legal question of whether groups, in addition to individuals, can have rights.[52] Except for the

[45] *See* Shapiro, *supra* note 40. In contrast to modern social contract theories (which first emerge with Hobbes and Locke in the 17th century) that posit individual natural rights, medieval Catholic conceptions of natural law were more rooted in organic and communal, but hierarchical, ideas of society. *See* O. Gierke, Natural Law and the Theory of Society, 2 vols. (E. Barker trans. 1934). *See generally* A.P. D'Entreves, *supra* note 39; J. Finnis, Natural Law and Natural Rights (1980); C.B. Macpherson, The Political Theory of Possessive Individualism: Hobbes to Locke (1962).

[46] *See* I. Berlin, Two Concepts of Liberty (1958).

[47] *See* R. Nozick, Anarchy, State and Utopia (1974).

[48] *See* R. Cover, Justice Accused (1975); D. Davis, The Problem of Slavery in the Age of Revolution, 1770–1823 (1975).

[49] Washington v. Davis, 426 U.S. 229 (1976), held that "specific intent" was necessary for proving discrimination. *See generally* Comment, *Proof of Racially Discriminatory Purpose Under the Equal Protection Clause:* Washington v. Davis, Arlington Heights, Mt. Healthy, and Williamsburgh, 12 Harv. C.R.-C.L. L. Rev. 725 (1977).

[50] *See* O. Fiss, *The Supreme Court 1978 Term—Foreword: The Forms of Justice*, 93 Harv. L. Rev. 1 (1979).

[51] *See* Horwitz, *The Jurisprudence of Brown and the Dilemmas of Liberalism*, 14 Harv. C.R.-C.L. L. Rev. 599, 608–09 (1979).

[52] *See* Fiss, *Groups and the Equal Protection Clause*, 5 Phil. & Pub. Affs. 107 (1976).

private corporation, our legal theory has been very resistant to recognizing group rights. Justice Powell's opinion for the *Bakke*[53] plurality explained that "the difficulties entailed in varying the level of judicial review according to a perceived 'preferred' status of a particular racial or ethnic minority are intractable."[54] He noted that the "concepts of 'majority' and 'minority' necessarily reflect temporary arrangements and political judgments,"[55] and that the "white 'majority' itself is composed of various minority groups, most of which can lay claim to a history of prior discrimination at the hands of the state and private individuals."[56] The Court was unwilling to accord "preferential treatment," because then "the only 'majority' left would be a new minority of White Anglo-Saxon Protestants."[57] Justice Powell could not find a principled basis for deciding which groups would merit 'heightened judicial solicitude' and which would not. He explained that:

> [c]ourts would be asked to evaluate the extent of the prejudice and consequent harm suffered by various minority groups. Those whose societal injury is thought to exceed some arbitrary level of tolerability then would be entitled to preferential classifications at the expense of individuals belonging to other groups. . . . As these preferences began to have their desired effect, and the consequences of past discrimination were undone, new judicial rankings would be necessary. The kind of variable sociological and political analysis necessary to produce such rankings simply does not lie within the judicial competence—even if they otherwise were politically feasible and socially desirable.[58]

Powell's conception of the individual nature of rights is an excellent example of how a non-communitarian conception of rights must inevitably come to regard the quest for substantive

---

[53] University of California Regents v. Bakke, 438 U.S. 265 (1978).
[54] *Id.* at 295.
[55] *Id.*
[56] *Id.*
[57] *Id.* at 296.
[58] *Id.* at 296–97.

equality itself as a threat to rights, and not as an indispensable foundation of true liberty and autonomy.[59]

Yet, as the Supreme Court begins to uphold and legitimate affirmative action programs,[60] it moves closer to understanding rights and entitlements as group based and their infringement as the result of systemic discrimination. It becomes correspondingly more difficult to conceive of the plaintiff as merely vindicating her own private rights and not as a private attorney general vindicating the rights of a coherent class or of the general public. As this model of the public law suit expands, we are inevitably drawn into thinking about more general and systemic questions involving the relationship between social equity and substantive justice.

Despite the recent expansion of group rights, Justice Powell's decision in *McCleskey v. Kemp*[61] is an example of how the individualistic spin of rights discourse continues to produce formalistic constructs that defy common sense. Although the Court recognized that the death penalty is disproportionately applied against blacks, the Court held that it is, nevertheless, not a violation of an individual black criminal's constitutional rights if he is sentenced to death. This type of conclusion requires one to believe that there is no "reality" to discrimination against groups—that discrimination is possible only against individuals—and that a high statistical correlation between race and the frequency of the death penalty contains no message about the existence of a societal structure of discrimination. The individualistic spin of rights discourse—and its strong tendency to see liberty and equality as in conflict—produces this narrow, tortured understanding of rights.

A second troubling aspect of natural rights discourse is its tendency to posit a sharp distinction between a public realm of

---

[59] *See* M. Sandel, Liberalism and the Limits of Justice (1982).

[60] *See* United States v. Paradise, 107 S. Ct. 1053 (1987) (holding that a court order requiring that 50 percent of promotions at the Alabama Department of Public Safety go to blacks was permissible under the equal protection clause of the fourteenth amendment in that it was justified by a compelling governmental interest in the eradication of discrimination which excluded blacks from various positions); Johnson v. Transportation Agency, Santa Clara County, 107 S. Ct. 1442 (1987) (holding that a county agency did not violate Title VII by taking a female employee's sex into account to promote her over a male employee with a higher test score as the decision was made pursuant to an affirmative action plan).

[61] 107 S. Ct. 1756 (1987).

coercion and a "natural," private realm of freedom.[62] But the public-private distinction is extremely malleable; it is in the nature of group and organizational life that state intervention can always be characterized either as an interference with the associational rights of the group or as a vindication of the rights of the individual members.[63] In family law, for example, we can speak of the state as intervening in the associational rights of the family or as vindicating the rights of the abused or deprived child or spouse.[64] In labor law, courts constantly fluctuate between emphasizing the private rights of association of labor unions as against state regulation and asserting the role of the state in protecting the private rights of members as against the exercise of power by the trade union.[65] Likewise, limitations placed on corporate spending for speech can be characterized as interference with a corporation's exercise of its free speech rights or as protecting the individual freedom of choice of the shareholders to express their diverse political views.[66]

The recent debate over pornography[67] emphasizes perhaps most clearly how difficult it is to believe in a realm of private rights independent of the social consequences of their exercise. One can, of course, structure the controversy as a conflict between the privacy rights of readers of pornography and the rights of women to regulate imagery that promotes the degradation of women. But the more fundamental difficulty is to what extent we should immunize a realm of "private" rights if it produces clearly deleterious social consequences.

A third troubling aspect of rights discourse is that its focus on fundamental, inherent, inalienable or natural rights is a way of obscuring or distorting the reality of the social construction

---

[62] *See Symposium: The Public-Private Distinction*, 130 U. Pa. L. Rev. 1289 (1982) [hereinafter *Symposium*].

[63] *See* Dewey, *The Historical Background of Corporate Legal Personality*, 35 Yale L.J. 655 (1926).

[64] F. Olsen, *The Myth of State Intervention in the Family*, 18 U. Mich. J. L. Ref. 835 (1984).

[65] *See* K. Klare, *The Public-Private Distinction in Labor Law*, in *Symposium*, *supra* note 59, at 1358.

[66] *See* Brudney, *Business Corporations and Stockholders' Rights Under the First Amendment*, 91 Yale L.J. 235 (1981).

[67] *Compare* MacKinnon, *Pornography, Civil Rights, and Speech*, 20 Harv. C.R.-C.L. L. Rev. 1 (1985) *with* the opinion of Judge Easterbrook for the court in American Booksellers Ass'n v. Hudnut, 771 F.2d 323 (7th Cir.), *aff'd* 106 S. Ct. 1172 (1986).

of rights and duties.[68] It shifts discussion away from the always disputable issue of what is or is not socially desirable. Rights discourse denies the assertion that a right is just a social interest to which we think it desirable to accord a privileged position in the law. It wishes us to believe instead that the recognition of rights is not a question of social choice at all, as if in the normative and constitutional realm rights have the same force as the law of gravity.

The powerful revival of rights discourse must be seen as a sort of fundamentalist reaction to the modernist picture of all social boundaries as socially constructed and all values as a product of social choice. Like all forms of fundamentalism, it substitutes dogmatism for the complexities of social life and insists on the existence of bright-line boundaries in a world of flux and ambiguity.

The most promising way to ensure that rights may be used on behalf of the socially weak, and to mitigate the three undesirable long-term risks of rights conceptions, is to ground rights theory in a substantive conception of the good society. The most important substantive question in our time is whether rights theories are conceived of as incorporating or as opposed to substantive ideals of equality. Thus, the meaning of *Brown v. Board of Education*[69] has been central to arguments about rights during the past 35 years. In one sense, all of the arguments are about how narrowly or broadly to read *Brown*: narrowly, as directed just to eliminating affirmative state-sanctioned discrimination or, broadly, as a fundamental statement of the presumptive moral superiority of the ideal of equality.[70] There are, of course, many positions in between.

During the past 35 years, much of the constitutional passion of conservatives has been focused on attacking any connection between rights discourse and equality.[71] If they are not positiv-

---

[68] *See* Kennedy and Michelman, *Are Property and Contract Efficient?*, 8 Hofstra L. Rev. 711, 751–53 (1980); Hohfeld, *Fundamental Legal Conceptions as Applied in Judicial Reasoning*, 26 Yale L.J. 710 (1917); Hohfeld, *Some Fundamental Legal Conceptions as Applied in Judicial Reasoning*, 23 Yale L.J. 16 (1913); R. Pound, *Liberty of Contract*, 18 Yale L.J. 454 (1908); Reich, *supra* note 12, at 771–74.

[69] 347 U.S. 483 (1954).

[70] *See* Black, *The Lawfulness of the Segregation Decisions*, 69 Yale L.J. 421 (1960); J. Rawls, A Theory of Justice (1971).

[71] *See, e.g.*, Kurland, *The Supreme Court 1963 Term—Foreward: "Equal in Origin*

ists who proclaim a sharp distinction between law and morals or between positive law and "subjective" higher law,[72] then they are often Kantians who seek to develop a language of rights free from any commitment to substantive equality.[73] But, *Brown v. Board of Education* has raised anew the relationship between social and political equality that liberal legal theory had sought to ignore. Whether it is now possible to incorporate an egalitarian ideal into a rights tradition that has been staunchly hostile to substantive equality is a serious question. The discourse of rights emerged within a tradition of liberalism that sharply distinguished between social and political equality.[74] One reading of *Brown* is that it recognized, more clearly than ever before, the intimate connection between the two. Separate but equal facilities were "inherently" unequal; the stigma was *not* the result of an interpretation that black people "chose" to put on segregation[75] but derived from the reality of a societal system of oppression. Broadly read, *Brown* reopened an issue that had been dominant at the time of the framing of the Constitution: that of the *social* conditions necessary for maintaining political equality.[76]

For most of American constitutional history, rights theories have been associated with protection of property against a more

---

and Equal in Title to the Legislative and Executive Branches of the Government," 78 Harv. L. Rev. 143 (1964).

[72] *See* Bork, *Neutral Principles and Some First Amendment Problems*, 47 Ind. L.J. 1 (1971).

[73] *See* C. Fried, Right and Wrong (1978); C. Fried, Contract as Promise (1981); Fletcher, *Fairness and Utility in Tort Theory*, 85 Harv. L. Rev. 537 (1972).

[74] That is the function of "state action" doctrine. *See* the Slaughterhouse Cases, 83 U.S.(16 Wall) 32 (1872).

In Coppage v. Kansas, 236 U.S. 1 (1915), the Court stated that:

> since it is self-evident that, unless all things are held in common, some persons must have more property than others, it is from the nature of things impossible to uphold freedom of contract and the right of private property without at the same time recognizing as legitimate those inequalities of fortune that are the necessary result of the exercise of those rights.

Id. at 17; *see also* F.A. von Hayek, The Constitution of Liberty (1960); G. de Ruggiero, The History of European Liberalism (trans. R.G. Collingswood 1927).

[75] The Supreme Court in Plessy v. Ferguson, 163 U.S. 537 (1896), had said that if the enforced separation of the two races stamps "the colored race" with a badge of inferiority, "it is not by reason of anything found in the act, but solely because the colored race chooses to put that construction upon it." *Id.* at 551.

[76] *See* Horwitz, *Republicanism and Liberalism in American Constitutional Thought*, 29 Wm. & Mary L. Rev. 57, 71–72 (1987).

just distribution of wealth and privilege. Even as an emancipatory conception of rights has emerged during the past half century, theories of rights have continued to represent a double-edged sword because of their lack of grounding in any substantive theory of social justice or the "good society." The question remains as to whether rights theories, still deeply rooted in the hostility of liberal individualism to ideals of substantive equality, can synthesize the two traditions and create a progressive conception of rights.

[4]

The Politics of Women's Wrongs and the Bill of "Rights": A Bicentennial Perspective

Mary E. Becker†

The language of the Bill of Rights is almost entirely gender neutral and its provisions have always applied to some women.[1] But free white men of property designed the Bill of Rights in a political process from which they excluded most Americans and all women. Not surprisingly, the Bill of Rights served and serves the interests of such men better than the interests of others.

Legal constitutional literature, whether from the right or the left, tends to be celebratory rather than critical.[2] But in looking back on the Bill of Rights during this bicentennial year, women and many men outside the propertied white male class should be ambivalent. In this Article, I assess the Bill of Rights from the per-

---

† Professor of Law, The University of Chicago Law School. This Article is the written version of the Katz Lecture given at The University of Chicago Law School on October 24, 1991. I thank Pauline Bart, Cynthia Bowman, Jill Fosse, Marcella David, Rochelle Dreyfus, Laurie Feldman, Stephen Gilles, Mary Ann Glendon, Wendy Gordon, Hendrick Hartog, Lynne Henderson, Jennifer Hertz, Linda Hirschman, Elena Kagan, Linda Kerber, Larry Kramer, Norval Morris, Judith Resnik, Carol Rose, Vicki Schultz, Kenneth Simmons, Geoffrey Stone, Cass Sunstein, Nadine Taub, Morrison Torrey, Robin West, John Wiley, and workshop participants at the Chicago Feminist Colloquium, UCLA Law School, Emory Law School, University of Miami Law School, NYU Law School, Northwestern Law School, and the University of Wisconsin Law School for helpful comments on earlier drafts and Paul Bryan, Jennifer Hertz, Elizabeth Rosenblatt, William Schwesig and Charles Ten Brink for research and other assistance. Research support was provided by the Russell Baker Scholars Fund and the Russell J. Parsons Faculty Research Fund of the University of Chicago and by the Morton C. Seely Fund and the Jerome S. Weiss Faculty Research Fund.

[1] The Bill of Rights is almost entirely free of gendered language. It speaks repeatedly of "person" or "people." The Fifth Amendment contains one "himself" and the Sixth Amendment one "him" and two "his's." Thus, one has the right not to be "compelled in any criminal case to be a witness against *himself*," US Const, Amend V (emphasis added); the right of the criminal defendant "to be confronted with the witnesses against *him*; to have compulsory process for obtaining witnesses in *his* favor, and to have the Assistance of Counsel for *his* defense," US Const, Amend VI (emphasis added). But the clauses containing these references were understood as applying to "free" women from the first.

[2] See, for example, John Paul Stevens, *The Bill of Rights: A Century of Progress*, 59 U Chi L Rev 13 (1992); Charles Fried, *The New First Amendment Jurisprudence: A Threat to Liberty*, 59 U Chi L Rev 225 (1992); Cass R. Sunstein, *Free Speech Now*, 59 U Chi L Rev 255 (1992); Michael W. McConnell, *Religious Freedom at a Crossroads*, 59 U Chi L Rev 115 (1992); and Kathleen M. Sullivan, *Religion and Liberal Democracy*, 59 U Chi L Rev 195 (1992).

spective of women and other outsiders, with special emphasis on its continuing impact on women's political participation. I offer three kinds of criticisms in discussing specific clauses.

First, and most important, I make a point that is not normative or prescriptive but merely critical: the Bill of Rights does less to solve the problems of women and nonpropertied men than to solve the problems of men of property, especially white men of property. Some clauses, such as the Fifth Amendment right to "property," originally did not help most women, or helped only trivially, or had vastly different meanings for women and men. Often this disparity continues. Some provisions overlook much more serious problems for women than the problems they address. Consider, for example, women's Fourth Amendment right "to be secure in their persons, houses, papers, and effects against unreasonable [governmental] searches and seizures."[3] The Fourth Amendment neither gives women security in their homes from husbands nor ensures that government treat marital rape like other rapes and assaults. Indeed, at the time the Fourth Amendment was adopted, and in many jurisdictions today, husbands and lovers could and can rape "their" women without criminal consequences.

Some provisions operate differently for women and men in the sense that they perpetuate women's subordinate status. Although many historical inequities would have persisted without the Bill of Rights, the Bill magnifies these inequities. For example, the Religion Clauses permit substantial subsidies from government to mostly-patriarchal religious organizations—organizations that continue to be important socializing institutions for children.

Second, although the Bill of Rights may not *cause* a given problem, it sometimes impedes legislative reform. We revere the Bill of Rights;[4] its invocation legitimates the status quo. For example, the Second Amendment assists the National Rifle Association in preventing stringent federal gun control legislation. Thus, although gun control might be good for women, and is favored by most women,[5] the Second Amendment impedes its adoption.

My third point concerns politics. Several provisions of the Bill of Rights have continuing political effects, impeding women's effec-

---

[3] US Const, Amend IV.

[4] See, for example, Hendrik Hartog, *The Constitution of Aspiration and "The Rights That Belong to Us All"*, 74 J Amer Hist 1013 (1987).

[5] Katherine M. Jamieson and Timothy J. Flanagan, eds, *Sourcebook of Criminal Justice Statistics* 110, Table 2.43 (US Dept of Justice, 1987).

tive political participation today. Consider, for example, *Buckley v Valeo*, which held unconstitutional spending limits on individuals directly engaging in political speech, thus constitutionalizing the right of the rich to participate in the political process more effectively than the poor.[6] And women are, of course, disproportionately poor.[7]

More fundamentally, the Bill of Rights is inadequate in guaranteeing women the exercise of governmental power. Given that women were excluded from the process that produced the Bill of Rights and that few women occupy high government positions today, we should question the legitimacy of our purported democracy. Surely we would question whether another government was truly democratic if a majority group, other than women, had never held the top executive position and comprised only six percent of the national legislature.[8] Only six percent of governors are women.[9] Women hold only eighteen percent of state-wide elective offices.[10] Women occupy only 18.1 percent of state legislative seats.[11]

Women are similarly under-represented in judicial positions at the state and federal levels. At the state level, only 2.8 percent of the law-trained trial court judges are women; 5.5 percent of intermediate appellate state judges are women.[12] On state supreme courts, 5.89 percent of justices are women; 0.56 percent are minority women.[13] At the federal level, women comprise only 4.07 percent of administrative law judges; seven percent of district court judges; eight percent of appellate judges; and 11.11 percent of the

---

[6] 424 US 1, 58-59 (1976).

[7] See, for example, 163 *Current Population Reports: Consumer Income: Poverty in the United States: 1987*, 118-19 (US Bureau of the Census, 1989).

[8] See Center for the American Woman and Politics (CAWP), *Fact Sheet: Women in Elective Office 1991*, Table 2 (Eagleton Institute, 1991) (on file with U Chi L Rev).

[9] *The World Almanac and Book of Facts 1992* 596-99 (World Almanac, 1991).

[10] CAWP, *Fact Sheet: Statewide Elective Executive Women 1991* 1 (Eagleton Institute, 1991) (on file with U Chi L Rev).

[11] Id.

[12] Telephone conversation with Dixie Noble, National Association of Women Judges, Williamsburg, Virginia (Oct 3, 1991) (notes on file with U Chi L Rev). This data was current as of the date of the call for the intermediate and appellate state courts. The data on trial court judges is from 1985. I have not been able to find data on minority judges in other categories.

[13] Id.

Supreme Court. No women serve as senior appellate judges and less than two percent of the senior trial judges are women.[14]

Two points recur in my criticisms of various clauses. The Bill of Rights incorporates a private-public split[15] with only negative rights under a limited government. As a result, women's activities and concerns—from economic rights to religion—seem beyond the proper scope of government. That women are poorer than, and subordinate to, men appears "natural" and pre-political. Because of the private-public split, the Bill of Rights protects a number of institutions that are not entirely good for women from governmental interference and effective reform, such as the media. Because the Bill of Rights incorporates only "negative" rights, it includes no provision guaranteeing, or even defining as an important concern of national government, the economic and educational rights so important to women as caretakers. Indeed, women in the United States have fewer economic and educational supports than in any other North Atlantic nation.

To a large extent, my criticisms could apply to any written set of cryptic, abstract, and negative rights enforced by judges. Any such scheme will better protect the powerful against government action harmful to their interests than the less powerful, who need protection against the powerful as well as against the government. In part, this is because abstract rights enforced by judges, regardless of their wording, are unlikely to make radical changes in the distribution of power and resources.[16] The less powerful need many concrete, positive rights. These rights require detailed implementation schemes and the expenditure of funds. Judges are not likely to order either when enforcing abstract clauses. For example, no matter how a constitution states its equality provision, it is unlikely that the provision would lead judges to restructure the social security system so as to provide equivalent old-age security to breadwinners and homemakers.[17]

---

[14] Id. For discussions of this problem, see Carl Tobias, *The Federal Judiciary Engendered*, 5 Wis Women's L J 123 (1990); Judith Resnik, *"Naturally" Without Gender: Women, Jurisdiction and the Federal Courts*, 66 NYU L Rev (forthcoming 1992).

[15] For a discussion of the inconsistencies in the way we look at the public-private split, see Frances E. Olsen, *The Family and the Market: A Study of Ideology and Legal Reform*, 96 Harv L Rev 1497 (1983).

[16] See, for example, Gerald N. Rosenberg, *The Hollow Hope: Can Courts Bring About Social Change?* (Chicago, 1991); Mary E. Becker, *Prince Charming: Abstract Equality*, 1987 S Ct Rev 201.

[17] See Mary E. Becker, *Obscuring the Struggle: Sex Discrimination, Social Security, and Stone, Seidman, Sunstein & Tushnet's* Constitutional Law, 89 Colum L Rev 264, 271-85 (1989).

We cannot, therefore, expect a piece of paper to produce justice for women or other disadvantaged groups.[18] I nevertheless suggest a number of ways in which the Bill of Rights could be improved through interpretation or amendment. For example, courts could redefine, or legislatures amend, the Religion Clauses of the First Amendment to prohibit government subsidies to religions that close the ministry to women. Courts could read the Free Speech Clause of the First Amendment to allow content-based governmental regulation of some sexist and racist speech, or subsidies for nonsexist speech.

Some of my points focus on the underclass, rather than women as such. It is impossible to separate the interests of women from those of their class and race. When, for example, justice is denied the urban underclass in the criminal "justice" system, women inevitably suffer even though most of those caught directly in the system are men. Women suffer the destruction of their communities as well as the destruction of the men and boys who are, or might have been, in their lives.

In the Conclusion, I make several general points not directed at specific provisions of the Bill of Rights. An ideal Constitution or Bill of Rights would contain a substantive sex equality provision. At a minimum, such a provision could require judges to take into account detrimental impact on women when approaching other constitutional provisions as well as legislation and other governmental action.[19]

In the Conclusion, I address more basic structural problems with the Constitution and the Bill of Rights. First, I note that our constitutional structure, with its emphasis on individual rights conceived in absolutist and negative terms, particularly property rights, contributes to a culture in which the kinds of economic rights women need are difficult to achieve. Mary Ann Glendon makes this point in her most recent book.[20] Absolutist individual rights are almost inevitably negative limits on government. Giving constitutional sanctity to negative rights only, with a central role for property rights, reinforces American faith in rugged individualism which is so incompatible with the needs of children and their caretakers.

---

[18] See, for example, Rosenberg, *The Hollow Hope* at 10-13 (cited in note 16): Becker, 1987 S Ct Rev 201 (cited in note 16).

[19] See note 301 and accompanying text.

[20] Mary Ann Glendon, *Rights Talk: The Impoverishment of Political Discourse* 14, 24-25 (Free Press, 1991).

I also discuss some of the ways in which our constitutional structure is countermajoritarian. The Framers deliberately devised a government that would protect the propertied minority from oppression by the propertyless majority.[21] We should see it as a problem of democracy that, to date, women have not exercised their share of governmental power. I suggest that other governmental structures and electoral systems might be more democratic.[22]

In as many sections, I discuss seven clauses or sets of clauses in the Bill of Rights: the Religion Clauses[23] and Free Speech Clause[24] of the First Amendment; the right to bear arms of the Second Amendment;[25] protections against misuse of the criminal justice system in the Fourth, Fifth, and Sixth Amendments;[26] the right to be secure in one's home under the Fourth Amendment;[27] the property right of the Fifth Amendment;[28] and the Due Process right of the Fifth Amendment, together with the jury provisions of the Sixth and Seventh Amendments.[29] I begin with the first two clauses of the First Amendment, which "guarantee" freedom of religion. I discuss the religion clauses in greater depth than the others because there have been so few explorations in the legal literature of the problems religion poses for women.[30]

I. Religious Freedom

The Bill of Rights begins with the First Amendment's Religion Clauses: "Congress shall make no law respecting an establishment of religion, or prohibiting the free exercise thereof."[31] All of my criticisms apply to both of these provisions. Religious freedom has meant, and means, vastly different things to women and men. In a number of ways this freedom secures to men rights superior to

---

[21] Jennifer Nedelsky, *Private Property and the Limits of American Constitutionalism: The Madisonian Framework and Its Legacy* 220-22 (Chicago, 1990).

[22] See notes 293-300 and accompanying text.

[23] See Section I.

[24] See Section II.

[25] See Section III.

[26] See Section IV.

[27] See Section V.

[28] See Section VI.

[29] See Section VII.

[30] For examples of articles that do discuss the patriarchal nature of religion, see Judith C. Miles, *Beyond* Bob Jones*: Toward the Elimination of Governmental Subsidy of Discrimination by Religious Institutions*, 8 Harv Women's L J 31 (1985); Kathleen A. McDonald, *Battered Wives, Religion, and Law: An Interdisciplinary Approach*, 2 Yale J L and Feminism 251 (1990); Judith Resnik, *On the Bias, Feminist Reconsiderations of the Aspirations of Our Judges*, 61 S Cal L Rev 1877, 1918-21 (1988).

[31] US Const, Amend I.

those secured to women. As I discuss below, religion perpetuates and reinforces women's subordination, and religious freedom impedes reform. The Religion Clauses allow substantial government subsidies of religion, such as exemptions from income and property taxes and awards of government contracts, thus assisting religion in perpetuating the subordination of women. Religious freedom also impedes women's effective political participation.

I divide the discussion of religion into four parts. I begin with a discussion of the ways in which religious practices and doctrine contribute to traditional attitudes towards women and their appropriate roles. Next, I discuss positive aspects of the relationship between religion and women: religion has often empowered women and has responded to and reflected the beliefs and values of women, who are, in general, more religious than men. Third, I consider empirical evidence on the relationship between religion and women's subordinate status. This evidence indicates that, despite the positive potential of religion and the ways in which women shape religion, mainstream Christian religions in the United States tend to contribute to women's subordinate status and to retard women's ability to participate fully and effectively in political life. I discuss several examples of current governmental subsidies of mostly-patriarchal religion. I conclude the Section by suggesting that the Religion Clauses be interpreted or amended to minimize their countermajoritarian effect while still preserving the positive potential of religion.

A. Religion and Patriarchy

The religious freedom clauses do not have the same meaning for women and men. For the Framers, the social reality of religious freedom meant their own freedom and the freedom of other men of their race and class to develop, govern, and control religion free of state interference. Even men of other races and classes could be religious leaders. For example, prior, even, to emancipation separate black churches developed led by black preachers.[32] These separate churches laid the foundation for an autonomous African-American Christianity.[33]

Religious freedom has not had this meaning for women. Religious leaders have been overwhelmingly male from the time the

---

[32] See, for example, Eugene D. Genovese, *Roll, Jordan, Roll: The World the Slaves Made* 255-79 (Pantheon, 1974).

[33] Id at 280.

Bill of Rights was passed until the present day. Many religious groups, including Mormons, Roman Catholics, and Orthodox Jews, still close the ministry to women. Other groups allow female ministers, but women still lead those groups in relatively low numbers, especially in the organizational hierarchy or at the head of large and important congregations.[34]

Male control of religious leadership has a number of negative effects. Only men are able to use positions as religious leaders to rise in the social hierarchy and to become leaders in their communities. The absence of women in leadership positions suggests to younger women and girls that women are not capable of leadership. Most important, because mainstream religious leadership has been and remains so dominated by men, mainstream religion inevitably incorporates male perspectives and bias against women. As one (male) student of comparative religion put it, "regardless of what a religion teaches about the status of women, or what its attitudes toward sex might be, if women are excluded from the institutions and positions that influence society, a general misogynism seems to result."[35] Religions thus contribute to women's subordinate status, not only within religious communities' hierarchies, but also in the broader culture.

At the time the Bill of Rights was passed, mainstream American religions taught the subordination of women openly and without embarrassment. For example, the Reverend Amos Chase described women's divinely ordained position of inferiority in a funeral sermon in Litchfield, Connecticut in 1791:

> A woman of fine feelings cannot be insensible that *her constitutional condition is secondary and dependant [sic] among men*. Nor can she long want conviction that the sure way to avoid any evil (to the thus dependant) [sic] is *to yield the front of battle to a hardier sex*.[36]

Religion was often used to legitimate the use of the state's power to enforce women's inferior social position. For example, in

---

[34] See, for example, Keith A. Roberts, *Religion in Sociological Perspective* 291-94 (Wadsworth, 2d ed 1990).

[35] Vern L. Bullough, *The Subordinate Sex: A History of Attitudes Toward Women* 134 (Illinois, 1973).

[36] Amos Chase, *On Female Excellence, or a Discourse in which Good Character in Women is Described, Occasioned by the Death of his Wife* 12 (delivered at Litchfield, March 6, 1791), as quoted in Nancy Falik Cott, *In the Bonds of Womanhood: Perspectives on Female Experience and Consciousness in New England 1780-1830* 99 (1974) (unpublished Ph.D. dissertation, Brandeis University (Waltham)) (on file with U Chi L Rev).

Bradwell v Illinois, the Supreme Court upheld a statute barring women from the practice of law, with three concurring justices using divine law to justify a man-made law by which men gave themselves a monopoly in the practice of law.[37]

Today, mainstream religions in the United States remain patriarchal in many ways. I begin with a discussion of substantive problems with religious doctrines and practices from the perspective of women.[38] The Religion Clauses have given men a comparatively greater ability to develop meaning, values, and morality based on an authority independent of government and made in their image. Although religion means much to women, it has not meant this.

1. Creation, male gods, and Eve.

All mainstream religious traditions in the United States replace the wonder of women's reproductive power with stories of creation by a male god.[39] In one of the two creation myths in Genesis, God created Eve out of Adam's rib to be his partner (rather than a being with her own purposes).[40] Eve tempts Adam and her reproductive power becomes a punishment for sin in the story of the fall.[41] Because of her sin, God declares Adam her master.[42] Christianity adds, as a prerequisite to true life, rebirth through redemption by a male god.[43]

Although there is an occasional use of female imagery in the Judeo-Christian tradition—in the Wisdom literature, for example[44]—the gods of that tradition are overwhelmingly male. The Christian "God the Father" is the ultimate male warrior: utterly

---

[37] 83 US (16 Wallace) 130, 132, 139 (1872).

[38] I have organized the discussion in the subsection in seven points, some of which apply to Jews and Christians, others of which apply only to Christians. Because most religious Americans are Jews or Christians, and because my space is limited, I examine only these traditions.

[39] Beverly Wildung Harrison, *Our Right to Choose: Toward a New Ethic of Abortion* 60-61 (Beacon, 1983); Mary Daly, *Gyn/Ecology: The Metaethics of Radical Feminism* 73-89 (Beacon, 1990).

[40] Genesis 2:18-23 (New English Bible). A less sexist version of creation is presented in the first story of creation. See Genesis 1:26-28.

[41] Genesis 3:16-19 (New English Bible):

> To the Woman he said: "I will increase your labor and your groaning, and in labour you shall bear children. You shall be eager for your husband, and he shall be your master."

[42] See id.

[43] Harrison, *Our Right to Choose* 59-61 (cited in note 39); Daly, *Gyn/Ecology* at 83-89 (cited in note 39).

[44] See, for example, The Wisdom of Solomon 10: 1-19 (New English Bible).

alone and without need for others or the ability to empathize with them, the unmoved mover.[45] More than the language ascribes maleness; the Old Testament God typifies the masculine warrior hero in western culture, violent and overpowering, striking down his enemies.[46] Jesus is, by contrast, often very feminine,[47] but his gender is clearly male. Although Mary sometimes has near-divinity status, she is a singularly passive and subservient god.

It is easy to dismiss this complaint as silly or unimportant. The effect of male gods goes unnoticed because it is so ubiquitous, and is effective because so consistent with male domination in our culture. If you look around, you will see widespread and severe under-representation of women in positions of power, as gods, in the ministry, as heroes, and as authorities, whether in religion or sports or the military or the evening news. Some of these problems are discussed elsewhere in this article.[48] The cumulative effect is a double message to girls. On one level, they hear, "you're equal, you're equal, you're equal." But when they observe the world around them, on television, in their history books, in their story books, in literature or religion, girls receive a different message: "you're not, you're not, you're not." Almost exclusively, they see males as active heroes and in positions of power and honor. Not surprisingly, girls and young women have less self-esteem and confidence than boys and men.[49]

Men in our culture fail to appreciate the advantages of having gods in their image. But women who can imagine a female god, despite indoctrination in religions with male gods, can sense the power of such images. Someone raised in the white Judeo-Christian tradition has extreme difficulty imagining a female god. But

---

[45] For feminist insight on the vision of "God the Father" as a male figure, see Catherine Keller, *From a Broken Web: Separation, Sexism and Self* 38-40, 86-87 (Beacon, 1986); Carol P. Christ, *Laughter of Aphrodite: Reflections on a Journey to the Goddess* 93-101 (Harper & Row, 1987); Susan Brooks Thistlethwaite, *Sex, Race, and God: Christian Feminism in Black and White* 109-25 (Crossroad, 1989).

[46] See, for example, Psalm 7:12-13 (New English Bible): "He sharpens his sword,/ strings his bow and makes it ready./He has prepared his deadly shafts and tipped his arrows with fire."

[47] For a discussion of the more feminine Jesus, central to the devotional life of many Christian women, white and black, see text accompanying notes 87-88.

[48] See text accompanying notes 152-59, 200, for example.

[49] American Association of University Women, *Shortchanging Girls, Shortchanging America: A nationwide poll to assess self esteem, educational experiences, interest in math and science, and career aspirations of girls and boys ages 9-15* graph B (following p 5) (Greenberg-Lake Analysis Group, 1991) (in elementary school, girls' self-esteem is 79% of boys'; in middle school and high school, 60% (calculation from figures in graph B)).

just a glimpse of the Goddess can be startling and empowering.[50] Mainstream American religions have not offered women what they offer men: the ability as leaders to develop powerful images of gods like themselves.

2. Emphasis on family stability.

In addition, all mainstream religious traditions emphasize family stability. Inequities exist in most families today, however, where women generally work more hours a week than their husbands because of the husbands' failure to share the second shift—housework. Emphasis on family stability, at least without an equal emphasis on the need for change within families, reinforces current advantages of both power and leisure that men enjoy within families. Religion encourages women to live with the status quo rather than destabilizing it by insisting on equality. For battered women, this emphasis reinforces their tendency to think only of the needs of others[51] and to try to keep the "family together at all costs—even the woman's life."[52] Again, religion does not do the same thing for women and men.

3. Fundamentalism, orthodoxy, and women's subordinate status.

Today, fundamentalist and orthodox religious groups, such as fundamentalist Christians, continue to teach, explicitly or implicitly, that women should be subordinate to men. For example, fundamentalist Christians still often state overtly that wives should submit to husbands. In *The Total Woman*, Marabel Morgan describes the "biblical remedy for marital conflict": " 'wives must submit to [their] husbands' leadership in the same way [they] submit to the Lord,' " citing Paul's letter to the Ephesians.[53]

Orthodox Jews state less explicitly that wives should submit to husbands, but orthodox belief and practice implies women's inferiority in at least four different ways. First, Judaism is phallocentric:

[50] Catherine Keller discusses parallels between the opening of Genesis and earlier Babylonian creation myths and concludes that the earlier Goddess is reflected in certain words in Genesis. I was thrilled (and amazed at how thrilling it was) to find such a revelation in the words I had been taught to revere as a child. See Keller, *From a Broken Web* at 80-88 (cited in note 45).

[51] Robin West, *The Difference in Women's Hedonic Lives: A Phenomenological Critique of Feminist Legal Theory*, 3 Wis Women's L J 81, 98 (1987).

[52] Lenore E. Walker, *The Battered Woman* 164 (Harper & Row, 1979).

[53] Marabel Morgan, *The Total Woman* 69 (Revell, 1973) (quoting *The Living Bible* Ephesians 5:22 (Tyndale House, 1971)).

a mark on the penises of baby boys symbolizes "Abraham's everlasting covenant with his god." The phallus is thus sanctified.[54]

Second, Jewish marriage and divorce law do not treat women and men as equals.[55] In both, women are passive, men are active. In an Orthodox wedding, the bride says nothing. A divorce is something a man effects and gives to a woman; she cannot remarry unless he agrees to divorce her. Although she can demand a divorce, and he *should* then give it to her, among the strictly Orthodox she often has little recourse if he refuses.

Third, the obligation to worship and to study Torah, central to the lives of Orthodox men, is less important for women, though women should know enough Torah to be able to educate their children. Implicit is the message that she counts less. Indeed, for purposes of the minyan (the quorum needed for certain prayers), she does not count at all. Her husband begins the day by thanking God that he was not born a woman. (Thereby, according to the least objectionable meaning, expressing gratitude that he is called to worship God and study Torah).[56]

Fourth, the Jewish faith relegates women to serving others, rather than recognizing them as creatures with important spiritual lives.[57] Orthodox men serve God through prayer and study. Orthodox women serve God through serving others. For very Orthodox women, much of this service consists of cooking and cleaning under circumstances made onerous by dietary laws.[58]

Fundamentalist religious groups encourage or require women to fulfill traditional roles, including economic dependence on husbands and serving others in the home. Yet economic dependence on individual men weakens women's position within marriage. The combination of traditional roles and fundamentalists' unusually strong emphasis (relative even to other mainstream religious groups) on family stability lessens fundamentalist women's ability to object to traditional relationships between the sexes. Again, the

---

[54] Batya Bauman, *Women-identified Women in Male-identified Judaism*, in Susannah Heschel, ed, *On Being a Jewish Feminist: A Reader* 88, 91 (Schocken, 1983).

[55] Saul Berman, *The Status of Women in Halakhic Judaism*, in Elizabeth Koltun, ed, *The Jewish Woman: New Perspectives* 114, 115 (Schocken, 1976).

[56] Thena Kendall, *Memories of an Orthodox Youth* in Heschel, ed, *On Being a Jewish Feminist: A Reader* 96, 97-98 (cited in note 54).

[57] Berman, *The Status of Women in Halakhic Judaism* at 116 (cited in note 55).

[58] Kendall, *Memories of an Orthodox Youth* (cited in note 56). At the same time giving spiritual significance to women's work and the way it is done is in some ways positive, according importance and value to women.

main point is that religion does not offer women what it offers men.

4. The core of Christianity: forgiving and suffering.

All strands of Christianity urge forgiving. Christianity teaches that the virtuous person forgives even the unpardonable. Quoting Matthew 18:22, Marabel Morgan advises wives to forgive "seventy times seven."[59] Christianity also places a high value on suffering, the archetype being Jesus's suffering during the crucifixion.

Forgiving and valuing suffering are not effective strategies for an oppressed group to force social change. These activities reinforce existing power disparities and encourage the disempowered to accept their real-world disadvantages as spiritual advantages.

Forgiving and valuing suffering are particularly dangerous strategies for battered women.[60] Such teachings encourage battered women (who are all too likely to believe their batterers who ask forgiveness and swear they will never do it again) to stay in extremely destructive relationships. Religious counselors often advise battered women to "pray for guidance, become better women, and go home and help their husbands 'become more spiritual and find the Lord.' "[61]

Even more perversely, the Christian valuation of suffering encourages women to accept abuse. Christian theology glorifies victimization, posing special hazards to women because society, as well as Christianity, assigns them the "suffering-servant role."[62] Joanne Carlson Brown and Rebecca Parker make this point powerfully:

> Christianity has been a primary—in many women's lives *the* primary—force in shaping our acceptance of abuse. The central image of Christ on the cross as the savior of the world communicates the message that suffering is redemptive. If the best person who ever lived gave his life for others, then, to be of value we should likewise sacrifice ourselves. Any sense that we have a right to care for our own needs is in conflict with

[59] Morgan, *The Total Woman* at 144 (cited in note 53) (citing King James Version of the Bible).

[60] See McDonald, 2 Yale J L and Feminism 251 (cited in note 30).

[61] Walker, *The Battered Woman* at 23 (cited in note 52).

[62] Joanne Carlson Brown and Rebecca Parker, *For God So Loved the World?*, in Joanne Carlson Brown and Carole R. Bohm, eds, *Christianity, Patriarchy, and Abuse: A Feminist Critique* 1, 3 (Pilgrim, 1989).

> being a faithful follower of Jesus. Our suffering for others will save the world.[63]

Thus, the values at the core of the Christian tradition reinforce and contribute to women's suffering and subordination.

5. Female sexuality and mothering.

Traditionally, Judaism has linked women's bodies with uncleanliness, regarding menstrual blood and childbirth as polluting. Prior to menopause, the Jewish faith deems a woman unclean for two weeks of every month: while she is menstruating and for seven days thereafter until she has "undergone ritual purification in a mikveh" (ritual bath).[64] After childbirth, purification of the woman's body is also necessary.[65] Instead of celebrating women's reproductive power, Judaism perceives women's bodies (and women themselves) as unclean and polluted.

Judaism nevertheless sees marriage (and sexuality) as a positive experience, a necessary part of life for an observant member of the community. The blessing given the newborn child is to grow up to Torah, marriage, and good deeds. Orthodox congregations do not hire unmarried rabbis nor do they usually hire unmarried cantors.

Christianity more consistently approaches women's bodies and sexuality negatively, linking women with sexuality and sexuality with imperfection and sin.[66] For example, Clement of Alexandria wrote that for women, "the very consciousness of their own nature must evoke feelings of shame."[67] The equation of women with sex may seem odd, since men seem more interested in genital sex than women do. But, from the perspective of heterosexual men who feel sexual desire but regard sexual intercourse as "filthiness" and "disgustingness" (the terms belong to St. Thomas Aquinas[68]), there is a certain logic in regarding women as the source of the evil. Were there no women, these men would not be tempted to engage in such repulsive activities.[69]

---

[63] Id at 2.

[64] Paula Hyman, *The Other Half: Women in the Jewish Tradition*, in Koltun ed, *The Jewish Woman* 105, 110-11 (cited in note 55).

[65] Heschel, ed, *On Being a Jewish Feminist: A Reader* 286 (cited in note 54) (glossary entry for *mikvah* at back of book).

[66] Bullough, *The Subordinate Sex* at 97-101 (cited in note 35).

[67] Uta Ranke-Heinemann, *Eunuchs for the Kingdom of Heaven: Women, Sexuality, and the Catholic Church* 127 (Doubleday, 1990) (quoting *Paedagogus* II, 33, 2.).

[68] Id at 194.

[69] Bullough, *The Subordinate Sex* at 84 (cited in note 35).

During much of Christian history, all sexual intercourse, even within marriage, was tainted. Augustine and Thomas Aquinas regarded original sin as transmitted via sexual intercourse (even when unaccompanied by pleasure).[70] For centuries, active sexuality ranked inferior to celibacy, and often was regarded as sinful even within marriage.[71] For example, Augustine regarded any married person who requested sex for pleasure, rather than procreation, as committing a venial sin.[72]

The equation of women with sexuality and sexuality with impurity and sin remains strong in Roman Catholicism, with its all-male celibate clergy and its rejection of contraception (which permits sex for pleasure). Most other Christian denominations permit clergy to marry, regard the married life as consistent with holiness, and permit contraception. But traces of the equation of women with sex and sex with sin persist. For example, most Christian denominations still insist on a belief in the Virgin Birth. The Virgin Birth distances ordinary women from the Christian ideal: ordinary reproduction and mothering are tainted. If Mary is "pure" because she never had sex, all other mothers are impure because they did. Again, religious doctrine offers different things to women and men. In the areas of sexuality and reproduction, religion stresses female impurity and male creative power.

6. Christian sin and virtue.

Christianity defines as sin what is most likely to be the sin of men: putting one's own development and needs ahead of others. It defines as virtue self-sacrificing love.[73] But self-sacrifice is often women's sin. Christianity thus encourages women to do what society encourages them to do as caretakers and nurturers: hide their own talents and find fulfillment vicariously through service to the talents of others. This very sacrifice tends to be the sin of women, who are too likely to dissipate themselves "in activities which are merely trivial" in the service of others.[74] A woman's greatest temp-

---

[70] Ranke-Heinemann, *Eunuchs for the Kingdom of Heaven* at 192-93 (cited in note 67).

[71] Id at 27-28.

[72] Id at 95.

[73] There is only one gospel parable about failing to develop one's talents. See Matthew 25:14-30 (New English Bible). In contrast, the gospels are full of verses on the need for humility. Christian churches continue to define sin primarily as pride rather than hiding.

[74] Valerie Saiving, *The Human Situation: A Feminine View*, in Carol P. Christ and Judith Plaskow, eds, *Womanspirit Rising: A Feminist Reader in Religion* 25, 38 (Harper & Row, 1979). Keller carries this insight further, noting that "God the Father" is the embodiment of Christian (male) sin. See Keller, *From a Broken Web* at 38-40 (cited in note 45).

tation is to hide her talents rather than develop them, sacrificing her development as an autonomous self in order to serve others. A woman who does this is:

> guilty of the sin of hiding; inasmuch as she has poured herself into vicarious living, inasmuch as she has denied her sense of self in total submission to husband/father/boss or in total self-giving to children, job, or family, she has been guilty of the sin of hiding. As she has been afraid to dream a dream for herself as well as for others, and as she has trained herself to live a submerged existence, she has hidden from her full humanity.[75]

Thus, the dominant conceptions of both Christian virtue and sin discourage women from developing as autonomous beings. Focusing on men's sin as *the* sin and extolling women's sin as virtue is a likely result of male domination of a religious tradition. Theology, like theory, is in large part autobiography. For most men, Christianity has correctly identified sin and virtue. Following Christian teaching helps men to become better people. But men have neither the insight nor any incentive to define women's sin in a way that will encourage women to become more self-interested. Instead, men define sin in a way that encourages women to sin rather than to work against their real temptations. It is possible to have it both ways; Christianity could give equal emphasis to both women's sin (hiding) and men's sin (pride), stressing the need to avoid *both*. Had women participated equally as leaders in Christianity, it is likely that Christianity would do so rather than perpetuate "woman's bondage to her hiddenness."[76] To reiterate my major point, religion does not mean for women what it means for men.

7. Christianity and traditional roles for women: Mary the mother.

Mainstream Christian religions present, as ideal, traditional images of women as caretakers, nurturers, servants of others.[77] Mary, the most prominent woman, is the most traditional and submissive of women: "I am the Lord's servant; as you have spoken, so

---

See also Susan Nelson Dunfee, *The Sin of Hiding: A Feminist Critique of Reinhold Niehbuhr's Account of the Sin of Pride*, 65 Soundings 316 (1982).

[75] Dunfee, 65 Soundings at 321-22 (cited in note 74).

[76] Id at 322.

[77] See, for example, Jerome L. Himmelstein, *The Social Basis of Antifeminism: Religious Networks and Culture*, 25 J Scientific Study Religion 1, 8 (1986).

be it."[78] In contrast to the portrayal of women in a singular traditional role, men are seen in many roles: God, savior, prophet, religious leader, father, etc. Again religion offers different things to men and women. It offers men a greater range of more powerful roles.

These problems in mainstream religions, particularly Christian religions, are deeply embedded in religious belief and practice. These religions cannot eliminate the sexism easily; the use of gender-neutral language will not eradicate deeper problems. A number of commentators consider America's religious traditions "to be our most deep-seated cause of patriarchy."[79] Nevertheless, religion has been and is a positive influence in many women's lives. It is a source of meaning for women more than for men, despite its patriarchal nature. I next consider the positive aspects of the complex relationship between women and religion. This exploration balances my critical discussion of religion. It does not, however, detract from my main point. Religious freedom has not given women and men the same ability to develop an extra-governmental authority for meaning, values, and morality.

B. Religion as a Positive Force in Women's Lives

In this Section, I discuss two positive aspects of religion for women. First, I explore ways in which religion has empowered women. Second, I explore ways in which religion has been affected by and reflects women's beliefs and values.

1. Religion often empowers women.

Throughout history, religion has been a source of power for individual women. Like men, many women, from Joan of Arc to African American women preachers in the nineteenth century,[80] have found an authority in religion to support unconventional choices. Religious activities and organizations offered women

---

[78] Luke 1:38 (New English Bible) (Mary's reply to the angel Gabriel when informed that she will have a son, though she is a virgin).

[79] Anne Barstow Driver, *Religion*, 2 Signs 434, 434 (1976) (review essay). See also, for example, John Wilson, *Religion in American Society: The Effective Presence* 264 (Prentice Hall, 1978) ("Religion is probably the single most important shaper of sex roles."); Himmelstein, 25 J Scientific Study Religion at 7-12 (cited in note 77).

[80] For the stories of some of the latter, see, for example, Bert James Loewenberg and Ruth Bogin, eds, *Black Women in Nineteenth-Century American Life* (Penn State, 1976); William L. Andrews, ed, *Sisters of the Spirit: Three Black Women's Autobiographies of the Nineteenth Century* (Indiana, 1986); Jean McMahon Humez, ed, *Gifts of Power: The Writings of Rebecca Jackson, Black Visionary, Shaker Eldress* (Massachusetts, 1981).

meaningful and respectable work in public life when many women were otherwise relegated to their homes. Women in religious orders received educations and achieved independence denied to most women. Activists in the suffrage and abolition movements first organized and pushed for change through their churches.[81] Some religious groups, particularly Quakers, produced exceptionally high numbers of women leaders.[82] During the nineteenth century, women used movements with religious overtones and membership, such as the temperance, voluntary motherhood, and social purity movements, to try to better the condition of women in a variety of ways.[83] Although many of these women used religious networks and ideals in their organizing, they were rarely religious leaders as such. Their ability to restructure religious belief and practice was therefore limited.

Religion continues to play a positive role in the lives of many women today. Most religious Christian women today, and more women than men, regard their religious commitment as a positive experience.[84] In the next Section, I explore some of the reasons why Christianity, despite and even because of its sexism, appeals disproportionately to women.[85]

2. Religion reflects women's traditional roles and values.

Religious values are, in many ways, more consistent with women's roles than men's. A man's duty to support his family by succeeding in the competitive world of a market economy conflicts

---

[81] See, for example, Eleanor Flexner, *Century of Struggle: The Woman's Rights Movement in the United States* (Harvard, rev ed 1975); Marjorie Wall Bingham, *Women and the Constitution: Student Textbook* 23-24 (Communicorp, 1990); Nancy A. Hewitt, *Women's Activism and Social Change: Rochester, New York, 1822-1872* 43-44 (Cornell, 1984).

[82] Bingham, *Women and the Constitution* at 22-24 (cited in note 81).

[83] See, for example, Linda Gordon, *Woman's Body, Woman's Right: A Social History of Birth Control in America* 116-20, 131-32 (Penguin, 1977); Elizabeth B. Clark, *Religion and Rights Consciousness in the Antebellum Woman's Rights Movement*, in Martha Albertson Fineman and Nancy Sweet Thomadsen, eds, *At the Boundaries of Law: Feminism and Legal Theory* 188 (Routledge, 1991); Carolyn De Swarte Gifford, *Women in Social Reform Movements*, in Rosemary Radford Ruether and Rosemary Skinner Keller, eds, 1 *Women and Religion in America: The Nineteenth Century* 294 (Harper & Row, 1981); Nancy F. Cott, *The Bonds of Womanhood: "Woman's Sphere" in New England, 1780-1835* 149-54 (Yale, 1977).

[84] Robert Wuthnow and William Lehrman, *Religion: Inhibitor or Facilitator of Political Involvement Among Women?*, in Louise A. Tilly and Patricia Gurin, eds, *Women, Politics, and Change* 300, 302 (Russell Sage Foundation, 1990). Indeed, "[w]omen are 18 points more likely than men to say that their religious commitment has been a positive experience." Id.

[85] Jews are as likely to be men as women. See George Gallup, Jr., *Religion in America 50 Years: 1935-1985*, in The Gallup Report No 236 at 34 (1985).

somewhat with the virtues of mainstream Christianity. Christianity calls for humility, service to others, obedience to the laws of God (rather than the market), generosity to the poor and unfortunate, and forgiving and forgetting. These virtues better match women's traditional roles as mothers, nurturers, and enablers responsible for making home a "haven" from the heartless world of the market.

I noted earlier that Christian sin is sin for men: pride and putting oneself first. For women, real sin tends to be forgetting one's own needs and living through others, the sin of "hiding," of failing to use one's talents. Ironically, Christianity extols women's sin—self-sacrifice and vicarious fulfillment—as the primary virtue. But precisely because self-sacrifice is women's real sin, the Christian notions of sin and virtue resonate with women. Christianity gives positive meaning to women's behavior as subordinates and victims.

Women's culture and rules of conduct also identify and proscribe the sin of pride. In her recent book, *You Just Don't Understand*,[86] Deborah Tannen studied the ways groups of girls and groups of boys interact. For girls, interaction is about sharing feelings and experiences, about empathy. Girls tend to consider it socially inappropriate to put oneself forward as superior, to out-distance one's friends in any way. Unusual success is something one apologizes for or explains away. Boys tend to see interaction as essentially about establishing hierarchy, out-distancing one's friends both in games and in other activities, using words to demonstrate that because of one's success, one out-ranks another. Given these differences, Christian sin will seem odd to boys, and out of touch with reality. For girls, Christian sin resonates with their social norms, which proscribe precisely the same thing as Christian sin. In other words, Christian virtues of service and self-sacrifice resonate deeply with girls' culture and with what girls are told they should do in order to be good wives and mothers. They make less sense for boys because they are inconsistent with boys' culture and with the traditional breadwinner role in a rough-and-tumble market economy. Thus, the appeal of Christianity is precisely its danger for women. Had more Christian theologians and preachers been women, Christianity might give equal emphasis to women's sin, and resonate with women's culture no more than with men's.

---

[86] Deborah Tannen, *You Just Don't Understand: Women and Men in Conversation* (William Morrow, 1990).

In Christianity, the evangelical emphasis on inner feelings and the emotional cult of Jesus also appeals greatly to women. Evangelical movements dominated Protestantism in America in the nineteenth century and profoundly changed the content of all mainstream Christian denominations,[87] shifting the devotional focus of many from a macho "God the Father" incapable of empathy to a very feminine and empathetic Jesus. For many women, religion fills an important emotional void. Educated in heterosexual romance,[88] but unable to find a satisfactory male lover, women find in religion the romantic emotional union they long for and cannot find in a relationship with a man.

The Christian emphasis on suffering, as exemplified by the crucifixion, valorizes traditionally feminine masochism of the sort Freud would recognize. In part, the appeal of Christianity to women arises from its ability to give meaning to the suffering and pain of their own lives; to give meaning to all suffering and subordination.

Jewish traditions are feminine in another sense, one not shared by most Christian sects: religious rituals in the home are of great importance. Women are ultimately responsible for such rituals. This emphasis sanctifies the space traditionally reserved for women and gives significance to women's caretaking activities, especially as cooks and organizers of family holidays and rituals.

In addition, both Judaism and Christianity protect and support women in important ways. Both legitimate and value women's traditional roles. Both developed economic protections for wives and mothers. For example, canon law developed the obligations of a husband, separated from wife and children, to pay alimony and child support. These obligations became the basis of secular family law's economic supports for divorced women.[89] Orthodox Judaism provides a number of property protections for a divorced wife.[90] In addition, the secular idea of equality—which has been important

[87] See Claude Welch, 1 *Protestant Thought in the Nineteenth Century: 1799-1870* 22-30 (Yale, 1972); Cott, *The Bonds of Womanhood* at 128-37 (cited in note 83). For another view of Jesus as feminine, see Roberts, *Religion in Sociological Perspective* at 284 (cited in note 34).

[88] On the importance of romance to women, see, for example, Dorothy C. Holland and Margaret A. Eisenhart, *Educated in Romance: Women, Achievement and College Culture* (Chicago, 1990); Keller, *From a Broken Web* at 15-16 (cited in note 45).

[89] See Mary Ann Glendon, *State, Law and Family: Family Law in Transition in the United States and Western Europe* 312-13 (North-Holland, 1977).

[90] See, for example, Daniel I. Leifer, *On Writing New* Ketubot, in Koltun, ed, *The Jewish Woman* 50 (cited in note 55).

in giving women a basis for arguing for social change—may have its origins in Christian ideas and ideals.

Although many feminists have left patriarchal religions because of the difficulty of reconciling their beliefs about women with traditional religious beliefs and practices,[91] many other women and feminists work from within to make religions less sexist and more responsive to, and reflective of, the human condition. Within Jewish and Christian congregations, feminists are working in many ways and on many levels to make religions more responsive to women's needs. For example, feminists challenge the focus on the male sin of pride in Christianity to include the female sin of "hiding,"[92] which is the "underdevelopment or negation of self."[93] Feminists also bring insights to evangelical Christianity (including fundamentalist evangelical groups),[94] Roman Catholicism,[95] Judaism,[96] and the study of early Christianity.[97] This outpouring of feminist insights and criticisms of mainstream religions indicates the deep attachment many women feel toward religion, even when they see its sexism.

The positive aspects of the relationship between women and religion and women's deep attachment to religion do not negate my central concern: religious freedom has not meant the same thing for women and men. Indeed, this discussion has demonstrated the close link between religion's appeal to women and its danger for women. Religion values women's traditional roles, including subordination and even suffering. Religion also offers emotional fulfillment, rather than requiring women to find fulfillment through the development of their abilities. Thus, religion reinforces women's subordinate status. It does not, of course, have this effect for men, who dominate both religion and society in general. In the next Section, I explore the empirical literature on the effect of religion on

---

[91] Wuthnow and Lehrman, *Religion* (cited in note 84).

[92] See Dunfee, 65 Soundings 316 (cited in note 74). See notes 74-76 and accompanying text.

[93] Saiving, *The Human Situation* at 37 (cited in note 74). See also Keller, *From a Broken Web* at 12, 39-40, 190 (cited in note 45).

[94] See Judith Stacey, *Brave New Families: Stories of Domestic Upheaval in Late Twentieth Century America* 139-46 (Basic, 1990) (reviewing writings of evangelical feminists).

[95] See generally Anne E. Carr, *Transforming Grace: Christian Tradition and Women's Experience* (Harper & Row, 1988); Rosemary Radford Ruether, *Sexism and God-Talk: Toward a Feminist Theology* (Beacon, 1983).

[96] See, for example, Koltun, ed, *The Jewish Woman* (cited in note 55).

[97] See, for example, Elisabeth Schussler Fiorenza, *In Memory of Her: A Feminist Theological Reconstruction of Christian Origins* (Crossroad, 1983).

political issues important to women and on women's political participation.

C. Empirical Evidence: Religion and Women

Religious Christians are more likely than other Americans to take positions inconsistent with women's equality. Those who attend Christian services frequently are more likely to oppose abortion, the Equal Rights Amendment, paternity leave, affirmative action quotas, government support of day care, women keeping their birth name or using the title "Ms.," and allowing girls on boys' sports teams.[98] Indeed, Christian "church attendance is generally more strongly related to [these] antifeminist beliefs than are education, income, occupational status, class, age, residence, and most other social traits."[99] Findings like these have been replicated in study after study.[100]

The evidence on the relationship between Jewish religious commitment and attitudes toward women is ambiguous. Female supporters of feminism are likely to have had parents who were Jewish, atheist, or agnostic and are more likely to be Jewish, athe-

---

[98] Himmelstein, 25 J Scientific Study Religion 1, 9-10 (cited in note 77). In another study, Christian church attendance was found to be correlated with traditional answers to two questions about the desirability of a traditional division of labor and power with women taking the domestic, subordinate role, and with two traditional answers about the consequences for children of maternal employment. Karen Oppenheim Mason and Yu-Hsia Lu, *Attitudes Toward Women's Familial Roles: Changes in the United States, 1977-1985*, 2 Gender & Soc 39, 43, 49-51 (1988).

[99] Himmelstein, 25 J Scientific Study Religion at 13 (cited in note 77).

[100] See id (looking at data amassed in a number of studies, including data from general population surveys, and concluding that antifeminist attitudes are rooted in Christian religious networks); Merlin B. Brinkerhoff and Marlene M. MacKie, *Religious Denominations' Impact Upon Gender Attitudes: Some Methodological Implications*, 25 Rev Religious Research 365, 365 (1984) ("denomination, the typology, and attendance [at Christian religious services] tend to be more strongly correlated to gender attitudes than age or education"); Ross K. Baker, Laurily K. Epstein and Rodney D. Forth, *Matters of Life and Death: Social, Political, and Religious Correlates of Attitudes on Abortion*, 9 Amer Pol Q 89 (1981) (approval of abortion found to be "a function of intensity of religious adherence"); Mary Y. Morgan, *The Impact of Religion on Gender-Role Attitudes*, 11 Psych Women Q 301 (1987) (religious devoutness most important variable for predicting five measured dimensions of gender-role attitudes); Carol Mueller and Thomas Dimieri, *The Structure of Belief Systems Among Contending ERA Activists*, 60 Soc Forces 657, 664-65 (1982) (activist opponents of state ERA in Massachusetts in 1975 were all members of a church or parish; most proponents were not); Kent L. Tedin, *Religious Preference and Pro/Anti Activism on the Equal Rights Amendment Issue*, 21 Pac Sociol Rev 55, 64 (1978) (study of activists involved in state deliberations on national ERA in Texas in spring of 1975; anti-ERA activists tended to belong to conservative denominations).

ist, agnostic, or Unitarian themselves.[101] But these studies confound secular Jewish people who identify with their ethnic heritage and those who are religious. It is not clear whether religious Jews are less sexist than religious Christians.[102] Given the content of Orthodox belief and practice,[103] it is possible that at least some religious Jews possess more sexist views than secular Jews.

To be sure, there is some variation among Christian denominations with respect to issues important for women's equality.[104] For example, researchers using 1980 data found that 85.7 percent of Jews, 64.3 percent of Catholics, 59.8 percent of Fundamentalist Protestants, 59.2 percent of other Protestants, and twenty-five percent of Mormons supported the Equal Rights Amendment.[105] One study of students at Utah State University demonstrated that Mormon students have much less favorable attitudes toward nontraditional roles for women than do other students.[106] Across Christian denominations, however, researchers have "clearly, con-

[101] J.A. Dempewolff, *Some Correlates of Feminism*, 34 Psych Rep 671, 671 (1974). I have not found studies examining various strands of Judaism to see if they differ on this point. Even religious Jews may be relatively egalitarian as a result of stress on the Israeli norm of sexual equality (which exists at least on the level of American rhetoric). See Andrea Dworkin, *Israel: Whose Country Is It Anyway?*, Ms. 69, 73 (Sep/Oct 1990).

[102] Of those who identified themselves as Jewish in a 1975 study, only 38% were members of a synagogue and only 32% attended services. Steven M. Cohen, *American Modernity & Jewish Identity* 56 (Tavistock, 1983). In 1989, Christians were 21-26% more likely to attend service than Jews. See Tom W. Smith, *Counting Flocks and Lost Sheep: Trends in Religious Preference Since World War II*, in GSS Social Change Rep No 26, 53, 55 (National Opinion Research Center University of Chicago, 1991).

[103] See notes 58, 64-65 and accompanying text.

[104] See Himmelstein, 25 J Scientific Study Religion at 7 (cited in note 77) ("Jews and the unaffiliated are distinctly more liberal on both ERA and abortion than either Protestants or Catholics. Protestants tend to be slightly more supportive of abortion and less supportive of ERA than Catholics. Fundamentalist and conservative Protestants are more likely to oppose both than are liberal protestants."). Himmelstein reviewed a number of population studies. See also Brinkerhoff and MacKie, 25 Rev Religious Research at 374 (cited in note 100) (some variation in gender attitudes found by Christian denomination: Mormons and Pentecostals most traditional in terms of attitudes though in terms of division of household labor and family power, Mormons among most egalitarian); Val Burris, *Who Opposed the ERA? An Analysis of the Social Bases of Antifeminism*, 64 Soc Sci Q 305, 308-10 (1983); Baker, Epstein, and Forth, 9 Amer Pol Q at 99 (cited in note 100) (denominational variation only modest on approval of abortion; key factor found to be intensity of religious adherence).

[105] Burris, 64 Soc Sci Q at 309 (cited in note 104). See also Glenna Spitze and Joan Huber, *Effects of Anticipated Consequences on ERA Opinion*, 63 Soc Sci Q 323, 326 (1982) (national sample: Catholics, Jews, and those without a religious affiliation more favorable to ERA than Protestants).

[106] Moshe Hartman and Harriet Hartman, *Sex-role Attitudes of Mormons vs. Non-Mormons in Utah*, 45 J Marriage & Family 897, 899 (1983).

sistently"[107] found a strong correlation between church attendance and opposition to the ERA[108] and abortion:[109] "Religious involvement has a conservative effect [on ERA and abortion attitudes] no matter what the denomination or its doctrines (though the magnitude of the effect varies)."[110] Religious devoutness has greater predictive power with respect to five dimensions of gender-role attitudes among women undergraduates than self esteem, assertiveness, mother's education, or mother's employment. The greater the woman's devoutness, the more traditional her notions about sex roles.[111]

---

[107] Himmelstein, 25 J Scientific Study Religion at 7 (cited in note 77).

[108] See, for example, Burris, 64 Soc Sci Q at 309-10 (cited in note 104); Baker, Epstein, and Forth, 9 Amer Pol Q at 99-101 (cited in note 100) (survey of New Jersey voters: opposition to ERA correlates with strength of religious attachment, regardless of whether respondent Catholic or Protestant); Louis Bolce, Gerald De Maio, and Douglas Muzzio, *ERA and the Abortion Controversy: A Case of Dissonance Reduction*, 67 Soc Sci Q 299, 306, 310 (1986) (Center for Political Studies National Election Study Data: traditionalist early supporters of ERA reversed positions as they experienced cognitive dissonance; white religious people especially likely to switch from pro-ERA to anti-ERA); David W. Brady and Kent L. Tedin, *Ladies in Pink: Religion & Political Ideology in the Anti-ERA Movement*, 56 Soc Sci Q 564, 575 (1976) (study of anti-ERA activists in Texas: 98% church members; 66% Fundamentalist Protestant; 25% other Protestant; 92% religion very important).

There are feminist reasons why one might oppose the ERA. See generally Becker, 1987 S Ct Rev at 214-24, 215 n 49 (cited in note 16). The empirical research consistently finds a correlation between religious commitment and, not just opposition to the ERA, but more generally opposition to change in women's roles and status. See notes 98-116 and accompanying text. In fact, the states that refused to ratify the ERA were states in which women were generally worse off than the states in which the ERA was ratified. See David C. Nice, *State Opposition to the Equal Rights Amendment: Protectionism, Subordination, or Privatization*, 67 Soc Sci Q 315, 324-25 (1986) (states supporting ERA had lower divorce rates; better AFDC benefit levels; better control of domestic violence; were less likely to have women on death row; were less likely to have called for banning abortion; were less likely to have required school segregation). This suggests that opposition was not grounded on a commitment to women's welfare, but an opposition to increased status for women. Id at 326-27.

[109] See, for example, Baker, Epstein, and Forth, 9 Amer Pol Q at 99-100 (cited in note 100) (survey of New Jersey voters: opposition to abortion correlates with *strength* of religious attachment, rather than with being a Catholic or Protestant); Sharon Marmon and Howard A. Palley, *The Decade After Roe Versus Wade: Ideology, Political Cleavage, and the Policy Process*, in Gwen Moore and Glenna Spitze, eds, 2 *Research in Politics and Society: Women and Politics: Activism, Attitudes, and Office-Holding* 181, 194 (1986) ("Among Catholics and Protestants who are frequent and regular churchgoers, church attendance strongly correlates with opposition to abortion on demand, a correlation which is considerably stronger with respect to Catholics than to Protestants.").

[110] Himmelstein, 25 J Scientific Study Religion at 8 (cited in note 77). This author notes that "differences are more marked for Catholicism than for Protestants and for the more conservative protestants than the less conservative ones, but they are present across the board." Id at 7.

[111] Morgan, 11 Psych Women Q at 305-06 (cited in note 100). Morgan measured five gender-role attitudes:

Interestingly, the correlation between Christian religious commitment and sexist attitudes contrasts with the relationship between such commitment and racist attitudes. Although moderately active Christians are, on the average, more racist than those who do not attend church, the most committed church members are as tolerant of racial minorities as non-members.[112] By contrast, church members are more sexist than the nonaffiliated, and the most committed churchmembers are the most sexist.[113]

The reader may object that religious activities (or perhaps Christian religious activities) do not "cause" antifeminist or other political attitudes or acceptance of traditional women's roles. Rather, those with traditional attitudes are more likely to be members of religious groups, especially conservative religious groups. Thus, self selection explains the correlation between religious involvement and antifeminist beliefs.

But children are not born with either sex-role attitudes or religious commitments. Rather, they are socialized within religious communities and by parents with certain beliefs. There is a high correlation between one's religious training as a child and one's religious commitment as an adult. For example, ninety-one percent of those "raised as Baptists say they are Baptists today."[114] For Episcopalians, the figure is ninety percent; for Lutherans, eighty-nine percent; for Methodists, seventy-four percent; for Presbyterians, seventy-two percent; for Catholics, eighty-one percent; for Jews, eighty-six percent; for those with no religion, forty-four percent.[115] The fact that parents so successfully socialize their chil-

---

> (a) familial roles, i.e., mothers' and fathers' roles pertaining to household division of labor and care of children; (b) extrafamilial roles, i.e., roles of men and women regarding career commitment, decisionmaking, and leadership ability; (c) male/female stereotypes, i.e., beliefs about the innate characteristics of men and women such as male superiority and female dependency; (d) social change as related to sex roles, i.e., changes in social structure necessary for equality in male/female roles such as equal pay and equal job opportunities . . . ; and [(e)] gender-role preferences for role of wife, i.e., the role of a woman in relationship to her husband when she is working outside the home.

Id at 302 (citations omitted).

[112] Richard L. Gorsuch and Daniel Aleshire, *Christian Faith and Ethnic Prejudice: A Review and Interpretation of Research*, 13 J Scientific Study Religion 281, 285 (1974). "The more intrinsically religious, nonfundamentalistic, and theologically discriminating persons were also more tolerant." Id at 281. See also Keith A. Roberts, *Religion in Sociological Perspective* 261-79 (Wadsworth, 2d ed 1990).

[113] Roberts, *Religion in Sociological Perspective* at 280-300 (cited in note 112).

[114] *Public Opinion Report: America: Land of the Faithful* 96, 101 n (American Enterprise, 1990).

[115] Id (again, the figure for Jews would include both religious and secular Jews). I am not asserting that adults *never* choose religion. Fifty-six percent of those raised without

dren into their religion means that we cannot regard correlations between sexist attitudes and religious beliefs as the result of self-selection by autonomous adults. To the extent religious beliefs correlate with antifeminist beliefs, sexual equality for younger generations conflicts with religious freedom for older generations.[116]

Further, to the extent "autonomous" adults do chose religion, the correlation between church devotion and antifeminist political views should be troubling because of the unavailability of any nonsexist religious tradition in the American mainstream. Adults have only a limited set of options—a set that does not include any tradition in which women have been leaders in appropriate levels for any period of time (let alone the millenia over which mainstream religious traditions have developed). If a nonsexist religion *were* part of the American mainstream, we would live in a culture rather different from the present one, and "autonomous" adults in that culture would likely make quite different choices from those made by "autonomous" adults in this culture. That people choose from the options available to them cannot justify the range of options.

The studies already cited suggest that mainstream Christian religions contribute to women's subordinate status in society at large: churchgoers are more likely to take antifeminist positions on political issues important to women.[117] Mainstream Christian religions also impede women's success as politicians. Researchers have found a negative correlation between fundamentalist membership within a state and female representation in the state legislature.[118] A study of female candidates running for state and national office from New York city and two neighboring counties found Catholic women underrepresented and Jewish women overrepresented.[119]

Churches also engage directly in politics. Protestant and Catholic organizations are often used to rally opposition to feminist is-

---

religion nevertheless have a religious affiliation as adults. My point is that particular religious beliefs are passed on from one generation to the next; one cannot, therefore, assert that religious beliefs are the result of choice by "autonomous" adults. If all children were raised without religion, fewer would be associated with religious organizations as adults (and more would be feminists as adults).

[116] *Wisconsin v Yoder*, 406 US 205, 241-46 (1972) (Douglas dissenting in part) (pointing out that religious freedom of high school-age Amish children may conflict with their parents' religious freedom).

[117] See text accompanying notes 98-111.

[118] See, for example, Thomas J. Bolgy, John E. Schwarz, and Hildy Gottlieb, *Female Representation and the Quest for Resources: Feminist Activism and Electoral Success*, 67 Soc Sci Q 156, 161 (1986).

[119] Nikki R. Van Hightower, *The Recruitment of Women for Public Office*, 5 Amer Pol Q 301, 311 (1977).

sues, and thereby have a very direct impact on politics.[120] Catholic prelates have been more willing to criticize female Catholic politicians (as compared to men) for failing to follow official doctrine.[121] Yet many Protestant and Catholic organizations enjoy significant tax and postage advantages over women's political organizations such as NOW PAC.

The empirical work on religion and women examined in this Section shows that religion is a political problem for women. Christian religious values support the sexual status quo. Christians disproportionately favor antifeminist positions. In part, this is because sexism pervades religious doctrines and practices in content and effect. In part it is because religious organizations are political actors and are led by men. In the next subsection, I examine the extent to which government subsidizes religion despite its antidemocratic effects.

D. Government Support for Religion

In the United States, we have neither separation of church and state nor state neutrality toward religion. Rather, the government contributes significantly to religions. I briefly give three examples: 1) *Lynch v Donnelly*[122] ("the creche case"); 2) tax and postage advantages; and 3) income tax-free housing subsidies for "ministers of the gospel." In each of these examples, the governmental subsidy is troubling for two reasons. The first is a general objection: subsidies to mainstream religions contribute to women's subordinate status generally and within the political system. The second is an objection to more specific practices. In the creche case, the government subsidized a sexist image. In the case of tax and postal subsidies, religions, which mobilize opposition to feminist issues, receive benefits denied women's political organizations. And housing subsidies reinforce and magnify discriminatory employment practices within religious organizations.

The reader may object that the Bill of Rights does not *cause* the problems in these three areas: it does not mandate the display of sexist imagery on government property, require tax exemptions from generally applicable taxes, or require housing subsidies. In-

---

[120] See, for example, Kenneth D. Wald, Dennis E. Owen, and Samuel S. Hill, Jr., *Churches as Political Communities*, 82 Amer Pol Sci Rev 531, 533-34 (1988); Himmelstein, 25 J Scientific Study Religion at 8 (cited in note 77).

[121] See, for example, Geraldine A. Ferraro with Linda Bird Francke, *Ferraro: My Story* 222 (Bantam, 1985).

[122] 465 US 668 (1984).

deed, the housing subsidy may be unconstitutional under the Establishment Clause.[123] My point is that, except for the housing subsidy, the Bill of Rights does not *prohibit* these subsidies. When they are held unconstitutional, as in the housing subsidy case, it is not because they discriminate against women. Indeed, the conflict between religious freedom and equality for women is not even visible in the literature or caselaw of the First Amendment.

1. *Lynch v Donnelly.*

In *Lynch v Donnelly* the Supreme Court held that the Establishment Clause does not prohibit a merchants' association in Pawtucket, Rhode Island, from erecting a creche (along with a number of other symbols, including a clown, an elephant, and a teddy bear) in a public park.[124] This governmental subsidy for religion—allowing public property to be used for the display of religious symbols—is not neutral with respect to sex for two reasons. First, most religion is patriarchal and governmental subsidies of religion will, therefore, reinforce patriarchal traditions. Second, an image of the Holy Family displayed on government property raises a more particular set of problems.

The relationship between Mary and Jesus embodies a male fantasy of the ideal mother-son relationship. Jesus is more important; he is the son of God. Mary, as a mere mortal, exists to serve him. Jesus will grow to be a powerful and active male with an important mission. Mary plays only a passive supporting role. The birth of Jesus had nothing to do with his mother's sexual pleasure or even sexuality. The reproductive agency of "God the Father" overshadows the reality of female reproductive power.[125] Admittedly, the virgin Mary is a positive female image—it might be worse to have no women at all. Moreover, both men and women are supposed to emulate the ideal of submission to the will of God. But, as noted earlier, the message of submission to God's will addresses men's sin (pride) more than women's sin (passivity) and Mary's virginity is a denial of female sexuality and reproductive power.[126] This message is a barrier to women's equality and effec-

---

[123] See note 134 and accompanying text.

[124] 465 US at 685. The Court has subsequently held that a creche not surrounded by animals or other secular symbols cannot be constitutionally placed on government property. *County of Allegheny v ACLU*, 492 US 573, 621 (1989).

[125] See, for example, Daly, *Gyn/Ecology* at 83 (cited in note 39).

[126] See text accompanying notes 73-74, especially Saiving, *The Human Situation* (cited in note 74).

tive political participation because it reinforces men's superior status and political dominance.[127]

Of course, the sexism in the imagery of the creche is likely to have only trivial consequences, compared with much more harmful sexist imagery, such as pornography and advertising aimed at selling clothes or beauty products to women by making women feel inadequate. For this reason, I would not recommend excluding such religious symbols from government property because of the harm they cause to women. But the sexism in such symbols should not remain invisible in legal analysis. And perhaps such sexism should justify compensatory "affirmative" action.

2. Tax and postage breaks for religious organizations.

Although religious organizations and feminist political organizations both act politically on issues important to women, such as abortion, they do not receive equal treatment in terms of either taxes or postage rates. The Constitution permits the government to subsidize antifeminist religious organizations yet deny equal treatment to feminist political organizations.

To illustrate this point, I compare the treatment of the Catholic Church, a politically active religious organization, and the treatment of a feminist political action organization, NOW PAC. The government treats these two organizations similarly in terms of income tax on organizational income: both are exempt, since NOW PAC is a nonprofit organization.[128] But all states exempt the Catholic Church from paying property taxes for churches.[129] Many states exempt all church-owned property used exclusively for religious purposes.[130] Most states exempt the Catholic Church from

---

[127] See Section I.B.2.

[128] 26 USC § 527(a).

[129] Richard R. Hammar, *Pastor, Church & Law* 378 (Gospel Publishing, 1983). In order to qualify for federal income tax exemptions, a religious corporation must not intervene or participate directly in political campaigns at all (i.e., it cannot support or oppose specific candidates). Id at 340-41. Nor is the organization allowed to undertake "substantial efforts to influence legislation." Id at 336-40. There is no bright line for determining when such efforts are substantial. Id. The Catholic Church has never lost its tax exempt status despite the fact that it teaches a position on abortion inconsistent with legislation allowing women to choose and despite the use of church networks and events to rally opposition to abortion rights. Nor did the Catholic Church lose its status when prelates attacked Geraldine Ferraro because of her position on abortion. See Ferraro, *My Story* at 211-39 (cited in note 121).

[130] Hammar, *Pastor, Church & Law* at 378 (cited in note 129). Others exempt parsonages in addition to churches. Id.

sales taxes, use taxes, and personal property taxes as well.[131] NOW PAC must pay these taxes. Contributors to the Catholic Church can deduct their contributions from income in calculating income tax.[132] Contributors to NOW PAC cannot. The Catholic Church can take advantage of subsidized mail rates which are unavailable to NOW PAC.[133]

Subsidies to mostly patriarchal religions are not gender neutral in two obvious respects. First, they are equivalent to taxpayer funding of sexist institutions. Second, these subsidies have political effects that are detrimental to women.

3. Income tax treatment of housing for "ministers of gospel."

The Internal Revenue Code permits a "minister of the gospel" to exclude housing costs or a housing allowance from income for tax purposes.[134] As interpreted by the courts and the IRS, this exemption is available only to ordained ministers and those holding equivalent positions in congregations without ordained clergy.[135]

Like other governmental subsidies of religion, this policy is troubling on two levels. First, it subsidizes only institutions that are mostly patriarchal because it subsidizes only religious workers and not other people. Second, because of the specifics of the provision, it magnifies traditional discrimination by religious groups with respect to leadership positions, giving the benefit only to those religious workers who are likely to be male: people who are either ordained ministers or the functional equivalent.[136] Women's traditional roles in congregations—as teachers, support staff, etc.—do not qualify under this provision, even when the women are full-time employees.[137] Although this provision of the federal

---

[131] See *Texas Monthly, Inc. v Bullock*, 489 US 1, 29, 30 n 2, 32 n 3 (1989) (Scalia dissenting) (lists many state exemptions from sales and use taxes). The majority struck down a Texas exemption from sales and use taxes that applied only to religious periodicals and not to "similar" charitable or educational organizations. Id at 25.

[132] 26 USC § 170(b)(1)(A)(ii).

[133] See 39 USC § 3626 (1991). Second and third class rates are available at a discount to religious, educational, scientific, philanthropic, agricultural, labor, veterans, and fraternal organizations if they are nonprofit and meet other requirements. 39 USC § 3626(a)(1) (1991) (incorporating former code sections 39 USC §§ 4358, 4359, 4421, 4422, 4452, and 4554). Qualified political committees may also mail at the discounted third class rates, but must be part of a political party. See 39 USC §§ 3626(e)(1) and 3626(2)(A). NOW PAC would not qualify, nor would any other women's organization since no women's political party exists.

[134] 26 USC § 107.

[135] See IRS Rev Rule 78-301 (Jewish cantor qualified as "minister of the gospel").

[136] Treas Reg § 1.107-1(a).

[137] IRS Private Letter Ruling 8614010 (unordained teachers did not qualify).

tax code is probably vulnerable to constitutional challenge in light of a 1989 Supreme Court case holding that a tax exemption applicable *only* to religious activities is unconstitutional,[138] it remains in effect. And if the Court does overrule it, I doubt that discrimination against women religious workers will inform the decision.

There are no estimates of the total taxpayer subsidies for religious organizations through postage and tax breaks including the housing exemption, but the amount is quite large. One recent case involved over $100,000 in sales taxes imposed on the Jimmy Swaggart Ministries' sales of religious materials through the mail over a period of about eight years in a single state.[139] In fiscal year 1985, Congress appropriated $723.6 million to subsidize postage for qualifying organizations; about forty-five percent of the qualifying organizations were religious.[140] Total annual government subsidies to religious organizations in the United States as a result of exemptions and direct subsidies must be well in the billions.

I have discussed three ways in which government supports mostly patriarchal religions: through the display of religious symbols on government property; through tax and postage breaks for religious organizations; and through exemptions from income tax for housing allowances for ministers of the gospel. This is not, of course, an exhaustive list. Myriad federal and state laws and policies support religion. I mention two others briefly as illustrations of the breadth of the problem, though many more exist. First, governments routinely hire religious organizations to perform governmental services, such as caring for abused or neglected families and children, sometimes in religious institutions.[141] Second, the Supreme Court has permitted federal funding of religious counseling programs on teenage sexuality,[142] though such programs reflect religious organizations' sexist attitudes toward sexuality, especially those of the Catholic Church.

---

[138] *Texas Monthly*, 489 US at 25.

[139] See Brief for Appellant 8-9, *The Jimmy Swaggart Ministries v Board of Equalization of California* S Ct No 88-1374, 493 US 378 (1990).

[140] See Richard Kielbowicz and Linda Lawson, *Reduced-Rate Postage for Nonprofit Organizations: A Policy History, Critique, and Proposal*, 11 Harv J L & Pub Pol 347, 398-99 (1988).

[141] See, for example, *Catholic Agency to Operate Youth Shelter*, Chi Trib 3 (May 13, 1988) (describing temporary shelter and more permanent institution for abused or delinquent children to be run by Catholic Charities); *State Seeks to Overhaul its Shelters*, Chi Trib 5 (Jul 28, 1989) (describing a child intake center for young neglected or abused children run by Catholic Charities: Columbus-Maryville Reception Center).

[142] *Bowen v Kendrick*, 487 US 589, 621 (1988).

True, government receives services in exchange under these kinds of programs, but hiring sexist religious organizations to perform governmental functions is not sex-neutral. Such contracts support religion and increase its power. Indeed, such programs often give governmental power as well as money to religion.

In this Section, I have discussed both the positive and negative aspects of mainstream religion for women and the relevant empirical evidence. As I stressed in the Introduction, my major point is purely critical: the religion clauses of the First Amendment do not have the same meaning for women and men. These clauses have not empowered women as much as men to develop an autonomous source of authority, meaning, value, and morality independent of the state. Instead, these clauses shield from state regulation deeply patriarchal institutions which impede women's political effectiveness in a democracy. Indeed, the Religion Clauses, at least as currently interpreted, allow the government to magnify the subordinating effects of religion by subsidizing it and giving governmental power to religious activities. There has been too little appreciation of this point in the legal literature. I know of no other discussion of this point, though there is some appreciation of the conflict between religious freedom for parents and children's interests in education or health care.[143]

We cannot expect the Bill of Rights to establish all the social rights women need. I do, however, suggest a change that we could implement by interpretation or amendment. In interpreting the First and Fourteenth Amendments, the Court could hold unconstitutional tax subsidies, tax exemptions, or the award of government contracts to religions that discriminate overtly and admittedly on the basis of sex in hiring leaders.

On this view, the Constitution compels a *Bob Jones* approach to religions that discriminate on the basis of sex in leadership positions. In *Bob Jones*, the IRS denied charity status to a religious university that discriminated on the basis of race.[144] The religious university prohibited interracial dating because the religion disapproved of interracial marriage. The Supreme Court held that the denial of charity status to such an institution was statutorily permissible. The case is understood to indicate that the Supreme

---

[143] See, for example, *Wisconsin v Yoder*, 406 US 205, 242-46 (1972) (Douglas dissenting) (pointing out that religious freedom of high school-age children may conflict with their parents' religious freedom); *In re Eric B. v Ted B.*, 189 Cal App 3d 996, 1008-09 (1987) (blood transfusion ordered for child whose parents' religion would not permit it).

[144] *Bob Jones University v United States*, 461 US 574, 604-05 (1983).

Court does not regard the IRS interpretation of the statute as unconstitutional. If the Court had regarded the IRS interpretation as unconstitutional, it would have interpreted the statute to avoid the constitutional problem. Thus, a denial of a benefit to a religious organization that admittedly and overtly discriminates on the basis of race does not violate either of the Religion Clauses.

The Constitution may *compel* this approach in the context of race. The grant of a tax advantage to a racist university is state action. And in both *Shelly v Kraemer*,[145] involving government enforcement of a racially exclusionary covenant, and *Burton v Wilmington Parking Authority*,[146] involving the government's grant of a lease to a racially discriminatory restaurant, the Supreme Court held that similar private racial discrimination was impermissible when accompanied by similar state action.[147]

This approach could and should extend to banning tax exemptions and postal subsidies and the award of government contracts to religious organizations that close leadership positions to women. Like anti-miscegenation policies (*Bob Jones*), and segregation in housing (*Shelley*) and in places of public accomodation such as restaurants (*Burton*), keeping women out of leadership positions denies women the opportunity to participate in society as equals. Keeping women out of religious leadership positions precludes a necessary prerequisite for religious freedom to mean as much to women as to men. For example, the sexist imagery of the creche, whether on government property or elsewhere, is less likely to change if women are not religious leaders. At the same time, denying benefits to religions that overtly close leadership positions to women would not involve greater governmental entanglement with religion than denying benefits to religious universities with anti-miscegenation policies. Under this interpretation, the Constitution would prohibit benefits only to religions or religious institutions which overtly and admittedly deny women religious autonomy and free exercise.

Thus, the Court could regard a *Bob Jones* approach as constitutionally compelled when religions close leadership positions to women. Grants of tax exemptions or subsidies or government contracts to such organizations are state action and the state cannot discriminate on the basis of sex without an exceedingly strong justification. Religious liberty cannot justify the exemption, since

---

[145] 334 US 1 (1948).
[146] 365 US 715 (1961).
[147] *Shelley*, 334 US at 23; *Burton*, 365 US at 726.

these organizations deny women the religious liberty they offer men. To be sure, denial of such subsidies will "hurt" religions that close leadership to women just as the denial of tax exempt status hurt Bob Jones University.[148] Our unwillingness to take action with respect to this blatant sex discrimination reflects our priorities. At present, religious freedom for some men and women justifies affirmative support for institutions subordinating women and denying women full religious freedom. At the very least, we should rethink our decision to *foster* such institutions.

We could modify the Constitution to proscribe religious subsidies altogether, or even to require state regulation of religion to eliminate sexism. I would not, however, favor these approaches. I think that all people need sources of authority outside government. Too much government control would preclude the ability of religion to perform that function. My only suggested change in this area is, therefore, exceedingly moderate.

II. Free Speech and Press

Amendment I to the Constitution guarantees "freedom of speech" and freedom "of the press."[149] In a society with a mass culture, where institutions of the "press" wield immense power, the freedom of the press assumes particular importance. The First Amendment views the "press" (television, movies, videos, books, video games) as largely beyond the reach of government regulation. Yet the "press," particularly its most powerful organ, television, impedes the democratic functioning of our political system. I discuss this problem in terms of both race and sex.[150] In addition, a "free" market in speech means that the market, governed by ability to pay, determines who can speak.

Although white men are a minority in this country, television presents a world in which white men are the majority of the popu-

[148] For an argument that distinguishing between religions that overtly discriminate and those that do not is a violation of the Establishment Clause (and *Bob Jones* was therefore wrongly decided), see Miles, 8 Harv Women's L J 31 (cited in note 30) (arguing that all subsidies to religions should therefore end).

[149] US Const, Amend I.

[150] In each case, there can be no absolutely firm evidence of causation. For example, correlations are always ambiguous since television viewing may not cause the observed trait but rather be related to other factors that cause both the observed trait and television viewing. I assume, for this discussion, that television does influence viewers' attitudes, especially the attitudes of young viewers.

lation as well as socially dominant.[151] As one group of researchers expressed it, "[t]he prominent and stable overrepresentation of well-to-do white males in the prime of life dominates prime time."[152] In 1989, only twenty-nine percent of the leads in feature films were for actresses. And a number of those parts were prostitutes, though prostitutes are a very small part of the population of women.[153] Minorities and women rarely appear as authorities on television.[154] When women do appear as authorities, they frequently espouse positions regarded as anti-women.[155] Television and films *about* caretaking portray men more often than women in the lead caretaking roles, contributing to the invisibility and undervalvation of women as caregivers.[156]

Media sports pervade American culture, and almost all sports heroes are male. Women's team sports do not receive national television coverage. When women do appear in popular sports events, such as Olympic gymnastics or ice skating, aesthetics—watching the female body in motion in a revealing costume—dominate. Even women tennis stars (the most visible non-Olympic women athletes in the national media) are held to an aesthetic standard more demanding, especially with respect to weight, than that applied to men.[157]

The visual media (film, television, magazines) inevitably stress appearance. But for women, the standard of beauty is both more demanding and of more singular importance than for men. In part, this is because women are more often defined as sex objects. Even when not presented *solely* as sex objects (for example, when portrayed as a business person with a briefcase in a credit card advertisement), women are almost always young and beautiful. The

---

[151] See, for example, Matilda Butler and William Paisley, *Women and the Mass Media: Sourcebook for Research and Action* 78 (Human Sciences, 1980) (reporting that in the thirteen studies of the relative appearance of women and men over a twenty year period, the appearance of women became less frequent; overall, men were 72% of all characters and women 28%; one study found that 79% of all white characters were men and 90% of all black characters were men).

[152] George Gerbner, et al, *Charting the Mainstream: Television's Contributions to Political Orientations*, 32 J Commun 100, 106 (1982).

[153] Gene Siskel, *It's the Streep Mystique*, Chi Trib Arts 4 (Sep 2, 1990).

[154] For example, most voice overs in commercials are male voices. See Butler and Paisley, *Women and the Mass Media* at 69-70 (cited in note 148).

[155] See Sunstein, 59 U Chi L Rev at 284 (cited in note 2).

[156] See Judith Posner, *Where's Mom? With more men in the kitchen, TV mothers fade from the screen*, 49 Media & Values 6 (1989). On the undervaluation of women's caretaking in the context of child custody standards, see Mary E. Becker, *Maternal Feelings: Myth, Taboo, and Child Custody*, 1 S Cal Rev L & Women's Stud (forthcoming 1992).

[157] See John Feinstein, *Hard Courts* 201-02 (Villard, 1991).

ubiquitous message confirms reality: a woman's body determines her value, even as a business professional.[158] Advertising is particularly damaging to women; it sells products to women by making women feel inadequate.[159]

Pornography—sexually explicit material presenting women's subordination as sexy—exemplifies the politics of sexuality in the media. Andrea Dworkin states: "The major theme of pornography as a genre is male power, its nature, its magnitude, its use, its meaning. . . . Male power is the raison d'etre of pornography; the degradation of the female is the means of achieving this power."[160] And pornographic themes—that women are sex objects available for male pleasure at all times—pervade mainstream media such as MTV and visual advertising.[161]

Children's television programs are actually more sexist than programs for adults. A 1982 study found that women and minorities appeared even less in children's television than in prime time. When present, women were "portrayed in a more stereotyped manner in children's programming than in prime-time programming."[162] Children's television has not improved since 1982. As of late April, 1991, no Saturday morning children's show featured a girl heroine.[163] The networks had cancelled the only Saturday morning cartoon show with a female lead because only girls were watching the show.[164] Girls will watch shows with boys in leading roles, but boys will not watch shows with female leads.[165] Many shows, like *Garfield*, are essentially all male; others may have one female, under the "Smurfette principle." The Smurfette principle presents "a group of male buddies . . . accented by a lone female, stereotypically defined."[166] The message: "boys are the norm, girls the variation; boys are central, girls peripheral; boys are individuals, girls types."[167] Children's television also emphasizes the impor-

---

[158] See generally, Naomi Wolf, *The Beauty Myth: How Images of Beauty Are Used Against Women* (Morrow, 1991); Robin Tolmach Lakoff and Raquel L. Scherr, *Face Value: The Politics of Beauty* (Routledge & Kegan Paul, 1984).

[159] Wolf, *The Beauty Myth* at 276-77 (cited in note 158).

[160] Andrea Dworkin, *Pornography: Men Possessing Women* 24-25 (Dutton, 1989).

[161] See, for example, Fred Pelka, *"Dreamworlds": How the Media Abuses Women*, 21 On The Issues 20 (1991).

[162] John Corry, *Children's TV Found Dominated by White Men*, NY Times C14 (Jul 15, 1982).

[163] Lynn Hecht Schafran, *The Smurfette Principle*, NY Times 6-12 (Apr 28, 1991).

[164] Id.

[165] Bill Carter, *Children's TV, Where Boys Are King*, NY Times A1 (May 1, 1991).

[166] Katha Pollitt, *The Smurfette Principle*, NY Times 6-22 (Apr 7, 1991).

[167] Id.

tance of physical appearance for girls.[168] Children's video games are worse: when female humans appear, which is rare, they are in need of rescue by the male hero. Female figures in such games are rarely active.[169]

American media, particularly television, film, and video games, promote violence. Most of the empirical evidence on the effect of television and film violence indicates that it stimulates, rather than purges, aggression.[170] Media violence almost always takes place in the context of stereotypical sex roles. It is rare for a woman to use violence other than as an agent of a man or as a crazy person. Military video games present military activities in an abstract context, without blood or pain or suffering. The military use video "games" as training devices, and civilians use them as recreational activities.[171]

As a result of free speech in the media—as well as sexist speech elsewhere in the culture—women face three problems. First, the media silences women. This is true on the most literal level. For example, whether in news, sports, or other programs, it is overwhelmingly men who speak on television. When women do speak, they usually speak others' words rather than their own. And when women are authorities, they tend to espouse anti-women positions.[172]

The media free market is not a market without censors, though the censors are not governments. Women's speech is censored directly by media executives and by advertisers who control the substantive content of articles and programs in magazines and on television.[173] Women's speech is censored indirectly by media

---

[168] See Butler and Paisley, *Women and the Mass Media* at 150-51 (cited in note 151).

[169] Eugene F. Provenzo, Jr., *Video Kids: Making Sense of Nintendo* 61 (Harvard, 1991):

> In a sample of 100 video arcade games, [Terri] Toles determined that 92 percent of the games did not include any female roles, and that of the remaining 8 percent of the games, 6 percent had females assuming "damsel in distress" roles and 2 percent in active roles. Interestingly, in the case of the two females who do take active roles, neither is human—one being a Mama Kangaroo attempting to retrieve her child and the second a feminized blob, Ms. Pac-Man.

[170] See, for example, L. Rowell Heusmann and Neil M. Malamuth, *Media Violence and Antisocial Behavior: An Overview* 42(3) J Soc Issues 1 (1986).

[171] Provenzo, *Video Kids* at 132-35 (cited in note 169); Terri Toles, *Video Games and American Military Ideology*, in Vincent Mosco and Janet Wasko, 3 *Critical Communications Review: Popular Culture and Media Events* 207, 217-21 (Ablex, 1985).

[172] See text accompanying note 155.

[173] See Sunstein, 59 U Chi L Rev at 282 (cited in note 2); Gloria Steinem, *Sex, Lies & Advertising*, Ms. 18 (Jul/Aug 1990).

portrayals of feminists as irrational, unattractive, man-hating lesbians.[174]

Second, market speech harms women more than men by impeding women's ability to develop as autonomous individuals. In a world of inequality, where men control a disproportionate share of resources and women have a disproportionate need for resources because of their responsibility for children, it often pays for women to present themselves as attractive sex objects. But women also internalize the beauty standard and judge themselves inadequate. In a 1984 *Glamour* survey, seventy-five percent of women between the ages of eighteen and thirty-five believed they were fat, though only twenty-five percent were fat by medical standards. More "heartbreaking," and a greater barrier to women's autonomous selfhood, "respondents chose losing ten to fifteen pounds above success in work or in love as their most desired goal."[175] Because of the implicit and explicit messages they receive about their abilities and worth, women have lower self-esteem and confidence than men. Pornography teaches women through concrete physical experience and example that they are worthless and that they exist to service men.

The third problem for women is the media focus on violence and its glorification. This culture of violence is alien to more women than men. Men use violence against women more than women use it against men.[176] The media's glorification of violence, together with the video-game mentality visible during the Gulf War, encourages citizens to view United States military aggression as a spectator sport, one in which men dominate.

These problems exist not only for American women but also for women throughout the world, given the high levels at which we export American media. People in other cultures viewing western media are likely to associate feminism with the pervasive images of women in western media, and hence with the sexualization of women. As a result, women in other cultures encounter more difficulty in objecting to their status; they can easily be tarred as "feminists," decadent as well as disloyal because western. American media thus silences women in other societies, forcing them to betray

---

[174] See Paula Kamen, *Feminist Fatale: Voices from the "Twentysomething" Generation Explore the Future of the "Women's Movement"* 63-74 (Donald I. Fine, 1991).

[175] Wolf, *The Beauty Myth* at 185-86 (cited in note 158).

[176] See text accompanying notes 170-71.

either their sex or their culture.[177] In addition, the allure of western glamor makes it more difficult for many women and girls to become autonomous selves, rather than the playthings western media suggests women are.[178]

These problems impede women's political success in the United States and elsewhere. "Free" speech in a market means that those with the ability to pay are able to speak the most. This is true for political speech. Women are poorer than men and have greater economic responsibility for children. These realities mean men have more disposable income to spend on political speech. Current case law constitutionally protects this differential.[179]

Speech and effective communication are necessary preconditions for having one's needs recognized in the political process. Low self-esteem compounds this differential, since it translates into feelings that one is not entitled to more.[180] Particularly in an individualistic culture such as the United States, low self-esteem and feelings of disentitlement impede solutions which must be both structural and political, such as the support systems women need and enjoy in the rest of the North Atlantic community of nations.[181]

The media's cultivation of violence also has political effects. Women oppose violence more than men do; the glorification of violence impedes action to suppress it, such as passage of gun control legislation or refusal to go to war.

The reader may object that the Free Speech Clause protects feminist speech today just as it protects other speech, and that

---

[177] See, for example, Leila Ahmed, *Feminism and Feminist Movements in the Middle East, A Preliminary Exploration: Turkey, Egypt, Algeria, People's Democratic Republic of Yemen*, in Azizah al-Hibri, ed, *Women and Islam* 153, 162 (Pergamon Press, 1982).

[178] One writer has noted that the combination of Western exports of media violence and weaponry to third world countries "satiate[s] the Third World in patterns of brutality." Sissela Bok, *Alva Myrdal: A Daughter's Memoir* 346 (Addison-Wesley, 1991). In *A Daughter's Memoir*, Bok discusses her mother's acceptance of the Nobel Peace Prize in 1982. The speech discusses these themes generally. See Alva Myrdal, *Disarmament, Technology and the Growth in Violence*, reprinted in *Les Prix Nobel 1982: Nobel Prizes, Presentations, Biographies and Lectures* 222, 228 (Acmquist & Wiksell, 1983).

[179] *Buckley v Valeo*, 424 US 1 (1976) (invalidating campaign expenditure ceilings, ensuring that those with more funding have a larger political voice).

[180] See Linda Gordon, *What Does Welfare Regulate?*, 55 Soc Res 609, 623 (1988):

> Women's movements have had a particularly erratic, discontinuous history. This is because women's sense of entitlement is tenuous, easily reinterpreted as selfish, women being raised to define their virtue in terms of selflessness.

[181] See, for example, Sylvia Ann Hewlett, *When the Bough Breaks: The Cost of Neglecting Our Children* 173-82 (Basic, 1991); Sheila B. Kamerman and Alfred J. Kahn, *What Europe Does for Single-Parent Families*, 93 Pub Int 70 (Fall 1988).

without this protection, women pressing for change would be worse off. But a comparison of government censorship of feminist speech in England and the United States suggests that the American Free Speech Clause is not the critical factor when feminist speech is permitted. England has no written constitution and hence no Free Speech Clause. Historically, both England and the United States censored much feminist speech, even simple information about birth control, during the nineteenth and early twentieth centuries.[182] Neither country's government censors private feminist speech. The United States, however, does censor some feminist speech today: doctors receiving certain federal funding cannot mention abortion to a pregnant woman, even when abortion is the safest available treatment.[183] This comparison suggests that the source of government's unwillingness to censor private feminist speech is not the Free Speech Clause.

The Free Speech Clause does not, in and of itself, cause the problems "free" speech creates for women. England, for example, has no Free Speech Clause and yet has sexist speech. My main point is that the Free Speech Clause does more for men than for women, protecting speech that supports patriarchy. In addition, the Free Speech Clause impedes needed reform. It makes many direct forms of regulation of sexist speech unconstitutional. It also gives constitutional legitimacy to opponents' arguments even when the Constitution might not bar such reform.

I suggest a number of ways in which we could interpret or amend the Free Speech Clause to avoid or lessen the problems discussed in this Section. We could redefine or amend the Free Speech Clause to allow more equitable limits on spending for political speech.[184] The Free Speech Clause could be redefined or amended to allow government to regulate speech in ways suggested by Andrea Dworkin, Catharine MacKinnon, Mari Matsuda, and Cass Sunstein. For example, Dworkin and MacKinnon would give those harmed by pornography a right to damages.[185] Matsuda suggests that the United States should limit racist hate speech, as do

[182] Elizabeth Barrett Browning was censored in the United States (Boston) and England. Contraceptive information was banned in both countries. Anne Lyon Haight, *Banned Books: Informal Notes on Some Books Banned for Various Reasons at Various Times and in Various Places* 49, 63-64, 74-75, 77 (Bowker, 1970).

[183] See *Rust v Sullivan*, 111 S Ct 1759, 1767 (1991).

[184] This interpretation would necessarily overrule *Buckley*, 424 US 1.

[185] See Andrea Dworkin and Catharine A. MacKinnon, *Pornography and Civil Rights: A New Day for Women's Equality* 139-41 (Dworkin/MacKinnon, 1988) (model anti-pornography ordinance).

other liberal democracies (including England).[186] Sunstein suggests that government intervention should be permissible if it does not abridge speech but rather expands the market in speech by subsidizing or otherwise enabling speech that would not otherwise be heard.[187] Under Sunstein's "New Deal for Speech," for example, it might be permissible for the FCC to take sexism or ownership by women into account in licensing.[188] In addition, Sunstein suggests that the free speech principle should be understood to be centered above all on political deliberation.[189] Under this approach, other forms of speech may be regulated for illegitimate reasons, but on the basis of a lesser showing of harm.[190]

Perhaps we should amend the Bill of Rights to make such reform seem possible. The African National Congress (ANC) draft Bill of Rights, for example, includes both a free speech provision[191] and a provision that "[e]ducational institutions, the media, advertising and other social institutions shall be under a duty to discourage sexual and other types of stereotyping."[192] In addition, the ANC draft Bill of Rights includes an affirmative action provision that would seem to permit government funding of, or preferences for, women's speech or nonsexist speech,[193] and another authorizing restrictions of racist or sexist speech.[194]

In this Section, I have discussed problems that "free" speech in a market economy poses for women. Women are silenced.

---

[186] Mari J. Matsuda, *Public Response to Racist Speech: Considering the Victim's Story*, 87 Mich L Rev 2320, 2346-47, 2380-81 (1989).

[187] Sunstein, 59 U Chi L Rev at 267-69 (cited in note 2).

[188] See *Metro Broadcasting, Inc. v FCC*, 110 S Ct 2997 (1990) (upholding constitutionality of requirement that transfers of certain "distress sale" licenses go to minority-controlled firms). The example is mine, rather than Sunstein's, and he might not agree.

[189] Sunstein, 59 U Chi L Rev at 301 (cited in note 2).

[190] Id.

[191] African National Congress, *A Bill of Rights for a Democratic South Africa—Working Draft for Consultation*, Art 4, § 1 (on file with U Chi L Rev) ("There shall be freedom of thought, speech, expression and opinion, including a free press which shall respect the right to reply.").

[192] Id at Art 7, § 5.

[193] Id at Art 13, § 1 ("Nothing in the Constitution shall prevent the enactment of legislation, or the adoption by any public or private body of special measures of a positive kind designed to procure the advancement and the opening up of opportunities, including access to education, skills, employment and land, and the general advancement in social, economic and cultural spheres, of men and women who in the past have been disadvantaged by discrimination.").

[194] Id at Art 14, § 4 (". . . the State may enact legislation to prohibit the circulation or possession of materials which incite racial, ethnic, religious, gender or linguistic hatred, which provoke violence, or which insult, degrade, defame or encourage abuse of any racial, ethnic, religious, gender or linguistic group.").

Women have difficulty developing as autonomous selves with as much confidence as men. And women live in a culture permeated by male violence. I have suggested a number of reforms that should be considered. If the First Amendment cannot be interpreted to allow such reforms, we should consider changing it, since the problems impede women's ability to participate effectively in the political system.

III. The Right to Bear Arms

The drafters of the Constitution saw the ability of armed citizens to oppose national government as an important check on the misuse of federal governmental power, with its "standing army of lackeys and hirelings (mercenaries, vagrants, convicts, aliens, and the like)."[195] The Second Amendment to the Constitution guarantees "the right of the people to keep and bear Arms."[196] This amendment has one of three meanings: either it grants states the right to organize citizens into state militias, or it grants individual citizens the right to bear arms (against the state and one another), or it grants both.[197] Each of these readings is troubling from the perspective of women.

A. State Militias

One reading of the Second Amendment is that it limits the ability of the federal government to limit state militias: citizens have the right to bear arms for the state.[198] But the right of states to organize militias of citizens has meant that only men may bear arms in military organizations, even after women received the vote and became, one might have thought, full citizens.[199] Women are still forbidden to bear arms in combat units, both in state militias and in the national armed services; women may serve in the militia

---

[195] Akhil Reed Amar, *The Bill of Rights as a Constitution*, 100 Yale L J 1131, 1163 (1991).

[196] US Const, Amend II.

[197] Wendy Brown, *Guns, Cowboys, Philadelphia Mayors, and Civic Republicanism: On Sanford Levinson's* The Embarrassing Second Amendment, 99 Yale L J 661, 662 (1989); Sanford Levinson, *The Embarrassing Second Amendment*, 99 Yale L J 637, 644-45, 648-51, 655-56 (1989); John E. Nowak, Ronald D. Rotunda, and J. Nelson Young, *Constitutional Law* § 10.2 n 4 (West, 3d ed 1986). Elaine Scarry has argued that the right of citizens to bear arms is inconsistent with the use of nuclear weapons. Elaine Scarry, *War and the Social Contract: Nuclear Policy, Distribution, and the Right to Bear Arms*, 139 U Pa L Rev 1257 (1991).

[198] Levinson, 99 Yale L J at 644-45 (cited in note 197); Brown, 99 Yale L J at 661-62 (cited in note 197).

[199] See Amar, 100 Yale L J at 1202-03 (cited in note 195).

and federal services only in limited numbers and in limited positions.[200]

Were women fully integrated in combat units in state militia, they would almost certainly serve in combat when state units are called up to fight at the federal level during national emergencies, given the integrated structure of the military. The state militia, together with the national army, navy, marines, and air force, form the United States military. Both the state militia and national armed services are delineated in Article I of the Constitution. It mentions the "organized"[201] state militia (or national guards) and the federal armed services. The state National Guards are under the command of the governors[202] unless called into the service of the United States by the President pursuant to his power under Article II, § 2.[203] The Congress has the power to organize, arm, and discipline the state militia (National Guard) and to govern "such Part of them as may be employed in the Service of the United States."[204] But the states have the reserved power to appoint officers to the militia (National Guard) and to train them "according to the discipline prescribed by Congress." In addition, Congress and the President have the power to raise and deploy federal armies. At the drafting of the Bill of Rights, the militia referred to male citizens drafted at the local or state level (citizen-soldiers) and the federal armies referred to volunteers (mercenaries).[205]

When the United States engages in war, the state National Guards are routinely called and integrated into active forces, both combat and noncombat. National Guard units served in World War I, World War II, the Korean War, Panama,[206] and the Gulf War. National Guard units have often played heroic roles in for-

[200] See, for example, *Women in Uniform*, Boston Globe 3 (Jun 19, 1991) ("Women constituted 11 percent of U.S. armed forces as of December 1990"); *Letters to the Editor* USA Today 11A (Jul 2, 1991) (52% of Army jobs open to women; 97% of Air Force jobs; 59% of Navy jobs; 20% of Marine jobs).

[201] There is also the unorganized militia, but it does not seem to be of any practical importance today. The unorganized militia is defined in the United States Code as consisting "of all able-bodied males" 17 to 44 who are, or have declared their intent to be, citizens of the United States unless they are members of the organized militia or of the federal armed forces. 10 USC §§ 311, 312 (1991).

[202] Richard Halloran, *With Roots in State and in Past, Guard Has Many Missions*, NY Times A16 (Aug 23, 1988).

[203] US Const, Art II, § 2. Article I, § 8 provides that Congress cannot appropriate money for the army "for a longer Term than two Years."

[204] US Const, Art I, § 8.

[205] Amar, 100 Yale L J at 1168 (cited in note 195).

[206] Halloran, NY Times at A16 (cited in note 202); Rudy Abramson, *U.S. Again Looks to the Reservists*, LA Times A1 (Aug 23, 1990) (only a few National Guard units served in

eign wars. For example, in World War I, the earliest troops in combat, and those who saw the most combat, were National Guards, including the famous "42d (Rainbow) Division composed of Guard units from many states, including the 69th Infantry Regiment from New York."[207] The government mobilized the National Guards for World War II prior to any draft, and over a year before the country entered the war. Many played important combat roles. For example, the 38th Infantry Division fought in the Philippines.[208] Today, the reserves play a central role in defense strategy. They are an integral part of any fighting force, capable of being quickly deployed and integrated with active troops, as illustrated by past wars.[209] Thus the full integration of women into the National Guard would mean full integration into the federal forces unless the various branches reorganized to limit women's integration into combat. That should be impermissible if women have a right to be treated as full citizen-soldiers.

As Akhil Amar has noted, militia service, along with jury service and voting, are political rights and obligations of citizens in a democracy.[210] Exclusion of women from militia service in combat denies women the obligations of full citizenship. This denial inevitably translates into disadvantaging women as citizens by depriving them of power they would otherwise share more equally with men. I discuss two concrete problems for American women.

First, keeping women out of combat maintains the image of the male warrior, who is superior to physically passive women who need his protection and cannot resist his violence.[211] This is important on many levels: in terms of the effect of these images on the culture in general and in terms of the lives of individual women and men. The military trains men to operate within a macho culture with the belief that they are superior to women. New male recruits are called "girls" and "ladies" until they earn a masculine label.[212] They march to a sexist and racist cadence: "I don't know

---

Vietnam, in part because of a perceived need to keep them available in the event they were needed in Europe).

[207] Halloran, NY Times A16 (cited in note 202).

[208] Id (this is the unit in which Vice President Quayle later served).

[209] Abramson, LA Times 1A (cited in note 206).

[210] See Amar, 100 Yale L J at 1202-03 (cited in note 195); Kenneth L. Karst, *The Pursuit of Manhood and the Desegregation of the Armed Forces*, 38 UCLA L Rev 499, 499-500 (1991).

[211] See generally Karst, 38 UCLA L Rev 499 (cited in note 210).

[212] Christine L. Williams, *Gender Differences at Work: Women and Men in Nontraditional Occupations* 69 (California, 1989).

but I've been told, Eskimo pussy is mighty cold."[213] They learn about venereal diseases from "Suzy Rottoncrotch."[214] Pictures of nude women are common.[215] In the late 1980s, Marine recruits at Parris Island, South Carolina, marched behind a sign with a naked woman on it and another with a skull and crossbones and the words "kill, rape, pillage, burn."[216] The boys and men trained in this system interact with women both within and outside the military. Men who chant these cadences and learn to consume pornography in the military become husbands, fathers, employees, employers, voters and politicians. Their experiences in the military are likely to make them less willing to accept women as leaders or to sympathize with the problems of women constituents.

The other side of this coin is that keeping women out of combat positions in the military supports the taboo against women using force, especially lethal force. The socialization of girls and women encourages them to be less physically aggressive than boys and men, and boys and men are socialized to expect girls and women to be passive in response to their violence.[217] It is revealing that current military rules do not exclude women from combat zones (i.e., do not keep women out of danger), but rather keep women from using lethal force.[218] Maintaining male control of le-

---

[213] Id.

[214] Id.

[215] Id. The author of this study reports that "[i]n the lounge of the student squadron where I interviewed female pilots, pictures of nude women and 'Playboy' insignias were tacked on the walls." In civilian life, such workplaces would constitute sexual harassment. See, for example, *Ellison v Brady*, 924 F2d 872 (9th Cir 1991); *Robinson v Jacksonville Shipyards, Inc.*, 760 F Supp 1486 (M D Fla 1991).

[216] *Marines' 'rape' slogan draws fire*, Wisc State J 7A (Oct 4, 1989).

[217] See Williams, *Gender Differences at Work* at 54 (cited in note 212) (policies that prohibit women from direct combat but expose them to indirect combat constitute a male protection racket); Pauline Burt and Patricia O'Brien, *Stopping Rape: Successful Survival Strategies* (Pergamon, 1985) (study of many connections between passivity and rape). See also Jalna Hanmer and Elizabeth Stanko, *Stripping Away the Rhetoric of Protection: Violence to Women, Law and the State in Britain and the U.S.A.*, 13 Intl J Soc L 357, 370 (1985) ("Essentially women in today's society are caught in a bind; male violence to women forces women to turn to men for protection.").

[218] See Williams, *Gender Differences at Work* at 54 (cited in note 212). During the Panamanian invasion, women drove other soldiers under sniper fire and one woman, Captain Linda Bray, led a military police company in a firefight. *2 Army Women Being Investigated for Disobeying Order in Panama*, NY Times A20 (Jan 21, 1990). An uproar followed over whether in fact Captain Bray had led troops in combat (in violation of military rules) and whether women *should* be allowed in combat positions. There was, however, no discussion of whether women should be kept out of combat zones as long as in noncombat positions, such as driving under sniper fire. See, for example, Tony Kornheiser, *Capt. Bray and a Dogged Assault*, Wash Post D1 (Jan 12, 1990); Judy Mann, *The Battle Has Just Begun*, Wash Post C3 (Jan 5, 1990). Several enlisted women in the military police were also in

thal force clearly preserves male interests both with respect to control of the military itself (a powerful institution in its own right) and with respect to men's power over women through physical intimidation throughout society.

Integrating women into the military would change the way we raise girls and decrease male violence against women. We treat girls and boys differently even as infants and children. As babies, boys are more likely to be tossed about. We expect boys to be tough and not to cry. We treat girls as more physically vulnerable and expect them to be less active physically. Girls' sports programs are different from boys': serious girls' sports are rarely aggressive contact team sports. Were women present in the military and in combat positions in proportion to their presence in the population, we probably would treat girls differently. There probably would be less violence against women, because women would be less passive physically and because military training would be less sexist. There is, for example, evidence that men who are or have been in the military are more likely to batter their wives.[219] Were women and men trained in the same system, they would be more likely to interact as equals elsewhere.

Women's exclusion from combat units in the military also increases the rate at which our soldiers rape women from the "other" side during war.[220] Our soldiers would be less likely to rape if half their comrades were women. Although we do not tend to hear much about this problem, it does happen many times in most wars.[221] We should consider it in assessing the costs and benefits of including women in the military.

The second major problem, and an extremely troubling one in a democracy, is that the exclusion of women from the draft and from combat positions in state militia and federal forces supports many barriers, erected by government itself, to women's participation in government and political life. The exclusion of women from combat means that women have less authority in government than

combat attacking Panamanian defense headquarters, thus raising controversy. See Wilson Ring, *Women Led U.S. Troops into Battle; Captain's Platoon Took PDF Target*, Wash Post A1 (Jan 3, 1990); Molly Moore, *Combat Role to be Sought for Women; Panama Experience Prompts Schroeder*, Wash Post A25 (Jan 4, 1990). See also Colman McCarthy, *Women at War, a Foolish First*, Wash Post F2 (Jan 14, 1990) ("What kind of society are we when similar opportunity in killing is the standard for equality.").

[219] See Del Martin, *Battered Wives* 52-53 (Glide, 1976); Walker, *The Battered Woman* at 36-37 (cited in note 52).

[220] Susan Brownmiller, *Against Our Will: Men, Women and Rape* 64-65 (Simon & Schuster, 1975).

[221] Id at 31-32.

men. Because of the exclusion, only men can be military heros. Women political candidates cannot boast of combat service, which voters regard as a credential for public office. Women within legislative bodies are regarded as having less authority on military matters than their male colleagues because they have not "been there;" they are regarded as less qualified to serve on military oversight committees and as having less authority if on such committees.

The military services deny women equal employment opportunities because they both limit the numbers of women in the services, and they deny women the combat experience necessary for promotion to high rank. Because they are so often present in token numbers, women in the services are subject to more sexual harassment than they would be in a more integrated organization.[222] No woman has ever been a member of the Joint Chiefs of Staff. Nor is any woman likely to be as long as women are not present in the military, in all positions, in proportion to their presence in the population.

It may be that women are more pacifist than men. If so, excluding women from combat disarms women's pacifism. Their resistance means less because it has fewer consequences. For example, women protesting the war in Vietnam had less authority because they did not have draft cards to burn and tended therefore (and for a host of other reasons) to be relegated to subservient positions in anti-war organizations.[223] Women in Congress who oppose military action have less authority because they have not been in combat. They, unlike Senator Kerrey, cannot oppose a military action with the authority of a recipient of the Congressional Medal of Honor who has lost a leg in combat.[224]

In addition, both federal and state governments have created a large number of preferences for veterans. Under these preferences, many positions in state and federal government are held mostly by men. For example, proportionately, even fewer federal administra-

---

[222] Karst, 38 UCLA L Rev at 525 (cited in note 210); Susanne Fowler, *Breaking Ranks: Rape, Harassment Claimed by Cadets* Chi Trib Womanews 1 (Oct 20, 1991) (allegations of sexual harassment in military training program at Texas A&M).

[223] Sara Ruddick has examined many of the arguments for including women in the military to serve peace and concludes that this is an inappropriate strategy because such interests can best be "cultivated in pacifist organizations." See Sara Ruddick, *Pacifying the Forces: Drafting Women in the Interests of Peace*, 8 Signs 471, 485-86 (1983). But, as Jennifer Hertz pointed out to me, Ruddick ignores the ways in which women's exemption from combat "disarms" them within pacifist organizations and denies them the same authority as pacifist men who have so much more to lose by resistance to military service.

[224] John Cassidy, *Democrats Run for Cover as Bush Fever Grips US*, Sunday Times 14 (London) (Mar 17, 1991).

tive law judges are women (5.41 percent) than federal Supreme Court (11.11 percent), federal Courts of Appeal (10.11 percent), or federal District Court judges (8.69 percent) because the federal veterans' preference applies to administrative law judges.[225] In many states, there are preferences for veterans in state employment as well.[226] Some state governments are almost entirely male at high levels for the same reason.[227] Thus, as a result of discrimination in military service, women are less likely to wield governmental power in nonelective offices.[228]

The reader may object that paying for military service is a valid governmental purpose, and that veterans' preferences are simply one form of compensation. But veterans' preferences for governmental employment are not the equivalent of compensation schemes. Such preferences give men an edge in running government and exclude women from power on the basis of a factor linked by government itself to sex. In addition, such policies are anti-democratic, creating a government based on a sort of military aristocracy rather than a government open to all.

I have discussed two ways in which the exclusion of women from combat hurts women. The exclusion contributes to cultural images and the social reality of violent male warriors and physically passive women in need of their protection. It also creates numerous barriers to women's participation in government and political life. As the framers of the Second Amendment realized, "ultimate political power" lies "with those who control the means of force."[229]

There are, of course, a number of arguments that can be made against full integration of women into the armed services and National Guard. Most women, even most women in the military today, oppose mandatory combat service. Most career military

---

[225] The data on women judges is based on a phone call to Dixie Noble, National Association of Women Judges, Williamsburg, Virginia (Oct 3, 1991) (notes on file with U Chi L Rev). 5 USC § 3105 (1991) authorizes agencies to appoint administrative law judges; 5 CFR § 930.203(e) (1990) instructs that agencies should accept highest rated applicants for Administrative Law Judge positions "augmented . . . by veteran preference."

[226] Veterans' organizations also receive postal subsidies denied to women's organizations. 39 USC § 3626 (1991).

[227] See, for example, *Personnel Administrator of Massachusetts v Feeney*, 442 US 256, 283 (1979) (Marshall dissenting) (majority upheld veterans' preferences in Massachusetts despite fact that 98% of veterans were male and virtually all desirable state civil service employment positions were consequently held by men).

[228] See id (as a result of Massachusetts's preference for veterans, "desirable state civil service employment [is] an almost exclusively male prerogative").

[229] David C. Williams, *Civic Republicanism and the Citizen Militia: The Terrifying Second Amendment*, 101 Yale L J 551, 553 (1992).

women want to engage in combat service, but ordinary enlisted women do not.[230] The military is perhaps the most masculinist institution in our society; its values and its focus on physical violence are alien to most women. Nevertheless, until women are full citizens—citizen soldiers on the same basis as men—women will have less power in government and outside it. They will lack power in waging peace as well as war, and will face restricted employment opportunities both in the military and in government.

Today's interpretation of the Bill of Rights does not require that women be accorded full citizenship. We should interpret the Second Amendment, especially in light of the Fourteenth and Nineteenth Amendments, as extending the right to bear arms in state militia to women. At a minimum, the Fourteenth Amendment should bar veterans' preferences in state employment as long as women do not receive equal treatment in the military. It is absurd to regard injury as justifying injury as when overt government discrimination against women in one area justifies non-merit based standards that exclude most women from many government jobs.

B. The Right of Individual Citizens to Bear Arms

The other possible meaning of the Second Amendment, either as an alternative reading or in combination with the reading given above,[231] is that it limits the ability of both the state and federal governments to regulate gun ownership. In other words, it grants individuals a right to bear arms, arms which may be used, perhaps illegally, against other individuals or the state.[232] Although it is extremely difficult to compare rates of violence internationally because of reporting differences, the United States is clearly much

---

[230] Most (about 75% of those interviewed by one reporter in Panama) female officers believed that women should be able to volunteer for combat. But only a quarter of that sample thought "that women should be compelled to enter combat units, just as men are." Charles Moskos, *Army Women* Atlantic Monthly 7, 77 (Aug 1990). In contrast, about 75% of enlisted women thought that women should not be allowed into combat. Only 25% thought that women should be able to volunteer for combat. No enlisted women "favored forcing women into combat assignments." Id.

[231] Amar argues, as noted earlier, that the Second Amendment means both the right of the individual citizen to bear arms and of the states to organize their citizens into militia. See Amar, 100 Yale L J at 1162-73 (cited in note 195).

[232] Although it is not clear whether the Second Amendment would ban legislation banning private ownership of guns (see, for example, Levinson, 99 Yale L J at 640 (cited in note 197)), the Second Amendment does appear to make even regulation more difficult, by giving those who want guns to remain unregulated a *constitutional* argument and rallying cry.

more violent than other countries.[233] Although there is no way to prove this point, it seems likely that the Second Amendment reflects and reinforces the unusual levels of violence in our culture. Moreover, violence harms women and other groups more than it harms men like the founding fathers.

Violence devastates poor inner city communities, which are made more deadly by the availability of guns. Women in the inner cities where crime is highest lead lives circumscribed by violence. Intolerable levels of violence victimize them and those they love. They must worry before going outside at night, or even during the day in some areas.[234] They worry about their children getting safely through the school day and back home. Many see their sons join the violent underworld of drugs and gangs with deadly results: "[T]he number one cause of death for African-American males between the ages of fifteen and twenty-four is murder."[235] Men like the founding fathers—propertied white men—do not live in these neighborhoods and are not as likely to be victims or perpetrators of violence as are poor women and men.

To the extent the Second Amendment protects individuals' rights to own guns, or assists the NRA in resisting effective gun control legislation, the Second Amendment is a countermajoritarian impediment to women's effective use of the political system. Men are not only more likely to own guns than women, they are also more likely to oppose gun control.[236] For example, in 1985, fifty percent of men but only twelve percent of women owned guns.[237] In 1986, fifty-five percent of women, but only thirty-nine percent of men, favored laws banning the sale and possession of handguns in their own community.[238] Women and men have conflicting interests and opinions concerning gun regulation, and the Constitution enshrines, at least on a rhetorical level, a male norm.[239]

---

[233] See, for example, James D. Wright, et al, *Weapons, Crime, and Violence in America: A Literature Review and Research Agenda* 2-4 (US Dept of Justice, 1981).

[234] Margaret T. Gordon and Stephanie Riger, *The Female Fear* 8-22 (Free Press, 1989).

[235] Randolph N. Stone, *Crisis in the Criminal Justice System*, 8 Harv BlackLetter J 33, 39 (1991).

[236] Katherine M. Jamieson and Timothy J. Flanagan, eds, *Sourcebook of Criminal Justice Statistics* 109-11, Tables 2.38-2.43 (US Dept of Justice, 1987).

[237] Id at 109, Table 2.38.

[238] Id at 110, Table 2.43.

[239] See Brown, 99 Yale L Rev at 663-64 (cited in note 197). For evidence tnat gun control laws can decrease violence, see Elisabeth Scarff, *Evaluation of the Canadian Gun Control Legislation: Final Report* 36, 39, 42, 53, 63, 65, 66, 68 (Ministry of the Solicitor General of Canada, 1983); *Gun Control Laws in Foreign Countries* 88-94, 135-36, 157-60 (Law Li-

Changes to the Second Amendment in light of my criticisms are easy to imagine. An amendment or new interpretation could allow effective national bans on gun ownership by individuals. Alternatively, if the Second Amendment affords citizens the right to bear arms in state militia, that right should be extended to all citizens, regardless of sex.

IV. Criminal Justice System Protections

The Bill of Rights contains a number of provisions designed to guard against governmental misuse of the criminal justice system. The Fourth Amendment proscribes unreasonable searches and seizures.[240] The Fifth Amendment provides for indictment by a grand jury for serious crimes and for due process in criminal trials.[241] The Sixth Amendment guarantees the accused a right to a trial by jury in criminal cases, and the assistance of counsel for his defense.[242] The drafters intended these provisions to guard against misuse of the criminal justice system by government, particularly criminal prosecution of government critics.[243]

Nothing in the Bill of Rights or the Fourteenth Amendment guards against systemic racism in the operation of the criminal justice system, or against its systematic misuse to "solve" problems associated with racism and poverty. In making these points, the emphasis in this section differs somewhat from the emphasis in other sections. Here, I stress that the Bill of Rights does less for poor minorities than it does for propertied white men. In other sections, I stress that the Bill of Rights does less for women than for men. This shift is appropriate even though my major concern is the latter. Although most of those caught in the criminal "justice" system are men, the problems with the way the system operates in poor minority communities pose major problems for women in those communities. One cannot separate the interests of poor minority women and men; their fates are intertwined in ways without precise parallel to white women and men, particularly propertied white women and men. Women who live in communities destroyed by drugs and by the "war" on drugs are devastated by the destruc-

---

brary, Library of Congress, 1981) (evidence from Britain mixed, but both Japan and Sweden, which have strict gun control laws, have low rates of murders involving firearms).

[240] US Const, Amend IV.

[241] US Const, Amend V.

[242] US Const, Amend VI.

[243] Amar, 100 Yale L J at 1175-99 (cited in note 195).

tion around them even though they themselves are less likely to go to prison than are their sons, lovers, and husbands.

At the time the Bill of Rights was enacted, whites were free to enter the home and batter, rape, or kill African Americans with impunity. This was particularly true for African Americans who were slaves, but even free or freed African Americans were often subject to white violence without the criminal law protection afforded white men (and white women in some contexts).[244] At the same time, black people, particularly slaves, were often punished for alleged crimes without any evidence of guilt. For African Americans in 1791, the criminal "justice" system was part of the problem, and the Bill of Rights did nothing to end these systemic abuses.

Racism persists within the criminal justice system.[245] African American women receive less protection from the criminal justice system than white women. When African American women are raped, their rapists are less likely to serve time than the rapists of white women.[246] Defendants in rape prosecutions often succeed by suggesting that the woman was a prostitute, and this may be especially effective when women live, as poor and African American women often must, in neighborhoods where prostitutes are on the streets. African Americans, women as well as men, more often fall into the police net because they fit the drug courier image,[247] are more likely to be treated roughly or beaten severely by the police,[248] and are more likely to be arrested. States are most likely to

---

[244] See, for example, *State v Weaver*, 3 NC 70, 71 (1798) (justifiable homicide for master to kill slave or freed servant who forcefully resists master's use of force to compel obedience).

[245] I only outline problems in the criminal justice system here. I am not an expert in criminal law and cannot provide the in-depth discussion these issues deserve. For a fuller discussion of these problems, I refer the reader to work by others. Stone, 8 Harv Black-Letter L J 33 (cited in note 235); Stephen J. Schulhofer, *Access to Justice for the American Underclass*, The World & I 463, 469-75 (Jun 1991); Sheri Lynn Johnson, *Unconscious Racism and the Criminal Law*, 73 Cornell L Rev 1016 (1988); Randall L. Kennedy, McCleskey v. Kemp*: Race, Capital Punishment, and the Supreme Court*, 101 Harv L Rev 1388 (1988); Samuel R. Gross, *Race and Death: The Judicial Evaluation of Evidence of Discrimination in Capital Sentencing*, 18 UC Davis L Rev 1275 (1985).

[246] Generalized from data that finds that black offenders are sentenced most harshly when their victims are white, Alfred Blumstein, et al, eds, 1 *Research on Sentencing: The Search for Reform* 101 (National Academic Press, 1983). See also Gary D. LaFree, *The Effect of Sexual Stratification by Race on Official Reactions to Rape*, 45 Am Soc Rev 842, 852 (1980).

[247] Editorial, *Bringing Sanity to Seizure Laws*, Chi Trib 2 (Sep 1, 1991).

[248] See, for example, Frank Clifford and John L. Mitchell, *Incident Gives City a National Black Eye; Image: Old Memories of Free-Swinging Cops Are Revived*, LA Times B1 (Mar 7, 1991) (reporting on Rodney Glen King police beating incident in Los Angeles).

impose the death penalty on African American defendants whose victims were white.[249]

Moreover, the criminal justice system is used today to "solve" problems caused by poverty—drugs and drug-related crime. As Randolph Stone has noted, "[t]he war on drugs has devastated the criminal justice system" as well as "some segments of the African-American community."[250] Today, "the judicial system has become an assembly line."[251] Most defendants do not receive trial by jury or the opportunity to confront witnesses against them.[252] Because judges are pressured to treat cases summarily, counsel is more important than ever. But effective assistance of counsel is often denied, particularly to the poor or those accused of drug-related crimes. Public defenders handle unmanageable caseloads.[253] In places without public defenders, poor defendants must rely on court-appointed counsel, who are often required to work pro bono or for token fees.[254]

Once dragged into the criminal "justice" net, the consequences can be devastating, even if police and prosecutors lack sufficient evidence to proceed to trial. Under federal law and many states' laws, if the police suspect that property is related to drugs, they can seize it on grounds as slight as those required for a search warrant:[255] probable cause to believe that the property was involved in illegal activities.[256] Seizure of property makes it more difficult to

---

[249] *McCleskey v Kemp*, 481 US 279, 286-87 (1987).

[250] Stone, 8 Harv BlackLetter L J at 36 (cited in note 235).

[251] Id at 34.

[252] For a description of the problem, see Schulhofer, *The World & I* at 474 (cited in 245) (As a result of our resource decisions, "85-90 percent of criminal convictions are obtained by guilty plea.").

[253] See Stone, 8 Harv BlackLetter L J at 34 (cited in note 235):

> Lawyers in our felony trial division [Cook County Public Defender's office] have one hundred pending cases, while those in our Homicide Task Force handle twenty-three pending murder cases each; one-third to one-half of those homicide cases are death penalty cases.

[254] See Schulhofer, The World & I at 469-75 (cited in note 245).

[255] See, for example, Walter J. Van Eck, *The New Oregon Civil Forfeiture Law*, 26 Willamette L Rev 449, 476-78 (1990); Thomas E. Payne, *An Introduction to Civil Forfeiture in Mississippi: An Effective Law Enforcement Tool or Cash Register Justice?*, 59 Miss L J 453, 463 (1989); Steven L. Kessler, *Quo vadis? Assessing New York's Civil Forfeiture Law*, 4 Touro L Rev 253 (1988).

[256] The federal civil forfeiture provision is at 21 USC § 881. For a discussion, see Barry Tarlow, *Forfeiture Trends*, 15 The Champion 42 (Nov 1991); Mark A. Jankowski, *Tempering the Relation-Back Doctrine: A More Reasonable Approach to Civil Forfeiture in Drug Cases*, 76 Va L Rev 165 (1990); G. Richard Strafer, *Civil Forfeitures: Protecting the Innocent Owner*, 37 U Fla L Rev 841 (1985); Gerard E. Lynch, *RICO: The Crime of Being a Criminal (parts III & IV)*, 87 Colum L Rev 920 (1987); Terrance G. Reed, *The Defense Case for RICO Reform*, 43 Vand L Rev 691, 701-11 (1990); Jeffrey M. Evans, *"Civil" For-*

hire counsel either to recover the property or for criminal defense. Given the fiscal crunch facing most law enforcement systems, these statutes create powerful incentives for misuse of seizure without trial.

Using the criminal justice system to battle problems caused by poverty and racism results in a prison population that is half African American men.[257] There are more African American men in prison than in college.[258] The incarceration rate in the United States is now the highest known in the world: 426 prisoners per 100,000 population. South Africa is second with a rate of 333 per 100,000 and the Soviet Union third with a rate of 268 per 100,000. Most of the world has much lower rates. For example, Western European rates are 35-120 per 100,000.[259]

Although poor pregnant addicts cannot find the in-patient medicaid-funded rehabilitation treatment they need, they are increasingly subject to criminal prosecution for delivering drugs to minors.[260]

The misuse of the criminal justice system to address problems of poverty and racism has political effects. People wrongly convicted of many crimes cannot vote in state elections while serving time and in most states even thereafter.[261] More importantly, keeping the poor impoverished—rather than dealing with poverty effectively—means keeping them politically ineffective. The poor, disproportionately, do not vote and do not participate in political life.[262]

The protections in the Bill of Rights against misuse of the criminal justice system do not "cause" these problems. But the Bill of Rights does less to guard against misuse of the criminal justice system to combat problems of poverty and racism than it does to guard against misuse of the criminal justice system to silence political dissidents. Furthermore, the misuse of the Bill of Rights to

---

feitures Under State RICO Laws: A Legislative Attempt to Circumvent the Constitution, 8 Crim Just J 293 (1986).

[257] Stone, 8 Harv BlackLetter L J at 35 (cited in note 235).

[258] Though one year in prison costs as much as an education at a four-year college. Id.

[259] Mark Mauer, *Americans Behind Bars: A Comparison of International Rates of Incarceration* 4-5 (The Sentencing Project, 1991). Incarceration rates have been dropping in the Soviet Union. Ten years ago they were estimated to be about 25% to 100% higher than current estimates. Id at 4, 6.

[260] See Michelle Oberman, *Sex, Drugs, Pregnancy and the Law: Rethinking the Problems of Pregnant Women Who Use Drugs*, Hastings L Rev (forthcoming 1992).

[261] *Shepard's Lawyer's Reference Manual* 575-95 table A-31 (1983) (survey of voter qualifications).

[262] See text accompanying notes 271-73.

facilitate the war on drugs has undermined specific constitutional guarantees as applied to poor minorities, especially those accused of drug involvement, by denying them a fair trial with effective assistance of counsel. Thus the general protections of the Bill of Rights against misuse of the system have been effectively destroyed by the drug war for many poor people, who are subjected to assembly-line justice without effective counsel. Finally, the Bill of Rights does not provide any affirmative economic or educational protections for the poor, protections which might ensure that problems of poverty be effectively addressed.

An interpretation of or amendment to the Bill of Rights might lessen these problems by directly addressing the economic and educational needs of the poor and by providing provisions more effective at ensuring justice for all within the criminal justice system. After discussing the "property" right enshrined in the Fifth Amendment, I suggest a number of positive economic and educational rights that we could incorporate in the Bill of Rights.[263] In addition, the Bill of Rights could include provisions guaranteeing effective assistance of counsel and fair trials. For example, we could interpret effective assistance of counsel as proscribing the seizure of assets used to pay counsel and as requiring reasonable caseloads for public defenders and reasonable fees for court-appointed counsel.[264] At a minimum, government should be prevented from seizing assets without a trial, and money paid to a lawyer prior to execution of a judgment should be no more coverable than money paid to any other creditor. We could obtain this result by reasonable interpretation of the Fifth Amendment's Takings Clause.

V. Security At Home

The Fourth Amendment provides that "[t]he right of the people to be secure in their persons, houses, papers, and effects, against unreasonable searches and seizures, shall not be violated." White male heads of family during the revolution and today face threats to physical security at home from two kinds of intruders: government actors and criminals. The criminal law has been used to protect against the latter, if not always effectively; the Fourth Amendment guards against the former.

---

[263] See text accompanying notes 274-80.

[264] For these and additional suggestions, see Schulhofer, The World & I at 475 (cited in note 245).

Women, by contrast, face a third major source of physical insecurity within the home: battery and rape by someone who lives in the home—their sexual partners. Yet we have never accorded protection against domestic violence at the level accorded other crimes of violence. The Fourth Amendment does not address domestic violence. The Fourth Amendment protects women against governmental assault, but leaves governments free to treat "domestic" assaults differently from other crimes. Indeed, the criminal codes of many states still deny equal criminal protection to wives who are raped by their husbands.[265] Although some states have eliminated this distinction, others have extended it to nonmarried cohabitants.[266]

These inequities have political consequences. Women who fear violence redefine themselves as wanting to give what might otherwise be taken away, instead of asserting their own interests,[267] particularly in a politically effective way. Women who are abused within their most intimate relationships are less able to assert their interests within those relationships. Abused women are unlikely to press strongly for change in the political arena, especially when their interests conflict with the interests of the abuser.

In large part, my criticism is simply that the Fourth Amendment does less for women than it has done for white men, who drafted it. Protected by the criminal justice system from attacks by criminals, they added the Fourth Amendment to protect themselves from governmental intrusion. The Fourth Amendment is much less thorough in providing the protections needed by women. It allows government, police, and prosecutors to treat domestic violence differently from other violence. Indeed, the Constitution allows government to treat marital rape as noncriminal. The Fourth Amendment may have affirmatively made women worse off by giving a constitutional foundation to the notion that a "man's home is his castle."

One can easily imagine improvements in the Bill of Rights from the perspective of violence against women. The Bill of Rights could include an equality standard for sex that would require the state to respond to domestic violence in the same way it responds to other crimes, and to proscribe marital rape.[268] Such constitu-

---

[265] See Robin West, *Equality Theory, Marital Rape, and the Promise of the Fourteenth Amendment*, 42 U Fla L Rev 45, 46-48, 46 n 6 (1990).

[266] See id at 48 n 11.

[267] See West, 3 Wis Women's L J at, 93-111 (cited in note 51).

[268] See generally West, 42 U Fla L Rev 45 (cited in note 265).

tional provisions would not by themselves revolutionize how police, prosecutors and jurors treat intersexual domestic violence, but they might contribute to changed attitudes. They would, moreover, ensure some of the prerequisites for effective control of domestic violence.

VI. Property

The Fifth Amendment provides that "[n]o person shall . . . be deprived of life, liberty, or property, without due process of law; nor shall private property be taken for public use without just compensation."[269] There are a number of problems with this provision from the perspective of minorities and women. First, and most dramatically, at the time the Bill of Rights was adopted in 1789, slaves *were* property. They were protected as property of others; they could have no property themselves. This provision of the Fifth Amendment was an instrument of oppression for African American women and men.

Second, at the time of the passage of the Bill of Rights, married women could not own or control property. Thus, the Fifth Amendment protected only the property of men and single women.

Third, the protection of "property" meant and means the privileging of existing distributions, no matter how dubious. Consider, for example, the property rights of the newly-freed people vis-a-vis the property rights of their former owners. The fields cleared and cultivated by the freed people belonged to the owners. The buildings and plantations built by the freed people belonged to the owners.

Fourth, while "property" has always included realty and the goods produced by the kinds of labor in which most men spend their working lives, we have never recognized women's reproductive and domestic labor as property. Women's caretaking impedes women's ability to accumulate property in three distinct ways: (1) caretaking itself does not tend to produce property; (2) caretaking tends to limit one's ability to earn property; and (3) caretaking tends to require consumption of property. As a result, women have fewer resources than men and are far more likely to be poor.[270]

Lack of property precludes effective political participation. The poor vote less often, are less politically active, and have fewer

---

[269] US Const, Amend V.

[270] See, for example, 163 *Current Population Reports: Consumer Income: Poverty in the United States: 1987* 118-19 (US Bureau of the Census, 1989) (slightly under 11% of all families are poor, though 34% of families headed by women are poor).

resources with which they can influence elections. It is more difficult for the poor to make contributions to candidates likely to represent their interests or to spend money themselves to advance candidates or political positions. Yet the Constitution protects the ability of the rich to spend more politically.[271] Although seventy-six percent of those making over $50,000 a year vote, only thirty-eight percent of those making less than $5,000 a year vote.[272] Registration is structured so as to discourage registration by the poor.[273]

Provisions in a Bill of Rights could lessen these problems. A Bill of Rights could provide for positive economic rights, ensuring women economic supports and safety nets as effective as those available to men. Such a Bill of Rights would be more detailed and specific, less elegant, brief, and abstract, than the Bill of Rights we have today. Against this aesthetic loss must be balanced the benefit to women and children, who form the majority of Americans. In addition, a society in which women have more power would be more democratic. Its government would have greater legitimacy.[274]

Affirmative economic rights could include a right to health care under a national and universal health care system (the details of which would be specified by legislation); a requirement of a family allowance (tied to some independent economic indicator, such as a fractional percentage of gross national product); caretaking leave with wage support as part of the unemployment insurance system (with support required at the level generally provided for unemployment compensation); government-financed child care; a requirement that social security benefits be, on average, the same for women and men (within a limited level of tolerance);[275] a right to a decent education (with a ban on financing schools through property taxes and a requirement that per pupil expenditures be uniform throughout the United States);[276] and a requirement that breadwinners and homemakers be treated the same with respect to

---

[271] *Buckley v Valeo*, 424 US 1 (1976).

[272] Garry Wills, *'New Votuhs'*, NY Rev Books 3, 3 (Aug 18, 1988).

[273] Id.

[274] See Linda Gordon, *What Does Welfare Regulate?* 55 Soc Res 609, 629 (1988).

[275] For a discussion of the many structural problems in the social security system, see Mary E. Becker, 89 Colum L Rev 264 (cited in note 17).

[276] In New Jersey, where the state supreme court has interpreted the state Constitution as banning differential school funding levels based on local property taxes, "per-pupil expenditures are still $2,880 in poor districts and $4,029 in wealthy districts." Hewlett, *When the Bough Breaks* at 58 (cited in note 181). See generally id at 56-61, 246-49.

all substantive standards for disability.[277] A ban on abortion should be seen as a taking (of women's reproductive labor) for government purposes without compensation.[278] The Bill of Rights should also include a right to abortion, fully paid by the state, in light of (inter alia) the economic consequences of childbearing for women.

Further, the Bill of Rights should make family law a matter within the control of the national government and not the states. Gender relations in the family are of primary importance for a just society.[279] Setting a framework for just relationships should be a priority for national government; living within such a framework should be a prerogative of national citizenship.[280]

Like other provisions of the Bill of Rights, the Takings Clause of the Fifth Amendment does much more for men than for women, favoring men's productive labor over women's reproductive labor. The Due Process Clause of the Fifth Amendment also favors men's experiences, by enshrining as the "rule of law" a legal system developed by and for elite white men. In the next Section, I examine this provision and contrast it with the jury provisions, which now provide for the participation of all in applying the laws developed by the few.

VII. Due Process and the Jury Provisions

The Fifth Amendment provides for "due process" before any person is deprived of "life, liberty, or property."[281] The Sixth and Seventh Amendments provide for a jury trial in criminal and civil cases.[282] The "due process" guaranteed by the Fifth Amendment thus entitled its framers, mostly elite white men, to the procedures

---

[277] Social Security has different substantive disability standards for homemakers and breadwinners. See Becker, 89 Colum L Rev at 269 (cited in note 17).

[278] In making this point, I do not suggest that women's reproductive ability should be treated in all respects like alienable property rights. Indeed, I think it a mistake to commodify women's bodies by creating a market for their reproductive labor. For a discussion of the problems with a market approach, see Margaret Jane Radin, *Market-Inalienability*, 100 Harv L Rev 1849 (1987); Cass R. Sunstein, *Neutrality in Constitutional Law (with Special Reference to Pornography, Abortion, and Surrogacy)*, 92 Colum L Rev 1 (1992). I am merely stating that government should not be able to take women's reproductive labor without compensation by banning abortion. Women's reproductive labor should, however, be inalienable.

[279] See generally Susan Moller Okin, *Justice, Gender, and the Family* (Basic, 1989).

[280] I am indebted to Hendrik Hartog for this idea.

[281] US Const, Amend V.

[282] US Const, Amends VI and VII. In civil cases, the right applies "where the value in controversy shall exceed twenty dollars." US Const, Amend VII.

and substantive rules of a legal system developed by and for people like themselves. At that time, women and African Americans could not participate as either lawyers or judges.

Today, the legal system remains one developed by and for propertied white men, with strong, built-in, conservative tendencies, in the form of well-developed substantive rules combined with rules favoring precedent.[283] As I have described,[284] the overwhelming majority of legislators and judges continue to be men. "Due process" continues to mean something quite different for propertied white men and other groups.

The Sixth Amendment provides that "[i]n all criminal prosecutions, the accused shall enjoy the right to a speedy and public trial, by an impartial jury. . . ."[285] At the time the Bill of Rights was enacted, neither women nor slaves were allowed on juries. As early as 1880, however, the Supreme Court held that states could not overtly exclude African Americans from juries under the Fourteenth Amendment.[286] But African Americans were effectively excluded throughout the South until relatively recently. Juries were drawn from voter rolls which—until the 1960s—included few African Americans. And in the North as well as the South, African Americans could be excluded on the ground of race from any particular jury prior to the Supreme Court's 1965 Fourteenth Amendment decision in *Swain v Alabama*[287] and its 1986 decision in *Batson v Kentucky*.[288] Since these cases, it has been unconstitutional to exclude African Americans or other racial minorities either from jury lists or from a particular jury because of race.

A more limited set of rules has developed with respect to sex.[289] The Supreme Court found overt limitations on women's presence in jury pools to be unconstitutional under the Fourteenth Amendment in 1975.[290] But several lower courts have refused to

---

[283] See, for example, Lois G. Forer, *Unequal Protection: Women, Children, and the Elderly in Court* (Norton, 1991) (retired judge discussing the many ways in which legal rules developed by white male judges adversely affect women, children, and the elderly).

[284] See text accompanying notes 8-14.

[285] US Const, Amend VI.

[286] *Strauder v West Virginia*, 100 US 303, 310 (1880).

[287] 380 US 202 (1965).

[288] 476 US 79 (1986).

[289] See generally Shirley S. Sagawa, Batson v Kentucky*: Will It Keep Women on the Jury?*, 3 Berkeley Women's L J 14 (1987/1988); Note, *Sex Discrimination in the* Voir Dire *Process: The Rights of Prospective Female Jurors*, 58 S Cal L Rev 1225 (1985).

[290] *Taylor v Louisiana*, 419 US 522 (1975). See also *Duren v Missouri*, 439 US 357 (1979). The Supreme Court has held that jury exclusions violate the Sixth Amendment only when capital sentencing occurs. See *Lockhart v McCree*, 476 US 162 (1986).

hold unconstitutional the exclusion of women from jury panels even if the exclusion is on the basis of sex.[291] Thus, the right to trial by a jury selected without discrimination on the basis of sex remains unavailable to women. Further, minority women remain without effective protection on the basis of race *and* sex.[292]

I suggest three changes to the Bill of Rights in the areas of due process and jury selection. First, in civil cases there should be the same protections against sex discrimination in jury selection as for race.[293] Second, women and minorities should be protected from sex or race discrimination by prosecutors in challenging jurors in criminal cases. Indeed, we might ban all peremptory challenges by prosecutors.[294]

Third, judges and legislators, as well as jurors, should represent the population. We require that juries be representative with respect to race and somewhat representative with respect to sex, but have no constitutional provisions regarding judges or legislators. This is so even though the law developed and applied by judges and legislators is all the process that is "due" in any dispute before a jury or a judge. For any group other than white men, who is on the bench or in the legislature is more important than who is on the jury.

The Bill of Rights could require that judges represent the population with respect to sex and race. The African National Congress (ANC) Draft Bill of Rights includes a provision that "the judiciary shall be transformed in such a way as to consist of men and women drawn from all sectors of . . . society."[295] The Bill of Rights could provide that women's representation in legislatures at appro-

---

[291] See, for example, *United States v Hamilton*, 850 F2d 1038, 1042 (4th Cir 1988); *State v Olivera*, 534 A2d 867, 870 (RI 1987). See also *State v Gilmore*, 511 A2d 1150, 1159 n 3 (NJ 1986). Even when women are on jury panels, they tend to be less influential than the men on the jury. See Nancy S. Marder, *Gender Dynamics and Jury Deliberations*, 96 Yale L J 593, 597-98 (1987).

[292] Minority women should, one would think, be entitled to *more*, not less, protection because of their dual disadvantages. See generally, Judy Scales-Trent, *Black Women and the Constitution: Finding Our Place, Asserting Our Rights*, 24 Harv CR-CL L Rev 9 (1989). See also Kimberle Crenshaw, *Demarginalizing the Intersection of Race and Sex: A Black Feminist Critique of Antidiscrimination Doctrine, Feminist Theory and Antiracist Politics*, 1989 U Chi Legal Forum 139.

[293] See *Edmonson v Leesville Concrete Co., Inc.*, 111 S Ct 2077, 2079 (1991) (race can not be basis for excluding juror in civil case). Structural changes may also be needed to accommodate women's different approaches to dispute resolution. See Laura Gaston Dooley, *Sounds of Silence on the Civil Jury*, 26 Valp U L Rev 405 (1991).

[294] See, for example, Albert W. Alschuler, *The Supreme Court and the Jury: Voir Dire, Peremptory Challenges, and the Review of Jury Verdicts*, 56 U Chi L Rev 153, 232 (1989).

[295] ANC, *A Bill of Rights for a Democratic South Africa* Art 14, § 7 (cited in note 191).

priate levels is of prime importance in a democracy, and authorize Congress to enact a Voting Rights Act for Women. Such an act could offset the political problems women face as a result of freedoms we all value, such as freedom of religion and speech. If we had separate voting districts for women and men, women would be represented in legislatures in rough proportion to their presence in the population.[296] Women tend to hold elective office in higher numbers in multi-member districts,[297] under proportional representation,[298] and with internal party quotas for women candidates.[299] Our parties already have internal sex-based quotas for their national committees, and the Democrats have experimented with quotas for convention delegates. Our parties could be encouraged to experiment with such quotas by government funding tied to the number of women running in open elections.[300]

Conclusion

The Bill of Rights serves the interests of those most like its drafters: relatively elite white men who tend to own more than their share of "property." Other groups—particularly women, the poor, and people of color—have fewer of their needs addressed by this revered document. I have shown three kinds of problems with the provisions of the Bill of Rights.

My major point has been critical: the Bill of Rights does less for other groups than it does for those in the class of propertied white men; often it perpetuates or even magnifies social inequities rather than eliminating them. When this happens, the Bill of Rights becomes part of the problem, rather than the solution. Second, the Bill of Rights is often an impediment to reform; this is

[296] This is more or less the result with respect to racial minorities under the remedial scheme of the Voting Rights Act. See, for example, Voting Rights Act Extension, S Rep No 97-417, 97th Cong, 2d Sess 1000-10 (1982).

[297] See, for example, Susan Welch and Albert K. Karnig, *Correlates of Female Office Holding in City Politics*, 41 J Pol 478, 486-87 (1979); Janet Clark, et al, *Women as Legislative Candidates in Six States*, in Janet A. Flammang, ed, *Political Woman* 141, 154 (Sage, 1984).

[298] See Anne Phillips, *Engendering Democracy* 80-83 (Pennsylvania, 1991). There are disadvantages to proportional representation. Proportional representation, like divided government, tends to mean weak government. See Arend Lijphart, *Democracies: Patterns of Majoritarian and Consensus Government in Twenty-One Countries* 107-26, 150-68 (Yale, 1984).

[299] Phillips, *Engendering Democracy* at 83-89 (cited in note 298).

[00] For example, the national parties could be given so much in federal funds for each woman in an open election for the House, double that amount for open Senate races, and triple that amount for open governor races.

particularly true for the First Amendment's Free Speech Clause and the Second Amendment insofar as it prevents gun control legislation. Third, the problems ignored or even perpetuated by the Bill of Rights have political consequences for women and other outsider groups. More fundamentally, the Bill of Rights has done too little to ensure that women, a majority group, can exert their interests effectively in the political system.

I have suggested a number of changes to the individual provisions of the Bill of Rights, changes that we could implement either as interpretations or as amendments. These changes would make the Bill of Rights more responsive to the needs of women and other outsider groups and should produce a more effective democratic structure.

In this Conclusion, I add three more general criticisms. First, part of the problem is that the Constitution contains no strong provision on sex discrimination. If such a provision were in the Bill of Rights, it might help judges balance other rights, such as free exercise of religion, against the right of women to social equality. Such a provision should be a right to substantive, not formal, equality.[301] In addition, as in the ANC Draft Bill of Rights,[302] the Bill of Rights should ban discrimination on the basis of sexual orientation, both because lesbian and gay people are a vulnerable group needing protection,[303] and because compulsory heterosexuality is a form of discrimination against women.[304]

---

[301] See, generally Catharine A. MacKinnon, *Toward a Feminist Theory of the State* 215-49 (Harvard, 1989); Catharine A. MacKinnon, *Reflections on Sex Equality Under Law*, 100 Yale L J 1281 (1991).

[302] See ANC, *A Bill of Rights for a Democratic South Africa*, Art 7 § 2 (cited in note 191) ("Discrimination on the grounds of gender, single parenthood, legitimacy of birth or sexual orientation shall be unlawful."). The European Human Rights Commission has interpreted the European Human Rights Convention as banning punishment for at least private homosexual acts between consenting adults. See Glendon, *Rights Talk* at 146-58 (cited in note 20).

However, I realize that a judicially enforced abstract right to sex equality would not do much for women. The drive for its adoption would drain scarce resources from more effective strategies for change. See, for example, Rosenberg, *The Hollow Hope* (cited in note 16); Becker, 1987 S Ct Rev 201 (cited in note 16). I do not, therefore, suggest we should seek such a right at the present time. I merely mention that, in a Constitution anywhere near ideal, we would have a substantive sex equality provision.

[303] See Bruce A. Ackerman, *Beyond* Carolene Products, 98 Harv L Rev 713, 730-31 (1985); Janet E. Halley, *The Politics of the Closet: Towards Equal Protection For Gay, Lesbian, and Bisexual Identity*, 36 UCLA L Rev 915, 916 n 5 (1989).

[304] See Sylvia A. Law, *Homosexuality and the Social Meaning of Gender*, 1988 Wis L Rev 187, 187 (1988); John Stoltenberg, *You Can't Fight Homophobia and Protect the Pornographers at the Same Time—An Analysis of What Went Wrong in* Hardwick, in Dorchen Leidholdt and Janice G. Raymond, eds, *The Sexual Liberals and the Attack on*

Second, the Bill of Rights and other provisions of the Constitution have created a structure posing obstacles to the implementation of the sorts of economic support systems and safety nets present in every other North Atlantic nation. Mary Ann Glendon makes this point powerfully and persuasively in her most recent book.[305] Several features of our Constitution have reinforced the individualism so dominant in our culture: the absolutist wording of individual rights in the Bill of Rights; the failure of the Bill of Rights to include any positive economic rights; and the focus of both the Constitution and the Bill of Rights on *limited* government as the guarantor of liberty. Given these elements in our constitutional structure, it is not surprising that initial attempts at social legislation in this country were declared unconstitutional as violations of the Contracts Clause, a variation on the property right protected in the Fifth Amendment.[306] We abandoned this approach during the New Deal,[307] but by then the United States was far behind the Continent in providing economic support systems. The gap persists today.[308] Had we *no* written constitution so that a *Lochner* era never happened we might live today in a more just society.[309]

My third and last general criticism has been made before by Jennifer Nedelsky, among others. Because the Framers focused on protection of private property as the key to liberty, they devised a "democratic" anti-majoritarian governmental structure. They saw the major problem of democracy as the "problem of majority oppression."[310] The solution was to create barriers to ordinary people's participation, including multiple levels of government and

---

Feminism 184 (Pergamon, 1990); MacKinnon, *Toward a Feminist Theory of the State* at 57 (cited in note 301); Adrienne Rich, *Compulsory Heterosexuality and Lesbian Experience*, in Rich, *Blood, Bread, and Poetry* 23 (Norton, 1986).

[305] See Glendon, *Rights Talk* at 106-08 (cited in note 20). For a discussion of the symbolic power of the Constitution, see Hendrik Hartog, *The Condition of Aspiration and "The Rights That Belong to Us All"*, 74 J Amer Hist 1013 (1987).

[306] See, for example, *Lochner v New York*, 198 US 45 (1905).

[307] *West Coast Hotel Co. v Parrish*, 300 US 379 (1937) (overruling *Lochner*).

[308] Glendon, *Rights Talk* at 32-46 (cited in note 20). For a brief discussion of economic supports in Europe, see Sheila B. Kamerman and Alfred J. Kahn, *What Europe does for Single-Parent Families*, 93 Pub Int 70 (Fall 1988).

[309] It is also possible that we would live in a fascist dictatorship. For an argument that a constitution should include provisions "designed to work against precisely those aspects of a country's culture and tradition that are likely to produce harm through that country's ordinary political process," see Cass R. Sunstein, *On Property and Constitutionalism*, 17 U Chi L Econ Working Paper No 3 (2d series 1991).

[310] Jennifer Nedelsky, *Private Property and the Limits of American Constitutionalism: The Madisonian Framework and its Legacy* 220-22 (Chicago, 1990).

rule by a distant elite.[311] In addition, the Constitution limited directly the ability of less-distant state governments to experiment with the basic structure of the economy.[312]

Seeing the problem of democracy as the problem of majority oppression of the propertied minority is particularly inappropriate from the perspective of women. Women are a majority of the population, who have never controlled or even exercised their proportionate share of influence. Surely we should regard men's domination of positions of power within government as at least *a* problem of democracy in light of women's ability to vote during the last seventy-one years.

We should consider whether other governmental structures and electoral systems would be more democratic. Three independent branches of government minimize governmental action, preserving the status quo. A requirement of coordination among three independent branches is countermajoritarian and conservative. Action is easier in parliamentary systems which integrate the legislative and executive power. We also should consider other electoral systems, such as the ones suggested above.[313]

These are not all pragmatic proposals for change. Members of our legislative bodies are not likely to change the way the game is played when they have won under existing rules. My point is that our governmental structure is not ideal from the perspective of women, other outsider groups, or, indeed, democracy. We could imagine better structures, and many are in place in some parts of the world. We should not be exporting ours, as is, to Eastern Europe.

How should we assess a constitutional structure or a Bill of Rights? I suggest that we should consider, along with other factors, how well the system facilitates women's political participation, poverty rates (especially for women and children), physical safety, and incarceration rates. Measured by these standards, our constitutional system must be found wanting.

---

[311] Id.

[312] Id.

[313] See text accompanying notes 295-300.

[5]

The Phenomenology of Rights-Consciousness and the Pact of the Withdrawn Selves

Peter Gabel*

I. Introduction

A main objective of the critical legal studies movement has been to develop a consciousness-based critique of the existing legal order, a critique that would show how prevailing legal ideas and institutions acquire social meaning and how this social meaning helps to constitute the social world.[1] This Article attempts to contribute to this effort by describing the way that existing legal thought both emerges from and helps to maintain the alienated character of our current social situation. Although my aim is to examine the relationship between the experience of alienation and the meaning of legal thought in general, I will place special emphasis on the meaning for alienated consciousness of believing in rights and the State. It will become clear that I do not think we ever are alienated entirely from one another, nor do I think legal concepts like "rights" by their very nature must have an alienated meaning; in fact, one of my goals in writing the Article is to clarify the relationship between the effort to overcome our alienation, which I see as a fundamental aim of all progressive social movements, and the struggle over the meaning of law that this effort inevitably entails. But my emphasis will be on the alienated meaning of existing legal thought, because this meaning remains dominant in our culture, and because the failure fully to understand it has played some part in limiting the gains of potentially emancipatory social movements up to this time.

My own view is that it is not possible to pursue an investigation of this type without using a method that allows us to reexperience the very phenomena that need to be investigated, in a way that brings to light essential aspects of these phenomena that are concealed from us in our everyday conscious activity. This effort to critically reexperience the

* Professor of Law, New College of California School of Law, San Francisco. I thank Gail Weiner, Karl Klare, Michael Lerner, Alan Freeman, Jack Schlegel, Bill Simon, and Andy Lichterman for critical comments and suggestions.

1. The best recent studies of this theme in critical legal studies scholarship are Gordon, *Critical Legal Histories*, 36 STAN. L. REV. 57 (1984) and Trubek, *Where the Action Is: Critical Legal Studies and Empiricism*, 36 STAN. L. REV. 575 (1984). *See also* Klare, *Law-Making as Praxis*, 40 TELOS 123 (1979).

phenomena of everyday life with an eye to illuminating their hidden meanings is commonly called the phenomenological method,[2] and its value for showing how law is "constitutive" of our social experience becomes apparent the moment we try to grasp what "the law" actually is. For example, to say that the law is "a set of rules and principles" could suggest that it is a thing made up of other things, but by reexperiencing the way these rules and principles normally appear to us when we use them, we "recognize" that they are not things but ideas. And if we once again reexperience our everyday use of these ideas, we discover through a new recognition that they form part of a whole complex of images, including a "State" that "creates" the rules and "rights" that we "have" because these rules "grant them to us." But what, then, is this "State" and how can "it" create something, since it appears to be only an image; and how can "rights" be granted to me by rules, since I appear to be thinking them into existence? To answer these questions, we must reexperience these ideas and images once again so as to gain a still clearer sense of their experiential quality (for example, I see that the State appears to be "above" me and rights appear to suggest "possible actions that I am allowed to do"). It is through the circular repetition of this process—supported by a critical intuition that allows us to transcend the way these phenomena normally appear in our unreflective consciousness—that we gradually can unveil their concealed everyday meaning. And when we realize that we routinely speak these ideas and images to each other while also thinking them in some way "together" and yet "by ourselves," we can begin to form an understanding of how the law is actually constitutive of our social existence.

The importance of using such a descriptive method is perhaps even more immediately evident if we are to understand a concept like

2. The phenomenological method has been most fully elaborated in the works of Heidegger, Husserl, Merleau-Ponty, and Sartre. Principal texts include M. Heidegger, Being and Time (1962); E. Husserl, Ideas (1952); M. Merleau-Ponty, The Phenomenology of Perception (1962); J.P. Sartre, Critique of Dialectical Reason (1976) [hereinafter cited as J.P. Sartre, Critique]; J.P. Sartre, Being and Nothingness (1956). Phenomenology means the study of being as it appears or is revealed to consciousness. Its theory of knowledge is based on an essential distinction between being and thought. Being encompasses the whole of our lived experience; thought is that aspect of being through which we reflect upon lived experience. In our being, we comprehend the intentional meaning of our actions "unreflectively"; even a new-born child "intends himself" toward gaining nourishment in a way that he comprehends in this unreflective sense, although he does not "know what he is doing" reflectively. The aim of critical thought is to gain access to these unreflective intended meanings by establishing an intuitive link between comprehension and intellection (or reflective knowledge). Phenomenology pursues truth, therefore, through a process of "unveiling description" rather than through explanation or rational analysis, and it seeks to be evocative rather than logical.

A good introduction to the relationship of phenomenology and critical social theory is M. Poster, Existential Marxism in Post-War France (1975).

alienation. While the law can, however mistakenly, be conceived as something that exists outside of us, alienation can refer only to a quality of our experience that exists inside of us, and whose meaning therefore can be revealed only "from the inside." It is precisely the weakness of most existing theories of alienation that they seek to "explain" our alienation from the outside, as if the quality of an experience could be illuminated or even "reached" by a set of explanatory concepts that purport to "account for" it. Thus whether one thinks of psychoanalysis, which posits an alienated ego resulting from the necessary renunciation of instinctual desires,[3] or of most forms of Marxism, which assert that alienation results from the system of production,[4] or of the various recent theories that "derive" alienation from the effects of language and other sign-systems upon the "constitution of the subject,"[5] we can never find *ourselves* revealed as living beings in the stories these theories purport to tell. This is not to deny that each of these perspectives hints at important truths that we can sometimes make *our* truth through a kind of "existential retranslation," but it is to say that they all suffer from a descriptive inadequacy that results from the dis-

3. *See, e.g.*, S. FREUD, THE EGO AND THE ID (1962). In spite of the many modifications psychoanalytic theorists since Freud have made to his original formulations, only two writers have produced theories that enrich the experiential texture of these formulations while retaining their full critical bite. (Many have done the former alone, *see, e.g.*, H. GUNTRIP, PERSONALITY STRUCTURE AND HUMAN INTERACTION (1961); G. KLEIN, PSYCHOANALYTIC THEORY (1976); H. KOHUT, THE RESTORATION OF THE SELF (1977); H. SULLIVAN, THE INTERPERSONAL THEORY OF PSYCHIATRY (1953), but at the cost of making social alienation vanish in the process.) The first is Jacques Lacan, whose descriptions of how the child's desire is skewed by cultural conditioning is a phenomenological advance over the abstractness of Freud's account, but whose insistence on the unintelligibility of desire leaves him as unable to capture what we are alienated *from* as Freud was. J. LACAN, ECRITS vii-ix (1977) (clarifying the biological concept of "instinct" to mean a psychic force or "pulsion" which is nonetheless inaccessible to phenomenological knowledge). The other is R.D. Laing, who has written very good experiential studies of how alienation is mediated through the family, but who has never tried to develop a theory of social being comparable in scope to Freud's. *See, e.g.*, R.D. LAING & A. ESTERSON, SANITY, MADNESS, AND THE FAMILY (1960); R.D. LAING, THE DIVIDED SELF (1960).

4. This is not to say that socioeconomic factors like the division of labor or the separation of the worker from the product of his or her labor-power are unrelated to the reproduction of alienation, *see* Marx, *Estranged Labour*, in THE MARX-ENGELS READER 70-81 (R. Tucker ed. 1978), nor is it to minimize the alienating effects of cultural factors like television, mass marketing, or dominant ideologies, all of which have been analyzed most fully within the Critical-Marxist tradition, *see, e.g.*, H. MARCUSE, ONE-DIMENSIONAL MAN (1964). It is merely to emphasize that the existential meaning of alienation in any of these contexts cannot be grasped from the external vantage point that most Marxist social theory adopts. For an important exception, see J.P. SARTRE, CRITIQUE, *supra* note 2, at 89-94 (discussing labor), 256-70 (discussing bus lines), 642-55 (discussing "other-direction" and the top ten).

5. I am referring to structuralism (alienation derived from the structural effects of language, family patterns, or production processes), semiotics (alienation derived from effects of cultural images located in signs), and poststructuralism (alienation derived from effects of circulating meaning-chains with no fixed origin).

For a good analysis of the writings in each of these traditions, see Heller, *Structuralism and Critique*, 36 STAN. L. REV. 127 (1984).

tance they put between the knowledge they produce and the only real world, the world of lived experience. None of them is rooted sufficiently in the experiential foundations of intersubjectivity, which are ontologically prior to all historical and cultural mediations and which infuse these mediations with their vital meaning.[6]

A phenomenological description of alienation is one that captures in a qualitative language what alienation feels like in its everyday manifestations, while also revealing the inner intentions that bring it into being. I will begin by giving such a description with enough detail to show how this alienation envelops us in a qualitative milieu of blocked connection, and how this experience of blocked connection leads us to want to create and then believe in legal ideas as "the law." My principal aim is to show that these ideas are intended[7] to convince us that we are "alienated as a matter of law," and to clarify the internal transformation of social relations that would be required to give these ideas a more emancipatory meaning. A second and more minor objective is to link the analysis I propose with other critical approaches to law (notably those that have criticized the reification and the indeterminacy of rights-discourse), and to suggest that this analysis may provide these critiques with a unifying theoretical foundation.

II. Alienation

A. Alienation as the Denial of Desire

Let me start by making a descriptive assertion that may be controversial but which seems to me nonetheless self-evidently true—we are constituted as social beings by the desire to be recognized by others in an empowering, life-giving way.[8] It is this fundamental experiential need that animates a baby's search for "eye-contact" with mother as well as the organizational efforts of adults who try to form into groups to vitalize their work-situations through the achievement of solidarity. While our actions are obviously also motivated by other factors (like

6. This is not to deny that cultural mediations exert a powerful influence on how we see ourselves and each other, as both a conduit of connectedness and a "co-efficient of adversity," J.P. SARTRE CRITIQUE, *supra* note 2, at 371. It is rather to say that we see each other "through" these mediations and not "in" them or "because of" them. For example, we do not speak to each other in a common language, but through this language on the basis of a connection that makes language itself possible.

7. Whenever I use the word "intended," I refer not to any conscious motive but to underlying intended meanings that are comprehended without being known. *See supra* note 2 (describing phenomenology).

8. The ideas in this section were influenced in various ways by J.P SARTRE, CRITIQUE, *supra* note 2, R.D. LAING, *supra* note 3, and the work of Martin Buber, *see, e.g.,* M. BUBER, THE KNOWLEDGE OF MAN (1965).

the baby's need for food or the workers' need for safer working conditions), it is the desire to *connect* through this confirming or genuine reciprocity that gives to our actions their distinctive social energy, impelling us out toward the other even when, as in the case of schizophrenics, the likelihood of success seems very small.

The problem is that we have lost confidence in the truth of this desire, for an historical reason that remains somewhat obscure.[9] Or to be more precise, each of us has lost confidence that this desire we feel within ourselves also motivates the others who approach us in direct encounters, or in more indirect encounters that take place through the media, through language, or even through material objects like flags or factories or school buildings. Each of us senses that others are determined to keep themselves at what one might call a threatening distance, desiring eye contact and yet forbidding this contact by hiding behind what I will call an as-if performance, a false appearance that demands to be taken as real.[10] And because this forbidding distance leads us to mistrust or lose confidence in the desire of the other, we seek to protect ourselves by installing this same forbidding distance in ourselves. We each become "one of the others" to each other, thus helping to create the very disconnection that we most wish others would allow us to overcome.

Alienation, therefore, is a paradoxical form of reciprocity between two beings who desire authentic contact with each other and yet at the same time *deny* this very desire in the way that they act toward one another. This denial is communicated through the medium of what we ordinarily call a "role," what I am describing here as an as-if performance. I approach a bank teller who affects a cheerful mood and who suggests in all her words and gestures that she is glad to see me. Yet I

9. The usual explanation within Marxism is that scarcity of the means of survival leads each person to see the other as both a mortal threat and a potential instrument whose labor can be exploited. *See* A. GOULDNER, THE TWO MARXISMS 186-89 (1980). But when Engels relies upon the empirical reality of scarcity to claim that "[t]he separation of society into an exploiting and an exploited class, a ruling and an oppressed class, was the necessary consequence of the deficient and restricted development of production in former times," Engels, *Socialism, Utopian and Scientific,* in THE MARX-ENGELS READER, *supra* note 4, at 714, he links a spiritual catastrophe with material circumstances in a way that I do not find wholly convincing, or at least not more convincing than the idea of a free betrayal that is metaphorically suggested in the theory of original sin. Even cannibalism under conditions of scarcity does not necessarily presuppose the alienating objectification of the other, any more than eating chickens does today.

10. Compare the following description of "collusion" by R.D. Laing:

> Collusion is always clinched when self finds in other that other who will "confirm" self in the false self that is trying to make real, and vice versa. The ground is then set for prolonged mutual evasion of truth and true fulfillment. Each has found an other to endorse his own false notion of himself and to give this appearance a semblance of reality.

R.D. LAING, SELF AND OTHERS 93 (2d ed. 1970).

detect in all these words and gestures an artificiality—her words are somehow "processed"; her gestures, ever so slightly delayed, have been "subject to review." In other words she is playing the role of being a bank teller, while acting as if her performance is real. As I move toward her from my place in line, I feel myself becoming a "customer" of "the bank," and she sees in me the same artificiality and delay-time she experiences in herself. But we are not robots. We each sense in the other the desire to recognize each other precisely through the amount of vigilant tension required to prevent this recognition from occurring. We may in fact make some minimal contact in "asides," in the interstices of our public performances, asides that we intentionally marginalize as private moments.[11] But on the whole we deny ourselves access to each other out of obedience to the demand implicit in the other's facade.

What then is the origin of this mutual mistrust that leads us to adopt a false self that denies its own falsity? For each of us individually, this mistrust originates in our childhoods—the alienated networks that constitute the social totality are introduced to us first through the mediation of our families, through direct relations with parents who themselves were conditioned within the "circle of collective denial" through which alienated reciprocities reproduce themselves. As a result of these early experiences of the distancing other, we internalize a memory of loss with which desire itself becomes permanently associated. Thus in the child's own development of a false or as-if self, we can see a compulsively repeated existential sequence: desire for connection—memory of loss—anxiety—self-falsification. Perhaps partly to avoid reexperiencing an original humiliation, perhaps partly to preserve the poignancy of unrealized love, the child "identifies" with his parents and plays the role of being himself, becoming "one of the others" in a family system that will prepare him for the school-system and beyond.

Thus the source of alienation is not to be found in the organization of production, or in some particular form of child-rearing,[12] or in a contradiction between self and other inherent in human nature:[13] it de-

11. For a more positive view of asides, see Duncan Kennedy's description in Gabel & Kennedy, *Roll Over Beethoven*, 36 STAN. L. REV. 1, 25 (1984) (arguing that freedom necessarily exerts itself in the interstices of structures).

12. *See generally* I. BALBUS, MARXISM AND DOMINATION (1982) (discussing the centrality of mother-centered childrearing to reproduction of domination, relying in part upon N. CHODOROW, THE REPRODUCTION OF MOTHERING: PSYCHOANALYSIS AND THE SOCIOLOGY OF GENDER (1978) and D. DINNERSTEIN, THE MERMAID AND THE MINOTAUR (1976)).

13. *See* Kennedy, *The Structure of Blackstone's Commentaries*, 28 BUFFALO L. REV. 205, 211-

rives instead from the incapacity of intersubjective desire to transcend the circular and self-reproducing constraint it has imposed upon itself in response to the fear of loss. The paradox is that the constraint itself reproduces the fear of loss it is designed to evade.

Yet however imposing the forces of denial appear from our isolated vantage-points, the truth is that alienation is extremely unstable because, unlike desire, it lacks a foothold in being. If we return to my encounter with the bank teller, we can see what this means and why it is so. For if her "good mood" seems processed[14] and the delay-time in her gestures gives her self-presentation a performance-like quality, then she and I both know, whether consciously or not, that she is not being herself but rather an ineffable "someone else"—a "bank teller." Her appearance manifests an *absence of being* intended to secure her anonymity in the face of my gaze, just as I enact myself as an anonymous "business-like customer" in the face of hers. Thus when I say that alienation lacks a foothold in being, I mean that the as-if performances through which it is constituted are makeshift phantoms that lack any ground, straining in "mid-air," you might say, to deny the other access to the withdrawn *someone* who we really are. And because our social existence is characterized by contingency, because every lived encounter perpetually opens out into a next moment that cannot be colonized in advance, the movement of desire perpetually threatens to dissolve the groundless appearances through which we hold ourselves at a distance.

B. *Ungroundedness and Belief in Authority*

This brings me to the law, and to the problem of rights that forms the basis of this Article. Although the law has a positive dimension to which I will return later, in its negative dimension it seems to me principally a kind of defense-mechanism intended to solve the problem of contingency by pretending that the next moment can be colonized in advance. Confronted at every moment with the instability of our as-if performances and the memory of loss that underlies them, we conspire to generate a "belief" (I use the term with all of its magical connota-

13 (1979) (discussing the fundamental contradiction between self and other). *But see* Gabel & Kennedy, *supra* note 11, at 15-16 (fundamental contradiction recanted as "reified abstraction").

14. Clerical workers in San Francisco have begun publishing a journal entitled *Processed World* containing articles, cartoons, and fantasies about their workplace existence. Recent numbers include *Power of Knowledge Against Power, Amazing Corporate Management Clone Program Pays Off!, Denizens of the Ice-Cube Tray, Workers Representation: New Carrot/Old Stick, It Reached Out and Touched Me,* and *The Office as Metaphor for Totalitarianism,* as well as regular features such as *Tales of Toil* and *Bad Girl.* The address for subscriptions is 55 Sutter St. #829, San Francisco, Cal. 94104.

tions) that our alienation is *dictated,* that there exists what could loosely be called a "sovereign" and a body of rules that give "outside support" to our assertion that our false selves express who we really are, and that these rules "govern" what I am calling the next moment, ridding this moment of its contingent character. You may say that these rules obviously do exist and you can take down a book and show them to me, but I am not contesting the fact that there exist verbal concepts, inscriptions on paper, filling thousands of volumes in thousands of libraries across the country. I am trying instead to capture the meaning of these concepts (and these libraries) in light of the conflict between the desire for connection and the need to deny this desire that is at the heart of our present existential situation. It is in this sense that "the law" does not exist, except as a projected conceptual schema designed to "cover" the open side of being with an appearance of false necessity.

To understand how the law is constructed to this end, we must begin by uncovering the origins in consciousness of "belief in authority," which is an existential constituent of all alienated cultural phenomena and which provides the foundation for the law's magical credibility. To do this, we must focus again on the ontological predicament of the false self—on its quality as an absence of being. For if we seek to keep the other at a distance by using gestures that are not real gestures and adopting moods that are not real moods, and if the other responds to us with the same intention and in the same way, how can we sustain our commitment to the reality of these performances in spite of the transparency of their falseness? We cannot manage this "on our own" because it is precisely the quality of the roles we "play" that we do not own them. They come to us from an experiential "outside" via the circle of collective denial that constitutes our cultural conditioning, and as a result they lack any anchorage with which to secure themselves, in a milieu of contingency, against the anxiety-producing movement of desire. To put this another way, our roles lack an "author" that would allow us to claim their authenticity with conviction.

To alleviate this predicament, we conspire to create such an author by inventing an authority whom we imagine to be the source of our performances and to whom we then attribute an *independent existence* so as to remove it from the realm of contingency. Returning to my interaction with the bank teller, we can see that as we play the roles of "teller" and "customer," we refer ourselves at every moment to a something "above us" that we in some sense "believe in" and "obey" by enacting ourselves as we do. The deference and caution that infect our gestures, as well as the conspiratorial quality of our private asides, reveal that we believe ourselves to be acting in accord with an authority that is not in us, but rather "elsewhere" as a third-party to whom we exist in relation. And if we were to look around ourselves, we would find this same deference reflected in the behavior of all of the others who co-constitute our gathering, from the secretaries, to the other tellers, to those others waiting on line, to the supervisors, to the vice-presidents, to the president. If we now try to specify who or what this third-party is that we believe ourselves to be "underneath" and to which we are in some sense enthralled, we discover a very odd thing—that it is the hallucinatory image of "the bank" itself that serves as our collective authority, upon which we confer the power to dictate our roles. Although this "bank" is a product of our own consciousness, we conspire to act as if it possessed an independent existence in order to give our pseudo-mutuality a pseudo-ground to stand on, so as to resist the threat of an immediate connection we feel too vulnerable to bear.

Belief in authority is thus a constituent element of alienation, and if we were to analyze the organization of the bank more carefully, we would discover that what we ordinarily call a hierarchy is actually an imaginary ordering of alienated reciprocities that allows a group to embody a unifying authority in a series of "top-down" gazes. In the bank, for example, it is the attribution of hierarchical difference to discrete role-performances that allows the imago of "the bank" to acquire its "thereness" for those who seek its authoritative security. I have written about this elsewhere[15] and will not do so here because my goal is not to describe the embodied hierarchies of the legal system (the social relations of the courtroom, for example), but rather to describe the existential foundations of legal consciousness itself as an authoritative form of thought that is mediated through these hierarchies in much the same way that "bank consciousness" is mediated through the imaginary "top-down" ordering of the social relations in a bank. Because the most fundamental constituent element of legal consciousness is the relationship between rights-bearing individuals (or groups) and the State, I will focus my discussion on what I will simply call "rights-consciousness," which is meant to refer to the belief in the existence of this relationship as the basis for the political organization of society.

15. *See* P. Gabel, Ontological Passivity and the Constitution of Otherness Within Large-Scale Social Networks (June 1, 1981) (unpublished manuscript on file with the *Texas Law Review*).

III. Alienation and Rights-Consciousness

A. *The Constitutional Thought-Schema*

Let me now review the inner experience of the alienated individual, placing special emphasis on certain qualitative concepts that will prove essential to understanding the phenomenology of rights-consciousness. Desiring the vitalizing intersubjective recognition that I have called authentic connection, the individual confronts a forbidding distance in the other which seems to require the denial of this desire. She therefore *withdraws* her own self and adopts a false self which projects a demand that it be taken as "who she really is." This false self or "role" expresses the quality of *anonymity*[16] insofar as she "performs" it with the intention of denying the other access to her being. In order to carry off this performance in spite of the pressure of desire in herself and the other, she continually must *observe* herself from the vantage-

16. Heidegger discusses the phenomenon of collective anonymity in a section of *Being and Time* entitled *Everyday Being-One's-Self and the 'They'.* M. HEIDEGGER, *supra* note 2, at 163-68. When we "level down" our being by "falling into theyness,"

> [e]veryone is the other, and no one is himself. The "*they*," which supplies the answer to the question of the "who" of everyday Dasein [translated literally as the "being-there" of consciousness in the world] is the "*nobody*" to whom every Dasein has already surrendered itself in Being-among-one-another . . . .

Id. at 165-66. Heidegger understood this phenomenon as resulting from a failure of will, *id.* at 166 ("In these modes one's way of Being is that of inauthenticity and failure to stand by one's Self."), rather than from a mutual distrust that becomes, to a significant extent, mutually coercive (which is what I mean to be saying).

A third position, which locates the source of this anonymity in the coercive effects of material conditions, is stated by Sartre in a passage describing what happens to people's internal reciprocity as they stand in line waiting for a bus:

> [T]o the extent that the bus designates the present commuters, it constitutes them in their *interchangeability*: each of them is effectively produced by the social ensemble as united with his neighbours in so far as he is strictly identical with them. In other words, their being-outside (that is to say, their interest as regular users of the bus service) is unified, in that it is a pure and indivisible abstraction, rather than a rich, differentiated synthesis; it is a simple identity, designating the commuter as an abstract generality by means of a particular *praxis* (signalling the bus, getting on it, finding a seat, paying the fare), in the development of a broad, synthetic *praxis* (the undertaking which unites the driver and conductor every morning in the temporalisation which is *one* particular route through Paris at a particular time). At this moment of the investigation, the unit-being (être-unique) of the group lies outside itself, in a future object, and everyone, in so far as he is determined by the common interest, differentiates himself . . . only by the simple materiality of the organism. . . . And, since all the lived characteristics which might allow some interior differentiation lie outside this determination, everyone's identity with every Other is their unity elsewhere, as other-being; here and now, it is their common [relation of separation]. Everyone is the same as the Others in so far as he is Other than himself.

J.P. SARTRE, CRITIQUE, *supra* note 2, at 259-60. Sartre intends this description to be simply a microexample of what occurs throughout a social order in which people have lost power over the conditions that shape their practical destiny. He thinks, in other words, that alienation results from the internalization of real, practical ends in a world in which these ends are coercively shaped by the inhuman "inertia" of productive forces (or what he calls "worked matter," *id.* at 153). But it seems to me that the reverse is true—that the inertia of "the system" exists and is sustained only by virtue of the reciprocal denial of desire that is at the heart of alienation itself.

pöint of her own withdrawn location. This self-observation gives her performance its slightly delayed quality, the appearance of having been *subject to review* in advance of expression. In order to assert a groundedness for her performance that can support its claim to authenticity in the face of the perpetual threat of exposure, she imbues her performance with the quality of *obedience to authority,* as if this authority were the *reviewing agency* responsible for the role that she is "allowed" to perform.

Now insofar as this inner experience is the experience of everyone within an alienated group, each person perpetually feels at once unconnected to everyone else and yet anxiously committed to the pretense of connection that is manifested in the reciprocity of roles. Thus everyone, from his or her own withdrawn vantage-point, comprehends that the common pretense of connection requires an "additional support" of some kind if each person is to sustain the claim, expressed through each person's false self, that the pretense of connection is an actual connection. This simply repeats the problem of contingency, of the open texture of social existence, as it appears at the level of "society as a whole" rather than at the level of a single institution or a two-person interaction.

How can a group haunted by an absence of connection reassure itself that it is characterized by the presence of connection? By conspiring to represent itself to itself as politically constituted, through the use of embodied rituals or symbolic objects or through the use of verbal concepts which tell the story of this constitution. In his or her heart (which I use as a synonym for the withdrawn "true self") no one ever believes in the truth of this story, but so long as each person manifests a belief in it as part of his or her performance, and sees this belief mirrored in the performance of the other, the false group can sustain its appearance as a real group.

For those of us gathered within the geographical borders of the United States, the verbal concepts that purport to constitute our group in this fashion are contained in "the Constitution,"[17] which signifies both an original moment in which we supposedly came together to form "a union," and the schema by which we are to reproduce our group connection through the reproduction of "the State," and through

17. The critical description of the Constitution and of legal thought contained in this section is aimed only at clarifying their alienated meaning, which I see as hegemonic to the degree that alienation itself is hegemonic, but which coexists in consciousness with a subordinate unalienated meaning that at certain historical moments plays a specific, though limited, role in counterhegemonic struggle. *See infra* subpart V(A). This unalienated meaning persists even within alienated consciousness as what I later call an "ethical memory." *See infra* Part VI.

"the following of laws" created and interpreted by this "State." These laws define how we are "allowed to act" in the form of "rights." If we now examine the relationship of this schema to the inner experience of the alienated individual that I have just summarized, we can discover how the schema is intended to "legalize" this experience and in so doing make the reproduction of alienation a condition of group membership.

First of all, it is essential to notice that, although this constitutional schema is inscribed somewhere on paper as a collection of word-artifacts, it is *lived* within consciousness as a form of representational thought, intentionally "brought to mind" in concrete existential moments. And whether one thinks of a civics class or a lawyer poring over a brief or a showing of the "People's Court," these moments seem to be generated as responses to or rehearsals for social conflict. But by conflict, I do not so much mean overt forms of social disruption as I do the existential conflict that is constitutive of alienation itself. Thus I would take something like a psychoanalytic view that this thought-schema is "brought to mind" at more or less regular intervals in order to "practice" containing the movement of desire and its threat to the preservation of the false self. In this respect, as I suggested earlier, the thought-schema resembles a collective defense mechanism through which the group allocates to various of its members the task of inducing in a controlled way the anxiety associated with the risk of reliving a shared loss, and then resolving the anxiety through the proclamation of correct thought.[18]

The first point to be emphasized about the very nature of this constitutional thought-schema is that it appears *within* consciousness as something observed *by* consciousness. In this sense it is properly called a "re-presentation" of the intersubjective life-world, which "works" as a defense precisely because it preserves the withdrawn character of the observing self. Just as the alienated individual safeguards his distance from the other in the realm of intersubjective action by repeatedly "watching" his as-if performances, so he retains this safeguard when observing the representations of his "legal thought." We can often detect this observing quality when watching lawyers "make arguments" to each other: it seems clear from their glassy eyes and rigid posture

18. *See* G. KLEIN, *supra* note 3, at 297-303 (asserting that the phenomenological basis for Freud's concept of neurotic "repetition-compulsion" derives from intentional reenactments of repressed wishes in symbolic behaviors which preserve the required inhibition of comprehension of their meaning).

that they are in some sense not here with us but rather are reading their thoughts aloud from somewhere deep inside.

If the quality of withdrawn observation characterizes what some philosophers call the noetic pole[19] of legal thought (meaning simply the location in consciousness from which this thought is generated), the representational schema itself which forms the noematic pole (or the ideas that are observed) reveals a distinctive distortion of the true existential quality of the intersubjective life-world. For while existential reality is always lived here and now as an experiential relation between a definite you and me, the "world" of legal thought is, you might say, drained of existential quality, which is to say of all vitality. We find an abstract something called "society" inhabited or "lived in" by a collection of disconnected and anonymous "individuals" who form another something called "the State," and so on. My point here is not to criticize the content of this world-view as being "too individualistic," but rather to emphasize its unreal, drained-of-any-life quality. Nor do I mean that the devitalized quality of this world results from its being devoid of any action, for it is clear that its inhabitants exist in a kind of time and that they engage in the activity of exercising their rights, in relation to each other and in relation to the group as a whole, denominated as the State.[20] My point, rather, is that these actions lack any

19. *See, e.g.*, E. HUSSERL, PHENOMENOLOGY AND THE CRISIS OF PHILOSOPHY 52 (1965). Since consciousness is always consciousness-of-something, every conscious act appears to itself as constituting (from its noetic pole) an intended object (at its noematic pole). A metaphor might be found in the relationship of a flashlight to the spot on the wall that its beam of light illuminates: if we think of this unscientifically (or from the flashlight's point of view), the light is both in the flashlight and on the wall.

20. A full phenomenological critique of our existing form of political democracy would require an investigation of the meaning of a whole series of such legal representations of collective actions not even touched upon in this Article. For example, it is somewhat remarkable that voting, which involves little more than sticking a pin through a piece of cardboard in secret once a year, should be regarded as the very essence of democratic participation. Yet if we try to understand this annual phenomenon as an expression of the group pretending to constitute itself in the service of maintaining alienation, we can begin to make sense of it.

In voting, we each designate ourselves as "Someone for a Day." We pretend to emerge from our anonymity by "going out into public" and becoming "one of the People" (although, by virtue of our anonymity, there is really no "People" to be "one of"). Through a ritualized transformation of public space (each "public polling place" was yesterday the garage or firehouse that we passed on our way home from work), we arrange to see each other act as if "everyone" believes in the State as the authentic repository of our collective will (although this "will" turns out to be a mere statistical object that can be "added up" via the anonymity of numerical methods). In one sense this is actually democratic. *See infra* subpart III(C) (discussing the "unity of the withdrawn selves"). Other phenomena in need of study include the formation of whom to vote for (political parties, polls) and the voyeuristic thrill of the moment in the voting booth (in which one gets to secretly touch the fetishized "name of the leader," and to participate, through a kind of sadistic reversal-fantasy, in choosing this leader rather than that leader).

None of this is to deny that voting-rights struggles have significant popular importance, or that voting is a source of some power through which we can affect events.

sense of the immediacy and contingency of truly lived encounters.

Yet if we recall the defensive intention that motivates the production of these images, we can see that their devitalized character results from a determination to "make it the law" that the real world be conceived as identical with its alienated appearance. First, in place of an intersubjective milieu characterized by experiential conflict between the desire for connection and the need to deny this desire, we are given discrete individuals whose desire has been denied *in advance* because their very discreteness severs the ontological link between self and other that is constitutive of real social existence. Second, the quality of anonymity that is characteristic of the alienated role-performance (as in concealing one's real self by adopting the gestures of a "bank teller") is presented as constitutive of each discrete individual's legal identity: he or she is not an existing someone but a "rights-bearing citizen," who exists as no-one-in-particular in relation to other individuals of the same type. You may say that this would be true of any attempt to refer to individuals apart from their concrete particularity, but this is not so. For the characterization of "rights-bearing citizen" has the intended effect of erasing the concrete and *common* reality in which we act on desire and replacing it with a blank and disembodied reality comprised of what we might call "empty vessels" who act only insofar as they have been filled with "rights." It is this empty-vessel quality of the "rights-bearing citizen" that represents "in law" the anonymous, absence-of-being quality of the alienated role-performance.

B. The Nature of Rights in Their Alienated Form

If we now turn our attention to the nature of rights themselves, we can see how they represent the field of social interaction in the service of legalizing its alienated appearances. A "right" has three phenomenological dimensions. First, to the extent that individuals are represented as "having" rights, these rights signify social experiences that are merely possible rather than the experiences themselves. To the extent that we think we have "the right to free speech," "the right to make contracts," and so forth, we represent each individual ontologically as being a passive locus of possible action, rather than as in action with others already. Second, these rights are conceived as being granted to the individual from an outside source, from "the State" which either creates them (in the positivist version of the constitutional thought-schema) or recognizes them (in the natural-law version) through the passage of "laws." Thus, insofar as the individual emerges from his passive station to act and interact with others on the basis of his rights, he does so because he has been "allowed" to do so in advance. Third, intersubjective action itself is conceived to occur "through" or "by virtue of" the "exercise" of these rights. The behavior of the bank teller who handles my deposit is represented in legal thought as resulting from or occurring as a consequence of the simultaneous exercise of a great many rights, including the right to perform certain functions as a bank employee (receiving money), the right to free speech (choice of words, gestures, and clothing), and perhaps even the right to seniority (if, because of the length of her employment, she is a teller instead of someone else). Seen as a whole, therefore, the "world" of this rights-based schema is one in which originally passive and disconnected individuals enter into relations with each other because they are allowed to, relations which have the quality of being "okayed in advance" because they occur only insofar as one is engaging in the right to do them.

It may now be self-evident that this picture of the world is but an abstract representation of our own alienated effort to distance ourselves from each other by representing our false selves as our real selves, as "who we really are." In "making it the law" that individuals are to be conceived of as originally passive and disconnected "empty vessels," we secure our effort to constrain the active movement toward connection that constitutes our true togetherness by denying that this movement exists. By replacing this active movement of desire with what we might call the "passive possibility" of "having rights," we place the immediacy of our lived experience in a kind of suspended animation that conforms precisely to the delay-time that self-observation inserts into our as-if performances. In equating "legal" action with being "allowed" to act on the basis of these rights, we make this self-observation a legal requirement of social action itself, just as self-observation is an existential characteristic of our alienated effort to be perpetually "on guard in advance" against the threat of excessive self-revelation. Finally, by representing the movement of the intersubjective life-world as the working of a legal order in which we interact through the "exercise" of these rights, we assert the legality of that quality in our as-if performances that suggests action at a distance from itself, thus attributing to this quality an "advance legitimacy" that is intended to make its illegitimacy invisible.

C. The State as the Unity of the Withdrawn Selves

What, then, are we to make of "the State" and of the relationship of the rights-bearers to it? If the idea that we act by being allowed to act derives from the self-observing quality of our role-performances, how is it that our own self-observation is represented in the constitutional thought-schema as "the State"? The answer to this question is found in the relationship between the nature of authority as I have earlier described it, and the common need within the alienated group to constitute itself in the first place. For insofar as our as-if performances require the projection of a common authority that is "believed in" as though it existed independent of this projection—a requirement that derives from the need to give these performances a foothold in being so as to deny their very as-if-ness—this authority must be represented in legal thought. And it is this authority that is represented in the form of a "State," which passes the laws that create (or recognize) our rights.[21] This is why we appear to ourselves in legal thought as existing "under" law: it is this representation of the "underneathness" of the rights-bearing citizens that corresponds to the obedient quality of our role-performances themselves. Yet the particular meaning that the State acquires as a *political* authority derives from the felt need to "constitute" ourselves as a defense against the experience of alienation itself, an experience of feeling "unconstituted," of feeling unconnected while pretending to be connected. And the way that we constitute ourselves through the State is revealed in the role that we allocate to it in legal thought, as the entity that "allows" us to act by granting us our rights. We constitute ourselves through the State by collectively agreeing to attribute to it our own powers of self-observation, thus making it the politically legitimate "reviewing agency" that serves as the authority for our alienated or "delayed" actions. It therefore seems accurate to say that the State acquires its political authority by representing the *actual unity of the withdrawn selves,* to the degree that we each, through a silent agreement, project onto it the power to constitute us as alienated beings.

D. *Legal Thought as Imagined Speech with Latent and Manifest Content*

If we now recall that this entire schema of representations does not simply "fill up" consciousness when it is thought, but is rather "brought to mind" and observed *by* consciousness like what we might call a "self-produced movie," we can gain a still deeper insight into the relationship of this thought to our alienated performances themselves. We discover that just as we "watch" these performances under the

21. Of course, the State is embodied in actual officials who are allocated special rooms and buildings to do the work of passing and interpreting these laws. But to say that they act as "State officials" is to say that they act as "representatives" of the projected image that I am describing.

pressure of the intersubjective pull of desire, we also "watch" our own thoughts that are intended to secure these performances by representing them as "already watched." It is one thing to say that legal thought acquires a self-observing quality when it is actually spoken in a social setting: we would have no difficulty recognizing this quality were we to examine the artificiality of, for example, someone playing the role of "lawyer" in a courtroom. This would just be the "bank teller" and the "business-like customer" all over again, with an as-if performance being thrown up to keep real others at a distance. But why must legal thought itself be watched, since it occurs within the safety of our own heads?

The answer to this question becomes apparent when we realize that the legal thought which we have been taking as a kind of object in consciousness is actually lived in experience as imagined speech. That is, when we think it, we are actually seeing ourselves speak it in the presence of an invisible other, as something like a dress rehearsal for the moment of expression itself.[22] And insofar as we *see* ourselves speaking it, we are adopting the same precaution we require of all our alienated performances—we withdraw our ownmost being from our appearance as an other to the other and secure our distance through the vigilance of perpetual self-observation. This may present a grim picture of our current situation because it leaves us neither able fully to realize our desire for connection nor able even to seek sanctuary from one another "in our heads." But then again it also affirms that our being is intersubjective in its very foundation, and that we are in it together even when we feel most alone.

Yet this very truth—that we are at all times constituted as social through the movement of desire, even though this connection is most often manifested through our denial of its existence—suggests that our investigation of the alienated foundations of existing legal thought still remains somewhat incomplete. For if this desire is truly ontological—if we do not even exist apart from its movement—then it also in some way must be realized in legal thought, just as it is partially realized through the feeling of "substitute connection" provided by our role-performances. We have already glimpsed the presence of this substitute connection in one way—in discovering that the State is constituted

22. All verbal thought is actually imagined speech. To discover this, try to catch yourself thinking in a distracted moment. As you realize that you are thinking "in your own voice," you may then say to yourself, "I am imagining I'm speaking." This thought will also be in your own voice.

This is not to say that all verbal thought expresses the same alienated intention that animates legal thought. It often expresses the effort to get through to somebody, just as actual speech does.

through the actual unity of our withdrawn selves. We have seen that however much our shared belief in the State is meant to divide us, it also connects us, somewhat paradoxically, as withdrawn observers. And there is no doubt that we feel this impoverished connection along a gradient of what might be called impoverished feelings that range from the pathetic to the grandiose. Thus on the one hand we feel the poignancy associated with the "tragic view of man" that seems to make the State necessary, while on the other we feel the "inflated-balloon" variety of solidarity that is manifested in the patriotism we experience in the presence of the flag.[23] These emotions reveal an obvious absence of connection and are manifestations of denial, but they also express our lived presence-to-each-other-at-a-distance that I am calling "substitute connection" so as to emphasize its contained or blocked quality.

As soon as we begin to look for it, we find this substitute connection throughout legal thought in what we might call the latent content of rights themselves. By representing our alienated performances as exercises of the rights to freedom of speech, freedom of contract, equality of opportunity, good faith cooperation, and so on, we "make it the law" that these performances be conceived as embodying the qualities that would characterize genuine connection. While at the purely rational, or manifest, level, these abstract rights signify only the universally allowed possible actions available to each individual in suspended form (we imagine we "have" these possible actions, and in acting "exercise" them, through a process of simple deduction[24]), at the irrational, or latent, level they link the totality of our current alienated experience with the realization of desire as a collective fantasy. To the extent that these legal images of our existing social life produce mere fantasies of connection, it seems accurate to say that through them we "use" our desire for connection to legitimize our real absence of connection, just as patriotism is often used to produce a feeling of unreal solidarity in order to deny our real experience of a lack of solidarity. Yet, as with patriotism, our production of these legal images in common from our dispersed and withdrawn locations reveals our residual ontological bond. Although we are absorbed in a collective fantasy, we are actually still together insofar as we are "watching the same movie."

We therefore can define the "substitute connection" provided by

23. It is possible to feel both extremes at once: "the last, best hope of mankind."

24. Rational deduction in legal thought actually involves a sequencing of narrative images; it is a way of telling a story. This idea is developed with examples in Gabel, *Reification in Legal Reasoning*, 3 RESEARCH L. & SOC. 25, 40-42 (1980).

legal thought as an impoverished form of actual connection: we participate in a collective fantasy of connection while comprehending that we are together in participating in it. And the distinctive significance of this feeling of substitute connection for making legal thought effective as a defense-mechanism is that it "takes care of desire," allowing us to support the assertion that we are alienated as a matter of law by generating a common feeling that denies that this alienation exists. Of course we comprehend that this feeling is "false" in the same way that we comprehend the artificiality of our role-performances, but nonetheless it assists us in keeping this comprehension out of awareness by linking what feeling of connection there is with what we might call the duty to remain unconscious. To be aware of the lack threatens us not only with reliving the original experience of loss, but with losing even the substitute sense of self through which we have managed to cover it up.

To now summarize the meaning of what I have alternately called legal thought, or the constitutional thought-schema, or simply "rights-consciousness," I would say that it is intended to secure the denial of desire in the face of contingency and the fear of loss by representing our false selves as legally compelled. We guard ourselves against the risk of taking existential action against our alienation by repeatedly telling ourselves that our alienation is inevitable, while at the same time denying that this alienation exists. And by acting toward each other as if we believe all this and that it must be believed, we coerce each other into remaining passive observers of our own suspended experience, hiding together inside the anonymity of artificial self-presentations that perpetually keep us locked in a state of mutual distance.

IV. Reification and Indeterminacy in Rights-Consciousness

Before turning to the positive dimension of legal thought, I want briefly to clarify the relationship between the critique I have been presenting and other elements in the critique of rights that have been emphasized in critical legal studies writings. I am referring specifically to what is sometimes called the "reification critique,"[25] which has shown the way that existing rights-thinking attributes a "falsely concrete" or frozen character to what are always contingent or merely possible social phenomena, and to the "indeterminacy critique,"[26] which

25. *See* Gabel, *supra* note 24; Gordon, *New Developments in Legal Theory*, in THE POLITICS OF LAW 281 (D. Kairys ed. 1982).

26. *See* Frug, *The Ideology of Bureaucracy in American Law*, 97 HARV. L. REV. 1277 (1984); Kelman, *Trashing*, 36 STAN. L. REV. 293 (1984); Kennedy, *supra* note 13; Mensch, *The History of*

has shown rights-arguments to be so inherently manipulable that they cannot by themselves provide authentic justifications for particular social results. These critiques can be and often are combined in studies which argue that the indeterminate character of rights-thinking is disguised through the process of reification,[27] as when it is asserted in a legal opinion, for example, that "the property rights of a shopping-center owner" (which can be shown to be indeterminate) "require the exclusion of picketers" (an illusion resulting from the reification of what is really a political judgment). Both critiques aim to expose the illusion of false necessity that is produced within legal thought as an attempt to deny the true political character of every normative judgment about social life.

While these critiques have been used effectively in a number of doctrinal areas to challenge the purported legitimacy of liberal legal thought,[28] thus far they have lacked a unifying theoretical method which could account for the meaning of reification and indeterminacy themselves as intentionally produced aspects of alienated thought. But if I have been right so far in my description of the experiential foundations of existing legal thought, then both the reification and the indeterminacy of rights-consciousness must reveal a common meaning that derives from our effort to maintain our alienation. This is perhaps easiest to see in the case of reification, because the attribution of a false concreteness to legal concepts simply "carries over" into legal thought an essential existential quality that appears in our as-if performances themselves—the "demand" that these performances be taken as real. I have already shown that this demand is incorporated into legal thought "in advance," in the very way that rights-consciousness represents our actions as *already* corroded by the "delay-time" and self-observation that characterizes our alienated lived experience; in this descriptive sense, our legal concepts represent our false selves as "already real" as a matter of law. But in order for these descriptive concepts to be convincing, we must experience them as real things—we must believe that we really "have" rights and that there really exists a State that allows us to act by exercising them. Reification is therefore but another word for

Mainstream Legal Thought, in THE POLITICS OF LAW, *supra* note 25, at 18; Olsen, *The Family and the Market: A Study of Ideology and Legal Reform*, 96 HARV. L. REV. 1497 (1983); Tushnet, *Critical Legal Studies and Constitutional Law: An Essay in Deconstruction*, 36 STAN. L. REV. 623 (1984).

27. *See, e.g.*, Frug, *supra* note 26; Kennedy, *supra* note 13.

28. Citations to articles on labor law, antidiscrimination law, torts, contracts, and various public-law doctrines can be found in Trubek, *supra* note 1, at 588.

the quality of "belief" itself,[29] through which we imbue legal concepts with their "law-like" power, and through which we deny the contingent and surpassable character of our current social existence.

Yet this description of reification is perhaps itself somewhat reified to the degree that it places too little emphasis on the emotional strain required to believe that something unreal is real,[30] and by reminding ourselves of the nature and source of this strain we can come to see the link between reification and indeterminacy. For reification is not a mere abstract characteristic of legal thought; it is *lived* as a difficult effort to keep out of awareness an underlying existential conflict between the desire for connection and the felt need to deny this desire. One aspect of this effort involves repression: we keep the conflict out of awareness by treating existing reality as fixed and embracing this idea with passion.[31] But a second aspect involves substitute gratification: we keep the conflict out of awareness by anxiously "keeping up" our absorption in the fantasies of substitute connection provided by the utopian imagery of legal thought. The carrying out of this second aspect requires that the cognitive or surface meanings of legal concepts be infinitely malleable because they are created and "believed in" precisely in order to resist (or to keep out of awareness) the underlying meaning that desire has in mind for them. In other words, for substitute gratifications to secure their substitute or unrealized character, the rights which embody them must be suspended in a permanent state of abstraction. They must be able to mean anything at the surface level in order that they not mean anything at the underlying level, where the desire for freedom and equality, for example, is embroiled in conflict. Thus the indeterminacy of what any right "really means concretely" results from our very intention that it should not mean anything concrete (or to put this more precisely, that it should not mean what it means). This idea that substitutive fantasies involve a constant juggling act in which conflictual wishes are perpetually kept out of awareness through the use of displacing imagery is a common theme in psychoanalysis—a child will allow his dream-thoughts to wander over an infinite series of symbolic objects in order not to think of his

29. *See* F. JAMESON, MARXISM AND FORM 296 (1971) (linking reification with fetishism and stating that "fetishism is a form of belief").

30. *See* Lawrence, *Justice or Just Us: Racism and the Role of Ideology* (Book Review), 35 STAN. L. REV. 831 (1983) (discussing emotional strain as a motivation for production of ideology).

31. *See* S. KIERKEGAARD, CONCLUDING UNSCIENTIFIC POSTSCRIPT 174 (1941) (stating, with regard to madness, that "[i]ts fixed idea is precisely some sort of objectivity, and the contradiction of madness consists in embracing this with passion").

Texas Law Review Vol. 62:1563, 1984

mother's breast.[32]

If indeterminacy is therefore an existential constituent of existing legal thought, intentionally produced in order to secure the substitute connection of our withdrawn selves (as well as the anonymity or ungroundedness of our role-performances), then the value of a critique which demonstrates this indeterminacy must be limited to delegitimizing the apparently determinate character that rights-thinking acquires through reification. Without negating the importance of this activity, I think it is nonetheless essential to recognize its paradoxical nature, because the critique itself presupposes that rights-thinking does not actually have to *be* determinate in order to convince those who intend to be convinced by it. In fact, just the opposite is the case if, as I believe, this thought is intentionally constructed to be both indeterminate and yet apparently determinate at the same time. The real question is how to make sense of this paradox—how does consciousness manage to play this trick on itself without being aware that it is doing so? To answer this question, we must recall that the feeling of substitute connection which makes legal thought partially gratifying is generated not by the rational or manifest content of rights, but by their latent content as unconscious fantasies. In other words, it is the fantasy of real freedom embedded in the idea of "freedom of contract" that accounts for our being attached to it (and "attached" through it), rather than any deep loyalty we have to the supposed set of "rational outcomes" that the right to freedom of contract "entails." If the reification of legal reasoning, and thus its apparent determinacy, derives from this emotional attachment to its latent content, then we can see quite clearly how reification and indeterminacy not only can coexist but also work together. Indeterminacy allows rights to possess an infinite number of surface meanings that serve (through a kind of perpetual flight into abstraction) to protect their fantastic nature from the call of desire to

32. This brief discussion of indeterminacy, including the description of the manifest and latent content of legal thought, owes a great deal to Freud's analysis of dreams. *See* S. FREUD, THE INTERPRETATION OF DREAMS ch. 6 (1965). That legal thought is indeterminate obviously does not mean that it is subject to no representational constraints. Like dreams, it is subject to what Freud called "considerations of representability," *id.* at 374, which in the case of dreams refers to the pictorial compatibility of sequential dream-images, and in the case of legal thought includes (among other factors) the appearance of narrative consistency, or "rationality." I understand the efforts of Al Katz and Duncan Kennedy to link transformations in legal thought with the "mediation of contradictions" as studies of representational constraints of this type. *See* Katz, *Studies in Boundary Theory: Three Essays in Adjudication and Politics,* 28 BUFFALO L. REV. 383 (1979); Kennedy, *supra* note 13; *see also* Freeman, *Antidiscrimination Law, A Critical Review,* in THE POLITICS OF LAW, *supra* note 25, at 96 (analyzing the Supreme Court's effort to reconcile result-oriented implications of antidiscrimination law with meritocratic images supporting class structure as a whole).

give them a realized meaning. Reification allows us to believe in the determinacy of *any* of these surface meanings through our very attachment to the fantasy of connection that each provides. As a consequence, the law does not have to be "really" rational for people to believe in it—in fact, this very "belief" is sustained by its nonrational or indeterminate quality.

We are now in a position to see how consciousness can both intend the meaning of a right to be infinitely manipulable and yet at the same moment believe that a particular application of that right is convincing. For it turns out that the feeling of being convinced by a particular rights-argument derives not from the argument's rational coherence, but from the "prerational" momentary gratification provided by the fantasy content of the images contained within it. Thus when we think something like "the right to freedom of contract requires that the acceptance match the terms of the offer," we are indifferent to the fact that the right to freedom of contract could just as easily mean that minor variations in the acceptance be ignored because "the intent to be bound by an agreement" was present. What convinces us is our latent and momentary attachment to the feeling that "we are all free to relate to each other just as we please." And because this feeling can be produced by *any* application of the right to freedom of contract, the indeterminacy of the right does not interfere with its power to convince us in any particular case. On the contrary, this indeterminacy allows us to be convinced to the degree that it reassures us that the right's concealed ontological meaning—the forbidden wish for the free and open reciprocity that would result from genuine social connection—will never be revealed or concretely realized.

Thus, from an ontological point of view it is not really true that the indeterminacy of rights is disguised by reification, because reification derives from the same commitment to fantasy that indeterminacy is intended to guarantee. And as a result the indeterminacy *critique* cannot really dissolve someone's "belief" in legal authority, any more than a psychotherapist can undo a client's defenses by trying to convince the client of their irrationality. Even if the client is convinced at a rational level that a particular defensive idea "makes no sense," he will either continue to believe in it (because he never really believed in it anyway), or he will come up with another one that serves the same purpose. This is not to deny that exposing the irrationality of a belief-system can to some extent undermine that aspect of it that relies upon rationality as a defense, but it is to say that so long as this critique remains only at the rational or manifest level, it will fail to engage the latent motivations that give rise to the intention to be defended, motivations that derive from the experiential foundations of alienation itself. Thus it seems quite possible for a believer to be persuaded that "the law is indeterminate" and that "everything is political" without ever abandoning his longing to defer to a senior partner, or the awe that he feels in the presence of a judge. He will give up these commitments only by participating in social experiences that give him the confidence to feel they are no longer necessary, including the experience of coming to understand why he gave himself over to them in the first place.

V. The Meaning of Rights During the Rising Period of Social Movements

A. *Rights-Struggles as an Effort to Transform Public Space*

The kind of disalienating experience to which I have just referred is often produced through the internal transformation of social relations that characterizes the rising period of a social movement. During such periods legal concepts like "rights" undergo a partial transformation of meaning that derives from the unique release of connection that constitutes the movement itself. I say "unique" release of connection to distinguish the movement experience from those sudden moments of connection that we often (or at least occasionally) feel in so-called "private life"—during an aside with a bank teller to take a relatively minor example, or when we fall in love to think of an obviously important one. The problem with such private moments is that we experience them as occurring "underneath" the weight of the alienated public facade, as if desire had somehow "sneaked through" its allowed constraints, and it is this illicit quality that I think accounts for the conspiratorial nature of the aside, as well as the somewhat hysterical and disbelieving quality that often accompanies falling in love.[33] In fact, the very idea that these moments are "private" is something of an illusion produced by their illicit quality because the truth is that the "whole public" has them, not just in the sense that we all experience them in roughly the same ways across our lifetimes, but that we act as a group to confer upon them their limiting "private" character. It is this limitation that social movements seek to surpass by challenging the experiential boundary that constitutes the public/private split with enough confidence to dissolve the fabric of performances that normally enclose the public world.

33. "Joy is a magical behavior which tends by incantation to realize the possession of the desired object as instantaneous totality." J.P. SARTRE, THE EMOTIONS 69 (1948).

Phenomenology of Rights-Consciousness

But the "mechanisms" of reciprocal denial that alienation itself produces make it very difficult for such movements to arise (for they amount to betrayals of the pact of the withdrawn selves), and the fact that alienation "enforces itself" in part through the reproduction of hierarchical differences virtually assures that such a movement will not arise the way it ought to—as a universal response to our common predicament. For insofar as the group as a whole imagines itself to be constituted through these differences (teller/supervisor, worker/owner, woman/man, black/white, student/teacher, child/parent, gay/straight, and so forth), it is much more likely that dispersed and withdrawn individuals will take the risk of releasing the movement of desire only when they can anticipate the reciprocation of those who they know already see themselves as suffering their ontological deprivation from "within the same difference." The paradox of the labor movement, or the women's movement, or the civil-rights movement is that they can acquire the ontological capacity to "gather steam" only through reciprocal recognition of a universal need, but they can achieve this recognition initially only through affirming a contingent and culturally produced particularity that is a badge of alienation itself. As we will see in a moment, the transformative (as opposed to "reformist") capacity of the movement depends upon its ability to overcome this paradox by gaining the confidence to link the surpassing of the particular "difference" that allowed it to form with the overcoming of alienation.[34] This universal need gives the movement its foundational energy, and it is only by sustaining this energy that the movement can transform the hierarchical conditions that caused it to come into being.

Thus when a movement manages to richochet into existence through an unpredictable convergence of "igniting" material and cultural circumstances combined with an irreducible element of free commitment by those who take the risk of reciprocation, it produces a

34. In one sense, the group's surpassing of its particularity is inherently linked to the overcoming of alienation. The group initially achieves its disalienating momentum by affirming its particularity in a new way: it becomes a movement precisely by taking over the alienated "otherness" that society has imposed upon it and regrounding this particularity on its own terms, or on the basis of its own autonomous self-constitution. When women demand *women's* liberation or blacks assert *black* power, they express the link between the particular and the universal as a contextual attempt to become the agents of their own conditioning (their affirmation of particularity, insofar as it involves a transformation of their internal reciprocity, is a disalienating negation of their prior inertia).

But in real life (as opposed to apocalyptic fantasies), this prior inertia is never fully overcome in the movement's rising period—why should a brief period of euphoria overcome the conditioning of an entire lifetime?—and for this reason the particularity of the movement's origins exerts a drag upon its transformative capabilities. This accounts for the paradox referred to in the text and for the necessity that the movement gradually build up an internal confidence in its autonomous self-constitution.

disalienating energy that wants to challenge everything that is (capitalism, patriarchy, hierarchy, "the system") and a set of specific demands for change that derive from the movement's particular origins and that are inspired, consciously or unconsciously, by its vision of the larger end. It is through its attempt to realize these demands that the movement comes up against "the law," not only because it wants to do things that are illegal and that can be prevented by force, but also because it wants to contest the very alienated consciousness through which the group as a whole defines how "we" are constituted. For while these demands for change always have a practical dimension, they must be understood in their ontological dimension as demands for recognition of the movement's desire to change the whole world, and as we have seen, it is precisely this transcendental desire that existing legal thought is constructed to deny. For the movement to succeed in driving its energy into public space, which it must do in order to sustain itself as a movement in the face of the anxiety and resistance that it provokes in the anonymous "public" and even within its own members, it must engage in a struggle with the existing legal "belief-system" over the very meaning of who "we" are and how we are really constituted as social beings.

As the movement begins to assert its rights at this moment of its internal development, therefore, we should understand these rights as motivated simultaneously by two intentions. The first is practical: when workers demand the right to engage in collective action on the shop floor, or women demand the right to safe abortions, or gays demand the right to dental care for "domestic partners" under employee-benefit plans,[35] they want to do things that are good in themselves and that will advance their practical aims (including the aim of building the movement). But the second and equally important motivation is to use these rights as a means for gaining a benchmark of recognition within public consciousness of the universal disalienating impulse that animates the movement itself. Thus all of the rights that I just mentioned claim their legitimacy not on the basis of each movement's particular and practical needs, but through an appeal to the universal and authentic meaning of freedom and equality as that meaning would be realized *for everyone* through the realization of each movement's particular demands. It is true that this message must be communicated in a somewhat muted way, through what we might call the repressed connotation that lies at the heart of existing legal thought, but it "comes across"

35. *See* Hinman v. Department of Personnel Admin., No. 308568 (Sup. Ct. of Sacramento County, Cal., filed Dec. 29, 1982).

nonetheless because the meaning of the movement itself resonates throughout the social order as an appeal for others to recognize themselves in it. It is therefore this second dimension of the rights-claim that allows the desire that is constitutive of the movement's internal bond to exert a pull upon the desire that lies submerged within the group as a whole in the form of a public claim that this desire is constitutive of who we all are, that it is "constitutional."

The meaning that rights like "freedom of speech" or "equal protection" acquire at such moments is not merely different from but actually opposed to the meaning normally given to them in alienated consciousness. For while these legal concepts are normally intended to deny our desire for genuine connection by "keeping up" the substitute connection engendered by their fantasy-content, they are intended by the movement to affirm the universal legitimacy of their true or realized meaning that the movement is trying to "bring into being" through the intersubjective vitality of its concrete practice. As a result, we should not call this contestation of meaning an "ideological struggle" to the degree that this term implies a battle of disembodied ideas over what legal concepts ought to mean "conceptually," but rather an ontological struggle over opposing ways of being that determine what these concepts do mean in their qualitative, lived dimension. The aim of the movement is to spread its way of being toward a universal realization rather than to create an improved set of concepts to be applied to everyone by a reconstituted authority, and it moves in this existential direction by "reversing" the normal meaning that rights have within the culture: it seizes upon the utopian imagery that is used to channel the universality of desire into collective, demobilizing fantasies and seeks to infuse this imagery with the desire-realizing meaning that is beginning to be lived out within the being of the movement itself. When workers claim during a rising period that their collective actions are expressive of the right to freedom of speech, they do not draw their meaning of freedom of speech from any "interpretation" of this idea that could be "found" within existing legal thought, as if this meaning could be seen as in some way "like" what corporations mean when they claim the right to make unrestricted contributions to election campaigns. Nor are they requesting recognition of their meaning from the hallucinatory projection we call "the State." They are rather speaking *through* these alienated forms from the vantage-point of their own disalienating experience, and they are seeking to provoke a recognition in what we might call the transcendental conscience of real other people. It is for this reason that the meaning of these rights is neither reified,

Texas Law Review Vol. 62:1563, 1984

nor indeterminate; it is rather *contingent* in the sense that it is rooted in the particularity of a concrete, lived experience, and *determinate* in the sense that it is expressive only of the existential quality of this experience, as this quality might be realized in its universality through an infinite number of particular, historical instances.

But the disalienating meaning of a right can survive only to the degree that the movement itself retains its vitality, and while a rights-victory can both strengthen the movement's confidence and awaken a feeling of possibility among a great many people, it can for these very reasons work to contain the movement and ultimately contribute to subduing its transformative potential. For the possibility that is either strengthened or awakened by such public victories (which are obviously not limited to rights-victories) is the possibility that "we" will actually have to change, and in a way that would require us both to open ourselves to each other in a new way and to abandon the forms of substitute connection through which we have defended ourselves against such an openness for a long time. The very success of the movement, therefore, evokes in a somewhat heightened way the fear of loss that the movement intends to surpass, and it does so not only in those who are most opposed to the movement, but also in those who constitute it. Thus far I have placed a somewhat exaggerated emphasis on the disalienating character of these movement-experiences in order to stress their emancipatory possibilities, but no one who has participated in such an experience can fail to recognize the ambivalence that corrodes it from within, an ambivalence that stems as much from what we might call a rotating lack of confidence in the commitment of the other as it does from the various forms of violence that are leveled against the movement from the outside.[36] While movements can fail to realize their deepest objectives for a great many reasons beyond their control, this incomplete confidence accounts in large part for the phenomenon of "cooptation," through which a movement gives up on these objectives with its own accord.

36. Michael Lerner has described this ambivalence as resulting from what he calls "surplus powerlessness." Lerner, *Surplus Powerlessness,* SOC. POL'Y, Jan. 1979, at 18, 18-19 (analyzing how this phenomenon contributed to the collapse of the new left). I would add in passing that neither his analysis nor mine is meant to imply some fundamental pessimism, as if it were inevitable that social transformation movements must collapse because of their own internal fragility. The point is to recognize the reality of this fragility in all of its crazy-making manifestations and to try to increase the common confidence by changing how we act toward one another in our respective capacities as one of the others to each other. This requires a combination of free will, compassion for the other's doubts, and concrete trust-building practices (what Morty Horwitz recently called a "mediating culture" at the last critical legal studies summer camp).

B. The Strategy of State Officials: Pseudo-Recognition and Containment by Interpretation

Rights-victories can facilitate a movement's cooptation by tempting the movement to "return" its power to the State in exchange for what I will call a pseudo-recognition of the movement's particular demands. I use the term "the State" here, just as I have earlier, to refer not to a collection of officials conceived as a conceptual unit, but to the projected image of authority that these officials "speak for" and that alienated consciousness "believes in" to provide itself with an illusory political foundation. This collectively believed-in authority serves as the political vehicle for opposing the internal development of the movement precisely to the degree that the group as a whole feels the need to resist the sense of possibility awakened by the movement's energy.

During the movement's rising period, the need to remain alienated continues to exist in each of us, including those at the movement's core, but its intensity is distributed throughout the group as a whole according to "social position," understood in a strictly experiential sense. For insofar as the movement initially finds the conviction to discover itself and "arise" through an affirmation of its difference from the rest of the group, it provokes a complex reaction in the group as a whole that depends in part upon how each person feels "positioned" in relation to the movement's particularity. While each movement *as a movement* aims at universality, the demands that emerge from its alienated particularity are aimed against others in their alienated particularity in a way that both mutes (in some locations) and accentuates (in other locations) the movement's transformative appeal. For example, a workers' movement may cause "management" and all those who identify with managerial "differentness" to want to "defend themselves"; yet the very fact that the workers have at first defined themselves against management may allow students who are beginning to discover themselves through their difference from teachers to "hear" the movement's deeper meaning. Blacks who organize against whites may cause whites to rigidify behind their difference, while striking a chord among women who are also coming to experience each other in a new way through their discovery of the social meaning of a common physical difference. While any true account of a movement's impact would require a narrative description with much greater phenomenological texture than I can produce here, it is through the totality of these ontological resonances, each acquiring its quality from the unique way that the movement aims at the disalienating universal through the alienated particular, that the movement influences the "consciousness-war" occurring within each one of us between the need to remain alienated and the desire to surpass this alienation.

In this early period it is virtually inevitable that the balance of forces within the group as a whole ("society") will tilt in favor of the loyalty to substitute connection that forms the inertia of the status quo, and the group tacitly will rely upon its State officials to cope with the heightened conflict that the movement has generated within it. The "social position" of these officials is somewhat unique because they are called upon to represent the constitution of the group to itself as it actually is (in the sense that their perceived legitimacy as "representatives" extends no further than the group's own dominant self-understanding), and yet they also help to constitute the balance of forces that forms this understanding in their capacity as real people who are part of the group. And as people they are likely to be relatively unavailable to the movement's transformative appeal because this appeal threatens the very "belief in the State" upon which their existing identities depend; they will be inclined to defend themselves against any movement, because movements by their very nature pose a challenge to the alienated universality that in their case constitutes their particularity. As a result, State officials are likely to play the part of "barometers on the side of alienation," seeking to recognize the movement's presence within the group to the extent necessary to maintain their legitimacy, but doing so in a way that sides with the tilt in the group as a whole toward preserving the collective belief in the authority of the State.

The cooptation strategy that these officials adopt—a strategy that may or may not be conscious as regards its form, but remains unconscious as regards its experiential meaning—is to calibrate their responses to the movement's demands so as to encourage the tendency already present in the movement to return to a state of quiescence. This strategy seems to involve roughly three stages[37] that take place across a time-span (often decades) dictated by the pulse of the movement itself. At first, these officials refuse to recognize the legitimacy of the movement's demands at all because they are inconsistent with existing law. This risks increasing the anger that forms part of the movement's strength and it may provoke destabilizing confrontations and

37. I use the word "stages" in the loosest possible sense to describe a process that commonly occurs but that has no lawlike or inevitable character. For a description of this process in the context of the history of a case, see Gabel & Harris, *Building Power and Breaking Images: Critical Legal Theory and the Practice of Law*, 11 N.Y.U. REV. L. & SOC. CHANGE 369, 384-89 (1983) (discussing Tinker v. Des Moines Indep. Community School Dist., 393 U.S. 503 (1969)).

demonstrations that increase the movement's visibility and appeal (for example, it may create a dispersed group of "sympathizers"). But this risk is a calculated one because it shores up the resolve of those who are opposed to the movement by backing up this resolve with an affirmation of what "the people" believe, while also tempting those within the movement to warp their own understanding of how the movement itself is constituted. Because the movement has achieved its disalienating reciprocity in part on the basis of a "surface recognition" of its common difference within the alienated social order, and because this new feeling of connection is as yet somewhat weak in light of the movement's incomplete internal confidence in its own autonomous and transcendental constitution, the movement suffers from an internal tendency to turn itself back into a group that is constituted "from the outside" on the basis of the inert particularity that as a movement it is seeking to surpass. When State officials refuse to recognize the legitimacy of the movement's demands, the movement may partially give in to this tendency by seeing itself less through its own eyes and more through the "eyes of the State," as if "the State" were the source of its being and for that reason ought to recognize it. The initial refusal of recognition by State officials, in other words, may begin to seduce the movement into deciding that "getting our rights" is the movement's ultimate objective rather than being but a moment of its own internal development. To that extent the movement's anger at the State may reveal a tendency toward compliance rather than transformation.

As the movement gathers momentum in this double direction—the one toward itself, the other away from itself and toward "the State"—the forces of alienation will begin to realign themselves to prepare for the second stage of the State's strategy, the stage of pseudo-recognition. Through a real intuition that spreads through the withdrawn selves on the basis of their existing organization of reciprocity (a phenomenological definition of "the social structure"), some people remain staunchly opposed to the movement because of their particular social relationship to it, while others begin to mediate the movement's relationship to the group as a whole (through "the media," for example) by recasting the movement's demands as a legitimate "rights-debate" with "difficult arguments on both sides." As leaders of collective experience, these oracles of the center seek to "mold public opinion" in a way that secures its anonymous or empty character against the risk that the desire unleashed by the movement could become a genuinely public force; their efforts are nervously aimed at reassuring the group as a whole that the images supporting our substitute connection can be reorganized to accommodate the movement's demands. These efforts are a measure of the movement's authentic impact. But they are also aimed at bombarding the movement itself with a false picture of its public success by suggesting that the movement is making headway because of its compatibility with the political foundations of the status quo (when exactly the reverse is the case). To the degree that the State's original refusal of recognition has already encouraged the movement to experience its own reciprocity as deriving from its external and role-based particularity, this shift toward mediation may further this temptation by implying that the "bad State" may be willing to back down and atone for its wrongs if the movement will abandon its transformative ambitions, or at least postpone them until an unrealizable future when these ambitions will be "allowed."

When State officials subsequently begin to recognize the movement's specific demands in the form of rights-victories, they do so with the hope that the movement will "trick itself" into equating these victories with its own internal ends. As State officials know perfectly well, it is not necessary or even conceivable that the movement will accept the acquisition of a few rights as all that it means to accomplish. It is necessary only that the movement divert itself from its authentic self-understanding enough to deceive itself into thinking that its objectives could eventually be realized through existing law, as if alienation could ever be overcome with its own agreement. For State officials comprehend in their being that once this diversion occurs, the movement will tend increasingly to see its own capacity to realize itself as located outside of itself in "the State," and to that degree its transformative momentum will tend to collapse from within for reasons described earlier: "belief in the State" itself derives from the reciprocal denial of desire that divides us from each other by our role-performances and that secures the apparent reality of these performances through our collective obedience to a projected authority. Thus the recognition of the movement's demands by State officials is actually a pseudo-recognition because it intends to strip these demands of their universal and transformative meaning and to induce the movement to grasp itself as a "recognized particularity," playing its part along with all of the others in the circle of collective denial that forms the alienated whole.

But just as the State's original refusal to recognize the movement may partly strengthen as well as weaken the movement's internal solidarity, the eventual recognition of the movement also has this dual potential: it runs the risk of giving the movement the foothold in public consciousness that partly inspired its struggle for rights in the first place. The consciousness-war can be quite fluid at the moment of recognition, with each side struggling over the meaning of what is happening, and struggling not only against each other but among themselves and *within everyone* insofar as these "sides" are lived as a universal conflict that pervades each person's relationship to others. When blue-collar workers win the right to strike, the bank teller may or may not be happy depending upon countless resonations that overdetermine each other in both directions without absolutely determining anything in advance (including her relationship to her mother, her husband's job, her loyalty to the bank, her "white-collar" identity, her sense of how women should respond to conflict, her vision of her children's prospects, and including what, if anything, happens in the bank that day). To control this fluidity, State officials, to the extent that they remain on the side of alienation, must rely on the third stage of their strategy, the stage of "interpretation," to stabilize a situation that they have had no choice but to help create.

This third stage has been discussed extensively in those critical legal studies writings[38] that have traced in specific historical instances how these officials attempt, through a process of doctrinal interpretation and legislative compromise elaborated over many years, to reconcile the movement's rights-victories with the pact of the withdrawn selves (as expressed through the intent of the framers, of the legislature, of the parties, of "the people"), and to distinguish these victories from their true social origins in the intent of the movement. During this extended period while the consciousness-war is waged with fluctuating intensity in countless microphenomenological contexts that mutually influence and totalize each other, these officials play a unique and constitutive role in equilibrating the conflict as a whole by purporting to universalize the meaning of each shift in direction through successive case-by-case revisions of what the Constitution says.[39] They absorb

38. *See, e.g.*, Freeman, *Legitimizing Racism Through Antidiscrimination Law,* 62 MINN. L. REV. 1049 (1978); Klare, *Judicial Deradicalization of the Wagner Act and the Origins of Modern Legal Consciousness, 1937-1941*, 62 MINN. L. REV. 265 (1978); Stone, *The Post-War Paradigm in American Labor Law,* 90 YALE L.J. 1509 (1981); *see also* J. ATLESON, VALUES AND ASSUMPTIONS IN AMERICAN LABOR LAW (1983).

39. Some writers have recently expressed doubts that legal ideology plays this unique and constitutive role, demanding empirical evidence. *See, e.g.,* Hyde, *The Concept of Legitimation in the Sociology of Law,* 1983 WIS. L. REV. 379 (1983). But it is a mistake to think that law starts out high up somewhere and then does or does not filter down to the masses in a way that could be studied empirically; it is rather a mishmash of symbolic fragments that are "manufactured, reproduced, and modified for special purposes by everyone, at every level, all the time." Gordon, *supra* note 1, at 123. But these "levels" exist only in consciousness, and one such level—we might call it the "up-there level"—is the level at which the mishmash gets "dressed up" in legal reasoning by people who are allocated the task of producing the group's idea-of-itself as an abstract universal entity. The study of doctrine is itself an empirical study of this level, which forms one aspect of

what they can of the social texture of these shifts, test it for available alienated image-content, write it up as a fantasy narrative that is vaguely consistent with prior chapters, and then feed it back into the group as a whole as the official interpretation of how they, the people, believe it should "come out."[40] But I think it is a mistake to understand this process as something that one group does to another, as if the State were trying to manipulate the movement into internalizing false consciousness by acting upon it in a one-way fashion. It is rather the final phase of a reciprocal and intersubjective struggle over the possibilities of social connection itself, as this struggle is mediated through a contest over the *ontological* meaning of legal concepts in their universal or constitutional dimension.

To the degree that the movement is successful in this universal sense, it can use a rights-strategy as part of its effort to leverage itself into public space with the ultimate aim of creating an experience of public community that could dissolve people's belief in and obedience to the State itself—it is only then that the judge can appear as a man in a tunic and "the law" can appear as something like his speech-impediment. But to the degree that the State is successful in using *its* rights-strategy to tempt the movement to substitute rights-*consciousness* for its own critical self-understanding, the movement's members will gradually find themselves losing each other in their legal reflection and becoming attached to this reflection as the medium through which they recognize one another. By their efforts they will have changed their material and cultural circumstances to the degree that their particular demands can be "balanced" with the common commitment to maintaining the stability of the hierarchical order. But they will experience a hemorrhage of being that will allow them to be reabsorbed into this order, first by depriving them of their unique public appeal in a way that will lead public space to reenclose around them, and finally by

the totality of "American consciousness." Empirical research on other aspects of legal consciousness, such as the way that workers on the shop-floor perceive collective bargaining or grievance procedures, is an equally important but different activity.

For a good analysis of the relationship between critical legal studies and empiricism, see Trubek, *supra* note 1.

40. I have written a brief description of how this process works in *The Mass Psychology of the New Federalism: How the Burger Court's Political Imagery Legitimizes the Privatization of Everyday Life*, 52 GEO. WASH. L. REV. 264 (1984). But the relationship of consciousness-control to image-manipulation is at least implicit in much critical legal studies writing. *See, e.g.*, Freeman, *supra* note 32 (analyzing the use of such background imagery as the "innocence" of those who do not "intend" to discriminate, "the ideology of vestedness," "merit," "luck," "fate," and "scientific measurement of ability"); Klare, *Critical Theory and Labor Relations Law*, in THE POLITICS OF LAW, *supra* note 25, at 65 (analyzing legal interpretations of "collective action," "industrial democracy," "labor-management partnership," and "quid pro quo").

hierarchizing themselves to secure the denial of desire upon which their continued acceptance within the group as a whole seems to depend.

VI. Conclusion

None of this is meant to deprecate the achievements of these movements even when they (we) cooperate in their own demise. Their particular gains reduce human suffering and may create new possibilities for popular mobilization, and the rights they win never entirely lose the resonance of authentic meaning that gives rise to their expression. For once this meaning has been realized in social experience even a little bit, we retain it as something like an ethical memory that is enveloped by its alienated meaning but not wholly erased by it.[41] Obviously "the right to freedom of speech" is good to the degree that prior generations have helped us to want to allow each other to dissent publicly from the many alienated forms of group coercion, and bad to the degree that we use it *mainly* to envelop ourselves in this coercion by calling it the exercise of this right. The same can be said of the right to freedom of contract if we recall at least part of its meaning from the serf's point of view, and even of the right to private property to the degree that it once meant that the barons couldn't kick people off their land, and to the degree that it still means the group will support you in a nice way, but in some circumstances and not others, when you ask your brother-in-law to leave your house.[42] No one that I know in critical legal studies is "against" civil rights or due process rights or workers rights or any rights to the degree that their meanings are linked in this way with their authentic foundations in experience. In this sense "the rights notion is a liberating accomplishment of our culture."[43]

But it is wrong to think that the critique of rights is "just a matter

41. This entire Article could be rewritten from this point of view, focusing on the ways that rights exert a positive force on social relationships in the form of such ethical memories. But I think it is better first to carry the critique as far as possible, so that we can make out just what this positive force is by knowing its limitations.

42. This example is taken, in slightly altered form, from Bob Gordon's description of why workers are likely to respect the property rights of the owner of a business:

> Take the ownership claim: the employees are not likely to think they can challenge that because to do so would jeopardize their sense of the rights of ownership, which they themselves exercise in other aspects of life ("I own this house, so I can tell my brother-in-law to get the hell out of it"); they are locked into a belief-cluster that abstracts and generalizes the ownership claim.

Gordon, *supra* note 25, at 287.

43. Embedded in the rights notion is a liberating accomplishment of our culture: the affirmation of free human subjectivity against the constraints of group life, along with the "paradoxical countervision of a group life that creates and nurtures individuals capable of freedom. We need to work at the slow transformation of rights rhetoric . . . rather than simply junking it." Kennedy, *Critical Labor Law Theory: A Comment*, 4 INDUS. REL. L.J. 503, 506 (1981).

of degree," or that all we need is to get the good meaning of rights into the law and get rid of the bad meaning, or that what we need are collective rights instead of individual rights or human rights instead of property rights. And it is also wrong to think that a transformation movement can be advanced by a conceptualized "combination" of rights-victories at the legal level and community organizing at the grass-roots level, as if we could produce a quantity of movement and then freeze it in stone, and then another and freeze that in stone, until we had the right to everything we wanted. To think any of these things is to participate in the illusion that the right to an experience can create the experience itself, and to reverse the true relationship between the meaning of verbal concepts and the qualitative or lived milieu out of which they arise. From my point of view, the critique of rights is a critique of that reversal; it is aimed at clarifying the possible existential meanings that rights can acquire once their true relationship to existence itself has been understood.

Because the emancipatory possibilities of rights-victories both arise from and remain located in the upsurge of connection that a movement brings into being, it seems clear that the problem of incomplete confidence places an internal limit on what we should expect these victories alone to produce. Not only are they double-edged in the sense that others will use them to exploit the movement's uncertainty about itself; they are also "just words"—their evocative power cannot be expected to go very far in carrying out the aim of strengthening the movement's bond by penetrating the boundaries of public space. This is why Paul Harris and I have argued elsewhere[44] that the movement's engagement with State officials (its "legal strategy") has got to subsume the goal of expanding its rights within a more general effort to expand its evocative appeal. It must attempt to reconstitute the very form of existing legal settings by using play, style, music, crowds, and anything else that can embody its message with enough life to erode the authoritarian quality of these settings and to get its message deeply across and deeply back in again in a way that legal arguments in their current form cannot do. Obviously this alone will not solve the problem of what I have called the rotating lack of confidence in the desire of the other that tends to weaken the movement from within. But the more that we can desanctify the forms of symbolic authority that are used by

44. *See* Gabel & Harris, *supra* note 37; *see also* Bellow, *Turning Solutions into Problems: The Legal Aid Experience,* NLADA BRIEFCASE, Aug. 1977, at 106 (relationship of "focused case-pressure" to popular mobilization); Simon, *Visions of Practice in Legal Thought,* 36 STAN. L. REV. 469 (1984) (relationship between working within and contesting the nature of the system).

others to generate the "belief" through which alienation becomes the law, the more likely it is that we can inspire others to inspire us that we know what we're talking about—that we can, you know, be ourselves, make contact, have a good time, "take control of the means of production," and generally come out from behind the fabric of appearances through which we make each other hostage to the illusion that it is distance rather than a good heart turned outward that the law in us requires.

[6]

Rights in Twentieth-Century Constitutions

Mary Ann Glendon†

Although this symposium has treated the subject of the Bill of Rights in the welfare state primarily within the context of American constitutional law, it is instructive and appropriate to compare the American experience with the experiences of other liberal democratic welfare states. Indeed, if a symposium on this subject had been held in 1991 at a university anywhere except in the United States, its approach almost certainly would have been cross-national from beginning to end. Most of the participants, no doubt, would have been invited to explore how some countries—for example, Canada, Denmark, France, Germany, Italy, Japan, Norway, and Sweden—have managed, more or less successfully, to remain simultaneously committed to political and civil rights, a well-developed welfare state, and a system of constitutional control of legislative and executive action. There would probably have been a session or two devoted to the transition of the East European countries from socialism to constitutional social democracy. Another major topic would have been how commitments made in international human rights instruments have affected national legal systems. Finally, in all likelihood, there would have been sessions devoted to two special cases: first, England, a welfare state without a system of judicial review or a bill of rights (in the modern sense); and second, the United States, a country with a venerable rights tradition and a strong system of judicial review, but with a minimalist welfare state.

In this article, I cannot present such an extended comparative survey. My goal is rather to advance the proposition that American thinking about rights and welfare would benefit from examining the experiences of other liberal democracies,[1] and to speculate about the insights that might emerge from such a comparative

---

† Professor of Law, Harvard University. The University of Chicago, B.A.; J.D.; M.Comp.L. This Article was prepared for *The Bill of Rights in the Welfare State: A Bicentennial Symposium*, held at The University of Chicago Law School on October 25-26, 1991. The helpful comments of Professor Aviam Soifer of Boston University Law School are gratefully acknowledged.

[1] In this Article, I concentrate mainly on nations whose experience is most similar to our own: countries at levels of social and economic development comparable to ours; and

analysis. I do not claim that we will find abroad any answers to the great questions debated by the participants in this symposium. Rather, the benefits I have in mind are more like those to which the great French historian, Fernand Braudel, was referring when he once said:

> Live in London for a year, and you will not get to know much about the English. But through comparison, and in the light of your surprise, you will suddenly come to understand some of the more profound and individual characteristics of France, which you did not previously understand because you knew them too well.[2]

Taking my cue from Braudel, I will reflect, first, on some of the "more profound and individual characteristics" of the United States that we often overlook—because we know them so well. I will then consider some of the special difficulties posed by our distinctive experience with rights and welfare. Finally, I will suggest that heightened awareness of how our country's experience is distinctive can alert us to opportunities for improvement—opportunities that seem, at least theoretically, to be more available to us than to policymakers elsewhere.

I. American Distinctiveness

Many of the issues vigorously debated at this symposium owe their very existence to the simple chronological fact that, when our Constitution and Bill of Rights were adopted, the welfare state as we know it was not even a twinkle in the eyes of the Founding Fathers. Because the overwhelming majority of the world's constitutions have been adopted within the past thirty years,[3] there are few other countries where scholars need to ask questions like the following: How does our eighteenth-century design for government fit with our modern regulatory state? Does it matter which branches of government take the lead in deciding what adaptations are necessary? Is it a problem that our welfare state, such as it is, continues to develop without any specific constitutional impetus?

---

countries where welfare states co-exist with a strong commitment to individual liberty and the rule of law.

[2] Fernand Braudel, *Histoire et Sciences Sociales: La Longue Durée*, Annales: Economies, Sociétés, Civilisations 725, 737 (1958).

[3] Three-quarters of the approximately 160 single-document constitutions in the world today have been adopted since 1965. Lis Wiehl, *Constitution, Anyone? A New Cottage Industry*, NY Times B6 (Feb 2, 1990) (citing Professor Albert P. Blaustein of the Rutgers Law School).

Or, does the deep structure of the Fourteenth Amendment—say, the idea of "protection"—provide a constitutional lodestar for the welfare state after all? The age of our Bill of Rights is thus foremost among the features that distinguish the United States with respect to rights and the welfare state. The first ten amendments to the Constitution, backed up by judicial review, were in place long before our legislatures began to attend systematically to the health, safety, and well-being of citizens. In most other liberal democracies, the sequence has been just the reverse. In Canada, France, and Germany, for example, the foundations of the welfare state were in place well before regimes of constitutional rights appeared.[4]

A second distinguishing feature is that the American Constitution, unlike the constitutions of most other liberal democracies, contains no language establishing affirmative welfare rights or obligations.[5] A third factor is the conspicuous unwillingness of American governments to ratify several important international human rights instruments to which all the other liberal democracies have acceded. And finally there is the unusual structure of our welfare state, which, much more than elsewhere, leaves pensions, health insurance, and other benefits to be organized privately, mainly through the workplace, rather than directly through the public sector. I will elaborate briefly upon the first three of these factors.

A. Rights Before Welfare

We Americans are justly proud of our long tradition of protecting individual rights, celebrated in this bicentennial year of the Bill of Rights. We also take patriotic satisfaction in that, prior to 1945, we were one of very few countries that protected constitutional rights through judicial review. However, it is worth recalling that American courts seldom exercised the power of judicial review

---

[4] Expanded suffrage in the French Third Republic and fear of militant socialism in Bismarck's Germany in the late nineteenth century led those countries to adopt factory legislation, rudimentary social welfare laws, and statutes regulating commerce and public utilities.

France adopted a limited form of constitutional control only in 1958, and Canada established judicial review only in 1982. In Germany, though some courts in the Weimar Republic had claimed the power to rule on the constitutionality of laws, constitutional review did not become a significant feature of the legal order until 1951, when the Federal Constitutional Court was established in what was then West Germany. Donald P. Kommers, *The Constitutional Jurisprudence of the Federal Republic of Germany* 6-11 (Duke, 1989).

[5] Louis Favoreu, *La Protection des Droits Economiques et Sociaux dans les Constitutions*, in *Conflict and Integration: Comparative Law in the World Today* 691-92 (Chuo, 1989).

claimed in *Marbury v Madison*[6] until the turn of the century, and then the courts deployed the power in a way that may well have impeded the development of the welfare state here for decades.[7] In the *Lochner* era, when the American Supreme Court engaged in its first sustained adventure with judicial review, legislators in the rest of the industrialized world were busily constructing their infant welfare states on the basis of statutes broadly similar in spirit to those our Court was striking down.[8]

It was not until the active period of constitution-making following World War II that other nations widely adopted bills of rights and institutional mechanisms to enforce them.[9] At that time, the majority of liberal democratic countries opted for variants of a system developed in pre-war Austria that has come to be known as the "European model" of constitutional control.[10] The principal feature that distinguishes the "European" from the "American" model is that, under the former, constitutional questions must be referred to a special tribunal that deals only or mainly with such matters. Constitutional adjudication is off-limits for other courts in such countries. It is only in the United States, and in the relatively small group of countries that have adopted the "American model," that ordinary courts have the power to rule on constitutional questions in ordinary lawsuits. Many nations that have adopted the European model are still further distanced from our system by the fact that constitutional questions may be presented to the consti-

---

[6] 5 US (1 Cranch) 137 (1803).

[7] As James Q. Wilson has noted,

> In the first seventy-five years of this country's history, only 2 federal laws were held unconstitutional; in the next seventy-five years, 71 were. Of the roughly 900 state laws held to be in conflict with the federal Constitution since 1789, about 800 were overturned after 1870. In one decade alone—the 1880s—5 federal and 48 state laws were declared unconstitutional.

James Q. Wilson, *American Government: Institutions and Policies* 83 (Heath, 3d ed 1986).

[8] See, for France, Leon Duguit, *Law in the Modern State* 32-67 (Allen & Unwin, 1919) (translated by Frida and Harold Laski); and for England, A.V. Dicey, *Lectures on the Relation Between Law & Public Opinion in England During the Nineteenth Century* 259-302 (Macmillan, 1914). See generally Alexander Alvarez, *Dominant Legal Influences of the Second Half of the Century*, in *The Progress of Continental Law in the Nineteenth Century*, 11 Continental Legal Hist Series 31, 52-56 (Little, Brown, 1918).

[9] For a concise survey of the development of judicial review, see Louis Favoreu, *American and European Models of Constitutional Justice*, in David S. Clark, ed, *Comparative and Private International Law: Essays in Honor of John Henry Merryman* 105 (Duncker & Humbolt, 1990).

[10] For a discussion of why the American model was widely regarded as unsuitable for transplant, see id at 106-11, and Mauro Cappelletti, *Judicial Review in the Contemporary World* 53-66 (Bobbs-Merrill, 1971).

tutional tribunal only by other courts *sua sponte*, or by political authorities, but not by private litigants.[11]

Even among the handful of countries that have adopted a form of the "American model" of judicial review—such as Canada, Japan, and the Republic of Ireland—the United States remains unique. For in those nations, neither the supreme courts nor the lower courts thus far have exercised their powers of judicial review with such frequency and boldness as their American counterparts have exercised at both the state and federal levels. Indeed, to foreigners, the recent burgeoning of state court constitutionalism and the innovative use of injunctions by federal district courts beginning in the 1960s are two of the most remarkable features of the American legal system. Even if judicial activism in the Supreme Court has subsided somewhat in recent years,[12] the relative readiness of American judges at all levels of jurisdiction to deploy their powers of judicial review in the service of a variety of social aims has made the United States the model of a particularly adventurous form of judicial rights protection.

B. What Counts as a Right?

A renowned European legal historian recently compiled a list he described as representing the "basic inventory" of rights that have been accepted by "most western countries" at the present time.[13] The list includes, first and foremost; human dignity; then personal freedom; fair procedures to protect against arbitrary governmental action; active political rights (especially the right to vote); equality before the law; and society's responsibility for the social and economic conditions of its members.[14] An American reader of this list is apt to be struck both by the omission of property rights, and by the inclusion of affirmative welfare obligations. Yet the list cannot be faulted as description of the law on the books of "most western countries." Welfare rights (or responsibili-

---

[11] Favoreu, *American and European Models* at 112-13 (cited in note 9). But Germany is an exception. There the bulk of the caseload of the Constitutional Court consists of constitutional complaints by private citizens. Kommers, *Constitutional Jurisprudence* at 32-33 (cited in note 4).

[12] I use the word "somewhat" advisedly. See, for example, *Missouri v Jenkins*, 110 S Ct 1651 (1990), in which the Supreme Court in dicta authorized a lower federal court, as part of a desegregation plan, to direct a local school district to levy taxes for capital improvements to schools, even without the normal requirement that the voters approve.

[13] Franz Wieacker, *Foundations of European Legal Culture*, 37 Am J Comp L 1, 29 (1989).

[14] Id.

ties) have become a staple feature of post-war international declarations[15] and have been accorded a place beside traditional political and civil liberties in the national constitutions of most liberal democracies.[16] It is the eighteenth-century American Constitution that, with the passage of time, has become anomalous in this respect.

As Gerhard Casper has pointed out, these differences regarding the rights that are accorded constitutional status in various countries are not merely a function of the age of the documents establishing those rights. To a great extent, the differences are legal manifestations of divergent, and deeply rooted, cultural attitudes toward the state and its functions.[17] Historically, even eighteenth- and nineteenth-century continental European constitutions and codes acknowledged state obligations to provide food, work, and financial aid to persons in need.[18] And continental Europeans today, whether of the right or the left, are much more

---

[15] See, for example, the *United Nations Universal Declaration of Human Rights*, adopted by the General Assembly on December 10, 1948:

> *Article 22*
>
> Everyone, as a member of society, has the right to social security and is entitled to realization, through national effort and international cooperation and in accordance with the organization and resources of each State, of the economic, social, and cultural rights indispensable for his dignity and the free development of his personality.
>
> *Article 25*
>
> Everyone has the right to a standard of living adequate for the health and well-being of himself and his family, including food, clothing, housing and medical care and necessary social services, and the right to security in the event of unemployment, sickness, disability, widowhood, old age or other lack of livelihood in circumstances beyond his control.

The *United Nations Covenant on Economic, Social and Cultural Rights* was opened for signature in December 1966 and came into force a decade later after being ratified by nearly ninety countries, but not, so far, by the United States. The United States did, however, sign the *Universal Declaration* and the *Helsinki Final Act of 1975* (which like the *Universal Declaration* calls for a nonbinding commitment to stated human rights). See generally Richard B. Lillich, *United States Ratification of the United Nations Covenants*, 20 Ga J Intl & Comp L 279 (1990); Louis B. Sohn, *United States Attitudes Toward Ratification of Human Rights Instruments*, 20 Ga J Intl & Comp L 255 (1990).

[16] The formulations vary from the bare recitation in the German Basic Law of 1949 that the Federal Republic of Germany is a "social" state (Article 20), to detailed lists of specific social and economic rights such as those contained in the constitutions of France, Italy, Japan, Spain, and the Nordic countries.

[17] Gerhard Casper, *Changing Concepts of Constitutionalism: 18th to 20th Century*, 1989 S Ct Rev 311, 318-19 (the Continental concept of the "state" is closer to the Anglo-American notion of the "welfare state" or the "administrative state"). See also Leonard Krieger, *The German Idea of Freedom: History of a Political Tradition* (Beacon, 1957).

[18] See Casper, 1989 S Ct Rev at 319-21 (cited in note 17). Early constitutions used the language of obligation rather than of rights: for example, "It is incumbent on the authorities of the State to create conditions which make it possible for every person who is able to work to earn his living by his work." Norwegian Constitution of 1814, § 110, reprinted in Gisbert

likely than Americans to assume that governments have affirmative duties actively to promote the well-being of their citizens.[19] The leading European conservative parties, for example, accept the subsidization of child-raising families, and the funding of health, employment, and old age insurance at levels most Americans find scarcely credible.[20] By contrast, it is almost obligatory for American politicians of both the right and the left to profess mistrust of government.

These divergent attitudes toward the state have found constitutional expression in what are sometimes called "negative" and "positive" rights. The American Bill of Rights is frequently described as a charter of "negative" liberties, protecting certain areas of individual freedom from state interference.[21] Judge Posner has succinctly stated the position: "The men who wrote the Bill of Rights were not concerned that the federal government might do too little for the people, but that it might do too much to them."[22] The Supreme Court, while willing to accord procedural due process protection to statutory welfare entitlements, has consistently declined to recognize constitutional welfare rights.[23] Chief Justice Rehnquist's opinion in *DeShaney v Winnebago County Department of Social Services* reaffirmed that the Due Process Clause of the Fourteenth Amendment was "a limitation on the State's power to act, not . . . a guarantee of certain minimal levels of safety and security."[24]

These statements contrast markedly with the attitudes of the post-World War II European constitution-makers who supple-

---

H. Flanz, *Norway*, in Albert P. Blaustein and Gisbert H. Flanz, eds, 13 *Constitutions of the Countries of the World* 8 (Oceana, 1976).

[19] "[The state achieves legitimacy] not so much through its constitution as through the active, welfare-providing administration." Casper, 1989 S Ct Rev at 325 & n 69 (cited in note 17) (quoting a treatise by a former constitutional law professor now serving on the German Constitutional Court).

[20] See William Pfaff, *Barbarian Sentiments: How the American Century Ends* 25 (Hill & Wang, 1989).

[21] See David P. Currie, *Positive and Negative Constitutional Rights*, 53 U Chi L Rev 864 (1986), which includes discussion of instances in which the U.S. Supreme Court has found "duties that can in some sense be described as positive" in negatively phrased provisions of the Constitution. Id at 872-80.

[22] *Jackson v City of Joliet*, 715 F2d 1200, 1203 (7th Cir 1983).

[23] See, for example, *Lindsey v Normet*, 405 US 56, 74 (1972) (no constitutional right to housing); *San Antonio Independent School District v Rodriguez*, 411 US 1, 30-31 (1973) (no constitutional right to education). The Court in this period did, however, extend procedural due process protection to certain forms of "new property." See, for example, *Goldberg v Kelly*, 397 US 254 (1970) (welfare entitlements); *Mathews v Eldridge*, 424 US 319 (1976) (social security disability benefits).

[24] 489 US 189, 195 (1989).

mented traditional negative liberties with certain affirmative social and economic rights or obligations. The idea of government underlying the "positive rights" in European constitutions has a complex history. In part, it represents a transposition to the modern state of the feudal notion that an overlord owed certain protection to his dependents in exchange for their service and loyalty. More proximately, it reflects the programs of the major European political parties—one large group animated by Christian social thought, and another by socialist or social democratic principles. As Casper has observed, it was only natural that peoples accustomed to the notion of a state with affirmative responsibilities would carry that idea forward when they added bills of rights to their constitutions.[25]

C. International Human Rights

In view of the long-standing American rights tradition, and the recent history of expansive judicial protection of a broad spectrum of individual and minority rights, the third aspect of American distinctiveness may at first glance seem puzzling. I refer to the dubious distinction of the United States as the only liberal democracy that has not ratified a number of important human rights instruments, notably the two United Nations Covenants on Civil and Political Rights, and on Economic, Social and Cultural Rights.[26] This reticence, no doubt, is due in large part to our prudent unwillingness to submit to the jurisdiction of international organizations dominated by critics of the United States. But, particularly where economic and social rights are concerned, our reluctance is also attributable to our prevailing ideas about which sorts of needs, goods, interests, and values should be characterized as fundamental rights. Another likely reason is that the American civil litigation system is not well-equipped to handle the potential consequences of characterizing a new set of interests as fundamental rights.[27]

II. Welfare Rights and Welfare States

The reaction of many Americans to the foregoing contrasts might be that we have little to learn from other nations about wel-

---

[25] Casper, 1989 S Ct Rev at 331 (cited in note 17).

[26] Alfred de Zayas, *The Potential for the United States Joining the Covenant Family*, 20 Ga J Intl & Comp L 299 (1990); Lillich, 20 Ga J Intl & Comp L 279 (cited in note 15).

[27] See notes 50-51 and accompanying text.

fare, and even less about rights. Other Americans, especially reformers who do not regard this American distinctiveness as a badge of honor, might be drawn in the opposite direction, toward viewing the rights or welfare arrangements in other countries as promising models for the United States to follow. Such reform-minded persons might ask: How have constitutional welfare rights worked out in practice? Do the "experiments" of other nations shed any light on what might have happened here had the Supreme Court in the late 1960s and early 1970s found a basis for welfare rights in the Fourteenth Amendment?[28] Though I will conclude that those questions lead almost to a dead end, it is instructive to examine why they do not open an especially fruitful line of inquiry.

As it happens, the contrast between the means of implementation of the American welfare system and other welfarist systems is less sharp than it initially appears. Though many countries have included welfare rights or obligations in their constitutions, no democratic country has placed social and economic rights on precisely the same legal footing as the familiar civil and political liberties. In most cases, the drafters have formulated the former somewhat differently than the latter.[29] In some countries, for example, the constitutional welfare language is so cryptic as to be meaningless without extensive legislative specification.[30] More commonly, the constitutions do specifically enumerate various social and economic rights, but present them merely as aspirational political principles or goals to guide the organs of government as they carry out their respective functions. For example, the Swedish Instrument of Government, in a section entitled "The Basic Principles of the Constitution," provides:

> Art. 2 . . . . The personal, economic and cultural welfare of the individual shall be fundamental aims of the activities of the

---

[28] See, for example, Frank I. Michelman, *The Supreme Court 1968 Term—Foreword: On Protecting the Poor Through the Fourteenth Amendment*, 83 Harv L Rev 7 (1969).

[29] "[T]here are two categories of fundamental rights: immutable and absolute rights that exist whatever the epoch or the reigning ideology; and other rights, known as economic and social rights, that 'carry a certain coefficient of contingency and relativity' and whose recognition is a function of the state of society and its evolution." Favoreu, *La Protection des Droits Economiques* at 701 (cited in note 5).

[30] For example, the German republic is a "social" state. German Basic Law of 1949, Art 20. The treaty of German reunification, however, obliges the legislature to consider adding a list of affirmative "goals of the state" to the traditional political and civil rights presently enumerated in the Basic Law. Fred L. Morrison, *Constitutional Mergers and Acquisitions: The Federal Republic of Germany*, 8 Const Comm 65, 70 (1991).

> community. In particular, it shall be incumbent on the community to secure the right to work, to housing and to education and to promote social care and security as well as a favorable living environment.[31]

Continental lawyers call such rights "programmatic" to emphasize that they are not directly enforceable individual rights, but await implementation through legislative or executive action, and through budgetary appropriations. Programmatic rights figure prominently in the constitutions of the Nordic countries, as well as in the French, Greek, Italian and Spanish constitutions.

The most interesting case in some ways is Japan, which accepted the American model of judicial review in 1947. In Japan, the catalog of constitutional rights (thanks to the New Dealers in the post-war occupational government) includes much of Franklin Roosevelt's "Second Bill of Rights,"[32] some of which are set forth in terms that are not, on their face, programmatic.[33] There is a right to decent minimum subsistence in Article 25, a right to receive an education in Article 26, and a right to work in Article 27.[34] In the drafting process, Article 25 was changed from a purely

---

[31] Gisbert H. Flanz, *Sweden*, in Blaustein and Flanz, eds, 17 *Constitutions* at 9-11 (cited in note 18).

[32] The "Second Bill of Rights," which Roosevelt urged in his 1944 State of the Union message, included the following:

> The right to a useful and remunerative job in the industries or shops or farms or mines of the Nation;
>
> The right to earn enough to provide adequate food and clothing and recreation;
>
> The right of every family to a decent home;
>
> The right to adequate medical care and the opportunity to achieve and enjoy good health;
>
> The right to adequate protection from the economic fears of old age, sickness, accident, and unemployment;
>
> The right to a good education.

See Cass R. Sunstein, *Constitutionalism After the New Deal*, 101 Harv L Rev 421, 423 (1987) (quoting Roosevelt's "Second Bill of Rights"). See also Cass R. Sunstein, *After the Rights Revolution: Reconceiving the Regulatory State* 21-22 (Harvard, 1990).

[33] See Akira Osuka, *Welfare Rights*, 53 L & Contemp Probs 13 (1990). See also Nobushige Ukai, *The Significance of the Reception of American Constitutional Institutions and Ideas in Japan*, in Lawrence Ward Beer, ed, *Constitutionalism in Asia: Asian Views of the American Influence* 114-27 (California, 1979).

[34] Property as such is not among the rights protected. It supposedly was excluded in order to conform the Japanese procedural guarantees to the American Due Process Clause as it stood *de facto* after the U.S. Supreme Court accepted "the necessity of direct state intervention in social and economic processes." Osuka, 53 L & Contemp Probs at 15-16 (cited in note 33). According to Osuka, the Japanese Constitution "substantially incorporate[d] the fruits of the New Deal." Id at 16. The Japanese Constitution of 1947 is set forth in Hiroshi Itoh and Lawrence Ward Beer, eds, *The Constitutional Case Law of Japan: Selected Supreme Court Decisions, 1961-70* 256-69 (Washington, 1978).

programmatic provision ("In all spheres of life, the State shall use its endeavors for the promotion and extension of social welfare and security, and of public health"), to a proclamation beginning with unvarnished American-style rights language ("All people shall have the right to maintain the minimum standards of wholesome and cultured living.").[35]

The adoption of the 1947 Constitution was quickly followed, however, by a Japanese Supreme Court decision holding that the right to a minimum standard of decent living in Article 25 was programmatic.[36] The government's constitutional welfare obligations, according to that decision, "must, in the main, be carried out by the enactment and enforcement of social legislation . . . . [The] state does not bear such an obligation concretely and materially toward the people as individuals."[37] In the years that followed, the Japanese Supreme Court has maintained the view that the welfare rights in the Constitution are not judicially enforceable individual rights. In a leading case, *Asahi v Japan*, decided in 1967, the Court held:

> [Article 25(1)] merely proclaims that it is the duty of the state to administer national policy in such a manner as to enable all the people to enjoy at least the minimum standards of wholesome and cultured living, and it does not grant the people as individuals any concrete rights. A concrete right is secured only through the provisions of the Livelihood Protection Law enacted to realize the objectives prescribed in the provisions of the Constitution.[38]

The *Asahi* decision went on to say that government officials would have to determine the minimum standard of living, subject to review for excess or abuse of power.[39] In Japan, then, as in the countries where constitutional welfare rights are explicitly programmatic, and as in countries like our own without any constitutional

---

[35] The original programmatic draft proposal was retained as Article 25(2), preceded by the right to a minimum standard of living in Article 25(1). Osuka, 53 L & Contemp Probs at 15 (cited in note 33).

[36] Id at 17.

[37] Id at 21.

[38] *Asahi v Japan*, translated and reprinted in Itoh and Beer, eds, *The Constitutional Case Law of Japan* 130, 134 (cited in note 34) (citation omitted).

[39] Id at 135.

welfare rights at all, the welfare state has been constructed through ordinary political processes.[40]

At this point, we might wonder whether the formal differences between the United States and other welfare states have any significance at all. After all, we too have a "program"—the New Deal statutes of the 1930s and 1940s, supplemented by the Great Society statutes of the 1960s—the cornerstones of our welfare state. Specifically, we have both aspiration and implementation in the Social Security Act of 1935, whose preamble declares that the statute is:

> [t]o provide for the general welfare by establishing a system of Federal old-age benefits, and by enabling the several States to make more adequate provision for aged persons, blind persons, dependent and crippled children, maternal and child welfare, public health, and the administration of their unemployment compensation laws . . . .[41]

Similarly, the Housing Act of 1949 calls for "the realization as soon as feasible of the goal of a decent home and a suitable living environment for every American family . . . ."[42]

Should we conclude, then, that the provisions of modern constitutions which commit the state to affirmatively protecting certain economic and social rights have little or no practical consequence? That conclusion seems too strong, if only because such rights at least endow statutes implementing the constitutional "program" with a strong presumption of constitutionality.[43] Moreover, the constitutional status of social and economic rights seems likely to have synergistically reinforced welfare commitments by influencing the terms, the categories, and the tone of public, judicial, and legislative deliberation about rights and welfare.[44] In

---

[40] Shortly after adopting the 1947 Constitution, Japan supplemented its pre-war social legislation with a series of important statutes in the areas of unemployment relief, social security, and child welfare. Osuka, 53 L & Contemp Probs at 16 n 5 (cited in note 33).

[41] Preamble, Social Security Act, 49 Stat 620 (1935), codified at 42 USC §§ 301 et seq (1988).

[42] Housing Act of 1949, 63 Stat 413 (1949), codified at 42 USC §§ 1441 et seq (1988).

[43] See Osuka, 53 L & Contemp Probs at 17-18 (cited in note 33).

[44] For an example of how the constitutional principle of the social welfare state has affected the interpretation of the equality principle in Germany, see the German Constitutional Court decision which held that medical schools could not impose numerical limits on admissions unless they had class size restraints. Numerus Clausus *Case I*, 33 BVerfGE 303 (1972), excerpted in Kommers, *Constitutional Jurisprudence* at 295-302 (cited in note 4). The Court explicitly stated,

> Any constitutional obligation [of the legislature] that may exist does not include the duty to supply a desired place of education at any time to any applicant.

countries with an already well-established welfare tradition, constitutional welfare commitments may well have strengthened that tradition, just as our Bill of Rights both emerged from and buttressed the Anglo-American rights tradition.

Nevertheless, there does not appear to be any strict correlation between the strength of constitutional welfare language and the generosity of welfare states, as measured by the proportion of national expenditures devoted to health, housing, social security, and social assistance.[45] For example, the United Kingdom, with no constitutional welfare rights, devotes proportionately more of its resources to social expenditures than its richer "neighbor" Denmark, where rights to work, education, and social assistance are constitutionally guaranteed. And analogous social expenditures consume considerably more of the budget of the Federal Republic of Germany, whose constitution merely announces that it is a "social" state, than they do in Sweden or Italy, whose constitutions spell out welfare rights in some detail.[46]

If there is a relationship between the constitutional status of welfare rights and the type and strength of a society's welfare commitment, it is only a loose relationship of consanguinity, with both

---

Id at 300 (bracketed text in excerpt). Of the constitutional right to education, the Court also said,

> [We] need not decide whether . . . an individual citizen can use this constitutional mandate as the basis for an enforceable claim [against the state] to create opportunities for higher study.

Id (bracketed text in excerpt).

[45] Percentages of central government expenditure devoted in 1988 to health, housing, social security, and welfare in selected countries with "high-income economies" are as follows:

Federal Republic of Germany	67.6%
Sweden	55.3
Norway	46.8
Italy	45.8
United Kingdom	44.5
United States	44.0
Canada	43.2
Ireland	42.7
Denmark	42.4

World Development Report 1990 198-99, Table 11 (Central Government Expenditure) (Oxford, 1990).

[46] Id. One cannot fit the United States readily into such comparisons because of the unique structure of our welfare state. But sophisticated analyses consistently rate us poorly, especially in assisting child-raising families. See Alfred J. Kahn and Sheila B. Kamerman, *Income Transfers for Families with Children: An Eight-Country Study* 182-95 (Temple, 1983); Samuel H. Preston, *Children and the Elderly in the U.S.*, 251 Scientific Amer 44 (Dec 1984); Timothy M. Smeeding and Barbara Boyd Torrey, *Poor Children in Rich Countries*, 242 Science 873 (Nov 1988).

the constitution and the welfare system influenced by such factors as the homogeneity or diversity of the population; the degree to which mistrust of government has figured in the country's political history; the vitality of political parties; the health of the legislative process; and the intensity of individualism in the culture. Such speculation leads only to the sort of conclusions that make sociology so unsatisfying to many people. It is difficult to become excited about the idea that a host of mutually conditioning factors, of which the constitutional status of welfare rights may be both cause and consequence, determine in numerous ways the shape of a given country's welfare state: its basic commitments, the priorities among those commitments, the spirit in which it is administered, the degree of support and approval it wins from taxpayers, and the extent to which it disables or empowers those who resort to it.

III. What If . . . ?

Still, a reform-minded American might consider the inconclusiveness of the foregoing analysis a source of encouragement. If the experience of other liberal democracies is any guide, the reformer might contend, according constitutional status to social and economic rights at least does not seem to cause any harm. At the margins, it may well exert a benign influence on the legislative process and on public deliberation by broadening the range of officially recognized social concerns, heightening their visibility, and underscoring their legitimacy. What a pity, the argument would go, that we have not bolstered the legal status of social and economic rights, either by recognizing them in our Constitution, as proposed to the Supreme Court in the 1960s and 1970s, or by ratifying the United Nations Covenant on Social, Economic and Cultural Rights, as the Carter administration advocated in the 1970s.

It would be risky, in my view, however, to draw those inferences from the foreign experience, for reasons that reside, not in the foreign experience, but in distinctive American attitudes toward rights. Americans, for better or worse, take rights very seriously. It is not just the term, but the very idea of "programmatic" rights that is unfamiliar and uncongenial to us. It is thus almost inconceivable that constitutional welfare rights, had they appeared in the United States, would have been regarded by the public or treated by the legal community as purely aspirational. An American, hearing of a "right" that merely represents a goal or ideal, is apt to react as Mark Twain did when he learned that a preacher was condemning the Devil without giving the Devil the opportunity to confront the witnesses against him. "[It] is irregular," he said. "It is un-English; it is un-American; it is *French*."[47] Most Americans, like Holmes and Llewellyn, believe that a right-holder should be able to call upon the courts to "smite" anyone who interferes with that right.[48] Furthermore, we take for granted that behind the courts' orders to respect that right are sheriffs, marshals, and the National Guard, if necessary.

As soon as we begin to imagine constitutional welfare rights that are other than programmatic, however, we start down a road that no other democratic country has travelled. That does not mean that we cannot make an educated guess about what consequences would be likely to follow if we made such a trip: recent history suggests that the most likely consequence of according constitutional status to social and economic rights would be something that has not occurred in the other liberal democracies—namely, a great increase in federal litigation.[49]

The crucial question for this symposium about that potential increase in federal litigation—a question whose answer is far from clear—is how private damage actions would affect the structure and performance of the welfare state. Some argue that such litigation would prod government agencies into action, that it would make them more responsive to the needs of the citizens. But it is at least equally plausible that the costs of defending such litigation, plus the occasional high damage award in Section 1983 actions, would prod financially strapped local providers in the other direction, toward cutting back services or eliminating some programs altogether. Unfortunately, there is little empirical data to evaluate the utility of private damage actions in promoting improved social services.

Still, comparing the United States to other countries does illuminate the problem. It demonstrates that we Americans place an unusual degree of reliance on our tort system (both ordinary personal injury litigation and constitutional tort actions) to perform certain social tasks that other advanced industrial nations handle with a more diversified range of techniques—for example, direct

---

[47] Mark Twain, *Concerning the Jews*, in 22 *The Writings of Mark Twain: Literary Essays* 263, 265 (Harper & Brothers, 1899).

[48] Oliver Wendell Holmes, Jr., *The Path of the Law*, 10 Harv L Rev 457, 460-61 (1897); Karl Llewellyn, *The Bramble Bush* 85 (Oceana, 1960).

[49] For example, since the 1960s, Section 1983 has been the second most heavily litigated section of the United States Code. Peter H. Schuck, *Suing Government: Citizen Remedies for Official Wrongs* 199 (Yale, 1983).

health and safety regulation and social insurance.[50] That reliance, in turn, suggests some further questions: Is our tort system well-suited for all the jobs we presently ask it to do? Do our substantive tort law and our civil litigation system adequately assure timely, fair, and cost-efficient disposition of legitimate claims, while effectively discouraging frivolous ones? If a major reason for court-centered reform efforts in the United States has been "legislative paralysis,"[51] can American legislatures ever be induced to take an active role in improving public services in the areas of health, education, and welfare?

IV. The Utility of Cross-National Comparisons

It may seem to follow from the discussion thus far that, contrary to what I asserted at the outset, Americans have little to gain from consulting other nations' experiences with rights and welfare. Certainly anyone who expects comparative studies to yield specific models for domestic law reform[52] is bound to be disappointed, for it is fairly clear that no other country has blazed a trail for the United States to follow. Nevertheless, the experiences of other countries may help us to find our own path by heightening our awareness of indigenous resources that we are inclined to overlook or underrate, because, as Braudel put it, we know them too well.

Beginning in the mid-1970s, economics became a constraint for all advanced welfare states. Even the Nordic countries (whose citizens are as proud of their famous cradle-to-grave welfare systems as we are of our Bill of Rights) began to sense that they had reached the limits of high taxation and direct public sector provision of services. In that climate, policymakers abroad have gazed with interest at our relatively greater capacity for governmental and non-governmental organizations to cooperate in the areas of health, education, and welfare, and at our ability, through our sort of federalism, to innovate and experiment with diverse approaches to stubborn social problems.

In some cases, tentative efforts at imitation have followed. In the area of industrial relations, for example, some countries have begun to experiment with American-style laws encouraging collec-

---

[50] Basil S. Markesinis, *Litigation-Mania in England, Germany and the USA: Are We So Very Different?*, 49 Cambridge L J 233, 243-44 (1990).

[51] Id at 242.

[52] For a critique of the use of comparative law as a source of "models," see Rodolfo Sacco, *Legal Formants: A Dynamic Approach to Comparative Law*, 39 Am J Comp L 1 (1991) (Installment I of II).

tive bargaining rather than the direct state regulation of the terms and conditions of employment that has been traditional in continental Europe.[53] Our innovative labor legislation of the 1930s—which has practically fallen into desuetude in the United States—has been seen in France and Germany as the prototype of "reflexive law" (legal norms that aim at facilitating and structuring private ordering, rather than imposing top-down state regulation).[54] And policymakers abroad have also begun to consider whether some types of social services can be delivered more efficiently and humanely by intermediate associations—churches, unions, community groups, and so on—than by the government. Our voluntary sector, shambles though it may appear to us, is still more vibrant than its counterparts in nations where excessive centralization has nearly extinguished non-governmental initiatives in the areas of health, education, and welfare.[55]

Ironically, these American institutions and experiences are attracting interest abroad just when they are showing the effects of long neglect at home. The United States represents a rare working example, albeit an imperfect one, of what European writers call the principle of "subsidiarity": the notion that no social task should be allocated to a body larger than the smallest one that can effectively do the job.[56] The legal apparatus that promotes and facilitates the subsidiarity principle includes federalism, reflexive legal norms that foster private ordering, and programs that use the mediating structures of civil society—such as churches and workplace associations—to help deliver social services.

These aspects of American law are attracting increased attention because every country in the democratic world is experiencing a tension between the two ideals that are linked together in the deceptively bland title of this symposium—a regime of rights and a welfare state. Every country is grappling with a set of problems that are in a general way similar: how to provide needed social aid without undermining personal responsibility; how to achieve the

---

[53] See Mary Ann Glendon, *French Labor Law Reform 1982-83: The Struggle for Collective Bargaining*, 32 Am J Comp L 449, 485-91 (1984).

[54] "Reflexive law" is an expression used by some legal sociologists to designate an alternative to direct regulation, in which legal norms shape procedures to coordinate interaction among social subsystems, rather than prescribe outcomes. See Gunther Teubner, *Substantive and Reflexive Elements in Modern Law*, 17 L & Society Rev 239, 276 (1983).

[55] For a comparison of non-governmental service organizations in the Netherlands, England, Israel, and the United States, see Ralph M. Kramer, *Voluntary Agencies in the Welfare State* (California, 1981).

[56] Markus Heintzen, *Subsidiaritätsprinzip und Europäische Gemeinschaft*, 46 Juristenzeitung 317 (1991).

optimal mix of markets and central planning in a mixed economy; and how to preserve a just balance among individual freedom, equality, and social solidarity under constantly changing circumstances. The problem of "the Bill of Rights in the Welfare State" is nothing less than the great dilemma of how to hold together the two halves of the divided soul of liberalism—our love of individual liberty and our sense of a community for which we accept a common responsibility.

Below the surface of that dilemma lies a more serious one. Neither a strong commitment to individual and minority rights, nor even a modest welfare commitment like the American one, can long be sustained without the active support of a citizenry that is willing to respect the rights of others; that is prepared to accept some responsibility for the poorest and most vulnerable members of society; and that is prepared to accept responsibility, so far as possible, for themselves and for their dependents. We should make no mistake about the fact that liberal democratic welfare states around the world are now demanding certain kinds of excellence in their citizens to a nearly unprecedented degree. They are asking men and women to practice certain virtues that, even under the best of conditions, are not easy to acquire—respect for the dignity and worth of one's fellow human beings, self-restraint, self-reliance, and compassion.

The questions that seldom get asked, however, are these: Where do such qualities come from? Where do people acquire an internalized willingness to view others with genuine regard for their dignity and concern for their well-being, rather than as objects, means, or obstacles? These qualities do not arise spontaneously in *homo sapiens*. Nor can governments instill them by fear and force. Perhaps there are alternative seedbeds of civic virtue besides families, neighborhoods, religious groups, and other communities of memory and mutual aid. If there are, however, history provides scant evidence of them. It is hard to avoid the conclusion that both our welfare state and our experiment in democratic government rest upon habits and practices formed within fragile social structures—structures being asked to bear great weight just when they are not in peak condition. The question then becomes: What, if anything, can the government do to create and maintain (or at least to avoid undermining or destroying) social conditions that foster the peculiar combination of qualities required to sustain our commitments to the rule of law, individual freedom, and a compassionate welfare state?

Conclusion

In a large, heterogeneous nation such as the United States, this question about the underpinnings of civic virtue is particularly urgent. It has been constantly repeated since Tocqueville said in the 1830s that America was especially well-endowed with moral and cultural resources—with vital local governments, and with a variety of associations that stood between citizens and the state.[57] As with our natural resources, however, we have taken our social resources for granted, consuming inherited capital at a faster rate than we are replenishing it. Indeed, like an athlete who develops the muscles in his upper body but lets his legs grow weak, we have nurtured our strong rights tradition while neglecting the social foundation upon which that tradition rests.

We Americans, with our great emphasis in recent years on certain personal and civil rights, have too easily overlooked the fact that all rights depend on conserving the social resources that induce people to accept and respect the rights of others. Perhaps it is time, therefore, to take a fresh look at our constitutional framework, and to recall not only that the Bill of Rights is part of a larger constitutional structure, but that its own structure includes more than a catalog of negatively formulated political and civil liberties. As Akhil Reed Amar has pointed out, scholars, litigators, and judges who concentrated single-mindedly in the 1960s and 1970s on judicial protection of individual and minority rights permitted other important parts of our constitutional tradition to fall into obscurity.[58] As it happens, those parts of the tradition that have been in the shadows—federalism, the legislative branch, and the ideal of government by the people—have an important bearing on maintaining the social capital upon which all rights ultimately depend.

And so, by a long and circuitous route, a cross-national approach to rights and the welfare state points back toward the American Constitution and toward the "Madisonian understanding that individual liberty and strong local institutions need not be at cross-purposes with one another."[59] If America's endangered social environments do indeed hold the key to maintaining simultaneously a liberal regime of rights and a compassionate welfare state, then we must start thinking about how both rights and welfare, as

---

[57] Alexis de Tocqueville, *Democracy in America* 126-33 (Oxford, 1953).

[58] Akhil Reed Amar, *The Bill of Rights as a Constitution*, 100 Yale L J 1131, 1133-37 (1991).

[59] Id at 1136.

currently conceived, affect those social environments. Reflecting upon our own tradition, moreover, should give us pause before indulging the disdain for politics that underlies so much current thinking about legal and social policy. One of the most important lessons of 1789 the world learned anew in 1989: that politics is not only a way to advance self-interest, but to transcend it. That transformative potential of the art through which we order our lives in the polity is our best hope for living up to our rights ideals and our welfare aspirations in the coming years.

[7]

THE CONSTITUTION OF THE PROCEDURAL REPUBLIC: LIBERAL RIGHTS AND CIVIC VIRTUES

*Michael J. Sandel**

PROFESSOR FLEMING: Good evening. I'm Professor Jim Fleming. On behalf of Dean John Feerick, along with Associate Dean Mike Martin and Professor Dan Capra, who are President and Secretary-Treasurer of the Fordham Chapter of The Order of the Coif, I would like to welcome you to The Order of the Coif Annual Lecture.

Our speaker is Michael J. Sandel, Professor of Government at Harvard University. His lecture is entitled "The Constitution of the Procedural Republic: Liberal Rights and Civic Virtues."

Let me say a few words about The Order of the Coif Annual Lecture Series. The Order of the Coif is an honorary scholastic society. Pursuant to its historic purpose of promoting excellence in legal scholarship, it sponsors a national lecture series designed to afford member schools additional opportunities to present lectures by outstanding speakers. The goals of the program are to encourage legal scholarship, to advance the body of legal knowledge, and to promote significant dialogue upon legal issues among scholars, members of the bench and bar, and law students. The brochure for this lecture contains a statement about the purposes of both The Order and the Annual Lecture Series.

Fordham University School of Law was awarded a chapter in The Order of the Coif in 1994, and it is pleased to present The Order of the Coif Annual Lecture by Professor Michael Sandel.

It is a privilege and a pleasure for me to introduce Professor Sandel. He is widely regarded as one of America's most important and provocative political and constitutional theorists and as a leading figure in the revival, or reinvigoration, of the civic republican strand of our political and constitutional tradition.

Professor Sandel is the author, most recently, of *Democracy's Discontent: America in Search of a Public Philosophy*, which has already

* This lecture draws upon my book *Democracy's Discontent: America in Search of a Public Philosophy* (1996). I would like to thank The Order of the Coif for sponsoring the lecture, and Dean John Feerick and the faculty of the Fordham University School of Law for their warm hospitality and probing questions. I am especially grateful to Professor James E. Fleming for his skillful arrangements and for leading the stimulating discussion that preceded and followed the lecture.

been highly acclaimed as a major work in countless reviews that span the political and constitutional spectrum. His earlier book, *Liberalism and the Limits of Justice*, is one of the most influential critiques of rights-based liberal theories associated with John Rawls and Ronald Dworkin. He is also a public philosopher of sorts, who regularly comments on American political and constitutional issues as a contributing columnist to the *New Republic*.

Finally, Professor Sandel is known as an outstanding speaker, typically drawing some 800 students in his undergraduate course at Harvard entitled "Justice." While I was a law student, I had the honor of serving as a teaching fellow in that great course and benefitted immeasurably from that experience.

Now, I give you Michael Sandel.

PROFESSOR SANDEL: Thank you very much for those very generous words of introduction from my friend, Professor Jim Fleming, and thank you all for having me. It's an honor to be here and an honor to speak under the auspices of The Order of the Coif.

My subject today is "The Constitution of the Procedural Republic." What I mean by the "procedural republic" is a certain way of thinking about politics and law. It describes a public philosophy—a vision of citizenship and freedom that is embodied in our legal and political practices.

What I'd like to argue is that the procedural republic is animated by a powerful and attractive vision of citizenship and freedom; and yet, it is flawed. Despite the attraction of the public philosophy of procedural liberalism, it gives up too much. It gives up on an older, more demanding understanding of citizenship and freedom connected with a rival tradition of political thought, a competing public philosophy. That competing public philosophy might be described as the civic, or the republican, tradition.

I. Liberal and Republican Freedom

Let me begin, before turning to our present political and constitutional circumstance, by saying something about these two traditions of thought and of practice. Let me first describe the public philosophy that informs contemporary political and constitutional discourse: the public philosophy of procedural liberalism. Why is it attractive, and why has it come to be the predominant public philosophy of our day?

According to procedural liberalism, to be free is to have the right to pursue my own values, interests, and ends, my own vision of the good life, whatever it may be, so long as I respect other people's right to do the same. According to the public philosophy of procedural liberalism, government shouldn't try to form in its citizens any particular purposes or ends, any particular virtues. Instead, government should be neutral among competing moral and religious outlooks.

Procedural liberalism worries about the danger of coercion; it worries about the danger of imposing on people values they may not share. That is why it insists that the Constitution must defend a framework of rights that is neutral among ends, neutral among the competing moral and religious convictions its citizens espouse.

The appeal of procedural liberalism is clear. We live, after all, in a pluralistic society. We know that people disagree on a great many moral and religious questions. So isn't it reasonable to try to bracket or set aside those moral and religious disagreements, those competing visions of the good life, when designing the basic structure of rights and duties that are enforced by law?

What is the rival picture? What is the more demanding notion of citizenship and freedom that procedural liberalism rejects? According to the civic—or republican—tradition, to be free isn't just to choose one's own ends or values or conception of the good life. To be free, according to the republican tradition, is to participate in self-rule, to share in self-government.

How is this conception opposed to procedural liberalism? In the following way: the republican tradition says that to share in self-rule, to participate in shaping the forces that govern the collective destiny, requires certain qualities of character, certain habits and dispositions. It requires that citizens possess or come to acquire certain civic virtues. What civic virtues? Adherents of the republican tradition have advocated a wide range of civic virtues, but among them, typically, are a knowledge of public affairs and a capacity to deliberate about the common good. The republican tradition emphasizes that this isn't the kind of skill that can be learned from books or lectures. It is the kind of skill that requires a certain moral disposition—a sense of belonging, a sense of identification with the community whose fate is at stake. The civic virtues typically include a sense of belonging that orients people away from sole concern with their individual interests toward the common good.

It may now be clear how there can arise a tension between these two understandings of freedom. For on the republican conception of freedom as sharing in self-rule, it is not enough to show up at the polls and express my preference once every four years or two years. On the republic conception, civic education matters because everyone has a stake in the moral and civic character of citizens. But that means that government can't be neutral; it means that politics and law can't be neutral with respect to the moral and civic character of its citizens.

The republican tradition accords to politics and to law a formative project. The formative project consists in worrying about the conditions of life—of social and cultural and political and economic life—that shape the virtues, the habits, and dispositions of citizens.

Once politics is accorded, as the republican tradition assigns it, a formative role, then it is possible to see why procedural liberals worry.

It is precisely the formative project that liberals see as containing the danger of coercion. That is partly what animates the liberal resolve to bracket morality and religion and character formation and virtue talk in politics.

I've described two public philosophies, two pictures of what it means to be a free citizen. But how do they bear on our actual political and constitutional life, and how does the embrace of procedural liberalism amount to a certain deflation of American ideals? How does it constitute a giving up on the aspiration to republican freedom?

I'd like to try to answer these questions by looking at some examples drawn from the American political and constitutional experience. What I'd like to suggest is that both of these public philosophies, both understandings of citizenship, have been present throughout the American political and constitutional tradition, but in shifting measure and relative importance.

Roughly speaking, republican understandings predominated earlier in the history of the Republic, from the time of the founding, through much of the 19th century, and into the early years of the 20th century; while the liberal procedural public philosophy, though present from the start, was at first a minor voice. It did not become predominant until the 20th century, especially in the decades since World War II.

I would like to suggest that the procedural understanding of freedom has gradually eclipsed the civic one; I would like also to show that the eclipse of the civic by the procedural understanding represents a loss—a loss of something indispensable to the project of self-government.

II. Procedural Liberalism in Constitutional Law

Consider some examples drawn from constitutional law. The Bill of Rights, which goes back almost to the founding, provides for the rights to freedom of speech and religious liberty. What's interesting, though, is that the interpretation of the rights to free speech and religious liberty, and more recently the interpretation of the right to liberty that has come to include the right to privacy, are products of recent decades. In fact, you can identify a moment that illustrates the shift from the civic to the republican understanding of citizenship if you consider the time when the Supreme Court changed its mind within three years, between 1940 and 1943, in the flag salute cases.

Minersville School District v. Gobitis[1] involved two children of Jehovah's Witnesses who were expelled from public school for refusing to salute the flag. The parents claimed the flag salute violated their religious beliefs. In an opinion by Justice Frankfurter, the Supreme Court upheld the flag salute. Frankfurter invoked the republican tradition, the formative project. He held that states can require the flag

1. 310 U.S. 586 (1940).

salute in order to inculcate in young citizens "the binding tie of cohesive sentiment" on which liberty depends.[2] This was Frankfurter's phrase, a phrase that affirms the formative ambition of the republican tradition.

Three years later, the Supreme Court heard another flag salute case, *West Virginia State Board of Education v. Barnette*,[3] and this time they struck it down. In doing so—and now it was Justice Jackson who wrote for the Court—they struck it down in the name of freedom, but in the name of a different conception of freedom. They didn't announce their shift from a formative to a procedural understanding of freedom. But in retrospect, the shift can clearly be seen.

According to Jackson's opinion, liberty depends not on cultivating virtue, but rather on identifying certain rights and placing them beyond the reach of majorities. Government can't impose on its citizens any particular conception of the good life. He puts it as follows: "If there is any fixed star in our constitutional constellation, it is that no official, high or petty, can prescribe what shall be orthodox in politics, nationalism, religion, or other matters of opinion . . . ."[4] Whenever a judge talks about a "fixed star" or a "fixed point," suspect that he or she is innovating. Jackson was innovating; in fact, his opinion in *Barnette* was a decisive departure. Not only was he overturning an opinion about flag salutes; he was announcing a new conception of liberty, a conception characteristic of the procedural republic: the idea that freedom consists in having certain rights that are beyond the reach of the majority, that it is the role of courts to enforce them, and that courts should interpret those rights according to the ideal of neutrality, an ideal that says no government or state or school board may impose any particular virtues or vision of the good life.

After World War II, shortly after the flag salute cases, in other areas of constitutional law, the Supreme Court began to take up its now-familiar role of protecting individual rights against majorities, against government infringement, in the name of being neutral toward competing conceptions of the good life.

In 1947, for the first time, the Supreme Court declared that government must be neutral toward religion.[5] In subsequent decades it defended this idea of neutrality toward religion in the name of the idea of choosing our religious beliefs for ourselves. Justice Stevens, in a 1985 case, gave articulate expression to the idea of freedom that animates the procedural republic when he said that "religious beliefs worthy of respect are the product of free and voluntary choice by the faithful."[6] Here you have the idea of rights in the name of neutrality,

2. *Id.* at 596.
3. 319 U.S. 624 (1943).
4. *Id.* at 642.
5. Everson v. Board of Educ., 330 U.S. 1, 18 (1947).
6. Wallace v. Jaffree, 472 U.S. 38, 53 (1985).

and neutrality for the sake of letting people choose their beliefs for themselves.

During this same period, from the 1940s to the 1970s, the Supreme Court broadened its protection of free speech and, more important, shifted the justification for free speech. Whereas previously the Court had emphasized the importance of speech to self-government, increasingly, through the 1950s, 1960s, and 1970s, the Court emphasized the importance of the right to free speech for self-expression, choosing and expressing one's own opinions—as one commentator put it, making "the choice of the speech by the self the crucial factor in justifying protection."[7] Here again we have a picture not just of rights, but of rights for the sake of neutrality, and neutrality as a way of respecting choice—choice of ends, values, or beliefs.

Finally, in a series of decisions from the 1960s to the 1980s, the Court comes to enforce, in the name of autonomy and freedom of choice, a right of privacy that prevents government from trying to legislate morality in areas like contraception and abortion.[8] So it is only in the 1940s and 1950s and 1960s that the language of neutrality, autonomy, and choice come to predominate in constitutional law, to inform the theory and practice of constitutional rights.

As I have described it so far, procedural liberalism seems to offer an attractive conception of freedom. After all, hasn't it expanded individual rights to religious liberty, free speech, and privacy, and thereby broadened freedom? Where, then, is the loss? Where is the deflation of ideals? What did we give up as we drifted toward a procedural republic? It's easier to answer this question, to see what we gave up, if we look beyond constitutional law and consider those aspects of political debate that engage more directly the question of how to form civic virtue in citizens.

III. The Political Economy of Citizenship

Consider, for example, debates about the economy: tax policy, trade policy, budget proposals, or regulatory reform. Most of the time, liberals and conservatives alike argue in the name of two values: increasing the general welfare, the size of the gross domestic product; and, to a somewhat lesser extent, worrying about how fairly the fruits of affluence are distributed. These are the two justifications that political figures advance when they argue for one or another economic policy.

But prosperity and fairness are not the only justifications that historically have been offered when Americans have debated economic affairs. There is a third consideration that goes back to Thomas Jefferson and that has faded only recently: What economic arrangements

7. C. Edwin Baker, Human Liberty and Freedom of Speech 256 (1989).
8. Roe v. Wade, 410 U.S. 113 (1973)(abortion); Griswold v. Connecticut, 381 U.S. 479 (1965) (contraception).

are more likely to cultivate in citizens the qualities of character that will equip them for self-government? This might be called the civic strand of economic argument or the political economy of citizenship.

Thomas Jefferson argued against big factories, against America becoming a manufacturing nation. He said we should remain an agrarian and a trading nation. The reason he advanced was not that greater prosperity would result if Americans stayed on the farm and traded with other countries; Jefferson's argument was about virtue. "Those who labor the earth are the chosen people of God," the embodiments of "genuine virtue."[9] Thinking of Manchester and the manufacturing cities of Europe, Jefferson feared that factory workers were bound to become a dependent, propertyless mob, unable to stand on their own two feet, incapable of talking back to government or to exercise independent judgment. They would, in short, lack civic virtue. "Dependence begets subservience and venality, suffocates the germ of virtue, and prepares fit tools for the designs of ambition."[10] Jefferson worried about the way in which economic arrangements shape civic character and civic virtue.

As we all know, Jefferson lost that debate. America became a manufacturing nation, and had already become one even as he advanced this argument. But the civic ideal underlying Jefferson's position persisted and informed American public debate through the 19th century and into the 20th.

Consider next the terms of political discourse in the Progressive era. Progressive reformers worried about the power of big business. By the early 20th century, the economy had become national, but democratic life was still organized locally, in cities and towns. American democracy, still dispersed and decentralized, was overpowered by an economy suddenly national in scope. Progressive reformers sought to ease the gap between the scale of economic life and the terms of political community. They worried about the effect of big business and concentrated economic power on the character of citizens. They feared that it was making American citizens servile and dependent in just the way that Jefferson had predicted a century earlier.

Progressives proposed a number of responses to this predicament. I would like to take a concrete example to bring out the way in which the political economy of the Progressive era differs from our own.

One response was the antitrust movement. Now, antitrust law persists to this day as an influential body of law. Lawyers in the Antitrust Division of the Department of Justice spend a lot of time bringing antitrust cases. What's striking is how different the rationale is for

9. Thomas Jefferson, Notes on the State of Virginia (1787) *reprinted in* Jefferson Writings 290-91 (Merrill D. Peterson ed., 1984).

10. *Id.* at 291.

antitrust law today from what it was when the Progressive reformers struggled with the power of trusts, monopolies, and big business.

One of the leading Progressive-era advocates of antitrust law was Louis D. Brandeis. Before he was appointed to the Supreme Court by Woodrow Wilson, Brandeis was an activist attorney and progressive reformer. His case against monopolies—he talked about the "curse of bigness"—was not that monopolies drive up consumer prices, and thereby decrease the general welfare; in fact, he didn't care, very much anyhow, about consumer welfare. His argument was a civic argument. He favored antitrust law as a way of reasserting democratic authority, as a way of enabling Americans to be citizens who could participate in self-rule and reach the sources of power. The only way to do that, Brandeis thought, was to break up the monopolies and the trusts so that a decentralized political system could exercise democratic authority over the economy.

Brandeis' argument reflected a long tradition of republican political thought. His was a producer ethic, not a consumer ethic. Consistent with a tradition going back to Jefferson and the Knights of Labor in the Gilded Age, he favored economic conditions that would enable farmers, artisans, small businessmen, and entrepreneurs to be citizens, civic leaders, people whose conditions of work afforded them the independence of mind and judgment to be effective citizens.

Brandeis' outlook contrasts sharply with the consumer-oriented reform movements of our day. Unlike the consumer movement of Ralph Nader, Brandeis was wary of consumers. His emphasis was on conditions of production. Brandeis' support for resale price maintenance illustrates the contrast between his case for antitrust and the contemporary consumer advocates' case for antitrust.

Resale price maintenance was a practice that enabled the manufacturer to prevent retailers from selling a product below a certain price. Consider the example of Gillette razors. If Gillette could fix the retail price of its razor, the price of Gillette razors would be higher than if Wal-Mart or the chain stores could discount them. But there was an advantage in this practice, Brandeis believed, because it would protect the local drug store from the cut-throat competition that the chain stores represented. "Every dealer," he wrote, "every small stationer, every small druggist, every small hardware man," can sell Gillette razors if you allow Gillette to fix the price.[11] Otherwise, the small retailer would be unable to compete with the chain store or the department store, which would monopolize the trade.

Brandeis considered it foolish for consumers to insist nonetheless on lower prices for Gillette razors. The effect would be to force small retailers out of business, leaving the big chains and department stores

11. Michael J. Sandel, Democracy's Discontent: America in Search of Public Philosophy 237-38 n.108 (1996) (quoting Brandeis' testimony before Congress).

to raise the price of Gillette razors. More important, the lower prices on Gillette razors would come at the expense of the political economy of citizenship; it would mean giving up on an economic structure of many small, local businesses that hold communities together and that cultivate not a nation of clerks, but a nation of entrepreneurs and small business people.

Jump ahead to the New Deal. Here we can see a moment of transition in antitrust policy comparable to the one we saw in the flag salute case. In 1938 Franklin Roosevelt appointed a man named Thurmond Arnold to be the head of the Antitrust Division of the Justice Department. Arnold had made a career heaping scorn on Brandeis-type arguments for antitrust. He thought it was a kind of hopeless nostalgia, a kind of old religion, to worry about the curse of bigness. Arnold argued that it was not possible to reverse the age of organization.

To his misfortune, Thurmond Arnold had also ridiculed Senator Borah, a great antitruster, who questioned Arnold during his Senate confirmation hearing. Arnold promised that he would be a vigorous advocate of antitrust prosecution. Senator Borah scratched his head, and he approved the nomination, but he did advise Arnold to revise the chapter in his book on trusts.

Arnold was true to his word. His was the most vigorous period of antitrust enforcement in American history. By the time he left in 1943, he had filed and won more antitrust cases than the Justice Department had initiated in all of its previous history. Wasn't this a great reversal of Arnold's stand against the antitrust tradition? Not really, because Arnold's revival of antitrust law was a revival with a difference: unlike Brandeis and the earlier antitrusters, Arnold didn't try to decentralize the economy for the sake of self-government, but rather to regulate the economy for the sake of lower consumer prices. For Arnold, the purpose of antitrust law was to promote economic efficiency and to keep consumer prices down, not to advance democracy or to cultivate civic virtue or to create a political economy of independent entrepreneurs. Americans should be enlisted to support antitrust enforcement, Arnold insisted, not out of hatred of big business, but out of interest in "the price of pork chops, bread, spectacles, drugs, and plumbing."[12]

So two antitrusters, Brandeis and Thurmond Arnold, both advocated the same policy, but for different reasons. In the change in justification, we see a shift from a political economy of citizenship to a political economy of consumer welfare. And in that shift we can glimpse a shift from the civic idea of freedom to a liberal idea—the liberal procedural idea—of freedom.

Concerned as he was with the welfare of consumers, Arnold gave up, in his antitrust policy, the old formative ambition. He worried

12. Thurman W. Arnold, The Bottlenecks of Business 123 (1940).

solely about productivity and prices. Giving up on the formative ambition is indicative of the shift from the political economy of citizenship to one premised on consumer welfare.

This shift occurred in antitrust policy at just about the same time that the Supreme Court changed its mind in the flag salute cases. Thurmond Arnold left the Justice Department in 1943, which was the very year—history is seldom so tidy—that Justice Jackson gave his famous opinion about the fixed star in our constitutional constellation and about the idea of government being neutral.

But the new public philosophy was also unfolding more broadly in American public life and political debate. The advent of Keynesian fiscal policy in the 1940s, 1950s, and 1960s was another instance of Americans giving up on old debates about the structure of the economy and the civic aspirations those debates reflected. The new political economy took consumer preferences as given, and sought to regulate the economy by manipulating macroeconomic demand.

In 1962, President John F. Kennedy articulated the appeal of moral neutrality implicit in Keynesian economic management. In retrospect, we remember John Kennedy for the great passage in his Inaugural Address, "Ask not what your country can do for you, ask what you can do for your country." That was a ringing expression of the civic ideal and of its demanding notion of citizenship. But in the actual conduct of his domestic policy, and especially of his economic policy, Kennedy articulated the new understanding, the new dispensation.

Here's what he said about modern economic debate in connection with his proposed tax cut of 1962, the high point of confidence in Keynesian fiscal management. "[M]ost of the problems, or at least many of them, that we now face," Kennedy declared, "are technical problems, administrative problems. They are very sophisticated judgments which do not lend themselves to the great sort of passionate movements which have stirred the country so often in the past."[13] "What is at stake in our economic decisions today is not some grand warfare of rival ideologies . . . but the practical management of a modern economy."[14] Kennedy urged the country to face technical problems without ideological preconceptions, to focus on the sophisticated and technical issues involved in keeping a great economic machinery moving ahead.[15]

Kennedy was articulating the received wisdom of the day. By 1962, the standard way of talking about economic policy was a way that abandoned old debates about the structure of the economy, its effect on democratic possibilities, on citizenship, and on the formative pro-

13. John F. Kennedy, Remarks to White House Conference on National Economic Issues (May 21, 1962) *reprinted in* 1962 Pub. Papers 422.

14. John F. Kennedy, Commencement Address at Yale University (June 11, 1962) *reprinted in* 1962 Pub. Papers 473.

15. *Id.*at 475.

ject. The new political economy of prosperity and fairness took consumer preferences as given, and pointed the way to the procedural republic.

IV. Reviving the Civic Project

What would it mean to revive the concern with civic virtue, the formative tradition, in our time? Some fear that it would mean embracing the kind of politics the Moral Majority and the Christian Coalition embrace. After all, they talk about virtue; they have a formative project; they want to legislate morality; they want government to take an interest in the moral character of citizens. Some would say that this demonstrates the danger of any attempt to revive the formative project.

If you look at current debates about welfare, you see this shift among conservatives. In the 1950s and 1960s, what was the conservative complaint against the welfare state? Recall the objections of Barry Goldwater and Milton Friedman to the welfare state: it coerces people; it violates the freedom of the taxpayer; it violates individual choice. That was an argument drawn from procedural liberalism: People should be free to spend their money as they choose, libertarian conservatives maintained; they shouldn't be coerced by the government to give to worthy causes, like school lunches, food stamps, or welfare.

Beginning in the 1980s, however, the conservative argument against welfare changed and began to draw on civic themes. Now conservatives argue that welfare is deplorable not because it violates the freedom of the taxpayer, though they may still think that, but because it breeds dependence, it corrupts the character of the recipient. This is a civic argument, reminiscent of the political economy of citizenship. Conservatives now oppose welfare on the grounds that it corrupts the character of citizens.

What is interesting, however—and this is a point I must make if I'm going to persuade many people in the room—is that the civic tradition, the formative project, is not inherently conservative and should not be regarded as such. In fact, even the argument about welfare that emphasizes its formative consequences and the dependence it induces did not originate with Ronald Reagan or Newt Gingrich or William Bennett.

Consider the following civic argument against welfare. Welfare was perhaps "our greatest domestic failure," because it rendered

> millions of our people slaves to dependency and poverty, waiting on the favor of their fellow citizens to write them checks. Fellowship, community, shared patriotism — these essential values of our civilization do not come from just buying and consuming goods together. They come from a shared sense of individual independence and personal effort.

The solution to poverty, this public figure argued, was not a guaranteed income paid by the government but "dignified employment at decent pay, the kind of employment that lets a man say to his community, to his family, to his country, and most important, to himself, 'I helped to build this country. I am a participant in its great public ventures.'" A guaranteed income "simply cannot provide the sense of self-sufficiency, of participation in the life of the community, that is essential for citizens of a democracy."[16]

Who do you think said that? It was Robert Kennedy shortly before he was assassinated. Robert Kennedy, of all of the politicians in recent decades who have groped to address the discontent that afflicts procedural liberalism, was alive to the civic strand of freedom. He was reviving this older tradition that goes back to Jefferson and to Brandeis, that worries about the social and economic and political conditions that foster effective citizenship. It is interesting that he appealed to blue collar conservatives, to those who had voted for George Wallace in the Indiana primary, and he also appealed to the left wing of the Democratic party.

What has happened, though, since 1968 is that for the most part it has been conservatives who have reached beyond the terms of political discourse made available by procedural liberalism. It is they who have spoken about virtue and about prayer in schools.

There are other precedents. Robert Kennedy isn't the only public figure on the left to invoke republican ideals. If you look back at the civil rights movement, Martin Luther King advanced civic arguments, moral arguments, and, sometimes, religious arguments. His "Letter from a Birmingham Jail,"[17] has all kinds of religious references as well as moral and civic arguments. At the time, there were those who insisted that religion and politics shouldn't mix, that they should be kept separate, that it was dangerous to mix them.

There was one Southern minister at the time who criticized Martin Luther King for bringing religious arguments into politics. This critic claimed that the role of a minister is to save souls, not to engage in politics, not to lobby for civil rights—to save souls. Religion, he maintained, is a private matter. The name of that Southern minister critical of Martin Luther King was Jerry Falwell. He changed his mind by 1980. I think Jerry Falwell was right the second time, after he changed his mind—not right about his politics, but right about the indispensable role of morality and religion in political discourse, right about the indispensability of the formative aspect of democratic life.

16. Robert F. Kennedy, Press Release, Los Angeles (May 19, 1968) *reprinted in* Edwin O. Guthman & C. Richard Allen, RFK: Collected Speeches 385-86 (1993).

17. Martin Luther King, Jr., I Have a Dream: Writings and Speeches That Changed the World 85 (James M. Washington ed., 1992).

So what would it look like to revive under present conditions this older civic ambition? How could it be other than the province of conservatives?

One of the things that conservatives have ignored is the market economy and its effect on virtue and on the habits and dispositions that orient citizens to the common good. The social and cultural conservatives emphasize Hollywood movies and television and sex and violence and rap music. And they are right, in my view, to criticize the coarse and corrupting and vulgar messages that flow from the popular culture. What cultural conservatives, however, often neglect are the formative effects of an unfettered market economy, which, in ways that Brandeis and Jefferson understood, can also undermine the stable communities and sources of moral authority that shape the habits and dispositions of citizenship.

Very little is said in our politics about the growing gap between rich and poor, which is more pronounced than at any time since the 1920s. One of the reasons it is difficult to talk about this inequality, I think, has to do with the narrowness of our political agenda. One argument that is sometimes made—and it hasn't been very effective politically—is that gross inequality is unfair to those at the bottom. That is an argument that can be made within the terms of procedural liberalism. Those at the bottom don't have the chance to choose their life plan, their way of life, their values, like everybody else.

But the civic tradition offers another way of thinking about the gap between rich and poor—not just from the standpoint of the individuals who find themselves at the bottom, and therefore less able to choose their ends, but from the standpoint of a common life. From Aristotle to Rousseau, republicans have worried about too great a gap between rich and poor if it leads to separate ways of life. For if fellow citizens become accustomed to living in separate neighborhoods, shopping in separate stores, taking different forms of transportation, not bumping up against one another in the course of their everyday life, then eventually they will find themselves unable to deliberate about the common good; they won't share enough to be able to think of one another as citizens with mutual obligations.

What we are seeing now is the evacuation of the public sphere. The affluent are able to buy their way out of public transportation and public schools, public institutions, public parks, and retreat to gated communities, or private enclaves. Here is one area in which the older tradition of the political economy of citizenship might provide a resource for criticizing—or at least talking about—a development in the American economy and in political patterns that is very difficult to capture within the terms of procedural liberalism alone.

The public philosophy of procedural liberalism, the one that emphasizes freedom of choice above all, holds out a liberating, even exhilarating, promise: what could freedom be if not the unfettered ability to choose my own way of life, my own conception of the good, without being imposed upon by government?

But what we're finding now in our public life—and here is where philosophy comes down to earth—is that the arrival of the procedural republic has coincided with a loss of mastery, a growing sense of disempowerment. Despite the expansion of rights in recent decades, Americans find to their frustration that they are losing control of the forces that govern their lives.

This may have something to do with the effects of the global economy, but it also has something to do with the self-image by which we live. The liberal image of the freely choosing self and the actual organization of modern social and economic life are sharply at odds. Even as we think and act as if we were freely choosing independent selves, we confront a world governed by impersonal structures of power that defy our understanding and control.

The public philosophy of procedural liberalism ill equips us to contend with our condition. Liberated though we may be from the burden of identities we haven't chosen, entitled though we may be to the range of rights secured by the procedural republic, we find ourselves overwhelmed as we turn to face the world on our own resources.

What kind of civic virtues, then, do we need today? How similar are they, and how different, from the ones that the philosophers of the republican tradition advanced? Since the days of Aristotle's *polis*, the republican tradition has assumed that self-government is an activity that must be rooted in a particular place, that must cultivate a comprehending loyalty to that place. We saw this, too, in Frankfurter's defense of the mandatory flag salute.

Self-government today, though, requires a politics that plays itself out not in a single place—whether nation or town or family or neighborhood or some transnational political community. It requires instead a politics that plays itself out in a multiplicity of settings, from neighborhoods, to nations, to the world as a whole. Politics today requires citizens who can live with the ambiguity of complex identities; it requires citizens who can think and act as multiply situated selves.

Here, then, is how we must translate republican ideals into terms relevant to our time: On the one hand, the formative project remains indispensable. We cannot do without the more demanding idea of citizenship to which, in their different ways, Aristotle, Rousseau, Jefferson, and Brandeis all aspired. But the civic virtue distinctive to our time is the capacity to negotiate our way among the sometimes overlapping and sometimes conflicting obligations that claim us and to live with the tensions to which multiple loyalties give rise.

It isn't easy to live with these tensions. Increasingly, our politics displays reactions against the demand that people live as multiply situated selves or as bearers of complex identities; we see recurring attempts to harden the distinction between "us" and "them," to assert sovereignty with a vengeance, to shore up borders. These are reactions against the demand to live as bearers of complex identities.

So while the content of civic virtue has to be complicated to reflect this feature of our condition, we cannot secure freedom without reviving the formative project of republican tradition. The global media and markets that shape our lives beckon us to a world beyond boundaries and beyond belonging. But the civic resources we need to master those forces—or at least to contend with them—are still to be found in the places and stories, the incidents and identities, that situate us in the world, that cultivate a sense of belonging and of mutual responsibility. The task for politics now, after and beyond the procedural republic, is to cultivate these resources, and to repair the civic life on which democracy depends.

Thank you very much.

QUESTIONS AND ANSWERS

QUESTION [FROM DEAN JOHN D. FEERICK]: I was wondering as you spoke whether Justice Jackson in that 1943 decision was influenced by the danger he saw in Germany, where certain content was sought to be developed among the people, and he was afraid of that if he went other than the way he went?

PROFESSOR SANDEL: Yes, I think he was. I think this was a powerful influence, especially when you think of the image of a flag salute in 1943 in relation to Nazi Germany. So I do think that was a powerful influence on him, given his experiences.

But the question is whether he drew the right conclusion — and not only with respect to flag salutes, but with the underlying rationale, which went far beyond the actual case. Jackson offered an eloquent statement, not just against mandatory flag salutes, but in favor of a certain picture of freedom and of the role of the Constitution in securing freedom.

For all its eloquence and influence, Jackson's opinion gave expression to a public philosophy that—so I've tried to argue, anyhow—goes wrong in important ways and gives up an aspect of freedom that I think is not so dispensable.

QUESTION [FROM DEAN FEERICK]: A second question. I find a certain ambiguity or paradox, in that during the time that this philosophy existed, women didn't vote, we had blacks that didn't vote, we had a very restricted franchise in this country that excluded many whites from voting. Does that suggest that those who argue the republican position from an historical standpoint have the burden, because we didn't see it working as one might have expected it to work, given the arguments for it as you stated?

PROFESSOR SANDEL: Yes, I think that does carry a burden. In fact, not only did restrictions on the franchise coexist with the republican public philosophy, but they drew their justification in many cases from the republican idea that only certain people possess the virtues necessary to deliberate well about the common good. These arguments were used to justify a wide range of exclusions, including property rights qualifications in early state constitutional debates, nativist arguments in the 19th century, arguments against immigration and against extending the vote to women and minorities. Any defender of the republican tradition has to own up to the burden that you rightly identify.

Republican arguments were also advanced by some Southern defenders of slavery. The Southern defenders of slavery criticized Northern wage laborers as being unfree. George Fitzhugh is a notoriously powerful example. He argued that Northern wage laborers were no freer than Southern slaves, since both lacked independence. While wage laborers possessed the liberal right to contract for their labor, Fitzhugh argued, they lacked the independence of condition and of mind and of judgment and of status that true participation in self-government requires. Now, he glorified and romanticized the kind of paternal authority that was exercised over Southern slaves, but Fitzhugh did have a trenchant critique of Northern wage labor, and it was a critique that drew on the republican idea of citizenship.

So the question is: Is it detachable from those dark episodes? In principle, I think it is detachable. There is nothing, I think, intrinsic to the republican idea that need regard virtue as fixed once and for all. To the contrary, some of the great early advocates of public education, such as Horace Mann in the 1830s, argued on republican grounds. Mann argued for the common school, not just on the grounds that we have an obligation to educate poor folks as well as rich folks, not just out of fairness—but, above all, for civic reasons: if everybody is going to vote in a democracy, everybody had better acquire the civic education necessary to deliberate well.

So the republican tradition does have its dark and exclusionary moments, but it has also animated (for the very same kinds of reasons) programs of public education and moral improvement. So I do not think it is intrinsically exclusive. It may run the risk of coercing people; that's the opposite worry—if you think about public education. The line between civic education and coercion may sometimes blur. The less exclusive republican citizenship becomes, the greater the danger of coercion. I think that risk does inhere in the republican tradition.

QUESTION [FROM PROFESSOR TRACY HIGGINS]: I'm impressed with the costs that you attribute to an increasingly so-called individualist interpretation of rights in your discussion of constitutional interpretation. Yet, it seems to me in the cases that you talk about, maybe with the exception of *Barnette,*[18] a Justice Sandel could have written a concurrence rather than dissent.

PROFESSOR SANDEL: Maybe even in *Barnette*. I'm not that enthusiastic about compulsory flag salutes. I don't think they're very effective, given the purpose.

QUESTION [FROM PROFESSOR HIGGINS]: So I'm wondering whether that's the case; and, if it is, whether you're concerned more about political discourse than about the outcome in that series of cases. The only case I could think of that might be a counter-example is *Buckley v. Valeo*,[19] where a more civic republican position would have affected the outcome possibly. But as Professor Fleming has pointed out, many liberals criticize *Buckley*.[20]

PROFESSOR SANDEL: Yes. My primary concern is more with the reasons and the terms of public discourse, than with the outcome of particular cases. Still, I think there would be some outcomes that would differ—in the area, for example, of religious liberty.

One of the expressions of procedural liberalism and the ideal of neutrality in the religion cases has been to give great weight to the non-establishment clause at the expense of the free exercise clause. Take, for example, a number of cases where the Court has refused to uphold laws making special accommodation for religious observance. In *Estate of Thornton v. Caldor, Inc.*,[21] the Court struck down a law that provided Sabbath observers the right to designate their day of rest. Everyone had one day off under the statute. An employer couldn't require any worker to work seven days a week, but Sabbath observers could have their day off coincide with their Sabbath. By 8-1 the Court struck it down as failing to be neutral to those who might have other, non-religious reasons for wanting a week-end day off. That seems to me a decision that reflects the philosophy of neutrality and choice and that gets the outcome wrong because it enforces a picture of religion as a matter of choice.

Another example would be the case about the yarmulke in the Air Force, *Goldman v. Weinburger*,[22] where the Court didn't even require the Air Force to show that its disciplinary objectives would be impaired by making an accommodation to a rule that prohibits the wearing of headgear by officers, in this case someone serving in a health clinic.

18. *See supra* text accompanying note 4.
19. 424 U.S. 1 (1976).
20. *See, e.g.,* James E. Fleming, *Constructing the Substantive Constitution*, 72 Tex. L. Rev. 211, 246-47 (1993) (discussing numerous liberal constitutional theorists criticisms of *Buckley*).
21. 472 U.S. 703 (1985).
22. 475 U.S. 503 (1986).

So there are a number of cases, *Smith*[23] being another one, where the emphasis on neutrality in the religion cases has led to an over-emphasis on the worry about establishment, even at a cost to accommodation of free exercise. That would be one set of cases where a critic of procedural liberalism might well reach a different outcome.

In the case of the privacy rights—the defect, I would say, in *Roe v. Wade*[24] is in the pretense of the Court to be neutral on the question of when life begins, on the moral status of the fetus. The Court held that no state may enact into law a particular theory of life, and then denied that it was endorsing a particular theory of life. The Court nonetheless proceeded to enunciate an elaborate, though reasonable policy about the trimesters and the relative interests of the state and the individual.

The problem was in pretending to a moral neutrality at odds with the right that it defended. Does that mean that the Court should have decided otherwise or that it should simply have been more willing to articulate and defend the moral judgment that underlies the right? In that case, I would be inclined to say that so abstemious a jurisprudence is mistaken and undesirable. It deprived that decision of much of its legitimacy. It eroded the legitimacy of the courts because it didn't own up to the moral, and partly theological, judgment that it depended on.

So the critique of procedural liberalism could make a difference either in the way the case is argued or, in some cases, in the outcome.

Could I offer one other example? In the free speech area, there may be a difference in the protection accorded commercial speech. If the FTC wants to regulate the number of commercials for sugared breakfast cereal that can be shown on Saturday children's cartoon shows, the First Amendment should not be interpreted to stand in the way. Shifting the emphasis away from neutrality and toward self-government in the free speech cases would lead, I think, to a number of different outcomes.

QUESTION [FROM PROFESSOR MICHAEL DORF]: Your answer on religious cases to Professor Higgins suggested to me a certain tendency to identify egregious aspects of the most procedural aspects of liberalism and call that liberalism. The kinder gentler points you identify as republican. If you take that pairing of cases, for example, the establishment of religion and free exercise cases, you will find for the most part the Justices who liked the establishment clause—that is to say, liked separation—also tend to like free exercise. Justice Stevens is the only exception that I can think of. So there is a real overlap.

23. Employment Div., Dep't of Hum. Resources of Oregon v. Smith, 494 U.S. 872 (1990).
24. 410 U.S. 113 (1973).

It struck me that this is especially true in your characterization of Justice Brandeis. I think about two of Justice Brandeis's most famous opinions. One is concurrence in *Whitney v. California*,[25] in which he says the Framers meant freedom—valued freedom—as both a means and an end, puts them together right there, so it's the liberal and the republican tradition. And then, when he comes to talk about the fear of government in his dissent in *Olmstead v. United States*,[26] what does he tell us? He tells us that government is the potent omnipresent teacher. So yes, he's concerned about morality, about citizenship, but he's also afraid that if government has certain kinds of powers that it's going to teach a very bad lesson. That, it seems to me, is exactly what Justice Jackson is getting at in *Barnette*; he is saying that of course government must inculcate values, but it can do it only in certain ways. So the more sympathetic view of liberalism is not that it wants to exclude moral arguments from the public domain, but that it wants to channel them in certain ways and say that they can only be given effect in certain ways because of a fear about government power, which is in some ways structurally similar to the fear about private power the progressives have, somewhat. Maybe the job of the future is to synthesize these two traditions along those directions.

PROFESSOR SANDEL: Well, any such attempt would have to decide a question of principle that does distinguish these two traditions. It would have to face the question: Is it permissible to attempt to shape the moral and civic character of citizens?

Now, some liberals would say yes, provided that the attempt to shape character observes certain restraints. Some liberals allow that government can try to cultivate certain qualities of character, certain virtues, provided they are restricted to liberal virtues like toleration, mutual respect, observing the rights of others—virtues that will uphold the procedural republic as a constitutional scheme and as a political practice.

But, says the liberal, those limited virtues of respect and toleration don't run the risk of coercing people because, they might say, very few life plans actually require anything at odds with those virtues; and if some fanatics or fundamentalists care a lot about other people's lives, we shouldn't credit that anyhow, so we don't have to worry.

But the question is whether the liberal's very limited soul-craft is sufficient or defensible. That's a question of principle, and it's one on which I suspect adherents of the liberal and republican traditions might disagree.

QUESTION [FROM EUGENE HARPER]: In your book, you start out with Aristotle and you cite Aristotle a fair number of times. To someone like myself who was educated here, at least in the pre-

25. 274 U.S. 357, 375 (1927) (Brandeis, J., concurring).
26. 277 U.S. 438, 472-79 (1928) (Brandeis, J., dissenting).

Council philosophy departments, not citing Aquinas in the book with so much reference to Aristotle looks like, to coin a phrase, something unnatural. I noticed in your subsequent article on judgmental toleration that appears in Robert George's collection you have a little piece about Aquinas.[27] I wondered whether or not you were jumping into this and looking more at viewing the perfectionist natural law tradition whole hog, much like MacIntyre,[28] or whether or not it's just off your screen; and, if you have rejected it, whether or not you have rejected it for fear of coercion and so forth.

PROFESSOR SANDEL: The broader question, as I understand it, is: what is the relation of the natural law tradition to the republican tradition that I'm emphasizing?

It's true the natural law tradition is at odds with the liberal tradition on grounds similar to the ones I've been advancing in the name of the republican tradition going back to Aristotle, but also on other grounds that I don't emphasize—perfectionist grounds, you say. I think there are perfectionist arguments to be made against liberal political philosophy, and I agree with them to a point. For purposes of trying to understand democratic life and the relation of constitutional law to democratic life, the more powerful contrast with the reigning liberal public philosophy is to be found, it seems to me, in the republican tradition.

I think the republican tradition is better equipped, despite worries to the contrary, to deal with a pluralist society, to deal with disagreement. It is often held against republicanism that it requires shared values. It doesn't really. It is a tradition that is teeming with disagreement about what counts as virtue, what kinds of citizens should be formed, what the formative project should aim at, just as the liberal tradition is teeming with disagreement about what it means to respect the right to choose one's values freely.

It is the openness of argument about virtue, about the conditions of self-government, about the qualities of character that democratic life requires, and the competing answers to those questions, that I think we need to restore, not a particular answer to that question. That is why I see the republican tradition as a more apt rival to the reigning public philosophy than the natural law tradition, though I know this could be the beginning of a long argument.

PROFESSOR FLEMING: Professor Sandel, thank you.

PROFESSOR SANDEL: Thank you.

27. Michael J. Sandel, *Judgmental Toleration*, *in* Natural Law, Liberalism, and Morality (Robert P. George ed., 1996).

28. *See* Alasdair MacIntyre, After Virtue (1981).

[8]

Moral Argument and Liberal Toleration: Abortion and Homosexuality

Michael J. Sandel†

People defend laws against abortion and homosexual sodomy in two different ways: Some argue that abortion and homosexuality are morally reprehensible and therefore worthy of prohibition; others try to avoid passing judgment on the morality of these practices, and argue instead that, in a democracy, political majorities have the right to embody in law their moral convictions.

In a similar way, arguments against antiabortion and antisodomy laws take two different forms: Some say the laws are unjust because the practices they prohibit are morally permissible, indeed sometimes desirable; others oppose these laws without reference to the moral status of the practices at issue, and argue instead that individuals have a right to choose for themselves whether to engage in them.

These two styles of argument might be called, respectively, the "naive" and the "sophisticated." The naive view holds that the justice of laws depends on the moral worth of the conduct they prohibit or protect. The sophisticated view holds that the justice of such laws depends not on a substantive moral judgment about the conduct at stake, but instead on a more general theory about the respective claims of majority rule and individual rights, of democracy on the one hand, and liberty on the other.

I shall try in this paper to bring out the truth in the naive view, which I take to be this: The justice (or injustice) of laws against abortion and homosexual sodomy depends, at least in part, on the morality (or immorality) of those practices.[1] This is the claim the sophisticated view rejects. In both its majoritarian and its liberal versions, the sophisticated view tries to set aside or "bracket" controversial moral and religious conceptions for purposes of justice. It insists that the justification of laws be neutral among competing visions of the good life.

---

† Professor of Government, Harvard University.

1. I do not defend the stronger claim that the morality (or immorality) of a practice is the only relevant reason in deciding whether there should be a law against it.

In practice, of course, these two kinds of argument can be difficult to distinguish. In the debate over cases like *Roe v. Wade*[2] and *Bowers v. Hardwick*,[3] both camps tend to advance the naive view under cover of the sophisticated. (Such is the prestige of the sophisticated way of arguing.) For example, those who would ban abortion and sodomy out of abhorrence often argue in the name of deference to democracy and judicial restraint. Similarly, those who want permissive laws because they approve of abortion and homosexuality often argue in the name of liberal toleration.

This is not to suggest that all instances of the sophisticated argument are disingenuous attempts to promote a substantive moral conviction. Those who argue that law should be neutral among competing conceptions of the good life offer various grounds for their claim, including most prominently the following:

> (1) the *relativist* view says law should not affirm a particular moral conception because all morality is relative, and so there are no moral truths to affirm; (2) the *utilitarian* view argues that government neutrality will, for various reasons, promote the general welfare in the long run; (3) the *voluntarist* view holds that government should be neutral among conceptions of the good life in order to respect the capacity of persons as free citizens or autonomous agents to choose their conceptions for themselves; and (4) the *minimalist*, or pragmatic view says that, because people inevitably disagree about morality and religion, government should bracket these controversies for the sake of political agreement and social cooperation.

In order to bring out the truth in the naive way of arguing, I look to the actual arguments judges and commentators have made in recent cases dealing with abortion and homosexuality. Their arguments, unfailingly sophisticated, illustrate the difficulty of bracketing moral judgments for purposes of law. Because their reasons for trying to be neutral among conceptions of the good life are drawn primarily from voluntarist and minimalist assumptions, I focus on these arguments. Finally, although much of my argument criticizes leading theories of liberal toleration, I do not think it offers any comfort to majoritarianism. The cure for liberalism is not majoritarianism, but a keener appreciation of the role of substantive moral discourse in political and constitutional argument.

I
PRIVACY RIGHTS: INTIMACY AND AUTONOMY

In the constitutional right of privacy, the neutral state and the voluntarist conception of the person are often joined. In the case of abor-

2. 410 U.S. 113 (1973).
3. 478 U.S. 186 (1986).

tion, for example, no state may, "by adopting one theory of life,"[4] override a woman's right to decide "whether or not to terminate her pregnancy."[5] Government may not enforce a particular moral view, however widely held, for "no individual should be compelled to surrender the freedom to make that decision for herself simply because her 'value preferences' are not shared by the majority."[6]

As with religious liberty and freedom of speech, so with privacy, the ideal of neutrality often reflects a voluntarist conception of human agency. Government must be neutral among conceptions of the good life in order to respect the capacity of persons to choose their values and relationships for themselves. So close is the connection between privacy rights and the voluntarist conception of the self that commentators frequently assimilate the values of privacy and autonomy: Privacy rights are said to be "grounded in notions of individual autonomy," because "[t]he human dignity protected by constitutional guarantees would be seriously diminished if people were not free to choose and adopt a lifestyle which allows expression of their uniqueness and individuality."[7] In "recognizing a constitutional right to privacy," the Court has given effect to the view "that persons have the capacity to live autonomously and the right to exercise that capacity."[8] Supreme Court decisions voiding laws against contraceptives "not only protect the individual who chooses not to procreate, but also the autonomy of a couple's association."[9] They protect men and women "against an unchosen commitment" to unwanted children, and "against a compelled identification with the social role of parent."[10]

In Supreme Court decisions and dissents alike, the justices have often tied privacy rights to voluntarist assumptions. The Court has thus characterized laws banning the use of contraceptives as violating "the constitutional protection of individual autonomy in matters of childbearing."[11] It has defended the right to an abortion on the grounds that few decisions are "more properly private, or more basic to individual dignity

4. Roe v. Wade, 410 U.S. 113, 162 (1973).

5. *Id.* at 153.

6. Thornburgh v. American College of Obstetricians & Gynecologists, 476 U.S. 747, 777 (1986) (Stevens, J., concurring).

7. Eichbaum, *Towards an Autonomy-Based Theory of Constitutional Privacy: Beyond the Ideology of Familial Privacy,* 14 HARV. C.R.-C.L. L. REV. 361, 362, 365 (1979).

8. Richards, *The Individual, the Family, and the Constitution: A Jurisprudential Perspective,* 55 N.Y.U. L. REV. 1, 31 (1980).

9. Karst, *The Freedom of Intimate Association,* 89 YALE L.J. 624, 641 (1980). For articles discussing the connection between privacy and autonomy rights, see also Henkin, *Privacy and Autonomy,* 74 COLUM. L. REV. 1410 (1974); Smith, *The Constitution and Autonomy,* 60 TEX. L. REV. 175 (1982); Wilkinson III & White, *Constitutional Protection for Personal Lifestyles,* 62 CORNELL L. REV. 563 (1977).

10. Karst, *supra* note 9, at 641.

11. Carey v. Population Services Int'l, 431 U.S. 678, 687 (1977).

and autonomy, than a woman's decision . . . whether to end her pregnancy."[12] Justice Douglas, concurring in an abortion case, emphasized that the right of privacy protects such liberties as "the autonomous control over the development and expression of one's intellect, interests, tastes, and personality," as well as "freedom of choice in the basic decisions of one's life respecting marriage, divorce, procreation, contraception, and the education and upbringing of children."[13] Writing in dissent, Justice Marshall found a regulation limiting the hair length of policemen "inconsistent with the values of privacy, self-identity, autonomy, and personal integrity" he believed the Constitution was designed to protect.[14] And four justices would have extended privacy protection to consensual homosexual activity on the grounds that "much of the richness of a relationship will come from the freedom an individual has to *choose* the form and nature of these intensely personal bonds."[15]

Although the link between privacy and autonomy is now so familiar as to seem natural, even necessary, the right of privacy need not presuppose a voluntarist conception of the person. In fact, through most of its history in American law, the right of privacy has implied neither the ideal of the neutral state nor the ideal of a self freely choosing its aims and attachments.

Where the contemporary right of privacy is the right to engage in certain conduct without government restraint, the traditional version is the right to keep certain personal facts from public view. The new privacy protects a person's "independence in making certain kinds of important decisions," whereas the old privacy protects a person's interest "in avoiding disclosure of personal matters."[16]

The tendency to identify privacy with autonomy not only obscures these shifting understandings of privacy; it also restricts the range of reasons for protecting it. Although the new privacy typically relies on voluntarist justifications, it can also be justified in other ways. A right to be free of governmental interference in matters of marriage, for example, can be defended not only in the name of individual choice, but also in the name of the intrinsic value or social importance of the practice it protects. As the Court has acknowledged, "certain kinds of personal bonds have played a critical role in the culture and traditions of the Nation by cultivating and transmitting shared ideals and beliefs; they thereby foster diversity and act as critical buffers between the individual and the power

12. Thornburgh v. American College of Obstetricians & Gynecologists, 476 U.S. 747, 772 (1986).

13. Doe v. Bolton, 410 U.S. 179, 211 (1973) (Douglas, J., concurring) (emphasis omitted).

14. Kelley v. Johnson, 425 U.S. 238, 251 (1976) (Marshall, J., dissenting).

15. Bowers v. Hardwick, 478 U.S. 186, 205 (1986) (Blackmun, J., dissenting).

16. Whalen v. Roe, 429 U.S. 589, 599-600 (1977).

of the State."[17] The Court's greater tendency, however, has been to view privacy in voluntarist terms, as protecting "the ability independently to define one's identity."[18]

II
FROM THE OLD PRIVACY TO THE NEW

The right to privacy first gained legal recognition in the United States as a doctrine of tort law, not constitutional law. In an influential article in 1890, Louis Brandeis, then a Boston lawyer, and his one-time law partner Samuel Warren argued that the civil law should protect "the right to privacy."[19] Far from later-day concerns with sexual freedoms, Brandeis and Warren's privacy was quaint by comparison, concerned with the publication of high society gossip by the sensationalist press, or the unauthorized use of people's portraits in advertising.[20] Gradually at first, then more frequently in the 1930s, this right to privacy gained recognition in the civil law of most states.[21] Prior to the 1960s, however, privacy received scant attention in constitutional law.

Two members of the Supreme Court first addressed the right of privacy as such in 1961 when a Connecticut pharmacist challenged the state's ban on contraceptives in *Poe v. Ullman*.[22] Although the majority dismissed the case on technical grounds,[23] Justices Douglas and Harlan dissented, arguing that the law violated the right of privacy. The privacy they defended was privacy in the traditional sense. The right at stake was not the right to use contraceptives but the right to be free of the surveillance that enforcement would require. "If we imagine a regime of full enforcement of the law," wrote Douglas, "we would reach the point where search warrants issued and officers appeared in bedrooms to find out what went on. . . . If [the State] can make this law, it can enforce it. And proof of its violation necessarily involves an inquiry into the relations between man and wife."[24] Banning the sale of contraceptives would be different from banning their use, Douglas observed. Banning the sale would restrict access to contraceptives but would not expose intimate relations to public inspection. Enforcement would take police to

17. Roberts v. United States Jaycees, 468 U.S. 609, 618-19 (1984).

18. *Id.* at 619.

19. Warren & Brandeis, *The Right to Privacy*, 4 HARV. L. REV. 193 (1890).

20. *Id.* at 195-96.

21. Prosser, *Privacy*, 48 CALIF. L. REV. 383 (1960) (discussing the ensuing recognition and development of a right to privacy).

22. 367 U.S. 497 (1961).

23. *Id.* at 509.

24. *Id.* at 519-21 (Douglas, J., dissenting).

the drugstore, not the bedroom, and so would not offend privacy in the traditional sense.[25]

Justice Harlan also objected to the law on grounds that distinguish the old privacy from the new. He did not object that the law against contraceptives failed to be neutral among competing moral conceptions. Although Harlan acknowledged that the law was based on the belief that contraception is immoral in itself, and encourages such "dissolute action" as fornication and adultery by minimizing their "disastrous consequence,"[26] he did not find this failure of neutrality contrary to the Constitution. In a statement clearly opposed to the strictures of neutrality, Harlan argued that morality is a legitimate concern of government.

> The very inclusion of the category of morality among state concerns indicates that society is not limited in its objects only to the physical well-being of the community, but has traditionally concerned itself with the moral soundness of its people as well. Indeed to attempt a line between public behavior and that which is purely consensual or solitary would be to withdraw from community concern a range of subjects with which every society in civilized times has found it necessary to deal.[27]

Though he rejected the ideal of the neutral state, Harlan did not conclude that Connecticut could prohibit married couples from using contraceptives. Like Douglas, he reasoned that enforcing the law would intrude on the privacy essential to the prized institution of marriage. He objected to the violation of privacy in the traditional sense, to "the intrusion of the whole machinery of the criminal law into the very heart of marital privacy, requiring husband and wife to render account before a criminal tribunal of their uses of that intimacy."[28] According to Harlan, the state was entitled to embody in law the belief that contraception is immoral, but not to implement "the obnoxiously intrusive means it ha[d] chosen to effectuate that policy."[29]

Four years later, in *Griswold v. Connecticut,*[30] the dissenters prevailed. The Supreme Court invalidated Connecticut's law against contraceptives and for the first time explicitly recognized a constitutional right of privacy. Although the right was located in the Constitution rather than tort law, it remained tied to the traditional notion of privacy as the interest in keeping intimate affairs from public view. The violation of privacy consisted in the intrusion required to enforce the law, not the restriction on the freedom to use contraceptives. "Would we allow the police to search the sacred precincts of marital bedrooms for telltale signs

25. *Id.* at 519.
26. *Id.* at 545 (Harlan, J., dissenting).
27. *Id.* at 545-46.
28. *Id.* at 553.
29. *Id.* at 554.
30. 381 U.S. 479 (1965).

of the use of contraceptives?," wrote Justice Douglas for the Court. "The very idea is repulsive to the notions of privacy surrounding the marriage relationship."[31]

The justification for the right was not voluntarist but unabashedly teleological; the privacy the Court vindicated was not for the sake of letting people lead their sexual lives as they choose, but rather for the sake of affirming and protecting the social institution of marriage.

> Marriage is a coming together for better or for worse, hopefully enduring, and intimate to the degree of being sacred. It is an association that promotes a way of life, . . . a harmony in living, . . . a bilateral loyalty . . . . [I]t is an association for as noble a purpose as any involved in our prior decisions.[32]

Although commentators and judges often view *Griswold* as a dramatic constitutional departure, the privacy right it proclaimed was consistent with traditional notions of privacy going back to the turn of the century. From the standpoint of shifting privacy conceptions, the more decisive turn came seven years later in *Eisenstadt v. Baird,*[33] a seemingly similar case. Like *Griswold,* it involved a state law restricting contraceptives. In *Eisenstadt,* however, the challenged law restricted the distribution of contraceptives, not their use. While it therefore limited access to contraceptives, its enforcement could not be said to require governmental surveillance of intimate activities. It did not violate privacy in the traditional sense.[34] Furthermore, the law prohibited distributing contraceptives only to unmarried persons, and so did not burden the institution of marriage as the Connecticut law did.

Despite these differences, the Supreme Court struck down the law with only a single dissent. Its decision involved two innovations, one explicit, the other unacknowledged. The explicit innovation redescribed the bearers of privacy rights from persons *qua* participants in the social institution of marriage to persons *qua* individuals, independent of their roles or attachments. As the Court explained, "It is true that in *Griswold* the right of privacy in question inhered in the marital relationship. Yet the marital couple is not an independent entity with a mind and heart of its own, but an association of two individuals each with a separate intellectual and emotional makeup."[35]

The subtler, though no less fateful change in *Eisenstadt* was in the shift from the old privacy to the new. Rather than conceiving privacy as freedom from surveillance or disclosure of intimate affairs, the Court

31. *Id.* at 485-86.
32. *Id.* at 486.
33. 405 U.S. 438 (1972).
34. In fact, the case arose when a man was convicted for giving away a contraceptive device at a public lecture. *Id.* at 440.
35. *Id.* at 453.

found that the right to privacy now protected the freedom to engage in certain activities without governmental restriction. Although privacy in *Griswold* prevented intrusion into "the sacred precincts of marital bedrooms,"[36] privacy in *Eisenstadt* prevented intrusion into *decisions* of certain kinds. Moreover, as the meaning of privacy changed, so did its justification. The Court protected privacy in *Eisenstadt* not for the social practices it promoted but for the individual choice it secured. "If the right of privacy means anything, it is the right of the *individual*, married or single, to be free from unwarranted governmental intrusion into matters so fundamentally affecting a person as the decision whether to bear or beget a child."[37]

One year later, in *Roe v. Wade*,[38] the Supreme Court gave the new privacy its most controversial application by striking down a Texas law against abortion and extending privacy to "encompass a woman's decision whether or not to terminate her pregnancy."[39] First with contraception, then with abortion, the right of privacy had become the right to make certain sorts of choices, free of interference by the state. The choice had also to be free of interference by husbands or parents. In *Planned Parenthood of Missouri v. Danforth*,[40] the Court struck down a law requiring a husband's consent, or parental consent in the case of unmarried minors, as a condition for an abortion. Since the state may not prevent even minors from having abortions in the first trimester, it cannot delegate to "a third party" such as a husband or parent the authority to do so.[41]

The voluntarist grounds of the new privacy found explicit statement in a 1977 case invalidating a New York law prohibiting the sale of contraceptives to minors under age sixteen.[42] For the first time, the Court used the language of autonomy to describe the interest privacy protects, and argued openly for the shift from the old privacy to the new. Writing for the Court in *Carey v. Population Services International*, Justice Brennan admitted that *Griswold* focused on the fact that a law forbidding the *use* of contraceptives can bring the police into marital bedrooms.[43] "But subsequent decisions have made clear that the constitutional protection

36. *Griswold*, 381 U.S. at 485.

37. *Eisenstadt*, 405 U.S. at 453. The Court's opinion in *Eisenstadt* camouflages the shift from the old privacy to the new with a false hypothetical premise: "If under *Griswold* the distribution of contraceptives to married persons cannot be prohibited, a ban on distribution to unmarried persons would be equally impermissible." *Id.* But *Griswold* did not hold that distribution to married persons cannot be prohibited.

38. 410 U.S. 113 (1973).

39. *Id.* at 153.

40. 428 U.S. 52 (1976).

41. *Id.* at 69, 75.

42. Carey v. Population Services Int'l, 431 U.S. 678 (1977).

43. *Id.* at 687.

of individual autonomy in matters of childbearing is not dependent on that element."[44] Surveying the previous cases, he emphasized that *Eisenstadt* protected the "*decision* whether to bear or beget a child,"[45] and *Roe* protected "a woman's *decision* whether or not to terminate her pregnancy."[46] He concluded that "the teaching of *Griswold* is that the Constitution protects individual decisions in matters of childbearing from unjustified intrusion by the State."[47]

Given the voluntarist interpretation of privacy, restricting the *sale* of contraceptives violates privacy as harshly as banning their *use*; the one limits choice as surely as the other. "Indeed, in practice," Brennan observed, "a prohibition against all sales, since more easily and less offensively enforced, might have an even more devastating effect upon the freedom to choose contraception."[48] Ironically, the very fact that a ban on sales does *not* threaten the old privacy makes it a greater threat to the new.

Later decisions upholding abortion rights also used the language of autonomy to describe the privacy interest at stake. The Court held in a recent opinion that "[f]ew decisions are . . . more properly private, or more basic to individual dignity and autonomy than a woman's decision . . . whether to end her pregnancy. A woman's right to make that choice freely is fundamental."[49]

Despite its increasing tendency to identify privacy with autonomy, the Court refused, in a 5-4 decision, to extend privacy protection to consensual homosexual activity. Writing for the majority, Justice White emphasized that the Court's previous privacy cases protected choice only with respect to child rearing and education, family relationships, procreation, marriage, contraception, and abortion. "[W]e think it evident," he held, "that none of the rights announced in those cases bears any resemblance to the claimed constitutional right of homosexuals to engage in acts of sodomy . . . ."[50] He also rejected the claim that Georgia's citizens could not embody in law their belief "that homosexual sodomy is immoral and unacceptable."[51] Neutrality to the contrary, "[t]he law . . . is constantly based on notions of morality, and if all laws representing

44. *Id.*
45. *Id.* (quoting *Eisenstadt*, 405 U.S. at 453) (emphasis added in *Carey*).
46. *Id.* (quoting *Roe*, 410 U.S. at 153) (emphasis added in *Carey*).
47. *Id.*
48. *Id.* at 688.
49. Thornburgh v. American College of Obstetricians & Gynecologists, 776 U.S. 747, 772 (1986).
50. Bowers v. Hardwick, 478 U.S. 186, 190-91 (1986).
51. *Id.* at 196.

essentially moral choices are to be invalidated under the Due Process Clause, the courts will be very busy indeed."[52]

Writing for the four dissenters, Justice Blackmun argued that the Court's previous privacy decisions did not depend on the virtue of the practices they protected but on the principle of free individual choice in intimate matters. "We protect those rights not because they contribute . . . to the general public welfare, but because they form so central a part of an individual's life. '[T]he concept of privacy embodies the "moral fact that a person belongs to himself and not others nor to society as a whole." ' "[53]

Blackmun argued for the application of earlier privacy rulings in the considerations of homosexual practices by casting the Court's concern for conventional family ties in individualist terms: "We protect the decision whether to have a child because parenthood alters so dramatically an individual's self-definition . . . . And we protect the family because it contributes so powerfully to the happiness of individuals, not because of a preference for stereotypical households."[54] Because the right of privacy in sexual relationships protects "the freedom an individual has to *choose* the form and nature of these intensely personal bonds,"[55] it protects homosexual activity no less than other intimate choices.

Defending the ideal of the neutral state, Blackmun added that traditional religious condemnations of homosexuality "give[ ] the State no license to impose their judgments on the entire citizenry."[56] To the contrary, the State's appeal to religious teachings against homosexuality undermines its claim that the law "represents a legitimate use of secular coercive power."[57]

Despite the Court's reluctance to extend privacy rights to homosexuals, the privacy cases of the last twenty-five years offer ample evidence of assumptions drawn from the liberal conception of the person. They also raise two questions about the liberalism they reflect: First whether bracketing controversial moral issues is even possible; and second

52. *Id.*

53. *Id.* at 204 (Blackmun, J., dissenting) (quoting Thornburgh v. American College of Obstetricians & Gynecologists, 476 U.S. at 777 n.5 (Stevens, J., concurring) (quoting Fried, *Correspondence*, 6 PHIL. & PUB. AFF. 288-89 (1977))).

54. *Id.* at 205.

55. *Id.*

56. *Id.* at 211.

57. *Id.* In striking down a similar sodomy law, the New York Court of Appeals clearly expressed the idea that government must be neutral among competing conceptions of the good. "[I]t is not the function of the Penal Law in our governmental policy to provide either a medium for the articulation or the apparatus for the intended enforcement of moral or theological values." People v. Onofre, 51 N.Y.2d 476, 488 n.3, 415 N.E.2d 936, 940 n.3, 434 N.Y.S.2d 947, 951 n.3 (1980), *cert. denied*, 451 U.S. 987 (1981).

whether the voluntarist conception of privacy limits the range of reasons for protecting privacy.

III
THE MINIMALIST CASE FOR TOLERATION: ABORTION

Unlike the voluntarist grounds for the neutral state, minimalist liberalism seeks a conception of justice that is political not philosophical, that does not presuppose any particular conception of the person, autonomous or otherwise. It proposes bracketing controversial moral and religious issues for the sake of securing social cooperation in the face of disagreement about ends, not for the sake of such "comprehensive" liberal ideals as autonomy or individuality.[58] One objection to minimalist liberalism is that the case for bracketing a particular moral or religious controversy may partly depend on an implicit answer to the controversy it purports to bracket. In the case of abortion, for example, the more confident we are that fetuses are, in the relevant moral sense, different from babies, the more confident we can be in bracketing the question about the moral status of fetuses for political purposes.

The Court's argument in *Roe v. Wade*[59] illustrates the difficulty of deciding constitutional cases by bracketing controversial moral and religious issues. Although the Court claimed to be neutral on the question of when life begins, its decision presupposes a particular answer to that question. The Court began by observing that Texas' law against abortion rests upon a particular theory of when life begins. "Texas urges that . . . life begins at conception and is present throughout pregnancy, and that, therefore, the State has a compelling interest in protecting that life from and after conception."[60]

The Court then claimed to be neutral on that question: "We need not resolve the difficult question of when life begins. When those trained in the respective disciplines of medicine, philosophy, and theology are unable to arrive at any consensus, the judiciary . . . is not in a position to speculate as to the answer."[61] It then noted "the wide divergence of thinking on this most sensitive and difficult question," throughout the western tradition and in the law of various American states.[62]

From this survey, the Court concluded that "the unborn have never been recognized in the law as persons in the whole sense."[63] Accord-

58. Rawls, *Justice as Fairness: Political Not Metaphysical,* 14 PHIL. & PUB. AFF. 223, 245 (1985); Rorty, *The Priority of Democracy to Philosophy*, in THE VIRGINIA STATUTE FOR RELIGIOUS FREEDOM 257 (M. Peterson & R. Vaughan eds. 1988).

59. 410 U.S. 113 (1973).

60. *Id.* at 159.

61. *Id.*

62. *Id.* at 160-62.

63. *Id.* at 162.

ingly, it argued that Texas was wrong to embody in law a particular theory of life. Since no theory was conclusive, it held that Texas erred in "adopting one theory of life . . . [which would] override the rights of the pregnant woman that are at stake."[64]

However, contrary to its professions of neutrality, the Court's decision presupposed a particular answer to the question it claimed to bracket.

> With respect to the State's important and legitimate interest in potential life, the "compelling" point is at viability. This is so because the fetus then presumably has the capability of meaningful life outside the mother's womb. State regulation protective of fetal life after viability thus has both logical and biological justifications.[65]

That the Court's decision in *Roe* presupposes a particular answer to the question it purports to bracket is no argument against its decision, only an argument against its claim to have bracketed the controversial question of when life begins. It does not replace Texas' theory of life with a neutral stance, but with a different theory of its own.

The minimalist case for neutrality is subject to a further difficulty: Even given an agreement to bracket controversial moral and religious issues for the sake of social cooperation, it may be controversial what counts as bracketing; and this controversy may require for its solution either a substantive evaluation of the interests at stake, or the autonomous conception of agency that minimalist liberalism resolves to avoid. *Thornburgh v. American College of Obstetricians & Gynecologists,*[66] a 1986 abortion case upholding *Roe,* offers an example of this difficulty.

Writing in dissent, Justice White urged the Court in *Thornburgh* to overrule *Roe v. Wade* and "return the issue to the people."[67] He agreed that abortion was a controversial moral issue, but argued that the best way for the Court to bracket this controversy was to let each state decide the question for itself. He proposed, in effect, to bracket the intractable controversy over abortion as Stephen Douglas proposed to bracket the intractable controversy over slavery—by refusing to impose a single answer on the country as a whole. "Abortion is a hotly contested moral and political issue," White wrote. "Such issues, in our society, are to be resolved by the will of the people, either as expressed through legislation or through the general principles they have already incorporated into the Constitution they have adopted."[68] For the Court to do otherwise is not

64. *Id.*

65. *Id.* at 163.

66. 476 U.S. 747 (1986).

67. *Id.* at 797 (White, J., dissenting).

68. *Id.* at 796.

to be neutral but to "impose its own controversial choices of value upon the people."[69]

Justice Stevens responded to White by arguing for a different way of bracketing. Given the controversial moral issues at stake, he urged that individual women, not legislatures, should decide the question for themselves. For the Court to insist that women be free to choose for themselves is not to impose the *Court's* values, but simply to prevent local majorities from imposing *their* values on individuals. "[N]o individual should be compelled to surrender the freedom to make that decision for herself simply because her 'value preferences' are not shared by the majority."[70] For Stevens, the basic question is not which theory of life is true, but "whether the 'abortion decision' should be made by the individual or by the majority 'in the unrestrained imposition of its own, extraconstitutional value preferences.' "[71]

What is striking is that both ways of bracketing are in principle consistent with minimalist liberalism: The practical interest in social cooperation under conditions of disagreement about the good offers no grounds for choosing one over the other. Even given agreement to bracket an intractable moral or religious controversy for the sake of social cooperation, it may still be unclear what counts as bracketing. Moreover, resolving that question—deciding between White's position and Stevens'—requires either a substantive view about the moral and religious interests at stake or an autonomous conception of the person such as the voluntarist view affirms. Both solutions, however, would deny minimalist liberalism its minimalism; each would implicate its putatively political conception of justice in precisely the moral and philosophical commitments that it seeks to avoid.

IV
The Voluntarist Case for Toleration: Homosexuality

The dissenters' argument for toleration in *Bowers v. Hardwick*[72] illustrates the difficulities with the version of liberalism that ties toleration to autonomy rights alone. In refusing to extend the right of privacy to homosexuals, the majority in *Bowers* declared that none of the rights announced in earlier privacy cases resembled the rights homosexuals

69. *Id.* at 790. Justice Harlan suggested a similar way of bracketing the moral controversy over contraception in Poe v. Ullman, 367 U.S. 497, 547 (1961) (Harlan, J., dissenting): "[T]he very controversial nature of these questions would, I think, require us to hesitate long before concluding that the Constitution precluded Connecticut from choosing as it has among these various views."

70. *Id.* at 777 (Stevens, J., concurring).

71. *Id.* at 777-78 (quoting *Id.* at 794 (White, J. dissenting)).

72. 478 U.S. 186 (1986).

were seeking: "No connection between family, marriage, or procreation on the one hand and homosexual activity on the other has been demonstrated . . . ."[73] Any reply to the Court's position would have to show some connection between the practices already subject to privacy protection and the homosexual practices not yet protected. What then is the resemblance between heterosexual intimacies on the one hand, and homosexual intimacies on the other, such that both are entitled to a constitutional right of privacy?

This question might be answered in at least two different ways—one voluntarist, the other substantive. The first argues from the autonomy the practices reflect, whereas the second appeals to the human goods the practices realize. The voluntarist answer holds that people should be free to choose their intimate associations for themselves, regardless of the virtue or popularity of the practices they choose so long as they do not harm others. In this view, homosexual relationships resemble the heterosexual relationships the Court has already protected in that all reflect the choices of autonomous selves.

By contrast, the substantive answer claims that much that is valuable in conventional marriage is also present in homosexual unions. In this view, the connection between heterosexual and homosexual relations is not that both result from individual choice but that both realize important human goods. Rather than rely on autonomy alone, this second line of reply articulates the virtues homosexual intimacy may share with heterosexual intimacy, along with any distinctive virtues of its own. It defends homosexual privacy the way *Griswold* defended marital privacy, by arguing that, like marriage, homosexual union may also be "intimate to the degree of being sacred . . . a harmony in living . . . a bilateral loyalty," an association for a "noble . . . purpose."[74]

Of these two possible replies, the dissenters in *Bowers* relied wholly on the first. Rather than protect homosexual intimacies for the human goods they share with intimacies the Court already protects, Justice Blackmun cast the Court's earlier cases in individualist terms, and found their reading applied equally to homosexuality because "much of the richness of a relationship will come from the freedom an individual has to *choose* the form and nature of these intensely personal bonds."[75] At issue was not homosexuality as such but respect for the fact that "different individuals will make different choices" in deciding how to conduct their lives.[76]

73. *Id.* at 191.

74. The phrases are from Griswold v. Connecticut, 381 U.S. 479, 486 (1965).

75. 478 U.S. at 205 (Blackmun, J., dissenting) (emphasis added).

76. *Id.* at 206.

Justice Stevens, in a separate dissent, also avoided referring to the values homosexual intimacy may share with heterosexual love. Instead, he wrote broadly of " 'the individual's right to make certain unusually important decisions' " and " 'respect for the dignity of individual choice,' "[77] rejecting the notion that such liberty belongs to heterosexuals alone. "From the standpoint of the individual, the homosexual and the heterosexual have the same interest in deciding how he will live his own life, and, more narrowly, how he will conduct himself in his personal and voluntary associations with his companions."[78]

The voluntarist argument so dominates the *Bowers* dissents that it seems difficult to imagine a judicial rendering of the substantive view. But a glimmer of this view can be found in the appeals court opinion in the same case.[79] The United States Court of Appeals had ruled in Hardwick's favor and had struck down the law under which he was convicted. Like Blackmun and Stevens, the appeals court constructed an analogy between privacy in marriage and privacy in homosexual relations. But unlike the Supreme Court dissenters, it did not rest the analogy on voluntarist grounds alone. It argued instead that both practices may realize important human goods.

The marital relationship is significant, wrote the court of appeals, not only because of its procreative purpose but also "because of the unsurpassed opportunity for mutual support and self-expression that it provides."[80] It recalled the Supreme Court's observation in *Griswold* that "[m]arriage is a coming together for better or for worse, hopefully enduring, and intimate to the degree of being sacred."[81] And it went on to suggest that the qualities the Court so prized in *Griswold* could be present in homosexual unions as well: "For some, the sexual activity in question here serves the same purpose as the intimacy of marriage."[82]

Ironically, this way of extending privacy rights to homosexuals depends on an "old-fashioned" reading of *Griswold* as protecting the human goods realized in marriage, a reading the Court has long since renounced in favor of an individualist reading.[83] By drawing on the teleological dimension of *Griswold,* the substantive case for homosexual privacy offends the liberalism that insists on neutrality. It grounds the right

77. *Id.* at 217 (Stevens, J., dissenting) (quoting Fitzgerald v. Porter Memorial Hospital, 523 F.2d 716, 719-20 (7th Cir. 1975), *cert. denied,* 425 U.S. 916 (1976)).

78. *Id.* at 218-19.

79. Hardwick v. Bowers, 760 F.2d 1202 (11th Cir. 1985), *rev'd,* 476 U.S. 747 (1986).

80. *Id.* at 1211-12.

81. *Id.* at 1212 (quoting Griswold v. Connecticut, 381 U.S. 479, 486 (1965)).

82. *Id.* at 1212.

83. For individualist readings of *Griswold,* see Eisenstadt v. Baird, 405 U.S. 438, 453 (1972) and Carey v. Population Services Int'l, 431 U.S. 678, 687 (1977).

of privacy on the good of the practice it would protect, and so fails to be neutral among conceptions of the good.

The more frequently employed precedent for homosexual rights is not *Griswold* but *Stanley v. Georgia,*[84] which upheld the right to possess obscene materials in the privacy of one's home. *Stanley* did not hold that the obscene films found in the defendant's bedroom served a "noble purpose," only that he had a right to view them in private. The toleration *Stanley* defended was wholly independent of the value or importance of the thing being tolerated.[85]

In the 1980 case of *People v. Onofre,*[86] the New York Court of Appeals vindicated privacy rights for homosexuals on precisely these grounds. The court reasoned that if, following *Stanley,* there is a right to the "satisfaction of sexual desires by resort to material condemned as obscene," there should also be a right "to seek sexual gratification from what at least once was commonly regarded as 'deviant' conduct," so long as it is private and consensual.[87] The court emphasized its neutrality toward the conduct it protected: "We express no view as to any theological, moral or psychological evaluation of consensual sodomy. These are aspects of the issue on which informed, competent authorities and individuals may and do differ."[88] The court's role was simply to ensure that the State bracketed these competing moral views, rather than embodying any one of them in law.[89]

The case for toleration that brackets the morality of homosexuality has a powerful appeal. In the face of deep disagreement about values, it seems to ask the least of the contending parties. It offers social peace and respect for rights without the need for moral conversion. Those who view sodomy as sin need not be persuaded to change their minds, only to tolerate those who practice it in private. By insisting only that each respect the freedom of others to live the lives they choose, this toleration promises a basis for political agreement that does not await shared conceptions of morality.

Despite its promise, however, the neutral case for toleration is subject to two related difficulties. First, as a practical matter, it is by no means clear that social cooperation can be secured on the strength of

84. 394 U.S. 557 (1969).

85. *Id.* at 564-66, 568 ("This right to receive information and ideas, *regardless of their social worth,* is fundamental to our free society. . . . [T]he States retain broad power to regulate obscenity; that power simply does not extend to mere possession by the individual in the privacy of his own home.") (emphasis added) (citation omitted).

86. 51 N.Y.2d 476, 415 N.E.2d 936, 434 N.Y.S.2d 947 (1980), *cert. denied,* 451 U.S. 987 (1981).

87. *Id.* at 487-88, 415 N.E.2d at 939-41, 434 N.Y.S.2d at 950-51.

88. *Id.* at 488 n.3, 415 N.E.2d at 940 n.3, 434 N.Y.S.2d at 951 n.3.

89. *Id.*

autonomy rights alone, absent some measure of agreement on the moral permissibility of the practices at issue. It may not be accidental that the first practices subject to the right of privacy were accorded constitutional protection in cases that spoke of the sanctity of marriage and procreation. Only later did the Court abstract privacy rights from these practices and protect them without reference to the human goods they were once thought to make possible. This suggests that the voluntarist justification of privacy rights is dependent—politically as well as philosophically—on some measure of agreement that the practices protected are morally permissible.

A second difficulty with the voluntarist case for toleration concerns the quality of respect it secures. As the New York case suggests, the analogy with *Stanley* tolerates homosexuality at the price of demeaning it; it puts homosexual intimacy on a par with obscenity—a base thing that should nonetheless be tolerated so long as it takes place in private. If *Stanley* rather than *Griswold* is the relevant analogy, the interest at stake is bound to be reduced, as the New York court reduced it, to "sexual gratification." (The only intimate relationship at stake in *Stanley* was between a man and his pornography.)

The majority in *Bowers* exploited this assumption by ridiculing the notion of a "fundamental right to engage in homosexual sodomy."[90] The obvious reply is that *Bowers* is no more about a right to homosexual sodomy than *Griswold* was about a right to heterosexual intercourse. But by refusing to articulate the human goods that homosexual intimacy may share with heterosexual unions, the voluntarist case for toleration forfeits the analogy with *Griswold* and makes the ridicule difficult to refute.

The problem with the neutral case for toleration is the opposite side of its appeal; it leaves wholly unchallenged the adverse views of homosexuality itself. Unless those views can be plausibly addressed, even a Court ruling in their favor is unlikely to win for homosexuals more than a thin and fragile toleration. A fuller respect would require, if not admiration, at least some appreciation of the lives homosexuals live. Such appreciation, however, is unlikely to be cultivated by a legal and political discourse conducted in terms of autonomy rights alone.

The liberal may reply that autonomy arguments in court need not foreclose more substantive, affirmative arguments elsewhere; bracketing moral argument for constitutional purposes does not mean bracketing moral argument altogether. Once their freedom of choice in sexual practice is secured, homosexuals can seek, by argument and example, to win from their fellow citizens a deeper respect than autonomy can supply.

---

90. Bowers v. Hardwick, 478 U.S. 186, 191 (1986).

The liberal reply, however, underestimates the extent to which constitutional discourse has come to constitute the terms of political discourse in American public life. While most at home in constitutional law, the main motifs of contemporary liberalism—rights as trumps, the neutral state, and the unencumbered self—figure with increasing prominence in our moral and political culture. Assumptions drawn from constitutional discourse increasingly set the terms of political debate in general.

Conclusion

Admittedly, the tendency to bracket substantive moral questions makes it difficult to argue for toleration in the language of the good. Defining privacy rights by defending the practices privacy protects seems either reckless or quaint; reckless because it rests so much on moral argument, quaint because it recalls the traditional view that ties the case for privacy to the merits of the conduct privacy protects. But as the abortion and sodomy cases illustrate, the attempt to bracket moral questions faces difficulties of its own. They suggest the truth in the "naive" view, that the justice or injustice of laws against abortion and homosexual sodomy may have something to do with the morality or immorality of these practices after all.

[9]

A PROGRESSIVE MORAL CASE FOR SAME-SEX MARRIAGE

by CHAI R. FELDBLUM*

There are different ways one can talk about the effort by gay individuals, and gay rights organizations, to convince courts and legislatures to recognize marriages for same-sex couples. The most common way to talk about this effort, certainly in political circles, is to talk about gaining "the right to marry." In an early advocacy piece, written by Tom Stoddard and entitled *Why Gay People Should Seek the Right to Marry*, Stoddard made the following point:

> First, and most basically, the issue is not the desirability of marriage, but rather the desirability of the *right* to marry. That I think two lesbians or two gay men should be entitled to a marriage license does not mean that I think all gay people should find appropriate partners and exercise the right, should it eventually exist.[1]

This way of talking about "the right to marry" is consistent with a widely-accepted form of liberal political theory that believes political discourse should be about "rights," not about conceptions of the "good." As Carlos Ball describes quite succinctly in a recent article: "A central component of contemporary liberalism has been to call for a moral bracketing in matters of public reasoning; namely, for a strict separation between the differing conceptions of the good held by individuals and the broader political discourse that seeks to define individual rights and formulate public policy."[2]

---

* Associate Professor of Law, Georgetown University Law Center. The author thanks the editors of the *Temple Political and Civil Rights Law Review* for sponsoring an interesting and informative symposium. This talk summarized here lays the basis for a longer piece, *The Moral Good of Same-sex Marriage* (manuscript available from author).

1. Tom Stoddard, *Why Gay People Should Seek the Right to Marry*, *in* SEXUAL ORIENTATION AND THE LAW 716, 720 (William B. Rubenstein ed., 1996) (*reprinting* OUT\LOOK NAT'L LESBIAN & GAY Q. (Fall 1989). Stoddard's piece was one of the earliest advocacy writings in only the latest round of discussion on this issue in the gay community. *See* WILLIAM N. ESKRIDGE, JR., THE CASE FOR SAME-SEX MARRIAGE 52-60 (1996) (describing history of debate on same-sex marriage in gay community).

2. Carlos A. Ball, *Moral Foundations for a Discourse on Same-Sex Marriage: Looking Beyond Political Liberalism*, 85 GEO. L.J. 1871, 1883 (1997). Ball argues that the "perfectionist liberalism" articulated by Joseph Raz is preferable to political liberalism because it "recognizes that some conceptions of the good are indeed more valuable than others precisely because they help individuals attain liberal ideals such as autonomy." *Id.* at 1882; *See* JOSEPH RAZ, THE MORALITY OF FREEDOM (1986); *see also* BRUCE A. ACKERMAN, SOCIAL JUSTICE IN THE LIBERAL STATE (1980); RONALD DWORKIN, TAKING RIGHTS SERIOUSLY (1977); JOHN RAWLS, A THEORY OF JUSTICE (1971); Milton C. Regan Jr., *Reason, Tradition, and Family Law: A Comment on Social Constructionism*, 79 VA. L. REV. 1515, 1518 n.12 (1993) ("Not all who regard themselves as liberals, of course, subscribe to neutrality liberalism. *See, e.g.*, WILLIAM A. GALSTON, LIBERAL PURPOSES: GOODS, VIRTUES, AND DIVERSITY IN THE LIBERAL STATE (1991).").

In these discussions, advocates of same-sex marriage neither assert, nor raise the fear, that once a right to marry is achieved, gay people will legitimately be expected by society to marry. To the contrary, while liberal advocates of marriage for same-sex couples may refer to the status of domestic partnership for gay couples as "second-class citizenship,"[3] such liberal advocates would also presumably support the right of gay people to *choose* such a status over marriage, were both marriage and domestic partnerships to be made available to gay couples.[4]

Gay rights advocates who oppose marriage for same-sex couples, or who oppose making recognition of marriage for same-sex couples a top priority for the gay rights movement, tend to speak in the same neutral liberal discourse. These advocates do not deny that government's legitimate role is to protect individual rights nor do they assert that gay people should affirmatively be denied such a right. Rather, they simply argue that achieving a right to marriage for same-sex couples will come at too high an ideological cost or pragmatic cost.[5] Thus, in their view, there are ideological and pragmatic reasons why *this* particular right should not be pursued with vigor by gay rights advocates at this time.

There is another manner in which individuals talk about marriage for same-sex couples. This way of talking is also familiar. It is used primarily by *opponents* of same-sex marriage, and it is replete with moral pronouncements. In the popular press, the assertion of moral harms that will inevitably result from recognizing same-sex marriages are often simply pronounced.[6]

3. *See, e.g.*, Evan Wolfson, *Crossing the Threshold: Equal Marriage Rights for Lesbians and Gay Men and the Intra-Community Critique*, 21 N.Y.U. REV. L. & SOC. CHANGE 567, 607 (1994).

4. *See, e.g.*, *id.* at 606 ("Like most non-gay people, most gay men and lesbians want the equal right to *marry*, not merely access to some other domestic status. If *all* were free to *choose* either domestic partnership or marriage, then it might be appropriate for the state to proffer such an additional status."). William Eskridge has recommended a "menu" approach to recognizing personal relationships: "If some couples crave the commitment and legal benefits of marriage while other couples prefer a less formal arrangement, one possible response would be for the American legal system to offer couples a menu of choices for their unions." ESKRIDGE, *supra* note 1, at 78.

5. *See, e.g.*, Sheila Foster, *The Symbolism of Rights and the Cost of Symbolism: Some Thoughts on the Campaign for Same-sex Marriage*, 7 TEMP. POL. & CIV. RTS. L. REV. 319, 322-24 (Spring 1998) (noting gay people need laws that will protect them from discrimination before they will avail themselves of seeking marriage license); Charles Pouncy, *Marriage and Domestic Partnership: Rationality and Inequality*, 7 TEMP. POL. & CIV. RTS. L. REV. 363 (Spring 1998) (noting ideological problems with pursuing marriage). Paula Ettlebrick and Nancy Polikoff have been two writers who have consistently warned of the costs in pursuing recognition of marriage for same-sex couples. *See* Paula Ettlebrick, *Since When is Marriage a Path to Liberation?*, OUT/LOOK NAT'L GAY & LESBIAN Q. (Fall 1989) *reprinted in* SEXUAL ORIENTATION AND THE LAW, *supra* note 1, at 723; Nancy D. Polikoff, *We Will Get What We Ask For: Why Legalizing Gay and Lesbian Marriage Will Not "Dismantle the Legal Structure of Gender in Every Marriage,"* 79 VA. L. REV. 1535, 1546 (1993).

6. For example, Linda Bowles wrote in the CHICAGO TRIBUNE: "Homosexual marriage requires the surrender of cherished principles and the abandonment of fundamental values. It makes a mockery of the natural family, corrupts the church, endangers our national health and further lowers the moral bulwarks that hold back a rising tide of human depravity." Ball, *supra*

In the legal academic world, people like John Finnis, Robert George, and Raymond O'Brien present a more sophisticated legal framework for the legitimate interaction between government and morality, and for the harms that are inherent in homosexual relations.[7] The bottom line of this analysis is that the intrinsic, basic good of marriage cannot be achieved through a homosexual relationship.[8]

The classic liberal political responses to these types of argument have been relatively simple: they either see these arguments as a vindication of their skepticism about marriage in the first place, or they find the arguments irrelevant. For people like Sheila Foster and Charles Pouncy,[9] one would imagine the valorization of traditional marriage by opponents of same-sex marriage would reinforce their concerns about rushing to join such an institution. And for political liberals who support same-sex marriage, individuals who are "new natural lawyers" proceed on an assumption most of these liberals disagree with in the first place: that is, that government appropriately legislates on the basis of morality. Thus, for these individuals, there is little practical reason to engage in a conversation that is premised on a faulty assertion.

From my perspective, there is a practical problem with this latter response. Many liberal advocates of marriage for same-sex couples take pains to assert that achieving the right to marry on the part of gay couples will not adversely affect any efforts to achieve alternative forms of family.[10] These advocates never affirmatively denigrate domestic partnership efforts; they simply characterize the success of those efforts as still achieving purely second-class citizenship for gay people. Moreover, these advocates never expressly valorize marriage over other forms of relationships. They do not

---

note 2, at 1880 n.42 (quoting Linda Bowles, *Tolerating Ourselves to Death*, CHI. TRIB., May 15, 1996, at 19.).

7. *See, e.g.*, JOHN M. FINNIS, NATURAL LAW AND NATURAL RIGHTS (1980); John M. Finnis, *Law, Morality, and "Sexual Orientation,"* 69 NOTRE DAME L. REV. 1049 (1994); Robert George, *Social Cohesion and the Legal Enforcement of Morals: A Reconsideration of the Hart-Devlin Debate, in* MAKING MEN MORAL (1993); Robert P. George & Gerard V. Bradley, *Marriage and the Liberal Imagination*, 84 GEO. L.J. 301, 305 (1995); Raymond O'Brien, *Single-gender Marriage: A Religious Perspective*, 7 TEMP. POL. & CIV. RTS. L. REV. 429 (Spring 1998).

8. *See, e.g.*, George & Bradley, *supra* note 7, at 305; *see generally* Ball, *supra* note 2, at 1909-19 (describing and critiquing "new natural lawyers"); Stephen Macedo, *Homosexuality and the Conservative Mind*, 84 GEO. L.J. 261, 272-93 (1995) (same).

9. *See supra* note 5 and accompanying text.

10. *See* Wolfson, *supra* note 3, at 605 n.167 ("Because I believe there is no inconsistency among these demands [for marriage and for domestic partnership], I have pressed for our right to marry at the same time as I have worked to win equal health benefits for the unmarried partners of gay and non-gay New York City employees.") (*citing* Gay Teachers Ass'n v. Board of Educ., No. 43069/88 (N.Y. Sup. Ct. Aug. 12, 1991), *aff'd*, 585 N.Y.S.2d 1016 (App. Div. 1992) (settled successfully Oct. 30, 1993) (on file with Lambda Legal Defense and Education Fund)).

At a roundtable meeting of gay rights litigators and policymakers in October 1997, Beatrice Dohrn, observed that Lambda had been devoting equal, if not more, resources to the effort to achieve domestic partnership recognition, as it had devoted to its Marriage Project. Conversation with Beatrice Dohrn, Legal Director of Lambda Legal Defense and Education Fund at Lambda Offices in New York, New York (Oct. 1997).

assert that people who are married are in a "better" status than those who are unmarried or in domestic partnership relationships. Indeed, such assessments—which reek of normative conceptions of the "good"—would be largely foreign to the rights model on which most liberal advocacy writings are based. Rather, these advocates simply argue that marriage is a "status" that a gay couple has as much of a *right* to enter into as a heterosexual couple—but not that marriage is necessarily a better status or even a good status.

But the fact that liberal advocates hardly, if ever, valorize marriage over other relationships does not undermine the concerns voiced by some that seeking the right to marry may ultimately result in denigrating the different forms of family that many gay rights advocates currently seek to have recognized. For example, Paula Ettlebrick, who with Tom Stoddard in 1989, started off the most recent debate within the liberal gay rights movement about the desirability of pursuing marriage,[11] voiced this concern about pursuing the right to marry:

> [P]ursuing the legalization of marriage for same-sex couples would be leading [the gay rights] movement into a trap; we would be demanding access to the very institution which, in its current form, would undermine *our* movement to recognize many different kinds of relationships. We would be perpetuating the elevation of married relationships and of "couples" in general, and further eclipsing other relationships of choice.[12]

Liberal advocates understandably get frustrated when they hear these concerns. They repeat, yet again, that they are not arguing in *favor* of marriage *over* some other form of relationship. But while such liberal advocates may never explicitly argue that the married state is a "better" status to be in than the unmarried state, the *society* around them certainly has made that judgment already. Indeed, it is precisely because society believes the married state is normatively better than the unmarried state, that so many practical, economic, and social benefits have been pegged to marriage.[13] Thus, unless advocates of marriage for same-sex couples affirmatively *distance* themselves from the normative judgment that being married constitutes a better status than being unmarried, the simple act of seeking the right to enter the married

---

11. *See* Ettelbrick, *supra* note 5, at 721.

12. *Id.* at 723. Nancy Polikoff echoed the same concern several years later:

> I believe that an effort to legalize lesbian and gay marriage would make a public critique of the institution of marriage impossible. Long-term, monogamous couples would almost certainly be the exemplars of the movement, sharing stories of adversity resulting from their unmarried status . . . . Marriage would be touted as the solution to these couples' problems; the limitations of marriage, and of a social system valuing one form of human relationship above all others, would be downplayed.

Polikoff, *supra* note 5, at 1546.

13. *See* David L. Chambers, *What If?: The Legal Consequences of Marriage and the Legal Needs of Lesbian and Gay Couples*, 95 MICH. L. REV. 447, 452-85 (1996) (documenting extensive economic and social benefits that accrue through status of marriage).

status could understandably be understood as *acquiescing* in the normative judgment that marriage is better than other relationships.

In an article I published in 1996,[14] and in a recent essay in a New York University *Law Review* memorial issue dedicated to Tom Stoddard,[15] I argue that avoidance of a discussion about normative goods may not, in the long run, help achieve full social equality for gay people. My primary concern in those pieces was not the practical difficulty of unforeseen ramifications, which I have just discussed with regard to seeking the right to same-sex marriage, but rather the concern that avoiding a discussion of normative goods may leave us in a weakened position when we try to make a case for substantive equality and full acceptance of gay people and gay relationships.[16] In particular, it may lead us to avoid making the normative argument about the substantive moral equivalence between homosexual and heterosexual sex.[17]

Professor Milton Regan, in a comment to a paper delivered by Professor William Eskridge in 1993, pointed out that the social constructionist arguments presented by Eskridge could be used to force a "reinterpretation of tradition" that would require extending marriage to same-sex couples "based on an affirmation of a particular view of marriage, not simply a way of vindicating the neutral principle of individual choice."[18] I agree with Regan's observations that a case for same-sex marriage could be based more strongly on principles other than liberal neutrality. Indeed, in a recent article, *Moral Foundations for a Discourse on Same-Sex Marriage: Looking Beyond Political Liberalism*, Carlos Ball does a superb job of carrying out such an effort.[19]

Ball correctly assesses that, of all issues concerning gay equality, the effort to achieve marriage for same-sex couples most dramatically highlights the necessity to engage in a moral discourse.[20] As Ball correctly observes: "[T]he national debate [concerning marriage for same-sex couples] has centered around philosophical and moral issues about homosexuals and whether their relationships are *normatively* equivalent to heterosexual relationships."[21] Moreover, with regard to same-sex marriage, Ball cogently assesses the limits of political liberal arguments. He notes that opponents of same-sex

---

14. *See* Chai R. Feldblum, *Sexual Orientation, Morality, and the Law: Devlin Revisited*, 57 U. PITT. L. REV. 237, 298-304 (1996) [*hereinafter* Feldblum, *Devlin Revisited*].

15. *See* Chai R. Feldblum, *The Moral Rhetoric of Legislation*, 72 N.Y.U. L. REV. 992, 992 (1997) [*hereinafter* Feldblum, *Moral Rhetoric of Legislation*].

16. *See* Feldblum, *Devlin Revisited*, *supra* note 14, at 304-06, 311-12; Feldblum, *Moral Rhetoric of Legislation*, *supra* note 15, at 1007-08. My thinking in this regard was first stimulated by Michael Sandel. *See* Michael J. Sandel, *Moral Argument and Liberal Toleration: Abortion and Homosexuality*, 77 CAL. L. REV. 521, 521-22 (1989).

17. *See* Chai R. Feldblum, *Keep the Sex in Same-Sex Marriage*, 4 HARV. GAY & LESBIAN REV. 23, 25 (Fall 1997) [*hereinafter* Feldblum, *Same-Sex Marriage*] ("[T]he struggle to achieve recognition of marriage for same-sex couples offers us an opportunity—if we choose to take it. It gives us the chance to make the case for the normative moral equivalence of gay and heterosexual sex—an argument that is hardly ever heard in political circles.").

18. Regan, *supra* note 2, at 1532.

19. *See* Ball, *supra* note 2, *passim*.

20. *See id.* at 1878.

21. *Id.* at 1880.

marriage often argue that if "society can ban polygamy, why can it not also ban, or at least greatly discourage, homosexual conduct?,"[22] and then observes:

> A political liberal, relying solely on notions of equality, tolerance, and privacy, cannot satisfactorily respond to this argument. A polygamous marriage and a monogamous homosexual marriage can only be differentiated (or equated) by engaging in normative assessments regarding the *value* (whether intrinsic or instrumental) and the societal costs, if any, of these types of human arrangements. The traditional liberal response that arguments relating to the morality of homosexuality (or polygamy) are irrelevant to the policies that should be pursued by public institutions is ineffective and unrealistic.[23]

"Exactly so" is my reaction. In his article, Ball describes and critiques the political liberalism of Rawls[24] and Dworkin,[25] and then describes, and ultimately adopts, the "perfectionist liberalism" of Joseph Raz[26] as an alternative political theory framework that would allow us to discuss the normative good of same-sex marriage in political discourse.[27]

In my view, Ball has helped move this conversation forward significantly. For both practical and theoretical reasons, I believe it is useful that the liberal political mode of analysis is not the only one shaping the discourse today on the issue of gay equality in both the popular and academic press (although it is, of course, still the predominant one). Now I want to take the conversation a few steps further. I want to propose an alternative vision of the moral good of marriage, what I term here a "progressive moral case" for same-sex marriage, that will take into account the lessons of feminism and psychology. This vision would have a different set of ramifications for both gay people and for society at large than visions of marriage currently propounded by some advocates of same-sex marriage.

In order to come up with a description of marriage as a moral good, I believe an assessment would need to proceed as follows: First, one must ask, what is the purpose of marriage? Unlike some writers, I would not dismiss love as a relevant social policy goal.[28] I would incorporate some of the insights of psychology in describing the complex human emotional system that

---

22. *Id.* at 1878.
23. *Id.* at 1878-79 (footnotes omitted).
24. *See id.* at 1884-89.
25. *See id.* at 1896-99, 1902-07.
26. *See id.* at 1920-30.
27. *See id.* at 1941-42.
28. For example, Jonathan Rauch notes that while love is certainly

> a desirable element of marriage . . . [i]t cannot . . . be the defining element in society's eyes" [since] "[y]ou may or may not love your husband, but the two of you are just as married either way . . . . Love helps make sense of marriage from an emotional point of view, but it is not terribly important . . . in making sense of marriage from the point of view of social policy.

Jonathan Rauch, *Who Needs Marriage*, NEW REPUBLIC, 1996, *reprinted in* BEYOND QUEER: CHALLENGING THE GAY LEFT ORTHODOXY 298 (Bruce Bawer ed., 1997).

marriage between two equal partners can create. It is a human system that creates a haven of support, love, and nurturing. It is about two people coming together—bringing all their unique vulnerabilities and frailties—and supporting each other as each one grows and confronts the emotional and physical challenges of life. It is the stories of hope and commitment that are apparent in every one of the twenty-seven stories that make up the book *Ceremonies of the Heart: Celebrating Lesbian Unions*.[29]

In some cases, a marriage can actually be transformational—as two partners help each other overcome wounds and losses of the past. A recent issue of the *Family Therapy Networker*, a magazine geared to family therapists, included an article on Imago, a relatively new therapy process for couples.[30] The author, who went through the therapy for purposes of writing the article observed:

> Harville Hendrix (the creator of Imago) is neither the first nor the only person to suggest that the committed, intimate partnership carries the potential for transformational inner shifts . . . . Others too have proposed that a deeper purpose of love may be its power to touch in us the raw, frightened places that need most to heal and grow. Unquestionably, it is a process of unfolding that requires great daring: we must be ready to break open our hearts to admit a partner's pain and truth and, just as harrowing, allow ourselves to be fully seen.[31]

This view of marriage is similar to one articulated by Professor Milton Regan, in his book *Family Law and the Pursuit of Intimacy*.[32] In Regan's view, marriage is a key component of "relational selfhood."[33] As Regan observes:

> One's very sense of both a meaningful universe and a coherent self are dependent in crucial ways upon relationships with other family members. From this perspective, marriage . . . is a web of interdependence, "a shared history in which two people are bound together in part by what they have been through together."[34]

In this view, then, "the moral aspiration that marriage has expressed is not heterosexual intimacy per se, but the more general vision of responsibility based on the cultivation of a relational sense of identity."[35]

I believe there is a moral good in the creation of a relational community by two individuals. A second, and fully independent question for me, then, is whether monogamy—that is, strict sexual fidelity between the two people—is

29. CEREMONIES OF THE HEART: CELEBRATING LESBIAN UNIONS (Becky Butler ed., 1997).

30. *See* Marian Sandmaier, *Love for the Long Haul*, FAM. THERAPY NETWORKER, Sept./Oct. 1997, at 22.

31. *Id.* at 35.

32. MILTON C. REGAN, JR., FAMILY LAW AND THE PURSUIT OF INTIMACY (1993).

33. *Id.*

34. *Id.* at 95-96 (quoting R. BELLANE ET AL., HABITS OF THE HEART 103 (1985)).

35. *Id.* at 120. As Regan later pointed out, evidence of same-sex unions throughout history "provides the basis for a claim that a better interpretation of our marital tradition is as the provision of social support for those who wish to make a commitment to emotional interdependence." *See* Regan, *supra* note 2, at 1532.

essential for achieving the full normative good of this relational community. In a recent essay in the *Harvard Gay and Lesbian Review*, I argue that gay people who seek the right to marry must be able to articulate a coherent position on the question of monogamy.[36] The implication in my essay was that the position should be one in favor of monogamy.[37] The more I have contemplated this issue, however, the more complex it appears.

Monogamy seems, to me, to be a very useful mechanism for ensuring that each partner stays truly *present* in the relationship, and for helping to maintain the vulnerability and trust on which this relationship rests. But I am not sure whether the attributes of commitment and loyalty, which I see as the true essential attributes for achieving the normative good in the relationship, must necessarily foreclose any and all sexual play with others outside the relationship. I truly do not know. Certainly, the experience of many gay male couples and some lesbian couples, where sexual play with others is agreed to by both parties, and where the couples have maintained a very committed and loyal relationship over a number of years, throws some doubt for me on the normative assessment that true commitment and loyalty in a relationship must always, and in every case, necessarily include strict sexual fidelity.

It may be we are asking the wrong question when we focus on monogamy. There may be more important questions to determine whether a marriage constitutes a moral good than: "Are the spouses faithful to each other sexually?" Questions such as: "Does each partner truly understand and accommodate the vulnerabilities of the other?," and "do the partners help each other grow and meet life's challenges?" may be more important ones to ask. I am not sure. I think it is necessary to explore this issue if we are to establish the contours of the normative good of marriage. The key point for me in this talk is: what *allows* us to *have* such a conversation in the first place is a discussion (and a political theory) that enables us, and indeed *requires* us, to affirmatively engage with conceptions of the "good."

After determining the purpose of marriage as creating a relational community between two people, I would then ask: "Is marriage a preferable set-up to other relational arrangements? Should it be privileged and valued over other types of relationships?" My answer would be: "Not necessarily." My assessment of the moral good embodied in marriage does not assume marriage will serve as the centerpiece for an isolated, nuclear family. To the contrary, there are lessons the heterosexual society could well learn from the gay and lesbian community in terms of constructing a family. Gay and lesbian couples have often, through dint of necessity, been pioneers in creating new forms of extended families made up of friends and (often) ex-lovers. Unlike nuclear families, who are often isolated and cast adrift in society, extended gay families can provide support and care beyond a community of two people.[38] In addition, because lesbian couples who have children often

36. *See* Feldblum, *Same-Sex Marriage, supra* note 17, at 23-25.

37. *See id.*

38. *See generally* KATH WESTON, FAMILIES WE CHOOSE: LESBIANS, GAYS, KINSHIP (1991).

involve known male sperm-donors, and gay male couples may involve surrogate mothers, these couples have often succeeded in having more than two individuals successfully carry out parenting roles and responsibilities. There is no empirical reason to assume these family arrangements are of any less value than a strict "community of two." Thus, there is no legitimate, moral reason to restrict practical and economic benefits solely to those whose marriages operate solely within the context of an isolated nuclear family.

Finally, a corollary to the question of whether marriage should be privileged over other relationships, is the following: "Assuming a community of two people, as embodied in marriage, is a moral good—even accepting that such a community may be enhanced or supplemented by extended family arrangements—is it not appropriate for society to *expect* individuals to enter marriages and to pressure individuals in society to get married?" My answer here is: "No." My normative argument about marriage is not that it is good for *society*; my argument is that it is good, indeed it can be transformational, for the two individuals who choose to enter that marriage. I do not think we *know* yet whether marriage for every single person is good for society. The sole assertion I feel comfortable with, at the moment, is that a "community of two" between two equal partners is a normative good for those two individuals. I see no basis for society to pressure all individuals to enter into such a community if particular individuals are not interested in doing so.

As I noted in the beginning of this talk, there are many ways to address same-sex marriage. I believe the moral bracketing imposed by political liberal theory is ultimately unsatisfactory in the effort to achieve societal recognition of same-sex marriages. Thus, I believe we would do better, in the long run, to adopt a political theory that enables us to discuss, *within* the context of litigation and legislation, the moral good that can be achieved in marriage for both heterosexual people and gay people. And to me, a key element in such a discussion must be an incorporation of the knowledge and insights some of us can bring as gay people and as feminists.

Once we begin such a discussion, I believe we will find that we can talk about the "good" of marriage, and not just the "right," without endorsing a cookie-cutter model of marriage as it has traditionally been understood. The moral good of marriage, as I see it, is an equal partnership between two people who enter the marriage for mutual love and support; a partnership that is valued by society, but not "privileged" or expected; and a partnership that can accommodate and interact with a rich range of extended family relationships.

I look forward to a further continuation of this conversation.

CAN CANADA SURVIVE THE *CHARTER*?

CHARLES TAYLOR*

Professor Taylor begins his analysis of Canada's current constitutional crisis by discussing two long-standing "existential" questions: why should Canada exist, and why should Quebec be part of Canada? The contradictory answers to these questions reflect contradictory understandings of the nature of rights, as reflected in the debate over the Charter of Rights and Freedoms. *Professor Taylor traces the roots of this debate in differing philosophical views of the nature of liberalism. He concludes by proposing a new kind of confederation in which these differing views could be accommodated.*

Le professeur Taylor commence son analyse de la crise constitutionnelle canadienne actuelle en traitant de deux questions «existentielles» de longue date: pourquoi le Canada devrait-il exister, et pourquoi le Québec devrait-il faire partie du Canada? Les réponses contradictoires reflètent la nature de notre compréhension des droits, comme l'indique le débat portant sur la Charte des droits et libertés. Selon le professeur Taylor, ce débat a ses origines dans des perceptions philosophiques différentes de la nature du libéralisme. Il conclut en proposant un nouveau type de confédération, où ces points de vue divergents pourraient coexister.

TABLE OF CONTENTS

I. INTRODUCTION

I apologize for my somewhat over-dramatic attention-grabbing title. If Canada breaks up, it won't be the *Charter* which does it alone, or even mainly. But I think the *Charter* has come to play an important role in the estrangement between the two parts of the country, especially among political elites, and it is worth trying to understand what is happening here.

In order fully to grasp what is going on, I think, we have to place the differences about the *Charter* in the context of the long-standing series of Canadian misunderstandings, the long struggle between French Canada and the rest of the country over a definition of Canada as a political entity. In a way, the divergences about the *Charter* constitute only the latest avatar of a running disagreement or misunderstanding which has plagued our federation from its beginning (or even before).

The disagreement emerges whenever we really face the question: what is a country for? That is, what ought to be the basis of unity around which a sovereign political entity

* Professor, Department of Philosophy, McGill University. This paper was presented on March 14, 1991 as the Third McDonald Lecture of the Centre for Constitutional Studies, University of Alberta.

can be built? This is a strange question, in a way; it is not one that would likely be asked in many countries. But it arises here because there are alternatives and, therefore, a felt need for justification. These alternatives exist for us — that is, in our understanding of our situation — even when they are not very likely, when they enjoy minimal support and are hardly in the cards politically. They can still exist as a challenge to self-justification, because they existed historically, and we retain the sense that our prevailing arrangements emerge out of a choice which excluded them.

II. WHY CANADA?

In Canada-outside-Quebec (COQ)[1] the alternatives are two: the country or bits of it could join, or could have joined the U.S.; and the bits could also have failed to join together — and indeed, could one day deconfederate again. So there are two "existential" questions for COQ which we can call the unity and distinctness questions respectively. For Quebec, there is one big question, which is too familiar, and too much on the agenda today to need much description. It is the issue whether to be part of Canada or not; and if so, how. I stress that neither of the "existential" alternatives may be strong options in COQ today, but that doesn't stop them functioning as reference points for self-definition, as ways of defining the question: what do we exist for? In a sense the existential questions of the two societies are interwoven. Perhaps COQ would not feel the need for self-definition to anything like the same degree if Quebec were not contemplating answering its existential question in a radical form. But once the country's existence is threatened in this way, all the suppressed alternatives rise to the surface in the rest of Canada, as well.

So what are the answers? It will be easier to set out the problem by taking "English Canada" first. The answer here used to be simple. Way back when it really fitted into our official name of British North America, the distinctness question answered itself; and unity seemed to be the corollary of the drive for distinctness in the face of the American colossus. But as the Britishness, even "Englishness," of non-Quebec Canada declines, this becomes less and less viable as an answer. We are all the Queen's subjects, but this seems to mean less to fewer people; and more awkwardly, it means quite a bit to some still, but nothing at all to others, and thus cannot be the basis of unity.

What binds Canada together outside Quebec is thus no longer a common provenance, and less and less a common history, but political institutions and ways of being. This is not a total break from the old identity, because Britishness also defined itself largely in terms of political institutions: parliamentary government, a certain juridical tradition, and

---

1 In Quebec we speak blithely of "English Canada," but the people who live there do not identify with this label. We need a handy way of referring to the rest of the country as an entity, even if it lacks for the moment political expression. In order to avoid the clumsy three-word hyphenated expression, I plan to use "COQ" henceforth in this paper. I hope the reader will not take this as a sign of encroaching barbarism or Québécois self-absorption (although it might partake in small measure of both).

the like. The slide has been continuous, and without a sharp break from the old to the new. There are even certain continuing elements, but the package is different.

Canadians feel that they are different from the Americans, because (a) they live in a less violent and conflict-ridden society. This is partly just a matter of lucking out. We do not have a history which has generated an undeclared, low-level race war continuously feeding itself in our cities. But it is also a matter of political culture. From the very beginning Americans have put a value on energetic, direct defense of rights, and therefore they are ready to mitigate their condemnation of violence. There is more understanding of it south of the border, more willingness to make allowances for it. And this has something to do with the actual level being higher there, as well as with a number of strange penchants of American society, such as that expressed in the powerful lobby for personal firearms. Canadians tend to put more value on "peace, order and good government." At least, this is how we see ourselves, which is perhaps what is important for our purposes; but there seems to be some truth in the perception.

As a consequence, there is more tolerance here of rules and restrictions which are justified by the need for order, more of a favourable prejudice (at least in English Canada), a free gift of the benefit of the doubt, to the police forces. Hence the relative absence of protest when the *War Measures Act* was invoked in 1970; hence also the strange reluctance of the Canadian public to condemn the RCMP, even after all the revelations of its dubious behaviour.

We might add that the Americans' tolerance of conflict extends into the domain of law, as well. They are more litigious than we are. They think that's a good thing, that it reflects well on them. No one should take any guff from anyone. We tend to deplore it. From an American point of view, we seem to have an endless appetite for guff. But perhaps the long term effect of the 1982 *Charter* will be to diminish this difference.

Related to this first point, Canadians (b) see their political society as more committed to collective provision, over against an American society which gives greater weight to individual initiative. Appeals for reduced government can be heard from the right of the political spectrum in both countries, but the idea of what reduced government actually means seems to be very different. There are regional differences in Canada, but generally Canadians are proud of and happy with their social programs, especially health insurance, and find the relative absence of these in the U.S. disturbing. The fact that poverty and destitution have been left to proliferate in American cities as they have during the Reagan years is generally seen here as a black mark against that society. Canadian practice may be not as much better as many of us believe; but the important point is that this is seen as a difference worth preserving.

(a) (Law and order) and (b) (collective provision) help to answer the distinctness question. They explain why we are and want to remain a distinct political unit. But what answers the unity question? Why be a single country, and what common goals ought to animate this country? In one sense, (a) and (b) can serve here as well, if one thinks (as many Canadians instinctively do) that we need to hang together in order to maintain this alternative political culture as a viable option in North America. And then (b) can be logically extended into one of the principal, declared common objectives of the Canadian federation in recent decades: (c) the equalization of life conditions and life chances between the regions. The solidarity of collective provision, which within each regional society generates such programs as medicare, can be seen as finding its logical expression in a solidarity of mutual help between regions.

And so Canadian federalism has generated the practice of large-scale redistribution of fiscal resources through equalization payments, and attempts have been made at regional development. This, too, contrasts with recent American practice and provides a further answer to the distinctness question. We perhaps owe the drive to equality to the fact that we have been confronted with existential questions in a way that our neighbours have not since 1865. The Canadian federal union has been induced to justify itself, and greater inter-regional solidarity may be one of the fruits of this underlying *angst*.

But this bonding principle has also been a worrying source of division, because it is widely seen as a locus of failed aspirations and disappointed expectations. The principles of regional equality and mutual help run against a perceived reality of Central Canadian domination in the outlying regions, a grievous mismatch of promise and performance. Recently it has become clearer that the disappointment takes two rather different forms, reflecting different ideas of regional equality. A source of disappointment in some parts, mainly Atlantic Canada, is the failure of federal programs actually to improve regional economic standards. The failure is one of mutual help. Elsewhere, mainly in Western Canada, the sense of grievance is mobilized around neglected interests: the regions are not listened to, their interests are ridden over roughshod by a dominant Central Canada. The failure is one of balance of power. In one version, the implicit contract which is seen as unfulfilled calls for redistribution to poorer regions. In the other version, it calls for a redress of power and influence in favour of the regions with less demographic and economic clout. In one case, the implicit promise is of equalized incomes; in the other it points to more equalized power between regional societies.

It is clear that this issue of regional equality is a very troubled one in Canada. That's because on one hand it is an indispensable part of the answer to the unity question, while on the other it seems to many so largely unrealized, and on top of it all, we agree less and less on what it actually means.

But even if things were going swimmingly in this domain, we still would not have a full answer to the unity question. "English" Canada has been becoming more and more diverse, less and less "English," over the decades. The fact that it has always been an immigrant society, i.e. one which functions through admitting a steady stream of new arrivals, on top of the fact that it couldn't aspire to make immigrants over to its original mould, has meant that it has *de facto* become more and more multicultural over the years. It could not aspire to assimilate the newcomers to an existing mould, because this was originally British, hence ethnic. In the United States, which has always operated on a strong sense that it incarnates unrivalled political institutions, the drive to make everyone American could proceed apace. It was never as clear what the Canadian identity amounted to in political terms, and insofar as it was conceived as British, it couldn't be considered normative for new arrivals. First, it was only the identity of one part of the country, and second, it couldn't but come to be seen as one ethnic background among others.

Canadians have seen their society as less of a melting pot than the U.S.A., and there has been some truth in this. In contrast to the neighbour society, people have spoken of a Canadian "mosaic." So this has even become for some a new facet of their answer to the distinctiveness question, under the rubric of (d) multiculturalism. This is also far from trouble-free. Questions are being posed in both the major cultures about the pace and even goals of integration, or assimilation of immigrants into the larger anglophone or francophone society. This is particularly troubling in Quebec which has much less of a historic experience of assimilating immigrants and a much higher proportion of whose francophone population is *pure laine*.

This makes even more acute the need for a further point of unity, a common reference point of identity, which can rally people from many diverse backgrounds and regions. In a quite astonishing way, (e) the *Charter of Rights* has come to fill this role in English Canada in recent years. It is astonishing, because nine years ago it didn't exist. Nor was there that much of a groundswell of support demanding its introduction before it became a bone of contention between federal and provincial governments in the run-up to the patriation of 1981-82. But the Meech Lake debate showed how important it has become in COQ not just as an additional bulwark of rights, but as part of the indispensable common ground on which all Canadians ought to stand. For many people, it has come in the space of a few years to define in part the Canadian political identity.[2] And since in COQ the national identity has to be defined in terms of political institutions for reasons rehearsed above, this has been a fateful development.

III. WHY QUEBEC?

How about Quebec? How can it go about answering its existential question? The terms are very different. In Quebec, there isn't a distinctness issue. The language and culture by themselves mark us off from Americans, and also from other Canadians. Much of (a) to (e) is seen as a Good Thing in Quebec. (a) People do not compare themselves a lot with the U.S., but there is no doubt that Quebeckers are spontaneously on the side of law and order, and are even more horrified by internecine conflict than other Canadians. The FLQ utterly and totally relegated themselves to irrecoverable history as

2. Alan Cairns has written very insightfully on this development. See in particular his "Constitutional Minoritarianism in Canada" in R.L. Watts and D.M. Brown, eds., *Canada: The State of the Federation 1990* (Kingston: Institute of Intergovernmental Relations, 1990) 71; and "Ritual, Taboo and Bias in Constitutional Controversies in Canada, or Constitutional Talk Canadian Style" (1990) 54 Sask. L. Rev. 121.

soon as they murdered Laporte. The present rather halfhearted attempts to romanticize their escapades on the 20th anniversary of the October crisis should not mislead in this regard. The reaction to the massacre at Polytechnique is also eloquent on this score. Quebec society reacted more like a wounded family than like a large-scale, impersonal political unit. (b) It goes without saying that people are proud of their social programs in the province, and want to keep them. (d) Multiculturalism is more problematic. As a federal policy, multiculturalism is sometimes seen as a device to deny French-speaking minorities their full recognition, or even to reduce the importance of the French fact in Canada to that of an outsize ethnic minority. And within Quebec itself, the growing diversity of francophone society is causing much heartburn and anxiety. (c) Regional equality is generally supported in Quebec, and even (e) the *Charter* was very favourably seen until it came to be perceived as an instrument for the uniformization of language regimes across the country. Even now its other provisions are widely popular.

But these factors do not go very far to answer the question, "what is a country for?" There is one obvious answer to this question, which has continued down through the decades for over two centuries: (f) you need a country to defend and promote the nation. The nation here was originally "la nation canadienne-française." Now without entirely abandoning the first formulation, it tends to be put as "la nation québécoise." This does not betoken any change in ethnic identity, of course. It reflects rather a sense which presents itself as realistic, but may be too pessimistic, that the really survivable elements of "la nation canadienne-française" are only to be found in Quebec.

But the real point here is that (f) makes the survival and flourishing of this nation/language one of the prime goals of political society. No political entity is worth allegiance which does not contribute to this. The issue, independent Quebec versus remaining in Canada, turns simply on different judgements about what does contribute to it. Put in terms of a possible formula for Canada, this means that from a Quebec perspective, (a) to (e) may be attractive features, but the absolutely crucial one, that Canada must have to possess a *raison d'être*, is that it contribute to the survival and furtherance of la nation canadienne-française.

This means in practice some kind of dualism. It was this, of course, which successive Quebec leaders always gave expression to when they described Canada as a pact between "deux nations" or "deux peuples fondateurs." Dualism in turn had to exist at two levels. (1) It meant that French had to be recognized as a language along with English in the federation. That is, French had to be given a status clearly different from that of an ethnic immigrant language, even if it were the most important among these. And (2) "la nation canadienne-française," or its major part, had to have some autonomy, some ability to act as a unit. Both these features were built to some degree into the original Confederation pact, but in the case of (1) in partial and somewhat grudging form. (1) and (2) are separate requirements, but also in a sense related. There is a certain degree of complementarity, in that the more freely and completely (1) is granted, in theory the less the need will be felt for autonomous action. It is perhaps the tragedy of Canada that (1) was eventually granted too late and too grudgingly, and that this established a high and irreversible pattern of demands on (2).

Both these requirements have been a source of difficulty. The extension of (1) beyond its original limits raised a problem because COQ in its developing multiculturalism was naturally led to accord English the status of a common language, and to split language from culture. That English was the main language was not meant to imply that people of English descent had privileges or were somehow superior. The hegemony of English had to be justified in purely utilitarian terms. Within this framework, the case for putting French alongside English was impossible to make. Outside Quebec, a special status for French was rarely justified by numbers, and certainly not by its indispensability as a medium of communication. It seemed like indefensible favouritism.

Secondly, both (1) and (2) met with resistance because of a perceived difference of Quebec from the values of the rest of Canada. This starts off as a dark prejudice in the mind of Orange Protestants, but it continues on in many another milieu because of the supposed appeal of illiberal modes of thought in Quebec. In particular, this militated against further concessions in the area of (2).

It has been one of the remarkable achievements of the last 30 years, and particularly of the Trudeau government, to have established (1) almost integrally. There has been a certain cost in resentment in some areas, and this may be fateful in the forthcoming negotiations. I shall return to this below. But there is no doubt that a big change has been brought about. On (2) as well, great progress has been made. First, the Canadian federation has proven a very flexible instrument, giving lots of powers to the provinces. And secondly, where Quebec's needs have been different from the other provinces, a large *de facto* special status has been developed. Quebec has its own Pension Plan, levies its own income tax, has a special immigration regime, and so on.

But where things have blocked is on the recognition of this. Giving Quebec the autonomy it needs without disbalancing the Canadian federation would involve giving Quebec a different kind of relation to the federal government and institutions. Although this has been worked *de facto* to a remarkable extent, there are powerful resistances to according it recognition in principle. This is because there is a deep clash of purpose between the two sides of Canada. Where the old clash of values seems to have disappeared, a new conflict of purposes, of answers to the question, "what is a country for?" has surfaced.

The demands of (2), of a special status for Quebec, run against those of regional equality (c) as these are conceived by many in COQ, and against a widespread understanding of the *Charter* (e). (c) has come to be defined for some as entailing an equality of the provinces. The great moral force of the principle of equity between regions has been mobilized behind the rather abstract juridical issue of the relative constitutional status of provinces. Now regional equity seems to be flouted if all provinces are not placed on the same footing. But a special status can be presented as a breach in this kind of equality.

More grievously, the special status for Quebec is plainly justified on the grounds of the defence and promotion of la nation canadienne-française (f). But this is a collective goal. The aim is to ensure the flourishing and survival of a *community*. Now the new patriotism of the *Charter* has given an impetus to a philosophy of rights and of nondiscrimination which is highly suspicious of collective goals. It can only countenance them if they are clearly subordinated to individual rights and to provisions of non-discrimination. But for those who take these goals seriously, this subordination is unacceptable. The *Charter* and the promotion of the nation, as understood in their respective constituencies, are on a collision course. The reactions to Bill 178 and much of the Meech Lake debate were eloquent on this score.

This difficulty arises with (2), where it didn't for (1). The provisions for bilingualism in federal legislation can be justified in terms of individual rights. They concern the guarantee that francophones can be dealt with and obtain government services in their language. Once French is given this status along with English, what is protected is the rights of individuals. The collective goal goes beyond this. The aim is not only that francophones be served in French, but that there still be francophones there in the next generation; this is the objective of (f). It cannot be translated into an assurance of rights for *existing* francophones. Indeed, pursuing it may even involve reducing their individual freedom of choice, as Law 101 does in Quebec, where francophone parents must send their children to French-language schools.

So the two halves of Canada have come onto a collision course because of the conflict between their respective answers to the question "what is a country for?" In particular, a conflict between (c) regional equality as widely understood and (e) the *Charter* as a symbol of unity on one hand, and (2) Quebec autonomy on the other. But before examining a bit more closely how this conflict works out in the case of the *Charter*, I want to look a little at the history of our national misunderstanding in order to see what is special about the present conjuncture.

IV. WHY NOW?

For one might well ask, why the collision course now? Surely the old "English" Canada, before the legislation about bilingualism and the Trudeau revolution, was even more inhospitable to the demands of Quebec. It balked not only at (2), but at (1) as well. Moreover, it penetrated much more within Quebec. In those days, the English minority, backed often by the federal government or pan-Canadian institutions like the CPR, maintained its own English-only forms of operation, excluding or marginalizing or down-grading the French language. Why didn't things fly apart then?

The answer is that separation did not seem a realistic option back then for all sorts of reasons. It started with a clear-sighted appreciation of the relation of forces, and a sense of what the English Canadian majority would tolerate. There was also a greater commitment to the francophone minorities outside the province than there now is. But an extremely important factor was the restricted economic role of French Quebeckers. The English still had a preponderant role in the economy. Big business spoke English; anglophones dominated the ranks of management and had more than their share of certain key economic professions like engineering. This was a source of grievance on many levels. In particular, it was what permitted English to arrogate to itself a place in the province which demographics would never justify. For instance, to take just one kind of instance, before the Quiet Revolution, again and again, union leaders would have to bargain in English with management on behalf of a work force which was 100% francophone. But at the same time, that imbalance contributed to a climate in which Quebec society felt incomplete, in which essential functions were being filled by outsiders. The relation was never articulated in this way at the time, but it helped to keep the option of a total break off the agenda. Separation wasn't a real option before 1960, even though it seems to have been toyed with as an eventual long-term destination by Abbé Groulx.

Paradoxically, as some of the most crying grievances were resolved, as the insulting and sometimes threatening marginalization of the French language was reversed, as francophone Quebeckers began to take their full place in the economy, at first through the public and para-public sectors (e.g. Hydro-Québec) and then the private sector, precisely in the wake of all these successes, the demand for independence gained strength; until it became one of two major constitutional options, on a par with its federalist rival, and since Meech even ahead. And all this while outside Quebec at the federal level, bilingualism is advancing and Quebeckers wield more power than ever before. These are the years of "French Power." Some westerners have the feeling that the federal government is run by Quebeckers. Why does break-up loom now? How is this paradoxical and even perverse result to be explained?

Part of the answer, implicit in the above, is that now for the first time the option looks conceivable, possible, even safe. In this regard, even the last decade has seen a change. In 1980, most Quebeckers still found sovereignty a somewhat frightening prospect. The referendum revealed that clearly. In 1990, this no longer seems to be so. A great deal of the difference seems to stem from the now perceived high-profile place of francophones as big players in our economic life. This change has been happening over a number of decades, but as is the way with media-driven public perceptions, the realization has come all in a rush. And with this realization, a great flush of confidence. As often with these media-driven perceptions, we go easily from one exaggeration to another. Quebeckers were not as powerless before as they thought, and they are not as powerful now as they think. Separation risks being much more economically costly than they now believe, even as it would have been less catastrophic than many thought in 1980. And we may even be in for another swerve of opinion as the present recession dims expectations. But the basic change is undeniable. Separation is really thinkable.

But that can't be the whole explanation. To claim this would be to say that Quebeckers never really wanted anything else, that they were just waiting for the moment when they could dare go for it. And nothing could be more false than that. Francophone Quebeckers are attached to this country by a great deal: first of all, the sense that the larger entity was the home of la nation canadienne-française, whose whole extent included more than Quebec; then a certain attachment to a constitutional home which had become familiar, and which their leaders had had a hand in building. But what was always missing was a genuine patriotism for Canada. That kind of sentiment was reserved for la nation canadienne-française. It has lately been transposed onto Quebec, as the viable segment of that nation, but never managed to spread from there onto the whole political unit. That is why people have often spoken of Canada as being for Quebeckers a *mariage de raison* (marriage of reason). This somewhat understates the case, because it doesn't take account of the multiform attachment to Canada I have just described, but it is emotionally true in the negative sense that a genuine patriotism for a bilingual, two-nation Canada never developed.

But this by itself still does not explain the strength of the independentist option today. After all, if Canada was a *mariage de raison*, why abandon it when it has never been so reasonable, when the deal seems the most favourable ever? Of course, many federalist Quebeckers are pleading the cause of Canada today in just these terms. But why does it not have more success? Why are even those who are making the plea profoundly ambivalent about it?

Here one can easily be misled, because the opponents of these partisans of "profitable federalism" seem to want to engage them on their own ground, and strive to prove that confederation is a bad deal for us. But in fact, the emotional drive behind independence is elsewhere. It is much more a failure of *recognition*. For decades, Quebec leaders explained that Confederation was a pact between two founding peoples, two nations. This was never the way the matter was understood outside the province. But the claim was not so much to the effect that this was the plain sense of the confederation pact, somehow perversely forgotten by the others — although that is how it was often put. It was much more an expression of the profound sentiment that this was the only form in which Confederation could be ultimately acceptable to French Canadians in a way which could engage their hearts and respect their dignity.

In reality it was necessary to live with compromises, in which the duality principle got a rather limited and grudging expression. It was necessary to operate in a country which for many purposes was run much more as a nation with one hegemonic culture, with more or less generous provision for minorities on a regional basis. Present-day Canadians, some of whom still may want to complain about the number of languages on their corn flakes boxes, have no idea of how exiguous the place of French was in the bad old days. In the '30s even the money was still unilingual English.

Canada had to be accepted, but never so as to engage the heart or respect dignity. It could not be accepted "dans l'honneur et l'enthusiasme," to use the phrase which has been so often repeated during the drama of Meech Lake. Below the rational acceptance of the *mariage de raison*, these denials bite deep. This is easy to lose sight of, because those who are frustrated in their desire for recognition understandably do not want to present their case in those terms. It is only when one is recognized that one is happy to avow the desire. So the phrase "dans l'honneur et l'enthusiasme" emerged when it looked as though that aspiration was at last met. But when it is denied, the opponents of federal Canada will pretend that no one was ever interested in mere symbols, that the calculus of independence is made in the realistic terms of power and prosperity, that the attitudes of the English-Canadian partner mean nothing to us. In all this, they do protest a little too much.

The present strength of independentism is thus due in part to the new confidence of Quebeckers, in part to the fact that Canada never gelled as a nation for them, but in large part it is due to the continued denial of their understanding of Canada, of the only terms on which it could have been fully accepted by them. These were articulated, among other forms, in the "two-nations" view of the country. Of course, this was unacceptable as it stood to the rest of the country, which did not itself feel like a "nation." Here there was an attempt by French-Canadians to foist a symmetrical identity on their partners. And this attempt is not yet abandoned, as one can see from much of the discussion in Quebec today, to which I will return below. But there was a basic demand which could be extricated from this presumptuous definition of the other. This was the demand that la nation canadienne-française be recognized as a crucial component of the country, as an entity whose survival and flourishing was one of the main purposes of Canada as a political society. If this had been granted, it wouldn't have mattered how the rest of the country defined itself.

In practice, the country has come to arrange itself not at all badly for this purpose, through federal bilingualism, through advances made by some French-speaking minorities elsewhere, and through a *de facto* administrative special status for Quebec. But what was missing was a clear recognition that this was part of our purpose as a federation. This is why Meech Lake was so important, and why its failure will have such dire consequences. If one just listens to what people say in Quebec, this can seem strange. Lots of Quebeckers never even admitted that they were in favour of Meech, or expressed lukewarm support. Basically, all the independentists took this line. Those who were sceptical about English Canada hedged their bets and never wanted to allow that the recognition mattered to them. But the depth of the reaction to its demise shows how little this represented how they felt.

Meech was important because it was the first time that Canada was writing into a statement of what it was about a recognition of Canadian duality and the special role of Quebec. The fact that the accord conferred no additional powers largely narrowed its significance to this one clear declaration of intent. The importance of this declaration can be understood only in the light of the years of non-recognition, of the *mariage de raison* that failed to engage the heart and reflect dignity. It can be understood in the context of a present generation which is quite free of the timidity of its ancestors before a possible break, which is even a little surprised, sometimes a trifle contemptuous of its predecessors, for having put up with non-recognition for so long. And its refusal when it was no more than a declaration of pure intent takes on fateful significance. (That's the point of the oft-repeated phrase that Meech constituted our "conditions minimales.")

With the demise of Meech, something snapped. I think it can be rather simply described. Quebeckers will no longer live in a structure which does not fully recognize their national goals. In the early '80s, after the defeat of the "yes" in the referendum, many toyed with the idea of accepting the *mariage de raison* and making a go of it with or without recognition. The new confidence could also have motivated this rather different stance, which marginalized the issue of recognition. After all, if you know your own worth, why do you need the other? But in a sense, Meech wiped out this possibility, just because it raised the hope of recognition. And now we are irretrievably on another track. (Not that I think the "reasonable" track could have lasted very long anyway; it was always at the mercy of some new development.)

What remains to be explained is the extraordinary euphoria which all observers noted among the crowds celebrating Quebec's national holiday, St. Jean Baptiste Day in 1990. Why did Quebeckers feel so united, and so relieved at being united, almost as though the demise of Meech had taken a great weight off them? I think it's because the long division and hesitation, between the "reasonable" acceptance of a structure which did not recognize them and the insistence on having their national purposes openly accepted, had at last been resolved. This was felt as a division between Quebeckers, and especially painfully at the time of the 1980 referendum, when families were often split. But is also divided many Quebeckers within themselves. At last the long conflict, the long hesitation, the long ambivalence was over. Quebeckers were clear on what they wanted to ask of any future political structure on the northern half of this continent. Consensus was recovered, but also a kind of psychic unity. A certain kind of compromise was forever over.

But what does this mean for the future? It means that demand (2) has become imperious and virtually non-negotiable. And this brings a real danger of breach between the two parts of the country. For it follows that Quebeckers will not accept any structure in which their collective aspirations are not fully and overtly recognized. Already this is expressing itself in the requirement that negotiation be one-on-one, because this is felt to reflect in itself the acknowledgement of Quebec's status as a distinct society. But all this is happening at the moment that COQ's newfound *Charter* patriotism is making it less capable of acknowledging the legitimacy of collective goals and as regional alienation is lending further strength to the principle of the equality of provinces. The common ground seems to be shrinking fast.

V. RIGHTS AND NATIONS

From the above discussion we can see that the impact of the *Charter* on our impending potential break-up fits into an already distressingly familiar pattern. What Quebec or French Canada has felt to be essential to its recognition seems in COQ to violate one of the conditions of national unity on a fair basis. Just as bilingualism seemed to many an unconscionable favouritism to one minority language, just because they saw Canada as a multicultural mosaic united around a lingua franca, English; so the recognition of collective goals for one province seems to violate the status of the *Charter* as the framework of rights enjoyed equally by all Canadians. And in fact the anti-Meech majority in COQ brought together these two kinds of opposition under one roof, even though many *Charter* patriots had been vigorous and courageous defenders of bilingualism.

But do we have to fight over the *Charter*? Is it all perhaps based on a misunderstanding? It is time to delve into the philosophical and political sources of the dispute.

At first sight, it might appear that the disagreement could have been avoided. Those who drafted the *Charter* were aware of the complexity of the Canadian political scene. They tried to strike a balance between individual rights and collective goals. The *Charter* not only entrenches the internationally recognized list of immunities, it also deals with language rights, which although they do not strictly figure as collective rights derive their political significance from the existence of communities striving to secure their survival. In addition, the document recognizes "aboriginal rights," which, although as yet undefined, will clearly have to incorporate some which are collective in nature.

But as the *Charter* entered public consciousness, this balance was progressively lost. This is not surprising if we take into account the whole movement towards entrenched rights and judicial retrieval which has been proceeding throughout western societies, and to some extent even on a world scale, since the Second World War. Our *Charter* in fact follows the trend of the last half of the 20th century and gives a basis for judicial review on two basic scores. First, it protects the rights of the individual in a variety of ways. And second, it guarantees equal treatment of citizens in a variety of respects; or alternatively put, it defends against discriminatory treatment on a number of irrelevant grounds, like race or sex. Our *Charter* consists of much more, as I have just mentioned, but the two themes I single out dominate in the public consciousness.

This is no accident. These two kinds of provisions are now quite common in entrenched schedules of rights which provide the basis for judicial review. In this sense, the western world, perhaps the world as a whole, is following American precedent. The Americans were the first to write out and entrench a bill of rights, which they did during the ratification process of their Constitution and as a condition of its successful outcome. One might argue that they weren't entirely clear on judicial retrieval as a method of securing those rights, but this rapidly became the practice. The first amendments secured individuals, and sometimes state governments,[3] against encroachment by the new federal

3. For instance, the First Amendment, which forbade Congress from establishing any religion, was not originally meant to separate state and church as such. It was enacted at a time when many states had established churches, and it was plainly meant to prevent the new federal government from interfering with or overruling these local arrangements. It was only later after the Fourteenth Amendment,

government. It was after the Civil War in the period of triumphant Reconstruction, and particularly with the Fourteenth Amendment which called for "equal protection" for all citizens by the laws, that the theme of non-discrimination became central to judicial review. But it is by now on par with the older norm of the defence of individual rights, and in public consciousness even perhaps ahead.

Now for a number of people in COQ, a political society's espousing certain collective goals threatens to run against both of these basic provisions of our *Charter*, or indeed any acceptable bill of rights. First, the collective goals may require restrictions on the behaviour of individuals which may violate their rights. For many non-francophone Canadians, both inside and outside Quebec, this feared outcome has already materialized with Quebec's language legislation. For instance, Law 101 prescribes the type of school to which parents can send their children; and in the most famous instance, it forbids certain kinds of commercial signage. This latter provision was actually struck down by the Supreme Court as contrary to the *Quebec Bill of Rights* as well as the *Charter*, and only re-enacted through the invocation of the notwithstanding clause.

But second, even if this were not the case, espousing collective goals on behalf of a national group can be thought to be inherently discriminatory. In the modern world it will always be the case that not all those living as citizens under a certain jurisdiction will belong to the national group thus favoured. This by itself could be thought to involve some discrimination. But beyond this, the pursuit of the collective end will in all likelihood involve treating insiders and outsiders differently. Thus the schooling provisions of law 101 forbid (roughly speaking) francophones and immigrants sending their children to English-language schools, but allow Canadian anglophones to do so.

This sense that the *Charter* clashes with basic Quebec policy was one of the strong grounds to opposition in COQ to the Meech Lake Accord. The worry here concerned the distinct society clause, and the common demand for amendment was that the *Charter* be "protected" against this clause or take precedence over it. There was undoubtedly in this a certain amount of old-style anti-Quebec prejudice, the continuing echoes of the old image of "priest-ridden Quebec." Thus various women's groups voiced the fear that Quebec governments in pursuit of higher birth rates might adopt Ceaucescu-type policies of forbidding abortions or making birth control more difficult. But even when one factors out the silliness, contempt and ill-will, there remains a serious point here. Indeed, there are two serious points. First, there is a genuine difference in philosophy concerning the bases of a liberal society; and second, there is a difference in view about the basis for national unity.

Let us take the philosophical difference first. Those who take the view that individual rights must always come first, and along with non-discrimination provisions must take

following the so-called "Incorporation" doctrine, that these restrictions on the federal government were held to have been extended to all governments, at whatever level.

precedence over collective goals, are often speaking out of a view of a liberal society which has become more and more widespread in the Anglo-American world. Its source is, of course, the United States, and it has recently been elaborated and defended by some of the best philosophical and legal minds in that society, for instance John Rawls, Ronald Dworkin, Bruce Ackerman, and others.[4] There are various formulations of the main idea, but perhaps the one which encapsulates most clearly the point which is relevant to us is Dworkin's way of putting things in his short paper entitled "Liberalism."[5]

Dworkin makes a distinction between two kinds of moral commitment. We all have views about the ends of life, about what constitutes a good life, for which we and others ought to strive. But then we also acknowledge a commitment to deal fairly and equally with each other, regardless of how we conceive our ends. We might call these latter "procedural" commitments, while those that concern the ends of life are "substantive." Now Dworkin claims that a liberal society is one which as a society adopts no particular substantive view about the ends of life. The society is rather united around strong procedural commitments, to treat people with equal respect. The reason why the polity as such can espouse no substantive view, cannot for instance allow that one of the goals of legislation should be to make people virtuous in one or another meaning of that term, is that this would involve a violation of its procedural norm. For, granted the diversity of modern societies, it would unfailingly be the case that some people and not others would be committed to the favoured conception of virtue. They might be in a majority; indeed, it is very likely that they would be, for otherwise a democratic society would probably not espouse their view. But nevertheless this view would not be everyone's, and in espousing this substantive outlook the society would not be treating the dissident minority with equal respect. It would be saying to them, in effect, "your view is not as valuable, in the eyes of this polity, as that of your more numerous compatriots."

There are very profound philosophical assumptions underlying this view of liberalism, which is very influenced by the thought of Immanuel Kant. Among other features, it understands human dignity to consist largely in autonomy, that is, in the ability of each person to determine for himself or herself a view of the good life. Dignity, that is, is connected less with any particular understanding of the good life, than it is with the power to consider and espouse for oneself some view or other. We are not respecting this power equally in all subjects, it is claimed, if we raise the outcome of some people's deliberations officially over that of others. A liberal society must remain neutral on the good life, and restrict itself to ensuring that however they see things, citizens deal fairly with each other and the state equally with all.

---

4. J. Rawls, *A Theory of Justice* (Cambridge, Mass: Belknap Press of Harvard University Press, 1971); "Justice as Fairness: Political not Metaphysical" (1985) 14 *Philosophy and Public Affairs* 223; Dworkin, *Taking Rights Seriously* (London: Duckworth, 1977); B. Ackerman, *Social Justice in the Liberal State* (New Haven: Yale University Press, 1980).

5. In S. Hampshire, ed., *Public and Private Morality* (Cambridge: Cambridge University Press, 1978).

The popularity of this view of the human agent as primarily a subject of self-determining or self-expressive choice helps to explain why this model of liberalism is so strong. But there is also the fact that it has been urged with great force and intelligence by liberal thinkers in the United States, and precisely in the context of constitutional doctrines of judicial review.[6] And so it is not surprising that the idea becomes accredited, well beyond those who might subscribe to a specific Kantian philosophy, that a liberal society cannot accommodate publicly-espoused notions of the good. This is the conception, as Michael Sandel has called it, of the "procedural republic"[7] which has a very strong hold on the political agenda in the United States, and which has helped to place increasing emphasis on judicial review on the basis of constitutional texts at the expense of the ordinary political process of building majorities with a view to legislative action.

But a society with collective goals like Quebec's violates this model. It is axiomatic for Quebec governments that the survival and flourishing of French culture in Quebec is a good. Political society is not neutral between those who value remaining true to the culture of our ancestors and those who might want to cut loose in the name of some individual goal of self-development. It might be argued that one could after all capture a goal like *survivance* for a proceduralist liberal society. One could consider the French language, for instance, as a collective resource that individuals might want to make use of and act for its preservation, just as one does for clean air or green spaces. But this cannot capture the full thrust of policies designed for cultural survival. It is not just a matter of having the French language available for those who might choose it. This might be seen to be the goal of some of the measures of federal bilingualism over the last 20 years. It is also a matter of making sure that there is a community of people here in the future which will want to avail itself of this opportunity. Policies aimed at survival actively seek to create members of the community, in assuring that the rising generations go on identifying as French-speakers or whatever. There is no way that they could be seen as just providing a facility to already existing people.[8]

---

6. E.g. L. Tribe, *Abortion: The Clash of Absolutes* (New York: Norton, 1990).

7. "The Procedural Republic and the Unencumbered Self" (1984) 12 *Political Theory*.

8. An ingenious argument has recently been put forward by Will Kymlicka in his brilliant book, *Liberalism, Community and Culture* (Oxford: Clarendon Press, 1989). He argues that what I have been calling procedural liberalism can be made compatible with the defense of collective rights and cultural survival in certain cases. Kymlicka, unlike the major American authors, writes in full knowledge of the Canadian scene and with a strong commitment to the defence of aboriginal rights in this country. While espousing a politics of "neutral moral concern," that is, a view of the liberal state as neutral between conceptions of the good life (at 76), he nevertheless argues that collective cultural rights can be defended on the grounds that the members of certain threatened communities will be deprived of the conditions of intelligent, self-generated decisions about the good life if the "cultural structures" through which they can grasp the options are undermined (at 165). If Kymlicka's argument really went through, it would close the gap between the two models of liberalism that I am contrasting in these pages.

Quebeckers therefore, and those who give similar importance to this kind of collective goal, tend to opt for a rather different model of a liberal society. On this view, a society can be organized around a definition of the good life, without this being seen as a depreciation of those who do not personally share this definition. Where the nature of the good requires that it be sought in common, this is the reason for its being an object of public policy. According to this conception, a liberal society singles itself out as such by the way in which it treats minorities, including those who do not share public definitions of the good, and above all by the rights it accords to all its members. But in this case, the rights in question are conceived to be the fundamental and crucial ones which have been recognized as such from the very beginning of the liberal tradition: such rights as to life, liberty, due process, free speech, free practice of religion and the like. On this model, there is something exaggerated, a dangerous overlooking of an essential boundary, in speaking of fundamental rights to things like commercial signage in the language of one's choice. One has to distinguish the fundamental liberties, those which should never at any time be infringed and which therefore ought to be unassailably entrenched, on one hand, from privileges and immunities which are important, but which can be revoked or restricted for reasons of public policy — although one needs a strong reason to do so — on the other.

A society with strong collective goals can be liberal, on this view, provided it is also capable of respecting diversity, especially concerning those who do not share its goals, and provided it can offer adequate safeguards for fundamental rights. There will undoubtedly be tensions and difficulties involved in pursuing these objectives together, but they are not uncombinable, and the problems are not in principle greater than those encountered by any liberal society which has to combine, for example, liberty and equality, or prosperity and justice.

Here are two incompatible views of liberal society. One of the great sources of our present disunity is that they have come to square off against each other in the last decade. The resistance to the "distinct society" which called for precedence to be given to the *Charter* came in part from a spreading procedural outlook in COQ. From this point of view, attributing the goal of promoting Quebec's distinct society to a government is to acknowledge a collective goal, and this move had to be neutralized by being subordinated to the existing *Charter*. From the standpoint of Quebec, this attempt to impose a procedural model of liberalism not only would deprive the distinct society clause of some of its force as a rule of interpretation, but bespoke a rejection of the model of liberalism on which this society has come to be founded. There was a lot of misperception by each society of the other throughout the Meech Lake debate, as I mentioned above. But here each saw something right about the other — and didn't like it. COQ saw that the distinct society clause legitimated collective goals. And Quebec saw that the move to give the *Charter* precedence imposed a form of liberal society which is alien, and to which Quebec could never accommodate itself without surrendering its identity. In this context, the protestations by *Charter* patriots that they were not "against Quebec" rang hollow.

This was one source of deep disagreement. There was also a second one, which was interwoven with it. The *Charter* has taken on tremendous importance in COQ not only because of the growing force of procedural liberalism, but also because in the steadily increasing diversity of this multicultural society people are looking for new bases of unity. COQ has seen its reason for existence partly in terms of its political institutions, for reasons discussed above. Even though the *Charter* offers a relatively weak answer to the distinctness question, because it makes us more like the U.S., it nevertheless can provide a convincing answer to the unity question. The two motives for *Charter* patriotism come together here. As the country gets more diverse, we are more and more acutely aware of the divergences in our conceptions of the good life. It then appears that what can and ought to bind us together are precisely the procedural norms that govern our interaction. Procedural liberalism not only begins to look more plausible in itself, but it also seems to be the only unquestionable common ground. But if so, then it is hard to accept that its meaning and application may be modulated in one part of the country by something like the distinct society clause, but not in others. The resistance to this clause of the Meech Lake Accord came partly from the sense that the *Charter* of all things had to apply in the same way to all Canadians. If the procedural bond is the only thing which can hold us together without ranking some above others, then it has to hold without exception.

VI. LEVELS OF DIVERSITY

Can this conflict be arbitrated? In a sense not. One side insists on holding the country together around a model of liberalism which the other cannot accept. If there is to be agreement, the first side has to give way. But ought it to give way? I can only offer an answer to this question by deserting all appearance of neutrality and taking an openly partisan stance. So let me throw off the mask and state my position.

It seems to me that the claim of proceduralist thinkers to define the very essence of liberalism is erroneous and in a sense arrogant. We have to acknowledge that there are other possible models of liberal society. This becomes pretty evident once one looks around at the full gamut of contemporary free societies in Europe and elsewhere, instead of attending only to the United States. Further, it should be evident to procedural liberals in COQ that their francophone compatriots wish to live by one such alternative. This should be clear to anyone with a modicum of knowledge of Quebec history and politics.

But once we accept these premises, then it is clear that the attempt to make procedural liberalism the basis of Canadian unity is both illegitimate and doomed to failure. For it represents an imposition of one society's model on another, and in the circumstances of late 20th century Canadian democracy this cannot succeed. The only way we can coexist is by allowing ourselves to differ on this. Does this mean that we can only coexist as two independent societies, perhaps loosely linked by supra-national institutions? That is the thesis of Quebec sovereigntists. But this has never seemed to me to be self-evident. It becomes true only to the extent that procedural liberals stand so firmly on principle that they cannot bear to share the same country with people who live by another model. Rigidity of this kind began to be evident during the Meech Lake debate. If this were to be COQ's last word, then indeed the independentists are right, and there is no solution short of sovereignty-association.

But do they have to be right? Is there something wrong with accommodating difference in this way?

In a way, accommodating difference is what Canada is all about. Many Canadians would concur in this. That is why the recent bout of mutual suspicion and ill-will in the constitutional debate has been so painful to many of our compatriots. It is not just that the sources of difference I have been describing are becoming more salient. Old questions may be re-opened. To some extent Trudeau's remarkable achievement in extending bilingualism was made possible by a growing sympathy towards the French fact among political and social elites in COQ. They pushed the process faster than many of their fellow citizens were happy with. For many people lower down in the hierarchy, French was being "stuffed down their throats," but granted the elite-run nature of the political accommodation process in this country they seemed to have no option but to take it.

But during the Meech debate the procedures of elite negotiation came under sharp criticism and challenge. Moreover, the COQ elites were themselves split on how to respond to the new package in a way they had not been on bilingualism. It was therefore not surprising that we began to see a rebellion against the accommodation of French. This might be the harbinger of greater resistance to come. Already one hears Westerners saying that Canadian duality is an irrelevancy to them, that their experience of Canada is of a multicultural mosaic. The very bases of a two-language federation are being questioned again. This important axis of difference is under threat.

But more fundamentally, we face a challenge to our very conception of diversity. Many of the people who rallied around the *Charter* and multiculturalism to reject the distinct society are proud of their acceptance of diversity. And in some respects rightly so. What is enshrined here is what one might call first-level diversity. There are great differences in culture and outlook and background in a population which nevertheless shares the same idea of what it is to belong to Canada. Their patriotism or manner of belonging is uniform, whatever their other differences, and this is felt to be a necessity if the country is to hold together.

But this is far from accommodating all Canadians. For Quebeckers, and for most French Canadians, the way of being a Canadian (for those who still want to be) is via their belonging to a constituent element of Canada, la nation québécoise, or canadienne-française. Something analogous holds for aboriginal communities in this country. Their way of being Canadian is not accommodated by first-level diversity. And yet many people in COQ are puzzled by the resulting sense of exclusion, because diversity is the only kind they are sensitive to, and they feel they fully acknowledge that.

To build a country for everyone, Canada would have to allow for second-level or "deep" diversity, where a plurality of ways of belonging would also be acknowledged and accepted. Someone of, let us say, Italian extraction in Toronto, or Ukrainian extraction in Edmonton, might indeed feel Canadian as a bearer of individual rights in a multicultural mosaic. Her belonging would not "pass through" some other community, although the ethnic identity might be important to her in various ways. But this person might nevertheless accept that a Québécois, or a Cree, or a Dene, might belong in a very different way, that they were Canadian through being members of their national communities. And reciprocally, the Québécois, Cree or Dene would accept the perfect legitimacy of the "mosaic" identity.

Is this utopian? Could people ever come to see this way? Could they even find it exciting and an object of pride that they belong to a country which allows deep diversity? Pessimists say no, because they do not see how such a country could have a sense of unity. The model of citizenship has to be uniform, or people would have no sense of belonging to the same polity. Those who say this tend to take as their paradigm the United States, which has indeed been hostile to deep diversity, and has sometimes tried to stamp it out as "un-American."

But these pessimists should bear in mind these things:

- Deep diversity is the only formula on which a united federal Canada can be rebuilt — once we recall the reasons (like (a) to (c) above) why we all need it.

- In many parts of the world today, the degree and nature of differences resemble Canada's rather than those in the U.S. If a uniform model of citizenship fits better the classical image of the western liberal state, it is also true that this is a straitjacket for many political societies. The world needs other models to be legitimated, in order to allow for more humane and less constraining modes of political cohabitation. Instead of pushing ourselves to the point of break-up in the name of the uniform model, we would do ourselves and some other peoples a favour by exploring the space of deep diversity. To those who believe in according people the freedom to be themselves, this would be counted a gain in civilization.

  In this exploration we would not be alone. Europe-watchers have noticed how the development of the European Community has gone along with an increased breathing space for regional societies — Breton, Basque, Catalan — which were formerly threatened with the steamroller of the national state.

- After dividing to form two polities with uniform citizenship, both successor states would find that they had failed after all to banish the challenge of deep diversity, because the only way that they can do justice to their aboriginal populations is by adopting a pluralist mould. Neither Quebec nor COQ could succeed in imitating the United States, or the European national states in their chauvinist prime. Why not recognize this now, and take the road of deep diversity together?

[11]

Rights and Politics[†]

JOSEPH RAZ[*]

It is an honour to join you today in celebrating Professor Jerome Hall. Professor Hall's work was ahead of its time. I did not know him, but his independence of mind and his spirited devotion to scholarship were striking in all I heard and read. Professor Hall's fame was at its height when I was beginning my research into the philosophy of law. And his name stood out as among the most distinguished American jurisprudential scholars. It stood out for his good sense, balanced judgment, and strong-minded convictions. His *Foundations of Jurisprudence* is thoroughly resistant to fashion.[1] It is an open-minded, undogmatic, and sympathetic exploration of a variety of intellectual trends and tendencies. His work on criminal law was an outstanding attempt at a thorough examination of a major branch of the law from a systematic and theoretical perspective. It set a standard for legal scholarship way above anything else accomplished in America at the time.

I do not know much about Professor Hall's private life, but there is a story which shows him to have been uniquely fortunate. As a young man practising law, so the story goes, Hall knew the great Clarence Darrow who gave him precious advice: "Swim with the current," he said, "and do only what you find interesting." The advice was opaque and bewildering, almost fitting the oracle at Delphi. Like some of that oracle's pronouncements, it appears to be designed to fail its receivers. However much they may try, they will not be able to fulfill it. But, so the story concludes, Professor Hall promptly acted on the advice, and never looked back. He abandoned legal practice and became an academic.

Only those whom the gods love can both swim with the current and do what they find interesting. And unlike Professor Hall, as my lecture today will illustrate, I am not one who, when doing what he is interested in, finds himself swimming with the current. In fact my aim is to swim against the current, or at least against a current. The main part of my talk is a challenge to two popular fallacies, which I will call the "Universalist" and the "Individualist" Fallacies. The Universalist Fallacy leads to the false belief that all rights derive from universal, and unchanging, rights. The Individualist Fallacy leads to the false belief that all rights—or more modestly, all important rights—are justified by concern for the rightholder and his interests. Having challenged these popular beliefs, I will say something about the way they have distorted our view of politics and our view of its relation to the law.

As I said, I will be swimming against powerful currents. But as is inevitable in matters of morality, political morality included, there are no currents without crosscurrents, or even countercurrents. It is not possible to discover completely new truths about fundamental moral questions like those upon which I will be touching. Such originality would imply that it is possible for all the people to be mistaken all the time about all basic moral beliefs. To suppose that that is possible is to misunderstand the nature of

---

† Presented on October 7, 1994, at the Indiana University School of Law-Bloomington, as the inaugural Jerome Hall Lecture.

* Professor of the Philosophy of Law, Oxford University and Fellow of Balliol College, Oxford. D. Phil., Oxford University 1967.

1. JEROME HALL, FOUNDATIONS OF JURISPRUDENCE (1973).

morality. So the path I will be following is not of my own making, and I trust that many of you will know its contours. This is helpful inasmuch as it is impossible in one talk to do more than scratch the surface.[2] Inevitably my aim today is modest. I will not argue for any rights, nor for any method of protecting rights. My purpose is to help focus the way we think about rights. While the substance of the talk is a critique of the two fallacies and the theses they support, I will conclude with some comments on the way rights should be seen and on the place, if any, of politics in judicial deliberations. Rights, I shall claim, should be thought of contextually, not universally, and as, in part, providing a framework for public life. Therefore, they cannot be totally separated from ordinary politics.

I. The Universalist Fallacy

A popular and deeply entrenched belief has it that little rights out of big rights grow. Or, in other words, relatively more specific rights are the application of universal rights to relatively specific circumstances. I will call it the "universalist thesis."

Rights are universal if (and only if) it is possible to specify the conditions for their application (*i.e.*, who has them and when) without using any singular referring expressions (*i.e.*, without the use of proper names, demonstratives, definite descriptions, or time and space coordinates). Otherwise they are, in the terminology I am using, more or less specific.[3] So my right to enter the university campus is a specific right, for it identifies its holder by reference to an individual, namely me. The right of every student of the university to enter the university campus is also specific, for the reference to a student of the university relates to a specific "thing," the university, and—by implication—also to certain authorities of it who admit students. I give these simple examples to emphasise that specific rights are not contrasted with general rights, but with universal rights. Specific rights can be general, and can enjoy various degrees of generality, for generality is a matter of degree. The right of American students of the university to vote in the election is less general than that of citizens of the United States to vote in the election, for the category of citizens of the United States is wider than that of students of the university. But both are specific rights, for the United States is also a specific "thing," a country, and the rightholders are identified through the reference to it by name.[4]

It goes without saying that many, if not all, legal rights are specific. For one thing, few legal systems claim, and none should claim, universal jurisdiction. With few exceptions (*e.g.*, some forms of international terrorism) the jurisdictional doctrines of most civilised countries limit the application of their law to people associated with them and/or to events which took place within their territory. Many other rights are confined to people who registered before certain dates, obtained permits or licenses, made agreements with

---

2. For a more in-depth discussion of these and related issues, see JOSEPH RAZ, THE MORALITY OF FREEDOM 165-263 (1986) [hereinafter RAZ, THE MORALITY OF FREEDOM]; JOSEPH RAZ, *Rights and Individual Well-Being*, *in* ETHICS IN THE PUBLIC DOMAIN 29-44 (1994) [hereinafter RAZ, *Rights and Individual Well-Being*].

3. These terminological distinctions are discussed and explained in R.M. HARE, FREEDOM AND REASON 7-50 (1963) and J.L. MACKIE, ETHICS 83-90 (1977).

4. For the purpose of my present discussion, I use "universal" to apply to any right the holders of which can be identified without reference to a specific item. According to this characterisation, the right of all human beings to enter the United States, should there be such a right, is a universal right, even though its object or content is to enter a specific territory. For various purposes it may be advantageous to tighten the condition and define a universal right as one which requires no reference to specific items in specifying either the rightholder or the content of the right.

others, and so on. Many nonlegal rights are similarly specific. Many rights arise out of agreements or special relations between people (*e.g.*, parents and children).

These facts notwithstanding, the universalist thesis seems compelling. First, we can put on one side all those cases in which the specificity of rights derives from jurisdictional considerations. These considerations, whatever their form—whether they limit the rights themselves, or the jurisdiction of the courts over disputes involving the rights, or over the entitlement rightholders have to pursue them in the courts—can rightly be said not to reflect the nature of the underlying rights. Rather, they arise out of considerations of the proper division of labour between different legal institutions: it is reasonable to think that legal rules and doctrines, legal rights included, are justified only if there are nonlegal considerations sufficient to justify holding them to be part of the law. It is further reasonable to sympathise with supporters of the universalist thesis in thinking that, to the extent that legal rights are restricted by jurisdictional considerations, they are justified by universal *moral* rights, plus other moral considerations (of civility between nations, of fairness to possible litigants, of assuring the correctness of judicial decisions, and others) which establish that the jurisdiction of institutions in adjudicating disputes should be delimited by geographical or personal criteria. That would show that jurisdictional considerations are consistent with the universalist thesis.[5]

To the Universalists, rights arising out of agreements or special relationships do not present a serious problem either. While all such rights are contingent on and particular to one individual or another, they all derive from general principles which establish universal rights: when I was a child I had a right against my parents to be taken care of by them. But it was an instance of a universal principle endowing all children with the right to be looked after by their parents (unless, for instance, the children were given for satisfactory adoption). My rights against the University of Oxford arise out of my contract of employment with the University. But they are merely an instance of a universal right that all employees have against all employers, for example, that the employers shall comply with the contract of employment, or that they shall obey occupational health and safety laws.

More generally, a powerful argument is liable to be invoked by defenders of the universalist thesis. Imagine that one person has a moral right which another does not possess, and that the only difference between them which explains why one has the right and the other does not is that one is the son of X, or that the other is an employee of Y, or that one was born on the first of January, or some other specific characteristic possessed by only one of them. Clearly that would be no explanation at all. If that is all the explanation there can be, then the difference between their moral rights is arbitrary. But the possession of moral rights cannot be arbitrary. I will refer to this as the "general argument" for the thesis. It purports to show that any right which neither is nor derives

5. An attenuated version of the universalist thesis holds that any right is either universal or it is the application of some universal right(s). In this form, the thesis allows that limits on the right can derive from considerations other than another's right. However, even the nonattenuated thesis is compatible with the existence of justified jurisdictional claims. My remarks in the text are to show that jurisdictional claims need not be viewed as limiting the right. They only limit the power of some institutions either to enforce it or to recognise it in some other way. I am relying on the fact that we can pierce through the official language (which in some cases may present jurisdictional claims as setting limits to the right itself) and interpret the law in ways which are morally sound. The degree to which this can be done cannot be discussed here.

Some rights may be geographically limited (*e.g.*, one may have rights to conduct oneself in certain ways in Oxford only). That is, there are such rights whose limitations are not based on jurisdictional concerns, and they can be applications of universal rights.

from a universal right is necessarily arbitrary. It is arbitrary because the difference between rightholders and those who do not have rights remains entirely unexplained and unexplainable.

To show its full strength, the universalist thesis should be elaborated and refined. Various objections to it are easily deflected. Some result from a misunderstanding of the thesis. Notice, for example, that it does not claim that we cannot know that a person, or people of a certain class, have a specific right unless we know what universal rights these specific rights instantiate. The universalist thesis is compatible with the following claims: (1) Often, or even always, we are justified in having greater confidence in our belief that a person has some specific right than in our belief that it is an instance of this or that universal right; and (2) Often we know that a person has a specific right, but we do not know of which universal right it is an instance.

All of this may well be the case, and it is entirely consistent with the universalist thesis. It is true that the thesis implies that, so long as we do not know of which universal right a specific right is an instance, we do not know the full justification of the specific right in question. But that does not mean that we need doubt its existence or refrain from protecting it. Nor does it mean that all reasoning about the existence of rights must be deductive reasoning, nor that it must proceed from the more to the less general, or from the abstract to the specific. Sometimes the best arguments about the existence of rights are analogical arguments proceeding from one specific case to another. Arguably, analogical reasoning is particularly important in the law.[6]

But I do not want to continue defending the universalist thesis. After all, my aim is to undermine it. I have spent some time defending it in order to be able to claim that, while the general argument for the thesis is based on a sound precept, that precept does not warrant accepting the thesis. The argument is fallacious. The sound precept is that (1) moral (or evaluative) differences are not arbitrary; (2) therefore, necessarily, if two cases differ in a particular moral or evaluative property there are other differences between them; and (3) to explain the difference, those further differences cannot be ones which must be expressed with the use of singular referring expressions. To explain a moral or an evaluative difference, one needs to invoke a universal property present in one case and not in the other.

So what is wrong with the argument? Why is it fallacious? The answer is simple. There is nothing in the precepts on which the argument rests to suggest that the explanation of a difference in the rights people have must depend on universal rights. The argument establishes only that moral differences must, on pain of arbitrariness, be susceptible to explanation, and that moral explanations derive from universal principles. It does not establish that these are universal principles of rights. Some may be. Others may be principles of duty, or some other universal moral considerations about the value of friendship, love, or gratitude, or any other universal moral precept.

Two ways of trying to reinforce the general argument in order to avoid my refutation can be quickly rejected. Some people believe that at its foundations there is nothing to morality except rights.[7] If so, then my suggestion that specific rights may derive from universal principles, which themselves are not principles of rights, can be dismissed. The thought that rights and rights alone are the ultimate moral consideration is encouraged

6. For an illuminating discussion, see Cass R. Sunstein, *On Analogical Reasoning*, 106 HARV. L. REV. 741 (1993).

7. I am not going to discuss here the claim that morality has foundations—a far-from-obvious claim.

by the fact that rights imply concern for the individual rightholder. Many people believe that morality is ultimately about the interests or well-being of individuals. Does it not follow that it is at bottom about rights? No, it does not. Concern for the individual expresses itself in love and friendship; it is reflected in the doctrine of virtue and in much else. But there is no right to have friends or to be loved, and none of the virtues can be understood in terms of rights. So, concern for the interests of individuals does not translate itself into principles of rights. At least it cannot be exhausted by them.

A second way of reinforcing the general argument in response to the refutation can also be readily rejected. Some people think that even if there is more to morality than rights, rights are lexically more important than any other matter of moral concern and therefore cannot be derived from other moral principles. There is no reason to accept this claim. Again, the examples of the virtues and of love and friendship seem to contradict it. And I believe that they do.

A related point concerns the relative importance of those rights which either are or derive from universal rights as against those which do not. Some people will concede that some rights are explained and justified by universal principles which are not themselves principles of rights. However, they will want to insist that universal rights are of greater importance and that they carry greater weight than any others. This view, too, is without support in any rational argument. Indeed, unless the thought can be sustained that universal principles of rights are more important than other universal moral principles and values, it is implausible to think that universal rights are necessarily or in fact more important than rights which may derive from other moral principles.

II. The Mistake of Individualism

So far my argument has been purely negative. I showed that the general argument for the universalist thesis is fallacious. That does not establish that the thesis is false. To do that one has to show that there are specific rights which derive from considerations other than those of other rights. So long as the argument remains negative, it remains incomplete and leaves open the possibility that some alternative reason for the universalist thesis may yet be found. So we have to move on to a closer look at the nature of rights and of the foundations of rights. When we do that we immediately encounter the second fallacy with which this talk is concerned, the Individualist Fallacy. Let me explain: *X* has a right to *Z* against *Y* if and only if his having *Z* or a right to it will protect or promote an interest of *X*, and if the case for protecting and promoting that interest of his through securing *Z* to him justifies the duty on *Y* not to interfere with *X* having *Z* or to help to secure his having it.[8] This definition is a variant of what is known as the "interest-based approach" to rights, since it regards rights as essentially protecting interests.

Given the definition, the individualist thesis seems inescapable. It regards rights as being by their very nature a way of protecting individual interests against the interests or claims of the public or collectivity, or against whatever reasons there are to promote

8. This is an abbreviated schematic definition. To make sense it cannot be unpacked or applied mechanically but has to be adapted to individual cases. For a more extensive discussion of the concept of a right, see RAZ, *Legal Rights*, *in* ETHICS IN THE PUBLIC DOMAIN, *supra* note 2, at 238-60; RAZ, THE MORALITY OF FREEDOM, *supra* note 2, at 165-92. Some other chapters in these books also explore themes which I repeat and develop here.

the general good.[9] The individualist view of rights is confrontational: Rights set the limits of the private sphere, in which each individual is sovereign over his or her own affairs, as against the public domain, where the public interest, as determined by political action, prevails. Rights protect individuals against demands that they contribute to the public good, or to the welfare of other individuals. Is not the individualist thesis, with its confrontational outlook, a logical implication of the fact that by definition only interests are protected by rights? The answer is a clear negative. To be sure, some rights do or can function in this way, and in some political cultures this function is prominent. But this does not warrant the individualist thesis, which is a thesis about the nature of rights in general. Two classes of rights provide a ready illustration of how the individualist's understanding of rights is narrow and, as a result, distorted.

First, groups as well as individuals possess rights. Group rights, the rights of nations, families, and the like, are based on the interests of these groups. Naturally, there is no intrinsic value in protecting the interests of groups. Their interests merit protection only to the extent that they serve individual interests. Whatever the ultimate justification of group rights, they are the rights of groups and not of individuals. Nor do they derive their justification from individual rights; rather, their proximate justification is in the interest of the group, and their ultimate justification lies in the service to individual interests of advancing the interest of the group.

Second, the rights of judges, of members of the legislature, and of all other legal officeholders are justified by the interest of the office. Whatever is necessary or useful for the efficient discharge of an office is in the interest of the office. But there is no intrinsic value in protecting these interests. The ultimate justification of the rights depends on the fact that in serving the interests of the officials they protect and promote the interest of the community as a whole; they protect and promote common goods.

Supporters of the individualist thesis usually dismiss these cases as marginal. It is difficult for the unblinkered to think of them as marginal given their prominence in public law, in commercial law, and in the law of obligations in general. The tendency to marginalise them is partly motivated by an empiricist and therefore individualist conception of social studies, which endorses methodological individualism, and a similar empiricist metaphysics endorsing ontological individualism. To an empiricist, corporations or officials are, if not fictions, at any rate less than completely real. They are a mere *façon de parler*, a mere figure of speech. Really, there are only people and their rights, and talking of corporations or of officials and their rights is just a convenient way of talking indirectly of people and their rights. In this way, the empiricist is an individualist, committed to the reduction of all rights to individual ones.

Empiricism is no longer unchallenged, and I need not feel guilty for my inability to tackle the distortions it brought in its wake to moral, political, and legal thought today. Nor need I rely on these examples to make my case. I mentioned them because even those who lost faith in empiricism have not always rid themselves of its mistaken consequences, and are sometimes prey to the individualist fallacy about rights.

Let me illustrate the same point through another example. The structure of all these cases is the same. All the nonindividualist examples depend on a simple fact: while every

9. The two most prominent supporters of the individualist thesis among political philosophers today, and the two who have done more than any other thinkers to propagate that way of understanding rights, are Ronald Dworkin and Robert Nozick. *See* RONALD DWORKIN, TAKING RIGHTS SERIOUSLY 81-130 (1977); ROBERT NOZICK, ANARCHY, STATE AND UTOPIA 28-33 (1974).

right protects or promotes an interest of the rightholder, the reasons for protecting those interests, and therefore the justification of the rights which provide the protection, are not confined to concern for the well-being of the rightholders. We saw how this factor works in the cases of group rights and the rights of officials. It obviously applies to the rights of guardians, trustees, and so on. But it applies to many rights, possibly to all the rights which merit legal recognition and enforcement. Consider, for example, rights which are protected by the criminal law. These include property rights protected by the criminal law through the institution of offences against theft, burglary, fraud, and many others. It is commonplace that the public interest in securing a society in which respect for property prevails is taken into account in apportioning punishment for these offences. That is, the punishment reflects the public interest in securing these rights, in securing a general atmosphere of respect for them.

The reason for caring about the violation of any one person's right to property therefore transcends concern for the interest of *that* person in his property. Moreover, it transcends the interest of all property owners in their property. Every person has such an interest inasmuch as (1) every person may become a property owner; and (2) every person benefits from the fact that property rights are secure. These benefits take many forms. They are not easy to specify exhaustively. They come close to being the interest that all people have in living in a civil society. My right in my property is based on my interest in having that property. But the weight given to my interest, the degree of protection it deserves, and the form that protection should take are morally determined by considerations which transcend concern for my interest in itself. They reflect the interest of other people in the common good of respect for property.[10]

Some people will try to resist this conclusion by denying that the criminal law protects the rights of the victims of crime. It is true, they will say, that in general whenever a property offence is committed a right of the owner of the property involved is violated. But that does not mean that the criminal law is there to protect that right. The right is protected by whatever private law remedies the victim has. Criminal law is concerned exclusively with protecting the public against crime. The proof is that the public interest rather than the interest of the victim dominates decisions involved in the criminal process. But this response seems to be motivated by nothing other than dogma. My suggestion is that the right which protects an individual's interest is justified and shaped in part by the fact that protecting his interest is in the public interest.[11] The objector sustains his rejection of this suggestion by arbitrarily denying that anything to do with the public interest is relevant to the right.

It is crucial to see that the objector's response is arbitrary. He could not possibly regard the fact that crimes against property consist of the violation of property rights as coincidental. So he must divide the protection of property rights into two elements: private law protects the right itself, and criminal law protects the public interest. This division is false to the facts, and in any case fails to support his objection. It is false to the facts as both private law remedies and criminal punishments are based on the dual

10. The fact that different conditions apply to criminal and civil liability (*e.g.*, the difference in the mens rea required for criminal and civil liability and the differences between the defence doctrines applicable in the different areas of law) is no more material to the argument of this essay than the fact that injunctions are available under different conditions than damages. Inevitably, if remedies and penalties are not to be unjust, conditions suitable to the nature of each have to be met before they become available. The fact that a defence of that kind exists does not show that the right was not infringed. It merely blocks the remedy or the punishment.

11. This interest is of the kind I call a "common good," as will be explained below. *See infra* part III.

concern for the rightholder and for the public. The existence of punitive and exemplary damages is but one small manifestation of private law's sensitivity to the public interest. The rights of victim and complainant under the criminal process is but one manifestation of the sensitivity of criminal law to the rights of victims. Tracing these crossings of concerns is a complicated task which cannot be undertaken here.

Let me turn to the fact that in any case the objector's alleged facts do not support his case. Suppose that the criminal law is concerned exclusively with public interest considerations, and private law exclusively with the interests of rightholders. That would be consistent with rights, even all rights, being based on both. It would simply indicate a division of labour according to which different branches of the law address themselves to different aspects of rights. To show that that is not so, the objector has to claim that the fact that offences against property infringe property rights is irrelevant to their justification. He has to show that, were property law to change and were the right which the conduct in question violates to be abolished, the case for criminalising that conduct as we now do would remain unaffected. I take this claim to be patently false. It follows that rights have a public interest aspect, as I claimed above.

Before leaving this part of the argument I will briefly indicate how it applies to constitutional rights. The argument is essentially the same. The practical importance of its application is, however, greater since individualist interpretations of constitutional rights have been particularly influential. We can take as our example "democratic rights"—rights like the right to vote, to stand for election, and to participate in political activities; the freedom of political association, demonstration, and assemblies; and those aspects of freedom of expression which are based on the fact that there is no democracy without free expression. I call these and their like "democratic rights" because of their justification. It is clear that they are not always identified as such in standard bills of rights. Rather, what I called democratic rights are often aspects of or parts of other constitutional rights.

I have a right to vote. I have an interest in being able to vote and the right is there to enable me to do so. But clearly its rationale is based not only on my interest. It is based on the common good of living under a democratic government. This is an interest shared by all, including those who—like young children—do not have a right to vote. It is the protection of that common good which gives special stringency to my right, a stringency it might not have enjoyed had my interest in it been the sole reason for it. Clearly the fact that the right is nonconvertible, that I cannot divest myself of it, nor commit myself for financial gain to exercise it one way or another, is based not on the fact that nothing can compensate me for the loss of the right to vote. Such paternalism is only rarely justified, and would be very dubious in this case. Rather, the nonconvertibility of the right reflects the fact that it is grounded in a common good of a distinctive kind which would be undermined were the right convertible. Hence, the interests which justify the right and which give it its shape and content are the interests of the public at large alongside the interests of the rightholder.

III. The Public Interest and the Common Good

The individualist and the universalist theses encourage —though they do not entail—an outlook which places the protection and enforcement of rights outside politics. Different accounts are put forward in support of that conclusion. A common one is that rights being universal cannot be subject to the vagaries of political fortunes. Moreover, rights protect the people who have them. That must mean, according to some writers, that rights protect people from being sacrificed for the sake of promoting the public interest. Promoting the public interest is the stuff of politics. Therefore, rights are outside politics. They mark the boundary beyond which individual interests cannot be sacrificed in the name of the public interest.

Rejecting the two theses removes the reasons for holding rights to be outside politics. Rights are justified in part by considerations of the public interest, and more specifically by considerations of the common good. And there are rights which change with time and which are neither mere applications of universal rights to particular circumstances nor less important or less stringent than universal rights.

At the same time, in my argument against the individualist thesis I was also arguing against a certain view of politics. The individualist thesis brings with it a confrontational view of rights. It is often associated with a confrontational view of politics in general. The preceding observations challenged the individualist thesis from time to time by invoking the common good as part of the rationale of rights. Some terminological clarification will bring out the implications of that point.

The public interest is, and is generally taken to be, a function of individual interests. So is the common good or the common interest. The common good differs, however, from the public one. The common good is a good which is in the interest of everyone in that society (though it need not benefit each one of them to the same degree). Here is an example. There is a public interest in the existence of a network of railway tracks in good repair. The interest is not merely that of railway users; many other members of the public, for example, consumers of goods transported by rail, share this interest. Yet some people may derive no benefit from this good, and quite possibly there are people whose interests are adversely affected by the maintenance of the railway networks. They may be affected by noise or air pollution, by decline in the value of their property, or in other ways, while not using the railway nor benefiting indirectly from its existence. So the judgment that the public interest is served by the existence of a railway network is based on the balance of good and evil, on a resolution of the conflicting interests of different people.

This is not so with the common good. If, for example, in a certain country the existence of a common language spoken by all its inhabitants is a common good, then (1) it serves an interest of every person; (2) it serves the same interest in the case of every person; and (3) that interest is served by the good in a noncompetitive way. Various public goods are common goods in this sense; for example, everyone benefits from unpolluted air. Everyone has a health interest which benefits from unpolluted air. The benefit is noncompetitive (one person's enjoyment is not at the expense of anyone else), and it is similar in nature for everyone (all enjoy it in the same way), since it serves the same health interest in every person's case (though people do not necessarily enjoy the benefit to the same degree).[12]

Another type of noncompetitive good is worth mentioning. Shared goods are goods whose benefit for people depends on people enjoying the good together and thereby

---

12. As the example illustrates, many common goods are public goods in the sense that term has in economic writings; that is, they are goods whose distribution is not subject to deliberate control, goods which no one has the power to deny to any individual (other than himself) without denying them to everyone in that society. However, I see no logical connection between the two notions.

contributing to each other's good. A simple example will illustrate the idea: A party or a dance is good (by being enjoyable) for its participants only because and to the extent that they enjoy it together. They enjoy having a good time together. While all shared goods are common goods in some group or another, they are not necessarily a common good in a society taken as a whole. As we know too well, they can contribute to setting one group against another. Yet one particularly important type of common good is the cultivation of a culture and a social ambience which make possible a variety of shared goods, that is, a variety of forms of social association of intrinsic merit. Shared goods are often neglected, although their role in modern societies deserves close study. But my remaining remarks will concern the importance of the wider category of the common good, and I will not pay shared goods special attention.

The importance, both theoretical and practical, of common goods is that they give the lie to the myth that politics is exclusively about the resolution of conflicts of interest. In part, and it is an important part, politics and political conflicts are about the provision of common goods; that is, about mobilising and coordinating the population to protect and promote interests which are common to all. But this conclusion and the case for it are complex and nuanced.

For example, it does not follow from the fact that a right serves a common interest that there is then no conflict of interests between the rightholder and others who have an interest served by the right. It is entirely possible that they also have other interests which conflict with their own interest which the right serves. If I am the owner of shares worth millions of pounds in companies which are the main contributors to air pollution, then, arguably, I not only have an interest in continued or increased air pollution, but that interest is my overall interest: it may outweigh my interest in clean air. So my interest in continued pollution conflicts with your interest in and your right (assuming you have one) to unpolluted air. By the same token, it conflicts with my own interest in, and my own right to, unpolluted air. This is no more than an instance of the general fact that, while rights protect interests of rightholders, those rightholders may also have other conflicting interests. Usually the result is that when rights do not serve the overall interest of the rightholders, they do not exercise them, or they waive them.

So the conclusion resulting from the fact that the protection of common goods is part of the justification of rights is not that rights inhabit a moral space in which conflict does not exist. They commonly embody a judgment about the way such conflicts are rightly resolved. Rather, the conclusion is that these conflicts are not between the rightholders and the rest, nor between the rightholder and the public interest. Rights and their boundaries demarcate the degree to which individual and common interests with (the protection of) which the rights under discussion are concerned are to be protected when they clash with other individual and common interests.

In some domains, politics is even further removed from conflicting interests than the considerations mentioned so far would suggest. Many goods are not independent of each other. Rather, many goods are interrelated through being embedded in more comprehensive structured goods. Take a simple example: I want to read Wood's book on Hegel's moral philosophy, for it will help me understand Hegel. I want to understand Hegel because he is a great philosopher and philosophy fascinates me. My interest in coming here and giving this talk, apparently so remote from my interest in Wood's book, is in fact but another aspect of my interest in philosophy.

In this example of the embeddedness of (many) goods, their connections may appear to depend on the structure of my interest in them, which is entirely up to me. But appearances are misleading. Philosophy has its own internal structure, and its own history. To be interested in philosophy, I have to be interested in it in the appropriate way: taking due account of its internal structure and of its history. Of course people who have a serious interest in philosophy do not have identical interests. A large latitude in emphasis is possible. But it is a limited latitude, limited by factors beyond the control of any individual. This objective structure of the subject and its history enables us to tell a genuine interest in the subject from a phony one, and also who is good at it and who is bad. The internal structure determines standards of success in the activity which guide the conduct of those engaged in it, and enable them and others to assess their progress.

What has all that to do with common goods? The interrelation of goods takes many forms, some very different from my example. In particular, the availability of certain goods is a precondition for the availability of many others. A property-respecting culture is a good, and it is a common good, common to the members of the society in which it is to be found. It is—and this is the point I want to emphasise—a precondition for all the goods which property makes possible. These include most of the economic activities we know of, but also many other features of the lifestyles familiar to us. They depend on much more than a property-respecting culture. But they will not exist without it. The dependence is so obvious that we do not often think of it. It is so pervasive and far reaching that we cannot trace accurately and exhaustively all the ways in which our lifestyles depend on the fact that we enjoy to a considerable degree the benefit of living in a more-or-less property-respecting society.

I will call goods the existence of which is a precondition for the existence of an adequate range of other goods in the society in which they exist "framing goods." I suspect that most of the goods available to people anywhere depend on framing goods; they depend on them in the sense that they would not be within people's reach unless those framing goods existed in their societies. Notice that I am not defining framing goods as those without which sufficient goods for human well-being will not exist. I want a concept of a type of goods which, while being the condition for the existence of a certain range of goods necessary for the well-being of people in the society in which goods of this type exist, can be replaced by other (framing) goods were they not to exist. The fact that private property is a framing good allows that there could be decent and flourishing societies without private property—societies in which only goods which do not presuppose private property exist (most of them different from goods available to us)—but that such goods could be sufficient for people's well-being.

The notion of a framing good is still very vague. But, as I do not intend to rely on it in complex, detailed argument, this may not matter. What does matter is that the availability of an adequate range of goods in a society is a common good, and to the extent that this availability depends on framing goods, the framing goods are also common goods. Moreover, the interest of members of the society in the existence of whatever framing goods exist in their society is more fundamental than most of their other interests. Even the market, that arena of economic competition and conflicting interests, presupposes market institutions (such as enforceable contracts) which are a common good, in that they provide everyone with the opportunity to benefit directly or indirectly from the advantages which accrue to free market economies.

There are other examples of common goods regarding which conflict of interests is limited, and where political controversy is primarily controversy about which goods are common goods and how best to serve them.[13] The extent to which we underestimate the importance of this aspect of politics may be due in part to a tendency to regard all disagreements about values as rationalisations that mask naked conflicts of interests. It may also be due to a misguided and narrow view of personal interests.

Disputes about the relation between religion and the state, or about the degree to which discrimination on the basis of sexual orientation violates people's rights, are prime examples of disputes over common goods. These are typically issues of constitutional law, though their ramifications will be felt in property law, contract law, and most other branches of the law. But do these issues concern common goods? In what way is it a common good to live in a tolerant society which does not discriminate against people on the basis of valuable aspects of their lifestyle which are central to their own sense of who they are? Is that not a matter which concerns only people who either discriminate or are discriminated against? The answer is that there are more ways in which we all benefit from living in a tolerant and nondiscriminatory society than can be discussed and illustrated here. A prejudiced and intolerant society affects adversely the options available to every one of its members. It colours the nature of the social relations each can have. It threatens to make each member complicitous with its bigotry through association with bigots, through involvement in projects which involve the display of prejudice and the practice of discrimination. It imposes duties actively to fight prejudice and discrimination in one's own society in order not to be tainted by its failures through membership in it; duties which are burdensome and limit one's ability to pursue other options. Alternatively, in order to avoid those duties one has to dissociate oneself from one's society, perhaps to emigrate. And that may leave one divided and torn.

I will not continue this list. It is clear that I am assuming that people have what one may call moral interests, as well as material, social, cultural, and other types of interests. The greatest obstacle to accepting the existence of such interests is that such acceptance makes it obvious that our interests can be adversely affected without our ever becoming aware of the fact. It assumes that one can have a life which is not worth having while being perfectly content with it. Controversial as that point may be, I am unable to defend it here. Once this point is agreed, the rest is a simple matter of exercising our moral imagination. In some ways it is more alert when we think of the failings of societies other than our own. Think of the way living in an apartheid system affects the life of all in that society. You will easily come up with more examples than I can survey here.

We are all aware that the politics of framing goods and of other common goods which serve the public interest are not free of controversy and conflicts of views. These controversies can be among those most bitterly fought in society. At the same time, we should not lose sight of the fact that no society can enjoy peaceful existence unless its members enjoy a considerable degree of agreement regarding common goods. In these days of so much talk about pluralism and multiculturalism, we tend to overlook the considerable measure of agreement on the nature and importance of common goods; an agreement that is no less secure for being often unspoken, consisting in what we so much take for granted that we do not notice it.

---

13. Let me interpose to clarify that I am not suggesting that politics is only about one or the other of these two. There is more to it than that.

IV. COMMON GOODS AND INDIVIDUAL RIGHTS

We are now in position to answer one objection to my main claim about rights. Individual rights protect the interest of the rightholder, and that is essential to their justification. But, I argued, the weight given to the interest of the rightholder in determining whether his interest is protected by a right, and how extensive that protection is, reflects not only our concern for the individual, but also our concern for the public interest which will be served by protecting the interest of the rightholder. One objection to this view is that it treats rightholders as means to the promotion of the public interest, rather than as ends in themselves.

The objection is misguided. It misses two vital aspects of my claim. First, rights are never justified just because they serve the public interest. They are justified because rights serve the interest of the rightholder and in doing so they also serve the common good. Far from it being the case that the interest of the rightholder is ignored or sacrificed for the common good, the fact that rights serve the common good justifies extra protection to the interest of the rightholder.

Second, to the extent that the rightholder's interest is given extra weight for reasons of the common good, these reasons are not altogether detachable from considerations of the rightholder's own interest. The common good is the good of all, including the good of the rightholder. By serving the common good, the right also serves the interest of the rightholder in that common good. There is here what I have called elsewhere a dual harmony between the interest of the rightholder and the interest of other people which is served by his right.[14] The right protects the common good by protecting his interest, and it protects his interest by protecting the common good.

Another objection to my account of rights is often made by those who claim the priority of rights over the good. They reject analyses of rights in terms of interests. They understand rights as expressing principles of respect for persons. In particular they are liable to say that, since people disagree about what is of value, the principles which lie at the foundations of a political community, including those asserting various fundamental rights, should not presuppose anything about value. They should be principles of respect.

The thought that general agreement about principles of respect is more likely than agreement on value is illusory. I, for example, tend to think that we respect people by respecting their interests. I suspect that those who deny this are motivated by a limited conception of people's interests. For example, they may think that being treated in a humiliating way is not against the interest of those so treated. If I am right in my understanding of respect for people, then disputes are as likely about respect as about value. But, since both my view and a range of other conflicting views about the nature of respect are prevalent in modern societies, there is no reason to think that controversy about principles of respect is less likely than controversy about value.

The existence of controversy over certain issues may well weigh against the state forcing one controversial view on a dissenting population. Political philosophy should explore the scope of restraint based on this consideration. But it should not elevate an illusory ideal of social agreement about the principles governing a political community

14. RAZ, *Rights and Individual Well-Being*, *supra* note 2, at 38.

to the status of an absolute and fundamental requirement. Political communities are held together primarily by ties of history and culture which determine people's identifications with one group or another, and which determine people's sense of who they are. Agreement on political principles is desirable and adds to the cohesiveness of a society. It is not, however, the fundamental determinant of that cohesiveness. Therefore, the justification of the fundamental principles of a political community is to be sought in general ethical considerations, assigning only a limited role to consensus.

V. CONSTITUTIONAL RIGHTS

These observations raise the last objection to my rejection of the individualist and the universalist theses to be considered today. Does not their rejection leave inexplicable the role of constitutionally entrenched rights, rights which cannot be overridden by ordinary legislation or common law?

It is not my claim that the type of common good protected by constitutional rights in and of itself provides the justification for entrenching constitutional rights. The importance of framing goods, or of other common goods, does not mean that they are permanent, unchanging fixtures in the life of any society. On the contrary, they are quite likely to be in continuous change. A simple example brings the point home: It is a good common to all who live in a democratic society that their society is democratic. But the character of any democracy is in a state of flux. In Britain in the years since the war, the role of the prime minister, the balance of power and responsibility between the prime minister and the cabinet, between the cabinet and parliament, between local and central government, between each party's members of Parliament and the party grass roots, as well as the party organisation, all have undergone radical changes. And I have not mentioned yet the considerable transfer of sovereignty to the European Union, as well as many other changes in the nature of British democracy.

Changes in common goods may be good, bad, or indifferent. But rarely are they catastrophic, by which I mean that rarely do they threaten the existence of common goods of sufficient diversity and richness to provide members of the society with adequate opportunities. Wars, drought, corruption, discrimination, and persecution pose such a threat. The changes that common goods undergo because of social, economic, technological, or cultural changes rarely have these catastrophic effects. Hence, while the continued existence of common goods—the kind which create the framework for the opportunities available in a society—is of vital importance, the desirability of one or another actual or possible change in them, while possibly a matter of consequence, is rarely of similar importance. There is no general reason to exclude deliberation about the legal regulation of framing or other common goods from the domain of ordinary politics.

My remarks will be confined to constitutional rights which, as is the practice in common law jurisdictions, include a power in the rightholder to sue for their enforcement or for damages for their violation. We are so used to legal rights coming together with powers of enforcement (as I will refer to them) that some writers take them to be an essential aspect of rights as such, or of legal rights.[15] But outside institutional settings—whether the law, universities, sport associations, or others—any talk of enforcement is out of place. Violators may indeed incur duties to compensate their victims, and the victim will then have a right to be compensated. But the victims do not have powers of enforcement. They can have words with the violator. They can avoid his company in the future. But the same is true of most other people. So-called "strangers" (who may in fact be closer to the violator than the victim: they may be family or friends) can also have words with him or shun his company. Outside institutional settings, there is very little that resembles the right to sue and enforce compliance, restitution, or damages, which is the feature of common law rights.

Nor do legal rights always come with powers of enforcement. Many legal systems recognise what can be called declaratory rights, which do not entitle their holders to sue for their enforcement. They may be purely declaratory, or they may be enforceable by other government institutions; even in common law countries, some remedies against the violation of rights are not available to the victim, but require government intervention.

Having said all that, let me return to the problem of constitutional rights. I will confine my remarks to rights regarding which the rightholder has powers of enforcement. I will further confine myself to the "bill of rights" type of rights, such as the freedoms of expression, conscience, religion, movement, and occupation. The moral nature of constitutional rights has been the subject of such exhaustive debate that all I can do is indicate which views are consistent with my refutation of the two fallacies. Formally, the rejection of the universalist and the individualist theses is consistent with the "human rights" view of constitutional rights, the view that constitutional rights are justified to the extent that they provide efficient protection for universal human rights. After all, I did not argue that there are no universal human rights, and possibly their protection is the sole role of the bill of rights part of constitutions. But you know by now that that is not my view. Constitutional rights have too much to do both with the foundations of democracy, without which the content of freedom of expression would be completely changed, and with nondiscrimination doctrines. And I have already argued that these do not derive from universal rights.[16]

The problem of justifying constitutional rights is not the question of why the law should recognise or confer such rights, though this is an important question. The problem is of justifying the constitutional character of the rights, assuming that there is a good cause for their legal recognition in some form. It is the question of justifying their special status, their constitutional entrenchment which makes them superior to ordinary legislation.

The difficulty is often supposed to be that, in constitutionally entrenching these rights, one is taking them out of the reach of democratic government. What could justify this limitation on the powers of democratic government? As I mentioned, the human rights

15. *See* H.L.A. HART, ESSAYS IN JURISPRUDENCE AND PHILOSOPHY 34-35 (1983) (advancing the view that enforcement powers are essential to legal rights); *see also* WILLIAM G. SUMNER, SUMNER TODAY 154-57 (1971); CARL WELLMAN, A THEORY OF RIGHTS 81-107 (1985) (taking legal rights to be paradigmatic examples of rights and consequently including power of enforcement as an essential feature of all or of some central categories of rights).

16. In fact I did less than that. I merely gave reason to suggest that certain rights should be viewed as at least partly justified by reference to the doctrine of democratic government or of nondiscrimination. *See supra* part I. I did not show that they are not also justified by reference to universal rights. Such a negative argument will take us into complex issues which cannot be explored here.

approach has a ready answer: since constitutional rights are (or should be) universal human rights, they cannot be changed by democratic processes.[17]

Stated like this, the answer is flawed even if one accepts that (justified) constitutional rights are all human rights, for it fails to address the real question: Assuming that governments should recognise and protect human rights and that they may not derogate from them, why should the courts, rather than parliaments, be trusted with this task? Supporters of the human rights approach are not, of course, short of attempted answers to this question. I am not denying that. The point is that once the debate is conducted in these terms, its centre of gravity has changed. It has become, as it ought to be, a debate about the distribution of power among different branches of government. The real issue to which constitutional rights give rise is of justifying the allocation of political power to various organs of government. When we think of constitutional rights we should think primarily of the role and powers of the courts versus other organs of government, not about whether the rights themselves are special. What makes them special is that it is best to let the matters they concern be settled by one organ of government rather than another, and not that they deal with immutable matters.

The fact that legal rights come with powers of enforcement turns them into sources of power. The allocation of rights is, among other things, a distribution of power, a way of empowering people and institutions, or of disempowering them. No less than allocating rights to government agencies, allocating them to individuals endows the individuals with power, which can be—again, among other things—political power. Its political character is particularly obvious when the rights in question are constitutional rights, especially if they are rights against the government. I believe that there is no possibility of a general account of the political role of constitutional rights. Different countries have different constitutional arrangements. The political significance of the constitution depends not only on the constitution, but also on the rest of the country's legal and political system, and on its political culture. But I want to point to one not unfamiliar feature which constitutional rights can have, and which I believe they do have in the United States.

Constitutional litigation, and the effects of people anticipating it, can become a second channel of political action, parallel to parliamentary politics. There are in various countries more channels of political action than these two. Strong, politically motivated trade unions, ready to take industrial action for social or political causes, may form another type of political arena. For present purposes, all that is required are a few remarks about the distinctness and importance of constitutional politics. The essentials of the case are simple.[18]

In the United States, we recently saw a clear example of how the same political goals can be pursued in parallel when the discrimination practised in the armed forces against gay people was coming under attack both in the courts and from the then-new Clinton administration. The case illustrates several important points. First, that often (though not always) the same objectives can be achieved through parliamentary politics or by the politics of constitutional rights. Second, the mechanism and the prospects of success in each political channel depend on very different factors. The mobilisation of public opinion in the streets and through the media with the aim of influencing Supreme Court decisions in the recent abortion cases, and the way the confirmation hearings for judicial

17. *See supra* note 16 and accompanying text.
18. I am relying here on my discussion of this point in my upcoming book LIBERTY AND TRUST (forthcoming).

appointments have developed in recent years, show that the difference should not be exaggerated. The failure of the Supreme Court to stand in the way of the wave of bigoted persecutions we know as McCarthyism shows that the politics of constitutional rights was never immune from the influences which shape ordinary politics. Nevertheless, even in the United States, and certainly in other countries, the politics of constitutional rights is marked by special features.

Three of them are very familiar. First, individuals whose rights were allegedly violated have the initiative in starting the legal process. In congressional politics, political processes are, of course, often initiated and controlled by interested organisations. But even so, they do, while the initiators of action in the politics of constitutional rights do not, need to mobilise support in the country at large, or among the major political organisations, or the main political pressure groups of the country. The politics of constitutional rights allows small groups easier access to the centres of power, including groups which are not part of the mainstream in society. Second, while the process is not free from unexplained decisions, characteristically it is conducted by the clash of arguments rather than through coalition-forming among powerful groups, and the outcome of litigation is meant to be justified by reference to the supposedly generally accepted principles of the constitution. Third, legal changes, once introduced by the courts, are normally less likely to alter with shifts in the climate of political opinion in the country.

All the points are a matter of degree. One particular misunderstanding of the nature of the politics of constitutional rights is to see its campaigns as aiming exclusively at winning a judicial decision supporting the propositions upheld by the campaigners. In fact, in many cases winning the support of the court is only a step on the hard road of securing one's political goals, as the court's decisions are often opposed by forces who do not shrink from subverting their implementation in any way they can, fair or foul. On the other hand, sometimes the campaigners can regard their action as successful even if they fail to obtain a decision supporting their cause. The publicity gained, the public sympathy aroused, and the implications of the decision to reject their claim may all play into the hands of the campaigners.

Much caution is needed in drawing conclusions from this list of three points. Political function is only loosely connected to formal legal structures. Not much can be said in general about the kind of issue which is suitable for treatment through constitutional politics, beyond the minimal observation that these should be matters admitting of greater stability, slower change, and of being settled by argument rather than through interest group coalitions.

Finally, I return to my first point. The politics of constitutional rights allows weak groups easier access to the centres of power; that is, groups with insufficient economic power, or with little social prestige, or groups who, because of their geographical dispersion or poor education or some other factor, find it difficult to have an impact in the coalition-building of congressional politics. Constitutional politics allows such weak groups access to the levers of power. This is not, I hope, a blue-eyed idealistic remark. I do not delude myself that a poor, ill-educated recent immigrant, or somebody similarly disadvantaged for other reasons, can find his way unaided to raise his grievances in the courts. But the cause-based groups which organise to fight their case in the arena of constitutional rights often represent people with no prospect of getting their case taken up through the coalition-building of congressional politics.[19] In that way, constitutional politics can empower people who are de facto politically disenfranchised. Of course, constitutional politics, like congressional politics, works within the limits set, vaguely and flexibly, by the country's political culture. And, of course, it is limited to issues which can be dealt with through constitutional litigation and the public opinion campaign which accompanies it. These areas differ in different countries, but they are always limited. Within these limits, constitutional politics can become a major political force.

I started the last part of my remarks by pointing out that constitutional rights should be perceived as akin— say—to the federalist provisions of federal constitutions; in other words, they should be perceived as concerned with the distribution of power among the various organs of government. I concluded by looking at the ability of constitutional rights not so much to strengthen the power of the courts as to empower the disenfranchised in society.

19. Am I not committed to saying that constitutional rights, in as much as they protect common goods, are in everyone's interests? Yes, but (1) constitutional rights may do more than just protect framing common goods; and more importantly (2) not everyone benefits equally from common goods. By and large, gay people benefit from the absence of homophobia more than nongays. And though everyone would benefit from the absence of homophobia, only the gays may have the will to try to fight it.

Part III
Aspirational Rights: Possibilities and Histories

[12]

ALCHEMICAL NOTES: RECONSTRUCTING IDEALS FROM DECONSTRUCTED RIGHTS

*Patricia J. Williams**

I. A Bit of CLS Mythodology

THE BRASS RING AND THE DEEP BLUE SEA

A. The Meta-Story

Once upon a time, tnere was a society of priests who built a Celestial City whose gates were secured by Word-Combination locks. The priests were masters of the Word, and, within the City, ascending levels of power and treasure became accessible to those who could learn ascendingly intricate levels of Word Magic. At the very top level, the priests became gods; and because they then had nothing left to seek, they engaged in games with which to pass the long hours of eternity. In particular, they liked to ride their strong, sure-footed steeds, around and around the perimeter of heaven: now jumping word-hurdles, now playing polo with the concepts of the moon and of the stars, now reaching up to touch that pinnacle, that fragment, that splinter of Refined Understanding which was called Superstanding, the brass ring of their merry-go-round.

In time, some of the priests-turned-gods tired of this sport, denounced it as meaningless. They donned the garb of pilgrims, seekers once more, and passed beyond the gates of the Celestial City. In this recursive passage, they acquired the knowledge of Undoing Words.

Beyond the walls of the City lay a Deep Blue Sea. The priests built themselves small boats and set sail, determined to explore the uncharted courses, the open vistas of this new and undefined domain. They wandered for many years in this manner, until at last they reached a place that was half-a-circum-

---

* Associate Professor of Law, CUNY Law School at Queens College. I am deeply indebted to the following people: my sister Carol Williams, whose research into our family's history gave me the idea for this piece; Richard Delgado, whose enthusiasm kept me going; the uniquely wonderful community of CUNY, past and present, faculty, students and staff; and, of course, Derrick and Jewell Bell, teachers, friends and inspiration to the many of us who are their students.

ference away from the Celestial City. From this point, the City appeared as a mere shimmering illusion; and the priests knew that at last they had reached a place which was Beyond the Power of Words. They let down their anchors, the plumb lines of their reality, and experienced godhood once more.

B. The Story

Under the Celestial City, dying mortals called out their rage and suffering, battered by a steady rain of sharp hooves whose thundering, sound-drowning path described the wheel of their misfortune.

At the bottom of the Deep Blue Sea, drowning mortals reached silently and desperately for drifting anchors dangling from short chains far, far overhead, which they thought were life-lines meant for them.

* * *

I wrote "The Brass Ring and The Deep Blue Sea" in response to a friend who asked me what Critical Legal Studies was *really* all about; the Meta-Story was my impressionistic attempt to explain. Then my friend asked me if there weren't lots of blacks and minorities, organizers and grass-roots types in an organization so diametrically removed from tradition. Her question immediately called to mind my first days on my first job out of law school: armed with fresh degrees and shiny new theories, I walked through the halls of the Los Angeles Criminal and Civil Courthouses, from assigned courtroom to assigned courtroom. The walls of every hall were lined with waiting defendants and families of defendants,[1] almost all poor, Hispanic and/or black. As I passed, they stretched out their arms and asked me for my card; they asked me if I were a lawyer, they called me "sister" and "counselor." The power of that memory is fused with my concern about the disproportionately low grass-roots membership in or input to CLS. CLS wields significant power in shaping legal strategies which affect—literally from on

[1] Few plaintiffs ever seemed to wait around as much as defendants did. In part, this was due to the fact that, in the courts in which I practiced, unlike, for example, a family court, the plaintiffs were largely invisible entities—like the state or a bank or a corporate creditor—whose corporeal manifestations were their lawyers.

high—the poor and oppressed. The irony of that reproduced power imbalance prompted me to complete "The Brass Ring and the Deep Blue Sea" with the Story.

In my experience, most non-corporate clients looked to lawyers almost as gods. They were frightened, pleading, dependent (and resentful of their dependence), trusting only for the specific purpose of getting help (because they had no choice) and distrustful in a global sense (again, because they most often had no choice). Subservience is one way I have heard the phenomenon described (particularly by harried, well-meaning practitioners who would like to see their clients be more assertive, more responsible, and more forthcoming), but actually I think it's something much worse, and more complexly worse.

I think what I saw in the eyes of those who reached out to me in the hallways of the courthouse was a profoundly accurate sense of helplessness—a knowledge that without a sympathetically effective lawyer (whether judge, prosecutor or defense attorney) they would be lining those halls and those of the lock-up for a long time to come. I probably got more than my fair share of outstretched arms because I was one of the few people of color in the system at that time; but just about every lawyer who has frequented the courthouse enough has had the experience of being cast as a saviour. I have always tried to take that casting as a real request—not as a literal message that I am a god, but as a rational demand that I work the very best of whatever theory-magic I learned in law school on their behalves. CLS has a good deal of powerful theory-magic of its own to offer; but I think it has failed to make its words and un-words tangible, *reach*-able and applicable to those in this society who need its powerful assistance most.

In my Story, the client-mortals reached for help because they needed help; in CLS, I have sometimes been left with the sense that lawyers and clients engaged in the pursuit of "rights" are viewed as foolish, "falsely conscious,"[2] benighted, or misled.[3] Such an attitude indeed gives the courthouse scenario a cast not just of subservience but of futility. More important, it may keep CLS from reaching back; or, more ironically still,

---

[2] A. Hyde, *The Concept of Legitimation in the Sociology of Law*, 1983 Wis. L. Rev. 379, 397.

[3] *See, e.g.*, Gabel & Kennedy, *Roll Over Beethoven*, 36 Stan. L. Rev. 1 *passim* (1984).

keep CLS reaching in the wrong direction, locked in refutation of formalist legal scholarship.

The present paper is an attempt to detail my discomfort with that part of CLS which rejects rights-based theory, particularly that part of the debate and critique which applies to the black[4] struggle for civil rights. There are many good reasons for abandoning a system of rights which are premised on inequality and helplessness; yet despite the acknowledged and compelling force of such reasons, most blacks have not turned away from the pursuit of rights even if what CLS scholars say about rights—that they are contradictory, indeterminate, reified and marginally decisive in social behavior[5]—is so. I think this has happened because the so-called "governing narrative,"[6] or metalanguage,[7] about the significance of rights is quite different for whites and blacks. For most whites, including the mostly-white elite of CLS, social relationships are colored by viewing achievement as the function of committed self-control, of self-possession. For blacks, including black lawyers, academics and

---

[4] I recognize that the categories of "black" and "white" do not begin to capture the richness of ethnic and political diversity which the debate actually contains; I do believe, however, that the simple matter of the color of one's skin so profoundly affects the way one is treated, so radically shapes what one is allowed to think and feel about this society, that the decision to generalize from this division is valid. Furthermore, I am at a loss as to how succinctly to describe the specifically racial perspectives and history which are my subject. "Disenfranchised" will not do, because part of my point is that a purely class-based analysis does not comprehend the whole problem. I don't like the word "minority" (although I use it) because it implies a certain delegitimacy in a majoritarian system; and if one adds up all the shades of yellow, red and brown which the term sweeps over, we are in fact not. "Oppressed persons" is rather more inclusive than I really mean; it would have to include all victims of religious, ethnic and sexual discrimination. I prefer, and use most frequently, the term "black" in order to accentuate the unshaded monolithism of color itself as a social force.

[5] *See* Trubek, *Where the Action Is: Critical Legal Studies and Empiricism*, 36 Stan. L. Rev. 575, 578 (1984).

[6] Governing narratives are "presiding fictions that allow us to behold ourselves and make sense of the historical world, and by them the status of knowledge is affected in intimate ways." Des Pres, *On Governing Narratives: The Turkish-Armenian Case*, 75 Yale Rev. 517, 517 (1986).

[7] Metalanguage is the language:

> used to talk *about* an object language and its component words. Thus if a treatise on the Russian language is written in English, Russian is the object language and English the metalanguage. If, however, we write about English using English, then English is both object language and metalanguage. The distinction between object language and metalanguage is entirely relative, since what may be used as a metalanguage in one discussion may become the object language in another.

A Dictionary of Philosophy 212 (A. Flew ed. 1979) (emphasis in original).

clients, on the other hand, relationships are frequently dominated by historical patterns of physical and psychic *dis*possession. In a semantic, as well as a substantive sense, then, I think that CLS has ignored the degree to which rights-assertion and the benefits of rights have helped blacks, other minorities, and the poor.

I by no means want to idealize the importance of rights in a legal system in which rights are so often selectively invoked to draw boundaries, to isolate, and to limit.[8] At the same time, it is very hard to watch the idealistic or symbolic importance of rights being diminished with reference to the disenfranchised, who experience and express their disempowerment as nothing more or less than the denial of rights.[9] It is my belief that blacks and whites do differ in the degree to which rights-assertion is experienced as empowering or disempowering. The expression of these differing experiences creates a discourse boundary, reflecting complex and often contradictory societal understandings.[10] The remainder of this article attempts to show how that

---

[8] Reconstruction cured most blacks of any idealization of property, authority and diligence:

> [T]he Reverend Henry Highland Garnet, a veteran black abolitionist, assured a gathering of freedmen, "The more money you make, the lighter your skin will be. The more land and houses you get, the straighter your hair will be." Even as they found their economic opportunities sharply curtailed, even as the deepening agricultural depression of the post-Reconstruction years drove thousands off the land, southern blacks were asked to pay obeisance to the same materialist deities, values, and goals that motivated the larger society. Success came ultimately to the hardworking, the sober, the honest, and the educated, to those who served their employers faithfully, who respected property and the sanctity of contracts, who cultivated habits of thrift, cleanliness, and temperance, who led moral, virtuous, Christian lives.
>
> In the experience of black southerners, such advice was as naive and mistaken in its assumptions as it was persistent.

Litwack, *"Blues Falling Down Like Hail": The Ordeal Of Black Freedom*, in New Perspectives on Race and Slavery in America, 109, 116 (R. Abzug & S. Maizlish, eds. 1986) (footnote omitted).

[9] *See* D. Bell, Race, Racism and American Law, (2d ed. 1980); Bell, *The Supreme Court, 1984 Term—Foreword: The Civil Rights Chronicles*, 99 Harv. L. Rev. 4 (1985); Bell, Bakke, *Minority Admissions, and the Usual Price of Racial Remedies*, 67 Calif. L. Rev. 3 (1979); Edley, *Affirmative Action and the Rights Rhetoric Trap*, 3 Harv. Blackletter J. 9 (1986).

[10] In another context, such a discourse boundary has been described as follows:

> [T]he women's movement has raised a fundamental question concerning everyone in complex systems: how communication is possible, how to communicate with "another" without denying the difference by power relations. Beyond the demand for equality, beyond the inclusion in the field of masculine rights, women are yet speaking of the right to difference and to "otherness." That is

opposition arises. It is my hope that in redescribing the historical alchemy of rights in black lives, the reader will experience some reconnection with that part of the self and of society whose story unfolds beyond the neatly-staked bounds of theoretical legal understanding.

II. A Tale With Two Stories

A. Mini-Story (In Which Peter Gabel and I Set Out to Teach Contracts in the Same Boat While Rowing in Phenomenological Opposition)

Some time ago, Peter Gabel[11] and I taught a contracts class together. Both recent transplants from California to New York, each of us hunted for apartments in between preparing for class and ultimately found places within one week of each other. Inevitably, I suppose, we got into a discussion of trust and distrust as factors in bargain relations. It turned out that Peter had handed over a $900 deposit, in cash, with no lease, no exchange of keys and no receipt, to strangers with whom he had no ties other than a few moments of pleasant conversation.[12] Peter said that he didn't need to sign a lease because it imposed too much formality. The handshake and the good vibes were for him indicators of trust more binding than a distancing form contract. At the time, I told Peter I thought he was stark raving mad, but his faith paid off. His sublessors showed up at the appointed time, keys in hand, to welcome him in. Needless to say, there was absolutely nothing in my experience to prepare me for such a happy ending.[13]

I, meanwhile, had friends who found me an apartment in a building they owned. In *my* rush to show good faith and trust-

---

> why they sometimes choose silence, because it is difficult to find words other than those of the dominant language.

Melucci, *The Symbolic Challenge of Contemporary Movements*, 52 Soc. Res. 789, 811 (1985).

[11] Peter Gabel was one of the first to bring critical theory to legal analysis; as such he is considered one of the "founders" of Critical Legal Studies.

[12] The people from whom Peter sublet did not want their landlord to know what they were doing—a not uncommon feature of New York life; they told him they wanted to minimize the "proof."

[13] In fact, I remain convinced that, even if I were of a mind to trust a lessor with this degree of informality, things would not have worked out so successfully for me; many Manhattan lessors would not have trusted *me*, a black person, enough to let me in the door in the first place—paperwork, references and credit check notwithstanding.

worthiness, I signed a detailed, lengthily-negotiated, finely-printed lease firmly establishing me as the ideal arm's length transactor.

As Peter and I discussed our experiences, I was struck by the similarity of what each of us was seeking, yet in such different terms, and with such polar approaches. We both wanted to establish enduring relationships with the people in whose houses we would be living; we both wanted to enhance trust of ourselves and to allow whatever closeness, whatever friendship, was possible. This similarity of desire, however, could not reconcile our very different relations to the word of law. Peter, for example, appeared to be extremely self-conscious of his power potential (either real or imagistic) as a white or male or lawyer authority figure. He therefore seemed to go to some lengths to overcome the wall which that image might impose. The logical ways of establishing some measure of trust between strangers were for him an avoidance of conventional expressions of power and a preference for informal processes generally.[14]

I, on the other hand, was raised to be acutely conscious of the likelihood that, no matter what degree of professional or professor I became, people would greet and dismiss my black femaleness as unreliable, untrustworthy, hostile, angry, powerless, irrational and probably destitute.[15] Futility and despair are very real parts of my response. Therefore it is helpful for me, even essential for me, to clarify boundary; to show that I can speak the language of lease is my way of enhancing trust of me in my business affairs. As a black, I have been given by this society a strong sense of myself as already too familiar, too personal, too subordinate to white people. I have only recently evolved from being treated as three-fifths of a human,[16] a sub-

[14] *See generally* Delgado, Dunn, Brown, Lee & Hubbert, *Fairness and Formality: Minimizing the Risk of Prejudice in Alternative Dispute Resolution*, 1985 Wis. L. Rev. 1359 [hereinafter *Fairness and Formality*].

[15]

> Whatever else they learned in school, black children came to understand, as their parents had, that their color marked them as inferior in the eyes of whites, no matter how they conducted themselves. "We came to understand," a black woman would recall of her youth, "that no matter how neat and clean, how law-abiding, submissive and polite, how studious in school, how church-going and moral, how scrupulous in paying our bills and taxes we were, it made no essential difference in our place."

Litwack, *supra* note 8, at 118 (footnote omitted).

[16] *See* U.S. Const. art. I, § 2.

part of the white estate.[17] I grew up in a neighborhood where landlords would not sign leases with their poor, black tenants, and *demanded* that rent be paid in cash; although superficially resembling Peter's transaction, such "informality" in most white-on-black situations signals distrust, not trust. Unlike Peter, I am still engaged in a struggle to set up transactions at arms' length, as legitimately commercial, and to portray myself as a bargainer of separate worth, distinct power, sufficient *rights* to manipulate commerce, rather than to be manipulated as the object of commerce.

Peter, I speculate, would say that a lease or any other formal mechanism would introduce distrust into his relationships and that he would suffer alienation, leading to the commodification of his being and the degradation of his person to property.[18] In contrast, the lack of a formal relation to the other would leave me estranged. It would risk a figurative isolation from that creative commerce by which I may be recognized as whole, with which I may feed and clothe and shelter myself, by which I may be seen as equal—even if I am stranger. For me, stranger-stranger relations are better than stranger-chattel.

B. Meta-Mini-Story (In Which I Reflect Upon My Experiences With Peter, Climb to Celestial Heights While Juggling the Vocabulary of Rights Discourse, and Simultaneously Undo Not a Few Word-Combination Locks)

The unifying theme of Peter's and my experiences (assuming that my hypothesizing about Peter's end of things has any

---

[17] As opposed to being a real part of the white estate. The lease of which I speak was for an apartment in Brooklyn; my search had started in Long Island, where two realtors had refused even to show me apartments in Port Washington and Roslyn.

[18] Peter describes "the law" of formalized hierarchical social arrangements as deriving from "externalized" and "totemic source[s] of unification" in which

> [e]ach person experiences his or her authentic being as a privatized non-self that is denied recognition and that is therefore "invisible" or unconscious: it is known or comprehended only through the experienced bodily tension that derives from not being-oneself and through a continual obsessive and preconscious fantasy life that reaches a dim awareness in moments of distraction. . . . The "visible" or conscious self that is enacted in behavior is experienced as a "public" or "outer" synthesis of as-if performances which is at once lived as passively undergone to the degree that it lacks any sense of its own agency and yet is "owned" to the degree that each person feels this self as "I."

Gabel, *The Bank Teller*, 2 Tikkun 44, 48 (1987).

validity at all) is that one's sense of empowerment defines one's relation to the law, in terms of trust-distrust, formality-informality, or rights-no rights (or "needs"). In saying this I am acknowledging and affirming points central to CLS literature: that rights may be unstable[19] and indeterminate.[20] Despite this recognition, however, and despite a mutual struggle to reconcile freedom with alienation, and solidarity with oppression, Peter and I found the expression of our social disillusionment lodged on opposite sides of the rights/needs dichotomy.

On a semantic level, Peter's language of circumstantially-defined need—of informality, of solidarity, of overcoming distance—sounded dangerously like the language of oppression to someone like me who was looking for freedom through the establishment of identity, the *form*-ation of an autonomous social self. To Peter, I am sure, my insistence on the protective distance which rights provide seemed abstract and alienated.

Similarly, while the goals of CLS and of the direct victims of racism may be very much the same, what is too often missing from CLS works is the acknowledgment that our experiences of the same circumstances may be very, very different; the same symbol[21] may mean different things to each of us. At this level,

---

[19] "Can anyone seriously think that it helps either in changing society or in understanding how society changes to discuss whether [someone is] exercising rights protected by the First Amendment? It matters only whether they engaged in politically effective action." Tushnet, *An Essay on Rights*, 62 Tex. L. Rev. 1363, 1370–71 (1984); *see also* The Politics of Law: A Progressive Critique (D. Kairys ed. 1982); G. Frug, *The Ideology of Bureaucracy in American Law*, 97 Harv. L. Rev. 1276 (1984); Gabel, *Reification in Legal Reasoning*, 3 Res. in L. & Soc. 25 (1980); Gabel & Harris, *Building Power and Breaking Images: Critical Legal Theory and the Practice of Law*, 11 N.Y.U. Rev. L. & Soc. Change 369 (1982–83); Kennedy, *The Structure of Blackstone's Commentaries*, 28 Buff. L. Rev. 205 (1979); Kennedy, *Form and Substance in Private Law Adjudication*, 89 Harv. L. Rev. 1685 (1976).

[20] *See* Tushnet, *supra* note 19, at 1375; *see also* Gordon, *Historicism in Legal Scholarship*, 90 Yale L.J. 1017 (1981); Trubek, *supra* note 5; Unger, *The Critical Legal Studies Movement*, 96 Harv. L. Rev. 561 (1983).

[21] I mean "symbol" in a very straightforward sense. I mean it as well, however, in its semiological sense:

> A *Symbol* is a sign which refers to the Object that it denoted by virtue of a law, usually an association of general ideas, which operates to cause the Symbol to be interpreted as referring to that Object. It is thus itself a general type or law, that is, a Legisign. As such it acts through a Replica. Not only is it general itself, but the Object to which it refers is of a general nature.

Peirce, *Logic as Semiotics: The Theory of Signs*, in Semiotics 1, 8 (R. Innis ed. 1985) (emphasis in original).

The word "sign," as it is used in linguistics, is a unit of meaning which joins a concept and a sound-image, which joins idea and form—or, in more mystical words,

for example, the insistence of Mark Tushnet, Alan Freeman and others[22] that the "needs" of the oppressed should be emphasized rather than their "rights" amounts to no more than a word game. It merely says that the choice has been made to put "needs" in the mouth of a rights discourse—thus transforming "need" into a new form of right. "Need" then joins "right" in the pantheon of reified representations of what it is that you, I and we want from ourselves and from society.

While rights may not be ends in themselves, it remains that rights rhetoric has been and continues to be an effective form of discourse for blacks. The vocabulary of rights speaks to an establishment that values the guise of stability, and from whom social change for the better must come (whether it is given, taken or smuggled). Change argued for in the sheep's clothing of stability (i.e., "rights") can be effective, even as it destabilizes certain other establishment values (i.e., segregation). The subtlety of rights' real instability thus does not render unusable their persona of stability.

What is needed, therefore, is not the abandonment of rights language for all purposes, but an attempt to become multilingual in the semantics of each others' rights-valuation. One summer when I was about six, my family drove to Maine. The highway was very straight and hot and shimmered darkly in the sun. My sister and I sat in the back seat of the Studebaker and argued about what color the road was. I said black. My sister said purple. After I had successfully harangued her into admitting that it was indeed black, my father gently pointed out that my sister still saw it as purple. I was unimpressed with the relevance of that at the time, but with the passage of years, and much more observation, I have come to see endless overheated highways as slightly more purpley than black. My sister and I will probably argue about the hue of life's roads forever. But, the lesson I learned from listening to her wild perceptions is that it

---

which joins signified and signifier. "[T]here is a tendency to interpret *sign* as signifier [alone], whereas [sign] is a two-sided Janus-like entity [of both signifier and signified]." R. Barthes, Elements of Semiology 39 (A. Lavers and C. Smith trans. 1964).

[22] *See* Tushnet, *supra* note 19; Freeman, *Legitimizing Racial Discrimination Through Anti-Discrimination Law: A Critical Review of Supreme Court Doctrine*, 62 Minn. L. Rev. 1049 (1978); *see also* D. Hay, P. Linebaugh, J. Rule, E. Thompson & C. Winslow, Albion's Fatal Tree (1975).

really is possible to see things—even the most concrete things—simultaneously yet differently; and that seeing simultaneously yet differently is more easily done by two people than one; but that one person can get the hang of it with lots of time and effort.

In addition to our differing word usage, Peter and I had qualitatively different *experiences* of rights. For example, for me to understand fully the color my sister saw when she looked at a road involved more than my simply knowing that her "purple" meant my "black." It required as well a certain "slippage of perception" that came from my finally experiencing how much her purple *felt* like my black:

> Wittgenstein's experiments in some of the passages of his *Zettel* teach us about multiple perception, ellipsis and hinging, as well as about seeing and saying. He speaks of "entering the picture," and indeed his tricks try out our picture as our thought. . . . Ambivalence is assumed. It is as if the imagination were suddenly to be stretched: "Suppose someone were to say: 'Imagine this butterfly exactly as it is, but ugly instead of beautiful'?!" The transfer we are called upon to make includes . . . stretching not just of the imagination, but of the transfer point: . . . "It is as if I were told: 'Here is a chair. Can you see it clearly?—Good—now translate it into French!'"[23]

In Peter's and my case, such a complete transliteration of each other's experiences is considerably harder to achieve. If it took years for me to understand fully my own sister, probably the best that Peter and I can do—as friends and colleagues, but very different people—is to listen intently to each other so that maybe our respective children can bridge the experiential distance. Bridging such gaps requires listening at a very deep level to the uncensored voices of others. To me, therefore, one of the most troubling positions advanced by some in CLS is that of rights' actual disutility in political advancement. That position seems to discount entirely the voice and the experiences of

[23] Caws, *Literal or Liberal: Translating Perception*, 13 Crit. Inq. 49, 55 (1986) (citations omitted).

blacks in this country, for whom politically effective action has occurred mainly in connection with asserting or extending rights.

The CLS disutility argument is premised on the assumption that rights' rigid systematizing may keep one at a permanent distance from situations which could profit from closeness and informality: "It is not just that rights-talk does not do much good. In the contemporary United States it is positively harmful."[24] Furthermore, any marginal utility to be derived from rights discourse is perceived as being gained at the expense of larger issues; rights are pitted against, rather than asserted on behalf of, the agencies of social reform.[25] This reasoning underlies much of the rationale for CLS' abandonment of rights discourse, and for its preference for informality—for restyling, for example, arguments about rights to shelter for the homeless into arguments about the "needs" of the homeless.[26]

However, such statements about the relative utility of "needs" over "rights" discourse overlook that blacks have been describing their needs for generations. They overlook a long history of legislation *against* the self-described needs of black people, the legacy of which remains powerful today. While it is no longer against the law to teach black people to read, for example, there is still within the national psyche a deep, self-replicating strain of denial of the urgent need for a literate black population ("*They're* not intellectual;" "*they* can't . . ."). In housing, in employment, in public and in private life it is the same story: the undesired needs of black people transform them into undesirables or those-without-desire ("*They're* lazy;" "*they* don't want to. . .").

For blacks, describing needs has been a dismal failure as political activity. It has succeeded only as a literary achievement. The history of our need is certainly moving enough to have been called poetry, oratory and epic entertainment[27]—but

---

[24] Tushnet, *supra* note 19, at 1386.

[25] "[T]he image of negative rights overshadows that of positive ones and may obstruct the expansion of positive rights." *Id.*

[26] Demanding that needs "be satisfied—whether or not satisfying them can today persuasively be characterized as enforcing a right—strikes me as more likely to succeed than claiming that existing rights to food and shelter must be enforced." *Id.* at 1394; *see also* Freeman, *supra* note 22.

[27] I do not mean to undervalue the liberating power for blacks of such poetry, oratory and epic; my concern is the degree to which it has been compartmentalized by

it has never been treated by white institutions as a statement of political priority. Some of our greatest politicians have been forced to become ministers or blues singers.[28] Even white descriptions of "the blues" tend to remove the day-to-day hunger and hurt from need and abstract it into a mood. And whoever would—how ever to—legislate against depression? Particularly something as rich, soulful and sonorously productive as black depression.

It may be different when someone white is describing need. Shorn of the hypnotic rhythmicity which blacks are said to bring to their woe, white statements of black needs suddenly acquire the sort of stark statistical authority which lawmakers can listen to and politicians hear. But from blacks, stark statistical statements of need are heard as "strident," "discordant" and "unharmonious"; heard not as political but only against the backdrop of their erstwhile musicality, they are again abstracted to mood and heard as angry sounds.[29]

For blacks, therefore, the battle is not deconstructing rights, in a world of no rights; nor of constructing statements of need, in a world of abundantly apparent need. Rather, the goal is to find a political mechanism that can confront the *denial* of need. The argument that rights are disutile, even harmful, trivializes this aspect of black experience specifically, as well as that of any person or group whose genuine vulnerability has been protected by that measure of actual entitlement which rights provide.[30]

---

whites as something other than political expression. For a discussion of the transformative significance of black music and literature, see Matsuda, *Looking to the Bottom*, 22 Harv. C.R.-C.L. L. Rev. 323, 335–37 (1987).

[28] "The various means of *purifying* the abject—the various catharses—make up the history of religions, and end up with that catharsis par excellence called art, both on the far and near side of religion." J. Kristeva, Powers of Horror 17 (1982) (emphasis in original).

[29] Mythologically speaking, black anger inspires white fear, and fear is the one mood to which white legislators have responded, but that's a story which has nothing to do with black need.

[30] How helpful, how *utile*, are deconstructionist observations like the following:

> It might be argued that, although busing violates the traditional . . . ideal relationship of school to neighborhood and is terribly inconvenient and expensive and often promotes only friction, it does do at least three things: (1) it allows blacks to believe something is being done for them; (2) it allows liberals to believe they are doing something for blacks; (3) it safeguards the continued segregation of the neighborhoods by quarantining integration inside the school. However, when liberals and conservatives quarrel over busing, we have an-

For many white CLSers, the word "rights" seems to be overlaid with capitalist connotations of oppression, universalized alienation of the self, and excessive power of an external and distancing sort. The image of the angry bigot locked behind the gun-turreted, barbed wire walls of his white-only enclave, shouting "I have my rights!!" is indeed the rhetorical equivalent of apartheid.[31] In the face of such a vision, "token bourgeoisification"[32] of blacks is probably the best—and the worst—that can ever be imagined. From such a vantage point, the structure of rights is akin to that of racism in its power to constrict thought, to channel broad human experience into narrowly referenced and reified stereotypes. Breaking through such stereotypes would naturally entail some "unnaming" process.

For most blacks, on the other hand, running the risk—as well as having the power—of "stereo-typing" (a misuse of the naming process; a reduction of considered dimension rather than an expansion) is a lesser historical evil than having been unnamed altogether. The black experience of anonymity, the estrangement of being without a name, has been one of living in the oblivion of society's inverse, beyond the dimension of any consideration at all. Thus, the experience of rights-assertion has been one of both solidarity and freedom, of empowerment of an *in*ternal and very personal sort; it has been a process of finding the self.

These differences in experience between blacks and whites are not, I think, solely attributable to such divisions as positive/negative, bourgeois/proletariat; given our history, they are differences rooted firmly in race, and in the unconsciousness of racism.[33] It is only in acknowledging this difference, however, that one can fully appreciate the underlying common ground of the radical left and the historically oppressed: the desire to heal

---

> other instance of the false squabbles which must precede every illusory reconciliation. . . .

W. Gass, Habitations of the Word 240 (1985). Is the integration of neighborhoods, classes, societies or ourselves likely to be any less inconvenient, costly, or filled with "false" squabbling?

[31] The word "apartheid" is, according to Jacques Derrida, "the archival record of the unnameable." Derrida, *Racism's Last Word*, 12 Crit. Inq. 290, 291–92 (P. Kamut trans. 1985).

[32] Freeman, *Antidiscrimination Law: A Critical Review*, in The Politics of Law: A Progressive Critique 96, 114 (D. Kairys ed. 1982).

[33] *See* Lawrence, *The Id, the Ego, and Equal Protection: Reckoning with Unconscious Racism*, 39 Stan. L. Rev. 317 (1987).

a profound existential disillusionment. Wholesale rejection of rights does not allow for the expression of such essential difference.

The white left is perhaps in the position of King Lear, when he discovered in himself a "poor bare forked animal"[34] who *needed* no silks, furs or retinue, only food, water and straw to sleep on. The insight of this experience also freed him to see the weight, the constrictions, which his due as king had imposed upon him.[35] Similarly, the white left may feel that words and rights "have only the meaning that power wishes them to have."[36] In this context, relationships of trust (which require neither speech nor "rights") are replaced by the kind of "sufferance with which force condescends to weakness."[37] From this perspective, the Olympus of rights discourse indeed may be an appropriate height from which those on the resourced end of inequality, those already rights-empowered, may wish to jump.

Blacks, however, may symbolize the King Lear who was pushed to the point of madness, who did not find his essential humanity *while* retaining some reference point to an identity as social being temporarily lost in the wilderness, but who ultimately lost everything, including a sense of self.[38] The black slave experience was that of lost languages, cultures, tribal ties, kinship bonds, and even of the power to procreate in the image of oneself and not that of an alien master. That sort of confron-

---

[34] "Is man no more than this? Consider him well. Thou ow'st the worm no silk, the beast no hide, the sheep no wool, the cat no perfume. . . . [T]hou art the thing itself; unaccommodated man is no more but such a poor, bare, forked animal as thou art." W. Shakespeare, King Lear, Act III, Scene IV.

[35]

O! reason not the need; our basest beggars
Are in the poorest things superfluous:
Allow not nature more than nature needs,
Man's life is cheap as beast's. . . .

Id. Act II, Scene IV.

[36] M. Ignatieff, The Needs of Strangers 37 (1984).

[37] *Id.*

[38]

Through tatter'd clothes small vices do appear;
Robes and furr'd gowns hide all.
Plate sin with gold,
And the strong lance of justice hurtless breaks;
Arm it in rags, a pigmy's straw does pierce it.

W. Shakespeare, *supra* note 34, Act IV, Scene VI.

tation with the utter powerlessness of status which is the true and full condition of the wilderness is what ultimately drove King Lear from insight into madness. Reduced to the basic provisions of food, water and a straw pallet, *kings* may gain new, perhaps profound, insight into those needs they share with all humankind. For others, however—for slaves, sharecroppers, prisoners and mental patients—the experience of poverty and need is fraught with the realization that they are dependent "on the uncertain and fitful protection of a world conscience" which has forgotten them as individuals, a collective mind which considers them (if it considers them at all) "examples of the universal abstraction Man."[39] For the historically disempowered, the conferring of rights is symbolic of all the denied aspects of humanity: rights imply a respect which places one within the referential range of self and others, which elevates one's status from human body to social being. For blacks, then, the attainment of rights signifies the due, the respectful behavior, the collective responsibility properly owed by a society to one of its own.

C. *Mega-Story* (In Which, by Virtue of My Own Mortality, I Am Dragged From a Great Height in Order to Examine the Roots of My Existence)

Another way of describing the dissonance between blacks and CLS is in terms of the degree of moral utopianism[40] with which blacks regard rights. I remember, for example, going to a family funeral in Georgia, where, in the heat of summer and the small church, fans with pictures of Martin Luther King, Jr. on them were passed out—as they still are in many black churches around the country. This icon of King is a testament to the almost sacred attachment to the transformative promise

---

[39] M. Ignatieff, *supra* note 36, at 53.

[40]

> Every social system contains a certain amount of moral and totalizing expectations toward happiness, justice, truth, and so on. These claims do not have social attributions, do not involve specific social interests or practical-historical projects. They live on the borders of great religions or great cultural and political waves, in the form of small sects, heretical cults, theological circles. The great collective processes offer a channel to express this moral utopianism, which otherwise would survive in marginal enclaves.

Melucci, *supra* note 10, at 803.

of a black-conceived notion of rights, which exists, perhaps, somewhat apart from the day-to-day reality of their legal enforcement, but which gives rise to their power as a politically animating, socially cohesive force.

For blacks, the prospect of attaining full rights under the law has always been a fiercely motivational, almost religious, source of hope. It is an oversimplification to describe that hope as merely a "compensation for . . . feelings of loss," rights being a way to "conceal those feelings. . . ."[41] Black "loss" is not of the sort that can be "compensated" for or "concealed" by rights-assertion. It must be remembered that from the *experiential perspective of blacks*, there was and is no such thing as "slave law."[42] The legal system did not provide blacks with structured expectations, promises, or reasonable reliances of any sort. If one views "rights" as emanating from either that body of "legal" history or from that of modern bourgeois legal structures,[43] then of course rights would mean nothing because blacks have had virtually nothing under either. And if one envisions "rights" as economic advantages over others, one might well conclude that "because this sense of illegitimacy [of incomplete social relation] is always threatening to erupt into awareness, there is a need for 'the law.'"[44] Where, however, one's experience is rooted not just in a "sense" of illegitimacy but in *being* illegitimate, in being raped, and in the fear of being murdered, then the black adherence to a scheme of negative rights—to the self, to the sanctity of one's personal boundaries—makes sense.[45]

The individual and unifying cultural memory of black people is the helplessness, the uncontrollability of living under slavery. I grew up living in the past: the future, some versions of

---

[41] Gabel, *supra* note 19, at 28.

[42] M. Tushnet, The American Law of Slavery 37–42 (1981). Tushnet's analysis is premised, in part, on an understanding of the law of slaveholders as creating a system of enforceable expectations and limited rights for slaves.

[43] *Id.*

[44] Gabel, *supra* note 19, at 29.

[45]

> In the discussion of law there is an ever-renewed conflict between those who see it as a functional necessity and others who invest it with hope and promise. The former accept law as given, as fact, at best as an instrument of practical problem-solving. For the legal idealist, on the other hand, law connotes a larger moral achievement.

Selznick, *Law, Society and Moral Evolution*, in Readings in Jurisprudence and Legal Philosophy 931, 936 (Schuman ed. 1979).

which had only the sheerest possibility of happening, was treated with the respect of the already-happened, seen through the expansively prismatic lenses of what had already happened.[46] Thus, when I decided to go to law school, my mother told me that "the Millers were lawyers so you have it in your blood."[47] Now the Millers were the slaveholders of my maternal grandmother's clan. The Millers were also my great-great-grandparents and great-aunts and who knows what else. My great-great-grandfather Austin Miller,[48] a thirty-five-year-old lawyer, bought my eleven-year-old great-great-grandmother, Sophie, and her parents (being "family Negroes," the previous owner sold them as a matched set).[49] By the time she was twelve,[50]

---

[46] "It is by now a trite observation that oppressed peoples have an acute sense of their past. Well they must: it is the crucible of their identity and their cohesion. Without it their present oppression becomes either meaningless or natural." Wiecek, *Preface To The Historical Race Relations Symposium*, 17 Rutgers L. Rev. 412 (1986).

[47] Of course Mother did not mean that law was literally part of my genetic makeup; she meant that law was an intimate part of the socially constructed reality into which I had been born. She meant that dealing with law and lawyers was something with which my ancestors were all too familiar. Mother was probably aware of the belief that "[t]he improvement of the blacks in body and mind in the first instance of their mixture with the whites, has been observed by every one, and proves that their inferiority is not the effect merely of their condition of life." T. Jefferson, Notes on Virginia 141 (Peden ed. 1955). However, Mother also knew that

> [e]verything depends therefore on encountering thought at its source. Such thought is the reality of man's being, which achieved consciousness and understanding of itself through it. . . . My own being can be judged by the depths I reach in making these historical origins my own. There is no palpable criterion for this in outward appearances. Such true thinking goes through history as a mystery which can reveal itself, however, to everyone with understanding, for this hidden thinking was once reality. Having been written down, it can be rediscovered: at any time it can spark a new blaze.

K. Jaspers, *On My Philosophy*, in Existentialism From Dostoevsky to Sartre 158, 161 (W. Kaufmann ed. 1975).

[48] In an earlier essay I wrote on this subject, Austin is incorrectly referred to as "Peter." *See* P. Williams, *A Brief Comment, with Footnotes, on the Civil Rights Chronicles*, 3 Harv. Blackletter J. 79, 79–80 n.1 (1986). While a great deal is known about the Miller family (they stayed pretty much in control of my mother's people until my grandmother's generation), his first name had to be retrieved from a census report that was both nearly illegible and confusingly organized. *See* Census of Hardeman Cty., Tenn., Aug. 29, 1850 (on file in National Archives, Roll 881, Sched. 2 (Slave Inhabitants of Bolivar)).

[49] By way of ironic counterpoint, see M. Tushnet *supra* note 42, at 15. "We know, however, that at least some slaves maintained nuclear families over long periods of time, which indicates that the slave code did not, as Goodel argued, state the best behavior that could be expected of slaveholders." *Id.* (footnote omitted).

[50] Knowledge of her youth enabled me to identify her in the Census listing. My mother and her siblings and cousins are pretty unanimous that Sophie was a child at the time she was purchased. On the Census, which of course does not give the names of slaves, there was only one very young female of childbearing age—younger than all

Austin Miller had made Sophie the mother of a child, my great-grandmother Mary.[51] He did so, according to family lore, out of his desire to have a family. Not of course, a family with my great-great-grandmother, but with a wealthy white widow whom he in fact married shortly thereafter. He wanted to *practice* his sexual talents on my great-great-grandmother. In the bargain, Sophie bore Mary, who was taken away from her and raised in the Big House as a house servant, an attendant to his wife Mary (after whom Sophie's Mary, my great-grandmother, had been named) and to his legitimated white children.[52]

In ironic, perverse obeisance to the rationalizations of this bitter ancestral mix, the image of this self-centered child molester became the fuel for my survival during the dispossessed limbo of my years at Harvard; the *Bakke* years, the years when everyone was running around telling black people that they were very happy to have us there, but after all they did have to lower the standards and readjust the grading system, but Harvard could *afford* to do that because Harvard was Harvard.[53] And it worked. I got through law school, quietly driven by the false idol of the white-man-within-me, and I absorbed a whole lot of the knowledge and the values which had enslaved me and my foremothers.

I learned about images of power in the strong, sure-footed arms' length transactor. I learned about unique power-enhancing lands called Whiteacre and Blackacre, and the mystical fairy rings which encircled them, called restrictive covenants. I learned that excessive power overlaps generously with what is seen as successful, good, efficient and desirable in our society.

I learned to undo images of power with images of powerlessness; to clothe the victims of excessive power in utter, bereft naiveté; to cast them as defenseless supplicants raising—*plead-*

---

the others by at least two decades—and she is listed as the mother of a female infant. Census of Hardeman Cty., Tenn., *supra* note 48.

[51] No lesser legal authority than Thomas Jefferson would undoubtedly attribute this to slaves' "own judgment in favor of the whites, declared by their preference of them, as uniformly as is the preference of the Oran-ootan for the black women over those of his own species." T. Jefferson, *supra* note 47, at 138.

[52] This information comes from my mother, who says that her grandmother told her. It was confirmed to me separately by my mother's cousin, whose own mother, my great-aunt (another Mary), was taken from the ages of five to thirteen into the Miller household to be the (unpaid) servant and companion to the Miller children.

[53] I do not mean this as a criticism of affirmative action, but of those who tried to devalue the presence and contributions of us, the affirmatively active.

ing—defenses of duress, undue influence and fraud.[54] I learned that the best way to give voice to those whose voice had been suppressed was to argue that they had no voice.[55]

D. Meta-Mega-Story (In Which I Attempt to Rescue My Great-Great-Grandmother From the Cruel Word-Bondage in Whose Circuity She Has Been Held Captive)

Some time ago, a student gave me a copy of *Pierson v. Post*[56] as reinterpreted by her six-year-old, written from the perspective of the wild fox. In some ways it resembled Peter Rabbit with an unhappy ending; most importantly it was a tale retold from the doomed prey's point of view, the hunted reviewing the hunter. I had been given this story the same week that my sister had gone to the National Archives and found something which may have been the contract of my great-great-grandmother Sophie's sale (whether hers[57] or not, it was someone's) as well as the census accounting which listed her, along with other, inanimate evidence of wealth, as the "personal property" of Austin Miller.[58]

In reviewing those powerfully impersonal documents, I realized that both she and the fox shared a common lot, were either owned or unowned, never the owner. And whether owned

[54] A quick review of almost any contracts text will show that most successful defenses feature women, particularly if they are old and widowed; illiterates; blacks and other minorities; the abjectly poor; and the old and infirm. A white male student of mine once remarked that he couldn't imagine "reconfiguring his manhood" to live up to the "publicly craven defenselessness" of defenses like duress and undue influence. *See* M.J. Frug, *Re-reading Contracts: A Feminist Analysis of a Contracts Casebook*, 34 Am. U.L. Rev. 1065 (1985); Klare, *Contracts Jurisprudence and the First-Year Casebook*, 54 N.Y.U. L. Rev. 876 (1979).

[55] *See* MacKinnon, *Feminism, Marxism, Method and the State: An Agenda for Theory*, 7 Signs: J. of Women in Cult. and Soc. 515 (1982); Olsen, *The Family and the Market: A Study of Ideology and Legal Reform*, 96 Harv. L. Rev. 1497 (1983).

[56]

> Post, being in possession of certain dogs and hounds under his command, did, "upon a certain wild and uninhabited, unpossessed and waste land, called the beach, find and start one of those noxious beast called a fox," and whilst there hunting, chasing and pursuing the same with his dogs and hounds, and when in view thereof, Pierson, well knowing the fox was so hunted and pursued, did, in the sight of Post, to prevent his catching the same, kill and carry it off.

3 Cai. R. 175, 175 (N.Y. Sup. Ct. 1805).

[57] I use the term "hers" intentionally, although her object-relation to such a contract technically would make it other than hers; a record of her, the possessory interest *in* others.

[58] Census of Hardeman Cty., Tenn., *supra* note 48.

or unowned, rights over them never filtered down *to* them; rights to their persons never vested in them. When owned, issues of physical, mental and emotional abuse or cruelty were assigned by the law to the private tolerance, whimsy or insanity of an external master.[59] And when unowned—i.e., free, freed, or escaped—again their situation was uncontrollably precarious, for as objects *to be* owned, they and the game of their conquest were seen only as potential enhancements to some other self.[60] They were fair game from the perspective of those who had rights;[61] but from their own point of view, they were objects of a murderous hunt.[62]

This finding of something which could have been the contract of sale of my great-great-grandmother irretrievably personalized my analysis of the law of her exchange. Repeatedly since then, I have tried to analyze, rationalize and rescue her fate, employing the tools I learned in law school: adequacy of valuable consideration,[63] defenses to formation, grounds for discharge and remedies (for whom?). That this was to be a dead-end undertaking was all-too obvious, but it was interesting to

---

[59] Perhaps this is what Mark Tushnet meant to say in this perplexing passage: "Cruelty thus was not tolerated in slave society, nor was the relationship of master and slave truly founded upon force alone. Rather, it was simply that *courts* could recognize no foundation other than force, and that control of cruelty must, and did, occur outside of the law." M. Tushnet, *supra* note 42, at 62.

[60] In *Pierson*, the dissent described the contest as between the "gentleman" in pursuit and the "saucy intruder." 3 Cai. R. at 180–81 (Livingston, J., dissenting). The majority acknowledged that Pierson's behavior was "uncourteous" and "unkind" but decided the case according to broader principles of "peace and order" in sportsmanship. *Id.* at 179.

[61] "Although societal acquiescence may be a practical necessity for rights to be legally respected, no individual or group need consent to . . . appropriation of previously unowned resources or their use for . . . rights to *morally* vest." Barnett, *A Consent Theory of Contract*, 86 Colum. L. Rev. 269, 297 (1986).

[62] *See* United States v. The Amistad, 40 U.S. 518 (1841), a suit for, among other things, the "salvage value" of a shipload of Africans who revolted during their passage to America. *See also* W. Breyfogle, Make Free: The Story of the Underground Railroad (1958), for descriptions of the elaborate rituals of slave-hunting, the history of the Fugitive Slave Act and the Underground Railroad.

[63] How much value, I wonder. Just how did the value break down? Did they haggle? Was it a poker game, a trade, a promissory note? How much was she *worth*? At one extreme, the New York Public Library's Shomberg Center (Shivery Papers) has in its archives a contract in which a young woman was sold for a dollar. In contrast, a review of the literature on the slave trade from Africa shows that the death of one-fourth to two-thirds of every cargo ship's population still provided slave traders "a good return on their investment." P. Finkelman, Slavery in the Courtroom: An Annotated Bibliography of American Cases 211 *passim* (1985). With what literalism must my philosophizing be alloyed: "There is something in me which might have been great, but due to the unfavorable market, I'm only worth a little." S. Kierkegaard, *quoted in* K. Jaspers, *supra* note 47, at 203.

see how the other part of my heritage, Austin Miller, the lawyer, and his confreres, had constructed their world so as to nip quests like mine in the bud.

The very best I could do for my great-great-grandmother was to throw myself, in whimpering supplication, upon the mercy of an imaginary, patriarchal court and appeal for an exercise of its extraordinary powers of conscionability and "humanitarianism."[64] I found that it helped to appeal to that court's humanity, and not to stress the fullness of her own. I found that the best way to get anything for her, whose needs for rights were so compellingly, overwhelmingly manifest, was to argue that she, poor thing, had no rights.[65] It is this experience of having, for survival, to argue our own invisibility in the passive, unthreatening rhetoric of "no-rights," which, juxtaposed with the CLS abandonment of rights theory, is both paradoxical and difficult for minorities to accept.

The discussion thus far may prompt the argument that this last paradox is the direct product of rights discourse itself. But, in addition, I tried arguing my great-great-grandmother's fate in terms more direct, more informal, more descriptive and more substantive. I begged, pleaded, "acted out" (the New Age way of describing the New Black Activism[66]) and cried. I prayed loudly enough for all to hear, and became superstitious.[67] But I

---

[64] *See* S. Elkins, Slavery: A Problem in American Institutional and Intellectual Life 237 (2d ed. 1963), in which the "conduct and character" of slave traders is described as follows: "Between these two extremes [from "unscrupulous" to "guilt-ridden"] must be postulated a wide variety of acceptable, genteel, semipersonalized, and doubtless relatively *humane* commercial transactions whereby slaves in large numbers could be transferred in exchange for money." *Id.* (emphasis added).

[65] *See* D. Bell, *Social Limits on Basic Protections for Blacks*, in Race, Racism and American Law 280 (1980).

[66] Many staunch white CLS-ers, attendees of every conference in the past, did not attend the one in January 1987, whose subject was Racism and Critical Legal Studies, and at which an earlier version of this paper was presented. In discussion groups addressing this issue, the low white attendance was reported to be attributable to fears that minorities would just "act out" their "displaced rage," or "guilt-trip" white participants, or make them feel like they were "in a confessional."

[67]

> When, striving for access to the word and to time, [woman] identifies with the father, she becomes a support for transcendence. But when she is inspired by that which the symbolic order repressed, isn't a woman also the most radical atheist, the most committed anarchist? In the eyes of this society, such a posture casts her as a victim. But elsewhere?

J. Kristeva, *About Chinese Women*, in The Kristeva Reader 158 (1986).

didn't get any relief for Sophie's condition; my most silver-tongued informality got her nothing at all.[68]

The problem, as I have come to see it, is not really one of choice of rhetoric, of formal over informal, of structure and certainty over context, of right over need.[69] Rather, it is a problem of appropriately choosing signs within any system of rhetoric. From the object-property's point of view (e.g., that of my great-great-grandmother and the nameless fox) the rhetoric of certainty (of rights, formal rules and fixed entitlements) has been enforced *at best as though* it were the rhetoric of context (of fluidity, informal rules, and unpredictability).[70] Yet the fullness of context, the trust which enhances the use of more fluid systems, is lost in the lawless influence of cultural insensitivity. So while it appears to jurisdictionally-recognized and invested parties that rights designate outcomes with a clarity akin to wisdom, to the object-property, the effect is one of existing in a morass of unbounded irresponsibility.

But this failure of rights discourse, much noted in CLS scholarship, does not necessarily mean that informal systems will lead to better outcomes.[71] Some structures are the direct products of people and social forces who wanted them that way.[72] If one assumes, as blacks must, not that the larger world wants to overcome alienation,[73] but that many heartily embrace it, driven not just by fear but by hatred and taboo,[74] then one is

[68] For a succinct summary of the political complexities involved in too-strict adherence to either formalism, informalism or "anti-informalism," see Simon, *Legal Informality and Redistributive Politics*, 19 Special Issue, Clearinghouse Rev. 384 (1985).

[69] *Id.*; *see also*, J. Auerbach, Justice Without Law? (1983); Johnson, Jr., *The Justice System of the Future: Four Scenarios for the Twenty-First Century*, in Access to Justice and the Welfare State 183 (M. Cappelletti ed. 1981).

[70] *See* Simon, *supra* note 68.

[71] *See* R. Abel, *The Contradictions of Informal Justice*, 1 Politics of Informal Justice: The American Experience 267 (1982); *Fairness and Formality*, *supra* note 14.

[72]

> There are two explanations for the unconscious nature of our racially discriminatory beliefs and ideas. First, Freudian theory states that the human mind defends itself against the discomfort of guilt by denying or refusing to recognize those ideas, wishes, and beliefs that conflict with what the individual has learned is good or right. . . .
>
> Second, the theory of cognitive psychology states that the culture—including, for example, the media and an individual's parents, peers, and authority figures—transmits certain beliefs and preferences. Because these beliefs are so much a part of the culture, they are not experienced as explicit lessons. Instead, they seem part of the individual's rational ordering of her perceptions of the world.

Lawrence, *supra* note 33, at 322–23 (citations omitted).

[73] *Cf.* Gabel, *supra* note 19.

[74] By this I do not mean to suggest a Hobbesian state of nature, but a crust of

compelled to recognize the degree to which informal systems as well as formal systems are run by unconscious and/or irrational forces. "Human nature has an invincible dread of becoming more conscious of itself."[75]

This underscores my sense of the importance of rights: rights are to law what conscious commitments are to the psyche. This country's worst historical moments have not been attributable to rights-*assertion*, but to a failure of rights-*commitment*. From this perspective, the problem with rights discourse is not that the discourse is itself constricting, but that it exists in a constricted referential universe. The body of private laws epitomized by contract, including slave contracts, for example, is problematic not only because it endows certain parties with rights, but because it denies the object of contract any rights at all.

The quintessential rule of contract interpretation, the parol evidence rule, illustrates the mechanics by which such constriction is achieved. It says, in relevant part, that "[t]erms with respect to which the confirmatory memoranda of the parties agree . . . may not be contradicted [by extrinsic evidence] . . . but may be explained or supplemented . . . by evidence of consistent additional terms. . . ."[76] If this rule is understood as a form of social construction, the words could as well read: "Terms with respect to which the constructed reality (or governing narrative) of a given power structure agree, may not be contradicted, but only supplemented or explained."

Such a social construction applied to rights mythology suggests the way in which rights-assertion has been limited by delimiting certain others as "extrinsic" to rights-entitlement: "Europe during the Discovery era refused to recognize legal status or rights for indigenous tribal peoples because 'heathens' and 'infidels' were legally presumed to lack the rational capacity necessary to assume an equal status or exercise equal rights under the European's medievally-derived legal world-view."[77] The possibility of a broader referential range of considered types

---

cultural habit and perception whose power shelters as it blinds: "Light am I; ah, that I were night!" F. Nietzche, Thus Spake Zarathustra 105 (W. Kaufmann ed. 1954).

[75] C. Jung, Psyche and Symbol 214 (V. de Laszlo ed. 1958).

[76] U.C.C. § 2-202 (9th ed. 1978).

[77] R. Williams, Jr., *The Algebra of Federal Indian Law: The Hard Trail of Decolonizing and Americanizing the White Man's Indian Jurisprudence*, 1986 Wis. L. Rev. 219, 290; *see also* Dred Scott v. Sandford, 60 U.S. 393, 407 (1857).

of rights may be found by at least adding to, even contradicting, traditional categories of public and private rights-recipients.[78]

Such an expanded reference, first made controversial by Christopher Stone's famous article, "Should Trees Have Standing?"[79] is premised on the degree to which rights do empower and make visible:

> We are inclined to suppose the rightlessness of rightless "things" to be a decree of Nature, not a legal convention acting in support of some status quo. It is thus that we defer considering the choices involved in all their moral, social and economic dimensions.
>
> . . .
>
> The fact is that each time there is a movement to confer rights onto some new "entity," the proposal is bound to sound odd or frightening or laughable. This is partly because until the rightless thing receives its rights, we cannot see it as anything but a *thing* for the use of "us"—those who are holding rights at the time.[80]

One consequence of this broader reconfiguration of rights, again in the context of contract, is to give voice to those people or things which, by virtue of their object relation to the contract,

---

[78] Imagine, for example, a world in which a broader range of inanimate objects (i.e., other than corporations) were given rights—as has not been done with regard to the looting of American Indian religious objects. Spurred by a booming international art market and virtually no fear of prosecution, raiders have taken

> ceremonial objects and ancient tools . . . [as well as] the mummified remains of Anasazi children. . . . [T]he asking price for quality specimens starts at $5,000. The best of these are said to have been preserved by casting them into acrylic blocks, an expensive, high-tech procedure. . . . The looting has struck a painful nerve for Native Americans. "To us," says Marcus Sekayouma, a Hopi employee of the Bureau of Indian Affairs, "the removal of any old object from the ground is the equivalent of a sacrilege."

Goodwin, *Raiders of the Sacred Sites*, N.Y. Times, Dec. 7, 1986 (Magazine), at 65.

[79] Stone, *Should Trees Have Standing?—Toward Legal Rights for Natural Objects*, 45 So. Cal. L. Rev. 450 (1972).

[80] *Id.* at 453, 455.

historically had no voice. Allowing this sort of empowerment opens up the *égoïsme à deux* of traditional contract, and increases the limited bipolarity of relationship which characterizes so much of Western civilization.[81] Analogizing from a contractual framework to social constructions generally,

> human action is an open work, the meaning of which is "in suspense." It is because it "opens up" new references and receives fresh relevance from them, that human deeds are also waiting for fresh interpretations which decide their meaning. All significant events and deeds are, in this way, opened to this kind of practical interpretation through present *praxis*.[82]

Listening to and looking for interests beyond the narrowest boundaries of linear, dualistically reciprocal encounters is characteristic of gift relationships, networks of encompassing expectation and support.[83] As my colleague Dinesh Khosla described it, "[i]n the circularity of gift, the wealth of a community never loses its momentum. It passes from one hand to another; it does not gather in isolated pools. So all have it, even though they do not possess it and even though they do not own it."[84]

Such an expanded frame of rights-reference is the premise of a philosophy of more generously extending rights to all crea-

---

81

> In bourgeois ideology, history is negated by the process of exchange: in the equalization brought about by the need to determine that one ware is worth another ware, and everything has its price, that this = that, history is replaced by an eternal stasis where values remain constant in an ideological tit for tat where the equal sign ensures a never-ending binary equilibrium in which a change on one side of the equation is always balanced by the algebraically obligatory change on the other. Everything becomes a perfect metaphor for everything else, for in the end all equations say the same thing and all equations say nothing. The emptiness behind the binary opposition is the emptiness behind the equation 0 = 0. One thing is opposed to another thing in a two-fold opposition incapable of accommodating marginalities, third forces, or syntheses.

Brockman, *Bitburg Deconstruction*, 7 Phil. For. 159, 160–61 (1986).

82 P. Ricoeur, Hermeneutics and the Social Sciences 208 (J. Thompson ed., tr. 1981).

83 *See* L. Hyde, The Gift: Imagination and the Erotic Life of Property (1983).

84 Khosla & P. Williams, *Economies of Mind: A Collaborative Reflection*, 10 Nova L. Rev. 621 (1986).

tures, whether human[85] or beast.[86] It is the basis of those theories of constantly returning cycles which are at the root of environmental reform,[87] and which give "utility" to maintaining the earth in an unexploited form.[88]

III. Conclusion (In Which I Attempt to Rescue From Silence Feelings for Which There Are No Words)

One lesson I never learned in law school, the one lesson I had to learn all by myself, was the degree to which black history in this nation is that of fiercely interwoven patterns of family, as conceived by white men. Folklore notwithstanding, slaves were not treated "as though" they were part of the family (for that implies a drawing near, an overcoming of market-placed distance): too often the unspoken power of white masters over slaves was the covert cohesion *of* family.[89] Those who were, in fact or for all purposes, family were held at a distance as strangers and commodities: strangers in the sense that they were

---

[85] Think, for example, how different the outcome might have been in the Tuskegee Syphilis Experiment, in which illiterate black men were deliberately allowed to go untreated and uninformed of the nature of their disease from 1932 until 1972, so they could be observed by doctors from the U.S. Public Health Service. Approximately 400 diseased men, with 200 more serving as controls, were allowed to degenerate and die; doctors told them only that they had "bad blood." J. Jones, Bad Blood (1981).

[86] Every year one reads in the newspapers about millions of cattle who are periodically destroyed for no other purpose than to drive up the price of either milk or beef. One also reads about the few "bleeding hearts" who wage a mostly losing war to save the lives of the hapless animals. Yet prior to the time of the Reformation, the bleeding heart was the Christian symbol of one who could "feel the spirit move inside all property. Everything on earth is a gift and God is the vessel. Our small bodies may be expanded; we need not confine the blood." L. Hyde, *supra* note 83, at 139. Today, on the other hand, the "'bleeding heart' is . . . the man of dubious mettle with an embarrassing inability to limit his compassion." *Id.*

[87] "Increasingly, the death that occupies each human's imagination is not his own, but that of the entire life cycle of the planet earth, to which each of us is as but a cell to a body." Stone, *supra* note 79, at 500.

[88] As ought to have been done in *Peevyhouse v. Garland Coal & Mining Co.*, 382 P.2d 109 (1962). There, the Oklahoma Supreme Court refused to enforce a contract provision requiring Garland Coal Company to rehabilitate leased farm and grazing land destroyed by the process of strip-mining. The court's rationale was that

> where the contract provision breached was merely incidental to the main purpose in view, and where the economic benefit which would result to lessor by full performance of the work is grossly disproportionate to the cost of performance, the damages which lessor may recover are limited to the diminution in value resulting to the premises because of the non-performance.

Id. at 114. The restoration of the land, the land's "voice," was viewed as extrinsic, unimportant; since it was not part of the "main purpose" for which the parties had been "righted" (i.e., money-making), that "voice" was permanently silenced.

[89] *See* K. Stampp, The Peculiar Institution 250–61 (1982).

excluded from the family circle at the hearth and in the heart, and commodities in the sense that they could be sold down the river with no more consideration than the bales of cotton they accompanied.

In the thicket of those relations, the insignificance of family connection was consistently achieved through the suppression of any image of blacks as *capable* either of being part of the family of (white) man[90] or of having family of their own.[91] The recognition of such a threshold is the key to understanding slavery as a structure of denial—a denial of the generative independence of black people. Instead, a substitution occurred: rather than black motherhood being the generative source for black people, master-cloaked white manhood became the generative source. Although the "bad black mother" is even today an archetypal way of describing what ails the black race, the historical reality is that of careless white fatherhood. Blacks are thus, in full culturally imagistic terms, not merely an unmoth-

---

[90] *See* Dred Scott v. Sandford, 60 U.S. 393 (1857), in which blacks were adjudged "altogether unfit to associate with the white race, either in social or political relations; and so far inferior, that they had no rights which the white man was bound to respect; and that the negro might justly and lawfully be reduced to slavery for his benefit." *See also* S.A. Cartwright, The Dred Scott Decision: An Essay on the Natural History of the Prognathous Race of Mankind (1859) (on file with Harvard Civil Rights-Civil Liberties Law Review), in which blacks were likened to "ourang outangs" and determined to be the descendants of Canaan.

> Noah, a tiller of the soil, was the first to plant the vine. He drank some of the wine, and while he was drunk he uncovered himself inside his tent. Ham, Canaan's ancestor, saw his father's nakedness, and told his two brothers outside. Shem and Japheth took a cloak and they both put it over their father's nakedness. When Noah awoke from his stupor he learned what his youngest son had done to him. And he said: "Accursed be Canaan. He shall be his brothers' meanest slave."

Genesis, 9:20–25 (New Jerusalem Bible, 1985).

[91]

> Since slaves, as chattels, could not make contracts, marriages between them were not legally binding. . . . Their condition was compatible only with a form of concubinage, voluntary on the part of the slaves, and permissive on that of the master. In law there was no such thing as fornication or adultery between slaves; nor was there bastardy, for, as a Kentucky judge noted, the father of a slave was "unknown" to the law. No state legislature ever seriously entertained the thought of encroaching upon the master's rights by legalizing slave marriages.

K. Stampp, *supra* note 89, at 198. Anti-miscegenation laws also kept blacks outside the family of those favored with rights; laws restricting the ability of slaveholders to devise property or freedom suspended blacks in eternal illegitimacy. *See generally* M. Tushnet, *supra* note 42.

ered race, but a badly fathered race, abused and disowned by whites.[92]

I am therefore not one of those who believes that the future and well-being of blacks lie solely with ourselves. Although I don't always yet trust this imagery of dependence, I think it is the reality, and necessity, if balanced coexistence is to occur. Blacks cannot be alone in this recognition, however. Whites, too, must learn to appreciate the communion of blacks in more than body, as more than the perpetually neotenized, mothering non-mother.[93] They must recognize us as kin. They must want to confer upon us the property of larger community, the integrated selfhood of owning up to family (as opposed to having, using and disowning). They must learn to listen and speak to the grieving, *enraged* black-people-within-themselves and within our society.

> Conscious realization or the bringing together of the scattered parts is in one sense an act of the ego's will, but in another sense it is a spontaneous manifestation of the self, which was always there. Individuation appears, on the one hand, as the synthesis of a new unity which previously consisted of scattered particles, and on the other hand, as the revelation of something which

[92] Certainly, the companion myths to this woeful epic are to be found in the brutalization of the archetypes of black male (as so indiscriminately generative as to require repression by castration) and of white female (as so discriminatingly virginal as to wither in idealized asexuality). *See generally* W. Jordan, White Over Black, 136–78 (1968) ("[C]astration [for blacks] was dignified by specific legislative sanction as a lawful punishment in Antigua, the Carolinas, Bermuda, Virginia, Pennsylvania, and New Jersey." *Id.* at 154); J. Dollard, Caste and Class in a Southern Town, 134–72 (1937) (Published originally in 1937, the author ominously and ambiguously says that the "reports" of exaggerated black potency are "further suspect because the same point seems to be coming up with respect to the Jews in Germany. . . ." *Id.* at 161); *see generally also* J. Mitchell, Woman's Estate (1973); E. Wolgart, Equality and the Rights of Women (1980).

[93] For example, the Mammy whom "W.E. B. DuBois . . . described . . . as 'one of the most pitiful of the world's Christs . . . was an embodied Sorrow, an anomaly crucified on the cross of her own neglected children for the sake of the children of masters who bought and sold her as they bought and sold cattle.'" Genovese, "Don't Mess with Mammy," Wash. Post, Oct. 27, 1974, at C5, col. 4. Mammy-exploitation persists—abounds—to this day in the too-familiar image of grossly underpaid but ever-so-*loved* black female "help." The going rate for black female full-time live-in baby-sitter/maids in New York City is as low as $150 a week. "Haitians come cheaper. Their starting salary ranges from $100 to $125 a week. . . . A Hispanic woman . . . is likely to start at $200 a week, since she's white." Laurino, *"I'm Nobody's Girl,"* Village Voice, Oct. 14, 1986, at 18.

> existed before the ego and is in fact its father or creator and is also its totality.[94]

Whites must confer upon blacks their recognition of black need and black identity, for is not "what we have in common precisely what is given to each of us as something exclusively his?"[95]

To say that blacks never fully believed in rights is true; yet it is also true that blacks believed in them so much and so hard that we gave them life where there was none before. We held onto them, put the hope of them into our wombs, and mothered them—not just the notion of them. We nurtured rights and gave rights life. And this was not the dry process of reification, from which life is drained and reality fades as the cement of conceptual determinism hardens round—but its opposite. This was the resurrection of life from 400-year-old ashes;[96] the parthenogenesis of unfertilized hope.

The making of something out of nothing took immense alchemical fire: the fusion of a whole nation and the kindling of several generations. The illusion became real for only a very few of us; it is still elusive and illusory for most. But if it took this long to breathe life into a form whose shape had already been forged by society and which is therefore idealistically if not ideologically accessible, imagine how long would be the struggle without even that sense of definition, without the power of that familiar vision. What hope would there be if the assignment were to pour hope into a timeless, formless futurism? The desperate psychological and physical oppression suffered by black people in this society makes such a prospect either unrealistic (i.e., experienced as unattainable) or other-worldly (as in the false hopes held out by many religions of the oppressed).

It is true that the constitutional foreground of "rights" was shaped by whites, parcelled out to blacks in pieces, ordained in small favors, as random insulting gratuities. Perhaps the predominance of that imbalance obscures the fact that the recursive

---

[94] C. Jung, *supra* note 75, at 214 (footnote omitted).

[95] I. Calvino, Mr. Palomar 14 (W. Weaver trans. 1983).

[96] "You must teach your children that the ground beneath their feet is the ashes of our grandfathers. So that they will respect the land, tell your children that the earth is rich with the lives of our kin. . . ." Chief Seattle of the Suquamish, 1854 speech in response to U.S. offer to enter into treaty for tribal lands, quoted in R. Williams, Jr. *supra* note 77, at 292 n. 275.

insistence of those rights is also defined by black desire for them, desire not fueled by the sop of minor enforcement of major statutory schemes like the Civil Rights Act, but by knowledge of, and generations of existing in, a world without any meaningful boundaries. And "without boundary" for blacks has meant not untrammelled vistas of possibility, but the crushing weight of totalistic—bodily and spiritual—*intrusion*. "Rights" feels so new in the mouths of most black people. It is still so deliciously empowering to say. It is a sign for and a gift of selfhood that is very hard to contemplate reconstructing (deconstruction is too awful to think about!) at this point in history. It is the magic wand of visibility and invisibility, of inclusion and exclusion, of power and no-power. The concept of rights, both positive and negative, is the marker of our citizenship, our participatoriness, our relation to others.

In many mythologies, the mask of the sorcerer is also the source of power. To unmask the sorcerer is to depower.[97] So CLS' unmasking rights mythology in liberal America is to reveal the source of much powerlessness masquerading as strength. It reveals a universalism of need and oppression among whites as well as blacks.

In those ancient mythologies, however, unmasking the sorcerer was only part of the job. It was impossible to destroy the mask without destroying the balance of things, without destroying empowerment itself.[98] Therefore, the mask had to be donned

---

[97] The "unmasking" can occur in a number of less-than-literal ways: killing the totemic animal from whom the sorcerer derives power; devaluing the magician as merely the village psychotic; and, perhaps most familiarly in our culture, incanting sacred spells backwards. C. Levi-Straus, The Raw and the Cooked 28 (1979); M. Adler, Drawing Down the Moon 321 (1979); W. La Barre, The Ghost Dance 315–19 (1970). Almost every culture in the world has its share of such tales: Plains Indian, Eskimo, Celtic, Siberian, Turkish, Nigerian, Cameroonian, Brazilian, Australian and Malaysian stories—to name a few—describe the phenomenon of the power mask or power object. *See generally* L. Andrews, Jaguar Woman and the Wisdom of the Butterfly Tree, 151–76 (1985); J. Halifax, Shamanic Voices (1979); Anatolii, *Beliefs About Spirits and Souls of the Dead*, in Raven's Bones 67 (A. Hope, III ed. 1982); J. Frazier, The Golden Bough 810 (1963).

[98]

> The dissolution of the contraries—life and death, light and dark, male and female—and reconstitution of the fractured forms is one of the most consistent impulses in the initiation and transformation process as experienced by the shaman. To bring back to an original state that which was in primordial times whole and is now broken and dismembered is not only an act of unification but also a divine remembrance of a time when a complete reality existed.

Halifax, *supra* note 97, at 22.

by the acquiring shaman, and put to good ends. As rulers range from despotic to benign, as anarchy can become syndicalism, so the power mask in the right hands can transform itself from burden into blessing.[99]

The task for CLS, therefore, is not to discard rights, but to see through or past them so that they reflect a larger definition of privacy, and of property: so that privacy is turned from exclusion based on *self*-regard, into regard for another's fragile, mysterious autonomy;[100] and so that property regains its ancient connotation of being a reflection of that part of the self which by virtue of its very externalization is universal.[101] The task is to expand private property rights into a conception of civil rights, into the right to expect civility from others.[102]

99

> Human existence, suffering, and death are rendered by shamans into a system of philosophical, psychological, spiritual, and sociological symbols that institutes a moral order by resolving ontological paradoxes and dissolving existential barriers, thus eliminating the most painful and unpleasant aspects of human life. The perfection of the timeless past, the paradise of a mythological era, is an existential potential in the present. And the shaman, through sacred action, communicates this potential to all.

Id. at 34.

100

> [I]n exactly the same way that the South imagines that it "knows" the Negro, the North imagines that it has set him free. Both camps are deluded. Human freedom is a complex, difficult—and private—thing. If we liken life, for a moment, to a furnace, then freedom is the fire which burns away illusion.

J. Baldwin, Nobody Knows My Name 116 (1961).

101

> The Yehudi and Peretz his disciple were crossing a meadow. Cattle put out to pasture there were lowing, and where it was watered by a stream a flock of geese rose from the water with a great cackling and beating of wings. "If only one could understand what all of them are saying!" cried Peretz. "When you get to the point of understanding the very core of what you yourself are saying," said the rabbi, "you will understand the language of all creatures."

M. Buber, *Speech*, in Tales of the Hasidim: Later Masters 228–29 (1948).

102

> He had to choose. But it was
> not a choice
> Between excluding things. It was not a
> choice
> Between, but of. He chose to include the
> things
> That in each other are included, the whole
> The complicate, the amassing harmony.

In discarding rights altogether, one discards a symbol too deeply enmeshed in the psyche of the oppressed to lose without trauma and much resistance. Instead, society must *give* them away. Unlock them from reification by giving them to slaves.[103] Give them to trees. Give them to cows. Give them to history. Give them to rivers and rocks. Give to all of society's objects and untouchables the rights of privacy, integrity and self-assertion; give them distance and respect. Flood them with the animating spirit which rights mythology fires in this country's most oppressed psyches, and wash away the shrouds of inanimate object status, so that we may say not that we own gold,[104] but that a luminous golden spirit owns us.[105]

Stevens, *Notes Toward a Supreme Fiction*, in The Collected Poems of Wallace Stevens 403 (1981).

[103] "[T]hough the modern state is too large a group to take its power from bonds of affection, still, the ideology of the socialist nations begins with the call for community. 'Labor should not be sold like merchandise but offered as a gift to the community,' Che Guevara used to say." L. Hyde, *supra* note 83, at 67.

[104]

If he walked in golden shoes
Cold his heart would be and stony.
Humble folk he would abuse
He wouldn't know me. . . .

B. Brecht, The Caucasian Chalk Circle, Scene VI.

[105]

Let him be afraid of hunger
Not of the hungry man's spite
Let him be afraid of darkness
But not fear the light.

Id.

[13]

CONSTITUTIONAL SCEPTICISM

Robin L. West*

Introduction: Constitutional Meaning and Value

Interpretive constitutional debate over the last few decades has centered on two apparently linked questions: whether the Constitution can be given a determinate meaning, and whether the institution of judicial review can be justified within the basic assumptions of liberalism. Two groups of scholars have generated answers to these questions. The "constitutional faithful" argue that meaning can indeed be determinately affixed to constitutional clauses, by reference to the plain meaning of the document,[1] the original intent of the drafters,[2] evolving political and moral norms of the community,[3] or the best political or moral philosophical theory available[4] and that,

---

* Professor of Law, Georgetown University Law Center. I would like to thank Walter Sinnott-Armstrong, Mark Tushnet, Michael Seidman, Vicki Jackson, and Fred Schauer for comments on early drafts of this article. I would also like to thank the participants in the Johns Hopkins "Law and Literature" seminar, the Georgetown Faculty Workshop, and the Dartmouth College Constitutional Interpretation Seminar for thoughtful comments and criticisms.

[1] *See, e.g.*, Planned Parenthood v. Casey, 112 S. Ct. 2791, 2874 (1992) (Scalia, J., joined by Rehnquist, C.J., White & Thomas, JJ., concurring in the judgment in part and dissenting in part).

> The issue is whether [abortion] is a liberty protected by the Constitution of the United States. I am sure it is not. I reach that conclusion . . . because of two simple facts: (1) the Constitution says absolutely nothing about it, and (2) the longstanding traditions of American society have permitted it to be legally proscribed.

Id.

[2] For examples of originalist interpretation and defenses of originalism, see Raoul Berger, FEDERALISM: THE FOUNDER'S DESIGN (1987) (advocating the doctrine of original intent for constitutional interpretation); Raoul Berger, *Against an Activist Court*, 31 CATH. U. L. REV. 173 (1982) (rejecting an activist theory that the judiciary was given unlimited, unaccountable power, checked only by judicial "self-restraint"); Raoul Berger, *New Theories of "Interpretation": The Activist Flight from the Constitution*, 47 OHIO ST. L.J. 1 (1986) (rejecting activist theories and defending original intent); Robert H. Bork, *Original Intent: The Only Legitimate Basis for Constitutional Decision Making*, 26 JUDGES' J. 12 (Summer 1987) (arguing that judges must follow the intention of the framers); Robert H. Bork, *The Constitution, Original Intent, and Economic Rights*, 23 SAN DIEGO L. REV. 823 (1986) (arguing that framers' intent is the only legitimate basis for constitutional decisionmaking and binds judges); Antonin Scalia, *Originalism: The Lesser Evil*, 57 U. CIN. L. REV. 849 (1989) (asserting that framers' intent is the necessary method by which to interpret the Constitution).

[3] For an example of "consensualist" interpretation, see Penry v. Lynaugh, 492 U.S.

because of that determinacy, judicial review can indeed be brought within the rubric of liberalism. Taking issue with the constitutional faithful is a group who might be called "constitutional sceptics." Scholars in this group see, in every constitutional phrase or doctrine, the possibility of multiple interpretations, and in the application of every constitutional method the possibility of multiple outcomes. It follows from this indeterminacy that judicial review cannot be easily justified by reference to liberal assumptions, because the power of the interpreting judge irreparably compromises the stability and rationality of the "Rule of Law" so central to liberal ideals.[5]

As important as the debate over constitutional determinacy may be, its prominence in modern constitutional theory over the last thirty years has carried with it serious opportunity costs. Specifically, the prominence of the debate over the Constitution's *meaning*, whether it can be said to have one, and the implications for the coherence of liberalism that these questions of interpretation seem to raise, has pushed to the background an older and possibly more important debate about the Constitution's *value*. By asking relentlessly whether the Constitution's meaning can be made sufficiently determinate to serve the Rule of Law—by focusing almost exclusively on whether constitutionalism is *possible* within liberal theory and whether liberalism is possible, given an indeterminate Constitution—we have neglected to ask whether our Constitution is *desirable*. Does it further the "good life" for the individuals, communities, and subcommunities it governs?

We might pose these evaluative questions in any number of ways. Has the Constitution or the Bill of Rights well served the communities and individuals they are designed to protect? Are the visions of individualism, community, and human nature on which the Bill of Rights rests, and the balances it strikes between rights and responsibilities, or civic virtue and freedoms, noble conceptions of social life, true accounts of our being, hospitable to

302 (1989) (holding that interpretation of Cruel and Unusual Punishment Clause depends upon community consensus).

[4] Those adopting this view include Bruce Ackerman, Ronald M. Dworkin, and John H. Ely. *See generally* BRUCE ACKERMAN, RECONSTRUCTING AMERICAN LAW (1984); BRUCE ACKERMAN, SOCIAL JUSTICE AND THE LIBERAL STATE (1980); BRUCE ACKERMAN, WE THE PEOPLE (1991); RONALD M. DWORKIN, TAKING RIGHTS SERIOUSLY (1977); JOHN H. ELY, DEMOCRACY AND DISTRUST: A THEORY OF JUDICIAL REVIEW (1980).

[5] *See, e.g.*, MARK TUSHNET, RED, WHITE, AND BLUE: A CRITICAL ANALYSIS OF CONSTITUTIONAL LAW 6-11 (1988) (contrasting some of the main elements of the liberal and republican traditions); Paul Brest, *The Misconceived Quest for the Original Understanding*, 60 B.U. L. REV. 204, 224-37 (1980) (rejecting originalism and defending nonoriginalist adjudication, which accords presumptive weight to the text and original history, but does not treat them as authoritative or binding). For an impassioned argument against the "indeterminacy thesis" on this ground, see Owen Fiss, *Objectivity and Interpretation*, 34 STAN. L. REV. 739, 742-62 (1982) (arguing against a new nihilism that insists that objectivity is impossible and that interpretation is based on the judge's own values).

societal and individual attempts to live the good life? More specifically, does the First Amendment, for example, well serve its core values of free expression, individual actualization, and open political debate? Assuming that it does, are those values good values to have? Are they worth the damage to our social cohesion, our fragile sense of fraternity with others, and our attempts at community that they almost undeniably cause? Are the Fourteenth Amendment's sweeping and majestic guarantees of "liberty" and "equal protection of the law," appearances notwithstanding, in fact unduly stingy? Do they simply, and cruelly, fail to guarantee a liberty that would meaningfully protect against the most serious constraints on peoples' liberties, or an equality that would even begin to address the grotesque material inequities at the very heart of our social and economic life? Do those guarantees perversely *protect*, rather than guarantee against, those constraints and inequities? Similarly, but from a quite different political orientation, are Fourth Amendment guarantees simply not worth their cost in law enforcement? Is it unwise to let eighteen-year-olds vote? Is the Second Amendment the height of foolishness?

These questions—about the value, wisdom, decency, or sensibility of constitutional guarantees—do of course receive some attention in contemporary legal scholarship, but nevertheless, it seems fair to say that in spite of the legal academy's supposed obsession with "normativity," normative questions about the Constitution have not been at the heart of constitutional discourse of the last thirty years. By contrast, normative questions of precisely this sort constitute the great bulk of scholarship in other areas of law. Scholars question the value of the holder in due course doctrine in commercial transactions, the negligence doctrine or strict liability in tort law, the rules governing acceptance of unilateral contracts in contract law, and insanity defenses in criminal law. But normative questions are neither the subject of constitutional "grand theory" nor, more revealingly perhaps, the subject of doctrinal constitutional scholarship. Instead, while theoretical constitutional scholarship centers on questions about the *meaningfulness* of the Constitution and its implications for the possibility or impossibility of liberalism, doctrinal constitutional scholarship centers on questions of the Constitution's *meaning*, rather than questions of its *value*. Thus, for example, rather than debate whether the First or the Fourteenth Amendment is a good idea, doctrinalists debate what the First Amendment or the Fourteenth Amendment means, and theorists debate whether they have any meaning and what it means to assert that they do or do not have meaning. In short, neither theoretical nor doctrinal constitutional scholarship places the value, rather than either the meaningfulness or the meaning, of the Constitution at the heart of constitutional analysis.

That we lack an explicitly normative debate about the Constitution's value might be evidenced by the visible effects of that absence in our substantive constitutional arguments. Let me cite a few examples, simply to convey the flavor of what I suggest is missing. One debate between constitutional scholars arising over the last few years, and of great interest to political progressives, concerns the constitutionality under the First Amendment of the attempts made by some cities and universities to control, through disciplinary sanctions, the intimidation and subordination of racial, ethnic, and sexual minorities by use of "hate speech." Those contributing to the small explosion of scholarly writing on this topic have generally taken one of two polar positions: one group of scholars and litigators (generally liberal) argues that hate speech regulations are simply unconstitutional under the First Amendment[6] while a second, more or less minority (and generally progressive), position argues that they are constitutional, either by virtue of the similarity between hate speech regulations and traditionally accepted limits on the First Amendment, or because of limits we should imply into that amendment through the "penumbral" and balancing, or counterbalancing, effect of the Fourteenth Amendment's equality clause.[7] The position that seems to have no adherents is that hate speech regulations are desirable, for progressive reasons, but are nevertheless unconstitutional, but shouldn't be, and that this shows that, at least from a progressive perspective, the First Amendment is morally flawed. But again, this position seems to have no adherents. Instead, those who think hate speech regulations are a good idea generally think they are constitutional while those who think they are not a good idea generally find them unconstitutional. No one seems to find them both desirable and unconstitutional, and hence exemplary of a problem with the First Amendment. No one, in other words, is led by a commitment to the desirability of hate speech regulations and a fair reading of the Constitution to take a progressive and morally sceptical stance toward the Constitution.

A second and structurally similar example involves the constitutionality of anti-pornography ordinances. Despite the wide range of conflicting feminist and libertarian positions on this issue, no one advances the apparently

[6] *See, e.g.*, George P. Fletcher, *Constitutional Identity*, 14 CARDOZO L. REV. 1, 26-27 (1992) (college speech codes undesirable, unconstitutional, and at odds with our constitutional identity); Suzanna Sherry, *Speaking of Virtue: A Republican Approach to University Regulation of Hate Speech*, 75 MINN. L. REV. 933 (1991) (arguing against the use of university hate speech regulations); Nadine Strossen, *Regulating Racist Speech on Campus: A Modest Proposal*, 1990 DUKE L.J. 484 (arguing that unless words are covered by "fighting words" exception to First Amendment ordinances suppressing them are unconstitutional).

[7] J. Peter Byrne, *Racial Insults and Free Speech Within the University*, 79 GEO. L.J. 399 (1991) (arguing that the Constitution can and should be read to afford universities the authority to prohibit racial insults by member of the academic community); Richard Delgado, *Campus Antiracism Rules: Constitutional Narratives in Collision*, 85 NW. U. L. REV. 343 (1991) (analyzing antiracism rules in terms of both a First Amendment and a Fourteenth Amendment problem); Charles Lawrence, *If He Hollers, Let Him Go: Regulating Racist Speech on Campus*, 1990 DUKE L.J. 431 (regulations both desirable and constitutional); Mari Matsuda, *Public Response to Racist Speech: Considering the Victim's Story*, 87 MICH. L. REV. 2320 (1989) (proposing legal sanctions for hate speech and thus rejecting an absolutist First Amendment position).

logical, and initially plausible, position that these ordinances are eminently desirable, but unconstitutional, revealing a serious problem with the First Amendment. Instead, those who view these ordinances as unconstitutional generally view them as objectionable,[8] while those who view the ordinances as desirable generally find them constitutional as well.[9] Again, no one is led by a commitment to the value of anti-pornography regulations and a fair reading of the Constitution to take a morally sceptical stance toward the Constitution, or at least toward the First Amendment.

Although this paper focuses primarily on the absence of progressive sceptical arguments about the Constitution's value, the same point holds regarding the absence of sceptical stances toward the Constitution reflective of other political or moral commitments. Thus, one finds few people arguing that the Constitution does indeed protect a woman's right to an abortion and, therefore, over-protects privacy, because abortion rights are morally unjustifiable. Few argue that the Constitution protects the individual's choice of sexual lifestyle and, therefore, over-protects individual choice, because homosexuality is an immoral way to live. No one seems led by a conservative commitment to the value of regulating private morality and a fair reading of the Constitution as prohibiting that regulation to the conclusion that the Constitution is morally and politically flawed. On the other hand, no one seems to believe that the Constitution does indeed fail to protect reproductive or gay rights, but that these rights should be granted, and that this shows the Constitution's inadequacy. Again, those who view abortion rights as desirable generally view them as constitutionally protected, and those who view them as unprotected generally view them as undesirable. No one seems led by virtue of their political views on abortion or sexuality combined with a fair reading of the Constitution to the conclusion that the Constitution is flawed.

The absence of these arguments in the legal literature evidences the more basic privation noted above: there is no general tradition, at least in the legal literature, of *normatively* sceptical constitutionalism from a liberal, progres-

---

[8] *See* Ronald Dworkin, *Liberty and Pornography*, 38 N.Y. REV. BOOKS, Aug. 15, 1991, at 12; Barry W. Lynn, *"Civil Rights" Ordinances and the Attorney General's Commission: New Developments in Pornography Regulation*, 21 HARV. C.R.-C.L. L. REV. 27, 48-56 (1986) (concluding that supporters of sex discrimination ordinances do not advance principles acceptable to society that truly support free expression and personal privacy).

[9] CATHARINE MACKINNON, *Pornography: On Morality and Politics*, *in* TOWARD A FEMINIST THEORY OF THE STATE 195-214 (1989) (condemning pornography as that which exploits sexual and economic inequality for gain); Catharine MacKinnon, *Not a Moral Issue*, 2 YALE L. & POL'Y REV. 321, 336-40 (1984) (arguing that First Amendment should not protect pornography because pornography suppresses women); Catharine MacKinnon, *Pornography, Civil Rights and Speech*, 20 HARV. C.R.-C.L. L. REV. 1, 22-32 (1985) (defining pornography as a civil rights violation and arguing for the constitutionality of an anti-pornography ordinance); Catharine MacKinnon, *Pornography: Social Science, Legal and Clinical Perspectives*, 4 LAW & INEQ. J. 17, 38-49 (1986) (part of a panel including Edward Donnerstein, Cheryl A. Champion, and Cass R. Sunstein).

sive, conservative, or any other developed political or moral perspective. Regardless of political viewpoint, constitutional scholars are peculiarly reluctant to see either the Constitution or a particular constitutional guarantee as being at odds with our political or moral ideals, goals, or commitments.[10] We tend to see the Constitution as an inappropriate object of criticism, and this may be even more true today than it was thirty, forty, or fifty years ago. Even in post-critical, post-modern, post-structuralist, post-feminist times, we lack a developed body of legal scholarship that takes a morally critical stance toward the Constitution and the rights it purports to protect.

The main purpose of this paper is simply to draw attention to this absence and initiate movement toward reversing the trend. By elaborating both a progressive argument against constitutionalism and a responsive progressive argument for it, I hope to show, by example, that we should develop normative arguments, grounded in politics and morality, for and against constitutional fidelity.

My second aim, however, is to try to account for the absence of normative constitutional debate. Why isn't there a recognizable body of constitutional scholarship criticizing the Constitution, on moral or political grounds? Why do so few advocates endorse the positions noted above: that hate speech regulation or anti-pornography ordinances are desirable but unconstitutional; that the Constitution protects abortion rights, but shouldn't; that the Constitution does, but shouldn't, protect reproductive or gay rights; or doesn't, but should, allow the regulation of private morality?

There is, of course, a "psychoanalytic" or "socioanalytic" explanation for the absence of constitutional doubt in the literature. Theorists, like the rest of the culture, and across the political spectrum, may find it sociologically or psychologically difficult to view the Constitution as morally problematic, or indeed even morally flawed. Either because there is so little else that binds us together as a civic culture, or, perhaps, simply out of a psychic need to identify some sort of authority in our lives who will love us as well as authoritatively guide us, we all may have a hard time seeing the Constitution itself—rather than its erroneous interpretation by a pernicious, dishonest, overly-conservative, or unduly activist Court—as being "the problem," the

---

[10] Indeed, constitutional scholars may be more reluctant to take a critical stance toward the Constitution than the general public. This might explain why constitutional scholars tend to be more sceptical of the wisdom of constitutional amendments than the latter. For example, a number of liberal constitutional scholars testified to both the constitutionality and desirability of a federal law to ban flag-burning, apparently in part because they feared that the alternative was a far more egregious constitutional amendment. *See Statutory and Constitutional Responses to the Supreme Court Decision in* Texas v. Johnson: *Hearings Before the Subcommittee on Civil and Constitutional Rights of the Committee on the Judiciary, House of Representatives*, 101st Cong., 1st Sess. 55-64, 107-24, 222-26, 444-47 (1989) (statements of Walter Dellinger, Laurence Tribe. Charles Fried, and Cass Sunstein).

obstacle to the attainment of some desired political or moral goal. We have trouble seeing the Constitution as part of the problem rather than part of the solution, and as a consequence, we tend, both in popular consciousness and at the level of theory to blur constitutionality with morality—to see the Constitution as more or less in line with moral and political virtue. It may be that because we have this difficulty, we are disinclined to oppose the Constitution itself, rather than its erroneous interpretation, to some moral ideal, to some cherished utopian vision, or more baldly, simply to some political ambition. Although this explanation may have some merit, it also sounds a bit dated, and even nostaligic: whatever may have been the case in the past, it is difficult to believe that in the fractured, relativist, nihilist, minimally *pluralist* moral climate in which we presently live and argue, that we are all still afflicted with an irrational and deeply emotional affection for a foundational legal document.

The explanation advanced in this paper for our continuing constitutional fidelity is considerably less global: at least one reason for our modern reluctance to generate constitutional criticism, I will argue, might stem from the preemptive logic of the "interpretation debate" that has dominated scholarship over at least the last two decades. As mentioned at the outset, the absence of normative debate can be viewed as a simple "opportunity cost" of the prominence of interpretive debate. Thus, whatever may be the effects of our psychic or social attraction to the Constitution, the logic of the interpretation debate alone, I will endeavor to show, has made sceptical arguments regarding the Constitution's value extremely difficult to even articulate, much less debate, even among political radicals who almost assuredly bear no excessive patriotic, civic, or psychic loyalty to the United States Constitution. I will try to show that our focus on questions of constitutional interpretation and methodology has minimally diverted our attention from questions of constitutional value, but the logic of that debate has also made questions of constitutional value difficult, for various reasons, to even raise.

The first section of this paper sketches one possible basis for a morally sceptical stance toward the Constitution. The sceptical position is grounded, again, not in the "indeterminacy thesis," but instead in a rejection of the *morality* (rather than coherence) of the liberalism that informs constitutional decisionmaking, and in an affirmation of a progressive and egalitarian political and moral orientation. This section argues, very simply, that our Constitution is fundamentally and possibly irreversibly at odds with progressive egalitarianism, and that because of that it is a seriously flawed document.

The second section examines why, with only a few exceptions—notably Derrick Bell's[11] and Alan Freeman's critical race theory,[12] Mark Tushnet's

---

[11] DERRICK A. BELL, AND WE ARE NOT SAVED: THE EXCLUSIVE QUEST FOR RACIAL JUSTICE (1987) (examining the intricacies of the barriers to racial equality established in law).

[12] Alan Freeman, *Antidiscrimination Law: The View from 1989*, 64 TUL. L. REV. 1407 (1990) [hereinafter Freeman, *Antidiscrimination Law*] (examining antidiscrimina-

"rights critique,"[13] and Mary Becker's[14] feminist analysis of the Bill of Rights—this form of constitutional scepticism—what might be called "progressive constitutional scepticism"—has not been elaborated in constitutional scholarship, despite the large numbers of constitutional writers and advocates who unquestionably hold egalitarian and progressive moral and political commitments. My argument will be that the logic of the dominant interpretive debates precludes articulation and elaboration of sceptical evaluative argument. This section then examines the costs—to progressivism as well as to constitutional discourse and theory—of the absence of this form of constitutional scepticism.

The last section sketches one possible response to the progressive constitutional scepticism laid out in section one. The response, however, is grounded neither in liberalism nor in a commitment to indeterminacy, but in the same progressive political orientation as that of the sceptics, and in a relatively determinate view of constitutional meaning. It thus rejects both liberal values and the indeterminacy critique of liberalism's most prominent contemporary critiques. This position, which I will call "progressive constitutional faith," seeks to rebut progressive scepticism not by exploiting the contradictions and ambiguities in liberalism (and hence in received constitutional interpretation), but rather by retelling the story of constitutionalism, emphasizing its convergence, rather than divergence with progressive politics. This position, unlike progressive scepticism, has received some doctrinal and theoretical elaboration in the literature, primarily in the emerging feminist and critical race theoretical movements. Mari Matsuda's groundbreaking characterization of "outsider jurisprudence,"[15] Akhil Amar's and

tion laws as evolved in Supreme Court opinions since 1954); Alan D. Freeman, *Race and Class: The Dilemma of Liberal Reform*, 90 YALE L.J. 1880 (1981) (book review of Derrick Bell's *Race, Racism and American Law* examining to what extent anything can significantly be done about the unique problem of racism without focusing on class structure and the forces that maintain it); Alan D. Freeman, *Race, Class and the Contradictions of Affirmative Action*, 7 BLACK L.J. 270, 270-74 (1982) (discussing racism, not as just another form of oppression, but in terms of problems of interdependence, remedial programs, and class struggle); Alan D. Freeman, *Race, Rights and the Quest for Equality of Opportunity: A Critical Legal Essay*, 23 HARV. C.R.-C.L. L. REV. 295, 316-25 (1988) (responding to the symposium entitled *Minority Critiques of the Critical Legal Studies Movement* and discussing two arguments, the "indeterminacy critique" and the "contradiction critique" of the movement); Alan D. Freeman et al., *A Hurdle Too High: Class Based Roadblocks to Racial Remediation: A Panel*, 33 BUFF. L. REV. 1, 4-10, 15-17 (1984) (analyzing the barriers to ending racial discrimination).

[13] Mark V. Tushnet, *An Essay on Rights*, 62 TEX. L. REV. 1363 (1984) (developing a version of the critique of rights and also exploring the epistemological basis of that critique).

[14] Mary E. Becker, *The Politics of Women's Wrongs and the Bill of "Rights": A Bicentennial Perspective*, 59 U. CHI. L. REV. 453 (1992).

[15] Mari Matsuda, *When the First Quail Calls: Multiple Consciousness as Jurisprudential Method*, 11 WOMEN'S RTS. L. REP. 7, 8-10 (1989) (arguing for multiple conscious-

Ruth Colker's historical writings about the original meaning of the Bill of Rights and the Reconstruction Amendments,[16] Catharine MacKinnon's progressive interpretation of the Constitution's general equality mandate,[17] and several critical race theorists' writings on the constitutionality of ordinances, statutes, or university regulations prohibiting hate speech[18] are all seminal contributions to a progressive constitutional faith. This third section articulates a set of premises for this developing body of scholarship and discusses its relation to both progressive constitutional scepticism and liberal constitutional faith.

As will be apparent, both "progressive constitutional scepticism" and "progressive constitutional faith" rest not only on a rejection of the ideals of liberalism, but also on a rejection of the indeterminacy thesis propounded by its critics or, to put it positively, on an *affirmation* of the determinacy of the Constitution's meaning. Thus, the progressive sceptical position holds that the relatively ascertainable and determinate meaning of the Constitution is radically inconsistent with progressive ideals, and the progressive faithful position holds that that meaning is in some deep historical or utopian sense consistent with non-liberal progressive politics. Both positions obviously depend upon some degree of constitutional determinacy: for the Constitution to be pernicious or salutary, its meaning must be determinate.

This paper does not defend the claim that the Constitution has a determinate meaning, whether that meaning is fatally inconsistent or deeply consis-

---

ness, a deliberate choice to see the world from the standpoint of the oppressed, as a jurisprudential method).

[16] Akhil R. Amar, *Our Forgotten Constitution: A Bicentennial Comment*, 97 YALE L.J. 28 (1987) (analyzing how history is used to interpret our supreme law and how we can make history by changing it); Akhil R. Amar, *Philadelphia Revisited: Amending the Constitution Outside Article V*, 55 U. CHI. L. REV. 1043 (1988) (asserting that constitutional amendments need not be limited by the Article V amending process or judicial review and that, instead, amendment should be by direct appeal to, and ratification by, the people); Akhil R. Amar, *The Bill of Rights as a Constitution*, 100 YALE L.J. 1131 (1991) (proposing an integrated overview of the Bill of Rights, illustrating the interaction between that document and the Constitution as originally drafted and refuting the notion that they represent two very different types of regulatory strategies); Amar & Widawsky, *Child Abuse as Slavery: A Thirteenth Amendment Response to* DeShaney, 105 HARV. L. REV. 1359 (1992) (arguing that child abuse is analogous to slavery and that the Thirteenth Amendment therefore imposes an affirmative obligation on the state to prevent it); Ruth Colker, *Antisubordination Above All: Sex, Race and Equal Protection*, 61 N.Y.U. L. REV. 1003, 1058-66 (1986) (proposing a new model for equal protection analysis, antisubordination, which finds it inappropriate for certain groups in society to have subordinated status because of their lack of power in society as a whole and would eliminate power disparities between groups).

[17] Catharine MacKinnon, *Reflections on Sex Equality Under Law*, 100 YALE L.J. 1281, 1282-97 (1991) (interpreting the Constitution's general equality mandate to combat the problem of sex inequality).

[18] *See supra* note 6.

tent with progressive ideals. It suggests instead that if we must first put aside doubts about whether the Constitution has an ascertainable meaning to debate, question, or affirm the Constitution's value from non-liberal political perspectives, then, in the spirit of pragmatism, we should put those doubts aside and see what may follow. Perhaps the doubts and faiths that may then come to the surface—doubts about the Constitution's worthiness rather than about its objectivity—might prove as central, innervating, and imperative as the questions of meaning and interpretation that continue to preoccupy our critical energies.

I. Progressive Constitutional Scepticism

Progressives have both substantive and methodological reasons to be sceptical about the Constitution's value. I define "progressivism," *in part*, by its guiding ideal: progressives are loosely committed to a form of social life in which all individuals live meaningful, autonomous, and self-directed lives, enriched by rewarding work, education, and culture, free of the disabling fears of poverty, violence, and coercion, nurtured by life-affirming connections with intimates and co-citizens alike, and strengthened by caring communities that are both attentive to the shared human needs of its members and equally mindful of their diversity and differences. Much of this guiding ideal, however, is shared by liberals. What *distinguishes* progressives from liberals is that while liberals tend to view the dangers of an over-oppressive state as the most serious obstacle to the attainment of such a world, progressives, while agreeing that some obstacles emanate from the state, argue that *for the most part* the most serious impediments emanate from unjust concentrations of *private* power—the social power of whites over blacks, the intimate power of men over women, the economic power of the materially privileged over the materially deprived. From a progressive perspective, it is those concentrations of private power, not state power, that presently riddle social life with hierarchic relationships of mastery and subjection, of sovereignty and subordination. Hence, it is those concentrations of private power that must be targeted, challenged, and reformed by progressive political action. That action, in turn, will often involve state intervention into the private spheres within which hierarchies of private power are allowed to thrive, and that simple fact will commonly pit the progressive strategy of ending private domination against the liberal goal of minimizing the danger of an oppressive state.

This difference between progressives and liberals largely accounts for the degree of conflict between their respective analyses and goals. For example, liberals and progressives generally agree, and lament, that the freedom of gays and lesbians to form and maintain nurturing intimate relationships is threatened by discriminatory state action. At the same time, progressives, far more than liberals, are sensitive to the degree to which that freedom is threatened by the continuing and seemingly unshakable hegemonic rage of an intolerant, abusive, and often violent minority of heterosexual private citizens. That hegemonic rage, not just state action, must somehow be challenged and transformed if gays and lesbians are to thrive. Similarly, liberals and progressive feminists agree, and lament, that the freedom of women to engage simultaneously in well-compensated work, in public life, and in a rewarding home and family life is threatened by discriminatory state law. Still, the dramatic and well-publicized split between liberal feminists and progressive feminists reflects the extent to which progressive feminists, unlike liberal feminists, realize that women's lives and freedom may be endangered more by private, intimate, economic, and social systems of power and control than by pernicious or discriminatory state action: by, for example, a family structure that saps women's time, energy, and self-esteem with unequal distributions of demanding and unpaid domestic labor; the social acceptability of private sexual violence and coercion in marriage and intimacy that threatens women's safety and drains women's sense of self-possession and self-will; and the prevalence of unequal compensation for work of comparable responsibility and difficulty that deprives women of material security, self-esteem, and independence. If we call these systems of private coercion, intimate violence, and economic disempowerment "patriarchy," then it seems that patriarchy exists and perpetuates itself to a considerable degree independent of "state action," discrimination or otherwise. Awareness of, and concern about, that social fact distinguishes progressive from liberal feminists.

Similarly, from a progressive perspective, African Americans and other ethnic minorities are hindered in their search for meaningful freedom and full civic equality, not so much by discriminatory state laws or actions as by the continuing and escalating presence of a virulent white racism in virtually all spheres of private, social, and economic life. Awareness of, and concern about, that complex social fact in large part distinguishes progressive "critical race theorists" from their one-time liberal allies. To take one final example, the poor in this society are hurt not nearly so much by pernicious or discriminatory state actions as by concentrations of private economic power. Again, concern over the centrality of this social fact distinguishes progressive from liberal politics on issues of class. Generally, what defines a progressive political perspective is simply the awareness that the greatest obstacles to enjoyment of the good life valued by liberals and progressives alike are not actions of any sort taken by states or state officials, but concentrations of *private* power, whether of a patriarchal, racist, homophobic, or capitalist sort.

If that progressive insight is basically correct, then at least two problems exist with the scheme of individual rights and liberties protected by the Constitution. First, the Constitution does not prohibit the abuse of private power that interferes with the equality or freedom of subordinated peoples. The Constitution simply does not reach private power, and therefore cannot possibly prohibit its abuse. Even the most far reaching liberal interpretations of the Reconstruction Amendments—the only amendments that *seemingly* reach private power—refuse or fail to find either a constitutional prohibition of private societal racism, intimate sexual violence, or economic coercion or a constitutional imperative that the states take affirmative action to eradicate it. Justice Harlan's famous liberal dissent in *Plessy v. Ferguson*,[19] for example, made painfully clear that, even on his reading of the amendment (which, of course, would have outlawed Jim Crow laws), the Fourteenth Amendment does not challenge the sensed or actual cultural and social superiority of the white race. More recently, Justices Brennan and Marshall's argument in their dissent in *City of Richmond v. J.A. Croson Co.*,[20] that the state *may* remedy private discrimination if failure to do so would enmesh the state in those discriminatory practices, did not suggest that the Constitution *requires* the state to address private discrimination. Similarly, virtually no liberal judges or commentators have read the Constitution and the Reconstruction Amendments to require that states take affirmative action to address the unconstitutional maldistribution of household labor, with its serious, well-proven, and adverse effects on women's liberty and equality. No liberal court or commentator reads the Constitution to require that states or Congress take action to protect against homophobic violence and rage, or to protect against the deadening, soul-murdering, and often life-threatening effects of homelessness, hunger, and poverty. The Constitution apparently leaves untouched the very conditions of subordination, oppression, and coercion that relegate some to "lesser lives" of drudgery, fear, and stultifying self-hatred. For that reason alone, the Constitution appears to be fundamentally at odds with progressive ideals and visions.

The incompatibility, however, of progressivism and the Constitution goes deeper. Not only does the Constitution fail to prohibit subordinating abuses of private power, but, at least a good deal of the time, in the name of guaranteeing constitutional protection of individual freedom, it also aggressively *protects* the very hierarchies of wealth, status, race, sexual preference, and gender that facilitate those practices of subordination. Thus, the Constitution seemingly protects the individual's freedom to produce and consume hate speech, despite its propensity to contribute to patterns of racial oppression. It also clearly protects the individual's right to practice religion, despite the demonstrable incompatibility of the religious tenets central to all three dominant mainstream religions with women's full civic and political equality. It protects the individual's freedom to create and use pornography, despite the possible connection between pornography and increases in private violence against women. It protects the privacy and cultural hegemony of the nuclear family, despite the extreme forms of injustice that occur within that institution and the maldistribution of burdens and benefits visited by that injustice upon women and, to a lesser degree, children. Finally,

---

19 163 U.S. 537, 552 (1896) (Harlan, J., dissenting) (stating that the Fourteenth Amendment targets discrimination by law, rather than societal discrimination).

20 488 U.S. 469, 528 (1989) (Marshall, J., joined by Brennan & Blackmun, JJ., dissenting) (arguing that the program setting aside a percentage of contracts for minorities is constitutional).

it protects, as a coincidence of protecting the freedom and equal opportunities of individuals, both the system of "meritocracy" and the departures from meritocracy that dominate and constitute the market and economy, despite the resistance of those systems to full participation of African Americans and hence despite the subordinating effects of those "markets" upon them. Very generally, the Constitution, incident to protecting the ideational, economic, and familial spheres of individual life against the intrusive effects of benign and malign legislative initiatives, protects that realm of private, intimate, social, and economic culture that creates and then perpetuates a spirit of intolerance toward, alienation from, and active hatred of subordinated persons. By so doing, the Constitution not only fails to protect against that subordination, but it also fails to exhibit neutrality toward it: it nurtures precisely those patterns and practices that are most injurious to the economic opportunities, the individual freedoms, the intimacies, and the fragile communities of those persons already most deprived in the unequal and unfree social world in which we live.

Finally, this incompatibility of the Constitution with progressive ideals is neither momentary nor contingent. It is not a product of false or disingenuous interpretation by a particular court or Justice hostile to progressive politics. Rather, the Constitution's incompatibility with progressive ideals stems from at least two theoretical and doctrinal sources that lie at the heart of our constitutional structure: first, the conception of liberty to which the Constitution is committed and, second, its conception of equality.

First, as is often recognized, the Constitution protects a strong and deeply liberal conception of what Isaiah Berlin has termed the "negative liberty"[21] of the individual to speak, think, choose, and labor within a sphere of noninterference from social, community, or state authority. As is less often recognized, however, the Constitution creates and protects these spheres of noninterference not only in preference to, but also *at the cost of*, the more positive conceptions of freedom and autonomy necessary for progressive change. The cultural, intimate, private, and economic spheres of noninterference protected by the Constitution are the very spheres of private power, control, and coercion within which the positive liberty of subordinated persons to live lives of meaning is most threatened. Thus, the Constitution protects the rights of producers and consumers of racial hate speech and pornography so as to protect the negative liberty of those speakers and listeners. By doing so, it not only fails to protect, but also actively threatens, the positive freedom of women and African Americans to develop lives free from fear for one's safety, the seeds of racial bitterness, the "clouds of inferiority,"[22] the interference with one's movements, and the crippling incapaci-

---

[21] SIR ISAIAH BERLIN, *Two Concepts of Liberty*, *in* FOUR ESSAYS ON LIBERTY 118 (1969) (distinguishing the "negative" liberty to do as one pleases within a designated sphere from the "positive" liberty to live a particular kind of life).

[22] MARTIN LUTHER KING, JR., WHY WE CAN'T WAIT 83 (1963) (describing the impact of racism on the self image of African American children).

ties to participate fully in public life occasioned by the constitutionally protected cultures of racism and misogyny. The negative liberty of the individual heralded and celebrated by liberalism is not only inconsistent with, but also hostile to the positive liberty central to progressivism, simply because protection of "negative liberty" necessarily creates the sphere of noninterference and privacy within which the abuse of private power can proceed unabated. The Constitution is firmly committed to this negative rather than positive conception of liberty, and is thus not only not the ally, but also a very real obstacle, to progressive ideals.

Second, the Fourteenth Amendment's mandate of equality, rather than being a limit to the Constitution's celebration of liberty, is also a bar to progressive progress, the heroic efforts of progressive litigators, judges, and commentators to prove the contrary notwithstanding. The "equal protection of the laws" guaranteed by the Fourteenth Amendment essentially guarantees that one's membership in a racially or sexually defined group will not adversely affect one's treatment by the state. As such, the mandate powerfully reinforces the liberal understanding that the only attributes that matter to the state are those shared universally by all members of the community: the possession of equal dignity, the power to form one's own plan of life, and the universal aspirations to autonomy and so forth. Precisely this understanding of equality, grounded in the liberal claim and promise of universality and equal treatment, however, renders the Equal Protection Clause an obstacle to progressive progress. The need to acknowledge and compensate for the individual's membership in profoundly non-universal subordinate groups—whether racially, sexually, or economically defined—is what distinguishes the progressive political impulse from the liberal. It is precisely that membership in non-universal groups, and the centrality of the non-universal attributes that distinguish them, that both liberalism and the liberally defined constitutional mandate of equality are poised not simply to ignore, but also to oppose. It is, then, both unsurprising and inevitable that the Fourteenth Amendment's Equal Protection Clause is understood as not requiring, and indeed forbidding, the state and public interventions into private, intimate, and economic spheres of life needed to interrupt the patterns of domination, subordination, and inequality that continue to define the lives of those within these protected private realms.

Methodologically, the Constitution is also hostile to political and moral progressivism, simply because it elevates one set of moral values above others, relegating non-constitutional ideals or visions to the sphere of the "merely political." The Constitution's peculiar status as a bridge between liberal morality and aspirations and positive law, although much heralded by liberal philosophers and constitutionalists, poses a triple danger to progressive ideals. First, because the Constitution is indeed *law*, and law in the ordinary as well as extraordinary sense, it imprints upon the liberalism on which it rests the imprimatur of positive legal authority. One set of political convictions hence receives not only the persuasive authority derived from its merits, but also the political, willed authority of the extant, empowered, positive sovereign. These ideals simply *are*, as well as ought to be; and they *are* in a way that makes compliance mandatory. Second, because the Constitution is law in the extraordinary as well as ordinary sense, the positive political authority imprinted upon the liberal morality of the Constitution is of a higher, permanent, and constitutive sort. It severely constrains moralities and aspirations with which it is inconsistent in the name of the community from which it purportedly draws its sovereign authority. Thus, it is not just "the law" that is hostile to non-liberal moral aspirations, such as progressivism. It is also, more deeply and meaningfully, "we the people"—all of us, the inter-generational community of citizens—for whom the Constitution speaks and from whom it draws its authority that is hostile to the ideals with which it is inconsistent. Third, because the Constitution is also undeniably a moral as well as legal document, the authority it embodies is exercised not only coercively—telling us who we must be—but also instructively—telling us who we ought to be. It defines and confines not just our options—as does any law, higher or lower—but our aspirations as well. For all three reasons, the Constitution is not just a peculiarly authoritarian legal document, but is also authoritarian in a peculiarly parental way. Like a parent's authority over the identity of his or her children, the Constitution both persuades us *to be* a certain way and it constitutes us *in* a certain way. It creates us as it defines a morality to which we will and should subscribe.

For all of these reasons, the Constitution is methodologically as well as substantively hostile to progressive politics. The moral authoritarianism at its core is in many ways conducive to the reverence for the individual and distrust of the mass so central to liberalism, but it is inimical to the egalitarian, inclusive, and largely communitarian methods—the grass roots politics at the local level and the participatory democracy at the national and state level—that must form the foundation of genuine progressive change. Effective political challenges to the subordination of some groups by others must rest on a fundamental change of human orientation in both the dominated and oppressing groups: the dominated must come to see their interests as both shared with each other and opposed to the interests of the stronger; and the stronger must come to embrace empathetically the subordinated as sufficiently close to their own identities to be "of their concern." Neither progressive end—the mounting of sufficient power within the ranks of the subordinated through cross-group organizing or the challenge to the received self-identity of the strong—is attainable through the legal, coercive imposition of a particular moral paradigm that characterizes constitutional methodology. In fact, the moral and legal authoritarianism at the heart of our constitutional method will almost invariably frustrate it.

These three attributes of our Constitution—its commitment to negative liberty at the cost of positive liberty, its individualist and universalist, rather than particularist and anti-subordinationist understanding of equality, and its moral authoritarian methodology—are just three possible grounds for scepticism about the Constitution's compatibility with progressive politics. If progressive politics are necessary for moral progress, then these three attributes are also grounds for scepticism about the compatibility of the Constitution with moral progress in this country.

This list is obviously not exhaustive. Other reasons grounded in progressive morality may exist for doubting the wisdom of the constitutional project. At the same time, the whole of the Constitution is certainly not adverse to progressivism, and some features of the Constitution, at least when properly viewed, may promote progressive projects. Nevertheless, it seems fair to say that *at least* the twin concepts of liberty and equality with which the Constitution is aligned, as well as our constitutional method, are not neutral toward progressive politics and ideals and collectively constitute a potent political, moral, and even social force against the realization of those aspirations.

II. The Absence of Progressive Constitutional Scepticism

Why is it that neither this progressive case against the value of the Constitution, nor any of its implications for particular issues, has a sizeable number of adherents in the legal profession, or has received more than occasional elaboration in constitutional scholarship? Although I have labelled the sceptical stance toward constitutionalism outlined above "progressive," it is by no means only those who think of themselves as political progressives who align themselves with some part of a progressive agenda. Political orientations generally are not monolithic, and progressivism in particular can be embraced in part by persons at virtually all points along the political spectrum. Thus, a sizeable number of liberals making up the mainstream of constitutional discourse, the vast majority of critical legal scholars, a probable majority of feminist legal theorists, most critical race theorists, and at least a few conservative legal theorists subscribe to some subset of "progressive" political commitments. The question posed above might be framed in this way: of the scores of constitutional writers favoring progressive political commitments,[23] why do only a handful *also* believe that these progressive initiatives are truly unconstitutional, revealing a serious moral failing in our constitutional scheme? Why are almost all of these more or less progressive writers, activists, and thinkers seemingly convinced that their beliefs are consistent with the Constitution? In contrast to whatever scepticism, nihilism, or simple pessimism progressives hold toward the Court, the public, Congress, and our public institutions, why are they so relentlessly optimistic about the Constitution itself? Why do so few think that, because of its deep incompatibility with progressive political and moral goals, the Constitution, although desirable at times, generally does more harm than good, and that we would be better off without it?

Perhaps the main reason is purely strategic. From a jurisprudential perspective, the absence of normative debate about the Constitution reflects a seemingly perverse refusal to apply the lessons of legal positivism to the doc-

---

[23] *See* discussion *supra* pp. 771-73.

ument applied as a matter of course in other areas of the law: we actually find it difficult to separate the Constitution "as it actually is" from our moral ideals of "what it should be," although we have few difficulties separating the law of negligence, the holder in due course doctrine, or the consideration doctrine from our ideals of what tort, commercial, or contract law should be. We have not achieved the positivist "separation of law and morality" in the constitutional sphere that we seem to embrace almost automatically in most other areas of law. But this may not be as surprising, or inconsistent, as it first appears. The positivist insistence on the separation of "the law" on the one hand and its merit or demerit on the other—the separateness of the actual and the ideal—ensures a clear perception of the law's true nature, a logical prerequisite to meaningful criticism and hence reform. Only by first understanding what the law is, the positivist argues, can we determine what it should be, and only after we see what it should be can we reform it. But, perhaps what is distinctive about the constitutional context is that there simply is no realistic chance of "reforming" the Constitution, and hence no sensible reform-based motive for insisting on the positivist separation of the Constitution "as it is" from the Constitution "as it ought to be." Given the permanence, the higher status, and the "constitutiveness" of constitutional law, what one achieves through insistence on the moral inadequacy of the Constitution is not the clear-headedness essential to its enlightened reform stressed by the classical legal positivists, but rather one's own exclusion from the community whose audience is sought.

From a purely strategic perspective then, there may simply be no gain and considerable cost from the positivist insistence on separating the constitutional "is" from the constitutional "ought." The Constitution is simply not amenable to the gradualist, piecemeal, liberal reform that positivism facilitates. Criticizing the Constitution may too closely resemble criticizing the earth for revolving around the sun. Although neither as natural nor as unchangeable as the law of the earth's rotation, the law of the Constitution is considerably more resistant to change than the criminal codes or private law regimes to which Bentham and his positivist followers directed their critical and reformist attentions. The costs of asserting the incompatibility of the Constitution with one's own moral and political values are high, and obvious. Once the unconstitutionality of a favored reform is conceded, marginality is virtually assured. Given the dominance of lawyers in constitutional discourse and their continuing commitment to change the world through law, the absence of a critical perspective that fails to achieve meaningful reform and delegitimizes the very values according to which the law is found wanting may not be so surprising.

Strategy alone, however, does not tell the entire story. After all, many, if not most, constitutional theorists are not litigators, or even aspire to be litigators. No matter how many of the last generation of grand constitutional theorists were one-time law clerks, there are now many contemporary constitutional theorists who have no secret or express urge whatsoever to tie their constitutional views to a potential argument for effectuating a desirable legal change. The absence of normative scepticism from constitutional discourse must have causes other than the strategic desire to back the winning horse, coupled with the obvious truism that an argument that concedes unconstitutionality to argue the immorality of the Constitution will lose in court every time.

In this section I will argue that the absence of normative scepticism from constitutional discourse is also attributable, at least in part, to the logic of the poles of the interpretive debates concerning the Constitution's meaning, its meaningfulness, or meaninglessness that currently dominate constitutional scholarship. Both the constitutional faithful—those who insist upon the determinacy of constitutional meaning and hence legitimacy of constitutional review within the framework of liberalism—and the constitutional sceptical—those who challenge the determinacy of the Constitution and hence the compatibility of judicial review with liberal theory—are, for different reasons, unlikely to pursue sceptical arguments about the Constitution's value, even if they adhere to the progressive political or moral premises on which that scepticism might be grounded. Thus, the absence of progressive scepticism about the Constitution might reflect the degree to which the now standard debate over interpretivism has captured the terms of constitutional discourse. Whatever the case concerning the wisdom of refraining from constitutional critique for strategic reasons, there is no good reason, I will argue, to allow the debate over interpretation to preempt debate over constitutional value. To the degree that the absence of a morally sceptical stance regarding the Constitution reflects a commitment to one or the other of the poles of debate over meaning, we should put aside, if we cannot resolve, the latter, so that we can again focus our attention on the former.

A. *The Progressive Critique and Liberal Constitutional Faith*

All members of the constitutionally faithful[24] pole of the debate adhering to the determinacy of constitutional meaning and to the compatibility of the constitutional enterprise with liberal premises will be disinclined to express progressive critiques of constitutionalism. For those purposes, the constitutionally faithful should be divided into two subgroups: the "traditional liberals" and a possibly larger group with mixed political commitments who might be called "progressive liberals."

First, of the sizeable number of the constitutionally faithful who are traditional or classical liberals, the disinclination to see whatever merit there is in the progressive case against the Constitution is fairly easy to explain. The traditional liberal, simply by virtue of his or her politics, will be relatively inattentive to the harms of subordination occasioned by the private sphere and insulated by constitutionalism. The progressive critique of the Constitution will, therefore, have no strong intuitive appeal. For this group, the constitutional commitment to the insularity of the private sphere converges

[24] *See supra* text accompanying notes 1-4.

perfectly with the political belief that the private sphere is the sphere of autonomy, growth, and self-actualization, rather than the "hellhole" of violation and subordination described by progressives. There is a perfect fit, in other words, of the coercive morality of the Constitution and the aspirational morality of traditional liberal politics. When the Constitution is correctly interpreted, it aligns with correct liberal moral commitments. There is simply no merit to the progressive critique.

This characterization of "traditional liberalism," however, obviously does not fairly describe the broad political commitments of persons within the "constitutionally faithful" camp of the interpretation debates. A sizeable number of the constitutionally faithful are committed to some aspect of progressive politics. The hard question, then, is not why the traditional liberal is blind to the progressive critique of constitutionalism, but why those who are committed to constitutional determinacy and method *but also* sympathize with at least some progressive goals and methods, nevertheless shy away from attacking directly the morality of the Constitution. For them, the refusal to see the unconstitutionality of politically desirable progressive proprosals as arguments against the Constitution must stem not from politics, but from a view of the Constitution as rooted in a higher, deeper, more "constitutive," or simply "prior" *morality*, and not simply a more coercive legal command. Hence, for this group, the unconstitutionality of proposals based on a politics incompatible with the constitutional mandate carries with it the moral justification of their demise. For the constitutionally faithful theorist who views some progressive proposals as politically wise, their unconstitutionality implies not the limits of the morality or justification of the Constitution, but rather the limits of the morality of the proposals themselves. It may be a politically and hence morally "good thing" to limit access to hate speech or pornography, but it must be a constitutionally and hence super-morally "better thing" to restrain our desires to do the (merely) politically right thing. For the constitutionally faithful, the Constitution provides a higher norm both positivistically and morally, and therefore the "lower" moralities with which it conflicts must simply give way. Their virtue cannot suggest fault with the Constitution itself.

The logic of constitutional faith, one might assume, eventually brings about a concrete reordering of moral and political priorities and a reordering of epistemological perceptions of the social world as well. To accommodate the moral and legal commitment to the priority of the constitutional norm in the face of an unconstitutional but desirable political proposal, the faithful constitutionalist must either elevate to new heights the stakes of departing from the constitutional norm or denigrate the evil the unconstitutional progressive proposal was designed to remedy. It is, then, not surprising that, in the hate speech and antipornography examples, the negative liberty of individual consumers of that speech achieves almost mystical status for faithful constitutionalists, while the harms caused by hate speech and pornography are trivialized. This simultaneous elevation of individual liberty and trivialization of group harm in turn affects the way the faithful constitutionalist sees the world. The harms occasioned by pornography, hate speech, and unequal distributions of domestic labor all become not just trivial, but even invisible. Their evil is "trumped" out of existence by the perceived evil of limiting a negative right. There is then no disabling conflict between the constitutional morality to which the faithful constitutionalist is definitionally committed and the political morality that may conflict with constitutional morality. The "moral dissonance" always present in the faithful constitutionalist's position is reduced to nothing through the altering of the perceptual landscape.

It is when this perceptual reordering becomes impossible that the faithful constitutionalist will switch sides and argue the constitutionality of progressive schemes designed to eradicate these harms. The harm may be so visible, concrete, and public that its trivialization requires just too great an act of will. Or, the presence of the evil may be as central to the theorist's world view as is the essential morality and determinacy of the Constitution. In either case, the moral dissonance between the Constitution and political morality must be reduced by some route other than trivialization of the harm or elevation of the constitutional value. The harm and the evil of purely private discrimination is one such example. The harm is simply too obvious and the evil too great to permit the "trumping" of this harm by the higher constitutional value of protecting the private sphere. For the faithful constitutionalist, however, even the undeniable harm of private discrimination cannot become an argument against the unassailable Constitution. Consequently, the faithful constitutionalist must find statutes or ordinances designed to remedy this evil compatible with the Constitution, either by carving exceptions to the private/public distinction or, more typically, by blurring the distinction between public and private. Not surprisingly, we have a huge body of liberal constitutional scholarship finding state action in almost any conceivable act of discrimination, but almost no liberal constitutional scholarship arguing that the prevalence and evil of constitutionally unassailable private discrimination shows that the state action requirement, itself firmly grounded in constitutional principle, is morally unjustified.

The constitutionally faithful theorist also harboring some commitment to progressive political methodology similarly risks moral dissonance created by the methodological incompatibility of the communitarian and collectivist methods of progressivism and the authoritarian methods of constitutionalism. As the faithful theorist reduces the risk of substantive dissonance by reorienting his perceptions of the social world to trivialize the private harms occasioned by subordination in the private sphere, he is inclined to minimize the risk of methodological dissonance by simply reorienting his perceptions of the virtues and vices of progressive methods. The vast majority of constitutionally faithful liberals harboring at least a fondness for the participatory democracy central to progressivism effect the accommodation between the Constitution's methods and the methods of progressive politics by simply attributing to participatory democracy the same majoritarian vices that constitutional methodology is perfectly poised to correct when directed against democratic excesses of a conservative or reactionary political hue. Whether the democratic wish being frustrated is the conservative desire to punish flag-burners or dispensers of contraception, or the progressive desire to punish or penalize hate speech or pornography, the constitutionally faithful liberal will argue that democracy has outreached its moral justification. In both cases she can readily conclude that constitutional methodology is perfectly designed to identify and rectify the excess. It just doesn't matter whether the democratic desire has come to fruition through the progressive methods of coalition building, consciousness raising, and democratic participation or through the politics of reaction and hate-mongering. In either case, the peculiar dangers to the individual and to the private sphere posed by majoritarianism are present, and in either case, the Constitution and the courts are poised with methodological perfection to eliminate them.

There is one major exception to the preceding descriptive account. Perhaps one of the most significant developments in legal academic thought over the last decade is that, for at least a few constitutionally faithful liberals committed to some progressive goals and methods, this traditional accommodation of constitutional method and participatory democracy has become untenable. This relatively new experience of an unacceptable degree of dissonance between the authoritarianism central to traditionally conceived liberal constitutional methodology and the participatory democracy celebrated and relied upon by progressive politics has given rise to the arguably oxymoronic academic movement known as "liberal civic republicanism." Liberal republicans are, perhaps, best defined by their insistence that the dissonance between the authoritarianism of traditional constitutionalism and the democratic methods of progressivism must be reduced in some way that does not simply denigrate the value of participatory democracy.[25] Two solutions have been fruitfully explored in neo-civic liberal-republican literature.

First, for some liberal republicans, notably Frank Michelman[26] and Owen Fiss,[27] the tension between the methods of constitutionalism and progressivism can be lessened by reconceiving the function, role, and content of judi-

---

[25] Frank Michelman, *Law's Republic*, 97 YALE L.J. 1493 (1988) (contending that only through a modern reconsideration of constitutional thought can we hope to make sense of the American belief that political liberty calls for a government "of the people, by the people"); Frank I. Michelman, *Foreword: Traces of Self-Government*, 100 HARV. L. REV. 4, 66-73 (1986) (exploring migration of self-government from the people to the Court); *see also* Cass R. Sunstein, *Beyond the Republican Revival*, 97 YALE L.J. 1539 (1988) (asserting that the common opposition between liberalism and republicanism is a false one).

[26] Michelman, *Law's Republic*, *supra* note 25; Michelman, *Foreword: Traces of Self Government*, *supra* note 25.

[27] Owen M. Fiss, *A Life Lived Twice*, 100 YALE L.J. 1117 (1991) (focusing on Justice William J. Brennan and his achievements as a liberal Justice on the Supreme Court); Owen M. Fiss, *Reason in All Its Splendor*, 56 BROOK. L. REV. 789 (1990) (examining the importance of procedural fairness before the deprivation of life, liberty, or property); Owen M. Fiss, *State Activism and State Censorship*, 100 YALE L.J. 2087 (1991) (stating

cial review to align with progressive politics. The methodological contradiction between progressivism and constitutionalism is, therefore, reduced by rethinking constitutional methodology. Constitutional processes can then be seen as actually doing the work of progressivism, and thus obviating the progressive politics with which constitutional methodology traditionally conceived is inconsistent. The judge, according to this view, should do precisely what, from a progressive point of view, would otherwise be done by coalition-building and consciousness changing: the judge should insist that law reflect public values that in turn reflect the good of the whole, rather than the elevation of private values and the private sphere, reflecting only the supremacy of an hegemonic group. The judge is not only the idealized progressive legislator, but also the speaker for the idealized outcome of a grass-roots progressive political campaign. She speaks for the mobilized subordinated and realigns and reorients the self-identity of the powerful, forging a new, more expansive community. The tension between constitutionalism and participatory, progressive democracy is lessened by casting the judge as the guardian of participatory democracy.

A second group of liberal neo-civic republicans, notably Cass Sunstein[28] and Paul Brest,[29] effects the accommodation of authoritarian constitutional methodology and participatory progressive method by identifying the representative branches of government, rather than the judiciary, as the primary locus of constitutional decisionmaking, or more simply, by democratizing constitutional method. For this group as well, the potential methodological clash between constitutionalism and progressivism is somewhat averted. The dissonance between participatory politics and authoritarian constitutionalism is reduced not by rendering the judge the spokesperson and guardian of the value of participation, but rather, by identifying the participatory branch of government as the site of constitutional decisionmaking.

Although strengthening the strategic resources of constitutionalism, this new development reinforces the basic point that, for all liberals and progressive-liberals committed to the determinacy of the Constitution and the legitimacy of the constitutional enterprise within liberal theory, the conflict between progressive political aspirations and constitutional substance and method will constitute not a challenge to the moral legitimacy of the Constitution, but instead, a constitutional, and hence moral, burden on progressiv-

---

that the principle of freedom that the First Amendment embodies is derived from the democratic nature of our society and is essential for collective self-determination).

[28] Sunstein, *supra* note 25.

[29] Paul Brest, *Congress as Constitutional Decisionmaker and Its Power to Counter Judicial Doctrine*, 21 GA. L. REV. 57 (1986) (exploring whether Congress has the ability to engage in constitutional interpretation); Paul Brest, *Constitutional Citizenship*, 34 CLEV. ST. L. REV. 175 (1986) (arguing that the Supreme Court is not authorized to decide issues of public morality); Paul Brest, *Further Beyond the Republican Revival: Toward Radical Republicanism*, 97 YALE L.J. 1623 (1988) (stating that we must abandon our obsession with courts and work toward decentralization and democratization).

ism itself. Consequently, even among the constitutionally faithful liberals sympathetic to progressive ends, progressive politics and progressive moral aspirations are to some degree delegitimized. This muting of the sceptical voice among liberal and progressive-liberal constitutionalists is unfortunate. As I will argue below, there are real costs from the muting of progressive doubts about the moral or political value of the Constitution. But it is also unfounded, and it is unfounded even within the assumptions of the very liberal tradition that presumably inspires constitutional faith.

The muting of scepticism is unfounded because there simply is no connection between the determinacy of the Constitution—the hallmark of constitutional faith—and the Constitution's *morality*. The notion that there is some connection, implicit in volumes of liberal writing on the Constitution and explicit in the remainder, rests on the fallacious argument that because the Constitution's *in*determinacy would imply its illegitimacy, and its illegitimacy in turn would imply its immorality, therefore, the Constitution's determinacy must imply both its legitimacy and morality. Not only is this wrong, but it is also profoundly illiberal. Conceding the necessity of determinacy to liberal legitimacy, it does not follow that the Constitution's determinacy is a *sufficient* condition of its ultimate political morality, for two reasons. First, determinacy may be a *necessary* but not a sufficient condition of legitimacy. Even a fully determinate Constitution might be illegitimate for reasons independent of its determinacy. Second, and more importantly, legitimacy may be a necessary but not a sufficient condition of morality. Even a fully "legitimate" constitutional enterprise—legitimate, for example, within the contours of either liberal or republican political theory—may be immoral for reasons independent of its legitimacy.

In otber words, only through conflation of determinacy with legitimacy, and then legitimacy with morality, does interpretive faith in the determinacy of the Constitution become moral faith in its ultimate justification. No conceivable grounds, however, justify that double conflation. Determinacy no more exhausts political legitimacy than political legitimacy exhausts moral justification. The mistaken notion that it does reflects either the profoundly illiberal view of the state as fully justified if "legitimate"—rather than as fully justified if, and only if, truly liberatory—or the equally illiberal view that that which has traditionally been valued must continue to be valued, regardless of our changing appreciation of the burdens and harms it inflicts, or, using the Deweyan phrase for the "nerve" of liberalism, regardless of our changing "intelligence" about the effect of that object on our felt, experienced lives.

B. *The Progressive Critique and Constitutional Scepticism*

Constitutional sceptics[30]—those who doubt the determinacy of constitutional phrases, and hence the compatibility of the Constitution with liberal

---

[30] *See supra* text accompanying note 5.

political theory—are also disinclined to embrace a progressive normative critique of the Constitution, even if they subscribe to progressive political and moral goals and methods. This fact alone is surprising because constitutional sceptics for the most part are members of the critical legal studies movement, a legal academic movement that itself may be defined by a commitment to progressive, left-wing, or radical politics. Thus, one may legitimately assume that most constitutional sceptics subscribe to most if not all of the progressive political commitments described above, and would therefore be inclined to assert the moral and political desirability of progressive political proposals designed to remedy abuses of power within the private, intimate, or social sphere. Yet, even from the sizeable number of progressive, feminist, or critical constitutional writers committed to the indeterminacy thesis and clearly supportive of progressive causes, one finds very little scholarship critical of the Constitution. The question remains, why?

The main reason may be strategic; but again, strategy alone cannot be the whole story. Although there may be others, one additional reason for the lack of criticism of the Constitution from constitutional sceptics may be that the logic of constitutional *scepticism* precludes moral *criticism*: for constitutional sceptics, neither the meaning nor the method of the Constitution is sufficiently determinate to be pernicious. If a text has potentially contradictory meanings, it can hardly be faulted for its substantive political implications, for it quite literally has none. Thus, for the sceptic, the Constitution's apparent incompatibility with progressive causes can hardly be attributed to the Constitution. Instead, the impulse to attribute these outcomes to the Constitution, the sceptic argues, rather than to its human interpreters and appliers, evidences the bad faith that the indeterminacy thesis is in part designed to uncover. The Constitution and the liberal tradition it purports to serve are sufficiently malleable to be susceptible to non-liberal, illiberal, conservative, tyrannical, or progressive interpretations. That it has received any particular interpretation or application, therefore, is a function not of its content, but of the constraining influences of the interpretive community or the political predilections of the interpreting judge. It follows that there is no reason, intrinsic to the constitutional text, for the Supreme Court's persistently non- and anti-progressive application and interpretation of the Constitution. Although the Court has generally read the Constitution to burden and limit the reach of affirmative action programs, for example, nothing in the document mandates that result. Consequently, the political inclinations of the judiciary, or the communities from which that group is drawn, must explain their interpretation. The Constitution itself can be read either to permit or to invalidate such plans. Similarly, the Constitution neither permits nor forbids hate speech ordinances. That it is read in such a way by liberal commentators and the Supreme Court, is not attributable to the language, content, or history of the Constitution, but rather to the constraints of the politics of the judge or community responsible for the interpretation.

The progressive critique of constitutional methodology is also obscured by the indeterminacy critique at the heart of constitutional scepticism. The authoritarianism of constitutionalism so antithetical to progressive political methodology simply disappears if the Constitution has no definitive meaning: if the indeterminacy claim is sound, the Constitution cannot be authoritative. A text that can mean either A or not-A can hardly be characterized as authoritative. If the indeterminacy thesis is right, the authoritarianism of constitutionalism cannot be attributed to the Constitution itself, although it might be attributable to the institutional forms, such as judicial review, responsible for its implementation. Not surprisingly, of the constitutional sceptics drawn to progressive political methods, few find any serious basis for moral, as opposed to epistemological, scepticism.

Here again, though, the inferences seem flawed. Constitutional scepticism no more obviates the need for normative constitutional criticism than constitutional faith undercuts its credibility. First, even if the Constitution is contradictory in precisely the way claimed by the sceptics—so any legal rule that is intended to specify results by reference to its content can be manipulated to reach contradictory results—it does not follow that the constitutional *tradition*, as opposed to the constitutional *document*, fails to render determinate results—results which, if history is a guide, are profoundly hostile to progressive politics. The indeterminacy thesis shows merely that the constitutional text, coupled with liberal theory, does not entail determinate results. But it does not follow that constitutional results are indeterminate. It only follows that it is not the text—the law—that does the determining. If we understand the constitutional tradition to be that which determines outcomes, and understand that tradition to include the politics of the community, the predilections of the judge, and in short the hegemonic and choice-denying inclinations of the judge's social context, then not only are constitutional outcomes determined, they are despairingly over-determined. They are over-determined, furthermore, by the very social and private forces of racism, misogyny, and classism that render progressive interpretations of the same document untenable. The felt determinacy of the Constitution and its felt incompatibility with progressivism hold *regardless* of the indeterminacy of the document and of liberalism itself.

Furthermore, it is worth noting that, to the extent that the indeterminacy critique is motivated by a European and existentialist impulse to unmask the otherwise denied responsibility of the judge for her political choices, the consequences of that critique are deeply paradoxical and self-defeating. On the one hand, the indeterminacy thesis, if true, precludes the judge from avoiding responsibility for the political and moral consequences of her decisions by cloaking them in the garb of a disingenuous legalism. On the other hand, however, the same critique exonerates the Constitution's authors. Peculiarly, the same indeterminacy critique that highlights the human responsibility of the present interpretive community or judge simultaneously obscures the equally human responsibility of the text's authors. Texts no less than interpretations have consequences, and one would expect a movement committed to demystifying the human authorship of, and hence responsibility for, institutional facts to be sensitive to the very real consequences of chosen words, and hence the responsibility for those consequences of the text's drafters. The indeterminacy critique muddles that responsibility as it denies the meaningfulness of the written text. It accordingly confuses the authority upon which that responsibility is predicated, and hence the moral dangers implied by the subsequent deference to textual authoritarianism so central to traditional constitutional method.

Whatever the merits of these arguments, however, it seems fair to say that constitutional sceptics view indeterminacy as obviating the need for progressive normative critique, just as constitutionally faithful liberals view constitutionalism as undermining the justification of progressive critique. For one group the critique is obviated; for the other its justification is undermined. All of this happens with no examination of the merits. The logic and framework of interpretive debates over the Constitution's meaning and meaningfulness have obscured debate over the Constitution's ultimate value by making the debate either illegitimate or moot. We might, therefore, be wise to consider putting aside our doubts about constitutional determinacy to look afresh at questions of constitutional value.

C. *Progressive Politics and Constitutional Discourse*

The absence of a tradition morally sceptical toward the Constitution from a progressive perspective has weakened progressivism, weakened our constitutional debates, weakened constitutional interpretation, and consequently, possibly weakened the Constitution itself. Progressivism is injured in at least two ways. First, there are obvious adverse political consequences if it is both true and unacknowledged that our constitutional guarantees of individual rights and liberties fail to guard against abuses of private power and affirmatively protect the spheres in which those abuses occur. The second type of damage, however, is more subtle and possibly more serious. The lack of a clear understanding of the obstacle to progressivism posed by constitutional guarantees further denigrates the "outlaw" position of the disadvantaged in this society simply because the advocacy of measures deemed both anti-communitarian and anti-individualist through their unconstitutionality is not consistently coupled with a critique of the Constitution that delegitimizes those initiatives. The tendency of all subordinated persons toward self-belittlement by trivializing the nature of their injuries is geometrically enhanced by the self-perception that their injuries do not exist because their infliction is constitutionally protected. To insist on the injustice of it is to injure, in a profound—because constitutional—sense, the entire community of which both the dominant and subordinate are a part. The understanding of the harms suffered by subordinated persons in the private realm is thereby frustrated when those injuries are perceived as having been the occasion of unconstitutional, and hence deeply immoral, legislative initiatives. The battle for passage of a progressive statute or ordinance, such as a hate speech regulation or an anti-pornography ordinance, destined to be found unconstitutional becomes the occasion not of greater public consciousness of the uniqueness, nature, and intensity of the suffering, but rather an occasion for obliterating difference by blurring the harm sustained by hate speech or pornography with other injuries sustained by other factions seeking ends at odds with constitutional guarantees. Greater understanding of the degree to which the Constitution frustrates progressivism would at least clarify the nature of the problem and might potentially demystify and hence dethrone and "untrump" constitutional morality.

A clearer understanding of the systemic threat to progressivism posed by constitutionalism that might be gained through a sustained debate over the value of constitutionalism might also enhance the quality of constitutional dialogue. Mainstream liberal constitutional discourse is presently characterized by an almost obsessive refusal to acknowledge or examine the nature of the costs of constitutional rights and liberties because of the logic and structure of rights themselves: the right exists to preclude precisely such cost-benefit analyses. Because there is no social cost that a right does not theoretically "trump," from a liberal perspective there is simply no reason to assess the costs of rights, and plenty of reason not to: assessment only threatens societal respect for the right in question. Nevertheless, this refusal to address the consequences of rights ultimately leaves them groundless, as well as dangerous. The right must implicitly, if not explicitly, rest on some intuition that in the long run the benefits of having a right—whether self-actualization, autonomy, intimacy, privacy, meritocratic treatment, or economic self-determination—outweigh any costs incurred by its possession. Failure to examine the wisdom of this balance in light of our expanding knowledge of the experience of persons most vulnerable to the harms occasioned by those rights, and failure to countenance the possibility that perhaps the balance ought to be re-struck, does not constitute "liberalism" in its best light; far from it. Instead, it constitutes a deeply conservative, traditionalist, and even reactionary posture toward the possibility of change and a profoundly illiberal rejection of the use of pragmatic knowledge to come to grips with an evolving social world.

The absence of a sustained tradition of normative constitutional scepticism also hurts the Constitution, in precisely the way that John Stuart Mill warned: unexamined institutions, ideas, and cultures become fossilized, non-vital, superstitiously worshipped, and then perversely discarded echoes of their original impulses.[31] This is surely as true of liberal ideals, institutions, and cultures as it is of the unexamined and uncriticized conservative traditions and religions that Mill ridiculed.

Finally, we should remember that the Constitution is merely difficult, not impossible, to change. It can be changed fundamentally through amendment, interstitially through judicial interpretation, and in fact if not form through patterns of practice occasioned through changes in consciousness. The strategic impulse to insist upon the constitutionality of unconstitutional

---

[31] J.S. MILL, ON LIBERTY (1859).

progressive initiatives, because of the sense that the Constitution itself cannot be changed, may be unduly pessimistic. Reform through critique is not utterly beyond the pale in constitutional dialogue or doctrine. Although the Constitution may be fundamental law, it is a fundamental charter of our self-understanding, as well, only if we permit it to be. Although a changed self-understanding is surely not a sufficient condition of change in a fundamental law, it is undeniably a necessary one. Failure to achieve it because of a sense of futility does nothing but render the immutability of an anti-progressive Constitution a self-fulfilling prophecy.

III. The Latent Possibility of a Progressive Constitutional Faith

Perhaps the greatest cost of the lack of a sustained tradition of normative constitutional scepticism on progressive grounds is that it has very likely impeded the development of a responsive tradition, which might be called a "progressive constitutional faith." Progressive constitutional faith might best be described in contrast to other constitutional approaches. First, unlike constitutionally faithful liberals, constitutionally faithful progressives would aim to tie the determinate meaning of the Constitution, ascertained through its text, history, and supporting moral philosophy, not to liberal hopes, fears, and ideals, but instead to progressive ones. But, unlike constitutional sceptics, progressive faithful constitutionalists would assert the possibility of a progressive interpretation of the Constitution not on the grounds of the Constitution's meaninglessness, but on the grounds of the position's fundamental correctness. The claim would be that the Constitution really means what the progressive insists, carries accordant obligations, and consequently mandates a progressive conception of community to which we all ought adhere. The possibility of a progressive interpretation of the Constitution, in other words, would rest not upon the real or perceived contradictions latent or explicit in liberalism and the potential for interpretive exploitation that those contradictions entail, but upon the Constitution itself—its progressive meaning, history, and text, and the political and moral philosophy against which it should and must be interpreted. Thus, unlike liberal faithful constitutionalists, with whom they share a belief in constitutional determinacy, progressive constitutionalists would ground constitutional meaning in progressive rather than liberal politics. And lastly, unlike constitutional sceptics with whom they share their politics, constitutionally faithful progressives would emphasize not the Constitution's indeterminacy, but rather those constitutional events and textual passages that support the claim that the Constitution is at least as concerned about the abuse of private and social power as it is patently concerned with the abuse of public and political power, and is at least as methodologically convergent with ideals of participatory democracy as it is explicitly concerned with the limits of majoritarian will.

On this view, the anti-progressive content and method of the Constitution that presently seem so inextricably interwoven with its text and history is revealed to be not just indeterminate, but *wrong*: a modern (as well as post-modern), transitory, and misguided moment. The identification of public, rather than private, power as the concern of the Constitution, the preference for negative over positive liberty at the heart of both the First Amendment and the Fourteenth Amendment's Liberty and Due Process Clauses, and the insistence on a formal rather than substantive understanding of the Equal Protection Clause is central not to the Constitution itself—whether understood as its text, its history, or the best political philosophy that might sustain it—but rather to the politics and felt contingent needs of the modern and post-modern world. Once seen as an unnecessary and false reading of the Constitution, the path is then cleared for a more accurate and progressive understanding of constitutional mandates and responsibilities.

Doctrinally, progressive constitutional faith would have to rest primarily on a rereading of the central message, meaning, and history of the Fourteenth Amendment. The modern understanding that the Fourteenth Amendment only reaches state action that operates injuriously upon subordinated groups, according to this view, is the result of a handful of erroneous opinions, beginning with the nineteenth century civil rights cases[32] and culminating with the modern state action cases.[33] Historically, the Fourteenth Amendment, like all the Reconstruction Amendments, was intended to ensure that the states refrain from inflicting injury upon subordinated groups and take affirmative action to guarantee that private power not be used to re-enslave the recently freed.[34] By principled extension, therefore, the amendments taken as a whole ought to be understood as requiring the states to guard against not only their own complicity in the domination of subordinate groups, but also the domination of those groups themselves, and to act affirmatively to end it. On this reading, "equal protection of the law" requires Congress to ensure that the states not only legislate in a fair and rational manner, but also that Congress protects against private subordination, whether that subordination occurs through the relationship of slave and master, of wife and husband, or of employee and employer when the parties possess radically unequal control of resources. The Due Process Clause fundamentally requires that the states ensure that

---

[32] *See e.g.*, Civil Rights Cases, 109 U.S. 3 (1883) (holding that Fourteenth Amendment claims require a showing of state action).

[33] DeShaney v. Winnebago County Dep't of Social Servs., 489 U.S. 189, 195-97 (1989) (holding that the Due Process Clause does not impose upon the states an affirmative obligation to protect a son from an abusive father).

[34] JACOBUS TENBROCK, THE ANTISLAVERY ORIGINS OF THE FOURTEENTH AMENDMENT (1951), *reprinted in* JACOBUS TENBROCK, EQUAL UNDER LAW (1969) ("[T]he national protection of men in their natural rights or of citizens in their privileges and immunities . . . extended to individuals without regard to the private or governmental character of the violator . . . ."); Robin West, *Reconstructing Liberty*, 59 TENN. L. REV. 441 (1992).

only the state be empowered to deprive people of their utterly positive liberty to work, live, participate in politics and culture, and sustain meaningful intimate relationships, and that the state only do so with due process *of law*. The amendment taken in its entirety, then, means that the states must take any necessary and possible action to guarantee that private social life will not regress to anything resembling either the relationship of enslavement of the slave era or the private exploitation and coercion that followed it. If the Fourteenth Amendment was intended to mean that its clauses are at least as concerned with the abolition of private relationships of subordination as with public abuses of political power, then the constitutionality of progressive proposals designed to eliminate patterns of subordination logically follows. Indeed, they are not simply constitutional, but also constitutionally mandated.

Methodologically, progressive constitutional faith would view the Constitution as mandating a method of decisionmaking and a style of discourse convergent with the progressive commitment to restrain majoritarian excess, bigotry, mistakes, or ill-will through the progressive tools of participatory democracy, collective political action, and social responsibility, rather than with the liberal commitment to correct those evils through an intellectual ideology that combines glorification of the abstract individual with contempt of the concrete majority, and an institution that imposes that ideology through coercion rather than through persuasion. It would claim that a reformed constitutionalism—one emphasizing legislative and citizen participation, persuasion over coercion, and anti-subordination—could shed itself of the authoritarianism of traditional constitutional discourse, yet retain the obligatoriness of constitutional meaning without which constitutionalism loses its value, whether to progressive or liberal self-understandings. To be *constitutional* as well as progressive, a progressive constitutional method would have to discover a means of ascertaining communal and communitarian self-understanding that implies the inclusion, unity, fraternity, sorority, mutual recognition, and obligation that makes constitutionalism a significant claim upon our social life and individual existence. To be progressive, the constitutional method must be respectful of dissent, non-coercive, non-authoritarian, and at least somewhat pluralist. The articulation of this constitutional method is a far greater challenge for a progressive constitutional faith, I think, than the historical, textual, and philosophical work required to justify a progressive interpretation of constitutional rights and liberties.

It remains to be seen whether a progressive constitutional faith could ultimately be sustained. It seems to me that there are enough "constitutional moments" in our political and social history to suggest that it could be, from the passage of the Reconstruction Amendments and their fundamental challenge to the most extreme forms of private subordination, to the attempt in the post-*Lochner* era cases to reject an interpretation of the Constitution prohibiting the states or Congress from addressing private subordination,[35] and to the Warren Court's decision in *Brown v. Board of Education*,[36] which at least arguably was concerned not only with state-ordered de jure segregation but also with the injurious consequences of private racism, inflicted through the protected and private spheres of speech, education, and the "culture" of racism.[37] Of course, if the Constitution—or at least the Fourteenth Amendment and the rights "incorporated" by it—is centrally concerned with private power, its abuse, and the injuries of racism, poverty, and sexism occasioned by its abuse, then the vast bulk of modern cases concerning those rights are wrong, and the legislative, adjudicative, and social work of implementing the true meaning of those amendments has not yet begun. That, however, ought not count against the plausibility of a progressive constitutional faith. It only restates two obvious and noncontentious points: first, at this point in history, any progressive constitutional faith would constitute a dissident tradition, and second, the Constitution articulates an aspirational morality that we have only occasionally glimpsed and that we have not yet begun to honor.

Now, for reasons easily summarized because they directly mirror those outlined above, the dominance of debate over the status of the Constitution's meaning has stymied the development of a progressive constitutional faith. Neither constitutionally faithful liberals nor constitutional sceptics have much stake in the articulation of a progressive constitutional faith and, for that reason alone, the dominance of interpretation debates focused on the coherence of liberalism has somewhat retarded progressive understandings of constitutional meanings. First, liberal constitutional faith is defined by its commitment to the proposition that the Constitution's meaning, as well as

[35] Day-Brite Lighting, Inc. v. Missouri, 342 U.S. 421, 429 (1952) (sustaining law requiring employers to give employees four hours off from work with pay for them to vote); Lincoln Fed. Labor Union v. Northwest Iron & Metal Co., 335 U.S. 525, 537 (1949) (upholding state "right to work" laws requiring that employment decisions not be based on union membership); Olsen v. Nebraska, 313 U.S. 236, 246-47 (1941) (upholding law fixing maximum employment agency fees as constitutional); United States v. Darby, 312 U.S. 100, 125-26 (1941) (upholding federal wage and hour requirements); United States v. Carolene Prods. Co., 304 U.S. 144, 154 (1938) (rejecting due process challenge to federal prohibition of interstate shipment of skimmed milk mixed with non-milk fats); West Coast Hotel Co. v. Parrish, 300 U.S. 379, 400 (1937) (sustaining state minimum wage law for women); Nebbia v. New York, 291 U.S. 502, 593 (1934) (upholding New York's Milk Control Board's minimum and maximum price fixing).

[36] 347 U.S. 483, 495 (1954) (holding that racial segregation of public schools violates the Fourteenth Amendment).

[37] Charles R. Lawrence III, *Education for Black Power in the Eighties: Present Day Implications of the* Bakke *Decision*, 10 NAT'L BLACK L.J. 58, 59-60 (1987) (arguing that *Brown* implies that all segregation in American public life is invalid); *see also* Charles R. Lawrence III, *If He Hollers Let Him Go: Regulating Racist Speech on Campus*, 1990 DUKE L.J. 431, 438-444 [hereinafter Lawrence, *Regulating Racist Speech*] (arguing that *Brown* supports the regulation of hate speech in the educational setting).

the justification for its imposition against the democratic will, must be drawn from the liberal tradition—a tradition that is generally hostile to progressive initiatives and understandings. A liberal faith then might share with a progressive faith a belief in the meaningfulness of the Constitution, but the meanings ascribed by the two movements are inevitably in near-diametrical opposition.

Second, constitutional sceptics, although sharing the politics of progressive constitutional faith, would have as little interest in the articulation of a view of the Constitution as essentially furthering progressive causes as they have in the articulation of a criticism of the Constitution as essentially hostile to those initiatives, for at least two reasons. First, if the Constitution's meaning is necessarily indeterminate, then it can no more be tied to progressivism than to liberalism. There is presumably no political commitment that does not share in the instability and the extreme contradictoriness of liberalism. Indeterminacy is, after all, a function not of particular politics, but of language and life. If the interpretive sceptic is right, therefore, progressive constitutional faith is *impossible*. Progressive, no less than liberal, constitutional faith is ruled out by the inevitable indeterminacy of the language with which the faith is constructed. Second, given the contradictions of liberalism, progressive initiatives can be argued to be either constitutional or unconstitutional. Therefore, progressive constitutional faith, and the determinate progressive politics on which it is predicated, is also strategically *unnecessary*. Indeterminacy is sufficient to facilitate progressive political goals.

Nevertheless, in spite of the preemptive nature of the interpretation battles, a small but growing number of progressive constitutional theorists subscribe in some form to a progressive constitutional faith. Much of it comes from critical race theory. Mari Matsuda's general characterization of "outsider jurisprudence"[38] as well as her particular reconstruction of the First Amendment to support the constitutionality of hate speech regulations[39] was seminal to this tradition, as was Charles Lawrence's interpretation of *Brown* as being centrally concerned with expressions of private racism, and hence supportive of the same conclusion.[40] Patricia Williams's[41] and Kimberlé Crenshaw's[42] early defense of rights as conducive to liberalism and to pro-

[38] Matsuda, *supra* note 15, at 9 (asserting that "the multiple consciousness I urge lawyers to attain is not a random ability to see all points of view, but a deliberate choice to see the world from the standpoint of the oppressed").

[39] Matsuda, *supra* note 7, at 2321 (arguing in favor of criminal and administrative sanctions as an appropriate response to racist speech).

[40] Lawrence, *Regulating Racist Speech*, *supra* note 37, at 439 (arguing that segregation was racist speech).

[41] Patricia Williams, *Alchemical Notes: Reconstructing Ideals from Deconstructed Rights*, 22 HARV. C.R.-C.L. L. REV. 401, 404 (1987) (arguing against the part of critical legal studies that rejects rights-based theory).

[42] Kimberlé W. Crenshaw, *Race, Reform and Retrenchment: Transformation and*

gressive racial goals, pre-visioned much of the direction of this movement. All of these essays stand in marked contrast not only to the liberal positions on the First Amendment or on the nature of rights that they are directly and doctrinally concerned to counter, but also to *both* the constitutional scepticism of the critical legal studies movement and the progressive scepticism of such critical race theorists as Derrick Bell,[43] Alan Freeman,[44] and, perhaps, Richard Delgado.[45] Against progressive scepticism, the progressive constitutional faithful argue that, properly read, the Constitution indeed supports and perhaps requires these regulations. Furthermore, against the constitutional scepticism of the critical legal studies movement, they assert that the Constitution requires precisely what they argue it requires, not because of the contradictions latent in its clauses or in the liberalism behind it, but because of the progressivism of the Constitution itself.

Feminists have also contributed to this tradition, none more so than Catharine MacKinnon.[46] Professor MacKinnon's argument that the Equal Protection Clause is directly concerned with a wide range of abuses against women, and directly requires the states to do something about them, stands in direct opposition to *both* liberal arguments limiting equal protection to rational categorizations of similarities and differences *and* to sceptical progressive claims that the Fourteenth Amendment's promise of equality is not merely irrelevant to women's progress, but indeed, hostile to it. Finally, it stands in striking opposition to the paradigmatic critical claim that, because of its indeterminacy, the Fourteenth Amendment has no meaning, pernicious or progressive, which can be effectively criticized or implemented.

All of these arguments, the positions they imply, and the twin premises of both constitutional fidelity and progressive politics on which they explicitly or implicitly rest, are richly suggestive of the possibility of a progressive constitutional faith. As paradoxical as it may sound, it seems to me that further

---

Legitimation in Antidiscrimination Law, 101 HARV. L. REV. 1331, 1336 (1988) (arguing that, because racism is a central ideological underpinning of American society, critical legal studies should focus on it as well as on legal consciousness).

[43] BELL, *supra* note 11 (using the mode of a fairy tale to explain why racial equality has not been achieved in the more than 30 years since *Brown v. Board of Education*).

[44] Freeman, *Antidiscrimination Law*, *supra* note 12, at 1408-09 (arguing that recent Supreme Court cases ruling against affirmative action programs are not the result of recent historical whimsy, but are "firmly rooted in the contradictory character of antidiscrimination law, the agenda of which was constrained at the outset by abstract principles of formal equality that would surely reassert themselves in time").

[45] Richard Delgado, *Norms and Normal Science: Toward a Critique of Normativity in Legal Thought*, 139 U. PA. L. REV. 933, 937 (1991) (arguing that critiques of normativity in legal studies "place[] the reformer in no worse position than he or she occupied before, and [are] no more threatening to the cause of social transformation than earlier critiques of law-as-logic or law-as-empirical-science").

[46] MacKinnon, *supra* note 17, at 1297 (arguing that because the "similarly situated" requirement controls equality claims, the laws of sexual assault and reproductive control have not been subject to constitutional attack).

development of this tradition is, at one and the same time, utterly futile, deeply utopian, absolutely necessary, terribly risky, and one of the most imaginative, fecund, and important shared enterprises presently ongoing in the legal academy. It is utterly futile because the particular positions regarding progressive legislation that a progressive constitutional faith implies will not prevail in the immediate or foreseeable future in any institutional form. It is deeply utopian in that it envisions a reconstructed understanding of our history and constructs an extraordinarily appealing vision of our distant, if not immediate, future. It is absolutely necessary because it may be impossible to attain progressive goals in this culture as long as the morality and the coercive power of the Constitution are understood, rightly or wrongly, as in direct opposition to those progressive goals. It is terribly risky because it may very likely be either tamed, co-opted, or, at worst, revealed to be in fact—as well as in the imaginations and arguments of modern liberals—nothing but the foundation of a new tyranny. It is imaginative, important, and fecund because it carries the possibility of a profoundly new understanding of our constitutional history and of constitutional meaning, and hence carries the possibility of a new and quite radical constitution.

Conclusion

The implications of a progressive constitutional scepticism are fairly obvious and quite momentous. If the Constitution is irreversibly and deeply hostile to progressive political action targeted at abuse of power in private, intimate, and economic spheres of life, it is imperative that at least progressives know that fact, and highly desirable that the rest of us know it as well. It should occasion strategic rethinking by the former and a sustained reexamination by the rest of the community of the relative costs, benefits, virtues, and burdens occasioned by the rights and liberties that we all, to varying degrees, either "enjoy" or suffer.

The implications of a progressive constitutional faith are also quite momentous. As Catharine MacKinnon, echoing Bruce Ackerman, has suggested, such a faith, if it can be sustained, mandates a rethinking of the identity of "We the People" in whose behalf the Constitution is implemented, and by whose hand it was, and is, recreated. This paper has argued definitively for neither of these opposed positions, but has offered instead the far more modest claim that both have merit, both need an elaboration that is presently more frustrated than furthered by the terms of contemporary constitutional debate, and both would contribute mightily to progressive politics and to our constitutional self-understanding.

At the risk of courting paradox, I would like to suggest that it is not at all unthinkable or even irrational for individual progressive theorists, litigators, or political actors to harbor both sceptical and faithful attitudes and beliefs regarding constitutional fidelity. Catharine MacKinnon's work stands as a stunning example of the possibility of rationally subscribing to both a constitutional faith and scepticism. She has authored some of the most devastating and insightful progressive criticisms of the liberal Constitution *and* some of the most convincing arguments that the Constitution can, and must, be read to require progressive initiatives intended to end patriarchy. This is not self-contradiction, but an example of pragmatic wisdom. Whether the Constitution can be interpreted to promote progressive politics, or whether it is implacably hostile to such efforts, is a momentous question that need not be resolved in a moment or a lifetime. It certainly is a question that matters, and it is one we ought not lose sight of, nor allow to be muffled by the seemingly endless debates over the Constitution's ultimate compatibility with a more liberal, but arguably less appealing, political vision.

[14]

Liberal Individualism and Liberal Neutrality*

Will Kymlicka

A distinctive feature of contemporary liberal theory is its emphasis on "neutrality"—the view that the state should not reward or penalize particular conceptions of the good life but, rather, should provide a neutral framework within which different and potentially conflicting conceptions of the good can be pursued. Liberal neutrality has been criticized from many angles, but I will be concerned here only with the connection critics draw between neutrality and individualism, particularly in the context of Rawls's theory of justice. One of the most persistent criticisms of Rawls's theory is that it is excessively individualistic, neglecting the way that individual values are formed in social contexts and pursued through communal attachments. I will distinguish three different ways that critics have attempted to connect neutrality and individualism and argue that all rest on misinterpretations of Rawls's theory. However, there are important aspects of the relationship between individual values and social contexts which Rawls does not discuss, and I hope to show that the dispute over liberal neutrality would be more fruitful if both sides moved away from general questions of "individualism" toward more specific questions about the relationship between state, society, and culture in liberal democracies.

DEFINING LIBERAL NEUTRALITY

What sort of neutrality is present, or aspired to, in Rawls's theory? Raz distinguishes two principles which he believes are present, and inadequately distinguished, in liberal writings on neutrality. One, which Raz calls "neutral political concern," requires that the state seek to help or hinder different life-plans to an equal degree—that is, government action should have neutral consequences. The other, which Raz calls the "exclusion of ideals," allows that government action may help some ways of life more than others but denies that government should act in order to help some ways of life over others. The state does not take a stand on which ways of life are most worth living, and the desire to help one way of life over another

* I would like to thank G. A. Cohen, Sue Donaldson, Les Green, Amy Gutmann, Dave Knott, and Arthur Ripstein for helpful comments on an earlier draft.

Ethics 99 (July 1989): 883–905

is precluded as a justification of government action. The first requires neutrality in the consequences of government policy; the second requires neutrality in the justification of government policy. I will call these two conceptions consequential and justificatory neutrality, respectively.

Which conception does Rawls defend? Raz argues that Rawls endorses consequential neutrality,[1] and some of Rawls's formulations are undoubtedly consistent with that interpretation. But there are two basic tenets of Rawls's theory which show that he could not have endorsed consequential neutrality. First, respect for civil liberties will necessarily have nonneutral consequences. Freedom of speech and association allow different groups to pursue and advertise their way of life. But not all ways of life are equally valuable, and some will have difficulty attracting or maintaining adherents. Since individuals are free to choose between competing visions of the good life, civil liberties have nonneutral consequences—they create a marketplace of ideas, as it were, and how well a way of life does in this market depends on the kinds of goods it can offer to prospective adherents. Hence, under conditions of freedom, satisfying and valuable ways of life will tend to drive out those which are worthless and unsatisfying.

Rawls endorses such a cultural marketplace, despite its nonneutral consequences. Moreover, the prospect that trivial and degrading ways of life fare less well in free competition is not something he regrets or views as an unfortunate side effect. On the contrary, the liberal tradition has always endorsed civil liberties precisely because they make it possible "that the worth of different modes of life should be proved practically."[2]

Consequential neutrality is also inconsistent with Rawls's explanation of the role of "primary goods." They are supposed to be employable in the pursuit of diverse conceptions of the good. But not all ways of life have the same costs, and so an equal distribution of resources will have nonneutral consequences. Those who choose expensive ways of life—valuing leisure over work, or champagne over beer—will get less welfare out of an equal bundle of resources than will people with more modest tastes. This is unlike an equality of welfare scheme, in which those with expensive tastes would be subsidized by others in order to achieve equality of welfare. On an equality of welfare scheme, resources would be unequally distributed so that every way of life is equally helped, no matter how expensive—those who wish beer get enough money for beer, those who wish champagne get enough money for champagne.

Rawls favors equality of resources, despite its nonneutral consequences and, indeed, because it prohibits excess demands on resources by those with expensive desires:

> It is not by itself an objection to the use of primary goods that it does not accommodate those with expensive tastes. One must argue

1. Joseph Raz, *The Morality of Freedom* (Oxford: Oxford University Press, 1986), p. 117.
2. J. S. Mill, *On Liberty*, ed. David Spitz (New York: Norton, 1975), p. 54.

> in addition that it is unreasonable, if not unjust, to hold people responsible for their preferences and to require them to make out as best they can. But to argue this seems to presuppose that citizens' preferences are beyond their control as propensities or cravings which simply happen. Citizens seem to be regarded as passive carriers of desires. The use of primary goods, however, relies on a capacity to assume responsibility for our ends. This capacity is part of the moral power to form, to revise, and rationally to pursue a conception of the good. . . . In any particular situation, then, those with less expensive tastes have presumably adjusted their likes and dislikes over the course of their lives to the income and wealth they could reasonably expect; and it is regarded as unfair that they now should have less in order to spare others from the consequences of their lack of foresight or self-discipline.[3]

Since individuals are responsible for forming "their aims and ambitions in the light of what they can reasonably expect," they recognize that "the weight of their claims is not given by the strength or intensity of their wants and desires."[4] Those people who have developed expensive tastes in disregard of what they can reasonably expect have no claim to be subsidized by others, no matter how strongly felt those desires are.[5]

So the two fundamental components of liberal justice—respect for liberty and fairness in the distribution of material resources—both preclude consequential neutrality. However ambiguous his terminology is, Rawls has to be interpreted as endorsing justificatory neutrality.[6] As

3. John Rawls, "Social Unity and Primary Goods," in *Utilitarianism and Beyond*, ed. Amartya Sen and Bernard Williams (Cambridge: Cambridge University Press, 1982), pp. 168–69; see also Rawls, "Fairness to Goodness," *Philosophical Review* 84 (1975): 553.

4. John Rawls, "Kantian Constructivism in Moral Theory: The Dewey Lectures 1980," *Journal of Philosophy* 77 (1980): 545.

5. This principle of responsibility is also central to Dworkin's equality of resources scheme: the cost to others of the resources we claim should "figure in each person's sense of what is rightly his and in each person's judgment of what life he should lead, given that command of justice" (Ronald Dworkin, "What Is Equality? Part 2," *Philosophy and Public Affairs* 10 [1981]: 289). Indeed, Dworkin's scheme does a better job than Rawls's difference principle of distinguishing the costs that people are responsible for from the costs that are an unchosen part of people's circumstances. Some people argue that an accurate assessment of individual responsibility requires going beyond either primary goods or equality of resources to "equal opportunity for welfare" (Richard Arneson, "Equality and Equal Opportunity for Welfare," *Philosophical Studies* 55 [1989]: 79–95), or "equal access to advantage" (G. A. Cohen, "On the Currency of Egalitarian Justice," *Ethics*, in this issue). While these critiques of Rawls's account of primary goods are important, they are not moves away from justificatory neutrality.

6. Although I cannot argue the point here, I believe that the other major statements of liberal neutrality must similarly be interpreted as endorsing justificatory neutrality—e.g., Bruce Ackerman, *Social Justice in the Liberal State* (New Haven, Conn.: Yale University Press, 1980), pp. 11, 61; Charles Larmore, *Patterns of Moral Complexity* (Cambridge: Cambridge University Press, 1987), chap. 3, esp. pp. 44–47; Ronald Dworkin, "Liberalism," in *Public and Private Morality*, ed. Stuart Hampshire (Cambridge: Cambridge University Press, 1978), p. 127, and *A Matter of Principle* (London: Harvard University Press, 1985), p. 222; Robert Nozick, *Anarchy, State and Utopia* (New York: Basic, 1974), pp. 272–73 (for an extended exegetical discussion of these passages, see David Knott, *Liberalism and the Justice of Neutral*

Rawls puts it, government is neutral between different conceptions of the good, "not in the sense that there is an agreed public measure of intrinsic value or satisfaction with respect to which all these conceptions come out equal, but in the sense that they are not evaluated at all from a social standpoint."[7] The state does not justify its actions by reference to some public ranking of the intrinsic value of different ways of life, for there is no public ranking to refer to. This kind of neutrality is consistent with the legitimate nonneutral consequences of cultural competition and individual responsibility. Indeed, and I'll return to this point, one might think that good ways of life are most likely to establish their greater worth, and individuals are most likely to accept responsibility for the costs of their choices, when the state is constrained by justificatory neutrality—that is, when individuals cannot "use the coercive apparatus of the state to win for themselves a greater liberty or larger distributive share on the grounds that their activities are of more intrinsic value."[8]

NEUTRALITY AND POSSESSIVE INDIVIDUALISM

I now want to consider three versions of the claim that liberal neutrality, as envisioned by Rawls, is excessively individualistic. The first version, advanced separately by Schwartz and Nagel shortly after the publication of *A Theory of Justice,* focuses on the content of people's aims and ambitions. Rawls claims that a state which gives each individual the largest possible share of resources and liberties to pursue their disparate ends, consistent with the claim of others to an equal share, lives up to the requirements of justificatory neutrality. But, according to Schwartz and Nagel, this presupposes a kind of possessive individualist theory of human motivation. It suggests that what people want in life is to maximize their share of social resources (rather than promote the good of others), and indeed to maximize their material good (rather than promote their spiritual or emotional well-being). Such a theory of motivation may suit the self-

---

Political Concern [D.Phil. thesis, Oxford University, 1989], chap. 2.) Hence, I will be using "liberal neutrality" and "justificatory neutrality" interchangeably. It is quite possible that 'neutrality' is not the best word to describe the policy at issue. Rawls himself has avoided the term until recently because of its multiple and often misleading meanings—e.g., neutrality in its everyday usage usually implies neutral consequences (John Rawls, "The Priority of Right and Ideas of the Good," *Philosophy and Public Affairs* 17 [1988]: 260, 265; cf. Raz, chap. 5). He has instead used the term "priority of the right over the good." But that too has multiple and misleading meanings, since it is used by Rawls to describe both the affirming of neutrality over perfectionism, and the affirming of deontology over teleology. These issues need to be kept distinct, and neither, viewed on its own, is usefully called a matter of the "priority of the right"; see my "Rawls on Teleology and Deontology," *Philosophy and Public Affairs* 17 (1988): 173–190, for a critique of Rawls's usage of "priority of the right." Given the absence of any obviously superior alternative, I will continue to use the term "neutrality."

7. Rawls, "Social Unity," p. 172; cf. Rawls, *A Theory of Justice* (London: Oxford University Press, 1971), p. 94.

8. Rawls, *Theory of Justice,* p. 329.

seeking and materialistic culture of contemporary capitalist cultures, but it penalizes those who value other ends. "Consider a socialist somewhat in the lines of the early Marx. This individual believes that a good life must rest on self-realization through labor . . . and that a person is morally harmed by the possession of more than a certain minimal amount of wealth."[9] Such a socialist will claim "that his good is furthered by just enough wealth so that he is decently fed, housed, and clothed" and that

> he would be harmed by living in a society based on a preference for a greater rather than a lesser amount of wealth. He could say that living in such a society he would devote valuable time to thinking about material wealth and trying to decide whether or not to avoid the temptation of attempting to acquire more possessions. . . . In addition, the socialist could claim that a system based on a preference for a greater amount of wealth would be against his interest since it would prevent him from forming strong ties of affection with other human beings. He could claim that, in such a system, people would tend to be more interested in wealth than in other people.[10]

Now this might seem at first glance to be attacking the idea of consequential neutrality, since Schwartz emphasizes that not all ways of life will fare equally well in a Rawlsian society. But the objection is not simply that communal ways of life will fare less well. After all, they might fare badly, not because primary goods are less useful for communal ways of life, but simply because most people choose not to use them for that purpose. Rather, the claim is that primary goods (beyond a certain point) are only useful for individualistic ends, and so Rawls's demand that society aim to increase the share of primary goods available to individuals reflects a decision that individualistic ways of life should be promoted at the expense of nonindividualistic ways of life, a decision which violates justificatory neutrality. The problem is not simply that communal ways of life do less well but, rather, that the reason they do less well is that Rawls's account of primary goods is arbitrarily and unfairly biased against them, since that account is based on (nonneutral) assumptions about people's individualistic aims.[11]

But this critique misinterprets Rawls's justification for the importance of primary goods.[12] Rawls does not assume anything like a possessive

9. Adina Schwartz, "Moral Neutrality and Primary Goods," *Ethics* 83 (1973): 302.

10. Ibid., p. 304; cf. Jurgen Habermas, *Communication and the Evolution of Society*, trans. Thomas McCarthy (Boston: Beacon, 1979), pp. 198–99.

11. Thomas Nagel, "Rawls on Justice," *Philosophical Review* 82 (1973): 228–29.

12. Both Schwartz and Nagel use the issue of individualistic conceptions of the good to make broader claims about Rawls's theoretical project. According to Schwartz, this issue is one example of the way in which Rawls invokes more than "minimalist" assumptions about reason and morality; according to Nagel, this issue is one example of the way in which Rawls exaggerates the relationship between impartiality and choice under ignorance. Both of these broader claims could be true even if, as I will argue, the particular example they cite is misconceived.

individualist theory of motivation. On the contrary, one of the things that people can do, and indeed are expected to do, with their resources and liberties is to join or create meaningful associations and attachments, including spiritual and emotional ones. Schwartz claims that material resources (above a certain minimum) are not useful in the pursuit of nonmaterialistic ends, and so Rawls's primary goods scheme is biased against the socialist who sees the good life as self-realization through labor and views material wealth as positively harmful. But Schwartz's discussion here is far too quick. The socialist needs resources in order to pursue a life of self-realizing labor—she needs access to land or other raw materials and to the technology which enables work to be creative and variable rather than merely onerous and repetitive. Someone who only has enough wealth to be decently clothed has no way to ensure that her labor is self-realizing, since the conditions under which she works will be determined by the exigencies of nature or by the aims of those who own the land and tools. Even if she wishes to live in harmony with nature and use only simple tools and techniques (perhaps the socialist is converted to deep ecology), she must still have control over resources. The desire to keep an ecological habitat in its natural condition requires restrictions on the way other people use not only the immediate habitat but also the surrounding land, air, and water. These nonindividualistic and nonmaterialistic ways of life require that substantial amounts of social resources be set aside for their purposes. It is entirely wrong to suppose that the less materialistic someone is, the less of an interest she has in Rawls's primary goods.[13]

Indeed, it is difficult to imagine a viable way of life which is genuinely harmed by, or even indifferent to, increases in the availability of material resources. One would not need resources if there was nothing in one's life which could go better or worse, nothing which would count as success

13. Schwartz's claim that material resources are harmful depends, I think, on confusing equality of resources with equality of income. People should be free to decide how and when their labor, or the fruits of their labor, will be sold in the economic marketplace, and many valuable ways of life will seek partial or total exclusion from it. People will not sacrifice all their leisure, or accept the degradation of their work conditions, in return for additional income, and some people put leisure and quality of work well above income in their scale of priorities. But this emphasis on values other than income, far from conflicting with a desire for resources, requires access to resources. We all want to do things, or produce things, which are not marketable, but these activities require resources which other people desire for conflicting purposes. The socialist prefers developing her personal skills, and the monk prefers celebrating God, to selling goods and services in the market. But the socialist and monk require land and other resources to pursue their nonmaterialist ends. One way to legitimately acquire those resources is to spend part of one's time acquiring income through the provision of goods and services others desire. But the more one desires to pursue nonmarketable activities, and to avoid income-producing activities, then the more dependent one is on acquiring resources through one's claim to a fair division of society's wealth. The groups which are least interested in earning income for a materialistic life-style are precisely the groups which are most dependent on their fair share of society's wealth.

or failure in the pursuit of one's goals. But so long as there are things that matter in one's life, things that are worth defending and promoting, then there will be threats to the promotion of those values. Resources help one to exercise some control over the social and natural environment, and hence control the direction and consequences of those environments for the pursuit of one's values.

There may be some ways of life which are not aided by increased amounts of Rawls's primary goods. Rawls cites the case of religious lifestyles which include a vow of personal poverty, although that too may be a little quick. Monks committed to personal asceticism often belong to monastic orders that have large land holdings, revenues from which help pay for the land, buildings, and maintenance of their community and which are used in promoting their good works. Moreover, the vow of poverty is often understood as a renunciation of their legitimate entitlements under a theory of fairness, not, as Schwartz and Nagel require, a renunciation of things which they think should not be part of a legitimate theory of fairness. In any event, such examples do not show that access to primary goods harms these ways of life, or favors individualistic and materialistic ways of life.[14]

Rawls's emphasis on what individuals are entitled to may seem misplaced for people who deploy their resources in group relations and activities. But a theory of individual entitlement is required, even for communally oriented people, because it teaches each person what is available for the pursuit of their attachments. As Dworkin says, "We are free to make decisions [about our attachments] with respect to the resources that are properly assigned to us in the first instance, though not, of course, to dispose in this way of resources that have been assigned, or rather are properly assignable, to others. Equality enters our plans by teaching us what is available to us, to deploy in accordance with our attachments and other concerns."[15] Rawls invokes a standard of individual entitlement, not because of an individualistic theory of motivation, but because of his principle of individual responsibility. If people are to be legitimately held responsible for any expensive aims and attachments they may have, then there must be a standard of individual entitlement in the light of which they can adjust those aims.

This requirement of justice holds just as much for communally oriented people as for materialistic people. Communally oriented socialists can have expensive desires. The Marxian socialist wants a piece of land on which to labor cooperatively so as to "humanize" the natural world.[16] But the naturalist wants the same land left unhumanized, and the monk

14. Rawls, *Theory of Justice,* pp. 142–43.

15. Ronald Dworkin, "In Defense of Equality," *Social Philosophy and Policy* 1 (1983): 31.

16. Karl Marx, *Economic and Philosophical Manuscripts* (London: Lawrence & Wishart, 1977), pp. 306–9.

wants it for sacred purposes, to build a community that will honor God. Each of these aims has costs for other people, who must forgo their aims with respect to that land. It is naive to expect that the desired land will automatically be available for one's preferred purposes, and it is selfish to demand that it be automatically available. The test of what is properly available for the pursuit of these ends is given by the difference principle. The naturalist may want more resources set aside than is allotted him under the difference principle, but he is responsible for adjusting his claims to the rightful claims of others, and to demand excess resources for his naturalist aims would be just as unfair as it would be for a materialistic person to demand excess resources in order to purchase consumer goods. The nonindividualistic content of their aims does not excuse socialists or naturalists from taking into account the legitimate claims of others.

Schwartz and Nagel might accept that we should take into account the cost of our choices for other people but claim that the problem with Rawls's theory is that the costs are assessed in a biased way, since a Rawlsian society produces people whose basic preference is for more wealth. Costs would be assessed differently in a society that is designed to produce socialist individuals: the socialist's desire for land would not be as costly, since fewer people would have conflicting desires.

But while it is true that Rawls's theory makes the costs of a particular choice dependent on the extent to which other people's aims coincide or conflict, that does not show that the primary goods scheme is biased against communal ways of life. For the extent to which other people share one's ends will depend on the judgments the others freely make when considering the various ways of life available to them. If socialists are unable to convince others of the worth of that way of life, then it will be difficult to acquire the resources necessary to start up a socialist community. On the other hand, if materialists are unable to convince people of the value of a high income and a consumer life-style, then they will have difficulty attracting people to choose income over leisure, or monotonous but productive labor over enjoyable but less productive labor. These are indeed problems which materialists have faced when promoting consumerism in various cultures, and Marx predicted that they will reoccur when people can acquire a decent standard of living in a shortened workday. Rawlsian neutrality does not prejudge the relative value of self-realizing labor and consumer goods, and the relative difficulty of pursuing these different ways of life is determined by the choices the members of a given society freely make at a given moment. Schwartz and Nagel do not explain how socialists are disadvantaged by this arrangement, or why their choices should be subsidized regardless of how costly they are for others, and regardless of how attractive the members of a society find that way of life. As Rawls says, communal ends that cannot flourish under this arrangement should not "be upheld by the coercive apparatus of the state. If socially collective communitarian aims could survive in no other way, why should we regret their demise, and consider the original position unfair and biased against them?"[17]

Schwartz and Nagel note that socialists are disadvantaged by Rawlsian neutrality in contrast to a society which is designed to produce as many socialists as possible. But every way of life would do better in a society designed to ensure that no one had conflicting preferences. That does not establish a legitimate grievance, since no one has the right that other people be socialized so as to best fit one's own way of life (other people are not resources to be distributed or molded so as to promote one's ends). Fairness for the adherents of different ways of life requires that people be guaranteed a fair share of resources to pursue their way of life, and the freedom to seek out new adherents. It does not require that each way of life be guaranteed a certain number of adherents, and indeed fairness precludes treating people as resources to be distributed or molded so that each way of life fares equally well. The question is whether socialists are disadvantaged by Rawls's scheme with respect to the things which they have a legitimate claim to—that is, resources and liberties, but not other people's preferences—and Schwartz and Nagel do not establish this.[18]

One respect in which communally oriented people may be disadvantaged is that they must coordinate the deployment of resources distributed to individuals, and this coordination involves costs and effort that individualistic people avoid. Communally oriented people would prefer that resources be distributed directly to groups and then allow individualistic people to withdraw their resources from the group (this would involve costs for individualistic people that communally oriented people avoid). This problem would be solved if there were mechanisms for communally oriented people to receive benefits communally and for individualistic people to receive benefits individually. And this is indeed what Rawls endorses. He proposes that one branch of the state be organized so as to facilitate such coordination.[19] Rawls would not object if various

17. Rawls, "Fairness to Goodness," p. 551. Rawls has recently retracted the claim that there is no reason to regret the loss of life-styles which cannot sustain themselves in a free society. As he rightly says, these ways of life may well have had considerable value. An aristocratic life-style may have value, even if would-be aristocrats cannot find people in a free society who are willing to be their subordinates. But while the loss of aristocratic life-styles may be a cause for legitimate regret, it is not a cause for legitimate grievance, for it is not the product of arbitrary biases (Rawls, "Priority of Right," pp. 266–67). See also Dworkin's explanation of the fairness of liberal neutrality in "What Is Equality? Part 3: The Place of Liberty," *Iowa Law Review* 73 (1987): 1–54, where he notes that neutrality "allows each person's social requirements—the social setting he claims he needs in order successfully to pursue his chosen way of life—to be tested by asking how far these requirements can be satisfied within an egalitarian structure that measures their cost to others" (p. 31).

18. Rawls, "Priority of Right," pp. 265–66.

19. Rawls, *Theory of Justice*, pp. 282–84. This passage refers only to the exchange branch of government, but the same reasoning seems equally applicable to distribution (p. 280).

marital and cultural groups pay taxes, and receive benefits, collectively, where the members have so agreed.

It is true that any collective provision of benefits requires the ongoing consent of individuals. But this requirement reflects Rawls's commitment to autonomy, not any commitment to individualistic aims. According to the "ideal of the person" underlying Rawls's theory, individuals "do not regard themselves as inevitably bound to, or identical with, the pursuit of any particular complex of fundamental interests that they may have at any given moment."[20] People are capable not simply of pursuing their given ends, but also of reflecting on the value of those ends, considering alternatives, and revising even their most deeply held beliefs about what is worthwhile in life:

> As free persons, citizens recognize one another as having the moral power to have a conception of the good. This means that they do not view themselves as inevitably tied to the pursuit of the particular conception of the good and its final ends which they espouse at any given time. Instead, as citizens, they are regarded as, in general, capable of revising and changing this conception on reasonable and rational grounds. Thus it is held to be permissible for citizens to stand apart from conceptions of the good and to survey and assess their various final ends.[21]

According to Rawls, this ability for autonomous choice is one of our two fundamental moral powers, and respect for autonomy requires that individuals retain the right to opt out of any particular communal practice (and corresponding communal provision of benefits). Hence Rawls's two principles of justice are designed to ensure that individuals can "stand apart" from their current ends—the liberties and resources distributed by Rawls's two principles do not preempt or penalize the attempt by individuals to form and revise their conceptions of the good, or to acquire the information needed to make those judgments rationally and intelligently. Since individuals can come to question their ends, they must have access to resources which are flexible, which can be translated into the goods and services appropriate for other ways of life, including, of course, other communal ways of life.[22]

20. John Rawls, "Reply to Alexander and Musgrave," *Quarterly Journal of Economics* 88 (1974): 641.

21. Rawls, "Kantian Constructivism," p. 544.

22. This feature of Rawls's theory is discussed in Allen Buchanan, "Revisability and Rational Choice," *Canadian Journal of Philosophy* 5 (1975): 395–408; and Dworkin, "In Defense of Equality," pp. 24–30. Rawls's view of the self as able to stand apart from its ends has been vigorously criticized by communitarians—e.g., Alasdair MacIntyre, *After Virtue: A Study in Moral Theory* (London: Duckworth, 1981), chap. 15; Michael Sandel, *Liberalism and the Limits of Justice* (Cambridge: Cambridge University Press, 1982), pp. 150–65. They argue that this view of the self as "unencumbered" by social attachments is at odds with our "deepest self-understandings." I believe the communitarians are simply wrong here (see my "Liberalism and Communitarianism," *Canadian Journal of Philosophy*

Rawls's commitment to the importance of primary goods, therefore, is not evidence of possessive individualism, but rather of two distinct ideas: (*a*) our way of life should reflect our autonomous choice, and so the resources available to us must be flexible; and (*b*) we are responsible for the costs of our choices, and hence there must be some standard which teaches us what is available to us to use in accordance with our attachments. Neither of these is primarily concerned with the content of people's ends. Rather they concern the relationship between the individual and her ends—an individual's ends are not fixed or imposed by others but, rather, are the objects of her autonomous and responsible choice.

NEUTRALITY AND ATOMISTIC INDIVIDUALISM

The second and third versions of the claim that neutrality is excessively individualistic accept Rawls's emphasis on the capacity for autonomous choice. But autonomous choices are only possible in certain contexts, and these two objections claim that liberal neutrality is incapable of ensuring the existence and flourishing of that context. While both objections attribute this failure of neutrality to a certain kind of atomistic individualism, they locate the failure in different places—the second objection centers on the need for a shared cultural structure that provides individuals with meaningful options, and the third centers on the need for shared forums in which to evaluate these options.

Neutrality and a Pluralist Culture

The second objection claims that liberal neutrality is incapable of guaranteeing the existence of a pluralistic culture which provides people with the range of options necessary for meaningful individual choice. Autonomy requires pluralism, but "any collective attempt by a liberal state to protect pluralism would itself be in breach of liberal principles of justice. The state is not entitled to interfere in the movement of the cultural market place except, of course, to ensure that each individual has a just share of available necessary means to exercise his or her moral powers. The welfare or demise of particular conceptions of the good and, therefore, the welfare or demise of social unions of a particular character is not the business of the state."[23] The state is not allowed to protect pluralism, yet if the cultural marketplace proceeds on its own it will eventually undermine the cultural structure which supports pluralism. Neutrality may ensure

18 [1988]: 181–203), but Rawls himself wishes to remain agnostic on the question of whether our self-understandings are or are not bound to any particular complex of ends. He now argues that people can accept his account of the self for the purposes of determining our public rights and responsibilities, without necessarily accepting it as an accurate portrayal of our deepest self-understandings (John Rawls, "Justice as Fairness: Political not Metaphysical," *Philosophy and Public Affairs* 14 [1985]: 240–44; cf. "Kantian Constructivism," p. 545). I raise some questions about the possibility and/or desirability of this agnosticism in *Liberalism, Community, and Culture* (Oxford: Oxford University Press, 1989), pp. 58–61.

23. Wesley Cragg, "Two Concepts of Community," *Dialogue* 25 (1986): 47.

that government does not denigrate a way of life that some individuals think is worthy of support, but "whatever else can be said about this argument one point is decisive. Supporting valuable ways of life is a social rather than an individual matter . . . perfectionist ideals require public action for their viability. Anti-perfectionism in practice would lead not merely to a political stand-off from support for valuable conceptions of the good. It would undermine the chances of survival of many cherished aspects of our culture."[24] The problem, then, is not that liberal neutrality fails to achieve its aim of genuine neutrality (as the possessive individualism objection claimed) but, rather, that neutrality undermines the very conditions in which it is a worthwhile aim.

Liberal neutrality is therefore self-defeating. There seem to be two possible ways out of this dilemma. One is to deny that the value of autonomous choice depends on a viable and flourishing culture. This is the "atomist" route which accepts "the utterly facile moral psychology of traditional empiricism,"[25] according to which an individual's capacity for meaningful choice is self-sufficient outside of society and culture. This route is inadequate, since our dependence on the cultural structure for worthwhile ways of life is undeniable, and few if any liberals have ever been "concerned purely with individual choices . . . to the neglect of the matrix in which such choices can be open or closed, rich or meagre."[26]

The second response is to accept that meaningful autonomous choice requires a viable culture but insist that good ways of life will sustain themselves in the cultural marketplace without state assistance.[27] But this too is an inadequate response. In conditions of freedom, people are able to assess and recognize the worth of good ways of life and will support them. But the interests people have in a good way of life, and the forms of support they will voluntarily provide, do not necessarily involve sustaining its existence for future generations. My interest in a valuable social practice may be best promoted by depleting the resources which the practice requires to survive beyond my lifetime. Even if the cultural marketplace can be relied on to ensure that existing people can identify valuable ways of life, there is no reason to assume that it can be relied on to ensure that future people have a valuable range of options.

So let us grant Raz's argument that state support may be needed to ensure the survival of an adequate range of options for those who have not yet formed their aims in life. Why does that require rejecting neutrality?

24. Raz, *Morality of Freedom*, p. 162.

25. Charles Taylor, *Philosophy and the Human Sciences: Philosophical Papers* (Cambridge: Cambridge University Press, 1985), vol. 2, p. 197.

26. Ibid., p. 207. See, e.g., Rawls, *Theory of Justice*, pp. 563–64; Dworkin, *A Matter of Principle*, pp. 220–24.

27. Rawls, *Theory of Justice*, pp. 331–32; Jeremy Waldron, "Autonomy and Perfectionism in Raz's *Morality of Freedom*," *University of Southern California Law Review* 62 (1989), in press; Robert Nozick, "Commentary on 'Art as a Public Good,' " *Art and the Law* 9 (1985): 162–64.

Consider two possible cultural policies. In the first case, the government ensures an adequate range of options by providing tax credits to individuals who make culture-supporting contributions in accordance with their personal perfectionist ideals. The state acts to ensure that there is an adequate range of options, but the evaluation of these options occurs in civil society, outside the coercive apparatus of the state.[28] In the second case, the evaluation of different conceptions of the good becomes a political question, and the government intervenes, not simply to ensure an adequate range of options, but to promote particular options. Now Raz's argument simply does not address this choice. What is "decisive" in Raz's argument is that one or the other of these policies must be implemented, but he has not given a decisive reason, or any reason at all, to prefer one policy over the other.

A perfectionist state might hope to improve the quality of people's options by encouraging the replacement of less valuable options by more valuable ones. But it is worth repeating that liberal neutrality also hopes to improve the range of options, and the cultural marketplace is valued because it helps good ways of life displace bad. Each side aims to secure and improve the range of options from which individuals make their autonomous choices. What they disagree on is where perfectionist values and arguments should be invoked. Are good ways of life more likely to establish their greater worth when they are evaluated in the cultural marketplace of civil society, or when the preferability of different ways of life is made a matter of political advocacy and state action? Hence the dispute should perhaps be seen as a choice, not between perfectionism and neutrality, but between social perfectionism and state perfectionism—for the flip side of state neutrality is support for the role of perfectionist ideals and arguments in civil society.[29]

28. This is endorsed by Dworkin in *A Matter of Principle,* chap. 11. This use of tax credits would only be fair if the distribution of resources in society was in fact just. Indeed, it might not be fair even if the difference principle was honored, since it gives disproportionate power in shaping cultural development to those who are endowed with (undeserved) natural talents, as they are likely to have more disposable income. I assume there are ways to ensure that this operates fairly while still leaving the evaluation of cultural options outside the political sphere. For a discussion of the problem of fairness in influence over culture, in the context of the neutrality/perfectionist debate, see Amy Gutmann, *Democratic Education* (Princeton, N.J.: Princeton University Press, 1987), chap. 9, esp. pp. 263–64.

29. Failure to recognize this undermines Beiner's argument against liberal neutrality, which he concludes by saying: "Even if the state is or tries to be neutral (which likely proves impossible), in any case the wider social order in which the individual is nourished *is not.* Liberal 'neutralism' is therefore a mirage. It is hard to see why the *state* is constrained to be neutral (whatever that might mean) if social life as a whole is and must be, however much denied by liberals, strongly partial towards a particular way of life" (Ronald Beiner, "What's Wrong with Liberalism?" in *Law and Community,* ed. Leslie Green and Alan Hutchinson [Toronto: Carswell, in press]). This is entirely off target. The best reason for state neutrality is precisely that social life is nonneutral, that people can and do make discriminations among competing ways of life in their social life, affirming some and rejecting others, without using the state apparatus. If individuals are unable to make these judgments in

Neutrality and Collective Deliberations

The third and final objection accepts that liberal neutrality recognizes the necessity of having a secure cultural structure. But it claims that a different sort of atomistic individualism is found in the liberal account of how cultural options should be evaluated. The liberal preference for the cultural marketplace over the state as the appropriate arena for evaluating different life-styles stems from an individualistic belief that judgments about the good should be made by isolated individuals, whose autonomy is ensured by protecting them from social pressures. Liberals think that autonomy is promoted when judgments about the good are taken out of the political realm. But in reality individual judgments require the sharing of experiences and the give and take of collective deliberations. Individual judgments about the good always depend on, and flow from, the collective evaluation of shared practices. They become a matter of purely subjective and arbitrary whim if they are cut off from collective deliberations:

> Self-fulfillment and even the working out of personal identity and a sense of orientation in the world depend upon a communal enterprise. This shared process is the civic life, and its root is involvement with others: other generations, other sorts of persons whose differences are significant because they contribute to the whole upon which our particular sense of self depends. Thus mutual interdependency is the foundational notion of citizenship . . . outside a linguistic community of shared practices, there would be biological *homo sapiens* as logical abstraction, but there could not be human beings. This is the meaning of the Greek and medieval dictum that the political community is ontologically *prior* to the individual. The polis is, literally, that which makes man, as human being, possible.[30]

Or, as Crowley puts it, state perfectionism is "an affirmation of the notion that men living in a community of shared experiences and language is the only context in which the individual and society can discover and test their values through the essentially political activities of discussion, criticism, example, and emulation. It is through the existence of organised public spaces, in which men offer and test ideas against one another . . . that men come to understand a part of who they are."[31] The state should be the proper arena in which to formulate and pursue our visions of the

---

social life, then state perfectionism might be the appropriate way to enable people to discriminate among different conceptions of the good (although it is unclear how moving from the cultural marketplace to the state would remove the disability). So the argument for state neutrality presupposes, rather than denies, social nonneutrality.

30. William Sullivan, *Reconstructing Public Philosophy* (Berkeley: University of California Press, 1982), pp. 158, 173.

31. Brian Lee Crowley, *The Self, the Individual, and the Community: Liberalism in the Political Thought of F. A. Hayek and Sidney and Beatrice Webb* (Oxford: Oxford University Press, 1987), p. 282; see also Beiner, *Political Judgment* (London: Methuen, 1983), p. 152.

good, because the good for individuals requires collective interaction and inquiry—it cannot be pursued, or even known, presocially.

But this misconstrues the sense in which Rawls claims that the evaluation of ways of life should not be a public concern. Liberal neutrality does not restrict the scope of perfectionist ideals in the collective activities of individuals and groups. Perfectionist ideals, although excluded from a liberal state, "have an important place in human affairs" and, hence, an important place in a liberal society.[32] Collective activity and shared experiences concerning the good are at the heart of the "free internal life of the various communities of interests in which persons and groups seek to achieve, in modes of social union consistent with equal liberty, the ends and excellences to which they are drawn."[33] Rawls's argument for the priority of liberty is grounded in the importance of this "free social union with others."[34] He simply denies that "the coercive apparatus of the state" is an appropriate forum for those deliberations and experiences: "While justice as fairness allows that in a well-ordered society the values of excellence are recognized, the human perfections are to be pursued within the limits of the principle of free association. . . . [Persons] do not use the coercive apparatus of the state to win for themselves a greater liberty or larger distributive shares on the grounds that their activities are of more intrinsic value."[35]

Unfortunately, civic republicans, who make this objection most frequently, rarely distinguish between collective activities and political activities. It is of course true that participation in shared linguistic and cultural practices is what enables individuals to make intelligent decisions about the good life. But why should such participation be organized in and through the state, rather than through the free association of individuals? It is true that we should "create opportunities for men to give voice to what they have discovered about themselves and the world and to persuade others of its worth."[36] But a liberal society does create opportunities for people to express and develop these social aspects of individual deliberation. After all, freedom of assembly, association, and speech are fundamental *liberal* rights. The opportunities for collective inquiry simply occur within and between groups and associations below the level of the state—friends and family, in the first instance, but also churches, cultural associations, professional groups and trade unions, universities, and the mass media. These are some of the "organized public spaces of appearance" and "communication communities" of a liberal society.[37] Liberals do not deny that "the public display of character and judgment and the exchange

32. Rawls, *Theory of Justice,* p. 543.
33. Ibid.
34. Ibid.
35. Ibid., pp. 328–29.
36. Crowley, p. 295.
37. Ibid., pp. 7, 239.

of experience and insight" are needed to make intelligent judgments about the good, or to show others that I "hold [my] notion of the good responsibly."[38] Indeed, these claims fit comfortably in many liberal discussions of the value of free speech and association.[39] What the liberal denies is that I should have to give such an account of myself *to the state*.

A similar failure to confront the distinctive role of the state weakens radical critiques of liberalism, like that of Habermas. Habermas, in his earlier writings at least, wants the evaluation of different ways of life to be a political question, but unlike communitarians and civic republicans, he does not hope or expect that this political deliberation will serve to promote people's embeddedness in existing practices.[40] Indeed, he thinks that political deliberation is required precisely because in its absence people will tend to accept existing practices as givens and thereby perpetuate the false needs and false consciousness which accompany those historical practices.[41] Only when existing ways of life are "the objects of discursive will-formation" can people's understanding of the good be free of deception. Rawls's view of distributive justice does not demand the scrutiny of these practices and, hence, does not recognize the emancipatory interest people have in escaping false needs and ideological distortions.

But why should the evaluation of people's conceptions of the good be tied to their claims on resources, and hence to the state apparatus? Communities smaller than the entire political society, groups and associations of various sizes, might be more appropriate forums for those forms of discursive will formation which involve evaluating the good and interpreting one's genuine needs. While Habermas rejects the communitarian tendency to uncritically endorse existing social practices as the basis for political deliberations about the good, he shares their tendency to assume that anything which is not politically deliberated is thereby left to an individual will incapable of rational judgment.

So the liberal commitment to state neutrality does not manifest abstract individualism either in regard to the importance of a shared cultural

38. Ibid., p. 287.

39. See, e.g., Thomas Scanlon, "Freedom of Expression and Categories of Expression," in *Pornography and Censorship*, ed. David Copp and Susan Wendell (Buffalo, N.Y.: Prometheus, 1983), pp. 141–47; Loren Lomasky, *Persons, Rights, and the Moral Community* (Oxford: Oxford University Press, 1987), p. 111.

40. Habermas seems to endorse this position when he says that the need for a "discursive desolidification of the (largely externally controlled or traditionally fixed) interpretation of our needs" is the heart of his disagreement with Rawls (Habermas, *Communication and the Evolution of Society*, pp. 198–99). However, he now rejects the idea of politically evaluating people's conceptions of the good (Jürgen Habermas, "Questions and Counterquestions," in *Habermas and Modernity*, ed. Richard Bernstein [Cambridge, Mass.: MIT Press, 1985], pp. 214–16). For discussion of the (apparent) shift, see Seyla Benhabib, *Critique, Norm, and Utopia* (New York: Columbia University Press, 1986), chap. 8; and Nanette Funk, "Habermas and the Social Goods," *Social Text* 18 (1988): 29–31.

41. Habermas, *Communication and the Evolution of Society*, pp. 198–99; Benhabib, pp. 312–14.

context for meaningful individual options, or in regard to the importance of the sharing of experiences and arguments for meaningful individual evaluation of those options. Liberal neutrality does not deny these shared social requirements of individual autonomy but, rather, provides an interpretation of them.

EVALUATING THE NEUTRALITY DEBATE

I have argued that liberal neutrality is not excessively individualistic, either in terms of the way it conceives the content of people's ends, or in the way that people evaluate and pursue those ends. Of course neutrality may be indefensible for other reasons. Neutrality requires a certain faith in the operation of nonstate forums and processes for individual judgment and cultural development, and a distrust of the operation of state forums and processes for evaluating the good. Nothing I have said so far shows that this optimism and distrust are warranted. Indeed, just as critics of neutrality have failed to defend their faith in political forums and procedures, so liberals have failed to defend their faith in nonstate forums and procedures. The crucial claims have not been adequately defended by either side.

In fact, it is hard to avoid the conclusion that each side in the neutrality debate has failed to learn the important lesson taught by the other side. Despite centuries of liberal insistence on the importance of the distinction between society and the state, communitarians still seem to assume that whatever is properly social must become the province of the political. They have not confronted the liberal worry that the all-embracing authority and coercive means which characterize the state make it a particularly inappropriate forum for the sort of genuinely shared deliberation and commitment that they desire. Despite centuries of communitarian insistence on the historically fragile and contingent nature of our culture, and the need to consider the conditions under which a free culture can arise and sustain itself, liberals still tend to take the existence of a tolerant and diverse culture for granted, as something which naturally arises and sustains itself, the ongoing existence of which is therefore simply assumed in a theory of justice. Hegel was right to insist that a culture of freedom is a historical achievement, and liberals need to explain why the cultural marketplace does not threaten that achievement either by failing to connect people in a strong enough way to their communal practices (as communitarians fear), or conversely, by failing to detach people in a strong enough way from the expectations of existing practices and ideologies (as Habermas fears). A culture of freedom requires a mix of both exposure and connection to existing practices, and also distance and dissent from them. Liberal neutrality may provide that mix, but that is not obviously true, and it may be true only in some times and places. So both sides need to give us a more comprehensive comparison of the opportunities and dangers present in state and nonstate forums and procedures for evaluating the good.

While both sides have something to learn from the other, that is not to say that the truth is somewhere in between the two. I cannot provide here the sort of systematic comparison of the empirical operation of state and nonstate forums and procedures that is required for a proper defense of neutrality, but I want to suggest a few reasons why state perfectionism would have undesirable consequences for our society. I will assume, for the moment, that the public ranking of the value of different ways of life which a perfectionist state appeals to would be arrived at through the collective political deliberation of citizens, rather than through the secret or unilateral decisions of political elites.

What are the consequences of having a collectively determined ranking of the value of different conceptions of the good? One consequence is that more is at stake when people publicly formulate and defend their conception of the good. If people do not advance persuasive arguments for their conception of the good, then a perfectionist state may take action which will make their way of life harder to maintain. In a liberal society with a neutral state, on the other hand, people who cannot persuade others of the value of their way of life will lose out in the competition with other conceptions of the good being advanced in the cultural marketplace, but they will not face adverse state action.

Why is that an undesirable consequence? In principle, it is not undesirable—it may simply intensify the patterns of cultural development, since the pros and cons of different ways of life might be revealed more quickly under the threat of state action than would occur in the cultural marketplace, where people are sometimes reluctant to confront opposing values and arguments. However, I believe that state perfectionism would in fact serve to distort the free evaluation of ways of life, to rigidify the dominant ways of life, whatever their intrinsic merits, and to unfairly exclude the values and aspirations of marginalized and disadvantaged groups within the community.

First, state perfectionism raises the prospect of a dictatorship of the articulate and would unavoidably penalize those individuals who are inarticulate. But being articulate, in our society, is not simply an individual variable. There are many culturally disadvantaged groups whose beliefs and aspirations are not understood by the majority. Recent immigrants are an obvious example whose disadvantage is partly unavoidable. But there are also groups which have been deliberately excluded from the mainstream of American society, and whose cultural disadvantage reflects prejudice and insensitivity. The dominant cultural practices of our community were defined by one section of the population—that is, the male members of the upper classes of the white race—and were defined so as to exclude and denigrate the values of subordinate groups. Members of these excluded groups—women, blacks, Hispanics—have been unable to get recognition for their values from the cultural mainstream and have developed (or retained) subcultures for the expression of these values, subcultures whose norms, by necessity, are incommensurable with those of the mainstream. It is unfair to ask them to defend the value of their way of life by reference to cultural standards and norms that were defined by and for others. Even where these historical factors are absent, the majority is likely to use state perfectionism to block valuable social change that threatens their preferred cultural practices. This cultural conservatism need not be malicious—the majority may simply not see the value of cultural change, partly due to incomprehension, partly from fear of change.

State perfectionism would also affect the kinds of arguments given. Minority groups whose values conflict with those of the majority often put a high value on the integrity of their practices and aim at gaining adherents from within the majority slowly, one by one. But where there is state perfectionism, the minority must immediately aim at persuading the majority, and so they will describe their practices in such a way as to be most palatable to the majority, even if that misdescribes the real meaning and value of the practice, which often arose precisely in opposition to dominant practices. There would be an inevitable tendency for minorities to describe and debate conceptions of the good in terms of dominant values, which then reinforces the cultural conservatism of the dominant group itself.

In these and other ways, the threats and inducements of coercive power would distort rather than improve the process of individual judgment and cultural development. Some of these problems also arise in the cultural marketplace (i.e., penalizing the inarticulate, social prejudice). Insensitivity and prejudice will be problems no matter which model we choose, since both models reward those groups who can make their way of life attractive to the mainstream. But state perfectionism intensifies these problems, since it dictates to minority groups when and how they will interact with majority norms, and it dictates a time and place—political deliberation over state policy—in which minorities are most vulnerable. State neutrality, on the other hand, gives culturally disadvantaged groups a greater ability to choose the time and place in which they will confront majority sensitivities and to choose an audience with whom they are most comfortable. There will always be an imbalance in the interaction between culturally dominant and subordinate groups. State neutrality ensures that the culturally subordinate group has as many options as possible concerning that interaction, and that the costs of that imbalance for the subordinate groups are minimized. State perfectionism, I think, does just the opposite.

Some of these problems could be avoided if the public ranking of ways of life was determined by political elites, insulated from popular debate and prejudice. Indeed, an enlightened and insulated political elite could use state perfectionist policies to promote the aims and values of culturally disadvantaged groups. Just as the Supreme Court is supposed to be more able to protect the rights of disadvantaged groups because of its insulation from political pressures, so an insulated political elite may be able to give a fairer hearing to minority values than they get in the cultural marketplace. But this raises troubling questions about accountability and the danger of abuse (after all, if majority groups are insensitive to minority aspirations, why won't they elect leaders who are similarly insensitive?). And, in any event, why shouldn't the aim of the political elite be to counteract the biases of the cultural marketplace, which affect the public evaluation of all minority values, rather than deciding for themselves which minority values are worth promoting? Using state power to counteract biases against minority values may be legitimate, not because of a general principle of perfectionism, but because of a general principle of redressing biases against disadvantaged groups.

These are some of the reasons why liberals distrust state perfectionism for our society.[42] Communitarians are right to insist that we examine the history and structure of a particular culture, but it is remarkable how little communitarians themselves undertake such an examination of our culture. They wish to use the ends and practices of our cultural tradition as the basis for a politics of the common good, but they do not mention that these practices were historically defined by a small segment of the population, nor do they discuss how that exclusionary history would affect the politicization of debates about the value of different ways of life. If we look at the history of our society, surely liberal neutrality has the great advantage of its potential inclusiveness, its denial that marginalized and subordinate groups must fit into the historical practices, the "way of life," which have been defined by the dominant groups. Forcing subordinate groups to defend their ways of life, under threat or promise of coercive power, is inherently exclusive. Communitarians simply ignore this danger and the cultural history which makes it so difficult to avoid.[43]

42. There are other reasons for opposing state perfectionism. I have been discussing the difficulty of finding acceptable procedures for formulating a public ranking of different ways of life. There are also difficulties about how the state should go about promoting its preferred ways of life, once those are identified. Even if the state can be relied on to come up with an accurate ranking and can get people to pursue the right ways of life, it may not be able to get people to pursue them *for the right reasons*. Someone who acts in a certain way in order to avoid state punishment, or to gain state subsidies, is not guided by an understanding of the genuine value of the activity (Waldron; Lomasky, pp. 253–54). This criticism is important and precludes various coercive and manipulative forms of perfectionism, but it does not preclude short-term state intervention designed to introduce people to valuable ways of life. One way to get people to pursue something for the right reasons is to get them to pursue it for the wrong reasons and hope they will then see its true value. This is not inherently unacceptable, and it occurs often enough in the cultural marketplace. Hence a comprehensive defense of neutrality may need to focus on a prior stage of state perfectionism—i.e., the problems involved in formulating a public ranking of conceptions of the good.

43. On the exclusionary tendencies of communitarianism, see Amy Gutmann, "Communitarian Critics of Liberalism," *Philosophy and Public Affairs* 14 (1985): 318–22; Don Herzog, "Some Questions for Republicans," *Political Theory* 14 (1986): 481–90; H. Hirsch, "The Threnody of Liberalism: Constitutional Liberty and the Renewal of Community," *Political Theory* 14 (1986): 435–38; Nancy Rosenblum, *Another Liberalism: Romanticism and the Reconstruction of Liberal Thought* (Cambridge, Mass.: Harvard University Press, 1987), pp. 178–81.

While liberalism need not be committed to neutrality in all times and places, the relationship between the culture and the state in our society makes neutrality particularly appropriate for us. However, certain features of that relationship also make neutrality particularly difficult to implement. I have discussed different ways a neutral state might protect and promote its culture. But if we look at actual states and actual cultures, we will quickly notice that most liberal democracies contain more than one cultural community. Most countries contain many cultures, like the French, English, and aboriginal cultures in Canada. When we say that the cultural context can be enriched or diminished, whose culture are we discussing? Whose language should be used in the schools and courts and media? If immigration policy should give consideration to the consequences of immigration on the cultural structure, as most liberals have agreed, then shouldn't we accept demands by Francophones in Quebec, or the Inuit in Northern Canada, to have some control over immigration into their cultural communities? What does liberal neutrality require when the state contains more than one culture?

The dominant view among contemporary liberals, to which Rawls apparently subscribes, is that liberalism requires the "absence, even prohibition, of any legal or governmental recognition of racial, religious, language or [cultural] groups as corporate entities with a standing in the legal or governmental process, and a prohibition of the use of ethnic criteria of any type for discriminatory purposes, or conversely for special or favored treatment."[44] But this view, which achieved its current prominence during the American struggle against racial segregation, has only limited applicability. Once we recognize the importance of the cultural structure and accept that there is a positive duty on the state to protect the cultural conditions which allow for autonomous choice, then cultural membership does have political salience. Respect for the autonomy of the members of minority cultures requires respect for their cultural structure, and that in turn may require special linguistic, educational, and even political rights for minority cultures. Indeed, there are a number of circumstances in which liberal theories of equality should recognize the special status of minority cultures (as prewar liberal theories often did).[45] The attempt to answer questions about the rights of cultural communities with the formula of color-blind laws applying to persons of all races and cultures is hopelessly inadequate once we look at the diversity of cultural membership which exists in contemporary liberal

44. Milton Gordon, "Toward a General Theory of Racial and Ethnic Group Relations," in *Ethnicity: Theory and Experience*, ed. Nathan Glazer and Daniel Moynihan (Cambridge, Mass.: Harvard University Press, 1975), p. 105.

45. Minority rights were a common feature of prewar liberalism, both in theory (e.g., L. T. Hobhouse, *Social Evolution and Political Theory* [New York: Columbia University Press, 1928], pp. 146–47) and practice (e.g., the League of Nations). I attempt to provide a liberal theory of the rights of minority cultures in "Liberalism, Individualism, and Minority Rights," in *Law and Community*, ed. Leslie Green and Alan Hutchinson (Toronto: Carswell, 1989), and *Liberalism, Community, and Culture*, chaps. 7–10.

democracies.[46] However, the alternatives have rarely been considered in contemporary liberal writings, which are dominated (often unconsciously) by the model of the nation-state.[47]

CONCLUSION

The real issue concerning neutrality is not individualism: nothing in Rawls's insistence on state neutrality is inconsistent with recognizing the importance of the social world to the development, deliberation, and pursuit of individuals' values. It is commonly alleged that liberals fail to recognize that people are naturally social or communal beings. Liberals supposedly think that society rests on an artificial social contract, and that a coercive state apparatus is needed to keep naturally asocial people together in society. But there is a sense in which the opposite is true—liberals believe that people naturally form and join social relations and forums in which they come to understand and pursue the good. The state is not needed to provide that communal context and is likely to distort the normal processes of collective deliberations and cultural development. It is communitarians who seem to think that individuals will drift into anomic and detached isolation without the state actively bringing them together to collectively evaluate and pursue the good.[48]

46. Even in a genuine "nation-state," there are questions about how to deal with immigrants from other cultures. Liberals have historically disagreed over the extent to which respect for the autonomy of existing members of the polity requires restrictions on immigration which might damage the cultural structure. They have also disagreed over the extent to which respect for the autonomy of immigrants requires encouraging or compelling their assimilation to the cultural structure of the new country. Again, the requirements of liberal neutrality are not at all obvious.

47. The assumption that the political community is culturally homogeneous is clear in a number of passages in Rawls and Dworkin—e.g., John Rawls, "The Basic Structure as Subject," in *Values and Morals,* ed. Alvin Goldman and Jaegwon Kim (Dordrecht: Reidel, 1978), p. 55, and "On the Idea of Free Public Reason" (1988, photocopy), p. 8; Dworkin, *A Matter of Principle,* pp. 230–33. While revising that assumption would affect the conclusions they go on to draw about the distribution of rights and responsibilities, Rawls and Dworkin never discuss what changes would be required in culturally plural countries. Indeed, they do not seem to recognize that any changes would be required. For a criticism of Rawls's inattention to cultural pluralism, see Vernon Van Dyke, "Justice as Fairness: For Groups?" *American Political Science Review* 69 (1975): 607–14.

48. For example, Crowley says that politics makes possible "a context within which our own self-understandings *may* be articulated and compared with others" (p. 290; my emphasis). But it would be more accurate to say, as he indeed goes on to say, that "politics both *makes* us test dialogically the adequacy of our present self-awareness and makes us aware of other dimensions articulated by other people" (p. 290; my emphasis). Since Crowley never discusses this shift, it seems that he believes that individuals are only able to deliberate collectively when they are made to do so. A similar belief may explain why Sullivan thinks that state perfectionism is needed to ensure that no one is "cut off" from collective deliberations (Sullivan, p. 158). Since people in a liberal society are only cut off from the associations and forums of civil society if they cut themselves off, state perfectionism is needed only if one is assuming that uncoerced people will choose not to participate in collective deliberations. Liberals make the opposite assumption that uncoerced individuals

The question is not whether individuals' values and autonomy need to be situated in social relations but whether the relevant relations are necessarily or desirably political ones. This should be the real issue in debates over neutrality, and settling that issue requires a closer examination of the relationship between society, culture, and the state than either defenders or critics have so far provided.

---

will tend to form and join collective associations, and participate in collective deliberations (the suggestion that nonpolitical activity is inherently solitary is also present in Sandel's claim that under communitarian politics "we can know a good in common that we cannot know alone" [Sandel, p. 183]).

[15]

RELIGION, RIGHTS, AND DIFFERENCE IN THE EARLY WOMAN'S RIGHTS MOVEMENT

*Elizabeth B. Clark**

The meeting of feminists at Seneca Falls in July of 1848 marked the nominal beginning of the movement which in the nineteenth century was labeled "woman's rights." For us that term has become commonly interchangeable with "suffrage," and we often assume that "woman's rights" describes a seventy-odd year campaign to gain civil and political power and protection from a government which—although it had perpetrated outrages against women and blacks—had an unquestioned legitimacy as the guarantor and enforcer of rights.

Historical interpretations of the woman's movement have reaffirmed this picture, stressing the republican origins of women's claims and their easy fit within the tradition of American constitutionalism. The movement's biographers have placed feminists' arguments well within the secular political tradition of the nineteenth century. They have treated "natural rights" as a form of "super-right"—more emphatic, an appeal to historical tradition, but not qualitatively different from constitutional claims—and natural law language as formulaic fist shaking.[1] Ellen DuBois, the foremost historian of the movement's early period, has stressed suffrage as the activists' most radical and most mature demand, and the highest evolution of women's political consciousness. For DuBois, the quest for the ballot reflected a rights consciousness rooted in the secular, enlightened, liberal tradition of the American Revolution. She labels suffrage as the primary goal from the beginning for the right-thinking portion of the movement as represented by Elizabeth Cady Stanton and the National Woman Suffrage Association (NWSA), and sees the more conservative Woman's Christian Temperance Union's endorsement of the vote in the 1880s as a measure of the NWSA's success in setting a liberal agenda for the woman's movement as a whole.[2]

Historians have overstated both the secular identity of antebellum feminism and the centrality of suffrage to that movement, emphasizing the roles of Elizabeth Cady Stanton and Susan B. Anthony to the exclusion of scores of other activists more representative of the movement's main-

---

* J.D. from Michigan University, Ph.D. in Legal History pending from Princeton University.

1. Aileen Kraditor takes this tack in The Ideas of the Woman Suffrage Movement, 1890-1920 (1965).

2. *See* Ellen C. DuBois, Feminism and Suffrage: The Emergence of an Independent Woman's Movement in America, 1848-1869 (1978); *and The Radicalism of Woman Suffrage: Notes Toward the Reconstruction of Nineteenth-Century Feminism*, Feminist Studies, vol. 3 no. 3 (1975), at 63-71.

stream. The rather abstract language of rights used by the Founding Fathers was common currency in America, and women drew on it for help in fashioning their arguments and in making public appeals. But feminists did not don the Founders' philosophy of rights as a perfectly fitting suit of mail. Many were initiated into organized feminism through the philosophies of liberal Protestantism so prevalent in antebellum reform thought. The content of their rights thinking was informed by a deeply religious sensibility which stressed the interconnections between rights and responsibilities, between civil and domestic relations, and between the workings of the state and of the home. Suffrage did not automatically take pride of place in the panoply of rights women sought in the period before the Civil War, but stood as one goal among many, and not the most important. Further, rights consciousness was originally rooted in domestic concerns for many women, who saw them as a means of achieving protection for themselves and their families while pursuing the ends of social justice. Such an understanding of rights was in full accord with the liberal Protestant imperative for the full development of the individual and his or her full participation in society. The demand for rights did not emerge theoretically full-blown from any woman's head, but was born the usual way, amid a welter of personal and familial concerns.

Finally, although "equality" was the watchword of the movement, in the antebellum period it referred largely to a negative proposition; the removal of the false and artificial restraints of woman's sphere, restraints which prevented her full entry into public life. "Equal" was not "like," and although feminists ideally hoped that the destruction of spheres could bring about the growth of common sympathies between men and women, their attitudes toward male culture were rooted in the genuine, material differences in men's and women's lives which existed in education, opportunity, political entitlement, and social expectation in nineteenth-century America. Although women demanded equality, they also predicated their entry into the political world on a moral sensibility which most saw as uniquely feminine, and which served as the basis for their political agenda and their theory of rights.

The Christian Understanding of Politics and Power

To understand what significance "law" and "rights" had for mid-nineteenth-century female activists, we must interpret their concepts of power and governance according to the Protestant ethos which informed their world vision. Within this Christian framework, the possession of power was construed in a peculiar way. Both evangelical revivalists and Garrisonian abolitionists—two groups which influenced budding feminist thought profoundly—were suspicious of power and of its potential for corruption in human hands, where it could so easily work against God's designs. The power of the husband, the father, the slaveowner, the legislator, the judge—all were potentially abusive, or abusive by the fact of their existence, as intrusions between God and the individual.[3] For many Christians, morality remained sharply antithetical to concepts of power or human governance, an attitude which in many respects early woman's rights advocates shared.[4] Certainly in the 1850s the Christian ethos still shaped women's apprehension of power relationships, and of what kind of action they could most effectively undertake in the world.

Given the early woman's movement's understanding of power—apprehension over its direct exercise, fear and distrust of the institutions of government, seeing morality and official power as antithetical, belief in change worked from within rather than from without—it is difficult to interpret the demand for woman's rights strictly within the framework of secular liberal political theory. Most feminists were more pragmatic than the Garrisonians; they lacked the wild, intense piety which prepared that group to renounce all human organizations on the spot, including their own, in favor of some form of mutual self-government which their faith had not yet revealed. Still, a strain of anti-institutionalism was strong within feminism in the antebellum years. Women repeatedly resolved to "rely no longer on organizations of any kind—upon neither national or state, secret or public societies of any description . . . but to depend upon . . . (our) own energetic, determined, and individual effort for . . . the final triumph of our glorious principles"—hardly the stuff of legal positivism.[5]

The majority of feminists believed that legal and political change—changes in statutes, court rulings, the common law, interpretations of women's political rights—were symptomatic, and could only reflect deeper change on the level of public opinion worked by individuals coming to a real understanding of natural laws. Even Stanton, certainly one of the best versed of the feminists in legal matters and a fiery advocate of political measures, opined that "Public sentiment is higher than laws—laws in advance of the people are mere chaff."[6] Most reformers

---

3. *See* Lewis Perry, Radical Abolitionism: Anarchy and the Government of God in Anti-Slavery Thought (1973), especially chapter 2.

4. One of the grievances in the original Declaration of Sentiments drawn up at Seneca Falls includes the claim, "He has usurped the prerogative of Jehovah himself, claiming it as his right to assign for her a sphere of action, when that belongs to her conscience and to her God." *See Report of the Woman's Rights Convention Held at Seneca Falls, New York, July 19th and 20th, 1848*" (1848; reprint, 1969) (hereafter cited as *Seneca Falls*), at 7.

5. Lily, vol. 3 no. 3, at 21 (March 1851).

6. Lily, vol. 1 no. 11, at 86 (Nov. 1849); *see also*, vol. 2 no. 1, at 4 (Jan. 1850). At one national convention, Abby Kelly Foster and Ernestine Rose came into direct conflict over the question of whether laws shape people, or only follow public opinion, as reported in *Proceedings of the Woman's Rights Convention Held at Cleveland, Ohio . . . October 5th, 6th, and 7th, 1853*" (1854) (hereafter cited as *Cleveland*), at 81-82. Foster urged strongly that law was a creature of public sentiment. Rose's counter-statement, and her stance within the movement, are fascinating. A Polish Jew who grew to intellectual maturity in the free-thinking circles of enlightened Europe, Rose was probably the only atheist among the early feminist leaders. Much closer to the secular, European tradition which

believed that reeducation of the moral sentiments was the way to bring public opinion around, and that old laws could not withstand new leanings: "The ballot box is not worth a straw, until woman is ready to use it . . . The moment that woman is ready to go to the ballot box, there is not a constitution that will stand in the country."[7] Far from looking to government for remedies and favors, there was a strong emphasis on self-help and a belief that, by readying themselves and their neighbors, activists could bring about the desired transformation without seeking direct political change or soliciting governmental intervention.[8] Women strove, not for new laws to reshape public life, but to promote moral sentiments and their adoption by the whole community. Majoritarian democracy was not the standard of judgment here. The appeal was rather to communal consensus, to the "honest judgment of every member of the community," and to that community's right to formulate and prosecute its own laws according to its own communal mores, and so defend itself from harm.[9] Women judged progress, not by citizens' begrudging acceptance of a law eked out through determined assaults on the legislature, but by a re-orientation of each individual conscience toward God, and a consequent righting of public opinion.

This vision is at odds with the positivist view of law and government which plays an important part in our conceptualization of rights. Rights consciousness today implies at least a mediating state power to protect against encroachment, and usually looks to human government or a constitution as the source and guarantor of rights. Between 1848 and 1860, however, positive or positivist attitudes were not a major feature of women's legal repertoire, which held only a nascent recognition of the law's transformative potential. For the many who believed that divine and natural laws ruled the world in intimate detail, human legislation loomed small. Stanton spoke for many when she said admiringly of the New York abolitionist Gerrit Smith that he went to the Bible for his policies, and to Christ for his social, moral, and political creed, "over the heads of Popes, Cardinals and Bishops, Judges, Jurists . . . writers on law and jurisprudence . . . (and) over all laws, common and uncommon, codified and uncodified"—a fairly comprehensive listing.[10] The determined belief in law as a constitutive or transformative force grew as women became politicized and moved outward from the revival-style convention to engagement with

---

produced feminists like Mary Wollstonecraft and Frances Wright, Rose alone consistently denied any connection between rights and duties or any particular feminine qualifications for the franchise. She had the earliest and most emphatic vision of law as a strong, positive force in shaping human thinking and behavior. On the differences between European and American feminism *see* Alice Rossi, The Feminist Papers (1974), part 2.

7. *Cleveland, supra* n.6, at 168.

8. Speech of Abby Kelly Foster in *Woman's Rights Commensurate with Her Capacities and Obligations: A Series of Tracts* (1853).

9. Lily, vol. 3 no. 3, at 21 (March 1851); vol. 1 no. 1, at 4 (January 1849); vol. 2 no. 1, at 5 (January 1850); vol. 1 no. 8, at 62 (August 1849).

10. Lily, vol. 4 no. 5, at 39-40 (May 1852).

state and national legislatures. But in the early years, the shared wisdom was that law was a creature of public sentiment, and any legal revision which did not derive from an underlying shift in the common mindset had a futile career ahead of it.

For most, a budding hope that law would provide them redress or protection was seriously compromised by the belief that the vision of law as external authority instead of as self-government *constituted* the problem, and that genuine reform would entail the erosion of government which sought to coerce human behavior. Feminists identified human law with the "might makes right" fallacy, as Hannah Tracy Cutler suggested in a letter to the *Una* in 1853.

> Laws, among men, have been for the most part either the enactments of despots who have swayed by the physical force they commanded, or else the concessions which despots have reluctantly yielded to the counterbalancing physical force of their unwilling subjects. Hence it has been the exponent of what force would yield to force, rather than the free expression of the moral sentiments of a people . . . the old physical force law . . . still keeps women from an equal participation in its primary relations, even after the evangel of equal human rights has been proclaimed.[11]

Women viewed the evolution of society as entailing the ascendence of moral and mental over physical might, and the consequent withering away of the state as an instrument of control. Divorced from law and legal processes as they were, and with their understanding of the corrupt nature of humanly held power, antebellum feminists were not simply seeking inclusion in the revolutionary settlement, or in the system as it stood. When it came to law and governance, their attitude is best expressed by the text they so frequently quoted—"Behold, I make all things new."

The Problem of Difference

The idea of a distinctive woman's politics or legal culture has not received much play in the scholarship. For some women's historians, the glory of the woman's suffrage movement lies in the assertion of equality, and in the "philosophical tenet that women were essentially human and only incidentally female" which helped women activists break down a sexual differentiation that was tantamount to inferiority and confinement.[12] For many contemporary feminists the acknowledgement of assertion of difference, then or now, is deeply illiberal. They can conceive of women having full rights only in a system which treats men and women as

11. Una, vol. 1 no. 1, at 14 (Feb. 1853). For biographical information about particular feminists mentioned here *see* James, Edward T.; James, Janet Wilson; and Boyer, Paul S., eds., Notable American Women, 1607-1950: A Biographical Dictionary (3 vols., 1971).

12. DuBois, Feminism and Suffrage, *supra* n.2, at 36.

strictly fungible civil and legal personalities. Ellen DuBois has raised the quest for suffrage and the claim of equality as the standard for the nineteenth-century woman's movement as a whole, and classifies anything else as a type of "domestic feminism," an inferior variety which mounted no challenge to the male hierarchy.

Surely the claim to the vote was eye-openingly radical. But this rather simplistic assessment of the themes of equality and difference as they came into play in the movement requires dismissing a large part of what women said about their own campaign and about themselves. Many who agreed that they were "essentially human" did not consider themselves to be "only incidentally female," and entertained strong beliefs in equality, difference, and a womanly mission, simultaneously.[13]

The claim of equality between men and women, a staple of woman's rights rhetoric, contradicted deeply entrenched social thought on gender roles. Rarely has a society postulated such elemental differences between men and women as mid-nineteenth century American society did. Feminists' assertion that women had the same souls, same moral duties, same intellects and hopes as men opened the way to a more fully integrated public sphere than was ever possible before: we are still dining out on the capital of that ideal. The assertion of equality was a protest lodged against discrimination in both law and custom, against whatever rules or attitudes restrained women's natural energies or kept them in a dwarfed or crippled state. Women believed that, "possessing common natures, common rights, and a common destiny, society can never be harmoniously organized until the individuality and equality of each one is practically recognized."[14]

Equality was an ideal with political consequences, and feminists used it in an attempt to break down formal structures of restraint. In the early years they envisioned legal equality entailing the abolition of all laws which weighed disproportionately on women. After that, women's unobstructed energy would surely bring them into full parity. But while the ideal of equality held great meaning for women, it did not eradicate their understanding of their social and familial roles and their larger interests as being distinct from men's. In twentieth century society, where civil equality is held up as the highest stage of the citizen's development, justice is blind to individual characteristics, and the fungibility of the bearers is the measure of rights. This kind of equality—ignorant of gender, race, role, duty, station—was initially incomprehensible to most feminists. Instead, they argued in the name of equality for rights that would allow

13. Blanche Glassman Hersh says of Stanton, Susan B. Anthony, and Lucy Stone, "All three combined a belief in woman's special moral and domestic responsibilities with a vision of her obligations in the broader world." The Slavery of Sex: Feminist-Abolitionists in America (1978), at 80.

14. Lily, vol. 2 no. 10, at 73 (Oct. 1850); *see also*, vol. 3 no. 5, at 36 (May 1851); and *Proceedings of the Woman's Rights Convention Held at Syracuse, Sept. 8th, 9th, and 10th, 1852* (1852) (hereafter cited as *Syracuse*), at 31.

each to fulfill her role and attain her highest individual destiny decreed by God, whatever it might be. An important degree of difference was built into this idea of equality, which did not "mean either identity or likeness . . . of the two sexes, but equivalence of dignity, necessity, and use; admitting all differences and modifications which shall not affect a just claim to equal liberty in development and action."[15]

The apprehension of their own special interests and duties which imbued women's politics in the 1850s did create some friction in the elaboration of women's political empowerment. The popular cultural idealization of woman's superhuman goodness, her angelic nature, raised the hackles of those who suspected men of packing women off to heaven prematurely to limit their influence on earth. Feminists rejected the idea that they were "fine porcelain" to be laid on the shelf, and insisted on their right to "mingle with the rude stone jugs, mugs, and platters of humanized crockery."[16] One writer even ventured the opinion that, far from moral superiority, woman's goodness resulted from a lack of opportunity, and that when they had money and power they would become competent swindlers and bribe-takers like everyone else.[17]

But although they were prickly and resistant to what they considered demeaning characterizations on the part of men, women reformers had their own ideas of their goodness and what role it would play in a reformed society. It would have been extraordinary if they hadn't. Revivalism, liberal Protestantism, romanticism, reform—all tended toward an identification of femininity with morality, spirituality, and self awareness as a potent political force capable of containing the male tyranny of corruption and greed. Women may have claimed that they were equal to men, but not that they were like; and likeness could not be established by assertion, but only by a different kind of living together, a recognition of "mutual dependence, and separate fountains of reciprocal life."[18]

The utopian dream was the eventual blending of natures, so that "there will be but one code of morals, and of taste. Women will acquire the energy and self reliance of man, and man will emulate the purity and religious sincerity of woman."[19] In their vision of a "better Eden," men and women would grow more alike over time, taking on each other's qualities, thereby eradicating the oppressive imbalance which deformed contemporary government, and making communal self-government a reality.[20] The result would mean narrowing the gap between men and

---

15. Paulina Wright Davis, *On the Education of Females*, tract no. 3 in *Woman's Rights Commensurate with Her Capacities and Obligations, supra* n.8.

16. Lily, vol. 3 no. 6, at 46 (June 1851).

17. Una, vol. 1 no. 5, at 72 (June 1853); *see also, Una*, vol. 1 no. 1, at 11 (Feb. 1853); vol. 1 no. 4, at 72-73 (May 1853); Lily vol. 3, no. 6, at 46 (June 1851).

18. *Syracuse, supra* n.14, at 60.

19. *Cleveland, supra* n.6, at 52; *see also* Elizabeth Oakes Smith, Woman and Her Needs (1851; reprint, 1974), *passim*.

20. Hersh, *supra* n.13, at 139, suggests that the conception of interdependence is a tenet of Universalism.

women, allowing their like moral natures to eradicate the harmful differences of temperament and culture. Women often quoted a stanza of Tennyson to that effect: "The woman's cause is *man's*: they rise or sink/ Together, dwarfed or god-like, bond or free./ . . . The woman is not underdeveloped man/But diverse./Yet in the long years, *liker* they must grow;/The man be more or woman, she of man . . . ."[21]

Pleasant as this idyll was, in envisioning a political future women saw themselves endowing men with their own traits far more often than they saw themselves taking on the traits of men. In the years before the Civil War, woman's rights activists were inspired by a sense of equality; but they were also motivated by a discontent with the existing order which fell out along gender lines, and emphasized the differences, both natural and cultural, between the sexes. When arguments for women's rights came largely from abolitionism, equality was a natural focus. But as women, unlike slaves, developed their own well articulated positions, they began to enumerate their grievances with male management.[22] The belief in woman's moral mission to clean up politics and society was not interjected into the woman's movement by the entrance of the Woman's Christian Temperance Union into the suffrage movement in the late 1870s and the 1880s, as Ellen DuBois has suggested.[23] Rather, it was a position to which many women openly or tacitly adhered from the movement's beginnings. Difference was both the agent of change in this scheme, and the problem to be overcome. Woman's rights workers expected the integration of masculine and feminine to bring particularly beneficial results in the public realm, often picturing themselves in the role of redeemer, as when a correspondent to the national convention in Cleveland suggested that "the eye of the law is diseased, and women must . . . make that eye pure and single sighted."[24] Even the egalitarian Stanton recommended the "feminine element in humanity" to "save man from the bondage of his animal nature—the slavery of his own low appetites."[25] Women had little doubt that they would perform the duties of office better than men, firmly opposing poverty, intemperance, and their social roots, and promoting "all just and beneficent purposes."[26]

---

21. *Report of the Woman's Rights Meeting at Mercantile Hall, May 27, 1859* (1859) (hereafter cited as *Boston*), at 9.

22. Barbara L. Epstein, in The Politics of Domesticity: Women, Evangelism, and Temperance in Nineteenth-Century America (1981), sees women's religious culture as a vehicle for antagonism between the sexes, picturing religion more as a tool to express generalized gender antagonism than as a system of belief which interpreted and fostered political change.

23. DuBois, *The Radicalism of Woman Suffrage, supra* n.2, at 68-69.

24. *Cleveland, supra* n.6, at 8.

25. In *The Pleasures of Age: An Address Delivered by Elizabeth Cady Stanton on Her Seventieth Birthday* (1885); *see also*, Lily, vol. 4 no. 5, at 40 (May 1850); vol. 2 no. 4, at 29 (April 1850).

26. *Cleveland, supra* n.6, at 30; *see also, Cleveland*, at 91; *Syracuse, supra* n.14, at 63.

Nor does the movement's moral consciousness necessarily suggest that it was politically immature, insular, or domestic in its focus. If anything, it suggests broader concerns, a fuller life within the reform community, than was true of suffragism after the war, when narrower legal and political concerns took precedence. Many of the pacific dicates of liberal Christianity—"feminine submissiveness"—were known in another guise as politically oppositional stands taken by reformers convinced that problems like slavery and territorial aggression would diminish under their rule.[27] Calls to non-violence and reason in place of force were grounded in a Christian tradition, but served in the antebellum years as a potent charge against the government which perpetrated such crimes. By adding the feminine to the masculine element, women were rejecting the political sphere men were carving out for themselves, one seemingly cut loose from the constraints of traditional moral principles of governance. The absence of either element would bring "results fatal both to justice and morality. The civil and political departments are fair illustrations of these results."[28] Above all, women manifested a wish to substitute the principles of noncoercion, nonviolence, and consensual government for the Hobbesian arrangements of the day.

> Politics and statesmanship, still resting so much upon the force of armament, must come under the jurisdiction of simple justice, give up the employment of physical force, and rise to a sphere of mind and feeling fit for woman's administration . . . the policy of government, now so intricate, so dark a contexture of fraud and force that the worst men are its best ministers, will be redeemed and reformed, so that the acknowledged excellence of feminine morality and woman's directness and clearness of intellect, will be the highest qualification for national government.[29]

Women activists vigorously disputed their critics' charges that they were being unsexed through their political activities, and affirmed their own femininity and security in their roles as wives and mothers. No one rebutted those charges more effectively than Frances Gage when she complained, "They (men) cannot get up a picture of a woman's rights meeting . . . but they must put cigars and pipes in our mouths, make us sit cross-legged, or hoist our feet above their legitimate positions—making us behave as nearly as possible as disgustingly and unbecomingly as themselves . . . . They have . . . so long associated their vulgar thoughts and feelings with constitutional rights and privileges, that they seem to think them inseparable . . . ."[30] Gage in her pithy way put her finger on a thread which runs consistently through women's concerns in this period—resentment and dislike of male political culture, from which women

27. Una, vol. 1 no. 3, at 37, 41 (April 1853); *Cleveland, supra* n.6, at 92.

28. *Syracuse, supra* n.14, at 22; *see also, Proceedings of the Seventh National Woman's Rights Convention Held in New York City . . . Nov. 25th & 26th, 1856* (1856) (hereafter cited as *New York*), at 23.

29. Una, vol. 1 no. 3, at 41 (April 1853).

30. Lily, vol. 4 no. 2, at 14 (Feb. 1852).

were so excluded. Stanton, in a letter to the Syracuse Convention, castigates men who, "having separated themselves from women, in the business of like, and thus made their natures coarse by contact with their own sex exclusively, now demand separate pleasures too; and in lieu of the cheerful family circle . . . they congregate in clubs to discuss politics, to gamble, drink, etc. . . ."[31] Stanton often spoke of a lyceum lecture she longed to write on "The Antagonism of the Sexes."[32] Male opponents of the woman's franchise often argued that polling places were too rough for women; feminists deplored this self-confessed pollution of civic functions, finding man in his role as political animal repugnant, whether as lawyer, judge, voter, or clubman.[33]

This attitude translated into often made claims that male legislators could not represent women adequately, not because they would not, but because the difference in their natures and interests meant that men were not capable of such representation. Ernestine Rose argued cleverly that, if man's nature was different, he could not understand woman's needs sufficiently to make laws for her; and if the same, there was no reason to exclude women from full political participation.[34] Cool argumentation aside, even Stanton clearly felt the outrage and slight when she asked, "Shall the most sacred relations of life be called up and rudely scanned by men who, by their own admission, are so coarse that women cannot meet them even at the polls without contamination? . . . How can man enter into the feelings of. . . . (a) mother? Shall laws which come from the logical brains of man take cognizance of the violence done to the moral and affectional natures which predominate, as it is said, in woman?"[35]

Antoinette Brown Blackwell tended toward essentialist rather than cultural explanations of men's and women's differences, but her conclusion was the same: "The law is wholly masculine: it is created by our type or class of man nature. The framers of all legal compacts are thus restricted to the . . . thoughts, feelings, biases of men . . . we can be represented only by our peers."[36] The insult of being bound by masculine law was compounded by "the shamefulness of trying intelligent, educated, well-bred native born American women by juries of men made up of the riffraff from the monarchies of the old world."[37] Women were sure that if they served on juries they would be very lenient with woman defendants,

31. *Syracuse, supra* n.14, at 32; *see also, Cleveland, supra* n.6, at 38.

32. Lily, vol. 3 no. 11, at 82 (Nov. 1851); *see also*, letters of Sept. 1, 1877, *and* Dec. 15, 1886, Stanton papers, Douglass College Library, Rutgers University.

33. *Syracuse, supra* n.14, at 73.

34. *Cleveland, supra* n.6, at 36; *see also,* Lily, vol. 2 no. 5, at 38 (May 1850).

35. Elizabeth Cady Stanton, *Address to the Legislature of New York, Adopted by the State Woman's Rights Convention, Held at Albany . . . Feb. 14 and 15, 1854* (1854), at 7.

36. *Syracuse, supra* n.14, at 20-21.

37. Stanton, letter to Susan B. Anthony and Matilda Joslyn Gage, 1873, in the Stanton Papers, Douglass College Library, Rutgers University. *See also*, Lily, vol. 2 no. 5, at 38 (May 1850).

perhaps under the tutelage of woman lawyers who would either suggest more liberal interpretations of the law, or a whole new code of laws to replace those that currently disgraced the statute books.[38]

It was this dangerous isolation of the masculine from the feminine which feminists hoped to remedy, feeling that "so long as woman is required to take care of the morals of the community and men to take charge of the politics, having . . . separate interests in these two great matters, we shall have a strange and incongruous state of things."[39] Traditional networks of women's influence—local, personal, religious networks which operated through churches, voluntary organizations, and familial contacts—had been strong in pre-industrial America. Through these networks women had wielded social influence disproportionate to their formal standing. But the growing cult of electoral politics—male politics—and the shifting of power away from the local to more centralized levels, undermined women's leverage in the community.[40] The early feminist agenda is remarkable, not because it tried to vault women from the private into the public arena leaving the wall intact, as scholars have suggested, but because it sought to eradicate spheres entirely, and with them the growing and dangerous split between public governance and private morality. Such a distinction made little sense to women reformers. Rather, through the interdependence of the sexes they hoped to integrate public with private, legal with moral, in a common standard of universal governance. Women's denigration of male political life for its insularity and its brutishness betrays both resentment and understanding of the dangers which the isolation of politics posed for women, a politics conducted outside their scope of influence.

Law, Nature, and Rights

Feminism also evolved an articulate critique of the exclusive legal world, criticism informed by moral and religious concerns. Distaste for the profession of lawyering was rife in larger reform circles, as well; the Boston reformer Thomas Wentworth Higginson reported in *Cheerful Yesterdays* that, under the influence of "the Newness," there was a "wave of that desire for a freer and more ideal life which made (William Wetmore) Story turn aside from his father's profession to sculpture, and made (James Russell) Lowell forsake law after his first client." Higginson himself abdicated a legal course, emboldened by friends who characterized

38. Una, vol. 1 no. 4, at 63 (May 1853); *Syracuse, supra* n.14, at 77.

39. Una, vol. 1 no. 1, at 14 (Feb. 1853).

40. On this general topic, *see* Judith Wellman, *Women and Radical Reform in Upstate New York: A Profile of Grassroots Female Abolitionists*, in Clio Was a Woman: Studies in the History of American Women, ed. Mabel E. Deutrich and Virginia C. Purdy (1980); Nancy Hewitt, Women's Activism and Social Change: Rochester, New York, 1822-1872 (1984); and Paula Baker, *The Domestication of Politics: Women and American Political Society, 1780-1920*, American Historical Review, vol. 89 no. 3 (1984), at 620-647.

law as a "system of formalized injustice" and a branch of "knowledge that cannot be carried into any other stage of existence."[41] "The Newness" did not bring women the immediate privilege of renouncing a career in law in favor of one in sculpture. In fact, it was often urged at conventions and in periodicals that women take up the profession, both to protect their own interests and to reform the field. At the same time, the legal system came in for a constant barrage of criticism from feminists who occasionally took gratuitous swipes at other professions, but reserved their most biting criticisms for clerics and lawyers.

The *Lily*, in particular, hosted a string of female correspondents with a distinctly gender-based legal critique, an editorial policy which drew fire from some.[42] Indeed, at times it seems in reading the *Lily* that each of its 6,000 subscribers had contributed her mite against the "chicken hearted ministers of justice."[43] As in most law reform movements, corruption was often alleged against lawmakers, but it was corruption of a particular kind. Bribery was occasionally charged in the *Lily*, and the economic interests of legislators involved in the sale or manufacture of liquor was seen as creating conflict of interest problems.[44] More often, though, women depicted lawyers and judges as morally and spiritually corrupt, "winebibbers" with "bullet heads and red faces," "vulgar, rum-drinking . . . tobacco chewing men, thick lipped voluptuaries, gourmands and licentiates who disgrace our national councils with their grossness and profanity . . . who, instead of sound reason and strong argument, resort to fisticuffs and . . . duelling."[45] As they did with the church, women reformers castigated law as a human corruption of a divine institution. Law, however, represented a particularly egregious instance of *male* corruption. The drinking, swearing legislator who would rather resort to brute force than logic and reason was pictured as a throwback to a less advanced stage of civilization, and as the opposite of the "Christian Gentleman" who was many reformers' and evangelicals' manly ideal.[46] Wily, dissolute lawyers figured prominently in short pieces of fiction which also filled the pages of women's papers. Readers could hardly fail to see the moral in stories like that about the wife of a "half-educated Attorney at Law, a thorough-bred contemnor of the laws of God," who brings his family to an unhappy and impoverished end.[47]

Women revealed the level of frustration and outrage they felt with male legislators in many ways, proclaiming "let man cease to persuade

---

41. Thomas Wentworth Higginson, Cheerful Yesterdays (1899; reprint, 1968), at 78, 87.

42. D.C. Bloomer, Life and Writings of Amelia Bloomer (1895; reprint, 1975), at 155.

43. Lily, vol. 1 no. 7, at 55 (July 1849).

44. Lily, vol. 3 no. 4, at 29 (April 1851).

45. Lily, vol. 4 no. 5, at 39 (May 1852); *see also*, vol. 2 no. 2, at 13 (Feb. 1850).

46. *See* Charles E. Rosenberg, *Sexuality, Class, and Role in Nineteenth-Century America*, American Quarterly, vol. 25 no. 2, at 131-153 (1973).

47. Lily, vol. 2 no. 6, at 44 (June 1850).

woman by his sophistry and logic, or compel her by his cruel and unnatural statutes to act in violation of her will and conscience . . . ."[48] Law had placed women in an intolerable position and created a catch-22 of tragic proportions by refusing the legal right of divorce, while refusing at the same time legal protection of maternal rights, property, and earnings for wives of drunkards and insolvents; "woman cannot obey nature's first law of self-preservation without violating man's (laws)," a fact which inspired "indignation and hatred of our laws and law-makers."[49] Elizabeth Cady Stanton was fond of saying that law gave women such protection as "the wolf the lamb, or the eagle the dove."[50]

At least on paper, the *Lily* encouraged women in acts of self-help like the burning or trashing of their husbands' haunts, and congratulated one unusual woman on horsewhipping the barkeeper, citing it as a justifiable act of self-defense.[51] Abolitionists' manifestoes on human rights and natural law had laid a strong groundwork for a critique of human laws like those enabling slavery and rumselling as counter to the laws of God and Nature.[52] The *Lily's* correspondents boldly and repeatedly urged women to ignore the law's shabby cloak of legitimacy, and act according to higher right: "Resistance to tyranny is obedience to God . . . if the vampyres of the law will continue to suck the life blood of their fellow men and spread destruction and death all around them, then let women step boldly forward and take matters into their own hands."[53] The question of damage to taverns was dismissed with the argument that a tavern "ceases to be property when it is employed to destroy the people."[54]

Again, in the antebellum years women were brought to this pitch not as much by high-minded notions of equality as by a vivid apprehension of their wrongs. Here the problem of alcohol took on great significance. In licensing the liquor trade legislators were acting, not just to withhold rights, but to commit clear wrongs, with grave consequences for women. Woman's righters were uniformly temperance advocates as well, and felt that it was in permitting the sale of alcohol that government truly showed itself to be morally deformed. They castigated the rumseller, and begged him to "stop your unholy work. Tell us not that you have a license, and certificate of good moral character (from the legislature) to justify your deeds . . . . What will your license avail you against the curse of your

48. Lily, vol. 4 no. 7, at 58 (June 1852).

49. Lily, vol. 1 no. 6, at 46 (June 1849); vol. 2 no. 2, at 13, 15 (Feb. 1850).

50. Lily, vol. 2 no. 10, at 73 (Oct. 1850).

51. Lily, vol. 4 no. 9, at 77 (Sept. 1852); vol. 1 no. 8, at 61-62 (July 1849).

52. *For example*, William Hosmer, The Higher Law in Its Relations to Civil Government (1852; reprint, 1969); and Elisha P. Hurlbut, Essays on Human Rights and Their Political Guarantees (1845). Feminists reproduced such arguments about the inefficacy of human laws against divine ones; *see* Lily, vol. 2 no. 4, at 30 (April 1850).

53. Lily, vol. 4 no. 9, at 77-78 (Sept. 1852).

54. Lily, vol. 4 no. 7, at 59 (July 1852).

God? Is man greater than his maker? Shall he set the laws of the Almighty at defiance? Your license cannot shield you from guilt."[55]

Far guiltier than the rumseller, though, was the law, which "threw its arms around him who was causing the ruin . . . (with) *legalized* poison."[56] The pages of the *Lily* in these years entertained a lively debate over the comparative guilt of the legislator and the rumseller, who is described as the lawmaker's "agent"—a word used here with satanic rather than corporate overtones. For the misguided agent, some women initially entertained fond hope of reform—"Much rather would we take you by the hand, and greet you as friends and brothers, in the great cause of humanity."[57] But legislators received no quarter. In the best Protestant tradition the humble were guilty, but the "people . . . of wealth and standing in society" were guiltier still.[58] Women agitated for the repeal of licensing laws, not because they believed that *any* law could make the sale of liquor legal—it could not—but because removing that shield would publicly brand liquor traders for what they were, "immoral law breakers and law defyers."[59] Many of these writers felt that they should "challenge our legislators to an account of their stewardship," and they looked forward, not with sorrow, to the day when legislators must appear "at a greater tribunal . . . where they must answer for many crimes committed, for much blood shed, and for many lives destroyed."[60]

Women reformers in this period judged what they perceived as male law by a higher standard, and found it wanting. They could see little difference between "the guilt of killing a man by arsenic or alcohol, or between stealing his property by first stealing his reason, or breaking into his house at midnight, and carrying it off when the owner is in peaceful slumber." As one woman declared, "God did not say, 'Thou shalt not kill with a pistol.' "[61] In the one case, the law would punish the slayer; in the other it protected him, at the expense of the wives and children of drunkards. A great deal of time and energy went into redefining crimes, and comparing various statutory crimes to those of the rumseller. Was the highwayman who pulled the trigger guiltier than the one who held the horses? Were either more guilty than the man who sold drink to an alcoholic?[62]

A deeply Christian conception of moral consequences underlay this assessment of man's law. Women saw that with liquor, legislators were concerned, not with preventing or punishing wrong, but with limiting lia-

---

55. Lily, vol. 1 no. 1, at 5 (Jan. 1849).
56. Lily, vol. 1 no. 7, at 61 (July 1849).
57. Lily, vol. 1 no. 1, at 5 (Jan. 1849); vol. 2 no. 1, at 4 (Jan. 1850).
58. Lily, vol. 1 no. 2, at 14 (Feb. 1849).
59. Lily, vol. 2 no. 6, at 45 (June 1850).
60. *Syracuse, supra* n.14, at 17; Lily, vol. 1 no. 9, at 70 (Sept. 1849).
61. Lily, vol. 2 no. 6, at 45 (June 1850); vol. 1 no. 11, at 85 (Nov. 1849).
62. Lily, vol. 2 no. 2, at 15 (Feb. 1850); vol. 1 no. 5, at 37-38 (May 1849); vol. 2 no. 6, at 45 (June 1850).

bility. They felt strongly that legal doctrines of causation and the treatment of the liquor trade as an issue of economic regulation only obscured the nature of the transaction. Moral consequences could not be rightly limited by legal doctrine. "We touch not a wire but vibrates in eternity . . . we see not in this life the end of human actions. The influence reverberates."[63] This was as true for evil as for good, and for the *Lily's* writers it was impossible not to see the misfortunes of many homeless, abused, hungry women and children pouring straight from the rumseller's bottle in a chain of accountability which no legal sanction could interrupt. For "sin perpetuates itself forever. Like the ocean ripple, its influence is beyond all calculation . . . ." No amount of legal hair-splitting could excuse men from their Christian duty, nor protect them on the day when "God will call upon them to answer, 'WHERE IS THY BROTHER?' "[64]

This sense of woman's wrongs at the hands of the intemperate was extremely fertile ground for rights consciousness, as women felt an increasing duty to protect themselves, each other, and their children from man's depredations on their persons and property. Those who invoke "rights" usually endow them with transcendental qualities, but "rights" itself is not an ahistorical concept with constant meaning over time. Rather, it denotes a set of values or demands used in a particular political context which gives them meaning. Antebellum feminists seized the language of rights and transformed it with their own ideas and concerns. This does not mean that women rejected the republican ideals of the founding generation. Revolutionary rhetoric, the enlightenment vision of inalienable human rights, was a critical tool in helping women to envision a new status, and express their demands to a male public. But the language women spoke among themselves appealed to a larger sensibility.

A telling instance of this discrepancy occurred at a woman's rights meeting in Ohio which was held in 1850 for the purpose of influencing the work of that state's upcoming constitutional convention. The official "Memorial" written to be presented to the convention began, "(W)e believe the whole theory of the common law in relation to woman is unjust and degrading, tending to reduce her to a level with the slave, depriving her of political existence, and forming a positive exception to the great doctrine of equality as set forth in the Declaration of Independence." Citing the need for freedom and equality, for protection of maternal interests and property rights by the government, it is a businesslike appeal to republican sentiments, in which each mention of rights is specifically qualified as "political and legal"—protection of property, custodial privileges, and the vote. The "Memorial" contains no broad enumeration of personal or economic entitlements, and is devoid of any hint of rights as divinely derived, or any religious language.

By contrast, the corresponding "Address to the Women of Ohio"

---

63. Lily, vol. 1 no. 2, at 15 (Feb. 1849).
64. Lily, vol. 2 no. 7, at 51 (July 1850); vol. 1 no. 11, at 86 (Nov. 1849).

passed by the convention on the same issue opens with the sweeping assertion that "How the people be made wiser, better, and happier is one of the grand inquiries of the present age."[65] The "Address" exalts the role of God above that of the legislature in the creation and definition of rights. Dismissing the "cold sympathy and tardy efforts" of the "dough-faced serviles" in the legislature, the address is a paean to the "Rights of Humanity . . . . What is their design? How do we know them? They are of God . . . their design is happiness." In the "Memorial" woman's entitlement is predicated on "the great doctrine of Equality as set forth in the Declaration of Independence," without elaboration. In the "Address" by contrast a broad range of rights are cast as directly contingent on the dis charge of responsibilities, enabling individuals to "attain the end to which God the Father gave them existence." Ohio feminists urged women to seek not just political rights but education and occupation as well—"The full exercise of the heavenly graces . . . ." The fact that the business of women's rights was carried out in two distinct languages signifies that women themselves identified their values and politics as in some way separate from men's.

This adjustment of language to audience crops up repeatedly, and illustrates women's complex relationship to the American rights tradition. Early documents addressed to legislators predictably plead in a secular language of rights based on equality and the revolutionary settlement, commonly citing principles like "no taxation without representation." Female lobbyists occasionally invoked their duties as mothers in favor of their cause, but by and large their arguments were couched in the familiar phrases of the revolutionary settlement. Women's writing to women proved a far richer admixture, not limited to claims for political and legal rights, but seeking a range of economic, domestic and personal entitlements and opportunities. Religious language and imagery permeates their discourse, while arguments from liberal theology undergird their vision of total reform.

Feminists stood both within and without the republican tradition. While genuine in their appeal to the revolutionary heritage, there was also a strong strategic element in their choice of words. As opponents of despotism, arbitrary power, orthodoxy and hierarchy in church and state, they honored the Founders and valued dearly the philosophy which had so effectively countered those evils. But the revolutionary settlement was incomplete and had unjustly excluded both women and slaves. Further, mid-century reformers constituted a political opposition, and remained highly skeptical that the current crop of statesmen and legislators possessed the requisite virtue to pursue the goal of liberty in their own policies.[66] Using the unadorned language of legal and political rights, femi-

65. Both of these documents are to be found in the History of Woman Suffrage, ed. Elizabeth Cady Stanton, Susan B. Anthony, and Matilda Joslyn Gage, vol. 1 (1881), at 105-110.

66. Stanton illustrates this attitude in a letter to Anthony of July 4, 1858 (Stanton

nists were appealing to a critical common tradition, in the language—meaningful both to themselves and within larger political circles—they thought would best make their case. At the same time, their appeal was not to the actual creations of the Founding Fathers, but to a normative ideal of natural rights to which feminists gave unique definition. Most women themselves seemed more at home with the spiritualized discourse which is the argot of private letters and diaries as well as women's newspapers and public proceedings.[67]

For the ideology of woman's rights, unlike revolutionary rhetoric, was shaped in the fervor of millennial perfectionism. On closer scrutiny both the form and content of rights theories employed by feminists differed markedly from the traditional strain of republican rhetoric. Rights for women were definitely not conceived in the cool, secular dispassion of American constitutionalism. The end of the eighteenth century represented a low point in religious fervor and activity of all kinds: church attendance dropped precipitously; except in the West there was little by way of organized religious movement; and in the love feast of toleration which attended the church-state settlement, religious concerns receded formally and informally as a predominant force in the establishment of a public order. This tepid public piety did not fuel a fervent, God-centered view of natural law or natural rights. By the early federal period, natural rights was a concept which statesmen sought to contain, because of its volatile and potentially explosive reach. The exuberant rights language of early political documents was toned down, and the enumeration of precise and specific entitlements replaced the sweeping claims of the earlier period.[68]

Feminists did not tread in this cautious path.[69] In common with laborers, abolitionists, and other dissident groups, women sought to reopen the great constitutional questions of inclusion and entitlement, wielding a theory of natural rights which went well beyond the meager portion alloted in the state constitutions. The onset of the first woman's movement came after the Second Great Awakening had stirred the country to new

---

Papers, Douglass College Library, Rutgers University). In it she defends some men as admirable against a friend's attack on the sex. "But alas! when we read the views of average men, their laws, their Bibles, . . . when we listen to their everyday talk, to their decisions in the Courtroom, and to their sermons in the pulpit . . . then we feel that they richly deserve all that she says." *See also*, Lily vol. 2 no. 2, at 13 (Feb. 1850).

67. Some leaders of the antebellum feminist movement, political sophisticates like Stanton and Anthony, subscribed to a spiritualized view of the scope of rights and the nature of social change, but needed no direct religious sanction for political action. Writings in the Lily suggest that perhaps they and others also used religious arguments strategically as those most likely to move their audience of female political uninitiates.

68. Daniel T. Rodgers, Nation of Words (forthcoming, 1987), chap. 2; and Benjamin Wright, American Interpretations of Natural Law (1931), at 179.

69. On the general question of feminists' use of natural rights theory, *see* Hurlbut, *supra* n.52, chap. 8; Kraditor, *supra* n.1, chaps. 3 and 4; Wright, *supra* n.68, at 176-179; and T.V. Smith, The American Philosophy of Equality (1927), chap. 3.

heights of millennial passion and transformed the public's understanding of social change. Nineteenth-century reformers did not share their forebears' utilitarian vision of power as something to be balanced and shared.[70] The emphasis on free will, the belief in the possibility of perfection and the newly benevolent designs of a well-disposed God—all worked to dispel the fear of unchecked liberty which dominated political debate in the constitution-making era. Women showed unbounded faith in the workings of an inner law: "emancipate from external bondage and the internal law written upon every heart makes itself audible."[71] Such protean concepts as natural law and natural rights were plastic in the hands of feminists, who followed traditional rhetorical forms with conviction while giving them new meaning.

One innovation lay in feminists' perception of the relation of rights to natural laws. A concept of ancient lineage repeatedly refashioned by thinkers both within and without the church, natural laws in the revolutionary era diminished in importance while natural rights theory grew explosively.[72] In America, natural rights became a largely secularized concept. Its proponents did not derive such rights from a divine source, but looked increasingly to human government and constitutional guarantees for their provenance, rendering a system of natural laws quaint and redundant.

Natural law regained its rule in the philosophy of the early woman's rights movement, where all rights were immediately derived from a divinely sanctioned order governed by the system of natural laws which was a pillar of reformers' faith. To claim human government as the source of rights was to confuse the cart and the horse—"It is God that gives our rights. *Government is the offspring of rights, not the parent.*"[73] Feminists, abolitionists, and other disaffected antebellum reformers frequently dismissed the Constitution as but another human law to be judged by God's standards.[74] Women saw rights as springing directly from the divinely ordained natural order, proclaiming that "the true rights of humanity are founded in the laws of nature, and consequently are natural rights."[75] Rights claims for antebellum feminists were not in the nature of strict bids for inclusion in a grant of powers and protections from human government. Rather, they expressed the terms on which individuals could best live out God's designs for human happiness. In the years before the Civil War the vote itself was repeatedly described by the valise theory of suffrage—as a way of obtaining the rights to domestic protection, prop-

70. Rodgers, *supra* n.68, chap. 2.

71. Elizabeth Oakes Smith, *supra* n.19, at 34.

72. Wright, *supra* n.68, at 173 ff.

73. *Proceedings of the Woman's Rights Convention Held at Akron, Ohio, May 28 and 29, 1851* (1851; reprint, 1973) (hereafter cited as *Akron*), at 41; *see also*, Hurlbut, *supra* n.52, at 27.

74. *See* Hosmer, *supra* n.52, at 46-47 and chap. 14; Hurlbut, *supra* n.52, at 33.

75. Lily, vol. 4 no. 2, at 11 (Feb. 1852).

erty, education, remunerative work, personal autonomy, and all the other entitlements which women so desired.[76] The specific rights women sought heralded not an alteration but a transformation of society.

"Nature" in early feminist thought became a powerful normative force, a measuring stick rather than a descriptive tool.[77] What was "natural"—and this was almost always defined by what contributed to the full realization of human potential—became the ideal state toward which to strive. At the same time, nature—spruced up into a civil order by the Founding Fathers—regained an earthiness in feminist thought rooted in the physical functions of life itself. For feminists and abolitionists both faced the problem of elaborating compelling grounds on which full rights should be extended to women and slaves—a difficult task since the constitutional guarantees of inalienability, freedom, and equality had produced such partial entitlement. Women's passionate arguments from moral equality partly filled the bill. But both women and slaves, suffering from a lack of education, were commonly stigmatized as mentally deficient and without the proper intellect or character to cultivate civic habits. In response to their opponents, reformers also fashioned arguments from the lowest common denominator of physical life—needs common to all. Abolitionist tracts elevated "the right to see, or to eat, or to walk" to stand beside life and liberty as "conditions of being. We have them from God when we have existence, and so long as existence remains those rights must remain, unless taken away by Him who gave them."[78] The pursuit of "happiness," always a somewhat vague component of revolutionary philosophy, took on a new specificity in claims to food, clothing, jobs, education—claims measured by needs and wants. "The Creator . . . has endowed man with certain innate desires, emotions, and faculties, the gratification and exercise of which are the means of his happiness. Here is the consummation of man's rights—the right to gratify his natural desires; to supply his natural wants; to exercise his natural functions, as the means of attaining happiness."[79]

Such abolitionist writing—particularly Elisha Hurlbut's treatise on human rights—proved very influential for feminists, who agreed that natural rights "emanated from the nature and wants and emotions of mankind."[80] Women and slaves did not know Latin, but they could know hunger, and from the capacity for hunger sprang the entitlement to food—"that is to say, physical existence acknowledges a higher law,

76. Una, vol. 1 no. 4, at 59 (May 1853).

77. *See* Wright, *supra* n.68, at 3, 176-179; T.V. Smith, *supra* n.69, at 106 ff.

78. Hosmer, *supra* n.52, at 46-47.

79. Hurlbut, *supra* n.52, at 16.

80. Lily, vol. 2 no. 10, at 73 (Oct. 1850); *see also*, vol. 4 no. 2, at 11 (Feb. 1852); and History of Woman Suffrage, *supra* n.65, at 112-113. *For references* to Hurlbut, *see* History of Woman Suffrage, *supra* n.65, at 38; Una, vol. 1 no. 4, at 59 (May 1853); Lily, vol. 4 no. 7, at 59 (July 1852); and *Cleveland, supra* n.6, at 57. The Lily also printed extracts from Hosmer's work, vol. 3 no. 5, at 35 (May 1851); and from Hurlbut's work, vol. 4 no. 9, at 80 (Sept. 1852).

whether we intellectually and morally acknowledge it or not."[81] It was this assertion of the essential, physical fact of humanity as granting status that was behind Sojourner Truth's cry, "Ain't I a woman?" And the right to provide for these wants was guaranteed by the God who created them, for it was a critical aspect of the new, benevolent deity that he would impart no hunger, no yearning, without granting a means of its satisfaction.[82] This concept of rights as following physical function ordained by natural laws is at odds with the idea of inalienable rights as settled during the struggle for independence. But it provided far greater scope for claims to economic and social justice than the revolutionary model, which effectively limited feminists to claims to political rights.

Feminists' conception of rights can perhaps best be contrasted with revolutionary republican tradition by comparing the terms "underlying" and "overarching." For the Founding Fathers, natural rights were pulled down from the sky, a set of external restraints to limit the actions of human government. In the early reform movement, by contrast, much of the focus of natural rights shifted to the internal. In a return to an older tradition, natural rights were seen as emanating from natural laws discovered, not in anterior principles like "no taxation without representation" and "one man one vote," but in the ordinary patterns of everyday life. Women did not look to outside sources or rules to control human behavior, but sought to bring human behavior into harmony with an inner working which comprehended material and spiritual forces alike.

The belief that God gave no need and no capacity which he did not mean to be fulfilled was expanded on by woman's rights advocates, and became what was probably the most common argument of that group before the war. Frequently the rationale for the dismantling of "woman's sphere" and taking up rights and duties in the wide world was put in functionalist terms, rather than in the language of inalienable human rights. Lucy Stone in one convention offered her own definition of "natural": "when God made the human soul and gave it certain capacities, he meant that those capacities should be exercised. The wing of the bird indicates its right to fly; and the fin of the fish the right to swim. So in human beings, the existence of a power presupposes the right to its use, subject to the law of benevolence."[83] It was this functionalism that lay behind the recounting of the stories of reknowned and competent women popular in speeches and tracts. What *had* been done indicated an ability, and where there was an ability lay a God-given right to use it. This argument, of course, had certain dangerous implications, apparent to a few who feared a standard of duty or performance as a prerequisite to grants of civil or political rights. But early feminists exuded confidence in their untested

81. Hosmer, *supra* n.52, at 20.

82. Elizabeth Oakes Smith, *supra* n.19, at 116-118; Hurlbut, *supra* n.52, at 13, 16.

83. *New York, supra* n.28, at 42. This sentiment was so strongly felt that it had already been adopted into the resolutions at the Syracuse National Woman's Rights Convention in 1852; *see Syracuse, supra* n.14, at 76, and at 46, 48, 83.

powers and relied heavily on this definition of natural rights to break down the artificial limitations of sphere. Frances Gage described how she lost her woman's sphere, piece by piece: a chunk fell off when she learned to plough and was ploughed under; another disappeared during a medical emergency, several more while doing her chores around the farm.[84] More than in an ideological commitment to political rights, women first perceived of rights as originating in the capacities and talents handed out by God, which it was their duty as well as their pleasure to use fully.

Initially, power and rights were conceived in this context of self-development: "for what is power in the sense in which it is so often applied to women, but the liberty to employ one's facilities in one's own way unobstructed . . . ?"[85] The emphasis on individual calling, not determined by sex but by innate talent, of course meant practically that women should enter into whatever activity or profession she felt fitted to. As the Syracuse Convention resolved in 1852, "that in the great body politic, or in the great social body, each one, irrespective of sex, talent, or capability for a higher or lower function, fulfill the great ends of his or her being."[86] In the unfolding of their natural talents women saw no limit to their intellectual, moral, or social progress, developments which would make the woman's sphere obsolete. Indeed, the pulling down of these artificial boundaries was among the most articulate of women's demands.

Rights arguments were strongly addressed to the development of individual capacities in the context of the fulfillment of duties in the 1850s. No clear distinction was made in this period between rights stemming from concerns for family and social justice, and those which contributed to civic competence and personal development. Most often the two were pictured as mutually reenforcing, with woman's increased freedom enhancing her capacity to serve herself and others, including her family.[87] Stanton in a speech to the American Anti-Slavery Society in 1860 gave voice to a cherished reform belief that "rights never clash or interfere, and where no individual in a community is denied his rights, the mass are more perfectly protected in theirs."[88] Most feminists subscribed to the thesis that "A man has rights in order that he may do right."[89] The frequent pairing of "rights" and "duties" was not accidental. Women were sincere when they repeatedly argued that it was because of their equal moral accounta-

---

84. Lily, vol. 3 no. 3, at 20 (March 1851).

85. Una, vol. 1 no. 1, at 7 (Feb. 1853); Elizabeth Oakes Smith, *supra* n.19, at 116.

86. *Syracuse, supra* n.14, at 75.

87. *Syracuse, supra* n.14, at 62-63; *Boston, supra* n.21, at 8; *Cleveland, supra* n.6, at 8.

88. Elizabeth Cady Stanton, Susan B. Anthony: Correspondence, Writings, Speeches (1981), Ellen C. DuBois, ed., at 78. *See also*, Hurlbut, *supra* n.52, at 25-27, for the same argument based on the need to defend individual liberties from a tyrannical government.

89. Mark Hopkins, cited in Rodgers, *supra* n.68; *see also*, resolutions passed at the first convention, in *Seneca Falls, supra* n.4, at 4-5.

bility to God, and the resulting duties to themselves, their families, and society, that they deserved and needed rights.[90]

Since women's duties were so much concerned with family, it should not be surprising that there was a significant domestic component in the developing ideal of woman's rights, and that natural rights were often pictured as concrete ways for women to protect or further the interests of their families. The *Lily* and the *Una* were published, not just for the several hundred pioneers of the movement, but also for many thousands who were still puzzling out their positions. Its letters and articles chronicle the conversion of many women to politics on the ground that it was woman's right and duty to assert her claims for protection.[91] It was a common maxim among reformers that the main object of the law was to protect the weak from the tyranny of the strong, and in the *Lily*, one can trace the clear evolution of a doctrine of woman's rights through the arguments over temperance—"learning woman's rights by woman's wrongs."[92] The archetypal tale is of "poverty, desertion, and tyranny on the part of . . . worthless and drunken husbands . . . taking away from their wives and children every possible means of support . . . ." The number and intensity of these stories increase with the *Lily's* commitment to political solutions; one enlightened girl takes her flighty cousin for a walk through an impoverished neighborhood, pointing out women who are victims of intemperate husbands, low wages, and a lack of legal protection, and demands at last, "Has this woman had her rights?"[93]

Nor was this elaboration of woman's rights confined to some conservative wing of the movement; in the antebellum years there was considerable harmony of position. Although Stanton and Anthony moved from organized temperance to woman's rights in the mid-1850s, they and other woman's righters remained advocates of the temperance cause, finding it a "hard matter to speak of the cruel wrongs inflicted on women by the liquor traffic, without at the same time saying that her rights have been trampled upon . . . (and) difficult to depict the woes of the drunkard's wife . . . without saying that her rights have been recklessly invaded, and wrongfully withheld."[94] Many women initially resistant to the assertion of rights became enthusiastic converts: their new ideals were rooted, not in higher political theory, but in concrete concern for the "sacred ties of family relations." Mothers turned to rights for the sake of their children, seeking assurance that they would be able to feed and clothe them, and

---

90. Lily, vol. 2 no. 10, at 73 (Oct. 1850); Clarina I. Howard Nichols, On the Responsibilities of Woman, tract no. 6 in *Woman's Rights Commensurate with Her Capacities and Obligations, supra* n.8. *See also Syracuse, supra* n.14, at 23, 34, 63.

91. Lily, vol. 1 no. 10, at 77 (Oct. 1849).

92. *New York, supra* n.28, at 4, 76.

93. Lily, vol. 3 no. 5, at 34 (May 1851); *see also*, vol. 3, no. 11, at 86 (Nov. 1851); and *Boston, supra* n.21, at 24.

94. Lily, vol. 4 no. 3, at 22 (March 1852).

keep them nearby.[95] Many women sought "equal rights for (women) *in the family*, in order that its highest uses and harmonies may be insured."[96]

Nevertheless, this theoretical harmony between rights for the self and duties to others was not to survive the Civil War. Even before then the two strains had begun to be discernible. The broadest category of rights included "the general question of woman's Rights and Relations (which) comprehends such as: HER EDUCATION, *literary, scientific, and artistic* HER AVOCATIONS, *Industrial, Commercial, and Professional* — —HER INTERESTS, *Pecuniary, Civil, and Political* in a word, her RIGHTS as an *Individual*, and her FUNCTIONS as a *Citizen*."[97] Many middle class feminists stressed forcefully the incidents which contributed to personal freedom and development—the right of sexual autonomy within marriage, of education, work outside the home, independence—and were content to see economic parity rather vaguely as the inevitable consequence of women's personal and civil gains.[98] Stanton herself emphasized autonomy above suffrage, saying "When we talk of woman's rights, is not the right to her person, to her happiness, to her life, the first on the list? If you go to a southern plantation and speak to a slave of his right to property, to the elective franchise, to a thorough education, his response will be a vacant stare . . . . The great idea of his right to himself, to his personal dignity, must first take possession of his soul."[99]

As the movement developed, those activists who weighted issues of autonomy and personal development more heavily tended increasingly to align themselves behind the vote, re-envisioning it, not just as a lever to achieve social ends, but as a measure of autonomy and individual freedom in itself. A few others, who saw women's impoverishment as the paramount issue, urged economic measures over the quest for legal or civil entitlement.[100] Still, antebellum activists understood their rights and duties as a seamless web. Only in Stanton's work do we see fully foreshadowed the conflict between individual women's rights and the interests of family and community which was to split the suffrage movement so bitterly in the last years of the century.[101]

---

95. Lily, vol. 4 no. 5, at 35 (May 1852); vol. 4 no. 6, at 51 (June 1852); Una, vol. 1 no. 1, at 14-15 (Feb. 1853).

96. *Boston, supra* n.21, at 8.

97. *Syracuse, supra* n.14, at iv.

98. *Cleveland, supra* n.6, at 10, 17, 41, 55-56; Una, vol. 1 no. 1, p. 10 (Feb. 1853); Lily, vol. 3 no. 5, at 35 (May 1851); Hersh, *supra* n.13, at 189.

99. Letter to Susan B. Anthony, July 20, 1857, Stanton Papers, Douglass College Library, Rutgers University.

100. History of Woman Suffrage, *supra* n.65, at 233; *Syracuse, supra* n.14, at 9; Clarina I. Howard Nichols, *supra* n.90.

101. Even in this early period Stanton is beginning to develop her notion of rights as based in the psychological needs of the autonomous personality, an individualism far more pronounced than the liberal Protestant ideal of self-development. Although Stanton scholars have generally viewed her late address *Solitude of Self* as representing an evolution of

To the extent that it is possible to isolate two different strands of rights thought here, the question arises of whether one is superior to the other, or more truly feminist in outlook. Most scholars of women's movements have explicitly valued political rights over any claim for right to livelihood or protection of the home. They see the "home values" of later temperance union suffragists as a second-class feminism, an expression of "woman-oriented moral conservatism."[102] Ellen DuBois, Barbara Epstein, and others have denigrated the suffrage campaign of the Woman's Christian Temperance Union as instrumental because it sought the vote with clear public policy goals in view which addressed women's welfare as tied to the well being of the family under the wage labor system.[103] For DuBois the strength of the demand for suffrage is that it bypassed the private sphere altogether to focus on equality within the public sphere.[104] As a political feminist, she sees a relation between woman's oppression and her ideological association with the private sphere. By this standard, any claim other than the strict one for formal equality appears a manifestation of false consciousness, even though well intentioned. In fact, some of the temperance workers goals were highly repressive. This should not obscure the fact that the association of political power with social ends allows greater possibility for social change than viewing the vote as an abstract good.[105] Political rights, rightly considered, are not ends in themselves, but ways of allocating power and resources within the community. In a democratic society, at least theoretically, they are closely connected to maximizing benefits for all.

Even leaving aside contemporary debates, it is unclear that this standard can be usefully applied to nineteenth-century feminism. For one thing, what could "formal equality" mean to women in the absence of *any* federal or state regulatory mechanism to ensure it?[106] In the 1850s, the possibility of constitutional amendments like the fourteenth, fifteenth, or nineteenth, was remote. In many ways the woman's movement's political aspirations developed reciprocally with the growth of the government's capacity to administer equal protection standards. As we have seen, most

---

her thought, at least one unusual passage fully prefigures that address, though written forty years earlier; in it she says that woman is her own "self supporter, self defender and self protector, compelled to stand or fall, to live or die, alone." Lily, vol. 4 no. 5, at 40 (May 1852). *Solitude of Self* is reprinted in Elizabeth Cady Stanton, Susan B. Anthony: Correspondence, Speeches, Writings, *supra* n.88, at 246.

102. Epstein, *supra* n.22, at 6.

103. Even the sympathetic chronicler of the WCTU, Ruth Bordin, while vaunting the Union's effectiveness in engaging women in political activity, finds its agenda defective in emphasizing the uses and purposes of the woman's vote above absolute rights. *See* Woman and Temperance: The Quest for Power and Liberty, 1873-1900 (1981).

104. DuBois, *The Radicalism of Woman Suffrage, supra* n.2, at 63.

105. I imagine this abstract good as the majestic, solitary figure of Elizabeth Cady Stanton sailing through the universe with a star in one hand and a ballot in the other.

106. In this I follow Michael Grossberg's line in Governing the Hearth: Law and the Family in Nineteenth-Century America (1985), that "rights" women were gaining in family law doctrine were actually privileges granted at the discretion of the court.

antebellum feminists were initially highly skeptical of the power of government to work change by law; Hannah Tracy Cutler once declared that she never saw the words "law reform" or "revised statutes" without thinking happily of a bonfire.[107]

More important is the question of whether "domestic rights" really represented an inferior brand, and what consequences the repackaging of women's early broad vision into the demand for political rights had for the movement as a whole. One critic has charged that "The concept of 'rights' in general (is) a concept that is inherently static and abstracted from social conditions. Rights are by definition claims staked within a given order of things. They are demands for access for oneself, or for 'no admittance' for others; but they do not challenge the social structure, the social relations of production and reproduction."[108] While this may accurately diagnose a contemporary malaise, antebellum woman's rights claims spilled over legal categories: not limited to what governments could provide, they were the markers of a state of harmony with natural laws which mandated the satisfaction of all human wants. Their revolutionary character lay in representing, not claims to an established order, but new ways of reenvisioning social relations and the relations of power.

Nor did feminists see rights as any kind of absolute or unlimited entitlement. The linking of rights to responsibilities, and their firm placement within a system of natural laws, meant that rights were not seen as discrete, but as functioning within a larger context as a set of reciprocal obligations. Far from granting a power to be exercised against others, restraint was built in: "The great laws of our own beings demand justice to ourselves and justice to our neighbors. We cannot infringe either law without disorder and pain, and . . . the Infinite Creator looks benignly upon his creature who thus obeys the laws of his own nature, and reverences those appertaining to every other."[109] Yet such restraints were not galling. Perfect freedom still lay not in total autonomy but in acting out God's will, so that "the most free are the most bound."[110] Rights were a precious new license for women to employ their talents for themselves and others, and women saw them, not only as individual entitlements, but as the context for a happier and more fulfilled life for all human beings. Rights were not static entitlements, but the conditions of a dynamic new freedom: "right . . . will galvanize women into civil liberty: (and) you will find her capable of being in it, and sustaining it."[111]

---

107. Una, vol. 1 no. 3, at 41 (April 1853).

108. Rosalind P. Petchesky, Abortion and Woman's Choice: The State, Sexuality, and Reproductive Freedom (1984), at 7.

109. Elizabeth Oakes Smith, *supra* n.19, at 118.

110. *Syracuse, supra* n.14, at 81.

111. *Proceedings of the Woman's Rights Convention Held at . . . Rochester, New York, Aug. 2, 1848* (1870; reprint, 1969), at 7.

Conclusion

When the antebellum woman's movement took up the concept and language of rights, it was not a case of incorporating the meanings and usages of the Founding Fathers whole into women's vocabulary. Rights rhetoric evoked a political tradition meaningful to women as well as men, a set of promises for women as gender-blind as the assurances of the new God of liberal theology. But the genesis of rights, their meaning for women, lay initially in Christian-based concepts of social justice, the fulfillment of needs, and each person's development according to their divinely-ordained talents. In the early years the problem of power was itself a critical hurdle for women's activism. Understanding its corrupting nature, seeing the evidence all around them in the political arrangements of men, how could women justify their own accession to power? A good deal of argument within the broader movement was directed toward the idea, not of seizing or sharing power, but of its *dissolution*, on the theory that when men ceased their corrupt administration, the problem of power would resolve itself into a natural harmonious balance between the sexes. Much of the rest of the discussion was taken up by mutual assurances that, should women gain their political due, their natures would protect them from the misuse of power through corruption and greed.

Despite their hesitance about the assumption of power, the antebellum feminist campaign was a time of political maturation, overcoming scruples and fears about acting in the political world. Women reformers began to prepare themselves, not just to speak in the role of outcast-prophet, but to take up the tools of government for their own ends. In the spring of 1852 the *Lily* published separate short blurbs side by side on two cases at law successfully argued by women. In one, the woman is armed with nothing but her knowledge of right and faith in good justice; her appeal reaches past the minds and straight into the hearts of her listeners, who acknowledge that she has shown up their law as irrelevant and grant her the decision. In the second, the female advocate is beautifully prepared with a wealth of incisive arguments which dumfound her opponents and lead to her uncontested victory on highly technical points of legal doctrine.

These two cases represent a progression: the woman's movement in the 1850s is a microcosm of political change, a moment of transition in individuals' basic attitudes toward government. Despite their initial disaffection with government, workers in combined woman's and temperance movements came to recognize that politics and law were increasingly becoming creatures of the central state, and were passing out of local control. The potential of national government to protect woman's due was only dimly realized, but the admission that "we are in an age when the wrongs of society are adjusted at the courts and at the ballot box" dictated a new approach.[112] Women saw that politics was increasingly a man's

---

112. History of Woman Suffrage, vol. 1, at 14. The History of Woman Suffrage,

game, one played away from home. They resented their own exclusion, and distrusted the ability of male legislators sitting at a distance to represent their interests, and to meet the diverse needs of the banker, the housewife, and the drunkard. The impartiality and anonymity of legislation in this period was seen not as a possible protection, but as a failure of government to care for the whole individual. Relying on the ancient maxim, "salus populi suprema lex,"[113] women revealed their fears that in the brave new world of politics there was no place for the standard of moral accountability which pertained between relatives, friends, and neighbors, and that the law was not creating any new ethic whereby the bonds of community, loosely worn but still taut in times of need, could be maintained. The imperative for women's entry into politics became clearer and clearer to feminist reformers in the decade before the War.

Theirs was a romantic vision; its romanticism was partly redeemed and partly betrayed by the political maturation of its proponents, a process that started even before the war. In fact, the *Lily* illustrates that it was through the temperance activities of the 1850s that many women were brought around to the use of political means, including the ballot. The Maine liquor law of 1851 gave reformers a heady taste of the sweeping change which legislation could accomplish so much more effectively than the painful, uncertain process of personal conversion to abstinence which had been the temperance workers' model. The Maine law was the "philosopher's stone in the pocket," capable of effecting spiritual and behavioral regeneration instantly, and the *Lily* followed the progress of similar laws with intense interest.[114] Under Amelia Bloomer's management, editorials, articles, and letters in almost every issue starting in 1850 exhorted women to take up political tools to accomplish their social ends.[115]

Not all those sympathetic to woman's rights were converted to political means on the spot. The leaders of the woman's movement, the politically sophisticated, the speakers, became convinced early on that, rotten or not, women had to enter man's political world to effect change. For a much larger group of women, sympathetic but unsure how far to go, the transformation into political beings was piecemeal and slow. Again, the *Lily* is valuable in that it exposes us not just to the thought of the leaders, but of the rank and file as well. For a time, Stanton and Anthony served as leaders of the state woman's temperance organization in New York, of which the *Lily* served as the unofficial organ. They and like-minded co-

---

although an invaluable and bottomless source, is not a fully objective account of the early years of the movement. Unlike the convention proceedings themselves, it was edited and issued thirty years after the movement's beginnings by three of the earliest and most vehement proponents of women's political activity; it consistently emphasizes political themes at the expense of spiritual and religious arguments.

113. Lily, vol. 2 no. 6, at 47.

114. Lily, vol. 5, nos. 1 or 2 (page and date undecipherable), speech of Antoinette Brown.

115. *See, for example*, Lily, vol. 2 no. 10, at 73-74 (Oct. 1850); vol. 3 no. 10, at 79 (Sept. 1851); vol. 4 no. 5, at 33, 35-36, 39-42 (May 1852); vol. 4 no. 6, at 53 (June 1852).

workers exercised a tremendous influence on the shape of women's reform through the newspaper, as well as through the blizzard of publications and the exhaustive cross-country lecture circuits many undertook. Under their tutelage many women came to believe they could best assure their own chances for self-development and thereby help to bring society back into a natural order through the means of the vote. Over the years of the *Lily's* publication (1849-1856) readers of all persuasions wrote in to attest to their conversion to political methods, at least to the combination of legal and moral suasion. A growing number found that moral suasion alone "will not do," was "worse than useless," and made little impression on the legislators who, corrupt or not, were calling the shots.[116] Citing the inability of mothers to protect sons from the liquor "monster," one former anti-feminist found that "there came a complete change over my feelings on the subject." "A realizing sense of our weakness . . . (and) that we were warring with harmless weapons" brought many reform women to a more assertive political challenge to the supremacy of the male liquor cartel.[117]

The new philosophy of women's political power did not require women to jettison moral ideals, but it did require a transformation of the imagery of morality and power. Most importantly, it required the acknowledgement that the institutions of government were not inherently opposed to morality but with the right composition could act to improve social conditions. Many women urged the adoption of political tactics for the purpose of fulfilling obligations to others. One woman, deploring her lack of the vote, exhorted, "Arise, sisters, to your duty! Gird on the garment of love to your fellow creatures, and form the high resolve to crush the enemy which is stabbing them to the heart," a formulation which retains the rationale of social duty but endorses a different kind of action.[118]

After the Civil War the rights movement became a suffrage movement in earnest, with the ballot's earlier focus as a carrier of other rights downplayed. Because of the movement's fuller engagement with the political process, and the growing involvement of government in mediating and enunciating the rights of its citizens, women increasingly conceived of rights in legal terms. The emphasis on legal rights, narrowly conceived, diminished discussions of economic and social entitlement. Feminists like Antoinette Brown Blackwell found the movement's agenda narrowed after the war, too neglectful of issues like education and work.[119] Although the untested antebellum vision was probably naive, and certainly immature, in its conviction that the wellbeing of the community lay simply in the perfection of individual rights, the shift in focus toward legal remedies represented both a gain and a loss. Women gained a basic political

116. Lily, vol. 4 no. 5, at 39 (May 1852); vol. 1 no. 8, at 61 (July 1849).

117. Lily, vol. 3 no. 10, at 77 (Oct. 1851).

118. Lily, vol. 1 no. 9, at 69 (Sept. 1849).

119. Elizabeth Cazden, Antoinette Brown Blackwell: A Biography (Old Westbury, New York, 1983), at 138.

agenda, which could be pursued to ultimate success, and limited their claims for transformative social change inherent in their early vision.

[16]

FORTY ACRES AND A MULE: A REPUBLICAN THEORY OF MINIMAL ENTITLEMENTS

AKHIL REED AMAR**

Let me begin by mapping out what, for this Federalist Society audience, I take to be common ground. Pure socialism is bad. A system of private property, at least up to a point, is good. A regime in which the state controlled all resources would threaten both individual liberty and true democracy. Quite literally, in such a socialist society, the citizen would have no ground of her own on which to stand, to define herself, and to resist government tyranny.

I will now move from this common ground to stake out a position that for this group may seem far less obvious. Private property is such a good thing that every citizen should have some. Indeed, a minimal entitlement to property is so important, so constitutive, and so essential for both individual and collective self-governance that to provide each citizen with that minimal amount of property, the government may legitimately redistribute property from other citizens who have far more than their minimal share. But wait—there's more. The notion of minimal entitlements is not simply constitutive, it is constitutional—not just constitutionally permissible, meaning that the government *may* distribute or redistribute to insure every citizen a minimal stake in society, but constitutionally obligatory. The government *must* do so. The Constitution does not enact Mr. Herbert Spencer's *Social Statics*,[1] but it does enact Mr. Thaddeus Stevens's forty acres and a mule.

Now that I have your attention, let me explain. There is a tradition deep in American constitutional law that I shall refer to as the "R/republican tradition," with both a lowercase and a capital "R." This tradition was a driving force behind a number

---

* This panel was introduced by Stephen F. Williams, Judge, United States Court of Appeals for the D.C. Circuit.

** Professor of Law, Yale Law School.

1. *See* Lochner v. New York, 198 U.S. 45, 75 (1905) (Holmes, J., dissenting).

of significant political movements that helped shape the American political experience. These include Abraham Lincoln's Republican party in the 1860s (and before it the Free Soil party), Thomas Jefferson's Democratic Republicans at the turn of the Nineteenth Century, and before that, the ideological platform of a group of commonwealth writers, most prominently James Harrington, in England in the Seventeenth and Eighteenth Centuries.

In this R/republican tradition, there is a recognition that for one truly to be a citizen in a democracy and to participate in the democratic process, one needs a minimum amount of independence. Economic independence is necessary if the citizen is to be able to deliberate on the common good, the *res publica*, the thing public. (Hence the word republicanism.) According to this tradition, the problem of poor people is that, in a real way, they have no wills of their own. You may give them the right to vote, but they will alienate that right. They will sell it either to rich people or to foreign tyrants. They lack some minimal stake in society sufficient to connect their own personal interests with that of the larger public interest. This lack of individual independence is one of the reasons that Thomas Jefferson was so concerned about cities and so hostile towards them. He saw cities as breeding grounds for the kind of urban proletariat that had no real stake in the common venture.

I suggest that there are two basic ways of dealing with the R/republican notion that in order for a democracy to work, people must have a stake in society. The first way is the dark side—the exclusionary side—of the R/republican vision. It is the Athenian solution, and I would suggest the original American solution. That solution is to enslave people, to ruthlessly disfranchise people who do not have property, to adopt poll taxes and property qualifications. Indeed, human slavery led to a host of economic rights provisions and property provisions in the original Constitution. We see economic protection of slavery in the two clauses about importation of slaves.[2] We see it in the Fugitive Slave Clause[3] and the three-fifths rule,[4] and it is lurking behind several other clauses in the Constitution.[5]

2. U.S. Const. art. I, § 9, cl. 1; *id.* at art. V.
3. *Id.* at art. IV, § 2, cl. 3.
4. *Id.* at art. I, § 2, cl. 3.
5. *See generally* R. Cover, Justice Accused 150-53 (1975); Diamond, *No Call To Glory:*

These clauses are dramatic evidence that economic rights and property are not necessarily a good thing. We need to ask questions about their distribution. Who has economic rights? Who has rights to property? And to how much? And for what purpose?

Edmund Morgan, in his brilliant book *American Slavery, American Freedom*,[6] elaborated on the seeming paradox that in Seventeenth- and Eighteenth-Century America, radical language about liberty, equality, and the rights of man coexisted in the same society that enforced a regime of human slavery. But in a way, it was not a paradox at all because it was the enslavement of many people that provided the economic well-being of the rest who constituted the polity. Ironically, slavery provided a rough equality among whites—they were all equal in being free men—and enough economic rent to allocate to poor whites to make them economically independent.

This original R/republican solution was radically modified by the Civil War and the Thirteenth Amendment.[7] The solution to the problem is no longer the Athenian solution of enslavement. It is now an inclusionary solution, a solution that says We the People of the United States will not allow a degraded caste of people to exist in our society. It is a solution that provides people with inalienable property rights in their own persons. Moreover, I suggest, it is a vision that, especially under section two of the Thirteenth Amendment,[8] provides for forty acres and a mule. It is a vision that provides a right to sustenance and shelter: minimum sustenance, minimum shelter.

I submit that the standard legal discourse has deradicalized this Thirteenth Amendment vision, this inclusionary vision. The people who adopted the Thirteenth Amendment provided for rights against the world. A martian looking at our Constitution would probably see the Thirteenth Amendment as its most radical provision.[9] There is no state action requirement, unlike

Thurgood Marshall's Theory on the Intent of a Pro-Slavery Constitution, 42 VAND. L. REV. 93 (1989).

6. E. MORGAN, AMERICAN SLAVERY, AMERICAN FREEDOM (1975).

7. U.S. CONST. amend. XIII, § 1 ("Neither slavery nor involuntary servitude, except as a punishment for crime whereof the party shall have been duly convicted, shall exist within the United States, or any place subject to their jurisdiction.").

8. *Id.* at § 2 ("Congress shall have power to enforce this article by appropriate legislation.").

9. So does at least one comparativist. *See* Damaska, *Reflections on American Constitutionalism*, 38 AM. J. COMP. L. — (forthcoming 1990).

just about every other provision in the Constitution. We fought a civil war over the slavery issue. The Thirteenth Amendment radically changed the social and economic structure of our society. The people who adopted it did not know that the Fourteenth and the Fifteenth Amendments were going to follow. They thought the Thirteenth Amendment was quite broad. Moreover, I submit that, if anything, we should read the Thirteenth Amendment even more broadly in the wake of the later adoption of the Fourteenth and Fifteenth Amendments.

When the Reconstruction Amendments are viewed as a whole, a radically different vision of society emerges. Precisely because the Fifteenth Amendment gave former slaves the right to vote,[10] and the Fourteenth Amendment made them citizens by dint of their birth,[11] we should interpret the Thirteenth Amendment to guarantee each American a certain minimum stake in society. Otherwise, We the People of the United States really failed to set the slaves free—free from economic dependence. Without guaranteeing independence, it would have been both futile and dangerous under R/republican principles to have extended the rights of equal citizenship and equal votes to freedmen. Thaddeus Stevens and his allies, for example, had policies of subsidized public education, of land redistribution in the South—forty acres and a mule—and of homesteading in the West—160 acres in the Homestead Act.[12]

The connection is clear between the educational vision of *Brown v. Board of Education*[13] and that of Thaddeus Stevens. Equally clear is the fact that the new economic rights under the Reconstruction Amendments are redistributive, at least in part. Land reform in the South redistributed property rights. Indeed, the Thirteenth Amendment itself effected the most massive deprivation of slaveholder property without just compensation imaginable, notwithstanding the Takings Clause.[14] Public education can also be seen as redistributive.

10. *See* U.S. CONST. amend. XV, § 1.

11. *See id.* at amend. XIV, § 1.

12. The Homestead Act of 1862, ch. 75, 12 Stat. 392 (1862) (repealed 1976); *see* J. BLUM, E. MORGAN, W. ROSE, A. SCHLESSINGER, JR. & K. STAMPP, THE NATIONAL EXPERIENCE 362 (3d ed. 1973); *see also* MEMORIAL ADDRESSES ON THE LIFE AND CHARACTER OF THADDEUS STEVENS (1869).

13. 347 U.S. 483 (1954); *see id.* at 493 (education "is the very foundation of good citizenship").

14. U.S. CONST. amend. V; *see also id.* at amend. XIV, § 3 (voiding all claims for shareholder compensation).

Wealthy people pay more school taxes than poor people, but poor children are no less entitled to public education. In the West, we did not auction off lands to the highest bidder. Behind the homesteading provisions there was a distributional vision of giving subsidized land to folks if they were going to farm their own homesteads.

What happens when there is no longer enough land left? The availability of such land, of course, was assumed by John Locke in his famous Lockean proviso.[15] I suggest that there is a connection between the "safety valve" of western land 100 years ago and language about the "safety net" today, language about trying to create situations in which everyone has a minimum stake in society. It is interesting to note that soon after the closing of the West around 1890, Americans adopted the Sixteenth Amendment, which provides not simply for an income tax, but a predictably progressive—that is, a *redistributive*—income tax.[16]

Professor Epstein has made some arguments about how the Federalist Constitution was anti-redistributive.[17] His argument, as I understand it, is not so much textual as structural, looking to the ideological background of the Framers of the Constitution. If one is going to engage in that level of generality in constitutional interpretation for the original Constitution, then to be consistent, to be a principled interpretivist, one has to be willing to do the same thing when looking at the Thirteenth, Fourteenth, Fifteenth, and Sixteenth Amendments. One then has to recognize that these amendments were motivated by a rather different vision of economics and democracy than that of the original Constitution.

Let me end with several quick caveats, lest I be understood to be making an even broader argument than I intend to. First, the notion of minimal entitlements is not a notion that everyone should have an equal amount of property. It is more a Thirteenth Amendment vision than a Fourteenth Amendment vision. It is not an argument that equal protection under the Fourteenth Amendment means equal property, but rather that freedom under the Thirteenth Amendment implies a notion of some minimal entitlement. So to the extent that many members

15. J. Locke, The Second Treatise of Government, § 27 (T. Peardon ed. 1952) (1st ed. London 1690).

16. *See* Amar, *Our Forgotten Constitution*, 97 Yale L.J. 281, 291-92 (1987).

17. *See generally* R. Epstein, Takings: Private Property and the Power of Eminent Domain (1985).

of this audience find freedom a more compelling ideal than equality, they should welcome my invitation to shift our focus from the Fourteenth to the Thirteenth Amendment.

Second, this vision is not a socialist one. It celebrates the notion of private property but suggests that we have to extend the benefits of that institution to all citizens of society. This is the vision of Charles Reich in his classic article on the new property.[18] It might suggest some implications for the *Rodriguez* case[19] dealing with a right to a minimally adequate public education, or for voucher systems in employment and education—not a socialist system, in which people have equal property rights in each other's incomes.

Third, forty acres and a mule is not a dole It is not welfare. It is much more like workfare. Forty acres and a mule do not yield a harvest without labor, and in the process of laboring, a citizen can gain self-respect and the respect of others. We must remember that our goal is to create *independent* citizens. Ironically, many current welfare programs may have moved us away from that goal by perpetuating cycles of dependency. By contrast, the kind of education and job-training programs I am advocating here are designed to promote self-sufficiency and reward hard work.

Fourth, I have not, at least here, argued that this Thirteenth Amendment vision of forty acres and a mule is judicially enforceable under section one of the Thirteenth Amendment. There may very well be a variety of institutional limitations on courts that make them unsuitable for the task.[20] Rather, I would like to stress the obligation—not only a moral obligation, but a legal, a *constitutional* obligation—of Congress, under section two of the Thirteenth Amendment. Congress has both a constitutional right and a constitutional duty to implement this vision.

Perhaps the legal obligation argument can be pushed even further. Unlike virtually every other constitutional provision, the Thirteenth Amendment creates rights against, and thus imposes duties on, private citizens. Even if courts for institutional

18. *See* Reich, *The New Property*, 73 YALE L.J. 733 (1964).

19. San Antonio Independent School Dist. v. Rodriguez, 411 U.S. 1 (1973).

20. *See generally* Fiss, *Groups and the Equal Protection Clause*, 5 PHIL. & PUB. AFF. 107, 175-77 (1976); Michelman, *Welfare Rights in a Constitutional Democracy*, 1979 WASH. U.L.Q. 659; Sager, *Fair Measure: The Legal Status of Underenforced Constitutional Norms*, 91 HARV. L. REV. 1212 (1978).

reasons cannot directly and fully enforce these duties, each of us may well have an obligation as a citizen to help assure each of our fellow citizens some minimal entitlements. We might be able to discharge this obligation in any number of ways—for example, by giving our time or money to private programs and intermediate associations (churches, charities, schools, and so on) that seek to provide minimal entitlements of education and property to our co-citizens. But once again, perhaps this obligation to be "points of light" is not merely a moral one, but a legal, a *constitutional*, duty as well.

Finally, I am not rejecting, but simply modifying, the three basic procedural notions of prospectivity, generality, and non-discrimination, said by some to underlie our constitutional scheme of property protection. Prospectivity has to be complemented by a vision of substantive baselines. Prospectivity, or non-retroactivity, says that whatever existing property rights you have must be respected prospectively. But we need a theory about initial baseline entitlements—starting points. We need a theory about the birthrights of inheritance of every American citizen. That is what the Thirteenth, Fourteenth, and Fifteenth Amendments are all about: birthrights of every American citizen.

The proposition about generality must be supplemented by a vision of independence of citizens. The way to create that independence is to give every citizen a stake in society. This is good both for the individual and collective self-governance, much as freedom of speech can be derived from both an individual theory of personhood, autonomy, and self-expression, and also from a theory of democratic self-rule. So whether we begin with a vision of individual dignity and human rights, or (as I have here) stress the structural requirements of R/republican government, we are led to the idea of guaranteed minimal entitlements.

Last, the notion of nondiscrimination—which is often assimilated by people like Professor Epstein to non-redistribution—has to be qualified by the need to accommodate modest redistribution so that we can make real today the vision of forty acres and a mule for every American.

[17]

THE FIRST DUTY OF GOVERNMENT: PROTECTION, LIBERTY AND THE FOURTEENTH AMENDMENT

STEVEN J. HEYMAN*

* Assistant Professor of Law, Chicago-Kent College of Law, Illinois Institute of Technology. A.B. 1979, J.D. 1984, Harvard University. I wish to thank many friends and colleagues for their thoughtful comments on earlier versions of this Article, including Akhil Reed Amar, Alison Baldwin, Lance Banning, Anita Bernstein, Richard Collins, Jacob Corré, Michael Kent Curtis, Stuart Deutsch, David Gerber, Philip Hamburger, Linda Hirshman, Howard Klemme, Michael Knoll, James Lindgren, Kerry Macintosh, Joan Meier, Sheldon Nahmod, Dale Nance, Steven D. Smith, Margaret Stewart, Arthur Travers, Richard Warner, Marianne Wesson, and Richard Wright. Invaluable research assistance was provided by Shari Lefkoff, Regina Drexler, Anne Gerrity, Susan Laser-Baer, and Laura Finnegan. My work was supported by the Marshall D. Ewell Research Fund.

This Article is dedicated to the memory of Paul A. Freund.

"The first duty of the Government is to afford protection to its citizens." [1]

INTRODUCTION

On January 22, 1983, Joshua DeShaney, age four, was brought to the emergency room of a Wisconsin hospital with multiple bruises and abrasions.[2] Suspecting child abuse, the hospital staff notified the County Department of Social Services, which immediately obtained custody of Joshua, only to return him to his father's home a few days later. Over the next fifteen months, the Department received constant reports indicating that Joshua was being seriously abused, but it failed to take any further action to protect him. On March 8, 1984, Joshua's father beat him so severely that he suffered massive brain damage, leaving him profoundly retarded and confined to an institution for the rest of his life.

In *DeShaney v. Winnebago County Department of Social Services*,[3] the Supreme Court ruled that the Department's failure to protect Joshua

---

1. CONG. GLOBE, 39th Cong., 2d Sess. 101 (1867) (remarks of Rep. Farnsworth) (debating Reconstruction Act of 1867).

2. The facts in this paragraph are derived from the opinion of the Supreme Court in DeShaney v. Winnebago County Dep't of Social Servs., 489 U.S. 189, 191-93 (1989), and from the unpublished opinion of the district court below, DeShaney v. DeShaney, No. 85-C-310, slip op. at 3-14 (E.D. Wis. June 20, 1986), *reprinted in* Appendix to Petition for Writ of Certiorari at 50-61, *DeShaney* (No. 87-154).

3. 489 U.S. 189 (1989).

did not violate the Federal Constitution. Chief Justice Rehnquist maintained that nothing in the language or history of the Due Process Clause of the Fourteenth Amendment required a state to protect its citizens from private violence. That clause, he observed, "is phrased as a limitation": "It forbids the State itself to deprive individuals of life, liberty, or property without 'due process of law,' but its language cannot fairly be extended to impose an affirmative obligation on the State" to protect these interests "against invasion by private actors."[4] This interpretation was reinforced by the history of the Clause, which indicated that "[i]ts purpose was to protect the people from the State, not to ensure that the State protected them from each other."[5]

The broader constitutional theory underlying this interpretation was articulated by Judge Richard Posner of the Court of Appeals for the Seventh Circuit.[6] According to Posner, the Constitution is "a charter of negative rather than positive liberties,"[7] a view that is compelled by the original understanding:

> The men who wrote the Bill of Rights were not concerned that government might do too little for the people but that it might do too much to them. The Fourteenth Amendment, adopted in 1868 at the height of laissez-faire thinking, sought to protect Americans from oppression by state government, not to secure them basic governmental services.[8]

DeShaney thus has crucial implications for constitutional law and theory. In addition to rejecting a constitutional right to protection, *DeShaney* implies that the Constitution protects only negative liberty—freedom from governmental oppression—while imposing no positive obligations on government.

This Article challenges *DeShaney* on its own ground—the original understanding of the Fourteenth Amendment. As I shall argue, the congressional debates on the Fourteenth Amendment show that establishing a federal constitutional right to protection was one of the central purposes of the Amendment.

The principal aim of the Fourteenth Amendment was not to create new rights, but rather to incorporate into the Federal Constitution the fundamental rights that individuals already possessed under general constitutional theory, but that the states had failed to enforce adequately.

4. *Id.* at 195.
5. *Id.* at 196.
6. *See* DeShaney v. Winnebago County Dep't of Social Servs., 812 F.2d 298 (7th Cir. 1987), *aff'd*, 489 U.S. 189 (1989); Jackson v. City of Joliet, 715 F.2d 1200 (7th Cir. 1983); Bowers v. DeVito, 686 F.2d 616 (7th Cir. 1982).
7. *Jackson*, 715 F.2d at 1203.
8. *Id.*

For this reason, the Fourteenth Amendment must be understood against the background of constitutional and legal theory before the Civil War.

In Part I, I trace the origins and development of the right to protection in Anglo-American constitutionalism. With its roots in the common law tradition and social contract theory, the right to protection in life, liberty, and property became a central principle of American constitutional thought by the time of the Revolution. This principle was expressed in the first state constitutions and was implicit in the Federal Constitution, which divided the function of protection between the state and federal governments.

Part I also explores the conception of liberty in American constitutional and legal thought between the Revolution and the Civil War. Contrary to Posner's view, the classical conception of liberty was not merely negative, but had a crucial positive dimension—the protection of individual rights under law.[9]

As I show in Part II, the right to protection was not merely a matter of constitutional theory, but a doctrine with concrete legal meaning. In the common law tradition, the protection of the law implied both the recognition of fundamental rights by law, and the enforcement of such rights by government. The paradigmatic instance was the government's duty to protect individuals against violence. By the middle of the nineteenth century, this duty was understood to include not only the enforcement of civil and criminal law with respect to injuries already committed, but also the responsibility to prevent violence before it occurred.

In Part III, I turn to the congressional debates over the Fourteenth Amendment. As these debates show, the members of the Thirty-Ninth Congress fully shared the classical view on the right to protection. The widespread violence and discrimination against blacks in the South after the Civil War convinced most Republicans that the states could not be relied upon to protect the fundamental rights of all persons. A central purpose of the Fourteenth Amendment was to compel the states to fulfill this obligation, by incorporating it into the Federal Constitution and empowering the national government to enforce it.

The three clauses of Section 1 of the Fourteenth Amendment secured the right to protection in different ways. Protection was one of the fundamental rights of citizenship secured by the Privileges or Immunities

9. In this Article, I shall use the term "classical" to refer to American thought between the Revolution and the Civil War, and to the sources of that thought in the English tradition. As this usage suggests—and as I try to show in Parts I and II—American thought during this period expressed a set of common themes regarding the nature of individual rights and the ends of government.

Clause. It also was implicit in the Due Process Clause, which was understood in the classical tradition to guarantee the protection of law to an individual's rights to life, liberty, and property, except where those rights had been held forfeited by due process of law. Finally, the Equal Protection Clause commanded that the states afford protection to all citizens in an impartial manner. In short, the Fourteenth Amendment was understood to incorporate the right to protection, as that right was understood in the classical tradition, into the Federal Constitution.[10]

This conclusion may seem surprising. During the twentieth century, and especially since the New Deal, the positive functions of government have expanded dramatically. The modern state undertakes to afford not only protection, but also at least a modicum of income, housing, health care, education, and other services. From a contemporary perspective, it is natural to identify all of these positive functions with the modern welfare state, and to assume that constitutionalism before the twentieth century was concerned solely with negative liberties.[11]

As I shall show, however, this view is seriously misleading. Although the positive role of government has reached a zenith since the New Deal, it does not follow that the state had no positive functions before that time. The classical state had a crucial positive function—the protection of rights. This function was not regarded as a mere "service"

10. For earlier discussions of the Fourteenth Amendment and the right to protection, see JACOBUS TENBROEK, EQUAL UNDER LAW (rev. ed. 1965); Earl M. Maltz, *The Concept of Equal Protection of the Laws—A Historical Inquiry*, 22 SAN DIEGO L. REV. 499 (1985); Aviam Soifer, *Protecting Civil Rights: A Critique of Raoul Berger's History*, 54 N.Y.U. L. REV. 651 (1979). Unlike these works, which discuss the concept of protection in general terms, the present Article focuses on protection *against private violence*, the crucial issue raised in *DeShaney*. Moreover, I seek to explore both the constitutional background and the legal content of the right to protection in a more comprehensive way than have previous studies.

For a brief but powerful attack on Judge Posner's and Chief Justice Rehnquist's use of history in *DeShaney*, see Aviam Soifer, *Moral Ambition, Formalism, and the "Free World" of* DeShaney, 57 GEO. WASH. L. REV. 1513, 1521-26 (1989).

11. The assumption that a right to protection is antithetical to traditional legal theory is so pervasive that it appears to be shared even by many of *DeShaney*'s strongest critics. For example, Susan Bandes, while noting the historical arguments for a duty of protection, argues that the hostility toward affirmative duties derives from the Anglo-American common law tradition and Western liberal political philosophy. *See* Susan Bandes, *The Negative Constitution: A Critique*, 88 MICH. L. REV. 2271, 2308-26 (1990). Similarly, Laurence Tribe criticizes *DeShaney* as reflecting a premodern, Newtonian view of the legal universe, according to which the state is neutral and detached from a "natural, pre-political order" of private life. Appropriating the insights of twentieth-century physics, Tribe argues that the state inevitably shapes the world that it observes, and thus bears some responsibility for its impact on that world. *See* Laurence H. Tribe, *The Curvature of Constitutional Space: What Lawyers Can Learn from Modern Physics*, 103 HARV. L. REV. 1, 7-14 (1989). Presumably, American law before the twentieth century reflected the Newtonian view that Tribe criticizes.

on a level with other benefits a state might choose to provide, but rather as the most fundamental obligation the government owed to its citizens.

My aims in this Article are both critical and positive. From a critical point of view, I hope to demonstrate that the Posner-Rehnquist view is indefensible, and that the history of the Fourteenth Amendment in no way forecloses recognition of a constitutional right to protection. From a positive perspective, this Article is intended as a contribution to the current debate over whether such a right should be recognized. In exploring the original understanding, I do not mean to imply that original intent should be binding in constitutional interpretation.[12] Instead, the original understanding may be regarded as a starting point in a continuing debate over the meaning of the Constitution. As I shall argue, that understanding points strongly toward recognizing a constitutional right to protection.

I. The Right to Protection in the Anglo-American Constitutional Tradition

A. *The Origins of the Right to Protection*

"[E]very member of society," asserted the Pennsylvania Constitution of 1776, "hath a right to be protected in the enjoyment of life, liberty and property."[13] This declaration—which was soon echoed in the constitutions of Delaware, Massachusetts, and New Hampshire[14]—expressed a fundamental principle of American constitutional thought by the time of the Revolution.

---

12. For some leading contributions to the debate over the role of original understanding in constitutional interpretation, see JOHN H. ELY, DEMOCRACY AND DISTRUST 1-41 (1980); Paul Brest, *The Misconceived Quest for the Original Understanding*, 60 B.U. L. REV. 204 (1980); Richard S. Kay, *Adherence to the Original Intentions in Constitutional Adjudication: Three Objections and Responses*, 82 NW. U. L. REV. 226 (1988); Mark V. Tushnet, *Following the Rules Laid Down: A Critique of Interpretivism and Neutral Principles*, 96 HARV. L. REV. 781 (1983). Although the degree of weight to be accorded original understanding is intensely controversial, few deny that it is one important source of constitutional meaning. This view is shared even by many of those most critical of original understanding. *See, e.g.*, Brest, *supra*, at 205 (Text and original history should be accorded "presumptive weight," but should not be treated as "authoritative and binding.").

13. PA. CONST. of 1776, Declaration of Rights, art. VIII, *reprinted in* 8 SOURCES AND DOCUMENTS OF UNITED STATES CONSTITUTIONS 278 (William F. Swindler ed., 1973-1979) [hereinafter STATE CONSTITUTIONS].

14. *See* DEL. DECLARATION OF RIGHTS AND FUNDAMENTAL RULES of 1776, art. 10, *reprinted in* 2 STATE CONSTITUTIONS, *supra* note 13, at 198; MASS. CONST. of 1780, pt. I, art. X, *reprinted in* 5 STATE CONSTITUTIONS, *supra* note 13, at 94; N.H. CONST. of 1784, Bill of Rights, art. XII, *reprinted in* 6 STATE CONSTITUTIONS, *supra* note 13, at 345; *cf.* N.Y. CONST. of 1777, art. XL, *reprinted in* 7 STATE CONSTITUTIONS, *supra* note 13, at 179 ("it is the duty of every man who enjoys the protection of society to be prepared and willing to defend it"). Vermont's first constitution (and all subsequent constitutions) contained a similar provision. *See* VT. CONST. of 1777, ch. I, art. IX,

The right to protection did not originate in America, however, but was inherited from English constitutionalism. Its roots lay in the common law tradition and natural rights theory. It is necessary to explore these sources to understand the concept of protection in American constitutional thought.[15]

1. *The Common Law Tradition and the Original Contract.* The right to protection has deep roots in the English legal tradition. Under traditional doctrine, every loyal subject was entitled to the king's protection.[16] This doctrine received its classic expression in the writings of Sir Edward Coke. In *Calvin's Case*,[17] Coke defined the relationship between sovereign and subject in terms of a "mutual bond and obligation," under which the subject owed allegiance or obedience, while the sovereign was bound "to govern and protect his subjects."[18] According to Coke, these reciprocal obligations were inherent in the very nature of the relationship between king and subject.[19]

As Coke made clear, the king's duty of protection included the obligation to protect his subjects from violence.[20] The king afforded such protection through his laws and through the legal process, which provided means for the enforcement of rights.[21] Thus, to be under the king's protection was to be under the "protection of the law."[22]

---

reprinted in 9 STATE CONSTITUTIONS, *supra* note 13, at 490. Vermont was not admitted into the Union until 1791.

For further discussion of these state constitutional provisions, see *infra* text accompanying notes 79-90.

15. For a brief overview of these sources, see Earl M. Maltz, *Fourteenth Amendment Concepts in the Antebellum Era*, 32 AM. J. LEGAL HIST. 305, 320-21 (1988).

16. *See* ANTHONY FITZ-HERBERT, THE NEW NATURA BREVIUM *29H (translation of work first published in 1534). The origins of this doctrine, which was fully established by the end of the thirteenth century, are traced in FREDERICK POLLOCK, *The King's Peace*, *in* OXFORD LECTURES AND OTHER DISCOURSES 65, 88-90 (1890).

17. 7 Co. Rep. 1a, 77 Eng. Rep. 377 (1608). For an excellent discussion of *Calvin's Case* and its role in the growth of American citizenship, see JAMES KETTNER, THE DEVELOPMENT OF AMERICAN CITIZENSHIP, 1608-1870, at 7-8, 16-28 (1978).

18. 7 Co. Rep. at 4b-5a, 77 Eng. Rep. at 382. For Coke these reciprocal obligations were summed up in the maxim "*protectio trahit subjectionem, et subjectio protectionem*": protection implies subjection, and subjection protection. *Id.* at 5a, 77 Eng. Rep. at 382.

19. *See id.* at 4b-5a, 77 Eng. Rep. at 382.

20. *See id.* at 8a, 77 Eng. Rep. at 386 (The object of "the King's protection" is to ensure "that his subjects in all places may be protected from violence, and that justice may equally be administered to all his subjects."); *see also* 1 EDWARD COKE, INSTITUTES OF THE LAWS OF ENGLAND *130a (The subject's right to protection entails "the safetie of his person, servants and goods, lands and tenements, whereof he is lawfully possessed, from violence, unlawfull molestation or wrong.").

21. *See* 1 COKE, *supra* note 20, at *130a.

22. 3 *id.* at *126a ("[F]or the law and the kings writs are the things whereby a man is protected and aided, so as he that is out of the kings protection, is out of the aid and protection of the law."); *see also* 1 *id.* at *130a (same).

Coke's formulation of the reciprocal obligations of king and subject was soon accepted as a fundamental principle of English constitutionalism. Over the next century and a half, however, the basis of this doctrine was transformed. For Coke, the relationship between subject and ruler arose from the law of nature, and hence was immutable.[23] During the seventeenth and eighteenth centuries, political obligation came to be regarded as based not on nature, but on consent. Accordingly, in constitutional theory, Coke's doctrine was transformed into a conception of an "original contract" between king and people, under which the people promised obedience in return for the ruler's protection.[24] Under this conception, if the king failed to protect the rights of his subjects, their duty to obey was also at an end.

2. *The Social Contract and Locke's* Second Treatise. The second major source of the right to protection in Anglo-American constitutionalism was the theory of natural rights and the social contract. The most influential exposition of this theory was John Locke's *Second Treatise of Government*.[25] Whereas Coke based the right to protection on the natural bond of allegiance between king and subject, Locke based it on the consent of free individuals to enter into society and establish government for the preservation of their natural rights.[26]

According to Locke, individuals are not naturally subject to a sovereign. Instead, the state of nature is a "*State of perfect Freedom*," where each individual is free to act as he thinks fit, without depending on the will of others.[27] By the same token, the natural state of mankind is one of equality, in which free and independent individuals live without any "Subordination or Subjection."[28]

In a state of nature, men are not subject to positive laws, but only to the law of nature, which Locke identified with reason.[29] That law teaches "that being all equal and independent, no one ought to harm

23. *See Calvin's Case*, 7 Co. Rep. at 12b-14b, 77 Eng. Rep. at 392-94.

24. *See* 1 WILLIAM BLACKSTONE, COMMENTARIES ON THE LAWS OF ENGLAND *233 (St. George Tucker ed., 1803 & photo. reprint 1969). On the theory of the original contract in the mid-eighteenth century, see 2 JOHN P. REID, A CONSTITUTIONAL HISTORY OF THE AMERICAN REVOLUTION: THE AUTHORITY TO TAX 55-60 (1987); GORDON S. WOOD, THE CREATION OF THE AMERICAN REPUBLIC, 1776-1787, at 268-73 (1969).

25. JOHN LOCKE, TWO TREATISES OF GOVERNMENT (Peter Laslett ed., student ed. 1988) (3d ed. 1698). All references to the *Two Treatises* in this Article are to the *Second Treatise*.

26. *See* KETTNER, *supra* note 17, at 44-61 (discussing contrasting views of political obligation held by Coke and Locke).

27. LOCKE, *supra* note 25, § 4.

28. *Id.* For further discussion of Locke's conception of equality and its relation to equal protection, see *infra* text accompanying notes 367-76.

29. *See* LOCKE, *supra* note 25, § 6. In order to accurately represent the thought of Locke and other classical writers, I shall follow their use of masculine language in describing their writings.

another in his Life, Health, Liberty, or Possessions."[30] Locke maintained that, in a state of nature, every individual has the right to enforce the law of nature by restraining and punishing violations of natural rights.[31]

In a state of nature, however, an individual often lacks the power to defend himself against invasion by others, rendering the enjoyment of his rights "very unsecure."[32] For this reason, individuals agree to form a community "for the mutual *Preservation* of their Lives, Liberties and Estates," which Locke comprehensively termed "*Property*."[33] Under the terms of this compact, each individual gives up his natural power to act for his own preservation "to be regulated by the Laws made by the Society, so far forth as the preservation of himself, and the rest of that Society shall require."[34] In addition, he "engages his natural force . . . to assist the Executive Power of the Society, as the law thereof shall require."[35] In return, the individual obtains not only benefits from "the labour, assistance, and society of others in the same Community," but also "*protection from its whole strength.*"[36] In short, according to Locke, the end of government is to direct "the force of all the subjects of the commonwealth" for the purpose of "preserving the members of the commonwealth in peace from injury and violence."[37]

Locke emphasized that, because government is established for this purpose, it is "obliged" to secure every individual's life, liberty, and property.[38] When it acts contrary to this trust, the government is dissolved and the community regains the right to establish a new form of government.[39] Such dissolution occurs, in Locke's view, where the government invades the rights of subjects, or where it fails to use its power to secure those rights.[40] Locke implied that the Glorious Revolution of 1688, in which King James II was dethroned and replaced by William and Mary, was justified on these grounds.[41]

---

30. *Id.*

31. *See id.* §§ 7-12.

32. *Id.* §§ 123, 126.

33. *Id.* § 123.

34. *Id.* § 129.

35. *Id.* § 130.

36. *Id.* (emphasis added). For other references to protection as the end of society and government, see *id.* §§ 122, 140, 211, 227.

37. JOHN LOCKE, *Third Letter on Toleration*, *in* 6 COLLECTED WORKS 214 (1801), *quoted in* LOCKE, *supra* note 25, § 135 (editor's note).

38. *See* LOCKE, *supra* note 25, § 131.

39. *See id.* §§ 211-243.

40. *See id.* §§ 219, 221-222.

41. Locke published the *Two Treatises* with the avowed object of justifying the Revolution. In a passage evidently referring to James's withdrawal from the kingdom during the Revolution, Locke wrote that the government was dissolved:

Natural rights theory, which was radical at the time that Locke wrote,[42] was gradually absorbed into mainstream English thought during the following century. Moreover, it was forcefully articulated during that period by a small group of radical Whig opposition writers, who had a crucial impact on the development of American political thought in the decades leading up to the Revolution.[43] It was a canon of radical Whig thought that government existed to protect the natural rights of its subjects. As John Trenchard and Thomas Gordon wrote in *Cato's Letters*:

> [M]utual Protection and Assistance is the only reasonable purpose of all reasonable Societies. To make such Protection practicable, Magistracy was formed, with power to defend the Innocent from Violence, and to punish those that offered it . . . . In order to this . . . End, the Magistrate is intrusted with conducting and applying the united Force of the Community; and with exacting such a Share of every Man's Property, as is necessary to preserve the Whole, and to defend every Man and his Property from foreign and domestick Injuries.[44]

3. *Eighteenth-Century Constitutional Theory*. Thus, by the end of the seventeenth century, the most important theoretical bases of the right to protection had been articulated: the common law doctrine of allegiance and protection; the original contract between king and people; and the theory of natural rights and the social contract. By the mid-eighteenth century, each of these concepts had been incorporated into the mainstream of English constitutional theory. The classic articulation of this theory was the *Commentaries on the Laws of England* published by Sir William Blackstone between 1765 and 1769.[45]

> when he who has the Supream Executive Power, neglects and abandons that charge, so that the Laws already made can no longer be put in execution. . . . Where there is no longer the administration of Justice, for the securing of Mens Rights, nor any remaining Power within the Community to direct the Force, or provide for the Necessities of the publick, there certainly is *no Government left*. Where the Laws cannot be executed, it is all one as if there were no Laws.

Id. § 219.

42. *See* RICHARD ASHCRAFT, REVOLUTIONARY POLITICS AND LOCKE'S TWO TREATISES OF GOVERNMENT 521-89 (1986).

43. On the radical opposition writers and their influence, see BERNARD BAILYN, THE IDEOLOGICAL ORIGINS OF THE AMERICAN REVOLUTION 34-54 (1967).

44. CATO'S LETTERS NO. 62, at 245 (London 3d ed. 1733). On *Cato's Letters*, see BAILYN, *supra* note 43, at 35-36.

In recent years, radical Whig writers such as Trenchard and Gordon have often been portrayed as "classical republicans" who subordinated individual rights to the good of the community, in contrast to Lockean liberals who founded government on the protection of individual rights. *See, e.g.*, DANIEL A. FARBER & SUZANNA SHERRY, A HISTORY OF THE AMERICAN CONSTITUTION 11-13 (1990). As this passage indicates, however, these writers were in complete accord with Locke on the government's obligation to protect natural rights.

45. BLACKSTONE, *supra* note 24.

Blackstone's chapter on the king's duties began with *Calvin's Case*. It was "a maxim in the law," he observed, "that protection and subjection are reciprocal."[46] Following the prevailing eighteenth-century view, he identified these "reciprocal duties" with "the *original contract* between king and people,"[47] the violation of which by James II had led to the Glorious Revolution.

Blackstone set the doctrine of reciprocal allegiance and protection in the broader framework of social contract theory. Although he denied the historical reality of a state of nature or a formal compact, he maintained that there was an "original contract of society . . . [that] in nature and reason must always be understood and implied, in the very act of associating together."[48] This contract provided:

> [T]hat the whole should protect all its parts, and that every part should pay obedience to the will of the whole, or, in other words, that the community should guard the rights of each individual member, and that (in return for this protection) each individual should submit to the laws of the community; without which submission of all it was impossible that protection should be certainly extended to any.[49]

In this formulation, Blackstone combined the three strands of English constitutional thought that we have considered.

A close reading of Blackstone reveals the structure of classical thought on the positive and negative character of individual rights and duties. In a state of nature, an individual has a right to be free from interference by others. In this sense, natural liberty is negative.[50] According to social contract theory, however, society is formed to obtain the advantages of association with others.[51] In contrast to natural liberty, the benefits of society are positive in character.[52] One of the

---

46. *Id.* at *233 (citing *Calvin's Case*, 7 Co. Rep. 1a, 5a, 77 Eng. Rep. 377, 382 (1608)); *see also id.* at *123 ("Allegiance is the right of the magistrate, and protection the right of the people.").

47. *Id.* at *233.

48. *Id.* at *47-48.

49. *Id.* at *48.

50. For a fuller discussion of the classical conception of liberty, which contained both positive and negative elements, see *infra* Part I(C).

51. *See, e.g.*, 1 BLACKSTONE, *supra* note 24, at *45, *47-48.

52. It is important to distinguish two meanings of the term "positive." In one sense, it is opposed to "negative." A positive right or liberty is a right to act in a particular way, or to receive or possess a particular thing, whereas a negative right or liberty is a right to be free from interference or coercion. For contemporary accounts of the relationship between positive and negative liberty, see ISAIAH BERLIN, *Two Concepts of Liberty*, *in* FOUR ESSAYS ON LIBERTY 118 (1969); LIBERTY (David Miller ed., 1991); Robin L. West, *Reconstructing Liberty*, 59 TENN. L. REV. (forthcoming 1992).

In a second sense, "positive" is contrasted with "natural." A positive right is one that derives from the positive law of the state as distinguished from the law of nature.

The right to protection was a positive right in the first sense. Whether it also can be called a positive right in the second sense is somewhat more complex. For Coke, the right to protection was

principal benefits is the protection of one's rights by the community.[53] Protection is a positive right—a claim on the community to provide something to which the individual is entitled.

In return for the benefits of society, the individual assumes certain positive duties, which are summed up in the obligation of allegiance or obedience. These duties, Blackstone writes, require simply that the individual "contribute, on his part, to the subsistence and peace of the society."[54] Among other things, the citizen is obligated to pay taxes,[55] to aid in enforcing the laws,[56] and to defend the community against rebellion or invasion.[57] In this sense, the obligation of protection runs both ways: The subject not only has a right to protection from the community, but also has a duty to contribute to the protection of other citizens and the

---

a natural right, arising from the natural bond between king and subject. For Locke and American writers, on the other hand, the right to protection derived not from the law of nature but from the social contract. In this sense, the right to protection was a positive rather than a natural right. *Cf.* 1 ANNALS OF CONG. 437 (Joseph Gales ed., 1789) (remarks of Rep. Madison) (distinguishing between natural rights and "positive rights . . . [that result] from the social compact which regulates the action of the community, but which [are] as essential to secure the liberty of the people as any of the pre-existent rights of nature"), *reprinted in* CREATING THE BILL OF RIGHTS 81 (Helen E. Veit et al. eds., 1991). As Madison indicates, however, positive rights of this kind were fundamental rights deriving not from positive law enacted by the legislature, but from the social contract itself. Thus, they were not "merely" positive in the sense that they were granted—and thus could be limited or denied—by the legislature.

The central issue in *DeShaney*, of course, relates to constitutional protection for positive as opposed to negative rights and liberties. In this Article, I shall use the term "positive" in that sense (except where referring to "positive law").

53. As Blackstone expressed it:

> [T]he principal aim of society is to protect individuals in the enjoyment of those absolute rights, which were vested in them by the immutable laws of nature, but which could not be preserved in peace without that mutual assistance and intercourse which is gained by the institution of friendly and social communities.

1 BLACKSTONE, *supra* note 24, at *124.

54. *Id.* at *45 (describing the duties of the individual regarded as a citizen).

55. Blackstone characterized taxes as "a portion which each subject contributes of his property, in order to secure the remainder." *Id.* at *281; *see also id.* at *307 (same). Locke explained the need for taxation in similar terms. *See* LOCKE, *supra* note 25, § 140.

56. For example, at common law, an individual who had knowledge that a felony had been committed had the legal duty to inform the authorities as soon as possible; failure to do so made the individual guilty of misprision of felony. 4 BLACKSTONE, *supra* note 24, at *121. In addition, every person who was present when a felony was committed had the legal duty to arrest the offender. *Id.* at *293. Individuals also were obligated to join the *posse comitatus* when requested to do so by an authorized officer. *Id.* at *122; *see also* 1 *id.* at *343-44.

57. *See* 4 *id.* at *122.

community itself.[58] To put it another way, under the classical view, society is an association for *mutual* protection.[59]

The community fulfills its duty of protection through the making and enforcement of laws. According to Blackstone, the legislative power in a state has an obligation to enact laws for the protection of natural rights.[60] He implies, for example, that laws must be enacted against murder and theft.[61] Such laws do not make these acts wrongful, but are merely declaratory of the law of nature, which forbids violations of the natural rights of individuals.[62]

The state's duty of protection requires not only the enactment of laws by the legislature, but also their enforcement by the executive and the courts. Under the English constitution, the executive power was

58. John Stuart Mill, although he rejected social contract theory, expressed the substance of this view in *On Liberty*:

> [E]very one who receives the protection of society owes a return for the benefit, and the fact of living in society renders it indispensable that each should be bound to observe a certain line of conduct towards the rest. This conduct consists first, in not injuring the interests of one another; . . . and secondly, in each person's bearing his share . . . of the labours and sacrifices incurred for defending the society or its members from injury and molestation.

JOHN S. MILL, ON LIBERTY 75 (Stefan Collini ed., 1989) (1859).

59. *See* LOCKE, *supra* note 25, § 123.

60. *See* 1 BLACKSTONE, *supra* note 24, at *52-53 (stating that it is not merely the right, but the duty of the legislature to make laws for the direction of individuals); *id.* at *41 (arguing that all valid human laws derive their force and authority from the law of nature); *id.* at *124 ("[T]he first and primary end of human laws is to maintain and regulate these *absolute* rights of individuals.").

61. *See id.* at *42-43, *54. From Blackstone's perspective, the question is not whether the state must pass laws forbidding murder, but whether it may pass laws allowing it or requiring it. This difference in perspective is important for understanding the classical conception of the state.

According to Blackstone, the legislative power of society has not merely the right, but the duty to make laws:

> For since the respective members are bound to conform themselves to the will of the state, it is expedient that they receive directions from the state declaratory of that its will. . . . [I]t is therefore incumbent on the state to establish general rules, for the perpetual information and direction of all persons in all points, whether of positive or negative duty.

Id. at *52-53. Thus, the state's law is comprehensive in nature; in principle it contains directions with respect to all situations. Because the law is comprehensive, it cannot remain neutral with respect to the legality of an act, but must take a position either forbidding, allowing, or requiring it. In the case of murder, for example, the state's law, if it is to conform with natural law, must declare that act to be a crime. If it does not enact such a law, the state in effect has provided that murder is allowed.

This interpretation helps to explain Blackstone's statement that a human law would violate natural law if it "should *allow* or enjoin us to commit" murder. *Id.* at *43 (emphasis added). To a modern reader, the reference to a law "allow[ing]" the commission of murder seems odd. Under the conception of state action that prevails today—and that underlies the position taken by Judge Posner and Chief Justice Rehnquist in *DeShaney*—a state that failed to legislate against murder would have taken no action at all, but simply failed to intervene to prevent private conduct. Under the classical view, however, the state's failure to prohibit murder would, in effect, have allowed it, in contravention of the law of nature.

62. *See id.* at *42-43, *54.

vested in the king.[63] The function of the king as supreme executive was "to protect the community, and each individual therein, from every degree of injurious violence, by executing those laws which the people themselves . . . have consented to."[64]

To a large extent, the king enforces the laws through his courts.[65] Courts of justice, according to Blackstone, are instituted "[t]he more effectually to accomplish the redress of private injuries, . . . in order to protect the weak from the insults of the stronger, by expounding and enforcing those laws, by which rights are defined, and wrongs are prohibited."[66] Blackstone stresses that the state, through its courts, has a *duty* to dispense justice to individuals; the administration of justice is a matter not of discretion, but of right.[67]

As the above discussion suggests, there is an important connection between the duty of protection and two other central doctrines of classical liberal thought: the rule of law and the separation of powers. The rule of law implies, among other things, that the rights of individuals are not dependent for their protection upon the arbitrary will of the government, but are recognized and protected by law. The legislature has a duty to enact laws for the protection of individual rights, the executive has a duty to enforce them, and the courts have a duty to apply them.

B. *The Right to Protection in Early American Constitutionalism*

American thought during the Revolutionary era was deeply influenced by all of these sources—the common law tradition of Coke and Blackstone, the history of English constitutionalism and the Glorious

63. *Id.* at *190.

64. 4 *id.* at *127.

65. *See* 3 *id.* at *23-24 ("[C]ourts of justice . . . are the medium by which [the king] administers the laws.").

66. *Id.* at *2.

67. *See, e.g.*, 1 *id.* at *141; *id.* at *266 ("Justice is not derived from the king, as from his free gift, but he is the steward of the public, to dispense it to whom it is *due*."); 3 *id.* at *115 (The king is "officially bound to redress in the ordinary forms of law" wrongs committed between subjects.).

This classical conception of the administration of justice should be contrasted with the legal positivist view that became predominant in the late nineteenth century. One of the leading exponents of this view, Thomas M. Cooley (who himself was an editor and thoughtful critic of Blackstone's *Commentaries*), wrote as follows:

> [D]oing justice as between particular individuals, when they have a controversy before [a court], is not the end and object which were in view when [the] court was created . . . . Courts are created on public grounds; they are to do justice as between suitors, to the end that peace and order may prevail in the political society, and that rights may be protected and preserved. The duty is public: the individual advantage or loss results from the proper and thorough or improper and imperfect performance of a duty for which his controversy is only an occasion.

THOMAS M. COOLEY, A TREATISE ON THE LAW OF TORTS OR THE WRONGS WHICH ARISE INDEPENDENTLY OF CONTRACT *379 (1st ed. 1879).

Revolution, and the natural rights theory of Locke's *Second Treatise*.[68] What integrated all these sources into a coherent worldview for Americans, as Bernard Bailyn and Gordon Wood have shown, was radical Whig ideology.[69] As we have seen, it was a basic tenet of Whig ideology that protection was a primary purpose of government.[70]

In this way, the concept of protection became a fundamental principle of American constitutionalism. It played an important role in the Revolutionary controversy, and became a basic element of the newly formed governments.

1. *The Revolution*. The decision in *Calvin's Case* played an important role in the controversy between Americans and Great Britain leading up to the Revolution. The decision was relevant not only for its formulation of the relationship between subject and sovereign, but also because of the concrete issues that gave rise to that formulation.

The immediate issue in *Calvin's Case* was the status under English law of Scots born after the accession of James I of England, who already was King of Scotland. Coke held that as subjects of the same king, Scots were entitled to the same protection as his English subjects, and therefore were entitled to all the rights of subjects under English law, including the right to hold property. At the same time, however, Coke recognized that although they shared an allegiance to the same king, England and Scotland were separate realms, with separate parliaments and laws.[71]

Confronted with assertions of the absolute supremacy of Parliament over the colonies, Americans struggled during the decade before 1776 to define their status and rights within the British Empire. Gradually, they came to the view that their position was analogous to that of Scotland at the time *Calvin's Case* was decided. Following Coke's analysis of Scotland, they argued that the colonies were united to Great Britain only through their shared allegiance to a common king. Thus, Americans were not subject to the authority of Parliament at all, but only to their own legislatures and King George III.[72]

In this way, Coke's doctrine of reciprocal obligations came to the forefront of American constitutional thought. "The colonists," wrote James Wilson in an influential pamphlet, "ought to be dependent on the king, because they have hitherto enjoyed, and still continue to enjoy, his protection. . . . [O]bedience is founded on the protection derived from

68. *See* BAILYN, *supra* note 43, at 22-54; WOOD, *supra* note 24, at 6-10.
69. *See* BAILYN, *supra* note 43, at 34; WOOD, *supra* note 24, at 14-17.
70. *See supra* text accompanying note 44.
71. *See* KETTNER, *supra* note 17, at 13-28.
72. *See id.* at 131-72.

government: for protection and allegiance are the reciprocal bonds, which connect the prince and his subjects."[73]

Although they adopted Coke's theory of the British Empire, Americans rejected his view that the bond between subjects and sovereign was natural and immutable.[74] Instead, they described this relationship in terms of the original contract between king and people, in which the king was bound to protect the rights of his subjects in return for their allegiance.[75]

When Americans finally decided to break from Great Britain, they appealed to the precedent of the Glorious Revolution, in which James II was held to have "abdicated" government as a result of breaking the original contract.[76] Thus, the Declaration of Independence, after reciting a long list of grievances that the king had failed to redress, alleged that the king "has abdicated Government here, by declaring us out of his Protection and waging War against us."[77] Several state constitutions justified independence on the same ground.[78]

2. *The First State Constitutions*. After independence, Americans turned to the creation of new state governments.[79] In this context, the traditional image of a bond between subjects and rulers lost much of its force.[80] Instead, Americans viewed themselves as free citizens deliberating on the structure of their political life. In framing their new governments, they were strongly influenced by social contract theory.[81]

---

73. JAMES WILSON, CONSIDERATIONS ON THE NATURE AND EXTENT OF THE LEGISLATIVE AUTHORITY OF THE BRITISH PARLIAMENT (1774), *reprinted in* 2 THE WORKS OF JAMES WILSON 743 (Robert G. McCloskey ed., 1967). For another extensive discussion of the application of *Calvin's Case* to the Revolutionary controversy, see JOHN ADAMS, NOVANGLUS IX (1774), *reprinted in* 4 THE WORKS OF JOHN ADAMS 141-51 (Charles Adams ed., 1851).

74. *See* KETTNER, *supra* note 17, at 165.

75. *See id.* at 160-61, 165-67; WOOD, *supra* note 24, at 268-70.

76. *See* KETTNER, *supra* note 17, at 169-71; GARRY WILLS, INVENTING AMERICA: JEFFERSON'S DECLARATION OF INDEPENDENCE 52-55, 64 (1978); WOOD, *supra* note 24, at 270.

77. THE DECLARATION OF INDEPENDENCE para. 25 (U.S. 1776). In his draft of the Declaration, Jefferson had written "declaring us out of his allegiance & protection." *See* WILLS, *supra* note 76, at 376.

78. *See* N.J. CONST. of 1776, pmbl., *reprinted in* 6 STATE CONSTITUTIONS, *supra* note 13, at 449-50; N.Y. CONST. of 1777, pmbl., *reprinted in* 7 STATE CONSTITUTIONS, *supra* note 13, at 169; N.C. CONST. of 1776, *reprinted in* 7 STATE CONSTITUTIONS, *supra* note 13, at 404; PA. CONST. of 1776, *reprinted in* 8 STATE CONSTITUTIONS, *supra* note 13, at 277; S.C. CONST. of 1776, *reprinted in* STATE CONSTITUTIONS, *supra* note 13, at 464; VA. CONST. of 1776, *reprinted in* 10 STATE CONSTITUTIONS, *supra* note 13, at 52.

79. On the making of the state constitutions, see generally WILLI P. ADAMS, THE FIRST AMERICAN CONSTITUTIONS (Rita Kimber & Robert Kimber trans., 1980); WOOD, *supra* note 24, at 125-255.

80. *See* WOOD, *supra* note 24, at 282-83, 290.

81. *See* ADAMS, *supra* note 79, at 156-58; WOOD, *supra* note 24, at 282-91.

Most of the first state constitutions included a bill of rights,[82] which generally began by declaring the natural rights of mankind. For example, Virginia's Declaration of Rights, the first to be adopted, asserted:

> That all men are by nature equally free and independent, and have certain inherent rights, of which, when they enter into a state of society, they cannot, by any compact, deprive or divest their posterity; namely, the enjoyment of life and liberty, with the means of acquiring and possessing property, and pursuing and obtaining happiness and safety.[83]

This provision implied that society was founded on contract, a view that was made explicit in the Massachusetts Constitution of 1780:

> The body-politic is formed by a voluntary association of individuals; it is a social compact by which the whole people covenants with each citizen and each citizen with the whole people that all shall be governed by certain laws for the common good . . .; that every man may, at all times, find his security in them.[84]

With its basis in such a compact, the function of government was to protect the natural rights of its citizens. Thus, several states declared that "government is, or ought to be, instituted for the common benefit, protection, and security of the people."[85] As we have seen, a number of states expressly recognized protection as the right of every individual.[86] As the Massachusetts Constitution put it:

---

82. *See* CONN. CONST. ORDINANCE of 1776, art. I, *reprinted in* 2 STATE CONSTITUTIONS, *supra* note 13, at 143-44; DEL. DECLARATION OF RIGHTS of 1776, *reprinted in* 2 STATE CONSTITUTIONS, *supra* note 13, at 197-99; MD. DECLARATION OF RIGHTS of 1776, *reprinted in* 4 STATE CONSTITUTIONS, *supra* note 13, at 372-75; MASS. CONST. of 1780, pt. I, *reprinted in* 5 STATE CONSTITUTIONS, *supra* note 13, at 93-96; N.H. CONST. of 1784, pt. I, *reprinted in* 6 STATE CONSTITUTIONS, *supra* note 13, at 344-47; N.C. CONST. of 1776, Declaration of Rights, *reprinted in* 7 STATE CONSTITUTIONS, *supra* note 13, at 402-04; PA. CONST. of 1776, Declaration of Rights, *reprinted in* 8 STATE CONSTITUTIONS, *supra* note 13, at 278-79; VA. DECLARATION OF RIGHTS of 1776, *reprinted in* 10 STATE CONSTITUTIONS, *supra* note 13, at 48-50.

83. VA. DECLARATION OF RIGHTS § 1, *reprinted in* 10 STATE CONSTITUTIONS, *supra* note 13, at 49. For similar provisions, see MASS. CONST. of 1780, pt. I, art. I, *reprinted in* 5 STATE CONSTITUTIONS, *supra* note 13, at 93; N.H. CONST. of 1784, pt. I, art. II, *reprinted in* 6 STATE CONSTITUTIONS, *supra* note 13, at 344; PA. CONST. of 1776, Declaration of Rights, art. I, *reprinted in* 8 STATE CONSTITUTIONS, *supra* note 13, at 278.

84. MASS. CONST. of 1780, pmbl., *reprinted in* 5 STATE CONSTITUTIONS, *supra* note 13, at 92-93. The Massachusetts Constitution was drafted by John Adams. *See* ADAMS, *supra* note 79, at 92, 157. Adams's draft appears in 4 THE WORKS OF JOHN ADAMS, *supra* note 73, at 219-67.

85. VA. DECLARATION OF RIGHTS § 3, *reprinted in* 10 STATE CONSTITUTIONS, *supra* note 13, at 49. For similar provisions, see MASS. CONST. of 1780, pt. I, art. VII, *reprinted in* 5 STATE CONSTITUTIONS, *supra* note 13, at 94; N.H. CONST. of 1784, pt. I, art. X, *reprinted in* 6 STATE CONSTITUTIONS, *supra* note 13, at 345; PA. CONST. of 1776, Declaration of Rights, art. V, *reprinted in* 8 STATE CONSTITUTIONS, *supra* note 13, at 278; R.I. DECLARATION OF RIGHTS OF 1776, § 2, *reprinted in* 8 STATE CONSTITUTIONS, *supra* note 13, at 387; VT. CONST. of 1777, pmbl., *reprinted in* 9 STATE CONSTITUTIONS, *supra* note 13, at 487.

86. *See supra* text accompanying notes 13-14.

> Each individual of the society has a right to be protected by it in the enjoyment of his life, liberty, and property, according to standing laws. He is obliged, consequently, to contribute his share to the expense of this protection; to give his personal service, or an equivalent, when necessary; but no part of the property of any individual can, with justice, be taken from him, or applied to public uses, without his own consent, or that of the representative body of the people.[87]

This provision articulates the essence of the classical eighteenth-century doctrine of the right to protection. Every individual has a positive right to protection by society. This protection is afforded by the enactment and execution of laws for the security of life, liberty, and property.[88] In return for this protection, the individual owes positive duties to society. He is obliged to pay taxes to meet the expense of protection—with the Lockean reservation, however, that he may not be taxed without his consent or that of his representatives.[89] In addition, where necessary he must render personal service in defense of the community.[90]

3. *The Federal Constitution*. The view that government was formed to protect the life, liberty, and property of its citizens was fully shared by the Framers of the Federal Constitution.[91] As James Madison wrote in *The Federalist*, the "protection" of "the faculties of men," and of "the rights of property" to which these faculties give rise, "is the first object of government."[92] The advocates of the Constitution argued, among other things, that the rights of citizens would enjoy greater security under the proposed Constitution than under the Confederation.[93]

---

87. MASS. CONST. of 1780, pt. I, art. X, *reprinted in* 5 STATE CONSTITUTIONS, *supra* note 13, at 94.

88. In addition to article X, quoted in text, see the preamble to the Massachusetts Constitution: "It is the duty of the people, . . . in framing a constitution of government, to provide for an equitable mode of making laws, as well as for an impartial interpretation and a faithful execution of them; that every man may, at all times, find his security in them." *Id.* pmbl., *reprinted in* 5 STATE CONSTITUTIONS, *supra* note 13, at 93.

89. *See* LOCKE, *supra* note 25, § 140.

90. This point is expressed most clearly in the New York Constitution: "[I]t is the duty of every man who enjoys the protection of society to be prepared and willing to defend it." N.Y. CONST. of 1777, art. XL, *reprinted in* 7 STATE CONSTITUTIONS, *supra* note 13, at 179.

91. *See generally* JENNIFER NEDELSKY, PRIVATE PROPERTY AND THE LIMITS OF AMERICAN CONSTITUTIONALISM (1990).

92. THE FEDERALIST NO. 10, at 42 (James Madison) (Max Beloff ed., 2d ed. 1987). (All further citations to the *Federalist* will be to this edition.) For an excellent discussion of *The Federalist*, see DAVID F. EPSTEIN, THE POLITICAL THEORY OF THE FEDERALIST (1984).

93. *See, e.g.*, THE FEDERALIST NO. 51, at 267 (James Madison). In the fifty-first *Federalist*, for example, Madison argued in favor of establishing "the extended republic of the United States" by means of an analogy to the state of nature and the social compact:

> Justice is the end of government. It is the end of civil society. . . . In a society, under the forms of which the stronger faction can readily unite and oppress the weaker, anarchy may as truly be said to reign, as in a state of nature where the weaker individual is not secured against the violence of the stronger: And as in the latter state even the stronger individuals

Under the Constitution, the function of protection was divided between the federal government, which was to serve "general and national purposes," and the states, which retained authority over local affairs.[94] Thus, the national government was responsible for security against foreign danger.[95] In addition, the United States was obligated under the Constitution to "protect each of [the states] against Invasion; and on Application of the Legislature . . . against domestic Violence."[96] The states, on the other hand, were to retain their role as "the immediate and visible guardian[s] of life and property," a role that they performed through "the ordinary administration of civil and criminal justice."[97] Thus, Madison wrote, the powers reserved to the states extended "to all the objects, which, in the ordinary course of affairs, concern the lives, liberties, and properties of the people."[98]

In this light, it is hardly surprising that the federal Bill of Rights contained no guarantee of a right to protection similar to those found in the state constitutions.[99] The Bill of Rights, which was added to the Constitution largely in response to opponents' fears of arbitrary federal power, imposed restrictions only on the federal government.[100] Under the Constitution, however, it was the states, not the federal government, which were to provide general protection of life, liberty, and property.

> are prompted by the uncertainty of their condition, to submit to a government, which may protect the weak as well as themselves: so in the former state, will the more powerful factions be gradually induced by a like motive to wish for a government which will protect all parties, the weaker as well as the more powerful.

Id. at 267-68.

It should be observed that in this passage, Madison treats the oppression of faction as essentially a sort of *private* domination—domination by a group for the sake of its own private interest, even though a faction that constitutes a majority may accomplish that domination under the forms of republican government. He argues that the end of civil society requires that government be constructed in such a way as to protect against such domination. Similarly, Locke wrote that government was established to enact rules to "moderate the Dominion of every Part and Member of the Society." LOCKE, *supra* note 25, § 222.

94. THE FEDERALIST NO. 3, at 9 (John Jay); *see also* THE FEDERALIST NO. 10, *supra* note 92, at 46.

95. THE FEDERALIST NO. 45, at 234 (James Madison); *see also* THE FEDERALIST NO. 3, *supra* note 94; THE FEDERALIST NO. 41, at 204 (James Madison) (referring to "[s]ecurity against foreign danger" as "one of the primitive objects of civil society" and "an avowed and essential object of the American Union").

96. U.S. CONST. art. IV, § 4.

97. THE FEDERALIST NO. 17, at 80 (Alexander Hamilton).

98. THE FEDERALIST NO. 45, *supra* note 95, at 238.

99. *See supra* text accompanying notes 85-87 (discussing state constitutional provisions). As we shall see, however, the Due Process Clause of the Fifth Amendment can be interpreted to recognize a right to protection within the sphere of the federal government. *See infra* text accompanying notes 333-65.

100. For accounts of the framing of the Bill of Rights, see FARBER & SHERRY, *supra* note 44, at 219-45; ROBERT A. RUTLAND, THE BIRTH OF THE BILL OF RIGHTS, 1776-1791 (1955).

Thus, it would have made no sense for the Bill of Rights to recognize a general right to protection by the federal government.

It would have been possible, on the other hand, for the Constitution to have guaranteed a right to protection by the states. The original Constitution, however, imposed few restrictions on the states.[101] Although most of these restrictions were calculated to prevent state interference with the national objects committed to Congress, others related to individual rights. In addition to such negative rights as the safeguards against bills of attainder and ex post facto laws,[102] the Constitution secured certain positive rights to protection by the states. Two such rights were of particular importance. First, the ban on state laws "impairing the Obligation of Contracts"[103] implied that the states had a duty to enforce the lawful rights of creditors.[104] Second, the Comity Clause provided that "[t]he Citizens of each State shall be entitled to all Privileges and Immunities of Citizens in the several States."[105] The basic purpose of this provision was to require that a citizen of one state be accorded rights of citizenship when traveling or residing in other states. As we shall see, the courts interpreted this provision to include the right to protection by state government—an understanding that was later incorporated into the Privileges or Immunities Clause of the Fourteenth Amendment.[106]

Apart from these limited provisions, the original Constitution did not protect individual rights—negative or positive—in relation to the states. Instead, the founders apparently assumed that the states could be relied upon to protect adequately the rights of their citizens. As we shall see, the mid-nineteenth-century conflicts over slavery and civil rights led the Framers of the Fourteenth Amendment to reject this assumption, and to incorporate a right to protection by state government into the Federal Constitution.

C. *Protection and Liberty*

The right to protection was informed by the classical conception of liberty. Contrary to Posner's view, this conception was not merely one of

101. These restrictions are primarily found in Article I, Section 10.

102. U.S. CONST. art. I, § 10, cl. 1.

103. *Id.*

104. On the affirmative obligation imposed by the contract clause, see David P. Currie, *Positive and Negative Constitutional Rights*, 53 U. CHI. L. REV. 864, 874-75 (1986). For a summary of antebellum contract-clause jurisprudence, see THOMAS M. COOLEY, A TREATISE ON THE CONSTITUTIONAL LIMITATIONS WHICH REST UPON THE LEGISLATIVE POWER OF THE STATES OF THE AMERICAN UNION *273-94 (1868 & photo. reprint 1972).

105. U.S. CONST. art. IV, § 2, cl. 1.

106. *See infra* text accompanying notes 316-32.

negative liberty, but had an important positive dimension—the protection of individual rights under law.[107]

Blackstone's account once more provides the best starting point for analysis.[108] Following Locke, Blackstone begins with "natural liberty"—the freedom that would be enjoyed by individuals in a state of nature. He defines natural liberty as "a power of acting as one thinks fit, without any restraint or control, unless by the law of nature."[109]

This conception of natural liberty contains both positive and negative elements. The first branch of the definition is positive: "a power of acting as one thinks fit." Liberty is not merely a lack of constraint, but a power—the capacity to act according to one's own reason and free choice.[110] In this sense, liberty means "*Self-determination*" or "*Self-direction*."[111]

In a state of nature, the individual possesses the power to act "without any restraint or control."[112] It is true, as Blackstone adds, that this liberty is limited by "the law of nature."[113] But that law, lacking effective means of enforcement outside civil society, is a matter more of internal guidance than of external constraint.[114] In this respect, natural liberty comes close to being a pure form of negative freedom.

107. On the distinction between negative and positive rights and liberties, see *supra* note 52. For a valuable account of the eighteenth-century conception of liberty, see JOHN P. REID, THE CONCEPT OF LIBERTY IN THE AGE OF THE AMERICAN REVOLUTION (1988). Reid properly emphasizes the importance of common law ideas, but underrates the role of natural rights in eighteenth-century thought.

108. Blackstone's account of liberty is of particular importance for several reasons: it was representative of much contemporary thought, *see* REID, *supra* note 107; it had great influence on the conception of liberty within the legal tradition prior to the Civil War; and it was relied upon during the congressional debates leading to the adoption of the Fourteenth Amendment, *see infra* text accompanying note 254-55.

109. 1 BLACKSTONE, *supra* note 24, at *125. For a similar definition, see LOCKE, *supra* note 25, § 4.

110. On the eighteenth-century definition of liberty in terms of power, see WOOD, *supra* note 24, at 21-23. For example, in *Cato's Letters*, Trenchard and Gordon defined liberty as "the Power which every Man has over his own Actions, and his Right to enjoy the Fruits of his Labour, Art, and Industry." CATO'S LETTERS NO. 62, *supra* note 44, at 244. For the philosophical basis of this view, see JOHN LOCKE, AN ESSAY CONCERNING HUMAN UNDERSTANDING bk. II, ch. XXI (Peter H. Nidditch ed., 1975).

111. RICHARD PRICE, OBSERVATIONS ON THE NATURE OF CIVIL LIBERTY 3 (London, 1776). As Price makes clear, liberty in classical liberal thought is an attribute of the individual considered as an *actor*, not merely as the passive object of action by others. *See id.* (By natural or "physical" liberty, "I mean that principle of . . . *Self-determination*, which constitutes us *Agents*; or which gives us a command over our actions."); *see also* LOCKE, *supra* note 25, §§ 57-59 (discussing liberty of individual as "*a free and intelligent Agent*"). Self-determination is at the root of the positive concept of liberty. *See* BERLIN, *supra* note 52, at 131.

112. 1 BLACKSTONE, *supra* note 24, at *125.

113. *Id.*

114. *See id.* at *39-41, *125; *see also* LOCKE, *supra* note 25, § 136.

Such unrestrained liberty, however, is self-destructive: If no one is subject to any external restraints, then no one can have any security against the invasion of his liberty by others.[115] Thus, to secure their liberty and to obtain the other benefits of social life, individuals enter into society and agree to obey its laws. In so doing, they give up a part of their natural liberty—the unrestrained right to act as they think fit—but gain something more valuable: "civil liberty," which is the liberty that belongs to individuals as members of society.[116]

Blackstone defines civil liberty as "natural liberty so far restrained by human laws (and no farther) as is necessary and expedient for the general advantage of the public."[117] Again, this conception of civil liberty has both negative and positive elements.[118]

In its negative aspect, civil liberty requires that individuals be left free from state control except where necessary for the public good. Blackstone condemns "every wanton and causeless restraint of the will of the subject" as "a degree of tyranny" and "destructive of liberty."[119] Much of Blackstone's chapter on "the absolute rights of individuals" is devoted to English constitutional protections against governmental oppression, such as the writ of habeas corpus.[120] Similarly, much of Chancellor James Kent's corresponding discussion relates to the provisions of the American bills of rights that protect individual rights against the government.[121] This is the negative liberty that Posner emphasizes.

There was, however, a positive element in the concept of civil liberty that was no less essential. For the principal justification of legal restraints on conduct was to protect the rights of members of society.

---

115. *See* 1 BLACKSTONE, *supra* note 24, at *125.

116. *Id.* For a similar account of natural and civil liberty, see JAMES WILSON, *Speech Delivered on 26th November, 1787, in the Convention of Pennsylvania*, *in* 2 THE WORKS OF JAMES WILSON, *supra* note 73, at 765, 767.

Civil liberty was sometimes referred to by Blackstone and others as "political liberty." This term, however, soon came to mean the right to share in political power, especially in America. *See infra* text accompanying notes 129-30.

117. 1 BLACKSTONE, *supra* note 24, at *123 (citing J. INST. 1.3.1). For a similar view, see MONTESQUIEU, THE SPIRIT OF THE LAWS pt. 2, bk. 11, ch. 3, at 155 (Anne M. Cohler et al. trans. & eds., 1989).

118. Although Blackstone does not do so, one might distinguish between *private civil liberty* (the individual's liberty in relation to other individuals in civil society) and *public civil liberty* (his liberty in relation to the state). Private civil liberty includes the same elements as natural liberty, modified by civil society. In a positive sense, it means the power to act as one thinks fit, within the bounds of civil law; in a negative sense, it means freedom from all restraints not authorized by that law. *See* LOCKE, *supra* note 25, § 22. In the following two paragraphs, I discuss the classical conception of public civil liberty.

119. 1 BLACKSTONE, *supra* note 24, at *126.

120. *See id.* at *122-44.

121. *See* 2 JAMES KENT, COMMENTARIES ON AMERICAN LAW *1-37 (1826).

Thus, Blackstone argues, "the law, which restrains a man from doing mischief to his fellow-citizens, though it diminishes the natural, increases the civil liberty of mankind."[122] From this positive perspective, it may be said that "civil liberty, rightly understood, consists in protecting the rights of individuals by the united force of society."[123] Used in this way, liberty is virtually synonymous with protection.[124]

Thus, in contrast to a negative conception of liberty, which perceives law solely as a limitation on individual freedom, classical liberalism regarded law as essential to liberty.[125] As Locke wrote: "*Liberty* is to be free from restraint and violence from others which cannot be, where there is no Law"; thus, "however it may be mistaken, *the end of Law* is not to abolish or restrain, but *to preserve and enlarge Freedom*."[126]

Incorporating both the negative and the positive elements of civil liberty, Blackstone describes rights under the English constitution as "either that *residuum* of natural liberty, which is not required by the laws of society to be sacrificed to public convenience; or else those civil privileges, which society hath engaged to provide, in lieu of the natural liberties so given up by individuals."[127]

---

122. 1 BLACKSTONE, *supra* note 24, at *125-26.

123. *Id.* at *251. Similarly, the author of a British pamphlet asserted that "[t]rue political Liberty consists in the protection, safety, and defence of every one in the peaceable enjoyment of his own rights, guarantee'd and secured to him by the laws, to which a full and exact obedience and submission are due." CIVIL LIBERTY ASSERTED 30-31 (London, 1776), *quoted in* REID, *supra* note 107, at 68.

124. For other examples of this usage, see 1 BLACKSTONE, *supra* note 24, at *424 (Because slavery is not recognized by English law, "the instant [a slave] lands in England, [he] becomes a freeman; *that is, the law will protect him in the enjoyment of his person, and his property*.") (emphasis added); *id.* at *425 (The law of England "gives liberty, rightly understood, *that is, protection*" to all persons irrespective of religion.) (emphasis added).

A closely related usage identified liberty with security. *See, e.g.*, REID, *supra* note 107, at 68-71; WOOD, *supra* note 24, at 609 & n.22. As Montesquieu expressed it, political or civil liberty is "that tranquility of spirit which comes from the opinion each one has of his security, and in order for him to have this liberty the government must be such that one citizen cannot fear another citizen." MONTESQUIEU, *supra* note 117, pt. 2, bk. 11, ch. 6, at 157.

125. *See* REID, *supra* note 107, ch. 8; *see also* ADAMS, *supra* note 79, at 159-60; FORREST MCDONALD, NOVUS ORDO SECLORUM: THE INTELLECTUAL ORIGINS OF THE CONSTITUTION 159-60 (1985).

126. LOCKE, *supra* note 25, § 57.

127. 1 BLACKSTONE, *supra* note 24, at *129. As Michael Kent Curtis has suggested, this conception of constitutional liberty as including both the privileges of society and a residuum of natural liberty appears to be one precursor of the term "privileges or immunities," a concept that has a central place in the Fourteenth Amendment. *See* MICHAEL K. CURTIS, NO STATE SHALL ABRIDGE: THE FOURTEENTH AMENDMENT AND THE BILL OF RIGHTS 64 (1986). For further discussion of privileges and immunities, see *infra* text accompanying notes 316-32.

Americans accepted the classical definition of civil liberty as natural liberty bounded and protected by law.[128] In addition, they emphasized a third sort of freedom, often referred to as political liberty: the right to participate in self-government, in making the laws by which one was ruled.[129] As the Delaware Declaration of Rights expressed it, "the Right in the People to participate in the Legislature, is the Foundation of Liberty and of all free Government."[130] Political liberty constituted the right to self-determination of the community as a whole.

Articulating the American view in 1826, Kent wrote that civil liberty "consists in being protected and governed by laws made . . . by the representatives of the people, and conducive to the general welfare."[131] Thus, explained Francis Lieber, civil liberty meant "not only the absence of individual restraint"; instead, "when the term Civil Liberty is used, there is now always meant a high degree of mutually guaranteed protection against interference with [important] interests and rights . . . together with an effectual share in the making and administration of the laws as the best apparatus to secure that protection."[132]

II. The Legal Meaning of Protection

As I have shown above, the right to protection was a central principle of Anglo-American constitutionalism prior to the Civil War. This right was not merely a matter of constitutional theory, but was a concrete legal concept.

This Part explores the concept of protection in the classical legal tradition. That concept had three major elements. The first related to the *status* of the individual: To be under the protection of the law meant

128. *See, e.g.*, Bailyn, *supra* note 43, at 77; McDonald, *supra* note 125, at 159-60; Reid, *supra* note 107, at 61. For an excellent account of the American view of liberty and protection, in some respects similar to the account presented here, see Philip A. Hamburger, Equal Protection and Equal Civil Rights in Eighteenth Century America (unpublished manuscript) (Part I: The State-of-Nature Analysis and the Idea of Protection).

129. *See* Adams, *supra* note 79, at 156-57; Wood, *supra* note 24, at 24-25; Gordon S. Wood, *Classical Republicanism and the American Revolution*, 66 Chi.-Kent L. Rev. 13, 23 (1990).

130. Del. Declaration of Rights of 1776, art. 6, *reprinted in* 2 State Constitutions, *supra* note 13, at 198; *see also* Md. Const. of 1776, Declaration of Rights, art. V, *reprinted in* 4 State Constitutions, *supra* note 13, at 373; Adams, *supra* note 79, at 157.

131. 2 Kent, *supra* note 121, at *1.

132. Francis Lieber, Civil Liberty and Self-Government 24 (2d ed. 1859). For a late nineteenth-century expression of the same view, see Thomas M. Cooley, The General Principles of Constitutional Law (1880):

> Civil liberty may be defined as that condition in which rights are established and protected, by means of such limitations and restraints upon the action of individual members of the political society as are needed to prevent what would be injurious to other individuals, or prejudicial to the general welfare.

Id. at 226.

to have the status of a freeman and a citizen. A second aspect referred to *substantive rights*: Protection meant that the law recognized and secured an individual's rights to life, liberty, and property. Finally, the most basic meaning of protection referred to the *enforcement of rights*: the specific ways in which government prevented violations of substantive rights, or redressed and punished such violations.

A. *The Status of Freeman and Citizen*

As we have seen, the classical tradition identified liberty with protection.[133] In one sense, therefore, to be under the protection of the law meant to be a free person, one whose rights were recognized by the law. In relation to the state, it meant to be a subject or, in a republic, a citizen—a person entitled to protection as a member of the political community. In this way, the concept of protection was closely related to the ideas of legal personality and citizenship.[134]

In the classical tradition, the opposite of a free person was a slave. Slavery was both a political and a legal concept. As John Phillip Reid has explained, slavery in a political sense meant arbitrary government and "the absence of [the rule of] law: law that protected the individual and law that limited the authority of both private masters and public rulers."[135]

In a legal sense, slavery was subjection to the absolute power of a master, without protection under the law; slaves were regarded "as things or property, rather than persons."[136] In *Somerset's Case*,[137] Lord Mansfield declared that slavery was "so odious" that "it is incapable of being introduced on any reasons, moral or political; but only [by] positive law," and held that slavery was not recognized by the law of England.[138] For this reason, Blackstone wrote, "the instant [a slave] lands in England, [he] becomes a freeman; that is, the law will protect him in the enjoyment of his person, and his property."[139]

Slavery, of course, continued to exist by positive law in much of the United States. As Jacobus tenBroek and William Wiecek have shown,

---

133. *See supra* Part I(C).

134. On the relation between protection and citizenship, see generally KETTNER, *supra* note 17.

135. REID, *supra* note 107, at 48. On the political concept of slavery, see *id.* at 38-54; BAILYN, *supra* note 43, at 232-46.

136. 1 BLACKSTONE, *supra* note 24, at *423-24; *see also* 2 KENT, *supra* note 121, at *253.

137. Somerset v. Stewart, Loftt 1, 98 Eng. Rep. 499 (K.B. 1772).

138. *Id.* at 19, 98 Eng. Rep. at 510. On *Somerset's Case* and its importance in American law, see WILLIAM M. WIECEK, THE SOURCES OF ANTISLAVERY CONSTITUTIONALISM IN AMERICA, 1760-1848, at 28-45 (1977).

139. 1 BLACKSTONE, *supra* note 24, at *424; *see also* 2 KENT, *supra* note 121, at *248-49.

the right to protection became a central concept in anti-slavery constitutionalism prior to the Civil War.[140] As we shall see, extending the protection of the law to the former slaves was one of the principal objects of the Fourteenth Amendment.[141]

B. *Recognition of Substantive Rights*

To enjoy the status of a freeman and a citizen implied that one's rights were recognized. This leads to the second basic aspect of "protection": the recognition of substantive rights by the law. The law protected rights in this sense by declaring that persons had certain rights and directing that those rights be observed.[142]

The classical legal tradition distinguished between two sorts of substantive rights: "absolute" and "relative." Absolute rights were those that would belong to individuals in a state of nature.[143] By contrast, relative rights were those that were "incident to [persons] as members of society, and standing in various relations to each other."[144] Blackstone declared that "the first and primary end of human laws" was "to protect individuals in the enjoyment of [their] absolute rights"; the protection of relative rights was a secondary aim.[145]

The classical tradition identified the absolute rights of individuals as the rights of personal security, personal liberty, and private property.[146] Personal security was defined as "a person's legal and uninterrupted enjoyment of his life, his limbs, his body, his health, and his reputation."[147] Personal liberty was the power of moving "without imprisonment or restraint, unless by due course of law."[148] Finally, the right of private property consisted of "the free use, enjoyment, and disposal of all [one's] acquisitions, without any control or diminution, save only by the laws of the land."[149] Taken together, these three absolute rights were often referred to as "security of person and property."

---

140. *See* TENBROEK, *supra* note 10, at 51-54, 117-20; WIECEK, *supra* note 138, at 155-56, 267-70, 275.

141. *See infra* Part III.

142. *See* 1 BLACKSTONE, *supra* note 24, at *54-55.

143. *See id.* at *123-24.

144. *Id.* at *123. For example, personal liberty was an absolute right, whereas the relationship of master and servant gave rise to relative rights. *See id.* at *134, *422.

145. *Id.* at *124-25.

146. *Id.* at *129; 2 KENT, *supra* note 121, at *1.

147. 1 BLACKSTONE, *supra* note 24, at *129. American writers added such rights as freedom of religion and freedom of opinion to the category of absolute rights. *See, e.g.*, *id.* at *129 n.6 (Tucker ed. note); 2 KENT, *supra* note 121, at *34-37.

148. 1 BLACKSTONE, *supra* note 24, at *134.

149. *Id.* at *138.

To understand the classical notion of absolute rights, it is essential to recognize that "absolute" had a different meaning than it does in modern usage. In classical terminology, an absolute right was one that was inherent in the individual as such, and not derived from his relations as a member of society.[150] To say that a right was absolute, however, did not mean that it could never be restricted. Instead, absolute rights were subject to regulation for the public good, especially to protect the rights of others.[151] In other words, although absolute rights had their origin in nature, they were defined in terms of civil rather than natural liberty.[152]

As elements of civil liberty, absolute rights were not merely natural rights but *legal* rights—rights protected by law. This was reflected in Blackstone's definitions of the absolute rights. Personal security, for example, was defined not merely as a negative right against invasion of one's life and person, but as a positive right to "*legal and uninterrupted enjoyment*" of these interests.[153] Absolute rights were rights to the *security* of person and property; and this security was provided by law, whose end was the protection of rights.

Absolute rights were understood to apply not only against governmental oppression, but also against private violence.[154] This is clear from the fact that these rights originate in the state of nature, where there is no government.[155] Individuals enter society to secure their rights against private violence.[156] Accordingly, when Blackstone and Kent discussed the ways in which the law protected absolute rights,[157] they reviewed not only the barriers against governmental oppression contained in Magna Carta and the American bills of rights, but also the protections against private aggression afforded by civil and criminal law.[158]

---

150. *See id.* at *123-25; 2 KENT, *supra* note 121, at *1.

151. As Blackstone indicated, liberty and property might be limited by "due course of law" or "the laws of the land." 1 BLACKSTONE, *supra* note 24, at *134, *138. Even the right to life might be forfeited by the violation of laws enforced by capital punishment. *Id.* at *133.

152. *See supra* Part I(C) (discussing natural and civil liberty).

153. 1 BLACKSTONE, *supra* note 24, at *129 (emphasis added).

154. For example, the right to personal security could be violated by murder, as well as by unlawful execution. *Id.* at *133-34.

155. *Id.* at *123.

156. *Id.* at *125.

157. *See id.* at *122-144; 2 KENT, *supra* note 121, at *1-37.

158. *See, e.g.*, 1 BLACKSTONE, *supra* note 24, at *129-30 (abortion); *id.* at *130-31 (mayhem, duress); *id.* at *133 (homicide); *id.* at *134 (assault and battery, defamation); *id.* at *136-37 (false imprisonment); 2 KENT, *supra* note 121, at *15 (criminal and tort law); *id.* at *16-17 (defamation); *id.* at *26 (false imprisonment).

C. *Enforcement of Legal Rights*

As Blackstone observed, laws recognizing substantive rights would be a "dead letter" if there were no method for actually enforcing those rights.[159] In its most basic meaning, protection referred to the means by which the law enforced the observance of rights.

These means of protection evolved over time. In principle, the sovereign's duty of protection had always extended to the prevention as well as the punishment of violence. Prior to the nineteenth century, however, the state's capacity to prevent violence was quite limited. Accordingly, the traditional notion of protection focused on the government's obligation to respond to injuries already suffered by affording a civil remedy and imposing criminal punishment. From a very early period, however, the common law provided some means of preventing violence before it occurred, including the process of requiring security of the peace and the responsibility of officers to keep the peace. During the nineteenth century, modern police forces were created to prevent crimes and thus afford more complete protection to person and property. Thus, by the time that the Fourteenth Amendment was adopted, the concept of protection had developed to include the state's obligation to take reasonable measures for the prevention of violence. This development is explored below.

1. *Self-Defense*. Classical writers viewed the right to protection against the background of the natural law of self-defense. In any situation where the government was unable to protect against threatened violence, the law allowed the individual to defend himself.[160] In such situations, Blackstone observed, "the law of nature . . . [has] made [the individual] his own protector."[161] On the other hand, there was no right to use force in self-defense when a resort to the law was possible.[162]

2. *Civil Protection*. In the common law tradition, "the protection of the law" meant above all the ability to enforce one's rights in a civil action and thus obtain a remedy for their violation.[163] As Chief Justice

159. 1 BLACKSTONE, *supra* note 24, at *140-41; *see also id.* at *55-56.

160. *See, e.g.*, 3 *id.* at *3; 4 *id.* at *180, *183-84; 2 KENT, *supra* note 121, at *15.

161. 4 BLACKSTONE, *supra* note 24, at *30. Similarly, Kent wrote that, in such instances, "the law, with great propriety, and in strict justice, considers the individual to be under the protection of the law of nature." 2 KENT, *supra* note 121, at *15 (citation omitted). As Tucker explained, the individual "retains the right of repelling force by force; because that may be absolutely necessary for self-preservation, and the intervention of society in his behalf, may be too late to prevent an injury." 1 BLACKSTONE, *supra* note 24, at *145 (Tucker ed. note).

162. *See* 4 BLACKSTONE, *supra* note 24, at *183-84.

163. *See Calvin's Case*, 7 Co. Rep. 1a, 13b, 77 Eng. Rep. 377, 393 (1608) ("If a man be attainted of felony or treason, he hath lost the King's legal protection, for he is thereby utterly disabled to sue

Marshall declared in *Marbury v. Madison*:[164] "The very essence of civil liberty certainly consists in the right of every individual to claim the protection of the laws, whenever he receives an injury. One of the first duties of government is to afford that protection."[165]

According to Coke and Blackstone, the right to a remedy was secured by chapter 29 of Magna Carta, which provided that justice should not be denied.[166] Under this provision, Coke wrote, "[e]very subject . . . for injury done to him [in goods, lands, or person], by any other subject . . . may take his remedy by the course of law, and have justice, and right for the injury done to him, freely without sale, fully without any denial, and speedily without delay."[167] Coke's paraphrase of Magna Carta was incorporated in some form in most of the antebellum state constitutions.[168]

In one sense, the right to civil protection might be viewed as merely procedural, consisting in the right to bring a lawsuit. As Coke's statement indicates, however, the concept of civil protection had substantive content as well. In the classical legal tradition, it was axiomatic that "where there is a legal right there is also a legal remedy, . . . whenever that right is invaded."[169] Indeed, a central purpose of Blackstone's *Commentaries* was to show that the common law accorded with the law of nature in recognizing fundamental rights, and gave a remedy for all invasions of those rights.[170] Thus, the right to civil protection was substantive, not merely procedural or formal: It sought to ensure that individuals were actually able to obtain remedies for the invasion of their rights by others.

---

any action real or personal."); 1 COKE, *supra* note 20, at *130a; 1 BLACKSTONE, *supra* note 24, at *56 ("This is what we mean properly, when we speak of the protection of the law.").

164. 5 U.S. (1 Cranch) 137 (1803).

165. *Id.* at 163.

166. *See* Magna Carta ch. 29 (1225) (Eng.); 1 BLACKSTONE, *supra* note 24, at *141; 2 COKE, *supra* note 20, at *55.

167. 2 COKE, *supra* note 20, at *55.

168. *See, e.g.*, ALA. CONST. of 1819, art. I, § 14, *reprinted in* 1 STATE CONSTITUTIONS, *supra* note 13, at 32; CONN. CONST. of 1818, art. I, § 12, *reprinted in* 2 STATE CONSTITUTIONS, *supra* note 13, at 145; DEL. CONST. of 1831, art. I, § 9, *reprinted in* 2 STATE CONSTITUTIONS, *supra* note 13, at 217-18; FLA. CONST. of 1838, art. I, § 9, *reprinted in* 2 STATE CONSTITUTIONS, *supra* note 13, at 317.

169. 3 BLACKSTONE, *supra* note 24, at *23; *see also id.* at *86, *422 ("[E]very possible injury that can be offered to a man's person or property is certain of meeting with redress" in some court.).

170. *See id.* at *1-2. Of course, Blackstone recognized that in some respects the common law was defective. *See, e.g.*, 1 *id.* at *143 (right to petition when law is "too defective" to give remedy for injury); *id.* at *171-72 & n.n (laws not as perfect as he presents them as being). For present purposes, the important point is that classical legal theory held that it was necessary for the law to provide remedies for all injuries to fulfill its function of protection.

3. *Criminal Protection*. In addition to civil protection, the individual had a right to protection under the criminal law. As Kent expressed it, "the personal security of every citizen is protected from lawless violence by the arm of government and the terrors of the penal code."[171]

According to classical legal theory, criminal law has its foundation in the law of nature.[172] That law forbids violations of the natural rights of others, such as murder or theft.[173] In a state of nature, everyone has the power to punish offenses against the law of nature.[174] When they enter into the social contract, individuals give up this power of criminal punishment to the society, to be exercised for the protection of its members.[175]

As we have seen, the state's responsibility for providing this protection was shared among the three branches of government.[176] The legislature had an obligation to enact criminal laws for the protection of life, liberty, and property, while the executive and the courts had a duty to enforce those laws to protect the community and its members against violence. This enforcement function was known in traditional English law as the conservation of the peace.[177] As we shall see, it included the prevention of violence[178] as well as the arrest, prosecution, and punishment of offenders.[179]

The right to criminal protection was even more fundamental than the right to a civil remedy for injuries. Under the traditional common law, an individual who fled from justice was declared an outlaw, that is, one who was "out of the protection of the law."[180] Outlaws, and capital felons,[181] forfeited the protection of the law in a civil sense: They were

171. 2 KENT, *supra* note 121, at *15.

172. *See* 1 BLACKSTONE, *supra* note 24, at *41-43, *54.

173. *Id.* at *42-43, *54.

174. *See* 4 *id.* at *7-8; LOCKE, *supra* note 25, §§ 7-8.

175. *See* 4 BLACKSTONE, *supra* note 24, at *8; LOCKE, *supra* note 25, §§ 128-130. As Tucker explained:

> When a man quits the state of nature, and enters into a state of society, he resigns into the hands of society the right of punishing an offender, for an injury already done him, the society by the terms of the social compact, having engaged to punish every such offender for him.

4 BLACKSTONE, *supra* note 24, at *145 (Tucker ed. note).

176. *See supra* text accompanying notes 60-67.

177. *See* 1 BLACKSTONE, *supra* note 24, at *349-51, *353-54.

178. *See infra* text accompanying notes 185-241.

179. *See* 1 BLACKSTONE, *supra* note 24, at *266, *268, *270.

180. *Id.* at *284.

181. The protection of the law was forfeited upon conviction of a capital felony, 4 *id.* at *380, as well as of the crime known as *praemunire*, *id.* at *117-18.

disabled from suing for any private injuries they suffered.[182] Nonetheless, they continued to be under the protection of the law in the criminal context.[183] Thus, to kill an outlaw or a felon without lawful justification constituted murder.[184]

4. *Prevention of Injury*. As I have noted, the government's duty of criminal protection included the prevention as well as the punishment of violence.[185] The traditional common law provided two important means of prevention: the process of requiring security of the peace, and the authority of officers to keep the peace.

a. Security of the peace. "[E]very person," Kent observed, "is . . . entitled to the preventive arm of the magistrate, as a further protection from threatened or impending danger."[186] By "the preventive arm of the magistrate," Kent meant the common law process of requiring security for the peace.[187] Under this procedure, any person under the sovereign's protection who feared a violent attack by another had a right to apply to a justice of the peace to have his adversary bound to keep the peace.[188] The justice was bound to grant the application if the demandant showed just cause to fear death or bodily harm.[189] The justice also

182. *See* 3 *id.* at *284; 4 *id.* at *117.

183. *See* 4 *id.* at *117-18; *id.* at *319-20. Under early law, an outlaw forfeited the protection of the law in all respects, and might lawfully be killed. *See id.* at *320.

184. *See id.* at *178, *319-20. As defined by Blackstone, the crime of murder consisted of killing, with malice aforethought, any person "under the king's peace and protection." *Id.* at *195, *197-98.

185. *See supra* text accompanying notes 178-79; *see also* 4 BLACKSTONE, *supra* note 24, at *2, *251. Indeed, Blackstone, following Beccaria, maintained that "*preventive* justice is . . . preferable in all respects to *punishing* justice," which although necessary is often harsh. *Id.* at *251 (citing BECCARIA, CRIMES AND PUNISHMENTS ch. 41 (Albany, W.C. Little 1872) (1764)).

186. 2 KENT, *supra* note 121, at *15.

187. The law governing this process is described in 4 BLACKSTONE, *supra* note 24, at *251-57, and in 5 NATHAN DANE, A GENERAL ABRIDGMENT AND DIGEST OF AMERICAN LAW 301-05 (1824).

188. 4 BLACKSTONE, *supra* note 24, at *253, *255.

189. *Id.* at *255; 5 DANE, *supra* note 187, at 301. As Blackstone observed, wives had a right to demand security of the peace against their husbands, and vice versa. 4 BLACKSTONE, *supra* note 24, at *254; *see also* 1 *id.* at *442. In this and other respects, the process of the peace resembled the modern protective order in domestic violence cases.

In Balistreri v. Pacifica Police Dep't, 855 F.2d 1421 (9th Cir. 1988), the Court of Appeals for the Ninth Circuit held that the police department violated the Due Process Clause by refusing to enforce a protective order that the plaintiff had obtained against her estranged husband. The Supreme Court implicitly disapproved this holding in DeShaney v. Winnebago County Social Servs. Dep't, 489 U.S. 189, 197 n.4 (1989). As this history shows, however, the protective order is closely related to a procedure that was considered to be an integral part of the right to protection in the classical legal tradition.

had broad authority, on his own motion, to require security of the peace from persons who appeared likely to break it.[190]

A party who was bound to keep the peace was required to find one or more sureties, who together with the party entered into a bond or recognizance for a large sum to be forfeited to the state in the event that he committed a breach of the peace against the demandant.[191] A party who did not find adequate sureties could be committed until he did.[192]

As Kent's statement indicates, the right to security of the peace was viewed as an important aspect of the general right to protection by the government. Conversely, the availability of such legal protection imposed a limitation on the individual's natural right to self-defense, "for, instead of attacking one another for injuries past *or impending*, men need only have recourse to the proper tribunals of justice."[193] Accordingly, the right to self-defense was limited to cases where the threatened harm was "immediate" and there was no time to obtain "the assistance of the law."[194]

b. Protection by peace officers. In addition to security for the peace, traditional law provided another important means of preventing violence: the responsibility of officers to maintain the peace. As we have seen, the executive had a duty to enforce the criminal laws to protect the community and its members from violence.[195] This function was performed by officers known as "conservators of the peace," a category that included justices of the peace, sheriffs, and constables.[196] As their name indicates, it was the general duty of these officers to keep the peace.[197] That duty included preventing violence as well as apprehending offenders.[198] Where necessary, the sheriff and justices had authority to

190. 4 BLACKSTONE, *supra* note 24, at *254-55.

191. *Id.* at *252-53.

192. *Id.* at *255.

193. *Id.* at *184 (emphasis added).

194. *Id.*

195. *See supra* text accompanying note 64.

196. *See* 1 BLACKSTONE, *supra* note 24, at *349-50.

197. *See id.* at *350 (authority of conservators to keep the peace); *id.* at *354 (duty of justices of the peace); *id.* at *356 (duty of constable).

198. *See id.* at *343 (stating that the sheriff has the power to "apprehend, and commit to prison, all persons who break the peace, *or attempt to break it*") (emphasis added); *id.* at *353-54 (observing that, at common law, the power and duty of conservators of the peace included "suppressing riots and affrays, . . . taking securities for the peace, and . . . apprehending and committing felons and other . . . criminals"); 4 *id.* at *145 (noting duty of constable to keep the peace by suppressing affray).

For a late-nineteenth-century recognition of the duty of peace officers to protect citizens against violent assault, see *In re* Neagle, 135 U.S. 1, 69 (1890).

command the power of the county (*posse comitatus*) to assist them in performing their duties.[199]

An officer who failed to keep the peace was subject to criminal prosecution for neglect of duty.[200] At common law, however, an individual who sustained injury because of an officer's failure to prevent violence apparently had no remedy against either the state, the local government, or the officer. Although the state, through its officers, had failed to afford protection, it was exempt from liability under the doctrine of sovereign immunity.[201] One alternative was to bring suit against the local government. In statutes of incorporation, states delegated to municipal governments the responsibility to protect persons and property within their jurisdiction. During the mid-nineteenth century, suits were sometimes brought against local governments for failing to protect against violence. As we shall see, such claims were consistent with a long tradition of communal liability in England, and were specifically authorized by statute in several American states.[202] In the absence of statute, however, the courts rejected such claims on the ground that local governments were entitled to immunity when exercising "governmental functions" delegated by the state.[203]

A final alternative was to bring suit against the officer. Legal writers sometimes asserted in broad terms that public officers were liable for injuries caused by neglect of duty.[204] On the other hand, the common law

199. *See* 1 BLACKSTONE, *supra* note 24, at *343-44; 4 *id.* at *122.

200. *See* 4 *id.* at *140 (describing "the *negligence of public officers*," which was a misdemeanor at common law). In addition, a number of English statutes imposed fines on officers who failed to perform specific duties to keep the peace. *See, e.g.*, *id.* at *293-94 (describing statute making constable liable to fine for refusing or neglecting to make hue and cry).

201. On the doctrine of sovereign immunity, see 1 *id.* at *242-48; 3 *id.* at *254-55. The origins and development of the doctrine are briefly traced in PETER H. SCHUCK, SUING GOVERNMENT: CITIZEN REMEDIES FOR OFFICIAL WRONGS 30-41 (1983). The classic work on the subject is Edwin M. Borchard's multipart article, *Government Liability in Tort*, 34 YALE L.J. 1, 129, 229 (1924-1925); 36 YALE L.J. 1, 757, 1039 (1926-1927); 28 COLUM. L. REV. 577, 734 (1928).

202. *See infra* text accompanying notes 218-25.

203. *See, e.g.*, Prather v. City of Lexington, 52 Ky. (13 B. Mon.) 559 (1852); Western College of Homeopathic Medicine v. City of Cleveland, 12 Ohio St. 375 (1861). In *Western College*, for example, it was alleged that city officials had negligently failed to protect the college's building from destruction by a riot. Although acknowledging that "[i]t is the duty of the state government to secure to the citizens of the state the peaceful enjoyment of their property and its protection from wrongful and violent acts," the Ohio Supreme Court denied recovery on the ground that, in performing this function, the municipal government "represents the state," and thus should share its immunity. *Id.* at 377.

204. Dane, for example, declared that "[i]n every case in which an officer is intrusted by common law, or by statute, to perform a service, and *neglects* it, this action [for negligence] lies against him by the party injured." 3 DANE, *supra* note 187, at 33. Blackstone stated the principle in similarly broad terms. *See* 3 BLACKSTONE, *supra* note 24, at *165.

accorded immunity to officials exercising "judicial" functions.[205] Before the mid-nineteenth century, the issue of whether officials were subject to civil liability at common law for failing to protect against violence had never been resolved authoritatively.

The issue came before the Supreme Court during the 1850s in *South v. Maryland ex rel. Pottle*.[206] Jonathan Pottle, the real plaintiff, alleged that in June 1850 he was going about his lawful business in Washington County, Maryland, when he was set upon by certain persons who threatened his life and personal safety, and detained him until he should pay them a large sum of money. Pottle asserted that he then applied to the sheriff of Washington County, Daniel South, "to protect and defend him . . . from [such] unlawful conduct and threatened violence . . . , and to preserve and keep the peace of the State of Maryland," but that South, although he had the necessary power and authority, failed to do so.[207] Pottle claimed that as a result he was forced to pay his captors $2500 for his release.[208]

Pottle brought a diversity action in federal court against South and his sureties for damages caused by the sheriff's alleged failure to protect him. A jury trial resulted in a substantial judgment for the plaintiff. The defendants then brought a writ of error in the Supreme Court. After the case was initially argued, the Court ordered reargument, directing the parties to focus on the question of whether a conservator of the peace was subject to civil liability in such circumstances.[209]

In 1856, the Supreme Court issued a decision reversing the judgment. Writing for the Court, Justice Grier recognized that the sheriff had a duty to preserve the peace, but ruled that there was no civil liability at common law for a breach of this duty. The decision was based on a distinction between "ministerial" and "public" duties.[210] An officer acted in a ministerial capacity when he was "bound to render certain services to individuals, for a compensation in fees or salary."[211] A prime example was the execution of process on behalf of a party in a civil

---

205. *See generally* J. Randolph Block, Stump v. Sparkman *and the History of Judicial Immunity*, 1980 DUKE L.J. 879.

206. 59 U.S. (18 How.) 396 (1856).

207. *Id.* at 399.

208. *Id.* at 398-99. The record of the case in the Supreme Court sheds light on these allegations. Pottle, together with his partners, had invested in a mill in Washington County. After the mill owner defaulted on the debt, Pottle and his partners recovered a judgment against him. While accompanying a deputy sheriff to an execution on the mill, Pottle was detained by the mill's workers who demanded that he pay them wages that they claimed were due them. *See* Record at 9.

209. *South*, 59 U.S. (18 How.) at 396.

210. *See id.* at 402-03.

211. *Id.* at 402.

case.[212] When performing such functions, the officer was "liable for acts of misfeasance or non-feasance to the party who is injured by them."[213]

Under traditional common law doctrine, an officer was immune from civil liability where he acted in a judicial capacity. Although "[t]he powers and duties of conservator of the peace exercised by the sheriff are not strictly judicial," Justice Grier reasoned, "he may be said to act as the chief magistrate of his county, wielding the executive power for the preservation of the public peace."[214] Expanding the category of "judicial" duties to include other "public" duties—such as conservation of the peace—the Court declared as a general principle that, for the breach of a public duty, an officer is responsible to the public only, and thus is subject to criminal, but not civil, liability.[215]

It is important to recognize that *South* did not hold that a conservator of the peace had no duty to protect citizens against violence. On the contrary, the opinion indicates that he did have such a duty, and that he was subject to criminal punishment at common law if he neglected to perform it.[216] More broadly, *South* might be interpreted as implying that protection against violence was not a duty that the state owed to individuals as such, but only to the public at large. Such an interpretation, however, confuses the duty of the officer with that of the state. Under the *South* doctrine, an officer is responsible only to the public, that is, to the state, for failure to perform his public duties. Nothing in *South*, however, is inconsistent with the principle that the state owes a duty of protection to each of its members. But an individual has no legal remedy against the state because of the doctrine of sovereign immunity. In effect, *South* extends the state's immunity to public officers when they act as representatives of the state in performing such functions as conserving the peace.[217] Thus, the effect of the *South* rule, in combination with the doctrines of state and local government immunity, was to deny any remedy at common law for the government's failure to prevent criminal violence.

c. Communal liability. During the mid-nineteenth century, a number of states responded to the lack of an effective remedy by enacting statutes. These statutes typically imposed liability on cities and counties for property damage, and sometimes for personal injuries, caused by

212. *Id.*
213. *Id.* at 402-03.
214. *Id.* at 403.
215. *See id.* at 402.
216. *See id.* at 403.
217. *See id.* at 402 ("As conservator of the peace in his county or bailiwick, [the sheriff] is the representative of the king, or sovereign power of the State for that purpose.").

riots within their jurisdictions. Some of these statutes also made officers civilly liable when they failed to use their authority to prevent such harm.

In enacting such laws, American states were following a much older English tradition of communal liability for certain kinds of violence. Under legislation going back to the Statute of Winchester,[218] the local community known as the hundred was required to pursue felons, and to compensate victims of robberies within its jurisdiction in cases where the community failed to apprehend the thief.[219] Similarly, the Riot Act of 1714 made the hundred liable for property damage caused by riots.[220]

By 1868, when the Fourteenth Amendment was ratified, at least nine states had enacted riot laws similar to the English acts.[221] Pennsylvania's law, adopted in 1841, provided a model for later statutes.[222] The law authorized individuals to bring suit against the county to recover damages for the destruction of any real or personal property by any mob or riot within its jurisdiction. As a condition of recovery, the owner was required, if there was sufficient time, to notify a conservator of the peace of the attack on the property. Upon receipt of such notice, the officer had a "duty . . . to take all legal means to protect the property so attacked."[223] If the officer failed to perform this duty, he became civilly liable to the owner for damages to the property. If the plaintiff recovered against the county, the county was given an action over against the rioters, or against any officer who had failed to perform his duty to suppress the riot.

As the Pennsylvania statute makes clear, these state laws reaffirmed the community's duty of protection and made it the basis of a legal action. As the Pennsylvania Supreme Court explained, these acts recognized that "tax-payers have a right to be indemnified for losses occasioned by lawless outrage, whenever the public are unable or unwilling to protect property."[224] Similarly, in upholding the constitutionality

218. 13 Edw., stat. 2, ch. 1-3 (1285) (Eng.).

219. *See* 4 BLACKSTONE, *supra* note 24, at *293-94.

220. Riot Act, 1714, 1 Geo., ch. 5, § 6 (Eng.).

221. *See* 1868 Cal. Stat. ch. 344; 1855 La. Sess. Laws no. 51; 1835 Md. Laws ch. 137; 1839 Mass. Acts 54; 1854 N.H. Laws ch. 1519; 1864 N.J. Laws ch. 150; 1855 N.Y. Gen. Mun. Laws ch. 428; 1841 Pa. Laws no. 144, §§ 7-11; 1863 Wis. Laws ch. 211.

222. *See* 1841 Pa. Laws no. 144, §§ 7-11. The provisions summarized in this paragraph are found in section 8 of the act.

As originally enacted, the Pennsylvania statute applied only to the county of Philadelphia; it was subsequently extended to certain surrounding counties. *See* 1849 Pa. Laws 184, § 1; 1863 Pa. Laws 499, § 1. The riot statutes of other states applied statewide. *See supra* note 221.

223. 1841 Pa. Laws no. 144, § 8.

224. *In re* Pennsylvania Hall, 5 Pa. 204, 209 (1847) (applying a predecessor of the 1841 act). The case involved the burning of a hall used for abolitionist meetings.

of the New York law, the Court of Appeals of New York explained that the statute was intended to compensate:

> those who may be so unfortunate, as without their own fault to be injured in their property by acts of lawless violence of a particular kind which it is the general duty of the government to prevent; and further and principally . . . to make it the interest of every person liable to contribute to the public expenses to discourage lawlessness and violence . . . . These ends are plainly within the purposes of civil government, and indeed it is to attain them that governments are instituted.[225]

Thus, the state riot acts strongly confirm that, in nineteenth-century legal thought, the government's duty of protection was understood to include the prevention as well as the punishment of violence. Moreover, they show that some states provided a legal remedy in certain cases for the government's failure to afford such protection.

d. The creation of modern police forces. Law enforcement in England and America traditionally relied on the efforts of a few officers, with the assistance of citizens where necessary. By the nineteenth century, this reliance on a "haphazard collection of constables and night watchmen"[226] seemed increasingly inadequate, especially in urban areas. In response to growing concerns about riots and crime, major cities began to create modern police forces—relatively organized units whose purpose was to prevent crime.[227] The legislative debates over the creation of such forces in England and America reflect the view that an efficient police force might be essential for the protection of person and property.

---

225. Darlington v. City of New York, 31 N.Y. 164, 187 (1865). For other contemporary statements that the riot statutes were based on the duty of protection, see Ely v. Supervisors of Niagara County, 36 N.Y. 297, 300 (1867); Luke v. City of Brooklyn, 43 Barb. 54, 56-57, 58 (N.Y. App. Div. 1864); Curtis v. County of Allegheny, 1 Phil. Rep. 237, 239-40 (Pa. Dist. Ct. 1851).

This view was echoed by the Supreme Court half a century later in City of Chicago v. Sturges, 222 U.S. 313 (1911). In *Sturges*, the city challenged the Illinois riot act under the Due Process Clause of the Fourteenth Amendment. Rejecting this claim, the Court declared:

> [T]he obligation of the government to protect life, liberty and property against the conduct of the indifferent, the careless and the evil-minded may be regarded as lying at the very foundation of the social compact. . . . The law in question . . . rests upon the duty of the State to protect its citizens in the enjoyment and possession of their acquisitions, and is but a recognition of the obligation of the State to preserve social order and the property of the citizen against the violence of a riot or a mob.

Id. at 322.

226. LAWRENCE M. FRIEDMAN, A HISTORY OF AMERICAN LAW 287 (2d ed. 1985).

227. On the creation of modern police forces, see *id.*; KERMIT L. HALL, THE MAGIC MIRROR: LAW IN AMERICAN HISTORY 176-78 (1989); SAMUEL WALKER, POPULAR JUSTICE (1980). For leading studies of individual cities, see ROGER LANE, POLICING THE CITY: BOSTON, 1822-1885 (1967); WILBUR MILLER, COPS AND BOBBIES: POLICE AUTHORITY IN NEW YORK AND LONDON, 1830-1870 (1977); JAMES F. RICHARDSON, THE NEW YORK POLICE (1970); ALLEN STEINBERG, THE TRANSFORMATION OF CRIMINAL JUSTICE: PHILADELPHIA, 1800-1880 (1989).

The first modern police force was established in London by the Metropolitan Police Act of 1829.[228] In a speech introducing the Act in Parliament, the home secretary, Sir Robert Peel, argued that the existing nightwatch system was wholly inadequate to combat sharply increasing rates of crime.[229] Legislative action was necessary "not only to prevent such . . . outrage against the laws, but to provide more secure means of protecting the person and the property of the subject."[230] Responding to the objection that a more powerful police force would threaten liberty, Peel observed that liberty included the sense of security that one's life and property would not be assaulted.[231] It was "the duty of the legislature," he concluded, to "afford to the inhabitants of the metropolis . . . *the full and complete protection of the law*, and to take prompt and decisive measures to check the increase of crime."[232]

During the following decades, several American cities established police forces based on the London model. Philadelphia experimented with such a system as early as 1833; Boston established a police force in 1838; and New York followed in 1845.[233]

Congressional debates in 1858 over a proposal to reform the District of Columbia police make clear that Americans shared the view that protection might require a modern police force. The legislation's rationale was articulated by its Democratic supporters. It was "the object of government," observed one member, "to protect the people in their personal liberty, their personal security, and their rights of private property."[234] The "conservation of life and of property" was the function of a police.[235] Under existing legislation, it was the duty of the city authorities to maintain order, but they were either unwilling or unable to do so.[236] As a result, Washington was overwhelmed by an "epidemic of crime," in which murder and robbery were a "daily occurrence."[237] "[W]e all know," declared Senator Stephen A. Douglas, "that life is not safe in this city at present; men are cut down and shot at the doors of citizens, who

228. 10 Geo. 4, ch. 44 (1829) (Eng.).

229. *See* 21 Parl. Deb. (2d ser.) 867-84 (1829).

230. *Id.* at 875.

231. *See id.* at 882. On the identification of liberty with security in this context, see Miller, *supra* note 227, at 108-09.

232. 21 Parl. Deb. (2d ser.) at 882 (emphasis added). For a similar speech supporting the Act in the House of Lords, see *id.* at 1750-52 (speech of the Duke of Wellington).

233. *See* Friedman, *supra* note 226, at 287; Hall, *supra* note 227, at 176.

234. Cong. Globe, 35th Cong., 1st Sess. 1592 (1858) (remarks of Rep. Hughes).

235. *Id.* at 1594 (remarks of Rep. Cochrane) ("[T]he office of a police is concededly that of the conservation of life and of property.").

236. Report of the Senate Comm. on the District of Columbia, *printed in* Cong. Globe, 35th Cong., 1st Sess. 1460 (1858).

237. *Id.*; Cong. Globe, 35th Cong., 1st Sess. 1586 (remarks of Rep. Maynard).

dare not open their doors to rescue the wounded for fear of being killed themselves."[238] Democrats argued that it was the duty of Congress, as the exclusive legislative authority over the District, to afford protection against such violence.[239] Therefore, they concluded, Congress had an obligation "to provide for an adequate and efficient police in this city, so as to preserve the peace and secure the lives and property of individuals."[240]

5. *Conclusion.* The right of protection was thus a well established concept in antebellum legal thought. In addition to the right of self-defense, it included civil remedies and criminal protection, as well as the process of requiring security for the peace. By the middle of the nineteenth century, the concept of protection had developed to include the state's responsibility to take reasonable measures to prevent violence, such as the creation of a police force where necessary for the protection of life and property. As the Supreme Court explained toward the end of the century:

> It has in modern times become apparent that the physical health of the community is more efficiently promoted by . . . preventive means, than by the skill which is applied to the cure of the disease after it has become fully developed. So also the law, which is intended to prevent crime . . . by regulations, police organization, and otherwise, which are adapted for the protection of the lives and property of citizens, . . . is more efficient than punishment of crimes after they have been committed.[241]

III. The Fourteenth Amendment

Although the right to protection was a fundamental principle of general constitutional and legal theory, it had limited recognition in the original Constitution. Instead, in most respects, the Constitution left the protection of the rights of individuals under the control of the states.[242] Moreover, slavery meant that most blacks were denied all protection of their rights, a principle asserted by the Supreme Court in the *Dred Scott* case,[243] which declared that blacks had no rights that whites were bound to respect.[244]

---

238. Cong. Globe, 35th Cong., 1st Sess. 1461 (1858).

239. *See id.* at 1465 (remarks of Sen. Crittenden); *id.* at 1468 (remarks of Sen. Green); *id.* at 1572 (remarks of Rep. Singleton); *id.* at 1612 (remarks of Rep. Scales).

240. *Id.* at 1465 (remarks of Sen. Crittenden).

241. *In re* Neagle, 135 U.S. 1, 59 (1890).

242. *See supra* text accompanying notes 94-98.

243. Dred Scott v. Sandford, 60 U.S. (19 How.) 393 (1857).

244. *Id.* at 407.

A central purpose of the Fourteenth Amendment and Reconstruction legislation was to establish the right to protection as a part of the federal Constitution and laws, and thus to require the states to protect the fundamental rights of all persons, black as well as white. In establishing a federal right to protection, the Fourteenth Amendment was not creating a new right, but rather incorporating into the Constitution the concept of protection as understood in the classical tradition. The debates in the Thirty-Ninth Congress over the Fourteenth Amendment and the Civil Rights Act of 1866[245] confirm that the constitutional right to protection was understood to include protection against private violence.

A. *The Need for a Federal Guarantee of the Right to Protection*

In accordance with the antebellum tradition, members of the Thirty-Ninth Congress regarded the right to protection as axiomatic. It was a "self-evident" principle, declared Representative Samuel Shellabarger of Ohio, "that protection by his Government is the right of every citizen."[246] In support of this right, Republicans invoked both the traditional doctrine of allegiance and protection, and the theory of natural rights.

There was general agreement that the citizen was entitled to protection in return for obedience. "Protection and allegiance are reciprocal," asserted Senator Alvin Stewart of Nevada. "It is the duty of the Government to protect; of the subject to obey."[247] "[T]hese are the essential elements of citizenship," agreed Senator Justin Morrill of Vermont, "allegiance on one side and protection on the other."[248] Many other Republicans invoked the same principle.[249]

Republicans also appealed to the natural rights tradition as a basis for the duty of protection.[250] Relying on the Declaration of Independence, Blackstone, and Kent, they contended that the rights to

245. Ch. 31, 14 Stat. 27 (codified at 42 U.S.C. §§ 1981-1982 (1988)).

246. CONG. GLOBE, 39th Cong., 1st Sess. 1293 (1866).

247. *Id.* at 2799.

248. *Id.* at 570.

249. *See, e.g.*, *id.* at 1152 (remarks of Rep. Thayer); *id.* at 1263 (remarks of Rep. Broomall); *id.* at 1293-94 (remarks of Rep. Shellabarger); *id.* at 1757 (remarks of Sen. Trumbull); *id.* at 1832 (remarks of Rep. Lawrence); *id.* at 2918 (remarks of Sen. Willey).

250. Jacobus tenBroek and Howard Jay Graham explored the influence of natural rights thought in their classic studies of the Fourteenth Amendment. *See* HOWARD J. GRAHAM, EVERYMAN'S CONSTITUTION (1968); TENBROEK, *supra* note 10. In recent years, a number of other scholars have emphasized the natural rights background to the Fourteenth Amendment. *See, e.g.*, CURTIS, *supra* note 127; FARBER & SHERRY, *supra* note 44, at 253-319; Robert J. Kaczorowski, *Revolutionary Constitutionalism in the Era of the Civil War and Reconstruction*, 61 N.Y.U. L. REV. 863 (1986).

life, liberty, and property were "natural" and "inalienable."[251] The protection of "these great fundamental rights," declared Representative James Wilson of Iowa, is "the first and most important office of government."[252]

Following the classical view, the Framers also identified liberty with protection.[253] Thus, in the course of an important speech on the Civil Rights Act, Senator Lyman Trumbull of Illinois defined constitutional liberty in terms of Blackstone's conception of civil liberty, in which the individual's natural liberty was subject to limitation in return for "the protection which civil government gives him."[254] Freedom "does mean protection," agreed Senator James A. McDougall, Democrat of California. "Under all Governments that are free, freedom is perfect protection in life, liberty, and the enjoyment and pursuit of happiness."[255]

As McDougall's remarks indicate, the right to protection was recognized even by the Democrats and conservative Republicans who opposed the Civil Rights Act and the Fourteenth Amendment.[256] Conservatives insisted, however, that under the federal system "all the arrangements of life with regard to the protection of property and person" were exclusively committed to the states.[257] There was no reason, they argued, "to assume that a State will not do its duty to its citizens in these particulars."[258]

Most Republicans, however, believed that the states had failed to fulfill this duty, in the past as well as the present. No state, declared Representative John A. Bingham of Ohio, ever had a "right to deny protection to any free citizen of the United States within their limits in the

251. *See, e.g.*, CONG. GLOBE, 39th Cong., 1st Sess. 474-75, 1757 (1866) (remarks of Sen. Trumbull); *id.* at 1088 (remarks of Rep. Woodbridge); *id.* at 1117-18 (remarks of Rep. Wilson); *id.* at 1152 (remarks of Rep. Thayer); *id.* at 1159 (remarks of Rep. Windom); *id.* at 1832-33 (remarks of Rep. Lawrence); *id.* at 2798 (remarks of Sen. Stewart).

252. *Id.* at 1118.

253. *See supra* Part I(C) (discussing classical conception of liberty).

254. CONG. GLOBE, 39th Cong., 1st Sess. 474 (1866).

255. *Id.* at 393. In this speech, McDougall opposed the Freedmen's Bureau Bill on the ground that blacks should merely receive the ordinary protection of the law, rather than be treated as special wards of the federal government. *See id.*

256. *See, e.g.*, *id.* at 476 (remarks of Sen. McDougall) (stating that blacks "should be conceded" the rights to "protection [in] the enjoyment of life and liberty and the pursuit of happiness and the protection of the courts"); *id.* at 989 (remarks of Sen. Cowan) ("I hold that it is the duty of every Government to protect its subjects . . . ."); *id.* at 2919 (remarks of Sen. Davis) (acknowledging the "universal maxim" that "it is the duty of the Government to protect the citizen"). That this view was shared by Democrats as well as Republicans is made clear by the 1858 debates over police reform in the District of Columbia. *See supra* text accompanying notes 234-40.

257. CONG. GLOBE, 39th Cong., 1st Sess. 1123 (1866) (remarks of Rep. Rogers); *see also id.* at 1270 (remarks of Rep. Kerr).

258. *Id.* at 1270 (remarks of Rep. Kerr).

rights of life, liberty, and property."[259] Yet, as Representative John M. Broomall of Pennsylvania observed, during the intense national controversy over slavery between 1830 and 1860, "everybody knows that the rights and immunities of citizens were habitually and systematically denied in [the southern] States to the citizens of other States."[260] Since the war began, stressed Bingham, the Confederate states had flagrantly violated the rights of citizens who had remained loyal to the Union.[261]

Above all, the southern states had denied protection to blacks held as slaves. Under the laws of the slave states, Senator Jacob M. Howard of Michigan explained, a slave "was nothing but a chattel, subject to the will of his owner, and unprotected in his rights by the law of the State where he happened to live."[262] The status of slavery, Bingham agreed, meant that blacks had been refused "protection in life [and] property."[263]

The Emancipation Proclamation and the Thirteenth Amendment had abolished slavery, and had thereby made the slaves freemen. In late 1865, southern legislatures responded by enacting "black codes" that restricted the rights of blacks in a wide range of ways, including their freedom of movement and their rights to dispose of their own labor, to hold property, and to testify in court.[264] In the view of many Republicans, these laws were incompatible with the status of a freeman, and constituted an effort by southern states to reduce blacks to slavery in all but name.

During the latter half of 1865, the nation also began to receive reports from the South of widespread violence against blacks as well as white Unionists and Northerners.[265] These reports came from northern journalists, Freedmen's Bureau officials, travelers in the South, and white and black Southerners themselves.[266] Among the most influential accounts was that of Carl Schurz, who toured the region at the request of President Johnson to report on the prospects for Reconstruction.[267]

Most Southerners, Schurz found, acknowledged the fact of military defeat, but had not accepted the "social revolution" involved in the abolition of slavery and its replacement by free labor.[268] The efforts of planters to hold blacks in continued subjection were responsible for a "large

259. *Id.* at 1090.
260. *Id.* at 1263; *see also id.* at 1066 (remarks of Rep. Price).
261. *See id.* at 1090-91, 1093-94.
262. *Id.* at 504.
263. *Id.* at 1090.
264. *See* ERIC FONER, RECONSTRUCTION, 1863-1877, at 198-202 (1988).
265. *Id.* at 224-25.
266. *Id.*
267. *See* S. EXEC. DOC. NO. 2, 39th Cong., 1st Sess. 3 (1865).
268. *See id.* at 4-5, 38, 45-46.

proportion of the many acts of violence" perpetrated against them.[269] Moreover, "[n]ot only the former slaveholders, but the non-slaveholding whites . . . are possessed by a singularly bitter and vindictive feeling against the colored race," which led to a "very great" number of murders, maimings, and assaults.[270] Local officials and communities were either "not willing or not able to enforce peace and order."[271] As one Freedmen's Bureau agent had reported: "As to protection from the civil authorities, there is no such thing," other than as a direct result of the military presence of the Bureau.[272]

Although violence was most frequently directed against blacks, Schurz reported that outrages had also been committed against white Unionists and federal soldiers.[273] Indeed, in many parts of the South, general lawlessness prevailed, with the local authorities unable to maintain order and security.[274] In short, the South was "drift[ing] into anarchy."[275] In conclusion, Schurz strongly urged that the federal government retain military control over the South until the social revolution was completed, a system of free labor was firmly established, the

---

269. *Id.* at 17.

270. *Id.* at 20.

271. *Id.*

272. *Id.* at 19. The agent, Captain J.H. Weber, wrote to the assistant commissioner of the Bureau as follows:

> In the immediate vicinity of our military posts, and in locations that can readily be reached by the officers of this bureau, the citizens are wary of abusing the blacks; they are so because this bureau has arrested and punished people committing such offenses . . . . But in remote localities . . . the blacks are as badly treated as ever; colored people often report themselves to the sub-commissioners with bruised heads and lacerated backs, and ask for redress, protection, to be permitted to live at their former homes, and some assurance that they will not be treated in a like manner again if they return. But nothing can be done if their homes happen to be twenty or thirty miles from any office that will protect them. . . .
>
> . . . .
>
> As to protection from the civil authorities, there is no such thing outside of this city. There is not a justice of the peace or any other civil officer in the district, eight (8) counties, of which I have charge, that will listen to a complaint from a negro; and in the city, since the adjudication of these cases has been turned over to the mayor, the abuse of and impositions upon negroes are increasing very visibly, for the reason that very little, if any, attention is paid to any complaint of a negro against a white person.

Id. at 77-78.

273. *Id.* at 7-9.

274. *Id.* at 14. Schurz wrote:

> In many districts robbing and plundering was going on with perfect impunity; the roads were infested by bands of highwaymen; numerous assaults occurred, and several stage lines were considered unsafe. The [accompanying statements of several military officers] give a terrible picture of the state of things in the localities they refer to. It is stated that civil officers are either unwilling or unable to enforce the laws; that one man does not dare to testify against another for fear of being murdered, and that the better elements of society are kept down by lawless characters under a system of terrorism. From my own observation I know that these things are not confined to the districts . . . referred to. Both the governors of Alabama and Mississippi complained of it in official proclamations.

Id.

275. *Id.* at 37.

status of blacks as freemen was fully recognized, and the capacity of local authorities to maintain order was restored.[276]

At the instance of radical Republican Senator Charles Sumner of Massachusetts, the Senate obtained the Schurz report from President Johnson, and arranged for its printing and circulation.[277] The report also was published in full in many newspapers throughout the country.[278] Together with other accounts coming in daily from the South,[279] the Schurz report had a substantial impact on Northern public opinion and convinced many people that it was necessary for the federal government to protect the freedmen from discrimination and violence.[280]

In addition to Schurz's report, Congress periodically obtained from the executive branch the reports of Freedmen's Bureau officials stationed in the South. These reports, and the testimony on conditions in the South taken by the congressional Joint Committee on Reconstruction, contained evidence of extensive violence against freedmen and Unionists.[281] Summarizing this testimony in its final report, the Committee wrote that the "deep-seated prejudice against color [in the South] . . . leads to acts of cruelty, oppression, and murder, which the local authorities are at no pains to prevent or punish."[282]

This unrestrained violence, as well as the enactment of the black codes, confirmed the Republicans' belief that the states could not be exclusively relied upon to protect the rights of citizens. Instead, they concluded that it was necessary to provide federal guarantees of protection, either through legislation or through constitutional amendment.

B. *The Adoption of the Civil Rights Act and the Fourteenth Amendment*

At the beginning of the Thirty-Ninth Congress, radical Republican Senator Henry Wilson of Massachusetts introduced a bill for the protection of freedmen in the South.[283] The bill declared in broad terms that all laws in the southern states recognizing "any inequality of civil rights and immunities" based on race were void, and making it a misdemeanor

276. *See id.* at 14, 45-46.

277. *See* JOSEPH B. JAMES, THE FRAMING OF THE FOURTEENTH AMENDMENT 51-52 (1956).

278. *Id.*

279. *See supra* text accompanying notes 265-66.

280. *See* FONER, *supra* note 264, at 224-26; JAMES, *supra* note 277, at 51-52.

281. *See* REPORTS OF ASSISTANT COMMISSIONERS OF FREEDMEN'S BUREAU, S. EXEC. DOC. NO. 27, 39th Cong., 1st Sess. (1866); REPORT OF THE JOINT COMM. ON RECONSTRUCTION, H.R. REP. NO. 30, 39th Cong., 1st Sess. (1866).

282. REPORT OF THE JOINT COMM. ON RECONSTRUCTION, *supra* note 281, at XVII.

283. For the text of the bill, see CONG. GLOBE, 39th Cong., 1st Sess. 39 (1865).

to make or enforce such a law.[284] Senator Wilson urged that the bill be passed immediately, to annul the black codes and to protect the freedmen from "[t]he crimes, the wrongs, [and] the outrages" that were being perpetrated against them.[285] As evidence of this violence, he cited private correspondence and reports of Freedmen's Bureau officials.[286]

Senator Lyman Trumbull, a moderate Republican and chairman of the Judiciary Committee, responded that "[t]he bill does not go far enough, if what we have been told to-day in regard to the treatment of freedmen in the southern States is true."[287] Senator Wilson's bill was based solely on the war power.[288] Once the Thirteenth Amendment was ratified, Trumbull contended, congressional authority to protect the freedmen would be clear. At that time, Congress could pass "a bill that will be much more efficient to protect the freedman in his rights."[289] Trumbull announced that, if no one else did, he would introduce such a bill after the Thirteenth Amendment became law.[290]

On January 11, 1866, Trumbull reported two bills to the Senate on behalf of the Judiciary Committee.[291] The first, a temporary measure confined to the South, was to expand the powers of the Freedmen's Bureau, an agency within the War Department that was charged with giving assistance and protection to freedmen and refugees in the south.

The second bill, which was enacted as the Civil Rights Act of 1866, was a permanent measure entitled "An Act to protect all Persons in the United States in their Civil Rights, and furnish the Means of their Vindication."[292] As enacted, Section 1 declared that "all persons born in the United States" were citizens of the United States, and provided:

> [S]uch citizens, of every race and color . . . shall have the same right, in every State and Territory in the United States, to make and enforce contracts, to sue, be parties, and give evidence, to inherit, purchase, lease, sell, hold, and convey real and personal property, and to full and equal benefit of all laws and proceedings for the security of person and property, as is enjoyed by white citizens, and shall be subject to like punishment, pains, and penalties, and to none other, any law, statute, ordinance, regulation, or custom, to the contrary notwithstanding.[293]

284. *See id.*
285. *Id.* at 39-41 (remarks of Sen. Wilson).
286. *See id.* at 39, 41; *see also id.* at 111.
287. *Id.* at 43.
288. *See id.* at 39 (remarks of Sen. Wilson).
289. *Id.* at 43.
290. *See id.*
291. *Id.* at 184.
292. Civil Rights Act of 1866, ch. 31, 14 Stat. 27 (codified at 42 U.S.C. §§ 1981-1982 (1988)).
293. *Id.* § 1, 14 Stat. at 27.

Republicans explained the Civil Rights Act in terms of natural rights theory and the classical legal tradition. "What are civil rights?" asked Representative James Wilson of Iowa, the floor manager of the bill in the House. "I understand civil rights to be simply the absolute rights of individuals."[294] Following Blackstone and Kent, Wilson defined these "natural" or "absolute rights" as " '[t]he right of personal security, the right of personal liberty, and the right to acquire and enjoy property.' "[295] Other Republicans explained the Act in the same terms.[296]

In addition to natural rights, Wilson indicated, civil rights included other rights that were "necessary to complete defense and enjoyment of the specific right."[297] As Representative William Lawrence of Ohio explained, these "necessary incidents of . . . absolute rights" included such rights as "the right to make and enforce contracts, to purchase, hold, and enjoy property, and to share the benefit of laws for the security of person and property."[298]

Conservatives attacked the bill for invading the exclusive authority of the states to regulate the rights of citizens.[299] In response, supporters argued that Congress had authority to pass the legislation under the Thirteenth Amendment.[300] Following the classical tradition, Senator Trumbull explained that "[l]iberty and slavery are opposite terms; one is opposed to the other."[301] Thus, in abolishing slavery, the Thirteenth Amendment in essence had "declared that all persons in the United States should be free."[302] Under Section 2 of the Amendment, Congress had power to "give effect to that declaration and secure to all persons within the United States practical freedom," by ensuring that the former slaves possessed all of the "privileges which are essential to freemen."[303] These rights, Representative Wilson added, would be a "sure defense against efforts to reduce [blacks] to slavery."[304]

294. CONG. GLOBE, 39th Cong., 1st Sess. 1117 (1866).

295. *Id.* (quoting 2 KENT, *supra* note 121, at *1); *see also id.* at 1118 (quoting 1 BLACKSTONE, *supra* note 24, at *129, *134, *138).

296. *See, e.g.*, *id.* at 1152 (remarks of Rep. Thayer); *id.* at 1159 (remarks of Rep. Windom); *id.* at 1757 (remarks of Sen. Trumbull); *id.* at 1833 (remarks of Rep. Lawrence).

297. *Id.* at 1118-19.

298. *Id.* at 1833.

299. *See, e.g.*, *id.* at 478 (remarks of Sen. Saulsbury); *id.* at 1156-57 (remarks of Rep. Thorton); *id.* at 1270 (remarks of Rep. Kerr).

300. Some supporters also relied on Article IV, Section 2 of the Constitution as a basis for congressional authority to enact the Civil Rights Act. This provision is discussed *infra* at text accompanying notes 316-32.

301. CONG. GLOBE, 39th Cong., 1st Sess. 474 (1866).

302. *Id.*

303. *Id.*

304. *Id.* at 1118. As these arguments suggest, the Thirteenth Amendment provides another potential source for a constitutional right to protection. For an exploration of *DeShaney* from a

More broadly, proponents argued that the national government had inherent authority to protect its citizens. "Allegiance and protection are reciprocal rights," asserted Senator Trumbull:

> How is it that every person born in these United States owes allegiance to the Government? Everything that he is or has, his property and his life, may be taken by the Government of the United States in its defense or to maintain the honor of the nation; and can it be that . . . the people of our day have struggled through a [civil] war, with all its sacrifices and all its desolation, to maintain it, and at last . . . we have got a Government which is all-powerful to command the obedience of the citizen, but has no power to afford him protection?[305]

"American citizenship," Trumbull concluded, "would be little worth if it did not carry protection with it."[306] The nation must have authority to protect fundamental rights, Representative Wilson agreed, "or our Constitution fails in the first and most important office of government."[307]

Republicans further argued that because the national government had the power and duty to protect the rights of its citizens abroad, it would be anomalous for it to lack that power within its own jurisdiction. "If a citizen of the United States should go abroad," stated Representative Wilson,

> and while within the jurisdiction of a foreign Power be despoiled of his rights of personal security, personal liberty, or personal property contrary to the due course of law of the nation inflicting the wrong, this Government would espouse his cause and enforce redress even to the extremity of war. . . . [I]f all the terrible powers of war may be resorted to for the protection of the rights of our citizens when those rights are disregarded and trampled on beyond our jurisdiction, is it possible that our Constitution is so defective that we have no power under it to protect our citizens within our own jurisdiction through the peaceful means of statutes and courts?[308]

Most Republicans believed on these grounds that Congress had the constitutional authority to pass the Civil Rights Act. However, one leading Republican, Representative Bingham, strongly disagreed, denouncing the Act as an unconstitutional invasion of the province of the states.[309] Although he believed that the national government should

---

Thirteenth Amendment perspective, see Akhil R. Amar & Daniel Widawsky, *Child Abuse as Slavery: A Thirteenth Amendment Response to* DeShaney, 105 HARV. L. REV. (forthcoming 1992).

305. Cong. Globe, 39th Cong., 1st Sess. 1757 (1866).

306. *Id.*

307. *Id.* at 1118.

308. *Id.* at 1119; *see also id.* at 1757 (remarks of Sen. Trumbull). For further discussion of the Republican argument on the national government's inherent power of protection, see FARBER & SHERRY, *supra* note 44, at 302-04.

309. *See* CONG. GLOBE, 39th Cong., 1st Sess. 1290-93 (1866).

have the power to ensure protection of fundamental rights, Bingham argued that another constitutional amendment was necessary to give Congress such power.[310] Some of the Act's supporters also admitted having doubts about its constitutionality.[311] For this reason, Republicans decided to draft a constitutional amendment "to make assurance doubly sure."[312] Equally important, Republicans desired to enshrine the protections of the Civil Rights Act in the Constitution, where they would be beyond the power of a subsequent Democratic majority in Congress to repeal.[313]

As adopted, Section 1 of the Fourteenth Amendment provided:

> All persons born or naturalized in the United States, and subject to the jurisdiction thereof, are citizens of the United States and of the State wherein they reside. No State shall make or enforce any law which shall abridge the privileges or immunities of citizens of the United States; nor shall any State deprive any person of life, liberty, or property, without due process of law; nor deny to any person within its jurisdiction the equal protection of the laws.[314]

It was agreed on all sides that the constitutional amendment embodied the same basic principles as the Civil Rights Act.[315]

C. *The Right to Protection Under the Civil Rights Act and the Fourteenth Amendment*

The 1866 debates make clear that the Framers understood the Civil Rights Act and the Fourteenth Amendment to incorporate a fundamental right to protection by the government, with a corresponding obligation on the states to afford such protection. This right was secured in different but overlapping ways by the three clauses of the Amendment's first section. Protection was a substantive right of citizenship under the Privileges or Immunities Clause. It was also implicit in the injunction that no person should be deprived of life, liberty, or property without due process of law. Finally, the Equal Protection Clause mandated that the protection afforded to a state's citizens be equal to all.

---

310. *See id.*

311. *See, e.g.*, *id.* at 1293 (remarks of Rep. Shellabarger); *id.* at 2498 (remarks of Rep. Broomall).

312. *Id.* at 2498 (remarks of Rep. Broomall).

313. *See id.* at 2459 (remarks of Rep. Stevens); *id.* at 2462 (remarks of Rep. Garfield); *id.* at 2498 (remarks of Rep. Broomall).

314. U.S. CONST. amend. XIV, § 1.

315. *See* CONG. GLOBE, 39th Cong., 1st Sess. 2465 (1866) (remarks of Rep. Thayer). For other supporters, see *supra* note 313. For opponents, see CONG. GLOBE, 39th Cong., 1st Sess. 2467 (1866) (remarks of Rep. Boyer); *id.* at 2538 (remarks of Rep. Rogers).

1. *The Privileges or Immunities Clause*. After declaring all persons born in the United States to be citizens, Section 1 forbids the states to "abridge the privileges or immunities of citizens of the United States."[316] For a definition of privileges and immunities, Republicans looked to a leading 1825 decision, *Corfield v. Coryell*.[317]

In *Corfield*, Justice Washington, sitting on circuit, was called upon to interpret Article IV, Section 2 of the Constitution, which provides that "[t]he Citizens of each State shall be entitled to all Privileges and Immunities of Citizens in the several States."[318] Justice Washington held that this clause protected:

> those privileges and immunities which are, in their nature, fundamental; which belong, of right, to the citizens of all free governments; and which have, at all times, been enjoyed by the citizens of the several states which compose this Union . . . . [T]hese fundamental principles . . . may . . . be all comprehended under the following general heads: *Protection by the government*; the enjoyment of life and liberty, with the right to acquire and possess property of every kind, and to pursue and obtain happiness and safety; subject nevertheless to such restraints as the government may justly prescribe for the general good of the whole.[319]

Corfield thus recognized "[p]rotection by the government" as a fundamental right of citizenship on a par with the rights to life, liberty, and property.

Corfield was invoked by both Senator Trumbull and Representative Wilson, the managers of the Civil Rights Act, to explain the fundamental rights of citizenship secured by the Act.[320] Similarly, Senator Howard, presenting the Fourteenth Amendment on behalf of the Joint Committee

---

316. U.S. CONST. amend. XIV, § 1.

317. 6 F. Cas. 546 (C.C.E.D. Pa. 1825) (No. 3230). *Corfield* was discussed as the leading authority on the meaning of privileges and immunities by Chancellor Kent. *See* 2 KENT, *supra* note 121, at *71-72.

318. U.S. CONST. art. IV, § 2, cl. 1.

319. 6 F. Cas. at 551-52 (emphasis added). Without attempting a complete enumeration, Justice Washington proceeded to mention "some of the particular privileges and immunities" that were regarded as fundamental, including:

> [t]he right of a citizen of one state to pass through, or reside in any other state, for purposes of trade, agriculture, professional pursuits, or otherwise; to claim the benefit of the writ of habeas corpus; to institute and maintain actions of any kind in the courts of the state; to take, hold and dispose of property, either real or personal; and an exemption from higher taxes or impositions than are paid by the other citizens of the state . . . to which may be added the elective franchise, as regulated and established by the laws or constitution of the state in which it is to be exercised.

Id. at 552. As we have seen, the right "to institute and maintain actions . . . in the courts" was a paradigmatic instance of the right to protection in traditional legal thought. *See supra* text accompanying notes 163-70.

320. *See* CONG. GLOBE, 39th Cong., 1st Sess. 474-75 (1866) (remarks of Sen. Trumbull); *id.* at 1117-18 (remarks of Rep. Wilson). Another leading House Republican, William Lawrence of Ohio, also relied on *Corfield* for the meaning of privileges and immunities. *See id.* at 1835-36.

on Reconstruction, looked to *Corfield* for the meaning of "privileges and immunities."[321] Thus, as John Hart Ely has observed, the Framers "repeatedly adverted to the *Corfield* discussion as the key to what they were writing."[322]

The fundamental right to protection was emphasized by the Framers. Under Article IV, Section 2, Representative Wilson contended, "every citizen" was "entitle[d] . . . to security and protection of personal rights."[323] If the states would all observe this constitutional requirement, it would be unnecessary for Congress to pass a civil rights bill. Because the states failed to comply, however, "we must do our duty by supplying the protection which the States deny."[324]

In several speeches, Representative Bingham, the principal draftsman of Section 1, expressed a similar understanding. The right "to be protected in life, liberty, and property," Bingham asserted, was one of the "privileges and immunities" of citizens under Article IV, Section 2 of the Constitution.[325] In common with some other Republicans, Bingham apparently believed that that provision applied to a state's treatment of its own citizens as well as of the citizens of other states.[326] Thus, he declared, under the Constitution "there never was even colorable excuse . . . for any man North or South claiming that any State Legislature or State court, or State Executive, has any right to deny protection to any free citizen of the United States within their limits in the rights of life, liberty, and property."[327] The "want of the Republic," however, was that there was no provision in the Constitution that empowered the national government to compel states to perform their duty of protection.[328] The purpose of the Fourteenth Amendment, Bingham indicated, was to remedy this deficiency by giving Congress the power "to protect by national law the privileges and immunities of all the citizens of the Republic and the inborn rights of every person within its jurisdiction

321. *Id.* at 2765.

322. ELY, *supra* note 12, at 29.

323. CONG. GLOBE, 39th Cong., 1st Sess. 1118 (1866) (citing Campbell v. Morris, 3 H. & McH. 535 (Md. 1797)).

324. *Id.*

325. *Id.* at 2542.

326. *See* CURTIS, *supra* note 127, at 60-61, 115-16.

327. CONG. GLOBE, 39th Cong., 1st Sess. 1090 (1866). Although most of Bingham's examples of state denials of protection appear to involve affirmative state deprivations, such as confiscation of property and banishment, *see id.* at 1090-91, he gives at least one example involving a positive right to protection: the right of "a party aggrieved in his person within a State . . . to protection by prosecution of a suit, which by the organic law of the State was denied to him." *Id.* at 1064.

328. *See id.* at 1034, 2542 (remarks of Rep. Bingham).

whenever the same shall be abridged or denied by the unconstitutional acts of any State."[329]

Bingham emphasized that his proposed constitutional amendment was not intended to remove from the states "the care of the property, the liberty, and the life of the citizen."[330] Instead, it was meant to give the federal government power to punish state denials of protection in violation of the states' constitutional responsibilities.[331]

It seems clear, then, that protection was understood to be one of the principal rights of citizenship encompassed by the Privileges or Immunities Clause. This simply reflected the classical view of the relationship between citizenship and protection. As Representative Lawrence expressed it, "citizenship implies certain rights which are to be protected," in return for "the duty of allegiance and obedience to the laws."[332]

2. *The Due Process Clause*. As we have seen, the substantive rights to be secured by the Civil Rights Act and the Fourteenth Amendment were discussed primarily in terms of the privileges and immunities of citizenship. The Privileges or Immunities Clause, however, was rendered virtually a dead letter by the *Slaughter-House Cases*.[333] When the Supreme Court, beginning in the late nineteenth century, expanded its interpretation of the Fourteenth Amendment to include substantive rights, it relied not on that clause, but on the Due Process Clause. Thus, the controversy in *DeShaney* focused on the Due Process Clause. In rejecting a constitutional duty of protection, Chief Justice Rehnquist relied on both the history and the language of that provision.[334] Properly read, however, both of these sources support a right to protection under the Due Process Clause.

The history of the Due Process Clause sheds crucial light on its meaning. As the congressional debates reveal, the clause was understood to have a positive dimension. Referring to the Due Process Clause of the Fifth Amendment, which was to be incorporated into the Fourteenth, Representative Bingham stated that the Clause ensured "the protection of the laws";[335] it guaranteed the right "of all persons to be protected in

329. *Id.* at 2542.

330. *Id.* at 1090, 1292.

331. *See id.* In these statements, Bingham was talking about an earlier version of the proposed amendment. His remarks, however, seem equally applicable to the version of the Fourteenth Amendment that was finally adopted.

332. *Id.* at 1832.

333. 83 U.S. (16 Wall.) 36 (1873).

334. *See supra* text accompanying notes 3-5.

335. CONG. GLOBE, 39th Cong., 1st Sess. 1292 (1866).

life, liberty, and property."[336] Hence, it was a violation of the Due Process Clause for any state "to deny protection to any free citizen of the United States within their limits in the rights of life, liberty, and property."[337] This positive understanding of the Due Process Clause was also expressed by other members.[338]

This identification of the Due Process Clause with the right to protection of the law was not, as is often thought,[339] peculiar to Republican or antislavery ideology. Instead, it was central to the classical understanding of "due process of law" or "the law of the land" in both England and America.

The Due Process Clauses of the Federal Constitution trace back to chapter 29 of Magna Carta, which declared: "No Freeman shall be taken, or imprisoned, or be disseised of his Freehold, or Liberties, or free Customs, or be outlawed, or exiled, or any otherwise destroyed; nor will [the sovereign] pass upon him, nor condemn him, but by lawful Judgment of his Peers, or by the Law of the Land."[340] Most of the first state constitutions contained "law of the land" provisions based on this clause of Magna Carta.[341] In drafting the Fifth Amendment, Madison translated the medieval language of Magna Carta into the modern terminology of life, liberty, and property.[342] It was generally agreed, however, that there was no substantive difference between the ancient and modern

336. *Id.* at 1089.

337. *Id.* at 1090.

338. *See, e.g.*, *id.* at 1152 (remarks of Rep. Thayer) (asserting that the Fifth Amendment "guaranties to all the citizens of the United States their right to life, liberty, and property"); *id.* at 1294 (remarks of Rep. Wilson) (stating that under the Fifth Amendment "[t]he citizen is entitled to life, liberty, and the right to property"); *see also id.* at 227 app. (remarks of Rep. DeFrees) (contending that Section 1 of the Fourteenth Amendment "secures to all life, liberty, and property").

339. *See, e.g.*, William W. Crosskey, *Charles Fairman, "Legislative History," and the Constitutional Limitations on State Authority*, 22 U. CHI. L. REV. 1, 16-17 (1954).

340. Magna Carta ch. 29 (1225) (Eng.), 1 Stat. at Large 7-8 (London, 1763) (emphasis omitted).

341. *See, e.g.*, MASS. CONST. of 1780, pt. I, art. XII, *reprinted in* 5 STATE CONSTITUTIONS, *supra* note 13, at 94; VA. DECLARATION OF RIGHTS of 1776 § 8, *reprinted in* 10 STATE CONSTITUTIONS, *supra* note 13, at 49.

342. *See* ADAMS, *supra* note 79, at 157 (describing American translation of medieval constitutional language into modern natural rights concepts).

forms of the provision.[343] By the time of the Civil War, the provision appeared in some form in virtually every state constitution.[344]

In his *Commentaries*, Blackstone treated chapter 29 of Magna Carta as having positive content. That provision, he wrote, "protected every individual of the nation in the free enjoyment of his life, his liberty and his property, unless declared to be forfeited by the judgment of his peers or the law of the land."[345] This view was echoed by Daniel Webster in his argument in the *Dartmouth College* case[346]—the most widely quoted antebellum definition of "the law of the land" or "due process of law."[347] "By the law of the land," he declared, "is most clearly intended, the general law; a law, which hears before it condemns; which proceeds upon inquiry, and renders judgment only after trial. *The meaning is, that every citizen shall hold his life, liberty, property and immunities, under the protection of the general rules which govern society*."[348]

Thus, Webster and Blackstone both described the law-of-the-land clause as requiring protection in life, liberty, and property. Read narrowly, these statements might be taken to refer only to protection against intrusions by the government itself. Understood in the context of classical thought, however, the principle that they articulated had broader meaning. A citizen holds his life, liberty, and property under the protection of the law. The law secures rights on one hand, and specifies the conditions under which those rights are forfeited on the other. The due process or law-of-the-land provisions bar the government from depriving a citizen of his rights except under the conditions set forth by law, ascertained through a judicial proceeding. In the absence of a judicially determined forfeiture, the citizen is entitled to the protection of the law, including the right to appeal to the law for redress of any injuries he

343. *See* Murray's Lessee v. Hoboken Land & Improvement Co., 59 U.S. (18 How.) 272, 276 (1855); COOLEY, *supra* note 104, at *351-53; Robert E. Riggs, *Substantive Due Process in 1791*, 1990 WIS. L. REV. 941, 991-95.

Bingham viewed the Fifth Amendment as expanding the coverage of Magna Carta. *See* CONG. GLOBE, 39th Cong., 1st Sess. 1292 (1866) (remarks of Rep. Bingham) (The Framers of the Fifth Amendment "abolished the narrow and limited phrase of the old Magna Carta . . ., which gave the protection of the laws only to 'free men,' and inserted instead the more comprehensive words, 'no person.' ").

344. *See* COOLEY, *supra* note 104, at *351-53 & n.1 (citing provisions).

345. 4 BLACKSTONE, *supra* note 24, at *424. In addition, Blackstone observed that the reference to "outlawry" in chapter 29 meant that no freeman could be "put out of the protection and benefit of the laws, [except] according to the law of the land." 1 *id.* at *141.

346. Trustees of Dartmouth College v. Woodward, 17 U.S. (4 Wheat.) 518, 551-99 (1819) (argument of Daniel Webster for plaintiffs in error).

347. *See* COOLEY, *supra* note 104, at *353. The Supreme Court adopted Webster's language in Hurtado v. California, 110 U.S. 516, 535-36 (1884).

348. *Dartmouth College*, 17 U.S. (4 Wheat.) at 581 (emphasis added).

might suffer, whether from private parties or from the government itself.[349]

Leading mid-nineteenth-century writers followed Blackstone and Webster in identifying due process or law-of-the-land provisions with the right to protection.[350] Reflecting this view, some antebellum judicial opinions determined that a state might violate these provisions not only by directly taking life, liberty, or property, but also by denying legal protection to an individual or his rights. As one judge expressed it:

> [To hold] that the [due process] clause can apply only to cases where there is to be some manual interference [by the state] with the rights of person or of property . . . would virtually nullify the provision, as the most oppressive and tyrannical ends may be accomplished by simply withdrawing from individual rights the protection of the law.[351]

Thus, it was held that the clause was violated by legislation that denied a class of persons the right to sue in court,[352] or that denied all legal remedy for the violation of an existing right.[353] Articulating the general principle underlying these cases, Thomas M. Cooley wrote that "every

---

349. *See id.* at 569-70.

350. For example, Theodore Sedgwick, in his influential treatise on statutory and constitutional interpretation, wrote that the clause "guarantees to life, liberty, and property the protection of law." THEODORE SEDGWICK, A TREATISE ON THE RULES WHICH GOVERN THE INTERPRETATION AND CONSTRUCTION OF STATUTORY AND CONSTITUTIONAL LAW 534 (1857). Sedgwick's identification of due process with the right to protection is further reflected by the fact that the entry in the table of contents corresponding to the due process clause is "Protection of Law." *Id.* at xi.

Similarly, in his *Constitutional Limitations*, Thomas M. Cooley wrote that the due process clauses guaranteed "[t]he protection of the subject in the free enjoyment of his life, his liberty, and his property, except as they might be declared by the judgment of his peers or the law of the land to be forfeited." COOLEY, *supra* note 104, at *351. Cooley's treatise was published in 1868, the same year that the Fourteenth Amendment was ratified.

351. Wynehamer v. People, 13 N.Y. 378, 434 (1856) (opinion of Selden, J.).

352. *See* Wally's Heirs v. Kennedy, 10 Tenn. (2 Yer.) 554 (1831). The same result was reached under state constitutional provisions guaranteeing the right to a remedy for injuries. *See, e.g.*, Davis v. Pierse, 7 Minn. 13 (1862); *supra* text accompanying notes 166-68 (discussing these provisions).

353. *See* Newland v. Marsh, 19 Ill. 376, 383-84 (1857); Wynehamer v. People, 13 N.Y. 378 (1856). The best known case is *Wynehamer*, which held that a New York statute prohibiting the sale of intoxicating liquor violated the due process clause of the state constitution. Although the case focused on the constitutionality of prohibition laws, it also raised the issue whether a state could deny all remedies for an injury to an existing property right. Section 16 of the statute effectively denied the owner of liquor a remedy if it was taken or injured by others. The intermediate court held that this provision violated the state due process clause by impairing "the right to protection of the laws, and to redress by the legal tribunals." People v. Berberrich, 11 How. Pr. 289, 320-21 (N.Y. Sup. Ct. 1855) (opinion of Brown, J.), *aff'd sub nom.* Wynehamer v. People, 13 N.Y. 378 (1856). Several of the leading opinions in the court of appeals also relied in part on this denial of protection in holding the statute unconstitutional. *See Wynehamer*, 13 N.Y. at 396, 397, 399 (opinion of Comstock, J.); *id.* at 423 (opinion of A.S. Johnson, J.); *see also id.* at 434 (opinion of Selden, J.) (quoted *supra* text accompanying note 351). Two other courts reached the same conclusion, relying on state constitutional guarantees of the right to a remedy. *See* Preston v. Drew, 33 Me. 558 (1852); Opinion of the Justices, 25 N.H. 537, 540 (1852).

man is entitled to a certain remedy in law for all wrongs against his person or his property."[354]

Thus, the contemporary understanding of the due process clause was not limited to direct governmental takings of life, liberty, and property. Instead, that clause was understood in the antebellum legal tradition to guarantee these rights the protection of the laws. As the congressional debates show, this understanding was shared by the Framers of the Fourteenth Amendment.

We may now return to the language of the Due Process Clause as it appears in the Fourteenth Amendment. The Clause, Chief Justice Rehnquist argued,

> is phrased as a limitation on the State's power to act, not as a guarantee of certain minimal levels of safety and security. It forbids the State itself to deprive individuals of life, liberty, or property without 'due process of law,' but its language cannot fairly be extended to impose an affirmative obligation on the State to ensure that those interests do not come to harm through other means.[355]

Although on the surface this interpretation seems very powerful, it fundamentally distorts the meaning of the Due Process Clause by abstracting the language from its historical context. When the Clause is read in light of the contemporary legal understanding, a different meaning emerges.

First, as the congressional debates indicate, when the Framers referred to "life, liberty [and] property," they principally meant the *rights* to life, liberty, and property.[356] They identified these rights with "the absolute rights" of individuals recognized in the classical legal tradition:

The *Wynehamer* decision was widely known. The intermediate court's decision was discussed with approval by Sedgwick, including the holding that the denial of a remedy impaired "the right of protection belonging to the citizen." SEDGWICK, *supra* note 350, at 481.

Wynehamer's broader holding that prohibition laws were unconstitutional was rejected by most other state courts. *See* COOLEY, *supra* note 104, at *582-83 & n.3 (citing cases). These decisions did not disagree with the view that the due process clause would be violated by denying all remedy for the violation of a valid property right. Instead, they held that in the exercise of the police power, the state could legitimately abolish or restrict the substantive right to property in liquor.

354. COOLEY, *supra* note 104, at *362. Several decades later, the Supreme Court endorsed the view that the Due Process Clause of the Fourteenth Amendment included a right to protection. In Truax v. Corrigan, 257 U.S. 312 (1921), Chief Justice Taft wrote:

> The due process clause requires that every man shall have the protection of his day in court, and the benefit of the general law, . . . so that every citizen shall hold his life, liberty, property and immunities under the protection of the general rules which govern society. [The due process clause] makes a required minimum of protection for every one's right of life, liberty, and property, which the Congress or the [State] Legislature may not withhold.

Id. at 332 (citation omitted). For discussion of *Truax*, see Currie, *supra* note 104, at 876-78.

355. DeShaney v. Winnebago County Dep't of Social Servs., 489 U.S. 189, 195 (1989).

356. *See, e.g.*, CONG. GLOBE, 39th Cong., 1st Sess. 475 (1866) (remarks of Sen. Trumbull); *id.* at 1089-90 (remarks of Rep. Bingham); *id.* at 1117-18 (remarks of Rep. Wilson); *id.* at 1833, 1835 (remarks of Rep. Lawrence); *id.* at 3036 (remarks of Sen. Henderson).

the rights to personal security, personal liberty, and private property.[357] As we have seen, these rights were understood in the legal tradition not merely as negative rights against invasion by others, but also as positive rights to the security of life, liberty, and property under the law.[358]

Moreover, in traditional legal terminology, the term "deprive" may mean not only to take away a possession, but also to divest of a right. For example, the Virginia Declaration of Rights asserted that "all men . . . have certain inherent rights, of which, when they enter into a state of society, they cannot, by any compact, *deprive or divest* their posterity."[359]

Understood in this way, the Due Process Clause forbids the state to deprive any person of the *rights* to life, liberty, and property, that is, of security in those rights under the law. Of course, the state would violate this provision by executing or imprisoning a person, or by taking his property, without due process. But it would do so as well by refusing to protect a person in life, liberty, or property, thereby depriving him of security against the invasion of those rights by others. As Representative Lawrence explained, "there are two ways in which a State may undertake to deprive citizens of [their] absolute, inherent, and inalienable rights: either by prohibitory laws, *or by a failure to protect any one of them*."[360]

An alternative (but not necessarily inconsistent) interpretation of the Due Process Clause leads to the same conclusion. The Clause expressly forbids state deprivations of the absolute rights of life, liberty, and property. As Lawrence explained, however, whenever the law gives a right, it also gives "the means whereby [the right] may be possessed and enjoyed."[361] Thus, as Chairman Wilson argued, the Due Process Clause may be understood to encompass not only these absolute rights but also "those which are necessary for the protection and maintenance and perfect enjoyment of the rights thus specifically named."[362] As we have

357. *Id.* at 1833 (remarks of Rep. Lawrence); *see also id.* at 1117-18 (remarks of Rep. Wilson); *id.* at 1757 (remarks of Sen. Trumbull).

358. *See supra* text accompanying note 153.

359. VA. CONST. of 1776, Bill of Rights § 1, *reprinted in* 10 STATE CONSTITUTIONS, *supra* note 13, at 49 (emphasis added).

360. CONG. GLOBE, 39th Cong., 1st Sess. 1833 (1866) (emphasis added). Lawrence's reference to "prohibitory laws" reflects the Thirty-Ninth Congress's predominant concern with the threat posed by the newly enacted black codes. Of course, the Fourteenth Amendment has long been interpreted to apply to all state action, not only legislation. *See, e.g.*, Yick Wo v. Hopkins, 118 U.S. 356, 371-72 (1886).

361. CONG. GLOBE, 39th Cong., 1st Sess. 1833 (1866). Lawrence quoted from Coke's *Reports* the legal maxim that where " 'the law granteth anything to any one that also is granted without which the thing itself cannot be.' " *Id.* (quoting Oath Before the Justices, 12 Co. Rep. 130, 130, 77 Eng. Rep. 1405, 1405 (1612)).

362. *Id.* at 1294.

seen, the Framers believed that the right "to share the benefit of laws for the security of person and property" was among the "necessary incidents" of the three absolute rights.[363] Accordingly, state deprivation of that right violates the Due Process Clause. This interpretation is consistent with the Framers' understanding that the Fourteenth Amendment constitutionalized the Civil Rights Act;[364] that Act, as we shall see, expressly guaranteed the right to share in the benefit of laws for the security of person and property.[365]

3. *The Equal Protection Clause*. The Equal Protection Clause expressly recognizes a right to the "protection of the laws," but qualifies it with the term "equal." It could be argued that the Fourteenth Amendment does incorporate a right to protection, but only to "equal" protection. On this view, the state need not grant protection to anyone; if it chooses to do so, however, it must afford protection to all citizens on an impartial basis, without regard to race or other suspect criteria.[366]

There are two responses to this line of argument. First, although the Equal Protection Clause, taken by itself, may not establish a substantive right to protection, that does not mean that the Fourteenth Amendment as a whole does not confer such a right. As we have seen, the principal source of substantive rights in the Amendment was the Privileges or Immunities Clause. Protection was clearly regarded as among the basic privileges of American citizenship. Thus, the Privileges or Immunities and the Equal Protection Clauses are perfectly complementary. The former confers a substantive right to protection, whereas the latter requires that the protection given to all citizens be equal.

More fundamentally, the argument misunderstands the concept of equality in Reconstruction-era thought. Equality was not sharply distinct from the substantive rights to liberty and protection, but was essentially connected with them. At its most basic level, equality meant being fully recognized as a freeman and a citizen, with all the rights and obligations corresponding to that status.

The foundations of equal protection may be found, in part, in Lockean thought.[367] Locke begins, as we have seen, with the idea of natural

363. *Id.* at 1833 (remarks of Rep. Lawrence); *see supra* text accompanying notes 297-98.

364. *See supra* text accompanying notes 313, 315.

365. *See infra* text accompanying notes 382-402.

366. Judge Posner suggests this position in several of his opinions. *See, e.g.*, Jackson v. City of Joliet, 715 F.2d 1200, 1203 (7th Cir. 1983); Bowers v. DeVito, 686 F.2d 616, 618 (7th Cir. 1982). For a similar view, see RAOUL BERGER, GOVERNMENT BY JUDICIARY: THE TRANSFORMATION OF THE FOURTEENTH AMENDMENT 176-83 (1977).

367. For another account of the relationship between equal protection and natural rights theory, see Hamburger, *supra* note 128.

liberty.[368] In a state of nature, every man is free to direct his own actions, without depending on the will of any other man. Men who are free in this way are also equal because each is independent of the others. Locke defines natural equality in two ways. In negative terms, it means the absence of "Subordination or Subjection," whereby an individual is deprived of his natural freedom and subjected to the will of another.[369] In positive terms, natural equality means the equal right to one's natural liberty.[370] As Locke explains, although men differ in ability, age, and virtue,

> yet all this consists with the *Equality*, which all Men are in, in respect of Jurisdiction or Dominion one over another, which was the *Equality* I . . . spoke of, . . . being that *equal Right* that every Man hath, *to his Natural Freedom*, without being subjected to the Will or Authority of any other Man.[371]

When men enter civil society, they give up their natural liberty in return for protection.[372] Just as natural equality was the equal right to natural liberty, civil equality is the equal right to protection under the law.[373] Thus, Locke writes that the members of society are "equally Subjects of the same Law together," a law that is "common to every one of that Society," and that secures the natural rights of all its members.[374]

For Locke, the concept of equality has crucial substantive implications. It gives rise to one of the most basic principles of the law of nature: "[T]hat being all equal and independent, no one ought to harm another in his Life, Health, Liberty, or Possessions."[375] To harm another denies equality because it treats him as subordinate to my will and infringes his equal right to liberty.[376] It follows that for the law to treat persons as equals, it must protect each individual against the invasion of his rights by others.

In sum, Locke implies that every individual has an equal right to protection under the law. This right has a substantive as well as a formal

368. *See* LOCKE, *supra* note 25, § 4.

369. *Id.*

370. *See id.* § 54.

371. *Id.*

372. *Id.* §§ 131, 136.

373. As we have seen, legal writers such as Blackstone and Kent identified liberty with protection. *See supra* Part I(C). In these terms, it may be said that, just as natural equality is the equal right to natural liberty, civil equality is the equal right to civil liberty, i.e., the equal right to protection.

374. LOCKE, *supra* note 25, §§ 22, 59, 131; *see also id.* § 142 (The legislative power must "govern by *promulgated establish'd laws*, not to be varied in particular Cases, but to have one Rule for Rich and Poor, for the Favourite at Court, and the Country Man at Plough.").

375. *Id.* § 6.

376. *Id.* For another good statement of this view, see JAMES WILSON, Lectures On Law (1790-1791), *reprinted in* 1 THE WORKS OF JAMES WILSON, *supra* note 73, at 241.

dimension: It requires not only that the law apply equally to all, but also that the law protect individuals against violation of their rights by others.

This understanding of equality was shared by the Framers of the Fourteenth Amendment, a point that was brought out most clearly in an exchange between Senators Henry Wilson of Massachusetts and Edgar Cowan of Pennsylvania during the Senate's consideration of the Freedmen's Bureau Bill.[377] Responding to a challenge by Senator Cowan, Senator Wilson replied:

> Sir, the Senator from Pennsylvania asks me what I mean by the equality of men . . . . He asks whether I mean that one man shall weigh as much as another, or have as much money. Why are these questions put? Does he not know precisely and exactly what we do mean? Does he not know that we mean that the poorest man, be he black or white, that treads the soil of this continent, is as much entitled to the protection of the law as the richest and the proudest man in the land?[378]

In identifying equality with protection, Senator Wilson was simply articulating the common view, expressed by supporters and opponents alike.[379] Indeed, Senator Cowan himself had defined equality earlier in the debate in almost identical terms:

> What is meant by equality, as I understand it, in the language of the Declaration of Independence, is that each man shall have the right to pursue in his own way life, liberty, and happiness. That is the whole of it. It is not that he shall be an elector, it is not that he shall receive the especial favors of the community in any way; but it means that if he is assailed by one stronger than himself the Government will protect him to punish the assailant. It means . . . that if an intruder and trespasser gets upon his land he shall have a remedy to recover it. That is what I understand by equality before the law.[380]

As the exchange between Wilson and Cowan shows, equality was not merely a formal or "empty"[381] concept to the Framers, but an essential correlate of the substantive rights to liberty and protection. By equality, the Framers meant the equal right of every individual to protection in his natural rights of life, liberty, and the pursuit of happiness.

377. CONG. GLOBE, 39th Cong., 1st Sess. 342-43 (1866).

378. *Id.* at 343.

379. In addition to the statements of Senators Wilson and Cowan, quoted in the text, see *id.* at 1293 (remarks of Rep. Shellabarger) ("Innumerable authorities might be produced to show a self-evident thing, that protection by his Government is the right of every citizen, and that this right to protection is equal to all citizens . . . ."); *id.* at 2539 (remarks of Rep. Farnsworth) ("How can [an individual] have and enjoy equal rights of 'life, liberty, and the pursuit of happiness' without 'equal protection of the laws'?"); *id.* at 2962 (remarks of Sen. Poland) ("All the people, or all the members of a State or community, are equally entitled to protection; they are all subject to its laws; they must all share its burdens, and are all interested in its legislation and government.").

380. *Id.* at 342.

381. *See* Peter Westen, *The Empty Idea of Equality*, 95 HARV. L. REV. 537 (1982).

Protection, in turn, was a fundamental right, not a mere benefit that the state could arbitrarily bestow or withhold. Understood in this way, "equal protection" was not a limited form of protection, a right to merely equal rather than to full protection; instead, it meant the equal right of every person to the protection that states owe to their citizens.

D. *The Meaning of Protection*

The final issue concerns the content or meaning of the constitutional right to protection. This meaning may be gathered not only from the 1866 debates, but also from the provisions of the Civil Rights Act, which gave concrete legal expression to the concepts that were embodied in the Fourteenth Amendment. As we have seen, constitutionalizing the Civil Rights Act was a major purpose of the Fourteenth Amendment.[382] These sources show that the Framers understood protection in the same way that the concept was understood in the classical legal tradition.

The Framers sought to secure protection in the three senses in which the term was traditionally understood.[383] First, the most basic purpose of the Thirteenth and Fourteenth Amendments was to recognize the newly freed slaves as freemen and as citizens—persons entitled to protection of the law as members of the community.[384] Second, the Framers sought to ensure substantive recognition of the absolute rights of individuals to life, liberty, and property. These rights were secured by the Privileges or Immunities Clause and by the Due Process Clause. Finally, the debates and the Civil Rights Act show that the Framers understood protection to include the enforcement of legal rights by government. In this sense, protection included civil protection, criminal protection, and the prevention of injury by peace officers.

1. *Civil Protection*. For the Framers, "the right to protection by the prosecution of a suit, . . . either for the vindication of a right or the redress of a wrong,"[385] was a central instance of the right to protection. In *Corfield*, Justice Washington had mentioned the right "to institute and maintain actions of any kind in the courts of [a] state" as one of the particular privileges and immunities of citizens—a privilege evidently falling under the general category of "[p]rotection by the government."[386] Following *Corfield*, Senator Trumbull declared that "the right

382. See *supra* text accompanying note 313.

383. *See supra* Part II.

384. *See* Kaczorowski, *supra* note 250, at 898-99; *see also* West, *supra* note 52 (arguing that the positive liberties of autonomy and citizenship were at the core of the Fourteenth Amendment).

385. CONG. GLOBE, 39th Cong., 1st Sess. 1064 (1866) (remarks of Rep. Bingham).

386. Corfield v. Coryell, 6 F. Cas. 546, 551-52 (C.C.E.D. Pa. 1825) (No. 3230) (quoted *supra* in note 319). In addition to *Corfield,* Republicans cited state decisions such as Clarke v. Morey, 10

to enforce rights in the courts" was one of "the great fundamental rights . . . appertaining to every freeman" set forth in the Civil Rights Act.[387] As Senator Sherman put it: "To say that a man is a freeman, and yet is not able to assert and maintain his right, in a court of justice, is a negation of terms."[388]

The right to civil redress clearly was encompassed by Section 1 of the Act, which expressly secured the rights "to sue [and] be parties."[389] Although these rights might be purely procedural, the substantive right to a remedy for injuries was protected by the guarantee of "full and equal benefit of all laws and proceedings for the security of person and property."[390]

2. *Criminal Protection*. In common with the legal tradition, the Framers also understood the right to protection to include the right to share in the benefit of criminal laws for the security of life, liberty, and property. This understanding was expressed most clearly by Senator Cowan, a conservative Republican opponent of the Fourteenth Amendment. Although he rejected granting citizenship to non-whites, Senator Cowan acknowledged that they had a right to protection. Even an alien, he stated,

> is entitled, to a certain extent, to the protection of the laws. You cannot murder him with impunity. It is murder to kill him, the same as it is to kill another man. You cannot commit an assault and battery on him, I apprehend. He has a right to the protection of the laws; but he is not a citizen in the ordinary acceptation of the word.[391]

Other members also understood the concept of protection to include criminal protection.[392]

It seems clear that the right to criminal protection was included within the Civil Rights Act's guarantee of "full and equal benefit of all

---

Johns. 71 (N.Y. 1813), in which then-Chief Justice Kent held that this right belonged even to enemy aliens lawfully present in the state: "A lawful residence implies protection, and a capacity to sue and be sued." *Id.* at 72 (quoted in CONG. GLOBE, 39th Cong., 1st Sess. 1757 (1866) (remarks of Sen. Trumbull)).

387. CONG. GLOBE, 39th Cong., 1st Sess. 475 (1866).

388. *Id.* at 41; *see also id.* at 1160 (remarks of Rep. Windom) ("Is he free who cannot bring a suit in court for the defense of his rights?").

389. Civil Rights Act of 1866, § 1, 42 U.S.C. § 1981 (1988).

390. *Id.*

391. CONG. GLOBE, 39th Cong., 1st Sess. 2890 (1866) (remarks of Sen. Cowan); *see also id.* ("So far as the courts and the administration of the laws are concerned, I have supposed that every human being within their jurisdiction was in one sense of the word a citizen, that is, a person entitled to protection . . . .").

392. For Republicans who made statements reflecting this understanding, see, for example, *id.* at 1292 (remarks of Rep. Bingham); *id.* at 1295 (remarks of Rep. Wilson); *id.* at 1833, 1835-36 (remarks of Rep. Lawrence). For Democrats, see, for example, *id.* at 479-80 (remarks of Sen. Saulsbury).

laws and proceedings for the security of person and property."[393] In the legal tradition, the enactment and enforcement of criminal laws was recognized as one of the principal means of assuring the security of person and property.[394] Throughout the session, Republicans denounced the violence against freedmen and loyalists in the South and the inability or unwillingness of local authorities to suppress it, and stressed the urgent need for Congress to respond.[395] The Act's opponents, on the other hand, attacked it for invading what they regarded as the states' exclusive responsibility for protecting citizens against criminal offenses.[396] In response, supporters demanded to know whether the national government was powerless to protect its own citizens where states "undertake to authorize such offenses, *or deny to a class of citizens all protection against them*."[397] Senator Trumbull also implied that the right to criminal protection was covered by the Act.[398] It appears, therefore, that there was a general understanding that the right to protection under the criminal laws was secured by the Act.

The Act also expressly secured another right that was closely connected to civil and criminal protection—the right to give evidence.[399] The rationale for this provision was brought out in a colloquy between Representative Wilson and Representative Columbus Delano of Ohio, a conservative Republican opposed to the Act.[400] Challenged by Delano to explain how the right to testify could be considered "a necessary incident to freedom," Wilson responded that testimony might be "necessary to be given in court for the protection of life, liberty, and property."[401] Other

393. Civil Rights Act of 1866, § 1, 42 U.S.C. § 1981 (1988).

394. *See supra* text accompanying notes 171-84.

395. *See, e.g.*, CONG. GLOBE, 39th Cong., 1st Sess. 339, 373 (1866) (remarks of Sen. Creswell); *id.* at 340 (remarks of Sen. Wilson); *id.* at 631, 633 (remarks of Rep. Moulton); *id.* at 656-58, 2774-77 (remarks of Rep. Eliot); *id.* at 1008 (remarks of Rep. Clarke); *id.* at 1017-19 (remarks of Rep. Beaman); *id.* at 1799 (remarks of Sen. Wade); *id.* at 1833-35 (remarks of Rep. Lawrence); *see also supra* text accompanying notes 283-90.

396. *See, e.g.*, CONG. GLOBE, 39th Cong., 1st Sess. 479 (1866) (remarks of Sen. Saulsbury); *id.* at 1292 (remarks of Rep. Bingham).

397. *Id.* at 1835 (remarks of Rep. Lawrence) (emphasis added).

398. In a speech urging that President Johnson's veto of the Act be overridden, Trumbull quoted several military orders for the protection of the freedmen, including one that provided: "All injuries to the person or property committed by *or upon* freed persons shall be punished in the manner provided by the laws of [this state] for like injuries to the persons or property of citizens thereof." *Id.* at 1759 (quoting military orders issued by Major General Sickles on June 17, 1866) (emphasis added). Trumbull remarked that these military orders embodied "the very provisions of this bill." *Id.*

399. *See* Civil Rights Act of 1866, § 1, 42 U.S.C. § 1981 (1988).

400. *See* Cong. Globe, 39th Cong., 1st Sess. 158 app. (1866) (remarks of Reps. Delano and Wilson).

401. *Id.*

supporters agreed, stressing that the right to testify was necessary to punish offenses committed against loyalists, blacks, and other minorities.[402]

3. *Prevention of Injury*. In its final report on the Fourteenth Amendment, the Joint Committee on Reconstruction criticized the failure of local authorities in the South to "prevent or punish" offenses against blacks.[403] That the right to protection was understood to include the prevention of violence by peace officers is made clear by the congressional response to the Memphis riot of 1866.

The Memphis riot began with an altercation between white police and recently discharged black soldiers on May 1, 1866, which led to three days of mob violence by whites. At least forty-six blacks were killed and over one hundred homes, churches, and schoolhouses belonging to blacks were destroyed.[404] Word of the massacre reached Washington a few days later, on the eve of House approval of the Fourteenth Amendment.[405] The Republican leader, Thaddeus Stevens, denounced the "atrocity" during the final House debate on the Amendment.[406] Soon thereafter, the House voted, on Stevens's motion, to dispatch a select committee to Memphis to investigate the riot.[407]

The committee's report found that the mob had been led by the city's recorder and many of its policemen, and thus had "the sanction of official authority."[408] The committee clearly indicated its view, however, that the civil authorities had a duty not merely to avoid participating in violence, but to protect against it, as "the chosen guardians of the public peace, the sworn executors of the law for the protection of the lives, liberty, and property of the people, and the reliance of the weak and defenceless in time of danger . . . ."[409] The report criticized the civil authorities, including the mayor and sheriff, for their failure to suppress

402. For example, Representative Lawrence agreed with an editorial in favor of the right to testify that gave the example of "a riotous white attack on a colored school kept by a white woman." *Id.* at 1833. Similarly, Senator John Conness of California contended that the provision was necessary because of laws such as those of his own state, which prohibited Chinese persons from testifying. The result of these laws, he stated, was that the Chinese had been robbed and murdered "with impunity, for if a white man was not present no one could testify against the offender." *Id.* at 2892.

403. *See* REPORT OF THE JOINT COMM. ON RECONSTRUCTION, *supra* note 281, at XVII.

404. *See* REPORT ON MEMPHIS RIOTS AND MASSACRES, H.R. REP. NO. 101, 39th Cong., 1st Sess. 6-22, 34-36 (1866); FONER, *supra* note 264, at 261-62.

405. *See* CONG. GLOBE, 39th Cong., 1st Sess. 2544 (1866) (remarks of Rep. Stevens).

406. *Id.*

407. *Id.* at 2572.

408. REPORT ON MEMPHIS RIOTS AND MASSACRES, *supra* note 404, at 34.

409. *Id.*

the riot, as well as for their failure to take any steps to bring the perpetrators to justice.[410] These failures were instances of a more general denial of justice. Blacks, the committee reported,

> have had no protection from the law whatever. All the testimony [taken by the committee] shows that it was impossible for a colored man in Memphis to get justice against a white man. Such is the prejudice against the negro that it is almost impossible to punish a white man by the civil courts for any injury inflicted upon a negro.[411]

The committee concluded that neither blacks nor white Unionists would be safe in Memphis without the presence of federal troops "to uphold the authority of the government, and protect the lives, liberty, and property of citizens of the United States."[412]

The committee submitted its report to the House on July 18, 1866, only six weeks after final congressional approval of the Fourteenth Amendment.[413] In effect, the committee report was endorsed by the House, which voted to print the report over Democratic opposition.[414]

The congressional response to the Memphis riot—a response that was virtually contemporaneous with Congress's approval of the Fourteenth Amendment—confirms that the Framers understood the duty of protection to include protection against private violence. Moreover, it shows that this duty was understood to include the responsibility of government to prevent violence, not merely to remedy or to punish it after it occurred.

IV. Conclusion

In *DeShaney*, the Supreme Court held that states have no constitutional duty to protect their citizens against private violence. In this Article, I have sought to challenge *DeShaney* on its own terms—the original understanding of the Fourteenth Amendment.

As I have argued, the right to protection was a central doctrine of American constitutionalism prior to the Civil War. This doctrine, rooted in the common law tradition and social contract theory, held that the most basic obligation of government was to protect individuals against

410. *See id.* at 23-25, 27.

411. *Id.* at 30.

412. *Id.* at 27.

413. CONG. GLOBE, 39th Cong., 1st Sess. 3905 (1866).

414. *Id.* at 4159. The vote on the motion was 85-23. The House subsequently voted to print more than 10,000 extra copies, probably, as Democrats charged, with a view to the fall elections. *Id.* at 4159, 4264-66. The Memphis riot, together with an even more serious outbreak of violence in New Orleans 12 weeks later, in fact played an important role in the 1866 elections by discrediting President Johnson's Reconstruction policy. *See* FONER, *supra* note 264, at 262-63. In addition, Republicans pointed to the Memphis and New Orleans massacres in arguing for state ratification of the Fourteenth Amendment. *See* CURTIS, *supra* note 127, at 159.

violence. The right to protection was not merely a matter of constitutional theory, but had concrete legal meaning.

Under the original Constitution, the responsibility for protecting life, liberty, and property was left largely to the states. The history of slavery and suppression in the South before the War, together with the torrent of violence against blacks and Unionists after the War, convinced most Republican members of the Thirty-Ninth Congress that the states could not be relied upon to protect the rights of all persons. In response, the Republicans secured the adoption of the Civil Rights Act of 1866 and the Fourteenth Amendment. A central purpose of both measures was to incorporate the right to protection into the Federal Constitution, and thereby to empower the national government to compel the states to fulfill their duty of protection.

Protection was one of the most basic rights of citizenship secured by the Privileges or Immunities Clause. It was also implicit in the Due Process Clause, which the classical tradition identified with the right to protection of the law. Finally, the Equal Protection Clause mandated that protection be afforded equally to all of the citizens of a state. In accord with the classical tradition, the Framers understood protection to include not only the right to a civil remedy and to protection under the criminal law, but also the state's responsibility to prevent violence.

In short, the reasoning at the core of *DeShaney* is indefensible. Far from showing that the Fourteenth Amendment was intended to prevent only the "affirmative abuse of power,"[415] the congressional debates show that imposing a constitutional duty on the states to protect the fundamental rights of their citizens was a principal object of that Amendment.

More broadly, at the time of the adoption of the Bill of Rights and the Fourteenth Amendment, the Constitution was not regarded merely as "a charter of negative liberties."[416] Instead, classical thought identified liberty not only with the absence of governmental coercion, but also with the positive protection of rights by the community. In the classical tradition, negative and positive liberty were viewed as essentially related. This is the conception of liberty that underlies the Fourteenth Amendment.

415. DeShaney v. Winnebago County Dep't of Social Servs., 489 U.S. 189, 196 (1989) (quoting Parratt v. Taylor, 451 U.S. 527, 549 (1981) (Powell, J., concurring in the result)).

416. Bowers v. DeVito, 686 F.2d 616, 618 (7th Cir. 1982).

[18]

THE NEGATIVE CONSTITUTION: A CRITIQUE

*Susan Bandes**

* Professor of Law, DePaul University College of Law. B.A. 1973, State University of New York at Buffalo; J.D. 1976, University of Michigan. — Ed. I wish to thank Erwin Chemerinsky, Michael Jacobs, Martha Minow, and Stephen Siegel for their valuable comments, Janet Angstadt, Antonio D'Amico, Victoria Friedman, Renee Frisch, Timothy Knight, and Susan Narimatsu for their research assistance, and the Faculty Research Fund of DePaul Law School for its support. I would also like to thank the editors of the Michigan Law Review for agreeing to include the full names of authors in article citations. For articulate arguments in favor of this practice, see Carolyn Heilbrun and Judith Resnick, *Convergences: Law, Literature and Feminism*, 99 YALE L.J. 1913, 1913 n.*** (1990) and Joseph William Singer, *Persuasion*, 87 MICH. L. REV. 2442, 2442 n* (1989).

INTRODUCTION

No inquiry is more central to constitutional jurisprudence than the effort to delineate the duties of government. The courts' approach to this complex subject has been dominated by reliance on a simple distinction between affirmative and negative responsibilities. Government is held solely to what courts characterize as a negative obligation: to refrain from acts that deprive citizens of protected rights. Obligations that courts conceive to be affirmative — duties to act, to provide, or to protect — are not enforceable constitutional rights.[1]

This austere conception of the role of government is not new; it has a lengthy pedigree.[2] Recently, the Supreme Court has demonstrated its continuing loyalty to the conception, in contexts which vividly illustrate its flesh and blood consequences. In *DeShaney v. Winnebago County Department of Social Services,*[3] the Court left remediless the mother of a boy who had been beaten so severely he will require institutionalization for the rest of his life, despite an avoidable governmental failure to prevent the harm. In *Webster v. Reproductive Health Services,*[4] the Court upheld restrictions which will make abortions difficult or impossible for poor women to obtain. In both contexts the Court refused to hold that a governmental duty had been breached, on the ground that the Constitution does not impose affirmative obliga-

1. Professor Martha Minow has insightfully described the parallel between the Court's own refusal to protect and that which it condones on the part of government. *See* Martha Minow, Law and Violence (unpublished speech presented at the Harvard Medical School Continuing Education 5th Annual Conference on Abuse and Victimization in Life-Span Perspective, Mar. 24, 1989) (transcript on file at the Harvard Law School Library).

2. *See infra* text accompanying notes 199-246.

3. 109 S. Ct. 998 (1989).

4. 109 S. Ct. 3040 (1989).

tions on government.[5]

In these and other cases, the powerful talismanic quality of certain phrases is striking. The due process clause grants no affirmative rights.[6] Governmental inaction is not actionable.[7] The Constitution is a charter of negative liberties.[8] These phrases signal the end of discussion about constitutional protections. A conclusion has been reached and no further reasoning is necessary. Yet when a conclusory incantation permits so many harms to flourish unchecked by the Constitution, it should send the opposite signal: that the language, and the concepts it describes, must be scrutinized with care. This article undertakes that scrutiny.

Part I describes the current approach, which demands adherence to the notion of a negative constitution. Part II critiques the assumptions underlying the current approach and demonstrates its undesirable consequences in decisional law. Part III explores the tenacious barriers to recognition of affirmative governmental duties: the constitutional, philosophical, and common law roots of the notion of a negative constitution, as well as the belief that recognizing affirmative duties would be an invitation to chaos. Finally, Part IV proposes discarding the rhetoric of negative rights and suggests an approach for constructing a theory better designed to effectuate constitutional goals.

I. The Charter of Negative Liberties: The Conventional Wisdom

Traditionally, the protections of the Constitution have been viewed largely as prohibitory constraints on the power of government, rather than affirmative duties with which government must comply.[9] Although scholars have long challenged this view,[10] the courts have steadfastly adhered to it. Once a claim on government is cast as a request that it engage in, rather than refrain from, a particular activity, its dismissal is ordained. This Part seeks simply to describe the prevailing conception of the Constitution as solely a charter of nega-

5. *See DeShaney,* 109 S. Ct. at 1003; *Webster,* 109 S. Ct. at 3051.

6. *See, e.g., DeShaney,* 109 S. Ct. at 1003; *Webster,* 109 S. Ct. at 3051.

7. *See, e.g.,* City of Canton v. Harris, 109 S. Ct. 1197, 1208 (1989) (O'Connor, J., concurring in part and dissenting in part).

8. *See, e.g.,* DeShaney v. Winnebago County Dept. of Social Servs., 812 F.2d 298, 301 (7th Cir. 1987), *affd.,* 109 S. Ct. 998 (1989); Jackson v. City of Joliet, 715 F.2d 1200, 1203 (7th Cir. 1983), *cert. denied,* 465 U.S. 1049 (1984).

9. Seth F. Kreimer, *Allocational Sanctions: The Problem of Negative Rights in a Positive State,* 132 U. PA. L. REV. 1293, 1295 (1984); Laurence Tribe, *The Abortion Funding Conundrum: Inalienable Rights, Affirmative Duties, and the Dilemma of Dependence,* 99 HARV. L. REV. 330, 331 (1985); Mark Tushnet, *An Essay on Rights,* 62 TEXAS L. REV. 1363, 1392 (1984).

10. *See, e.g.,* articles cited *infra* note 20.

tive liberties; Part II will demonstrate the flaws in its central distinction.

The conventional wisdom distinguishes between negative rights to be free from governmental interference and positive rights to have government do or provide various things.[11] The conventional wisdom is that the Constitution recognizes[12] only the former. Individuals have no right to have government *do* anything at all; it must only refrain from harming or coercing them.

This sweeping statement encompasses a broad spectrum of possible claims against the government. At one end of the spectrum are narrow claims that particular government officials violated specific duties to known individuals. In its pure form, the conventional wisdom disclaims such duties. For example, in *Gilmore v. Buckley,*[13] the First Circuit found no liability when state officials released a dangerous mental patient they knew had threatened a specific individual, without warning the individual, leading to her murder the next day. In *Archie v. City of Racine,*[14] the Seventh Circuit upheld dismissal of a claim against a 911 dispatcher who gave incorrect advice and erroneously failed to dispatch an ambulance for a caller who then died.

According to the conventional wisdom, rejection of these claims follows from rejection of broader claims for government services. The conventional view holds that citizens have no constitutional right to government services. Government need not establish police[15] or fire departments;[16] it need not provide medical[17] or social services. From this premise follows another: that the greater includes the lesser.[18]

11. *See* Tushnet, *supra* note 9, at 1392.

12. Or claims to recognize; such a simplistic distinction is of course impossible to implement perfectly. *See infra* text accompanying notes 24-29 and 50-55.

13. 787 F.2d 714 (1st Cir.), *cert. denied,* 479 U.S. 882 (1986).

14. 847 F.2d 1211 (7th Cir. 1988), *cert. denied,* 109 S. Ct. 1338 (1989).

15. Jackson v. City of Joliet, 715 F.2d 1200, 1204 (7th Cir. 1983), *cert. denied,* 465 U.S. 1049 (1984).

16. Jackson v. Byrne, 738 F.2d 1443, 1446 (7th Cir. 1984).

17. *Archie,* 847 F.2d at 1222.

18. The greater-includes-the-lesser doctrine views services as gratuitous privileges which government chooses to provide, and reasons that the greater power to withhold a benefit includes the lesser power to grant it with conditions. The doctrine was widely used in the nineteenth century. In its pristine form, the doctrine held that since the greater always includes the lesser, if a man has an absolute right to do a thing (*e.g.,* stop dealing with his employer at will) he may qualify the exercise of that right by agreeing to relinquish it on condition. That this condition is, or even is intended to be, injurious to a third person is immaterial, for the court cannot inquire into the intention with which a lawful act is done. *See* G. HENDERSON, THE POSITION OF FOREIGN CORPORATIONS IN AMERICAN CONSTITUTIONAL LAW 140 (1918) (citing Allen v. Flood, App. Cas. 1 (1898)). Current jurisprudence assumes that the greater-includes-the-lesser doctrine is limited by the constraints of the Constitution. Thus it is subservient to the unconstitutional conditions doctrine, Sherbert v. Verner, 374 U.S. 398 (1963), and may not be used to permit government to withhold services based on impermissible factors such as race, Yick Wo v. Hop-

Because government has no duty to provide services, if it chooses to provide them, it need not do so competently.[19]

Justice Rehnquist's opinion in *DeShaney v. Winnebago Department of Social Services,* rejecting a due process claim[20] against a social service agency which negligently failed to protect a child from a brutal beating which inflicted irreversible injury, explains and reaffirms the conventional thinking about government duty to provide competent services:

> The [Due Process] Clause is phrased as a limitation on the State's power to act, not as a guarantee of certain minimal levels of safety and security. It forbids the State itself to deprive individuals of life, liberty, or property without "due process of law," but its language cannot fairly be extended to impose an affirmative obligation on the State to ensure that those in-

kins, 118 U.S. 356 (1886). But reconciling the greater-includes-the-lesser and unconstitutional conditions doctrines may not be so easy. *See* Kathleen M. Sullivan, *Unconstitutional Conditions,* 102 HARV. L. REV. 1415, 1458 (1989). *See generally Unconstitutional Conditions Symposium*, 26 SAN DIEGO L. REV. 175-345 (1989). *See infra* text accompanying notes 159-67.

19. Much of the articulation of this view has occurred in the courts of appeals. Based on this reasoning, in *Jackson v. City of Joliet* the court refused to hold police liable when, in the course of observing a burning car, they made no attempt to determine whether it was occupied or to call an ambulance, and two people, one six-months pregnant, died in the car. 715 F.2d 1200 (7th Cir. 1983), *cert. denied,* 465 U.S. 1049 (1984). In *Jackson v. Byrne,* police during a firefighters' strike barred firefighters from gaining access to a firehouse though a fire had broken out directly across the street. Two children died. The court refused to find governmental liability, reasoning that the Constitution creates no positive entitlement to fire protection. 738 F.2d 1443, 1446 (7th Cir. 1984). In *Bowers v. DeVito,* mental health officials released a patient who had killed before, and was known to be dangerous, and he killed again. The court held that "there is no constitutional right to be protected by the state against being murdered by criminals or madmen." 686 F.2d 616, 618 (7th Cir. 1982).

In particular, Judges Posner and Easterbrook of the Seventh Circuit have been zealous supporters of this view. *See, e.g.,* Archie v. City of Racine, 847 F.2d 1211 (7th Cir. 1988) (Easterbrook, J.; Posner, J., concurring); Jackson v. City of Joliet, 715 F.2d 1200, 1204 (Posner, J.); *Bowers,* 686 F.2d at 616 (Posner, J.); *see also* William M. Landes & Richard A. Posner, *Salvors, Finders, Good Samaritans, and Other Rescuers: An Economic Study of Law and Altruism,* 7 J. LEGAL STUD. 83 (1978) (arguing that imposing liability for failure to rescue would be economically inefficient).

20. When the courts speak of the Constitution as a charter of negative rights, the discussion in defense of this proposition often proves to be solely concerned with due process. *See, e.g.,* Jackson v. City of Joliet, 715 F.2d 1200, 1204 (7th Cir. 1983). Many scholars arguing that the Constitution contains affirmative rights have focused on the due process clause, often in conjunction with the equal protection clause. *See, e.g.,* Albert M. Bendich, *Privacy, Poverty, and the Constitution,* 54 CALIF. L. REV. 407 (1966) (arguing for a governmental duty of minimum protection); Archibald Cox, *The Supreme Court, 1965 Term — Foreword: Constitutional Adjudication and the Promotion of Human Rights,* 80 HARV. L. REV. 91 (1966) (same); Frank Michelman, *The Supreme Court, 1968 Term — Foreword: On Protecting the Poor Through the Fourteenth Amendment,* 83 HARV. L. REV. 7 (1969) (same). However, the arguments for positive rights are by no means confined to this approach. *See* Kreimer, *supra* note 9 (arguing that given pervasive government regulation, negative rights concept is inadequate); Arthur Selwyn Miller, *Toward a Concept of Constitutional Duty,* 1968 SUP. CT. REV. 199 (argument for positive rights from structure and purpose of Constitution as a whole); Laurence Tribe, *Unraveling* National League of Cities: *The New Federalism and Affirmative Rights to Essential Government Services,* 90 HARV. L. REV. 1065 (1977) (argument for affirmative rights from *Usery* decision); Tushnet, *supra* note 9 (agreeing that present balance of positive and negative rights is askew, but arguing that entire rights rhetoric should be abandoned).

> terests do not come to harm through other means. Nor does history support such an expansive reading of the constitutional text. . . . [The purpose of the Clause] was to protect the people from the State, not to ensure that the State protected them from each other. The Framers were content to leave the extent of governmental obligation in the latter area to the democratic political process.
>
> Consistent with these principles, our cases have recognized that the Due Process Clauses generally confer no affirmative right to governmental aid . . . . If the Due Process Clause does not require the State to provide its citizens with particular protective services, it follows that the State cannot be held liable under the Clause for injuries that could have been averted had it chosen to provide them.[21]

Finally, at the far end of the spectrum are broad claims that government must provide food to the starving, jobs to the unemployed. If courts are unwilling to recognize governmental duties toward specific endangered individuals, or duties by government agencies and employees to meet their job descriptions, then broadly worded claims for minimum subsistence seem doomed to failure. In their most utopian form, these claims are made only by scholars[22] or by judges warning that they are the inevitable result of embarking on the slippery slope of requiring governmental duties.[23]

If claims for minimum subsistence, or even increased police and fire protection, are the feared result, application of the conventional wisdom is thought to keep the courts off the slippery slope entirely. Like most legal constructs, however, the conventional wisdom rarely exists in its pure form. This is not to underestimate the power of the construct, which is considerable. Nevertheless, courts have often permitted liability for what might be classified as governmental inaction.

Some constitutional provisions clearly mandate affirmative governmental conduct. For example, the sixth amendment requires government to provide an accused a speedy public trial, compulsory process, assistance of counsel, and the opportunity to be informed of the nature of the accusation and confronted with the witnesses against him.[24] The equal protection clause requires that government sometimes take affirmative steps to ensure that certain groups are not treated unequally;[25] and has been held to mandate government provision of

21. DeShaney v. Winnebago County Dept. of Social Servs., 109 S. Ct. 998, 1003-04 (1989).

22. *See, e.g.,* Bendich, *supra* note 20 (arguing for a governmental duty of minimum protection); Cox, *supra* note 20 (same); Michelman, *supra* note 20 (same).

23. *See, e.g.,* Griffin v. Illinois, 351 U.S. 12, 34 (1956) (Harlan, J., dissenting); Archie v. City of Racine, 847 F.2d 1211, 1221, *cert. denied,* 109 S. Ct. 1338 (1989). *See infra* text accompanying notes 309-27.

24. U.S. CONST. amend. VI.

25. U.S. CONST. amend. XIV.

goods and services which individuals would otherwise be denied because of their poverty.[26] The conventional wisdom views these guarantees as aberrations; exceptions which prove the rule.[27] It asserts that their language contrasts with the negative phrasing elsewhere in the Bill of Rights. Moreover, the sixth amendment's affirmative protections are made necessary by its peculiar context: the government's initial deprivation of liberty.[28] Likewise, the equal protection clause simply says that once government has acted, either on behalf of a certain group, or to place a certain group at a disadvantage, it must ensure that its acts have not created an invidious inequality.[29]

It is difficult to distill a rule from these cases independent of the requisites of particular constitutional provisions. It would not be a correct characterization to say that once government has acted, it must act competently, or fairly, or continue to act at all. The public services cases have flatly rejected this formulation.[30] It is more accurate to describe the rule as saying that once government has acted to place a person in danger, it must protect him from that danger. Thus in *White v. Rochford*,[31] where police arrested the driver of a car and left the remaining passengers, two young children, in the car alone on a busy highway, the Seventh Circuit found liability. In situations where a plaintiff is in custody, or has been involuntarily committed, the courts more willingly find a duty to protect.[32] In cases in which the state is viewed as having done nothing to cause or worsen the plaintiff's situation, though it is aware of a danger to her which it could easily prevent, the courts are generally unwilling to find

26. *See, e.g.*, Boddie v. Connecticut, 401 U.S. 371 (1971) (access to divorce); Douglas v. California, 372 U.S. 353 (1963) (attorney for appeal of right); Griffin v. Illinois, 351 U.S. at 19 (1956) (trial transcript).

27. Of course, even rights which are phrased in the affirmative can be narrowly construed, and the Rehnquist Court's antipathy for governmental duties is evident even in regard to the rights whose affirmative nature is textually obvious. *See, e.g.*, Murray v. Giarratano, 109 S. Ct. 2765 (1989) (no constitutional right to appointment of counsel for collateral appeals for indigent prisoner in capital cases); United States v. Monsanto, 109 S. Ct. 2657 (1989) (sixth amendment not violated by government confiscation of accused's assets before trial though effect would be to prevent defendant from paying for an attorney); Skinner v. Railway Labor Executives' Assn., 109 S. Ct. 1402 (1989) (approving drug testing of railway workers after accidents); National Treasury Employees Union v. Von Raab, 109 S. Ct. 1384 (1989) (fourth amendment not violated by drug testing of customs workers despite lack of individualized suspicion); Teague v. Lane, 109 S. Ct. 1060 (1989) (federal court may not hear habeas petition presenting claim of a new constitutional right, except in rare instances when that right, if recognized, would be applied retroactively).

28. David Currie, *Positive and Negative Constitutional Rights*, 53 U. CHI. L. REV. 864, 873 (1986).

29. *See id.* at 880.

30. *See infra* text accompanying notes 294-99.

31. 592 F.2d 381 (7th Cir. 1979).

32. *See, e.g.*, *DeShaney*, 109 S. Ct. at 1006; Youngberg v. Romeo, 457 U.S. 307 (1982); Estelle v. Gamble, 429 U.S. 97 (1976).

liability.[33]

Consistent with a burgeoning trend in tort law,[34] courts, prior to the *DeShaney* decision, carved out an exception to the rule against affirmative duties when a special relationship was found to exist between the government and the injured party, such that government officials had undertaken to assist or protect particular individuals or classes.[35] However, the *DeShaney* holding seems to invalidate this approach, by holding that the only special relationship the Court recognizes is that between a custodian and a person in custody, and that it arises solely from the government's act of placing the person in danger or otherwise restraining his liberty.[36]

In short, the conventional wisdom rests on the efficacy of the distinction between government action and inaction. Government has no obligation to act, except, in limited circumstances, to ensure that no harm is caused by its previous actions. In order to make the distinction between action and inaction, it becomes crucial to determine what constitutes a governmental act, to distinguish the acts of government from those of private persons, and to delineate the circumstances in which the government has caused harm. Therefore, the distinction between action and inaction reappears in other forms: the public/private distinction; the penalty/subsidy distinction; and the rules of causation. Part II examines the application of the action/inaction distinction in its various forms, and seeks to demonstrate that it is unworkable and misguided.

II. The Charter of Negative Liberties: The Flawed Nature of the Conventional Wisdom

The conventional wisdom about governmental duties reflects an unfaltering belief in the rightness of certain distinctions. Moreover, it

33. *See* Archie v. City of Racine, 847 F.2d 1211 (7th Cir. 1988) (no liability where 911 dispatcher gave wrong advice to ill caller and erroneously failed to dispatch an ambulance, and caller then died), *cert. denied,* 109 S. Ct. 1338 (1989); Gilmore v. Buckley, 787 F.2d 714 (1st Cir.) (no liability where state knew of threat to specific individual yet released dangerous mental patient who murdered her the next day), *cert. denied,* 479 U.S. 882 (1986); Ellsworth v. City of Racine, 774 F.2d 182 (7th Cir. 1985) (no liability when police who were protecting a witness failed to do so adequately, resulting in attack); *see also* Restatement (Second) of Torts § 314 (1965). *But see* Doe v. New York City Dept. of Soc. Servs., 649 F.2d 134 (2d Cir. 1981) (liability where foster parent's abuse of child permitted by state agency's failure to monitor home adequately); Jackson v. City of Joliet, 465 U.S. 1049 (1984) (White, J., dissenting from denial of *certiorari*).

34. *See, e.g.,* Restatement (Second) of Torts §§ 314-24; 3 F. Harper, F. James & O. Gray, The Law of Torts § 18.7 (2d ed. 1986 & Supp. I 1990).

35. *See* Note, *Defining the Scope of the Due Process Right to Protection: The Fourth Circuit Considers Child Abuse and Good Faith Immunity,* 70 Cornell L. Rev. 940, 948-64 (1985).

36. *DeShaney,* 109 S. Ct. at 1005-06.

displays great faith in the ability of language to capture those distinctions.[37] Its method is to classify claims about governmental obligations according to a simple either-or system. Is the government being asked to act or to refrain from acting? To protect from the acts of private parties or from its own wrongful acts? To afford positive, affirmative rights or negative rights? If the former, relief is denied.

In short, major issues about the scope of constitutional protection are resolved by reference to a series of highly rigid and conceptualistic distinctions[38] which exalt negative over positive rights, and hold that, for government, only action is actionable. The purpose of this Part is to take a close look at these distinctions which the courts vest with such tremendous power. Section II.A argues that the distinction between action and inaction is far too arbitrary and simplistic to describe the complex web of acts and omissions through which government conducts its business. Sections II.B and II.C examines in detail two variations on the distinction between action and inaction: the public/private distinction, with particular attention to its misuse in the *DeShaney* decision; and the penalty/subsidy distinction, in the context of the abortion funding cases, most recently *Webster v. Reproductive Services.* My goal is to demonstrate that the Court has relied on conclusory labels about negative and positive rights instead of articulating, in a principled fashion, the difficult value choices these cases require.

A. *The Disappearing Distinction Between Government Action and Inaction*

In the conventional wisdom, positive rights are rights to have government do or provide something. Negative rights are rights to have government refrain from doing something. In cases as diverse as *DeShaney* and *Webster,* the Court has labeled the plaintiff's complaint as a claim for positive rights, or government action, and dismissed it with little additional analysis. Are the spheres of positive and negative, inaction and action, so self-contained that this complacency is justified?

The definitional difficulties in distinguishing action from inaction are manifold. It would be overstating the case slightly to say that the

37. *See* Martha Minow, *The Supreme Court, 1986 Term — Foreword: Justice Engendered,* 101 HARV. L. REV. 10, 35-36 (1987).

38. *See* Joseph William Singer, *The Legal Rights Debate in Analytical Jurisprudence from Bentham to Hohfeld,* 1982 WIS. L. REV. 975, 1014-18 (description of conceptualism as a belief that concepts at a high level of generality and abstractness correspond to elements of the real world and can form the basis for numerous and concrete subrules that can be deduced from them).

distinction is a useless one. It describes a common perception to say that a police officer who beats a suspect has acted, whereas a police officer who has decided not to interrupt his lunch break to aid an endangered citizen has not acted. However, the description alone cannot be used to determine the scope of constitutional protections: that determination requires a number of value choices. I argue in this section not that words like inaction and action should be stricken from the language, but that the distinction they describe is incapable of application without value choices, and ultimately is incapable of serving the purposes for which it is employed. It cannot itself justify the choices about government responsibility which are made in its name.

The term "act" is not self-defining. In fact, it is impossible to define without an understanding of the particular purpose for which the term is to be used. For example, an act could be defined, as it often is in common usage, as a voluntary physical movement, or a " 'willed muscular contraction.' "[39] Yet this definition is both atomistic and naive. It is atomistic in that it defines conduct as an isolated event apart from its effects on others. It is naive because it is simplistic and rests on unimportant differences. As Professor George Fletcher observes: "Conscious non-motion is a greater assertion of personality than casual acting. One can only be puzzled by the widespread belief that the distinction between motion and non-motion is of importance to the law."[40]

Whether one has acted might be defined by state of mind, so that a conscious decision to pursue or not pursue a certain course of conduct would qualify. For example, an act could be defined as an "external manifestation of the will."[41] Using this definition, such consciously caused harm as a deliberate refusal to make an elevator available to people attempting to escape from a mine would be classified as an act, though it lacks a physical component.[42]

What is apparent from attempts to focus on either physical or state-of-mind criteria is that it is difficult to consider the act apart from those whom it might affect, that is, apart from the harm it caused, was meant to cause, or was likely to cause. The law sometimes chooses to focus on the act apart from its consequences, as with

39. George Fletcher, Rethinking Criminal Law § 6.4.1, at 421 (1978).

40. *Id.* at 421-22.

41. Ernest J. Weinrib, *The Case for a Duty to Rescue,* 90 Yale L.J. 247, 252 n.24 (1980).

42. *Id.*

strict liability,[43] or attempt,[44] and more often chooses to focus on the act in relation to its consequences.[45] Which approach is chosen is a function of policy choices about duty, causation, fault, and remedy, not of the mechanical application of a definition of the term "act."

The definition of an act is also dependent on the way its scope is delineated. That is, whether a defendant has "acted" in the eyes of the law depends largely on how far back in the chain of events the court is willing to look.[46] In Prosser's well-known example of the difficulty of distinguishing action from inaction, "[f]ailure to blow a whistle or to shut off steam, although in itself inaction, is readily treated as negligent operation of a train, which is affirmative misconduct."[47] As this example illustrates, if a defendant has set a dangerous instrumentality in motion, the law must determine whether he should be liable for the consequences, though he has done nothing additional which could be classified as an immediate cause of harm.[48]

Perhaps it is common ground that the distinction between action and inaction is malleable. Even Judge Easterbrook, a zealous opponent of requiring affirmative duties, admits that "it is possible to restate most actions as corresponding inactions with the same effect, and to show that inaction may have the same effects as a forbidden action."[49] Especially in light of their fluidity, the question should be why these distinctions are important; what purpose they are meant to

43. *See, e.g.*, RICHARD A. EPSTEIN, A THEORY OF STRICT LIABILITY: TOWARD A REFORMATION OF TORT LAW 51-53 (1980) (arguing that strict liability is preferable to negligence theory in tort law).

44. G. FLETCHER, *supra* note 39, § 3.3.4.

45. *See id.* at § 6.4, at 420-46, § 8.2.1, at 588-93 (meaning of "act" in criminal law).

46. Weinrib, *supra* note 41, at 253-55; *see also infra* text accompanying note 337 (same point in context of causation).

47. W. PROSSER & W. KEETON, PROSSER AND KEETON ON THE LAW OF TORTS § 56, at 374 (5th ed. 1984) (footnote omitted).

48. *See, e.g.*, F. HARPER, F. JAMES & O. GRAY, *supra* note 34, § 18.6, at 719-22.

49. Archie v. City of Racine, 847 F.2d 1211, 1213 (7th Cir. 1988), *cert. denied*, 109 S. Ct. 1338 (1989). A few lower court cases, including *Archie* itself, illustrate the correctness of his observation. In White v. Rochford, 592 F.2d 381, 382-83 (7th Cir. 1979), the majority found the police liable because they had *abandoned* children on the highway and *deprived* them of adult protection. The dissent objected that the police had done nothing to the children themselves: it was not the children but their uncle whom the police took into custody. The officers simply failed to take affirmative steps to protect them. 592 F.2d at 390 (Kilkenny, J., dissenting). In *Archie*, 847 F.2d at 1214-20, a 911 dispatcher gave an ill caller incorrect medical advice and failed to send an ambulance. The majority construed this as a mere failure to send rescue services. The government did not "act" because it neither caused the illness nor interfered with the caller's ability to seek other medical help. The dissent argued that the defendant had affirmatively discouraged the caller from seeking other medical assistance. 847 F.2d at 1228-29 (Ripple, J., dissenting). In Bowers v. DeVito, 686 F.2d 616 (7th Cir. 1982), in which the department of mental health released a dangerous schizophrenic who then killed someone, the court construed the suit as a claim for state protective services, though the state's affirmative act of releasing the patient was obviously at issue.

serve. In the context of this discussion, the question is what the distinctions are asked to accomplish in the constitutional realm.

In constitutional law, the relevant question is whether the government has violated protected rights. The conventional wisdom holds that government cannot be held liable for its failure to act, but only for its affirmative acts, making it necessary to determine what constitutes an affirmative governmental act. In the governmental context, drawing a line between action and inaction is particularly problematic.

First, the determination of governmental liability under the Constitution must begin with its provisions, which rarely allow for a neat division between action and inaction. Even those constitutional duties which are most clearly phrased in the negative may be enforceable only through affirmative governmental exertions.[50] The first amendment exhorts only that "Congress shall make no law," but it has been obvious for some time that the mere failure to pass laws restricting speech will not relieve government of its responsibility for protecting the freedom of speech. Government may be required to take affirmative steps and allocate resources to ensure public access to forums and information.[51] It can be argued persuasively that the purpose of the fourth amendment was to keep government out of people's private affairs,[52] but enforcement of the protections against unreasonable search and seizure depend on the government's observance of affirmative duties to obtain warrants based on probable cause. The fifth amendment also speaks in terms of freedom from government coercion: "No person . . . shall be compelled in any criminal case to be a witness against himself."[53] Yet the Court correctly has recognized that to prevent this compulsion effectively, the government must take the affirmative step of warning the accused of their rights.[54] Although some members of the Rehnquist court disparage the *Miranda* warnings on the ground that they are not mandated by the fifth amendment, but are merely a way of enforcing it,[55] the elusiveness of this distinction is precisely the

50. As discussed earlier, many constitutional duties are phrased in the affirmative, a state of affairs which the conventional wisdom explains as anomalous. *See supra* text accompanying notes 24-29.

51. *See, e.g.,* Schneider v. State, 308 U.S. 147 (1939) (city must expend resources to clean up litter rather than deny leafletters access to a public forum); Downie v. Powers, 193 F.2d 760, 763-64 (10th Cir. 1951) (police have duty to protect speakers from mob action). Tribe notes that Professor Zechariah Chafee first identified the need for affirmative government action to facilitate expression in 1941. LAURENCE TRIBE, AMERICAN CONSTITUTIONAL LAW § 12-25, at 998 (2d ed. 1988).

52. *See* Anthony Amsterdam, *Perspectives on the Fourth Amendment,* 58 MINN. L. REV. 349, 395-409 (1974).

53. U.S. CONST. amend. V.

54. Miranda v. Arizona, 384 U.S. 436 (1966).

55. See, for example, Justice Rehnquist's opinion in New York v. Quarles, 467 U.S. 649, 654

point. Once it has been observed that some of the Bill of Rights is phrased in terms of positive commands[56] and some in terms of negative exhortations, the task of interpreting the guarantees remains. The scope of the rights, and the means of enforcing them, must be ascertained.

Second, the distinction between action and inaction fails to reflect the distribution of power and the ways in which government can cause harm in the modern welfare state. In the words of Professor Seth Kreimer:

> [T]he conception of negative rights as freedom from coercive violence has questionable value in shaping constitutional restraints on a government that more often exerts its power by withholding benefits than by threatening bodily harm . . . . The greatest force of a modern government lies in its power to regulate access to scarce resources.[57]

The assumption that government can deprive individuals of protected rights only by its actions does not take into account government's pervasive influence through regulatory action and inaction,[58] its displacement of private remedies, and, indeed, its monopoly over some avenues of relief.[59]

Government can harm by its inertia. When an individual fails to act, perhaps he harms only himself.[60] Like a dangerous instrumentality set in motion, when government fails to act, its momentum continues. It keeps collecting taxes; its employees continue to perform their jobs; its directives continue in force. In short, the bureaucracy continues to function. How it functions, whether it spends its money wisely, whether it promulgates rules, abides by them, or discards those which need to be discarded, whether it supervises its employees and disci-

(1984), and Justice O'Connor's opinion in Oregon v. Elstad, 470 U.S. 298, 305 (1985). For a discussion of the distinction between constitutional interpretation and constitutional common law, see Henry Monaghan, *The Supreme Court, 1974 Term — Foreword: Constitutional Common Law,* 89 HARV. L. REV. 1 (1975). *But see* Thomas S. Schrock & Robert C. Welsh, *Reconsidering the Constitutional Common Law,* 91 HARV. L. REV. 1117 (1978) (discussing dangers of assigning *Miranda* rules subconstitutional status).

56. *See, e.g.,* the sixth amendment protections, *supra* text accompanying note 24.

57. Kreimer, *supra* note 9, at 1295-96.

58. Sullivan, *supra* note 18, at 1451.

59. *See, e.g.,* Boddie v. Connecticut, 401 U.S. 371 (1971) (state monopoly over avenues for obtaining a divorce led to invalidation of requirement for payment of court fees); *see also* Sullivan, *supra* note 18, at 1451 (government has a monopoly on legitimate violence); Richard A. Epstein, *Unconstitutional Conditions and Bargaining Breakdown*, 26 SAN DIEGO L. REV. 189, 194-96, (1989) (government has monopoly over highways).

60. Whether he causes harm will depend on the definition of harm, which is linked to the question of duty. For example, if under modern tort principles he has a duty to rescue under certain circumstances, he will harm those he fails to rescue when those circumstances obtain. *See infra* text accompanying notes 338-39. Under most circumstances, this will not be a large group of people in comparison to the size of the group vulnerable to harm from governmental wrongdoing.

plines them when necessary, all depend on a continuing series of choices. Whether these are choices in favor of action or inaction, they will have consequences, and in either case the consequences may cause harm.[61]

Government can harm by its inaction and its inadequate action, as well as its direct action. Government can cause harm by failing to promulgate and enforce rules[62] and failing to supervise.[63] It can harm by allocating scarce resources in an arbitrary or discriminatory fashion.[64] It can harm by skewing incentives so that its employees find it more opportune to fail to protect or assist.[65] It can harm by displacing private services and failing to ensure adequate replacement services.[66] In short, it can harm by its ostensible omissions, as seriously as, and often more efficiently than, by its direct, tangible actions.[67]

I referred earlier to the importance of determining the scope of an act: the question of how far back in the chain of events a court is willing to look.[68] The fact of pervasive and longstanding government influence makes this issue particularly complicated when the government is the actor. If everything hinges on whether government *acted* to deprive an individual of rights, or simply *failed to act* by ignoring an existing deprivation, it becomes crucial to determine whether the deprivation occurred before government acted. The action/inaction distinction does not work in part because it fails to provide a baseline, or vantage point, for comparison. If the question is whether government conduct has placed an individual in a worse position than she would have been in otherwise, that conduct must be measured against some standard.[69] The conventional assumption is that the baseline should

61. The Court has held government inaction actionable in some circumstances, but has expressed hesitation in others. *See* Brandon v. Holt, 469 U.S. 464 (1985) (liability for failure to promulgate rules); City of Canton v. Harris, 109 S. Ct. 1197, 1204 (1989) (failure to supervise actionable only where motivated by deliberate indifference).

62. *See* Kenneth Culp Davis, *An Approach to Legal Control of the Police,* 52 TEXAS L. REV. 703, 713-14 (1974).

63. City of Canton v. Harris, 109 S. Ct. 1197 (1989).

64. Kreimer, *supra* note 9, at 1295.

65. As Professor Peter Schuck argues, in a bureaucracy incentives are automatically skewed in favor of inaction, since maintenance of the status quo is least likely to bring about visibility or personal risk. This natural skewing is greatly exacerbated by legal rules which not only do not penalize, but put a premium on, inaction. *See* PETER SCHUCK, SUING GOVERNMENT 59-81 (1983); *see also* Note, *A Theory of Negligence for Constitutional Torts,* 92 YALE L.J. 683, 688 (1983).

66. *See infra* text accompanying notes 91-94

67. Miller, *supra* note 20, at 209; Kreimer, *supra* note 9, at 1324-26.

68. *See supra* text accompanying notes 46-48.

69. Professor Kreimer suggests three baselines, which he calls history, equality and prediction. *See* Kreimer, *supra* note 9, at 1359-74 and Seth F. Kreimer, *Government "Largesse" and Constitutional Rights: Some Paths Through and Around the Swamp*, 26 SAN DIEGO L. REV. 229

be complete lack of government involvement. Although this choice of baseline is presented as "neutral and natural,"[70] it is a choice which is difficult to defend. Indeed, the portrayal of government as passive and uninvolved is sharply at odds with the reality of government as pervasive regulator and architect of a vast web of social, economic, and political strategies and choices.

Ultimately, mechanical use of the action/inaction distinction masks a failure to address the essential question of government's proper role under the Constitution. The distinction is merely a shorthand: it cannot assist in making the value choices necessary to determine the scope of constitutional protections. Consider the proposition that government inaction is not actionable because it is not an abuse of power. This conclusory proposition begs the question of why inaction is not an abuse of power. If government can do harm to constitutional values through its inaction, insulating that inaction from judicial scrutiny has no apparent justification. The question of whether the harm should be actionable simply cannot be answered without giving content to the concept of abuse of power and determining whether that content is contiguous only with government's actions, or with its inactions as well.

B. *The Public/Private Distinction*

The conventional wisdom holds that since the fourteenth amendment limits only government and not private action, the state action requirement should not be circumvented by permitting liability for official failure to prevent private activity.[71] This limitation is phrased in the language of state action, but it is the familiar governmental action/inaction distinction in slightly different linguistic clothing. The realm of state action is the realm in which the state has acted *affirmatively;* the private realm is that in which the state has failed to act to protect its citizens from harm by other forces.

This is a highly conceptualistic application of the state action doctrine. It seeks to identify the sphere of government responsibility through a simple bright line: government is accountable only when it

(1989). Although these baselines have been criticized, the insight that some baseline is needed has been widely accepted. *See* Louis Michael Seidman, *Reflections on Context and the Constitution,* 73 MINN. L. REV. 73, 78-80 (1988); Sullivan, *supra* note 18, at 1450 n.150 and Larry Alexander, *Understanding Constitutional Rights in a World of Optional Baselines*, 26 SAN DIEGO L. REV. 175 (1989).

70. Cass Sunstein, *Lochner's Legacy,* 87 COLUM. L. REV. 873, 887 (1987).

71. Currie, *supra* note 28, at 866.

acts visibly and directly.[72] It faithfully reflects the belief that the influences of the public and private spheres are neatly severable, and that the public sphere intrudes only by its tangible actions.

The state action doctrine buttresses the action/inaction distinction, as Dean Paul Brest perceived: "In our everyday life we notice change and movement, while things that do not change fade into the background. It is consistent that we perceive the state as involved in our affairs when it assists in changing the status quo, and not when it assists in maintaining it."[73]

Political philosophers have often emphasized the importance of a critical vantage point from which to distinguish public and private, noting the relativism and dependence on historical and social circumstances of the public/private distinction.[74] As a practical matter, under current conditions of pervasive government regulation, the state may be involved in every sphere in some way, whether actively or through tacit approval. It may nevertheless be important to distinguish the public from the private realms *for certain purposes,* for example to ensure that a sphere of individual privacy is protected.[75] But the decision to create these spheres has more to do with the substantive reach of constitutional protections than with "whether the government has *done* anything to which the Constitution speaks."[76] Ultimately, the question of the proper reach of governmental power must be faced on its own terms, and cannot be avoided through the fiction that the public/private distinction is a natural rather than a pragmatic construct.

I will discuss the reach of the public/private distinction, its premises, and its practical consequences in the context of the Court's recent

72. *See* Paul Brest, *State Action and Liberal Theory: A Casenote on* Flagg Brothers v. Brooks, 130 U. PA. L. REV. 1296, 1329 (1982).

73. *Id.* at 1322; *see also* Minow, *supra* note 37, at 22-25 ("neutral" action becomes non-neutral when government fails to recognize pertinent differences).

74. *See, e.g.,* ANDREW LEVINE, LIBERAL DEMOCRACY: A CRITIQUE OF ITS THEORY 108 (1981); John Dewey & James H. Tufts, ETHICS, *Moral and Social Problems,* ch. XVI, at 495, *reprinted as abr.* in SOCIAL AND POLITICAL PHILOSOPHY 495 (J. Somerville & R. Santoni eds. 1963).

75. The state action doctrine and the public/private distinction it has engendered have been criticized on many levels. Scholars have questioned the coherence of the rules applying the state action doctrine, *see, e.g.,* Charles Black, *The Supreme Court, 1966 Term — Foreword: "State Action," Equal Protection, and California's Proposition 14,* 81 HARV. L. REV. 69 (1967); Robert Jerome Glennon & John Nowak, *A Functional Analysis of the Fourteenth Amendment "State Action" Requirement,* 1976 SUP. CT. REV. 221; the wisdom of the doctrine itself, *see, e.g.,* Brest, *supra* note 72; Erwin Chemerinsky, *Rethinking State Action,* 80 NW. U. L. REV. 503 (1985); and the philosophical basis for distinguishing public from private action, *see generally Symposium on the Public/Private Distinction,* 130 U. PA. L. REV. 1289 (1982). The focus here is on the ways in which the distinction flows from, or reinforces, a theory of negative rights.

76. L. TRIBE, *supra* note 51, § 18-7, at 1720; *see also* Brest, *supra* note 72, at 1330.

decision in *DeShaney v. Winnebago County Department of Social Services.*[77] The *DeShaney* case is worthy of close scrutiny because it is a classic example of the conventional, conceptualist approach and because it places the questions about the legitimacy of that approach in sharp relief. It looks to bright lines like state action, causation and custody to answer wrenching questions about government responsibility. The viability of that approach is considered in the following three sections.

1. *The Question of Responsibility*

Joshua DeShaney, the child of divorced parents, was placed in his father's custody by a Wyoming court in 1980, when he was one year old. His father, Randy DeShaney, then took him to live in Winnebago County, Wisconsin. When Joshua was three years old, county officials began receiving reports that his father was physically abusing him, and the Department of Social Services (DSS) began investigating these reports. When Joshua was four, he was hospitalized with suspicious injuries, prompting the juvenile court to place him in temporary custody. The county soon remanded Joshua to his father's custody, with certain conditions. For the next fourteen months, the DSS caseworker assigned to Joshua's case received reports and made personal observations indicating that the abuse continued, and that the county's conditions had not been met, but took no action. In March 1984, Joshua's father beat him so brutally that he suffered irreversible brain damage and will be institutionalized for the rest of his life.[78] When told of this last beating, the caseworker said: "I just knew the phone would ring some day and Joshua would be dead."[79] Joshua's mother sued on his behalf for damages to assist her in paying for his institutionalization.

The Court, in an opinion by Chief Justice Rehnquist, rejected the claim that the county deprived Joshua of liberty without due process of law. Justice Rehnquist reasoned that the state was not implicated in the deprivation of Joshua's due process rights because "[the clause] forbids the State itself to deprive individuals of life, liberty, or property without 'due process of law,' but its language cannot fairly be extended to impose an affirmative obligation on the State to ensure that those interests do not come to harm through other means."[80] For Justice Rehnquist, the facts in *DeShaney* fall into a simple pattern: there

77. 109 S. Ct. 998 (1989).

78. 109 S. Ct. at 1001-02.

79. 109 S. Ct. at 1010 (Brennan, J., dissenting) (quoting 812 F.2d 298, 300 (7th Cir. 1987)).

80. 109 S. Ct. at 1003.

are the things which Randy DeShaney did to his son, Joshua, and there are the things the state did not do to help Joshua. The state simply failed to protect Joshua from private violence. Since the state is not required to provide services, it need not provide them competently. Since it did not itself act violently, it is absolved of responsibility.[81]

This version of events ignores the complex interaction between the state and private entities. The state interviewed Randy DeShaney upon receiving the first complaint of abuse. It placed Joshua in temporary custody after he was hospitalized. It convened a child protection team to consider Joshua's situation. It released Joshua to his father's custody, and placed conditions on that custody. It made regular visits to the home, and kept records of incidents observed on these visits and of the father's failure to meet the conditions. In short, the state made a series of conscious choices, and performed a series of affirmative acts. Throughout, the state also made a series of conscious decisions to take no action on its own findings and on reports from others.[82]

One way to explain the Court's assertion that the state did not act is to classify this series of its affirmative acts as beside the point. The sole act that mattered was the ultimate beating of Joshua. Since the state did not participate directly in this beating, it bears no responsibility for its occurrence.[83]

To dispute this parsimonious view of governmental responsibility, one need not argue that the state should be responsible for its failures to act, or for the acts of others from which it fails to protect. One need only hold the state responsible for the foreseeable consequences of its actions.[84]

Nevertheless, even the majority's version of the events leading up

81. 109 S. Ct. at 1004.

82. 109 S. Ct. at 1001-02; 109 S. Ct. at 1010-11 (Brennan, J., dissenting); *see also* Minow, *supra* note 1, at 8.

83. If the state had placed Joshua in a foster home and then taken the same series of steps, the result might have been different. The Court specifically declined to address the issue. 109 S. Ct. at 1006 n.9. Since the decision, lower courts have reached varying results on the issue. *See, e.g.*, Aristotle P. v. Johnson, 721 F. Supp. 1002 (N.D. Ill. 1989) (child in foster care is in state custody and has due process right to be free from unreasonable intrusions); B.H. v. Johnson, 715 F. Supp. 1387 (N.D. Ill. 1989) (same). *But see* Doe v. Bobbitt, 881 F.2d 510 (7th Cir. 1989) (for qualified immunity purposes, it was not clearly established in 1984 that public officials who place foster child at risk of violence have violated due process); Milburn v. Anne Arundel County Dept. of Social Servs., 871 F.2d 474 (4th Cir. 1989) (when foster child had been voluntarily placed by parents, state's failure to protect him from abuse did not violate due process). For pre-*DeShaney* cases holding that foster care constitutes custody for due process purposes, see cases cited in *DeShaney*, 109 S. Ct. at 1002.

84. The Court sidesteps this mainstream notion of responsibility by its use of a novel causation theory which I will discuss shortly. *See infra* text accompanying notes 95-115.

to the final injuries illustrates the artificiality of the distinction between state and private action. The state *acted* by returning Joshua to his violent home, which it judged to be safe only if certain conditions were met, and by undertaking to ensure that those conditions were indeed met.[85] There was a symbiotic relationship between the hospital, which often was the first to learn of Joshua's injuries, and the state. The state placed Joshua in temporary custody at the hospital, gathered information from its staff, and assumed the statutory responsibility to act on what it learned.[86] These facts belie the notion of a discrete series of private acts observed by a passive state. They instead describe an intricate series of interlocking acts and omissions by the state, private agencies, and citizens.[87]

Moreover, the Court's version of events cannot be accepted at face value. As Justice Brennan argued, assumptions about the starting point, or baseline, may preordain the conclusion about whether the state acted to cause harm.[88] In one sense, the Court was willing to trace the chain of events only to the time when the state began its efforts to protect Joshua. These failed efforts were the only state "actions" the Court was willing tc evaluate.[89] Yet for comparison purposes, the Court was willing to start at a time before social services existed: it posited a situation in which the state, when faced with reports of abuse, would provide no services at all, and concluded that Joshua was no worse off than he would have been at that time.[90]

The only starting point the Court did not assume was the descriptively accurate one. The *DeShaney* court failed to place the state actions at issue in the greater context of pervasive social regulation. DSS, like other social welfare agencies, has consolidated and, in many respects, supplanted, the preexisting web of educational, law enforcement and health institutions, relatives, friends and neighbors which used to attempt to assist abused children.[91] Whether agencies like

85. 109 S. Ct. at 1010-11 (Brennan, J., dissenting). Apparently, the subsequent failure to carry out this undertaking converted this series of acts into a mere failure to protect. 109 S. Ct. at 1006.

86. 109 S. Ct. at 1001-02.

87. Compare the liability of the auto driver who drives too quickly and then fails to brake. See *infra* text accompanying note 337.

88. 109 S. Ct. at 1008 (Brennan, J., dissenting). *See supra* text accompanying notes 69-70.

89. 109 S. Ct. at 1004. Professor Ernest Weinrib called this device "pseudo-nonfeasance": distortion of misfeasance to nonfeasance by starting in the middle, or focusing on only one phase of an action. Weinrib, *supra* note 41, at 253-55.

90. 109 S. Ct. at 1006.

91. *See* Brief for Petitioners at 27, *DeShaney v. Winnebago Dept. of Social Servs.,* 109 S. Ct. 998 (1989) (No. 87-154); *see also* Marsha Garrison, *Child Welfare Decisionmaking: In Search of the Least Drastic Alternative,* 75 GEO. L.J. 1745, 1746-57 (1987); Daley, *Treating Kin Like Foster Parents Is Straining a Child Agency,* N.Y. Times, Oct. 23, 1989, at A20, col. 5.

DSS have improved the situation is uncertain and perhaps irrelevant; the issue is that we cannot know what would have happened to Joshua before the state took over the business of child protection, and we cannot pretend it did not do so. In the context of the pervasive regulation of child abuse which does exist, DSS clearly made a series of "calamitous"[92] decisions which subjected someone dependent on its assistance to "private violence"[93] which he otherwise would have been spared. At this point, the line between private and public violence, private and public responsibility, blurs.[94]

2. *Causation: The Requirement for Making Things Worse*

When assessing government responsibility, the issue of causation is closely intertwined with the state action inquiry. The question is whether the government acted in a way that caused harm or whether that harm was caused by private parties.[95] The *DeShaney* court absolved the state of Wisconsin of responsibility because, although it "stood by and did nothing when suspicious circumstances dictated a more active role," it did not make things worse.[96] Judge Posner, the author of the lower court opinion, put the matter less delicately in *Archie v. City of Racine:* "[T]he victim [in *Deshaney*] . . . would probably have been no better off if the negligent caseworker had never intervened; he would simply have been beaten into a vegetative state by his father that much earlier."[97]

Judge Easterbrook seemed to take the proposition a step further, arguing that even when a state puts a person in danger its responsibility is to protect him "to the extent of ameliorating the incremental risk."[98]

The requirement for making things worse is rooted in early com-

92. 109 S. Ct. at 1007.

93. 109 S. Ct. at 1004.

94. As Martha Minow argues, the persistent failure of responsible social agencies and society in general to respond to such private violence implicates public patterns of conduct and morals. Minow, *supra* note 1, at 8.

95. For further discussion of causation, see *infra* text accompanying notes 330-41; *see also* Sheldon Nahmod, *Constitutional Accountability in Section 1983 Litigation,* 68 IOWA L. REV. 1, 24-29 (1982). The case of Martinez v. California, 444 U.S. 277 (1980), illustrates the intersection between these inquiries. In that case, the parents of a murdered girl sued the parole board of a mental hospital for releasing her murderer, a mentally ill man of known dangerous propensities. The Court held that the decision to release the parolee was state action, but that his action in killing the girl five months later was not, because it was too remote a consequence of the parole officers' actions. 444 U.S. at 284-85.

96. 109 S. Ct. at 1006-07.

97. Archie v. City of Racine, 847 F.2d 1211, 1225 (7th Cir. 1988) (Posner, J., concurring), *cert. denied,* 109 S. Ct. 1338 (1989).

98. 847 F.2d at 1223.

mon law notions. Prosser notes that the rationale behind the common law refusal to recognize liability for nonfeasance is that "by 'misfeasance' the defendant has created a new risk of harm to the plaintiff, while by 'nonfeasance' he has at least made his situation no worse."[99] Once the defendant undertook to rescue someone, his only duty at common law was to avoid acts which would make matters worse.[100]

Applying the requirement in the constitutional realm is problematic for a number of reasons. First, it relies on an oversimplified and static version of the common law. Even the early common law found liability for failure to rescue under certain circumstances.[101] In addition, the inexorable though slow trend in tort law has been to find ways of imposing liability for failure to rescue;[102] the no-duty rule may be "in the process of being consumed and supplanted by the widening ambit of the exceptions."[103]

In addition, as the courts repeatedly note, tort principles are not always congruent with the scope of constitutional protection. Although the courts usually use this incongruence to grant lesser protections in constitutional cases,[104] it may justify the granting of greater, or different protections, particularly when the defendant is not an individual but a governmental entity.[105] The imbalance of power between individual and government, and the nature of government itself, may justify a different assessment of its responsibilities.[106]

Two major problems arise from the requirement for making things

99. W. PROSSER & W. KEETON, *supra* note 47, § 56, at 373.

100. *Id.*

101. For example, in those failure to rescue cases in which the defendant had nonnegligently placed the plaintiff in peril and then failed to rescue, the early common law held the defendant strictly liable for the ensuing harm. R. EPSTEIN, *supra* note 43, at 53-54; James Barr Ames, *Law and Morals*, 22 HARV. L. REV. 97, 113 (1908).

102. *See, e.g.*, F. HARPER, F. JAMES & O. GRAY, *supra* note 34, § 18.6, at 720-24 (discussing enterprise liability, the duty on one who controls a dangerous instrumentality, the duty on volunteers to complete a rescue, and the growth of special relationships); *see also* Weinrib, *supra* note 41, at 248 (discussing limitation of contributory negligence to cases where plaintiff was reckless, fading of voluntary assumption of risk rule, use of reasonable foreseeability doctrine, and increase in number of special relationships).

103. Weinrib, *supra* note 41, at 248.

104. *See* Archie v. City of Racine, 847 F.2d 1211, 1217 (7th Cir. 1988), *cert. denied*, 109 S. Ct. 1338 (1989); Jackson v. City of Joliet, 715 F.2d 1200, 1203 (7th Cir. 1983), *cert. denied*, 465 U.S. 1049 (1984).

105. Monroe v. Pape, 365 U.S. 167, 196 n.5 (1961) (Harlan, J., concurring), *revd.*, 436 U.S. 658 (1978); Christina Whitman, *Government Responsibility for Constitutional Torts*, 85 MICH. L. REV. 225 (1986); Susan Bandes, Monell, Parratt, Daniels & Davidson, *Distinguishing a Custom or Policy from a Random, Unauthorized Act*, 72 IOWA L. REV. 101, 120-27 (1986); Thomas A. Eaton, *Causation in Constitutional Torts*, 67 IOWA L. REV. 443, 444 (1982). Tort law itself has an ambivalent attitude toward governmental defendants. *See infra* text accompanying notes 294-99 (discussing public duty doctrine).

106. *See infra* text accompanying notes 259-76.

worse. First, measurement is difficult. The question of whether the government has exacerbated the situation cannot be answered without both a baseline, or vantage point, for comparison, and a method of quantifying. The notion of "incremental harm" has no built-in time limits. For example, it might be logically extended to hold that the state need take no action to assist an abused foster child because he was also abused by his biological parents. If the question is whether Joshua DeShaney was made worse off by the government's conduct, the notion of "worse" is meaningless without determining "worse than things were at what point?" Worse than things would have been if DSS did not exist? If DSS always acted in a professional manner? If it had never released him to his father's custody? If the state of Wyoming had never awarded his father custody? If he had been removed from custody before his father hit him the second time, or the last time? We also need some way of quantifying. Would Joshua DeShaney have been better off had DSS not existed? Would a relative have taken him in had she not been discouraged or prevented from doing so because of the pervasive social welfare structure which seeks to displace such self-help remedies?

The Court routinely assumes, as it did in *DeShaney,* that the standard of comparison for government actions is whether they render the plaintiff worse off than she would have been at a time when government provided no services.[107] This assumption is based on a misapprehension of the nature of government, and certainly of modern government. In the aftermath of the New Deal, pervasive government regulation and services, rather than lack of government action, has been the norm. In light of pervasive government regulation and services, the baseline of governmental inaction has not described the status quo in at least half a century.[108]

Once inaction is rejected as the status quo, the Court's assumptions about state action become questionable. Recognition of pervasive government control would lead to an understanding that state action may consist, not only of direct state action, but of inaction as well. This is so because government is perpetual, and continually makes choices which affect its citizens. These choices create the conditions against which government's current actions and inactions are measured. When government chooses to maintain the status quo, it perpetuates a

107. *See supra* text accompanying notes 88-90.

108. This assumes that the baseline is used by the Court as a reflection of the status quo. It may instead be used normatively, as a description of what citizens are entitled to expect from government. *See infra* text accompanying notes 368-69.

condition for which it is largely responsible.[109]

Once government is viewed as ongoing, two things become clear. First, it can cause harm by its inaction, because its bureaucracy remains in motion and its actions and omissions continue to affect people. Second, it need not make matters worse than they were before government existed, since this is an improper baseline.

The tort law analogy on which courts often rely is that government will be charged with an affirmative duty to act only when it has first placed an individual in a condition of helplessness or otherwise invited reliance on its protection.[110] Even if this limitation is accepted, a realistic view of the ways in which government acts and causes harm demonstrates that in the realm of social services, as in numerous other realms, government has invited reliance on its protection through regulation and provision of services, and has induced dependence on the continuation of those services through displacement of private alternatives.[111]

The second problem with the requirement for making things worse is that it insulates government from responsibility for its complicity, or its contribution to constitutional injury. In state action language, the question should not be simply whether the harm would have occurred without private action, but whether the government's acquiescence in that action infringed constitutional rights.[112] As the Court has sometimes recognized,[113] state and private forces may act symbiotically.[114] In such cases, a test focused on sole or immediate cause is misleading. By focusing on immediate, physical causes, the Court deflects attention from its complicity in the plight of the powerless. In causation language, the question should be whether the government's conduct, whether immediate or ongoing, was a substantial factor in causing the harm. If so, the government ought not to escape liability simply because other factors also contributed.[115]

109. *See* Brest, *supra* note 72, at 1322; Sunstein, *supra* note 70, at 889. In Sunstein's example, the traditional treatment of poverty as "simply 'there' " is at odds with what is known about government's power to control wealth distribution.

110. *See* Currie, *supra* note 28, at 873 & n.54.

111. When the government's duty is framed in this way, it becomes clear that a government agency can be held responsible for its failure to act competently irrespective of whether it has a duty to exist in the first place. Whether, for example, DSS must exist to protect the children of Wisconsin is a much more difficult question, *see infra* note 326, and one whose consideration is completely unnecessary to the resolution of the *DeShaney* case.

112. *See* Burton v. Wilmington Parking Auth., 365 U.S. 715, 722 (1961); L. TRIBE, *supra* note 51, § 18-2, at 1692.

113. 365 U.S. at 724-25.

114. It can be argued that virtually any private action in which the state acquiesces implicates the state. Brest, *supra* note 72, at 1301; Chemerinsky, *supra* note 75, at 522.

115. Eaton, *supra* note 105, at 452-61. *But see* Mount Healthy City School Dist. Bd. of Educ.

Ultimately, the questions can be reduced to one: Did the government breach a constitutional duty to the injured party? This question can be answered only by reference to a normative conception of the scope of the due process clause. The search for bright lines based on rules of state action and causation is a poor substitute for asking the unavoidable question: Should this harm be chargeable to the state under our conception of its proper role in preventing governmental harms?

3. *The Custody Limitation: The Requirement for Forced Physical Restraint*

The final issue of government responsibility raised by *DeShaney* is the question of the form the state action must take. Can the state cause harm only by a tangible, direct and physical interference with liberty, such as a beating by a state officer or while the victim is in physical custody, or might less tangible forms of harm, coercion and restraint be actionable?

In this regard, the *DeShaney* court considered an argument by the plaintiff which sought to create an exception to the general rule that the state has no duty to protect against private dangers. The argument was that a special relationship arose between Joshua and the state because it knew he faced a special danger of abuse and promised to protect him against that danger, and that this relationship gave rise to a duty to protect. The Court held that this argument is available only to persons in custody.[116]

The first cases finding a constitutional duty to protect were custody cases. In *Estelle v. Gamble,*[117] the Court held that prison officials must provide adequate medical care to those in custody.[118] It reasoned that inmates must rely on prison authorities to provide medical care or not receive it at all; the failure to receive care could result in suffering violative of the eighth amendment.[119] In *Youngberg v. Romeo,*[120] the

v. Doyle, 429 U.S. 274 (1977). As Professor Eaton discusses in detail, the *Mount Healthy* standard, which the Court has used in mixed motive employment cases, rejects this notion in favor of a restrictive but-for test which imposes liability for discriminatory employment decisions only if the decisions would not otherwise have been reached. Eaton argues that this approach should not be extended beyond the mixed motive employment context, and that it is inconsistent with both common law tort causation principles and the goals of § 1983.

116. DeShaney v. Winnebago County Dept. of Social Servs., 109 S. Ct. 998, 1004-05 (1989).

117. 429 U.S. 97 (1976).

118. However, the failure to do so would be actionable only if it rose to the level of deliberate indifference to serious medical needs. 429 U.S. at 106.

119. 429 U.S. at 104. The eighth amendment states: Excessive bail shall not be required, nor excessive fines imposed, nor cruel and unusual punishments inflicted. U.S. CONST. amend. VIII.

120. 457 U.S. 307 (1982).

Court found a state duty to the involuntarily committed mentally retarded arising from the due process clause. It held that when a person is institutionalized and wholly dependent on the state a duty arises to provide certain minimal services.[121] In *Smith v. Wade,*[122] the Court found due process had been violated when a prison guard recklessly placed two prisoners who had harassed, beaten and sexually assaulted the plaintiff in a cell with him.[123]

The *DeShaney* court traced the origin of the affirmative duty to protect to the state's exercise of its power to restrain one's liberty through "incarceration, institutionalization, or [some] similar restraint."[124] Therefore, since the state did not take Joshua into custody or otherwise play a part in the creation of the dangers he faced, it had no duty to protect him.[125]

For a number of reasons, the custody limitation is a problematic bright line. As Justice Brennan responded in his *DeShaney* dissent, *Estelle* and *Youngberg* do not rely on the state's act of incarceration or commitment, but on the failure to provide services once that incarceration has occurred. It was not the initial, unchallenged, deprivation of liberty which gave rise to a duty, but the nature of the confinement: the fact that it deprived the individual of other sources of aid.[126]

By its emphasis on "involuntary commitment,"[127] on restraints which "*render* [one] unable to care for himself,"[128] and on taking an individual into custody "against his will,"[129] the Court casts doubt on the state's duty to care for those who are so seriously impaired they have no choice but to be institutionalized,[130] or for children who have

121. 457 U.S. at 324.

122. 461 U.S. 30, 56 (1983).

123. But see Davidson v. Cannon, 474 U.S. 344 (1986), in which the Court held that no due process claim was available to a prisoner who had been injured after he had warned prison officials that he had been threatened by another prisoner, when the officials' failure to follow the appropriate procedures to protect him was merely negligent. Like its companion case, Daniels v. Williams, 474 U.S. 327 (1986), *Davidson* presages *DeShaney*'s approach. The *Davidson* opinion focused on the prison officials' failures to act, and classified them as negligent, and thus not rising to the level of a deprivation of due process. 474 U.S. at 347-48. As in *DeShaney,* the Court failed to see the omissions as conscious choices of a course of action. *See* Bandes, *supra* note 105, at 110, 129.

124. 109 S. Ct. at 1006.

125. 109 S. Ct. at 1005-06.

126. 109 S. Ct. at 1008-09 (Brennan, J., dissenting).

127. 109 S. Ct. at 1005.

128. 109 S. Ct. at 1005 (emphasis added).

129. 109 S. Ct. at 1005.

130. As Justice Brennan notes in *DeShaney,* in Youngberg v. Romeo, 457 U.S. 307 (1982), Romeo had an "I.Q. of between 8 and 10, and the mental capacity of an 18-month-old child." 109 S. Ct. at 1009. Thus it was not the state that rendered him incapable of taking care of himself. *Id.*

been voluntarily turned over to foster care.[131] Yet these individuals are equally cut off by the state from other sources of aid, and dependent on the state for protection. It is this condition of dependence which requires state assistance to safeguard due process rights.

When the rationale for the imposition of duty is seen as the deprivation of other sources of aid,[132] the custody limitation becomes unworkable. When police left children alone on a busy highway by arresting their guardian, they deprived the children of aid, although they did not put them in custody or even place them on the highway.[133] Likewise, when the state undertook to help Joshua, within a regulatory structure which encouraged reliance on its promise to help him, it "effectively confined [him] within the walls of Randy DeShaney's violent home until such time as DSS took action to remove him."[134]

Even based on the Court's rationale that the state must have played a part in the creation of the danger, the custody limitation is unsatisfactory. When a parole board releases a prisoner it knows to be dangerous, it has performed an affirmative act which creates danger. Although admittedly the parole board did not *create* the dangerous prisoner, neither did it do so in *Smith v. Wade.*[135] It did create a changed situation, as the people who failed to protect themselves believing their tormentors were safely in jail would attest.[136]

---

131. *See, e.g.,* Milburn v. Anne Arundel County Dept. of Social Servs., 871 F.2d 474, 476 (4th Cir. 1989), a post-*DeShaney* case which held that no state-imposed restraint of liberty occurred when a plaintiff was voluntarily placed by his parents in foster care. It further held that since the foster parents' contract with the Department of Social Services did not contain a description of the expected foster parent-foster child relationship, the child's physical abuse could not be attributed to the state's failure to supervise. *Id.* at 476-79. This holding is not so surprising in light of the language the *DeShaney* court used in declining to decide whether foster care may constitute custody: "Had the State *by the affirmative exercise of its power* removed Joshua from free society and placed him in a foster home [he might be considered to be in custody]." 109 S. Ct. at 1006 n.9 (emphasis added). *But see* Parham v. J.R., 442 U.S. 584, 600 (1979) (acknowledging that children have liberty interests in not being institutionalized even when parents seek institutionalization).

132. *See* Note, *supra* note 35, at 950-55.

133. White v. Rochford, 592 F.2d 381 (7th Cir. 1979); *DeShaney,* 109 S. Ct. at 1008 (Brennan, J., dissenting). *See supra* text accompanying notes 29-33. In the lower court opinion in *DeShaney,* Judge Posner sought to distinguish *Rochford* by characterizing it as a case in which the police placed the victim in a situation of high risk. 812 F.2d 298, 303 (7th Cir. 1987). Whether they indeed placed the children in the situation, or merely left them in it, as the *Rochford* dissent argues, 592 F.2d at 392, (Kilkenny, J., dissenting), is exactly the sort of "tenuous metaphysical" debate which the action/inaction distinction necessitates, and which the *Rochford* majority declined to enter. 592 F.2d at 384.

134. *DeShaney,* 109 S. Ct. at 1011 (Brennan, J., dissenting).

135. 461 U.S. 30 (1983). *See* text accompanying notes 122-23.

136. Federal courts have uniformly refused to find a duty under federal law to protect the general public from released prisoners or mental patients. *See* Martinez v. California, 444 U.S. 277 (1980); Fox v. Custis, 712 F.2d 84 (4th Cir. 1983); Bowers v. DeVito, 686 F.2d 616 (7th Cir. 1982). Cases like *Martinez* have indicated that the result might be different where the state knew

The custody limitation is the product of the Court's preoccupation with state actions which are not only affirmative in the traditional sense, but *physically tangible.*[137] Although the custody limitation is too narrow even in light of these criteria, the criteria themselves bear no relationship to the concerns of due process. The state decided to leave Joshua in a violent home, subjecting him to known danger. Whether the state acted or failed to act, whether it placed him at risk or left him at risk, whether Joshua's confinement was physical or based on practical, social, economic and emotional forces,[138] the result is the same. The state abused its power by subjecting Joshua to a known risk without giving him the help it had ensured only it could offer.

C. *The Penalty/Subsidy Distinction*

Another, closely related assumption which flows from the action/inaction distinction is that although government may not penalize constitutionally protected activity, it is under no obligation to subsidize it. To illustrate the facile cruelty of this questionable distinction, I turn to the abortion funding decisions which engendered it.

In the first abortion funding cases, *Beal v. Doe,*[139] and *Maher v.*

---

of a specific threat to a known person. *See* 444 U.S. at 285; *DeShaney,* 109 S. Ct. at 1004 n.4; *see also* Tarasoff v. Regents of the Univ. of Cal., 17 Cal. 3d 425, 551 P.2d 334, 131 Cal. Rptr. 14 (1976) (duty of psychiatrist to warn person of specific threat grounded in tort). *But see* Estate of Gilmore v. Buckley, 787 F.2d 714 (1st Cir. 1986) (no federal liability where state knew of specific threat to victim yet released dangerous mental patient), *cert. denied*, 479 U.S. 882 (1986).

137. 109 S. Ct. at 1009 (Brennan, J., dissenting); *see also* C. Macpherson, *Berlin's Division of Liberty,* in Democratic Theory: Essays in Retrieval 117 (1973). As Professor Tribe points out, the custody cases fail to provide a helpful framework for resolving the *DeShaney* case because they do not recognize the harms a state can inflict, not merely on individuals, but systemically, as a result of its structure. Laurence Tribe, *The Curvature of Constitutional Space: What Lawyers Can Learn from Modern Physics,* 103 Harv. L. Rev. 1, 11-12 (1989).

138. In the context of upholding the practice of juvenile preventive detention, Justice Rehnquist evinced an understanding that custody need not be physical:

> [J]uveniles, unlike adults, are always in some form of custody. Children, by definition, are not assumed to have the capacity to take care of themselves. They are assumed to be subject to the control of their parents, and if parental control falters, the State must play its part as *parens patriae.*

Schall v. Martin, 467 U.S. 253, 265 (1984) (citations omitted). *See also The Supreme Court — Leading Cases,* 103 Harv. L. Rev. 174 (1989) (Court's recognition of state's broad *parens patriae* interest at odds with *DeShaney* Court's view of private sphere of child rearing insulated from state intervention).

Borrowing from fourth amendment law, the issue might be framed as whether Joshua was free to leave. The Court has long recognized that one need not be physically restrained to be seized or arrested: the question is whether under the circumstances a reasonable person would believe he was free to leave. United States v. Mendenhall, 446 U.S. 544 (1980). It is difficult to imagine where Joshua could have gone without state assistance. *See also* Palko v. Connecticut, 302 U.S. 319, 327 (1937) (liberty is more than just exemption from physical restraint).

139. 432 U.S. 438 (1977). *Beal* held that the Social Security Act does not require states that participate in Medicaid to provide funding for nontherapeutic abortions.

Roe,[140] the Court upheld governmental decisions to exempt funding for nontherapeutic abortions from comprehensive Medicaid coverage which included funding for childbirth. In *Harris v. McRae,*[141] the Court reached a similar result regarding Medicaid funding of certain medically necessary abortions. Most recently, in *Webster v. Reproductive Health Services,*[142] the Court upheld restrictions on the use of public facilities and employees to perform medically necessary abortions.

The abortion funding decisions, like the *DeShaney* decision, rest in large part on the Court's rejection of the concept of affirmative governmental duties. Just as the Court in *DeShaney* avoided imposing a duty to protect, in the abortion funding cases it avoided imposing a duty to assist women in obtaining medical care.

The *Webster* decision, for example, rejected a challenge to a Missouri statute which placed several regulations and limitations on the performance of abortions in the state.[143] Of relevance here is the Court's resolution of the challenge to a prohibition on the use of public facilities or employees to perform abortions. The challenged statutes made it unlawful "for any public employee within the scope of his employment to perform or assist an abortion, not necessary to save the life of the mother";[144] and "for any public facility to be used for the purpose of performing or assisting an abortion not necessary to save the life of the mother."[145]

Chief Justice Rehnquist began his discussion for the Court with a citation from the *DeShaney* opinion: "[O]ur cases have recognized that the Due Process Clauses generally confer no affirmative right to governmental aid, even where such aid may be necessary to secure life, liberty, or property interests of which the government itself may not deprive the individual."[146] The Court reasoned that although the

140. 432 U.S. 464 (1977). *Maher* held that the equal protection clause does not require a state participating in the Medicaid program to fund nontherapeutic abortions although it pays for childbirth. *See also* Poelker v. Doe, 432 U.S. 519 (1977) (equal protection clause does not require municipal hospitals to provide facilities for elective abortions although they do so for childbirth).

141. 448 U.S. 297 (1980).

142. 109 S. Ct. 3040 (1989).

143. Four sections of the Missouri Act were at issue: the preamble, which found that life begins at conception and that unborn children have protectable interests in life, health, and well-being (MO. REV. STAT. § 1.205.1(1),(2) (1986)); the prohibition on the use of public facilities or employees to perform abortions (MO. REV. STAT. §§ 188.210, .215 (1986)); the prohibition on public funding of abortion counselling (MO. REV. STAT. § 188.205 (1986)); and the requirement that physicians conduct viability tests prior to performing abortions (MO. REV. STAT. § 188.029 (1986)). 109 S. Ct. at 3049.

144. MO. REV. STAT. § 188.210 (1986).

145. MO. REV. STAT. § 188.215 (1986).

146. 109 S. Ct. at 3051 (quoting *DeShaney,* 109 S. Ct. at 1003).

State may not itself prevent a woman from obtaining an abortion, it need not assist her in obtaining one.

The Court saw its decision upholding the restriction as a logical outgrowth of *Maher v. Roe* and *Harris v. McRae.* In those cases, the Court held that a state may "make a value judgment favoring childbirth over abortion and . . . implement that judgment by the allocation of public funds."[147] The *Webster* court found it a logical next step to permit implementing the value judgment through allocation of other public resources, such as hospitals and medical staff.[148] Although the Court of Appeals had found that preventing access to a public facility went beyond demonstrating a political choice in favor of childbirth, and actually narrowed or foreclosed the availability of abortion to women,[149] Justice Rehnquist rejected this reasoning:

> [T]he State's decision here to use public facilities and staff to encourage childbirth over abortion places no governmental obstacle in the path of a woman who chooses to terminate her pregnancy . . . . Missouri's refusal to allow public employees to perform abortions in public hospitals leaves a pregnant woman with the same choices as if the State had chosen not to operate any public hospitals at all.[150]

Webster, like *Maher* and *Harris* before it, purports to apply the same simple principle that engendered the *DeShaney* result. The Court casts the claim as one for basic government services; here, medical services. The Court assumes that there is no constitutional right to medical services, and that the government can withhold all such services if it so chooses. This assumption provides the basis for comparison: the harm to indigent women is measured against a baseline of no services at all. The greater power to withdraw all medical services implies the lesser power to withdraw only some such services.[151]

In short, the decision to withhold funding or use of public facilities is cast as a failure to give affirmative aid: the mere withholding of a benefit or subsidy. It is not an act of government interference or coercion, but simply a legitimate choice by government not to help. The government has not interfered with the right of indigent women to obtain abortions; it has merely chosen not to subsidize the procedure.[152]

---

147. *Maher,* 432 U.S. at 474, *quoted in Harris,* 448 U.S. at 314.

148. 109 S. Ct. at 3052.

149. Reproductive Health Servs. v. Webster, 851 F.2d 1071, 1081 (8th Cir. 1988), *revd.,* 109 S. Ct. 3040 (1989).

150. 109 S. Ct. at 3052 (citation omitted).

151. As noted *supra* note 18, this power is limited by the unconstitutional conditions doctrine. As will be discussed *infra* at text accompanying notes 159-67, this doctrine poses considerable obstacles in the *Webster* context.

152. *See, e.g., Webster,* 109 S. Ct. at 3052.

In both semantic and legal terms, the Court's meaning in describing these restrictions as mere decisions not to subsidize is elusive.

One possible meaning is that the *result* of the restrictions is not to penalize at all. A second possible meaning is that the *intent* of the restrictions is not to penalize the exercise of the right to abortion; any penalty is only an innocent byproduct of the decision to fund childbirth in preference to abortion. The third is that even if the states do intend to penalize the right, they may accomplish this end through a passive failure to subsidize, but not through an active use of penalty.

In a very limited sense, the first meaning is correct: the Court did not see the loss of access to abortions for poor women as being a result of the funding restrictions. It recognized that many indigent women choosing abortions would no longer be able to obtain them once the restrictions were in force,[153] but attributed this not to the government restrictions themselves, but to the women's preexisting condition of indigency.[154] That is, it was not the government's action which caused this deprivation. This formulation rests on particular assumptions about state action, causation and the appropriate baseline for measuring deprivation which will be considered shortly.

As to the second meaning, if the Court meant to absolve the government of an intent to discourage abortion, it set itself an impossible task. The legislative history straightforwardly established that the legislation was motivated by the purpose of discouraging abortion.[155] Seemingly, the Court's own finding that the restrictions were meant to implement "a value judgment favoring childbirth over abortion"[156] establishes just such a purpose.

153. The restrictions upheld in *Harris* have had this effect. *See* Trussell, Menken, Lindheim & Vaughan, *The Impact of Restricting Medicaid Financing for Abortion*, 12 FAM. PLAN. PERSP. 120 (1980). The *Webster* Court's not very reassuring remark that "[t]he challenged provisions only restrict a woman's ability to obtain an abortion to the extent that she chooses to use a physician affiliated with a public hospital" (109 S. Ct. at 3052) recalls Captain Black's explanation to Milo Minderbender: "[T]his whole program is voluntary, Milo — don't forget that. The men don't *have* to sign [the] loyalty oath if they don't want to. But we need you to starve them to death if they don't. It's just like Catch-22. Don't you get it? You're not against Catch-22, are you?" JOSEPH HELLER, CATCH 22, at 113 (1955); *see also Webster*, 109 S. Ct. at 3052; *Harris*, 448 U.S. at 314; *Maher*, 432 U.S. at 474.

154. *Harris*, 448 U.S. at 314 (quoting *Maher*, 432 U.S. at 474); *Webster*, 109 S. Ct. at 3052.

155. As to *Harris*, see Michael Perry, *Why the Supreme Court Was Plainly Wrong in the Hyde Amendment Case: A Brief Comment on* Harris v. McRae, 32 STAN. L. REV. 1113, 1125-26 (1980); Richard A. Epstein, *The Supreme Court, 1987 Term — Foreword: Unconstitutional Conditions, State Power, and the Limits of Consent*, 102 HARV. L. REV. 5, 89-90 (1988). As to *Webster*, the Court of Appeals concluded that the Missouri legislature "intended its abortion regulations to be understood against the backdrop of its theory of life," which was that life begins at conception. *Webster*, 109 S. Ct. at 3068 n.1 (Blackmun, J., dissenting) (quoting 851 F.2d 1071, 1076 (8th Cir. 1988)).

156. *Webster*, 109 S. Ct. at 3052 (quoting *Maher*, 432 U.S. at 474).

This is where the penalty/subsidy distinction comes in: it enables the Court to finesse the intent problem. The reasoning might be reduced to the following: (1) The purpose of withdrawing the subsidy was to burden the exercise of the right to abortion. (2) The effect of the withdrawal may be to burden the exercise of the right. (3) But the first two propositions are irrelevant because the withdrawal was not a direct, coercive action by the government, but merely a failure to assist. In short, the third suggested meaning is the correct one: the government may accomplish the otherwise illegitimate end of purposefully burdening a protected right, so long as it achieves it by indirect subsidy, not direct penalty.[157]

The abortion funding cases, then, have made the difference between a penalty and a subsidy crucially important, and in fact outcome determinative.[158] Although it would seem incumbent on the Court to explain why the distinction is legally significant, the question

157. *See* Sullivan, *supra* note 18, at 1500-02 (decision "turned on the supposed absence of coercive acts, not on absence of rights-pressuring purpose").

158. The penalty/subsidy distinction has also been applied outside the abortion funding context. For example, in Buckley v. Valeo, 424 U.S. 1, 87-89 (1976) (per curiam) the Court upheld a provision of the Campaign Finance Act which approved reimbursement of up to two million dollars for expenses to major political parties, a lesser amount to minor parties, and no reimbursement at all to parties or candidates which could not qualify as minor. The *Maher* Court cited *Buckley* for the proposition that interference with a protected right is prohibited, but encouragement of an alternate activity is not. 432 U.S. at 475. *Maher* interpreted *Buckley* to hold that the subsidy provisions did not burden the rights of the nonqualifying candidates, but merely enhanced the opportunities of the eligible candidates. *Maher*, 432 U.S. at 475-76 n.9 (citing *Buckley*, 424 U.S. at 94-95). For criticism of this reasoning, see Marlene Nicholson, *Political Campaign Expenditure Limitations and the Unconstitutional Condition Doctrine*, 10 HASTINGS CONST. L.Q. 601, 616-17 (1983); *see also* Sunstein, *supra* note 70, at 883-84 (Court in *Buckley* assumes state must take disparities in wealth and consequent access to fora as "a part of nature for which government bears no responsibility").

The penalty/subsidy distinction has also been invoked in the context of congressional refusal to fund offensive art. In the wake of an outcry over a provocative photography exhibit which had been subsidized by a grant from the National Endowment of the Arts (NEA), Congress recently adopted a law which will enable it to withdraw such funding for exhibits the NEA judges to be obscene. *See* Pub. L. No. 101-121, 103 Stat. 701, 738 (1989). Its proponents defend the law as a simple refusal to subsidize. *See, e.g.*, Hilton Kramer, *Is Art Above the Laws of Decency?*, N.Y. Times, July 2, 1989, § 2, at 1, 7, cols. 1-5. There is some precedent for this position. *See* Advocates for Arts v. Thomson, 532 F.2d 792, 795 (1st Cir.) (upholding content based withdrawal of arts funding on the theory that it does not constitute suppression, but rather promotion of another's work in its stead), *cert. denied*, 429 U.S. 894 (1976). However, particularly in light of the overwhelming power government has to determine artists' access, not only to grants, but to fora for the display of their work, *see* Grace Glueck, *Border Skirmish: Art and Politics*, N.Y. Times, Nov. 19, 1989, § 2, at 1, 22, cols. 1-5, and Paul Mattick Jr., *Arts and the State: The N.E.A. Debate in Perspective*, THE NATION, Oct. 1, 1990, at 348, the issue of whether the government may withhold funding from first amendment activity based on content may not be so clear cut. *See, e.g.*, Kenneth Karst, *Public Enterprise and Public Forum: A Comment on* Southeastern Promotions Ltd. v. Conrad, 37 OHIO ST. L.J. 247, 255-59 (1976); Marlene Nicholson, *The Constitutionality of Contribution Limitations in Ballot Measure Elections*, 9 ECOLOGY L.Q. 683, 731-33 (1981); Kathleen Sullivan, *A Free Society Doesn't Dictate to Artists*, N.Y. Times, May 18, 1990, at A-31, col. 2.

is never addressed. Once the activity is labeled a mere subsidy, the Court treats the matter as closed.

The Court's treatment of the unconstitutional conditions doctrine, which would seem to pose an obstacle to the refusal to fund protected activity, is illustrative. The doctrine holds that government may not condition receipt of benefits on relinquishment of constitutional rights, even if the receipt of the benefits is otherwise a mere privilege.[159] The *Harris* court admitted that under the unconstitutional conditions doctrine a legislature may not withhold all Medicaid benefits from an otherwise eligible candidate simply because she has exercised her right to abortion. The Court reasoned, however, that a legislature may withhold the particular benefits which enable a woman to exercise that right, because "this represents simply a refusal to subsidize certain protected conduct . . . [which] . . . without more, cannot be equated with the imposition of a 'penalty' on that activity."[160] That is, "denial of funding that enables a person to exercise a constitutional right is not a penalty, but denial of other benefits because he or she chooses to exercise such a right would be considered a penalty."[161]

The distinction is baffling. The Court fails to explain why the refusal to subsidize protected conduct does not violate the unconstitutional conditions rule. The fact that the statute does not sweep more broadly to exempt unprotected conduct as well hardly clarifies the matter. The linchpin of the argument seems to be that a condition which would otherwise be unconstitutional is acceptable if it takes the form of a refusal to subsidize, rather than a penalty.[162]

In what way does the refusal to subsidize differ from a penalty on protected activity? The Court's response is to invoke the "greater-in-

159. Sherbert v. Verner, 374 U.S. 398, 403-06 (1963); L. TRIBE, *supra* note 51, § 10-8, at 681. Thus, the doctrine represented a rejection of the right-privilege distinction, which held that when one receives a privilege from government, it may be withheld absolutely, and therefore may be withheld conditionally, though the condition is otherwise unconstitutional. *See* Justice Holmes' opinion in McAuliffe v. Mayor of New Bedford, 155 Mass. 216, 29 N.E. 517 (1892); *see also* Sullivan, *supra* note 18; Epstein, *supra* note 155; William Van Alstyne, *The Demise of the Right-Privilege Distinction in Constitutional Law,* 81 HARV. L. REV. 1439 (1968); Nicholson, *supra* note 158, at 612-14; and *supra* note 18 (discussing the greater-includes-the-lesser doctrine).

160. 448 U.S. at 317 n.19.

161. Nicholson, *supra* note 158, at 615.

162. The Court may be saying that the refusal to subsidize abortion is germane to legitimate governmental objectives, but a withdrawal of all medicaid coverage for a woman who has exercised her right to choice would not be germane. If so, the Court's reasoning illustrates Professor Sullivan's point that germaneness "is a poor benchmark for distinguishing constitutional from unconstitutional conditions." (Kathleen M. Sullivan, *Unconstitutional Conditions and the Distribution of Liberty*, 26 SAN DIEGO L. REV. 327, 329-30 (1989)). If encouraging childbirth over abortion is a legitimate end, cutting off all medicaid benefits to women who choose abortion would be an effective way to accomplish it, and different only in degree from cutting off funding for the abortion itself. Conversely, if the right to abortion is constitutionally protected, it is not clear why either consequence should be acceptable.

cludes-the-lesser" argument. Since the government has no obligation to fund any medical procedures or provide any medical facilities, it may decide, *for any reason,*[163] not to fund particular procedures. This does not penalize because it leaves the woman in the same position she would have been in without any government intervention, and that position is fixed by her individual condition of poverty, rather than any affirmative act of the government.[164]

The Court's invocation of the greater-includes-the-lesser doctrine completes an argument of nearly perfect circularity. This doctrine, initially an attempt to claim governmental freedom from any restrictions on its largess, was severely limited by the ascendancy of the unconstitutional conditions doctrine.[165] As Justice Brennan pointed out in his dissent in *Harris,* the demise of the right-privilege distinction means that government may no longer premise a grant of gratuitous benefits on the relinquishment of constitutional rights.[166] The Court disingenuously responded that the government's withholding of funding had done nothing to force relinquishment of the right to choose abortion; it has merely made it more attractive not to exercise it.[167]

Several unstated assumptions underlie the Court's reasoning. First, there is the choice of a baseline. Justice Brennan argued that the Hyde amendment, at issue in *Harris,* imposed unconstitutional conditions because it deprived women of benefits to which they were otherwise entitled.[168] Thus, Justice Brennan judged the results of the legislation in comparison to the status quo ante, which included full coverage for medically necessary services.[169] In contrast, the majority used as its point of comparison a time before there was any subsidized health care at all. It treated the baseline of government inaction as the only logical point of comparison. When compared to a complete failure to subsidize, a government decision to fund childbirth but not abortion can only be seen as an expansion of opportunities for indigent women.[170]

The argument that government has taken no action, or at least no

163. This is the "greater includes the lesser" doctrine in its most archaic form. *See supra* note 18; *see also The Supreme Court, 1979 Term,* 94 HARV. L. REV. 75, 100 (1980) ("[a] state cannot refuse to extend benefits on a forbidden basis, even if the refusal creates no government obstacle to the exercise of a right").

164. Webster v. Reproductive Health Servs., 109 S. Ct. 3040, 3052 (1989).

165. *See* Sullivan, *supra* note 18, at 1458-61.

166. Harris v. McRae, 484 U.S. 297, 334-37 (Brennan, J., dissenting).

167. *Id.* at 315-16.

168. *See id.* at 336 n.6.

169. *See id.* at 332-37.

170. *See* Epstein, *supra* note 155, at 90.

coercive action, because it has not made women worse off than they were twenty-five years ago,[171] has some obvious flaws.[172] First, it assumes that the propriety of the government's conduct and motivation can be judged solely by reference to its results.[173] Second, it presents a woman's "choice" in the starkest possible terms, then concludes that forcing women to choose the lesser evil is not coercive. But the fact that women could be threatened with the loss of *all* subsidized medical care does not render voluntary their choice to lose only subsidized abortion.[174] Finally, it is simply impossible to know whether women would have been worse off twenty-five years ago. Pervasive subsidies have existed for a long time, and they have changed the landscape so irrevocably that it is no longer possible to know what health care options would have been open to poor women if subsidized care had not displaced them.[175]

Even assuming for the moment that "making things worse" should be the standard, the restrictions at issue in *Webster* would likely satisfy it. The ban on the use of public facilities defined "public" so broadly that, as Justice Blackmun pointed out, it would apply to the many privately owned facilities using property which is publicly owned, leased or controlled.[176] Here the government's role as landowner and

171. The Medicaid program was adopted in 1965.

172. Once again it should be noted that this argument has ramifications for both state action and causation: the question of whether the state, by its action, caused the harm, or whether it was caused by private forces. *See supra* note 95.

173. *See* Kennedy v. Mendoza-Martinez, 372 U.S. 144, 163-70 (1963) (need for motive analysis in due process context); Washington v. Davis, 426 U.S. 229, 239-42 (1976) (need for motive analysis in equal protection context).

174. *See* Seidman, *supra* note 69, at 78-79; SIR ISAIAH BERLIN, *Two Concepts of Liberty*, in FOUR ESSAYS ON LIBERTY 130, 130 n.1 (1970).

175. Since abortion was not legal in 1965, history provides no indication of what abortion facilities would have been available to poor women before the advent of subsidized medical care.

176. 109 S. Ct. at 3068 n.1 (Blackmun, J., dissenting). A four-member plurality voted to uphold §§ 188.200 and .215 of the Missouri statute. Justice O'Connor declined to consider a facial challenge to the provisions on the ground that they might have some constitutional applications. 109 S. Ct. at 3059 (O'Connor, J., concurring in part and concurring in the judgment). Even prior to *Webster*, there was evidence that the refusal by public hospitals to perform abortions may also exert pressure on the few completely private hospitals which might have provided abortion services. *See* L. Belkin, *Women in Rural Areas Face Many Barriers to Abortion*, N.Y. Times, July 11, 1989, at A1, col. 3; *see also* ACLU REPRODUCTIVE FREEDOM PROJECT, SUMMARY AND LEGAL ANALYSIS OF WEBSTER V. REPRODUCTIVE HEALTH SERVICES 25 (1989):

> The Court's approval of this provision will make other states more likely to attempt to prohibit abortion at public facilities. Restricting access to hospital-based abortion will harm women who require hospitalization for abortion services because of life-threatening medical conditions; women who need late abortions because they discover late in pregnancy that the fetus has severe anomalies; rural women and poor women who often depend on local public hospitals as their primary medical providers; and teenagers who tend to seek abortion later in pregnancy and who often face greater health risks than adult women. Worst of all, because many "public" hospitals are also teaching institutions, fewer and fewer practitioners will acquire the expertise either to perform abortions or to remedy the effects of botched abortions.

provider of monopoly utilities[177] provides a graphic illustration of the pervasive reach of its power, in the face of which the individual's ability to protect her own rights to access is severely compromised. The traditional conception of the government as a passive entity forbidden to provide services is at odds with its identity as a major economic player in its own right.[178]

As to the correctness of the "making things worse" standard itself, the criticisms of that standard were presented earlier.[179] The abortion funding cases show why the standard is insufficient in the context of indigency.

The requirement for making things worse is intertwined with the Court's assumptions about choice and fault. The assumptions are twofold: a woman's indigency is of her own making, or at least not the government's fault; and it is that indigency which prevents her from obtaining an abortion. Beginning with the latter assumption, it is a dangerous half truth. Certainly if a woman could afford an abortion she would not need government assistance or government facilities. But in the context of subsidized health care, her indigency is an impediment only because the government has acted to single out this procedure as one it will not protect from the vagaries of the free market.[180] Given that the right is constitutionally protected, a strong argument can be made that at minimum government is required to maintain a neutral stance toward its exercise, if not to make affirmative efforts to safeguard its exercise.[181] In any case, it defies common sense to argue that the government's choice is not a substantial cause of the woman's inability to obtain an abortion.[182]

The concept of the vagaries of the free market raises the former

---

See also Frances Olsen, *Comment: Unraveling Compromise,* 103 HARV. L. REV. 105, 105 n.5 (1989) (effect of *Webster* decision in Missouri has been to lead "public and private hospitals to refuse to allow abortions . . . and one state university to bar talk of abortion.").

177. The appellees and amici in *Webster* suggested that the ban was so broadly worded that it could be enforced against private hospitals using public water and sewer lines. *See* 109 S. Ct. at 3059 (O'Connor, J., concurring in part and concurring in the judgment).

178. *See* Regina Austin, *The Problem of the Legitimacy of the Welfare State,* 130 U. PA. L. REV. 1510, 1511 (1982) (government is both "the regulator and the competitor of private economic concerns").

179. *See supra* text accompanying notes 95-115.

180. Tribe, *supra* note 9, at 336.

181. *Id.* at 338-40; *see also* Perry, *supra* note 155, at 1122; Margaret Radin, *Market-Inalienability,* 100 HARV. L. REV. 1849, 1900-01 (1987). As the *Griffin-Douglas* line of cases has recognized in the equal protection context, government may under certain conditions be required to subsidize some services to ensure that the inability to afford them does not effect a forced waiver. *See* Griffin v. Illinois, 351 U.S. 12 (1956); Douglas v. California, 372 U.S. 353 (1963).

182. 448 U.S. at 333 (Brennan, J., dissenting). See discussion of causation and complicity *supra* text accompanying notes 112-15.

assumption: that a woman's indigency is of her own making, or not the government's fault. Professor Macpherson's critique of Berlin's division of liberty is relevant:

> Vulgar proponents of free enterprise [may argue that poverty and dependence are not the result of other people's arrangements]. But free enterprise theories of any standing from Adam Smith to Bentham to Mill . . . have recognized that it is indeed arrangements made by other human beings (as well as differences in native abilities and industriousness) that determine the distribution of wealth and poverty. . . . [This distribution] is a matter of social institutions, [which decide how property is to be held or controlled]. . . . [This] unequal access . . . diminishes . . . negative liberty, since dependence on others . . . diminishes the area in which [people] cannot be pushed around.[183]

The abortion funding cases are testimony to the fact that people without resources, dependent on government for the ability to exercise their constitutional rights, can be pushed around. *Webster* provides perhaps the most dramatic illustration of Macpherson's point, since it reveals the extent of government's control over property, and the ease with which, in denying access to that property, it can diminish essential liberties.

The response, that the loss of liberty is caused by the marketplace, not the government, is too facile. It is uncontroversial that government activity affects wages, prices and job and housing availability,[184] and protects certain entitlements but not others.[185] While the extent to which government activity affects the incidence of poverty is a subject of disagreement,[186] the Court's comfortable assumption that the woman unable to afford a private abortion has brought her plight upon herself with no help from her government does not bear close scrutiny.[187]

---

183. C. MACPHERSON, *supra* note 137, at 100-01; *see also* Frances Olsen, *The Family and the Market: A Study of Ideology and Legal Reform,* 96 HARV. L. REV. 1497, 1515 (1983) (laissez faire theory denies or particularizes and privatizes inequality).

184. *See* Bendich, *supra* note 20, at 413-14.

185. *See* Goldberg v. Kelly, 397 U.S. 254, 261-63 (1970); Morris Cohen, *Property and Sovereignty,* 13 CORNELL L.Q. 8 (1927); Charles Reich, *Individual Rights and Social Welfare: The Emerging Legal Issues,* 74 YALE L.J. 1245, 1255 (1965).

186. *See, e.g.,* Austin, *supra* note 178, at 1511; Richard A. Epstein, *The Uncertain Quest for Welfare Rights,* 1985 B.Y.U. L. REV. 201, 225-29; Robert H. Mnookin, *The Public/Private Dichotomy: Political Disagreement and Academic Repudiation,* 130 U. PA. L. REV. 1429, 1431 (1982); *see also* Passell, *Forces in Society, and Reaganism, Helped Dig Deeper Hole for Poor,* N.Y. Times, July 16, 1989, at 1, cols. 4-5; 12, cols. 6-8,.

187. *See* Goldberg v. Kelly, 397 U.S. 254, 265 (1970) ("We have come to recognize that forces not within the control of the poor contribute to their poverty."); L. TRIBE, *supra* note 51, § 16-49. *See also* Sullivan, *supra* note 18, at 1499 n.366 (although government does not create poverty, "it does create a hierarchy between women who are and are not dependent on public medical insurance when it enacts a selective subsidy"). Fran Olsen unmasks another wrong assumption about choice and fault in the abortion debate: that women almost always exercise a

Ultimately, the Court's holdings in *Harris* and *Webster,* whether cast in terms of due process or equal protection,[188] of state action, unconstitutional conditions, or causation, depend for their support on the proposition that a refusal to subsidize is per se permissible noninterference. What is never explained in the Court's opinions is the rationale for the foundation on which the entire abortion funding edifice is built: that there is a legally significant difference between a penalty and a subsidy.

Government cannot imprison or fine a woman for exercise of the right to abortion. Although government cannot fine her, perhaps it may charge her money, although it is providing all other medical services for free. This may be consistent with the Court's refusal to impose affirmative funding obligations.[189] But under what meaning of the word would this charge be anything other than a penalty?[190] It certainly imposes a tangible disadvantage on the woman by virtue of her choice of abortion over childbirth.[191] If the government itself may not levy a charge, the question arises whether it can exempt abortion from a comprehensive scheme of subsidized medical care for the indigent, when the effect will be identical: to impose a charge which the targeted women cannot afford to pay.[192] The crucial question, again, is under what theory this action avoids being called a penalty.[193]

free, uncoerced choice about whether to have sexual intercourse. Olsen, *supra* note 176, at 124-26.

188. In *Harris,* the equal protection claim fell based on the due process finding. Because the court found that a mere refusal to subsidize could not burden due process rights and that therefore no fundamental right had been violated, it saw no reason to use strict scrutiny in addressing the equal protection claim that the state had unfairly singled out abortions for differential treatment. Under minimal scrutiny, it upheld the claim. *See Harris,* 448 U.S. at 322-23. *But see* 448 U.S. at 341 (Marshall, J., dissenting); Robert Bennett, *Abortion and Judicial Review: Of Burdens and Benefits, Hard Cases and Some Bad Law,* 75 NW. U. L. REV. 978, 1009-17 (1981).

189. 448 U.S. at 318.

190. *See* JOEL FEINBERG, *The Idea of a Free Man,* in RIGHTS, JUSTICE AND THE BOUNDS OF LIBERTY: ESSAYS IN SOCIAL PHILOSOPHY 8 (1980).

191. "Penalty: A punishment imposed for breach of law, rule, or contract; a loss, disability or disadvantage of some kind . . . ; sometimes specifically the payment of a sum of money imposed in such a case . . . ." THE COMPACT EDITION OF THE OXFORD ENGLISH DICTIONARY (1971).

192. *Harris,* 448 U.S. at 347 (Marshall, J., dissenting).

193. *See* Sullivan, *supra* note 18, at 1497 n.358 (same danger is posed whether the state uses sanctions or bribes); Epstein, *supra* note 155, at 90 (*Harris* sidesteps bar on fines by offering financial inducements). *But see* Kenneth W. Simons, *Offers, Threats and Unconstitutional Conditions,* 26 SAN DIEGO L. REV. 289, 303-308 (1989) (arguing that an offer to increase benefits (or subsidize) is less troublesome than a threat to decrease them (or penalize), especially in context of government benefit programs). The use of the encourage/discourage dichotomy, see *Harris,* 448 U.S. at 315 (basic difference between interference with a protected activity and encouragement of an alternate activity), is equally elusive. There are many possible ways to encourage childbirth. *See* Brief for a Group of American Law Professors as Amicus Curiae in Support of Appellees at 28-29, Webster v. Reproductive Health Servs., 109 S. Ct. 3040 (1989) (No. 88-605) (States may encourage respect for human life by assuring that women do not become pregnant as a result of

The Court's only real answer to the question is to restate its conclusion. A failure to subsidize is not a penalty because it is not an act, it is a failure to act. It does not coerce, it does not place obstacles in a woman's way.

Yet the government can coerce and create obstacles by selectively withholding funding or access to public health care from those with no other viable options.[194] Although the imposition of legal control takes a more subtle form than a fine or imprisonment, the result, like the purpose, may be exactly the same.[195] The question the Court should have addressed in the abortion funding cases was whether the right to abortion is important enough to protect from the inevitable burdens imposed by the government's choices.[196]

It may well be that the Court did make a value choice about the protection to which the right to abortion is entitled, and therefore ratified the government choices it reviewed in *Harris* and *Webster*.[197] This is a substantially different matter from presenting the entire sequence as a series of failures to act. Just as government deliberately acted to discourage abortion, so did the Court make a decision to ratify these acts, a decision which will ensure that the obstacles remain in place, and which was not compelled by the nearly invisible distinction between a penalty and a subsidy.

III. The Charter of Negative Liberties: Loosing the Tenacious Grip of the Conventional Wisdom

The idea of the Constitution as a charter of negative liberties, which pervades the judicial way of talking about constitutional rights, is much more than a rhetorical flourish. It translates into a restrictive series of assumptions about governmental action which serves to exclude whole categories of government misconduct and individual suffering from the ambit of constitutional protection. These assumptions have been treated as virtually sacrosanct. To call the Constitution a

---

involuntary sexual relations, by making adequate contraceptive counseling available, enhancing health education and medical care, providing assurance of adequate support for lives of children against starvation and malnutrition, violence, abuse and disease, and by setting example through its own treatment of women and children.). The schemes in *Harris* and *Webster* appear to encourage childbirth through a different method: discouraging abortion.

194. *See* Tribe, *supra* note 9, at 332-34.

195. *See* J. Feinberg, *supra* note 190, at 8.

196. Tribe, *supra* note 9, at 335-36; Perry, *supra* note 155; Cass R. Sunstein, *Is There an Unconstitutional Conditions Doctrine?*, 26 San Diego L. Rev. 337, 343-45 (1989).

197. Had the Court made such a choice explicitly, it would have been forced to confront the fact that it was impermissible under Roe v. Wade, 410 U.S. 113 (1973). *See* Perry, *supra* note 155; *The Supreme Court, 1979 Term*, *supra* note 163, at 104-05; Sullivan, *supra* note 18, at 1457 n.358: *see also* Tribe, *supra* note 9, at 336.

charter of negative rights is to state a conclusion; yet the Court has mistaken conclusory rhetoric for the reasoning which should have preceded it.

This Part seeks to understand why the conventional wisdom about negative liberties has held constitutional jurisprudence in such powerful sway. It first examines the constitutional arguments against affirmative duties and concludes that they are only a small part of the explanation for their wholesale rejection. It then looks to the philosophical and common law sources of the conventional wisdom in order to trace the deeply entrenched assumptions underlying the rejection of affirmative duties. Finally, it examines the tenacious arguments against affirmative duties which can be loosely characterized as "slippery slope" objections.

This Part seeks to show that although the conventional wisdom about negative and affirmative rights presents itself as neutral and inexorable, rather than as a particular way of thinking, shaped by particular influences,[198] it is instead an amalgam of vestigial common law notions, individualistic political philosophy, originalist constitutional theory, and fear of the slippery slope. More accurately, it relies on deeply rooted notions about common law and philosophy and makes little attempt to understand the Constitution on its own terms. Yet major constitutional decisions have been based on an unquestioning belief in the rightness of this way of thinking.

It will argue that none of the traditional assumptions is entitled to a priori status. Each represents a choice: about the extent of reliance on the common law, and the interpretation of the common law relied on; about the particular philosophic tradition adhered to; about the allocation of resources, and, ultimately, about the values the Constitution should protect. When the assumptions are treated as neutral and inexorable, the result is choices which are unarticulated and unjustified.

A. *The Constitutional Source*

According to the conventional wisdom, the source of the refusal to recognize positive constitutional rights is the Constitution: its text and the intent of the Framers. In a recent article, Professor David Currie set forth the classic argument for the proposition that the conventional wisdom, at least in the due process context, is justified by the Constitution itself.[199] He argued that the lack of affirmative due process rights

198. Martha Minow says: "Unstated reference points lie hidden in legal discourse, which is full of the language of abstract universalism." Minow, *supra* note 37, at 44-45.

199. Currie argues that a distinction exists between positive and negative constitutional

could be inferred from the language and context of the clause: "the due process clause is phrased as a prohibition, not an affirmative command," in contrast to other constitutional guarantees, such as the right to counsel.[200] He further argued that the ratification debates support the idea that "the Bill of Rights was designed to protect against 'abuse of . . . power[]'. . ., and in particular to limit the powers of Congress" and not to help needy citizens.[201] In fact, he argued, the Framers were not even sure Congress had the power to help needy citizens.[202]

The conventional argument, then, is that the refusal to recognize affirmative governmental obligations is supported by the text of the Constitution and the Framers' intent. Both foundations are flimsy. The conventional wisdom portrays the text and Framers' intent as objective measures of the Constitution's meaning. However, text and intent lead to a rejection of affirmative governmental duties onlv when certain interpretational choices are made.

The argument from the Framers' intent assumes the legitimacy of an originalist mode of interpretation: that the Court should enforce only those values that are clearly stated in the text of the Constitution or intended by the Framers.[203] The conventional wisdom relies on the Framers' intent and the conditions which prevailed at the time the Constitution was drafted. The Framers' intent was neither monolithic nor crystal clear in this regard. Scholars have argued that even if the sole intent was to keep government from invading the private realm, the Framers sought to accomplish this goal by imposing on government affirmative obligations to provide certain safeguards. The purpose of these safeguards was to prevent government from dominating its citizens by virtue of its tremendous power.[204] On a more utopian note, scholars have argued that the Framers imposed affirmative obligations to enforce the social contract and to enable citizens to realize

---

rights, and that as a general rule only negative rights are protected by the due process clause. He notes, however, that the notion that the Constitution protects negative liberties should not be used as a "talisman capable of resolving a broad spectrum of problems against the existence of governmental duties that can in some sense be deemed affirmative." Currie, *supra* note 28, at 887.

200. *Id.* at 865.

201. *Id.* at 874.

202. Currie, *supra* note 28, at 865-66; *see also* Archie v. City of Racine, 847 F.2d 1211, 1221 (7th Cir. 1988) ("Amendments designed to protect the people from the government . . . adopted when governmental services were more likely to be viewed as forbidden than desirable . . . phrased as prohibitions on governmental action . . . are not a plausible source of mandatory rescue services.")

203. *See generally* RAOUL BERGER, GOVERNMENT BY JUDICIARY (1977).

204. *See* Tribe, *supra* note 9, at 333-34; Michelman, *supra* note 20, at 9.

the promises of the Declaration of Independence.[205]

Moreover, the extent of reliance on the Framers' intent involves choices. The originalist approach which interprets the Constitution based solely on the plain meaning of the text and the verifiable intent of the Framers has been criticized widely.[206] Even if the intent of the Framers is agreed to be the sole proper inquiry, it is necessary to decide whether their specific intent will be required, or their more general intent will suffice.[207] If, for example, the Framers' general intent was to disable government from dominating citizens by virtue of its unequal power, that intent may be effectuated through positive obligations to protect as well as negative constraints.[208]

Finally, even assuming the notion of a negative constitution accurately describes the late eighteenth century, any argument to impose it on the late twentieth century must reckon with the vast changes which have occurred since the 1930s. The welfare state, with its proliferation of government regulation and subsistence programs, little resembles the polity with which the Framers were familiar.[209] To construe current constitutional protections based on an antiquated world view is a choice which may be difficult to justify.[210]

The argument from the text of the Constitution suffers from similar disabilities. The text of the Constitution does not support the idea that, as a whole, it was meant to be solely a charter of negative rights. Although many of the rights it provides are phrased negatively,[211]

---

205. *See* Bendich, *supra* note 20, at 409; Charles Black, *Further Reflections on the Constitutional Justice of Livelihood,* 86 COLUM. L. REV. 1103 (1986); Peter B. Edelman, *The Next Century of Our Constitution: Rethinking Our Duty to the Poor,* 39 HASTINGS L.J. 1, 21 (1987); Miller, *supra* note 20, at 245-46.

206. *See, e.g.,* Paul Brest, *The Misconceived Quest for the Original Understanding,* 60 B.U. L. REV. 204 (1980).

207. *See* Paul Brest, *The Fundamental Rights Controversy: The Essential Contradictions of Normative Constitutional Scholarship,* 90 YALE L.J. 1063, 1085 (1981). Professors Wasserstrom and Seidman illustrate this point in the fourth amendment context. A rigid originalist approach might limit the reach of that amendment to the "general warrants that angered the colonists in the pre-Revolutionary period." A more flexible originalist might attempt to determine whether modern intrusions like wiretaps or drug tests serve as the "modern equivalent of general warrants." Silas J. Wasserstrom & Louis Michael Seidman, *The Fourth Amendment as Constitutional Theory,* 77 GEO. L.J. 19, 57-58 (1988); *see also* Amsterdam, *supra* note 52, at 395-409.

208. *See supra* text accompanying notes 24-29, 50-55.

209. Sullivan, *supra* note 18, at 1455 n.170; Sunstein, *supra* note 70, at 886-88; Kreimer, *supra* note 9, at 1295.

210. "Due process was not restricted to rules fixed in the past, for that 'would be to deny every quality of the law but its age, and to render it incapable of progress or improvement.'" Duncan v. Louisiana, 391 U.S. 145, 176-77 (1968) (Harlan, J., dissenting) (quoting Hurtado v. California, 110 U.S. 516, 529 (1884)); *see also* Wasserstrom & Seidman, *supra* note 207, at 58 (preference for Framers' preferences must be justified).

211. *See, e.g.,* U.S. CONST. art. I, § 9, cl. 3 (no Bill of Attainder or *ex post facto* law); art. I, § 9, cl. 5 (no tax or dutv on articles exported from anv state); art. I, § 9, cl. 8 (no title of nobility

many are also phrased affirmatively.[212] Even as to the rights which are phrased negatively, their enforcement may require the imposition of affirmative obligations on government.[213] The conventional wisdom treats the affirmative rights as exceptions to the general rule, but there is nothing inexorable about this conclusion.

More specifically, the language of the due process clause does not mandate the conclusion that it prohibits only affirmative acts, and not omissions. Although its language prohibits certain deprivations, it affirmatively demands that when the government does deprive, it must *afford* due process of law, something which only the government can provide.[214] Finally, to say that the clause protects against abuse of power says very little about the form such abuse must take, or specifically, about whether government can abuse by its inaction as well as its action.[215]

Invariably, assertions about the text of the Constitution and the Framers' intent seem to overlook the fourteenth amendment. The fourteenth amendment is the product of a radical shift in the perception of the duties of the federal government.[216] Its legislative history

shall be granted by United States); amend. I ("Congress shall make no law"); amend. II (the right to bear arms shall not be infringed); amend. VIII ("excessive bail shall not be required").

212. *See, e.g.,* U.S. CONST. art. I, § 2 ("House of Representatives shall be composed of"); art. I, § 9, cl. 2 (privilege of writ of *habeas corpus*); art. I, § 9, cl. 7 (regular statement and account of receipts and expenditures shall be published); art. II, § 1, cl. 8 (President will preserve, protect and defend the Constitution); amend. IV (warrant and probable cause requirements); amend. V (grand jury requirement); amend. VI (right to speedy, public jury trial; confrontation, compulsory process, counsel); amend. VII (right to civil jury trial); *see supra* notes 24-29 and accompanying text.

213. *See, e.g., supra* note 51 (discussion of the first amendment). Professor Arthur Selwyn Miller points out that any time the Court decides a norm-creating case, it is imposing affirmative duties on the organs of government to enforce that norm. *See* Miller, *supra* note 20, at 229-35. As I have argued, all judicial decisionmaking creates norms because it creates precedent. *See* Susan Bandes, *The Idea of a Case,* 42 STAN. L. REV. 227, 299 (1990). Thus, all decisions impose affirmative duties of enforcement. The remedial question of the form that enforcement must take (*e.g.,* preclusion of other courts, damages paid by offending entity, simple negative injunction or complex structural injunction against entity) must be kept distinct from questions about the existence of the enforcement duties themselves. *See infra* text accompanying notes 354-64.

214. The due process clause provides: "nor shall any State deprive any person of life, liberty, or property, without due process of law . . . ." U.S. CONST. amend. XIV. This seems little different from: If any State deprives a person of life, liberty, or property, it must *provide* due process of law. *See* J. TENBROEK, EQUAL UNDER LAW 121 (1965) (due process imposes affirmative obligations on government to protect against private action); ROBERT JENNINGS HARRIS, THE QUEST FOR EQUALITY 42-44 (1960) (same); Tribe, *supra* note 9, at 331 (government may have to make an affirmative exertion to protect rights, e.g., it cannot dispense with a hearing to save time or money).

215. *See, e.g.,* Miller, *supra* note 20, at 209 (government power to do nothing is itself a significant power); *see also* William Burnham, *Separating Constitutional and Common-Law Torts: A Critique and a Proposed Constitutional Theory of Duty,* 73 MINN. L. REV. 515, 567-70 (1989) (failure to act can constitute abuse of power); Sunstein, *supra* note 70, at 888 (whether there is a deprivation depends on antecedent conceptions of entitlement).

216. *See* L. TRIBE, *supra* note 51, § 7-2, at 550.

reflects that an overriding purpose of its passage was to require the federal government to protect its citizens in the face of the states' failure to do so. A strong argument can be made that both the equal protection and due process clauses were meant to impose on government an affirmative duty to protect against private action.[217]

In short, neither the language nor the history of the Constitution prohibits affirmative government duties. The arguments against affirmative duties are based on a series of choices: methodological choices on one level, but ultimately substantive choices about the role of government. In light of their indeterminacy, the arguments from the language and text of the Constitution might seem a flimsy basis for such sweeping choices about the scope of constitutional protection. The ease and tenacity with which these arguments have been accepted is partially explained by their pervasive presence in Western thought.

B. *The Philosophical and Common Law Sources*

The antipathy toward affirmative duties is drawn from the Anglo-American common law. The common law in turn reenacts and is supported by the conventional strain of Western political philosophy. Therefore, the constitutional rationales for this antipathy are profitably discussed in the context of the common law and Western political thought. This section analyzes the philosophical, political and common law roots of the conventional wisdom and the intersection among them.

1. *Philosophical Roots*

The proscription against affirmative duties has an impressive lineage. Professor Judith Shklar describes a conventional wisdom about justice, articulated by Aristotle, and accepted by Hobbes and Kant, which condemns only "active injustice"[218] and "ignores the ills that we cause by simply letting matters take their course."[219] However, this ancient reluctance to condemn inaction has always been counterpoised by an alternative way of thinking. The Platonic model of jus-

217. *See* J. TENBROEK, *supra* note 214, at 118-21; HARRIS, *supra* note 214 at 42-44; Michael Gerhardt, *The Ripple Effects of* Slaughterhouse: *A Critique of a Negative Rights View of the Constitution,* 43 VAND. L. REV. 409, 417 (1990) (intent of framers of the fourteenth amendment was to expand governmental power and create enforceable affirmative rights to due process and equal protection); Tussman & tenBroek, *The Equal Protection of the Laws,* 37 CALIF. L. REV. 341 (1949).

218. Judith Shklar, *Giving Injustice Its Due,* 98 YALE L.J. 1135, 1146 (1989).

219. *Id.* at 1142. Under this model, justice is achieved by adopting rules for distribution of goods, and then setting up institutions to maintain those rules in the course of private exchanges and to punish violators. Shklar refers to this as the "normal way of thinking about justice." *Id.* at 1136; *see also* Radin, *supra* note 181, at 1898 n.186.

tice developed alongside the Aristotelian, and, according to Shklar, was transformed by Cicero from a purely philosophical to a political conception.[220] This model viewed injustice not only as active misconduct, but as indifference to wrongdoing as well.

> When [the passively unjust man] sees an illegal action or a crime, he just looks the other way. If he is a public official his offence is very grave. He is the tyrant who condones injustice by ignoring it, or an indifferent ruler who does nothing to mitigate and prevent the social and natural disasters that afflict all of us.[221]

Before discussing why the conventional strain has continued to eclipse the alternative strain, it is helpful to first distinguish, as Shklar does, the philosophical and political versions of the conventional story. The philosophical version rests on the assumptions that individuals are atomistic and motivated by self interest, and that the optimal society is one in which each individual is left alone to do as he wishes so long as he causes no harm to others.[222] John Stuart Mill's often quoted definition of liberty as the freedom to engage in self-regarding conduct is the best known articulation of the purely individualistic view.[223] Sir Isaiah Berlin later called Mill's position the " 'negative' conception of liberty in its classical form": all coercion is bad, all noninterference is good.[224]

In its political version, the conventional story makes identical assumptions about the role of government. Its optimal role is noninterference, or at least the smallest amount of interference necessary to permit individuals to exercise the greatest degree of freedom without encroaching on others.[225] Berlin's essay, *Two Concepts of Liberty,*[226] is perhaps the most influential explication of the distinction between positive and negative liberty and the preference for the latter. For Berlin, a government which safeguarded negative liberty was simply one which created no external obstacles to individual freedom, whereas a government which sought to provide positive liberty was one which prescribed the nature or content of that freedom. He feared that

---

220. Shklar, *supra* note 219, at 1141-47.

221. *Id.* at 1142-43.

222. However, as Professor Olsen explained, a very different set of assumptions informed the "family sphere." This sphere, which was (or is) perceived as female and private, was thought to be motivated by woman's altruism and instinct to nurture. Thus a social order based on women's willingness to sacrifice their individual interests for the sake of male dominance of the family and for the sake of the children was seen as merely the way of nature. Olsen, *supra* note 183, at 1505.

223. JOHN STUART MILL, ON LIBERTY 13 (C. Shields ed. 1956) (1859); Lloyd L. Weinreb, *The Complete Idea of Justice,* 51 U. CHI. L. REV. 752, 791 (1984).

224. I. BERLIN, *supra* note 174, at 128.

225. *See* J. MILL, *supra* note 223, at 16-17.

226. I. BERLIN, *supra* note 174.

although the impulse to positive freedom might begin benignly as an attempt to remove internal obstacles to happiness by ensuring that government helped citizens, citizens helped each other, and citizens participated in government, it would eventually lead to totalitarianism. The only sure way to avoid this trap was to ask of government only that it leave its citizens alone.[227] Although the definition has always engendered controversy,[228] it has long exerted a powerful, even predominant, influence on legal thought. As Professor Mark Tushnet explained:

> [The preference for negative rights reflects] fear that others . . . will act to crush our individuality. . . . But we also know that we need other people to create the conditions under which we can flourish as social beings, and thus we need positive rights. In our culture, the fear of being crushed by others so dominates the desire for sociality that our body of rights consists largely of negative ones.[229]

Although philosophers have long debated whether man's essential nature tends toward autonomy or sociality, individualism or collectivism, the question as posed seems unanswerable.[230] A more concrete question, which cannot be fully considered here,[231] is why the individualist strain, rather than the collectivist, has, to all appearances, become ascendant. In brief, scholars have credited certain historical conditions, particularly in the eighteenth-century United States, with providing fertile ground for individualism to flourish. Both the psychology of the emerging nation and the needs of the industrial revolution contributed to its growth.

In John Dewey's words:

> [I]t was an easy step from the restrictions imposed on the colonies by Great Britain to the idea that all government by its very nature tends to be repressive, and that the great aim in political life is to limit the encroachments of governments in order to make secure the liberty of citizens.[232]

The conventional wisdom sees the public sphere as something to be

227. *Id.* at 130-70; MACPHERSON, *supra* note 137, at 105-16.

228. *See, e.g.*, J. FEINBERG, *supra* note 190; MacCallum, *Negative and Positive Freedom*, 76 PHIL. REV. 312 (1967).

229. Tushnet, *supra* note 9, at 1392.

230. On the merits, there seems no definitive way to resolve the debate about the essence of human nature. More to the point, the question as framed is unanswerable, because it rests on a false duality. John Dewey, *Reconstruction in Philosophy*, ch. VIII, at 474, *reprinted in* SOCIAL AND POLITICAL PHILOSOPHY, *supra* note 74 (social and individual tendencies inextricably intertwined). *See infra* text accompanying notes 248-51.

231. A detailed discussion of the historical roots of individualism is beyond both the scope of this article and the author's expertise.

232. Dewey & Tufts, *supra* note 74, at 492-93.

teared.[233] The articulated premise is the primacy of the value of individual autonomy over societal values like cooperation, participation and mercy. There is an equally strong, unarticulated, premise: that individuals are on equal footing and can fend for themselves without the assistance of government.[234] This is not to say that all people are equally strong, quick or intelligent, but that no structural imbalances or hierarchies exist which might require intervention.[235] If government will simply leave us alone, and we leave each other alone, the resulting order will be just.

The second fertile ground for individualism, according to Dewey, was the industrial revolution.[236] Certain laissez-faire doctrines were needed to help unshackle developing industry from limits imposed by feudal and agrarian customs.[237] It was most important to protect the freedom to contract and to retain the fruits of one's labor. As Dewey argues, these tenacious assumptions have long outlasted the conditions which gave rise to them. What might have begun as a recognition that these freedoms were needed to achieve certain immediate aims was generalized to a belief that governmental protection of contract and property is neutral and natural, or not government action at all. In contrast, governmental attempts to protect other interests, such as the right to a fair wage or job security, were viewed as political or artificial efforts to interfere with the natural order.[238]

233. Tushnet, *supra* note 9, at 1392; *see also* Austin, *supra* note 178, at 1517-18.

234. Dewey & Tufts, *supra* note 74, at 494; *cf.* Olsen, *supra* note 183, at 1527 (free market ideology legitimates status quo by asserting juridical equality).

235. *See* THOMAS HOBBES, LEVIATHAN, OR THE MATTER, FORM AND POWER OF A COMMONWEALTH ECCLESIASTICAL AND CIVIL 183 (C.B. Macpherson ed. 1968) ("Nature hath made men . . . equal . . . . [T]he weakest has strength enough to kill the strongest, at least in confederacy with others . . . .").

236. *See* Dewey & Tufts, *supra* note 74, at 494.

237. *See* Olsen, *supra* note 183, at 1513-15. Professor Olsen traces the stages of the market, arguing that in feudal times juridical equality was not assumed; rather, hierarchies were taken for granted. With the rise of the free market, the rules which had governed the hierarchy, and had also protected those on its lower rungs from the arbitrary will of their superiors, came to be seen as impediments to liberty. The assumption of equality was needed to justify the loss of those protections.

238. Dewey & Tufts, *supra* note 74, at 490-97; *see also* Monell v. New York City Dept. of Soc. Servs., 436 U.S. 658, 681 (1978) (noting that the nineteenth-century courts, while eschewing imposition of some affirmative duties upon the states, "vigorously enforced the Contract Clause against municipalities — an enforcement effort which included various forms of 'positive' relief, such as ordering that taxes be levied and collected to discharge federal-court judgments, once a constitutional infraction was found").

Professor Tribe recently suggested an additional source of, or metaphor for, the conventional approach: Newtonian physics. He argues that the Newtonian view lacked an understanding (later contributed by relativity theory and other developments in scientific thought) that objects do not simply exist in space; they bend and shape it so that space and objects cannot be viewed as independent from one another. Likewise, the Newtonian approach to law sees the state as a neutral, passive backdrop to human events and fails to recognize that the state, and the judiciary, shape the space in which events occur. Tribe, *supra* note 137, at 6-13.

2. *Effects on Common Law*

The effects of these philosophical assumptions on the development of the common law are readily apparent. The common law, at least in its early stages, assumed that we are atomistic beings, motivated by self interest, and that it was not its function to impose on us an alien morality.[239] As Prosser commented, the early common law "had no great difficulty in working out restraints upon the commission of affirmative acts of harm, but shrank from converting the courts into an agency for forcing men to help one another."[240] The common law paradigm is that a man may sit on a dock smoking his pipe and watch another man drown, though he could easily throw him a rope.[241] Thus the common law's antipathy toward affirmative duties has been called "an attitude of rugged, perhaps heartless, individualism."[242] The assumption of parity — that individuals are equally able to fend for themselves — made the end result of permitting the pursuit of self interest socially acceptable.

Even accepting as a given that people should not be legally bound to help one another, the question remains whether government should be legally bound to help its citizens. Two tenets of the conventional wisdom come together to provide a negative answer to this question.

The first tenet is the conventional common law assumption of parity, which the common law often employs even when one of the parties to a transaction is the government.[243] The second tenet, the deeply rooted fear of governmental encroachment on individual freedom, leads to the same result as the equation of government with an individual: theoretically, a severely limited governmental role. "That government is best which governs least."[244] Finally, the conclusion that government should not intrude is buttressed, in the conventional story, by assumptions about when government is or is not governing.

---

239. *See* Ames, *supra* note 101, at 97-103 (tracing unmoral character of early common law).

240. W. Prosser & W. Keeton, *supra* note 47, § 56, at 373.

241. Restatement (Second) of Torts, *supra* note 33, § 314 comment c.

242. F. Harper, F. James & O. Gray, *supra* note 34, § 18.6, at 719.

243. *See* Whitman, *supra* note 105, at 226-27; Bandes, *supra* note 213, at 282-83.

244. This quotation is commonly ascribed to Thomas Jefferson. However, according to Bergen Evans' Dictionary of Quotations 285 (1968) it reflects one strain of thought in Jefferson's First Inaugural Address, but no one has ever been able to find it in Jefferson's writings. Thoreau said it in "On the Duty of Civil Disobedience," *reprinted in* Social and Political Philosophy, *supra* note 74, at 282, but in quotation marks and without noting the source. The Oxford Dictionary of Quotations (3d ed. 1979) attributes it to John L. O'Sullivan in his introduction to The United States Magazine and Democratic Review (1837). As Evans says, the idea was in the air in the nineteenth century. Emerson in his Politics (1844) also said, "[T]he less government we have the better." R.W. Emerson, *Politics*, in 3 The Complete Works of Ralph Waldo Emerson 199, 215 (2d ed. 1979) (1844).

The common law notion that government should do nothing affirmative rests on the perception that government does not act when it protects certain entitlements in service of the status quo: specifically contractual and property rights.[245] Thus the philosophical ideal of governmental inaction is achieved through the fiction that preservation of the status quo is a mere failure to act. In addition, the common law's focus on the tangible leads to a failure to recognize that government may act, and cause harm, through means other than intentional, physical coercion.[246]

3. *Critique of the Use of Common Law and Philosophical Sources*

I do not wish to argue that the conventional philosophical and common law positions are completely without merit. My concern is with their influence on conventional thought about the scope of governmental duties under the Constitution. In that context, I offer three major criticisms of the conventional wisdom's reliance on these sources. First, the conventional wisdom presents the individualistic view as not merely the predominant, but the *only,* way of thinking about governmental duties, and thereby ignores the insights of countervailing philosophical and common law strains. Second, it reflexively adopts the assumptions of these sources even though constitutional concerns may not be contiguous with those of political philosophy or the common law. Third, and most fundamentally, the conventional wisdom is based on a set of dualities which are unworkable. The difficulty in rebutting the conventional wisdom, which posits a duality of negative and positive rights and exalts the former over the latter, lies in avoiding acceptance of its terms. Claude Levi-Strauss captured the difficulty when he said that "in attacking an ill-founded theory the critic begins by paying it a kind of respect."[247] This leads to an inherent tension in the arguments. As a result, I argue that the conventional wisdom has adopted a myopic focus on negative rights to the exclusion of positive rights and portrayed it as the only possible focus. But more fundamentally, I argue that the distinction is unworkable, and cannot bear the weight of the constitutional choices courts rely on it to make.

The first issue, then, is the myopic focus of the conventional wisdom on individualism. The philosophical sources on which conventional thought draws, such as Aristotle, Kant, and Hobbes, are

245. *See* Cohen, *supra* note 185, at 21; Dewey & Tufts, *supra* note 74, at 490-91; Sunstein, *supra* note 70, at 882.

246. *See* Macpherson, *supra* note 137, at 97-117.

247. CLAUDE LEVI-STRAUSS, TOTEMISM 15 (R. Needham trans. 1963).

counterpoised by an alternative philosophic strain. The individualistic notion that liberty can be defined solely in terms of autonomy, or "freedom from . . . ,"[248] and entails no positive obligations, has always existed in tension with more collectivist notions of liberty as the freedom to be part of a community, participate in government and pursue happiness.[249] However strong is the hold of Mill's individualism on current thought, few would argue that in its pure form it is a useful model for people who live in a community.[250] Political philosophers have long argued that it does not reflect the reality of a "community that recognizes . . . myriad interactions among persons and affirmative obligations of support."[251]

Likewise, the conventional wisdom about the role of government rests on complacent acceptance of the philosophic notion that government causes harm only by its actions, and more specifically, its tangible, intentional, physical actions. Yet this view is at odds with the Platonic, collectivist notion that wrongful inaction, particularly by government which is charged with preventing injustice, is as objectionable as wrongful action.

Just as conventional thought draws selectively from philosophical sources, so it relies on particular common law notions. The common law, however, is not monolithic or unchanging. Many of the attitudes which led to the charter of negative liberties are identified with the early common law. The common law is gradually evolving from a "formal and unmoral" state[252] toward a more humane concern for the protection of the powerless. Recently it has shown greater concern with the public interest,[253] which has led to increasing acceptance of

248. J. FEINBERG, *supra* note 190, at 4.

249. *See* I. BERLIN, *supra* note 174, at 131-71; Donald Elfenbein, *The Myth of Conservatism as a Constitutional Philosophy,* 71 IOWA L. REV. 401, 458-59 (1986); Weinreb, *supra* note 223, at 790-91.

250. *See* Weinreb, *supra* note 223, at 791 n.53 (citing James Stephen's comment that there is no significant self-regarding conduct while a community is intact: "The intimate sympathy and innumerable bonds of all kinds by which men are united, and the differences of character and opinions by which they are distinguished, produce and must for ever produce continual struggles between them . . . .").

A more current critique of the individualist perspective has been contributed by feminist scholars, who have identified it as a male construct, counterpoised by a female perspective which places a higher value on interpersonal relations. Minow's article, *Justice Engendered,* provides a detailed demonstration of the ways in which the male construct becomes the unstated norm. *See* Minow, *supra* note 37, at 61 n.242 and generally; *see also* Leslie Bender, *A Lawyer's Primer on Feminist Theory and Tort,* 38 J. LEGAL EDUC. 3, 8 n.16 (1988); Deborah L. Rhode, *Feminist Critical Theories,* 42 STAN. L. REV. 617, 618 (1990).

251. *See* Weinreb, *supra* note 223, at 791 n.53 (citing H. SIDGWICK, THE METHODS OF ETHICS 265 (7th ed. 1907)).

252. Ames, *supra* note 101, at 97.

253. W. PROSSER & W. KEETON, *supra* note 47, § 3, at 16-17 (5th ed. 1984); 3 F. HARPER,

affirmative duties,[254] and suspicion toward rules which immunize government misconduct.[255] Thus, reliance on the common law involves choices: if the Court relies on common law notions which the common law itself is gradually repudiating, it must justify this choice.[256]

The decision to rely on the common law is itself a choice which must be justified. The early common law was concerned largely with enforcing contract and property rights among individuals; whereas the Constitution is concerned largely with delineating the role of government in relation to the individuals it governs. This is not to say that constitutional interpretation should develop without reference to the common law. The point is that constitutional and common law concerns are often not contiguous,[257] and therefore common law attitudes should not be adopted reflexively.[258] That, for example, common law did not recognize affirmative duties does not resolve the issue whether the Constitution should recognize them.

In sum, the insights of political philosophy and the common law have the power to enrich constitutional discourse, under certain conditions. One condition is that the predominant strain must not be mistaken for a single, unanimous voice. Another is that the ultimate test of an assumption's worth must be its fidelity to constitutional principles, not its historical pedigree.

4. *Limits of the Common Law: The Failure To Recognize the Unique Role of Government*

The failure of the conventional wisdom to recognize the unique role of government in a constitutional system exemplifies the danger of a reflexive adoption of common law principles. The common law paradigm does not account for the imbalance between the "awesome

F. JAMES & O. GRAY, *supra* note 34, § 18.6, at 718-23 (increasing tendency to find special relationships requiring affirmative duties; enterprise and strict liability; duty to complete a rescue).

254. *See, e.g.,* Riss v. City of New York, 22 N.Y.2d 579, 584, 240 N.E.2d 860, 862, 293 N.Y.S.2d 897, 900 (1968) (Keating, J., dissenting).

255. *See, e.g.,* Ryan v. State, 134 Ariz. 308, 656 P.2d 597 (1982); Schear v. Board of County Commrs., 101 N.M. 671, 687 P.2d 728 (1984).

256. In response it might be argued that the relevant common law for constitutional purposes is the body of law which existed at the time of the Framers. *See supra* discussion at text accompanying notes 203-10.

257. *See* Whitman, *supra* note 105.

258. The belief that the Constitution is contiguous with the common law is reminiscent of the attitude which historians argue prevailed among the Framers and through the *Lochner* era, that the Constitution, like common law, was based on natural law. *See* Erwin Chemerinsky, *The Supreme Court, 1988 Term — Foreword: The Vanishing Constitution,* 103 HARV. L. REV. 43, 64-68 (1989); Suzanna Sherry, *The Founders' Unwritten Constitution,* 54 U. CHI. L. REV. 1127, 1130-35 (1987).

power"[259] of the government and the lesser power of the individual.[260] In addition, although the individual has an autonomy interest in being free from coercion, it makes no sense to ascribe a similar interest to the government.[261] Nevertheless, the common law tends to treat individual and government interchangeably when inveighing against affirmative rights.[262]

It should be evident that government does not act like an individual, and is not on an equal footing with individuals. It is self-perpetuating, it possesses massed power[263] and resources, it is stratified, and it speaks through numerous individuals, not with one voice.

These characteristics of government define the ways in which government can cause harm. Government harms are different from and in many respects more serious than individually caused harms, and these differences have important ramifications for the theory of positive and negative rights.

Government creates individual dependency on its services and resources. For example, it has asserted monopoly power to protect from crime and to enforce the laws.[264] It has the power to tax and to decide how tax dollars are spent.[265] It has monopoly control over access to certain resources, such as highways, legal proceedings, and government information.[266] It has displaced private alternatives and required or encouraged reliance on its own regulatory structure in

259. Wardius v. Oregon, 412 U.S. 470, 480 (1973) (Douglas, J., concurring).

260. Susan Bandes, *Taking Some Rights Too Seriously: The State's Right to a Fair Trial,* 60 S. CAL. L. REV. 1019, 1025 (1987).

261. Michael Wells & Thomas A. Eaton, *Affirmative Duty and Constitutional Tort,* 16 U. MICH. J.L. REF. 1, 4 (1982); *see also* Bandes, *supra* note 260, at 1026. *But see* Epstein, *supra* note 186, at 212.

262. Whitman, *supra* note 105, at 226; Bandes, *supra* note 213, at 282-83.

263. Whitman, *supra* note 105, at 253.

264. Government has a monopoly on "legitimate violence." Sullivan, *supra* note 18, at 1451. In addition, the Court has repeatedly held that government has the sole interest in seeing that laws are enforced. *See* Schlesinger v. Reservists Comm. to Stop the War, 418 U.S. 208 (1974); United States v. Richardson, 418 U.S. 166 (1974); Linda R.S. v. Richard D., 410 U.S. 614 (1973). This monopoly power is sometimes said to arise from the terms of the social contract under which citizens surrendered some natural rights to society in return for some protections. *See* SOCIAL CONTRACT: ESSAYS BY LOCKE, HUME AND ROUSSEAU (E. Barker ed. 1960). The social contract theory has given rise to arguments that the government owes its citizens a duty of protection. *See, e.g.,* Richard L. Aynes, *Constitutional Considerations: Government Responsibility and the Right Not to Be a Victim,* 11 PEPPERDINE L. REV. 63, 75-77 (1984).

265. A series of Supreme Court decisions have established that individuals have virtually no standing to challenge the tax expenditures of federal government. *See, e.g.,* Valley Forge Christian College v. Americans United for the Separation of Church & State, Inc., 454 U.S. 464 (1982); Massachusetts v. Mellon, 262 U.S. 447 (1923). *But see* Flast v. Cohen, 392 U.S. 83 (1968).

266. *See, e.g., U.S. Data on Abortion Censored, House Unit Says,* N.Y. Times, Dec. 11, 1989, at A20, col. 4.

numerous areas,[267] including licensing of professionals, inspection of buildings, food and drugs, and supervision of child welfare. In short, it has stripped citizens of self-help remedies in numerous areas.

Government exerts substantial control over the distribution of scarce resources. These include natural resources such as timber and water, but also resources like government benefits[268] and wealth.[269] With the control of wealth comes power over availability of jobs, the price of commodities and access to goods and services. Government can harm simply by withholding these resources.

Government's status as a major employer illustrates another way in which it differs from individuals. Even when government acts as a private individual, as landlord, employer, owner of hospitals or railroads, it does so on a much grander scale. Its decisions on the training and discipline of its employees affect not only its vast work force, but the untold numbers of people with whom it comes into contact. Its tremendous wealth and power enable it to place conditions on access to its holdings which few individuals could approximate, and to cause great hardship by its refusal of access.[270]

In light of state action requirements, government is the only entity that can violate the Constitution.[271] Action which is taken under color of law is more serious than a tort committed by an individual, because it is an abuse of power possessed by virtue of state authority.[272] The opportunity for abuse is greatly exacerbated by the fact that governmental harm often occurs on a systemic basis.[273]

Government, unlike an individual, is a bureaucracy.[274] This obvious fact is important in several respects. Government decisions are

267. *See generally* Richard Stewart, *The Reformation of American Administrative Law*, 88 HARV. L. REV. 1669 (1975).

268. *See* Kreimer, *supra* note 9, at 1295-97.

269. PAUL SAMUELSON & WILLIAM NORDHAUS, ECONOMICS 47, 568-69 (12th ed. 1985).

270. The government's freedom to place conditions is, of course, restricted to some extent by the Constitution. *See* discussion of the unconstitutional conditions doctrine, *supra* note 18, *supra* notes 159-67. *See also* Board of Regents v. Roth, 408 U.S. 564 (1972); Perry v. Sindermann, 408 U.S. 593 (1972); LAURENCE TRIBE, CONSTITUTIONAL LAW § 10-9, at 686. Once government has decided to distribute largess, it may not destroy entitlement without due process.

271. *See supra* text accompanying note 71. However, Congress has some power to regulate private conduct, such as conspiracy, which interferes with the exercise of fourteenth amendment rights. United States v. Guest, 383 U.S. 745 (1966).

272. Monroe v. Pape, 365 U.S. 167, 254-58 (1961) (Frankfurter, J., dissenting). One example of the dissonance between tort and constitutional concerns is the question of remedy. The tort model sees money damages as sufficient compensation for its wrongs. This conclusion does not necessarily hold true under the Constitution, which treats some harms as unacceptable, whether or not after-the-fact damages are available. *See* Whitman, *supra* note 105, at 226.

273. *See* Bandes, *supra* note 105, at 125-27; Bandes, *supra* note 213, at 310.

274. *See generally* P. SCHUCK, *supra* note 65; M. LIPSKY, STREET-LEVEL BUREAUCRACY: DILEMMAS OF THE INDIVIDUAL IN PUBLIC SERVICES (1980).

made by a series of individuals, sometimes in different branches.[275] Government is stratified, creating classes of supervisors and subordinates. The natural disincentives to act which exist in bureaucracies exist in government as well. Finally, governmental choices, however harmful, are more often made by the interaction of several people acting in good faith than by a single malevolent person, and they are, therefore, more likely to cause intangible harm than direct physical damage.

The analogy between individual and government harm is not only flawed, but pernicious. When government is treated as an individual, the many ways in which it can cause harm are overlooked because they do not neatly fit common law conceptions which focus on equally placed individuals who cause or suffer tangible physical harms.[276]

5. *The Unhelpful Distinction Between Positive and Negative Rights*

The more fundamental issue is the unworkable nature of the philosophical distinctions: their inability to assist in determining what the duties of government ought to be. Ultimately, the distinctions cannot work because positive and negative rights, like action and inaction, or state action and private action, are concepts which cannot be distinguished without a reference point, or a theory of values. In themselves, they tell us little which will assist in making difficult choices about the role of government.

Negative liberty, as Mill and Berlin saw it, was easily defined and applied. By limiting the role of government to safeguarding our right to be left alone, it avoided the complex value judgments about individual motivations and governmental duties which a theory of positive liberty would require.[277] However, the ease of application is based on a number of restrictive and ultimately untenable assumptions about individuals and government.

At its most restrictive, the concept of negative liberty is based on a Hobbesian notion of each person as an atomistic body, which goes on moving until physically impeded by the impact of another body.[278] Even in this view, government is needed to safeguard freedom from physical intrusion. If liberty means more than a life of constant fear of

---

275. *See* Owen v. City of Independence, 445 U.S. 622 (1980).

276. *See* discussion of the *DeShaney* Court's treatment of the custody issue, *supra* text accompanying notes 116-38.

277. I. BERLIN, *supra* note 174, at 132-70; Charles Taylor, *What's Wrong with Negative Liberty*, in THE IDEA OF FREEDOM 179, 187 (A. Ryan ed. 1979).

278. *See* T. HOBBES, *supra* note 235, at 88; Taylor, *supra* note 277, at 183; C. MACPHERSON, *supra* note 137, at 104; *see also* Tribe, *supra* note 137, at 7, calling this a Newtonian view.

physical harm in which only the strongest survive, some laws are necessary, and they will infringe on freedom to some degree.[279] It then becomes necessary to determine which physical intrusions will be permitted,[280] and whose freedom of movement will be protected at the expense of that of others.

The Hobbesian view is thus unsuccessful even on its own terms as a way to avoid value judgments about the role of government. But in any case its view of people as an atomistic beings who impinge on others' freedom only through physical coercion is crude and reductionist. Many commentators have noted that in modern society, in which we live together in a complex web of interdependencies, virtually any act has repercussions on others and impinges on their freedom.[281]

If *A* wishes to visit a beautiful valley, her freedom to do so, or at least to do so in solitude, may be impeded by *B*'s physical presence in the valley, or even by *B*'s threats of physical force. But her freedom will be more effectively impeded by *B*'s ownership of the valley. This latter impediment derives its efficacy from the force of law, which enables *B* to exclude others and restrict their freedom of movement and access.[282] In the Hobbesian view, *A* is coerced only in the former instance, yet her loss of freedom is the same in each, and in the second instance it is attributable, not only to an individual, but to an act of government.

In the conventional view, the government's act to protect property and certain other well-established entitlements through its laws is not coercive, and in fact is not an act at all.[283] The ownership of property is a *fait accompli,* and government would act only if it tried to interfere with it. This conception is traceable to the Aristotelian approach to justice described by Professor Shklar, in which there must be "primary rules settling what is due to whom, [and] there must be effective institutions to maintain the rules in the course of private exchanges and to punish violations. When these norms are not followed there is injustice, and that is all that can be said about it."[284]

Once everything is distributed, government's only duty is to main-

279. C. MACPHERSON, *supra* note 137, at 117.

280. Mill, for example, was troubled by the hypothetical case of a man about to walk unknowingly off a bridge, and questioned whether it would be permissible to grab him to prevent him from drowning. *See* Weinreb, *supra* note 223, at 791 n.53 (1984) (citing J. MILL, *supra* note 223, at 17).

281. *See, e.g.,* Singer, *supra* note 38, at 995-97; Weinreb, *supra* note 223, at 790.

282. *See* Cohen, *supra* note 185, at 11-12.

283. Sunstein, *supra* note 70, at 886-88

284. Shklar, *supra* note 219, at 1137.

tain the status quo. When it does so, its role is perceived as passive and noninterfering, and therefore consistent with the ideal of negative liberty. Negative liberty, once again, is an ideal because it leaves people free to pursue their own ends and because it keeps government out of the realm of value choices. Yet it becomes obvious that those goals cannot be achieved.

The initial distribution of goods and property was done according to a value system which may or may not have been fair. The decision to enforce the status quo, freezing the effects of the initial distribution, is a value choice. As Morris Cohen forcefully argued sixty years ago, the assumption that each person is entitled to keep his "own" property is only one of many possible principles of distribution. Moreover, it is not necessarily consistent with negative liberty's ideal of maximizing self-regarding conduct, since few people are solely responsible for accumulating their own wealth.[285] Finally, in protecting the initial distribution, government is complicit in excluding others and thereby impinging on their freedom of access. Its actions, in short, are based on value choices about whose freedom it will protect and whose it will obstruct.

In the conventional view, the concept of negative liberty is easy to apply because it forbids only external (other-imposed) constraints; whereas positive freedom also includes liberty from internal (self-imposed) constraints.[286] That is, if government were responsible for ensuring that people were not internally constrained, it would have to make dangerous determinations about whether they were acting in their own best interests. If government need only ensure that *it* does not obstruct them, it can do so simply by doing nothing.

In fact, whether a constraint originates with government or with the individual depends on where one draws the boundary between the two.[287] For example, although Berlin conceived of lack of education as an internally imposed constraint, pervasive government regulation and provision of education render this conclusion anachronistic.[288] If it was until recently nearly impossible to gain legally recognized unrestricted access to land in Hawaii, it was because government has

285. Cohen, *supra* note 185, at 15.

286. I. BERLIN, *supra* note 174.

287. *See* J. FEINBERG, *supra* note 190, at 5-7; Thomas Morawetz, *Persons Without History: Liberal Theory and Human Experience,* 66 B.U. L. REV. 1013, 1032 (1986); Weinreb, *supra* note 223, at 792-93.

288. *See* Plyler v. Doe, 457 U.S. 202 (1982) (striking down state law which barred illegal aliens from attending public schools); San Antonio Indep. School Dist. v. Rodriguez, 411 U.S. 1 (1973) (sustaining school finance scheme based on property tax despite disparate impact on poor districts).

long protected the entitlements of the few at the expense of the many,[289] not because the distribution was natural, just or efficient. If after *Webster* many Missouri women cannot obtain abortions because the government has deprived their doctors of access to public hospitals as well as to many private ones, it is because the Court has approved the state's determination that this constraint on access to medical care may be externally imposed. Much hinges on how the natural order is defined.

The question, unavoidably, is what functions *ought* to be external to government and what functions it *ought* to perform. Mechanistic formulae about what is positive or negative, what is internal or external, allow a pretense that this question need not be faced. It is a pretense, because in the end, the formulae are empty. They have no descriptive force, since the reality is much too complex to fit within polar categories. The formulae are said to be devoid of normative force: they are billed as an alternative to value choices. Thus although they rest on a series of value choices — to condemn only physical or tangible interference; to prefer the status quo; to protect certain entitlements while leaving the means for satisfying others to the vagaries of the open market — they do not justify them. In short, they fail to describe the way things are or the way things should be. It is a puzzle that our jurisprudence vests them with such power.

C. *The Fear of Chaos: Floodgates, Slippery Slopes, and Judicial Incapacity*

My focus thus far has been on the historical antecedents which have informed and misinformed constitutional thinking about affirmative and negative duties. In this final section I explore another set of tenaciously held beliefs which prevents clear thinking about the scope of governmental duties.[290] Broadly speaking, these arguments rest on a common belief that once the courts recognized any affirmative duties, they would lose control and chaos would reign. To state the converse, the arguments begin from the assumption that by recognizing only the negative governmental duty to avoid direct harm, courts avoid the need for difficult decisions about motivation, causation, duty, allocation of governmental resources, allocation of judicial resources and a host of other thorny issues. Although the arguments overlap, I consider three variations on the general theme that recognition of affirmative rights would lead to chaos. First, the floodgates and

289. *See* Hawaii Housing Auth. v. Midkiff, 467 U.S. 229, 232 (1984).

290. These beliefs also rest to a great degree on common law and other historical assumptions, as I will discuss throughout this part.

institutional competence arguments: recognition of affirmative duties would drain scarce resources and burden the courts with nonjudicial tasks. Second, the slippery slope argument: recognition of limited affirmative duties would inexorably lead to unwieldy, unenforceable and undesirable duties as well. Finally, the difficulty of application argument: affirmative duties destroy the convenient, containable and enforceable pairing of rights and duties and raise difficult questions about causation, motivation and enforcement.

1. *The Floodgates and Institutional Competence Arguments*

The floodgates argument, in its crudest form, expresses the fear that if we allow this case, too many others like it will arise. It is often paired with a more sophisticated institutional competence argument, which is an objection not merely to the number of cases, but to the legitimacy of judicial involvement in any cases of this type.

The nature of this objection to imposing governmental duties is that once a court has held that government has failed to perform some duty, for example that the police have failed to protect a citizen from a threat of violence or the fire department has sat idly by and watched a building burn to the ground, the court will become mired in questions about how each government employee should do her job, will have to allocate the resources of the various governmental agencies, and will virtually usurp the function of the agencies themselves.[291] Thus the court may be doing something inherently undesirable,[292] which, to make matters worse, will dominate the court's docket and crowd out meritorious claims. Consider the following representative language:

> Should a Court . . . be empowered to evaluate . . . the handling of a major fire and determine whether the hoses were properly placed and the firemen correctly allocated? Might a Court also properly entertain a tort claim over a school teacher's ability to teach seventh grade English or over a postman's failure to deliver promptly an important piece of mail?

Having raised the specter of unlimited judicial duties, the court described the feared consequences:

> The creation of direct, personal accountability between each government employee and every member of the community would effectively bring the business of government to a speedy halt, "would dampen the ardor of all but the most resolute, or the most irresponsible in the unflinching discharge of their duties," and dispatch a new generation of litigants to

291. *See, e.g.*, Archie v. City of Racine, 847 F.2d 1211, 1223-24 (7th Cir. 1988), *cert. denied*, 109 S. Ct. 1338 (1989); Jackson v. Byrne, 738 F.2d 1443, 1447 (7th Cir. 1984).

292. Thus, although the argument obviously has a slippery slope aspect to it, it does not make the "implicit concession" which, according to Professor Schauer, is the requisite of the slippery slope: that in the instant case, as opposed to the danger case, the result would be correct. Frederick Schauer, *Slippery Slopes*, 99 HARV. L. REV. 361, 368-69 (1985).

> the courthouse over grievances real and imagined. An enormous amount of public time and money would be consumed . . . [and] prudent public employees would choose to leave public service.[293]

Courts and legislatures have long found ways to prevent this accountability from coming to pass. One of the most effective ways has been sovereign immunity. In the tort context, even where sovereign immunity has waned, claims that government has failed to provide services in a nonnegligent manner often founder on the public duty rule, which states that the duty owed by government is to the public at large, and is unenforceable by individuals.[294] Although some courts have rejected the public duty rule as a back door form of sovereign immunity,[295] it lives on.[296]

The stated rationale for this rule is that the question of how a government will allocate its resources is political, and must be left to the discretion of elected officials.[297] This rationale is mirrored in constitutional law. The assumption behind the public duty rule, that a duty owed to many should be enforceable only at the polls, not through the courts, is a familiar tenet of the doctrines of generalized grievance and political question.[298] With a gloss of federalism, the assumption has been used to explain why federal courts should not require state government to provide competent services.[299]

There is an inherent ambiguity in the floodgates argument between the notion that every enforced public duty is undesirable, and the notion that the undesirability comes from the sheer number of such cases. To the extent the objection is to sheer numbers, it falls of its own weight.[300] It amounts to the crudest defense of the status quo: meritorious cases must be turned away because the courts are busy with other cases. The argument fails because it skirts examination of

293. Warren v. District of Columbia, 444 A.2d 1, 9 (D.C. 1981) (en banc). This case rejects a claim based on tort, not the Constitution. However, its language and concerns are representative of those in cases rejecting constitutional claims that government failed to provide adequate services. *See, e.g., Archie,* 847 F.2d at 1224.

294. *See, e.g.,* Riss v. City of New York, 22 N.Y.2d 579, 240 N.E.2d 860, 293 N.Y.S.2d 897 (1968).

295. *See, e.g.,* Schear v. Board of County Commrs., 101 N.M. 671, 673 (1984); Riss, 240 N.E.2d at 866 (Keating, J., dissenting).

296. *See* Riss, 240 N.E.2d 860; Warren v. District of Columbia, 444 A.2d 1 (D.C. 1981) (en banc).

297. *Riss,* 240 N.E.2d at 861; Wells & Eaton, *supra* note 261, at 5.

298. *See* United States v. Richardson, 418 U.S. 166 (1974); Schlesinger v. Reservists Comm. to Stop the War, 418 U.S. 208 (1974).

299. *See* Archie v. City of Racine, 847 F.2d at 1224; Webster v. Reproductive Health Servs., 109 S. Ct. 3040, 3053 (1989) (decision to prohibit abortion subject to public debate and approval or disapproval at the polls).

300. I have made very similar arguments against the bar to granting standing in generalized grievance cases. *See* Bandes, *supra* note 213, at 285-86.

the nature of those other cases and determination of docket priorities. The argument is crude for another reason: it erroneously assumes that the status quo includes no cases in which government breached a duty to its citizens. Courts inevitably review government practices which injure citizens; the question is whether they are excluding the most important ones.[301]

The more sophisticated, judicial competence, tenet of the argument holds that the idea of judicially enforced public duty is in itself undesirable. The myriad decisions by governmental officials and entities not to provide services should not be reviewed by the judiciary. Once the courts hold that government failed to exercise a duty, they will be in the business of running the government. Any breach by the government of its duties to provide services can be corrected by the political branches.

This argument assumes that by avoiding recognition of affirmative duties, the court is kept out of the political realm. On the contrary, the decision not to consider whether a duty has been breached is a decision to defer to, and *ratify,* the political choices government makes. Whether that ratification is correct is unavoidably a judicial question. As Chief Justice Marshall made clear in *Marbury v. Madison,*[302] the courts will not interfere with the discretion of the political branches, but they must determine whether those branches are transgressing the rights of individuals. Thus whether a governmental decision is discretionary or violative of protected rights is a judicial question.[303]

Professor Lucinda Finley made this point forcefully in the context of police response to domestic violence. As she noted, many of the public duty cases, including the notorious *Riss v. City of New York,*[304] turned away claims by women that police failure to respond to their requests for protection from threats of domestic violence led to their grievous injury. The court's response that it could not force police departments to change their priorities begged the precise question raised: whether those priorities should be judicially ratified.[305] Even-

301. *See* Riss v. City of New York, 22 N.Y.2d at 588-90, 240 N.E.2d at 865, 293 N.Y.S.2d at 903-05 (Keating, J., dissenting).

302. 5 U.S. (1 Cranch) 137 (1803).

303. *See* Owen v. City of Independence, 445 U.S. 622, 649 (1980) ("[A] municipality has no 'discretion' to violate the Federal Constitution; its dictates are absolute and imperative."); *see also* Bandes, *supra* note 213, at 277-79; Davis, *supra* note 62, at 706 (discretion should not be eliminated, but unnecessary discretion should); Miller *supra* note 20, at 225-28 (discussing individual duties, government duties and duty of the court as national conscience).

304. 22 N.Y.2d 579, 240 N.E.2d 860, 293 N.Y.S.2d 897 (1968).

305. Lucinda M. Finley, *A Break in the Silence: Including Women's Issues in a Torts Course,* 1 YALE J.L. & FEM. 41, 71-72 (1989).

tually, courts began to recognize constitutional infirmities in police department priorities, and to award damages for violation of individual rights.[306]

The solicitude for discretion leads to insulation of government practices, policies, and choices from meaningful constitutional scrutiny, unless they fit the conventional description of direct and tangible harm.[307] This is a normative choice about the role of the court and the political branches. It says that the judicial role is to defer to governmental inaction, and thus it is a choice in favor of inaction. Given the nature of government, the choice is dangerous: it reinforces incentives which are already skewed against supervisory control over government employees, and encourages the unbridled discretion which leads to unconstitutional conduct.[308]

2. *The Slippery Slope Argument*

Fear of the slippery slope is perhaps the most tenacious barrier to the recognition of affirmative duties. Every critic of affirmative duties invokes the slippery slope. In the philosophical realm, Berlin rejected the notion of positive governmental duties because of the specter of totalitarianism: once we begin allowing government to do anything but leave us alone, we will end with it coercing us to obey its idea of freedom.[309] In the constitutional realm, the argument is that once we

306. *Id.* at 72 (discussing Thurman v. City of Torrington, 595 F. Supp. 1521 (D. Conn. 1984) (equal protection violated when police treat domestic violence differently, and less seriously, than other types of crime)).

307. *See* Sunstein, *supra* note 70, at 918 (to leave governmental decisions to political determination spells an end to constitutionalism). An additional and complex issue is raised. Even if government agencies should be subject to judicial oversight to ensure that they discharge their duties, that oversight arguably can be achieved through state tort law rather than under the Constitution. One might argue, for example, that enforcement of affirmative duties is a tort function, whereas the sole constitutional function is to ensure that government discharges its negative duty to cause no harm. *See, e.g.,* Archie v. City of Racine, 847 F.2d 1211, 1215-19 (7th Cir. 1988). Although I do not wish to minimize the complexity of the federalism issues involved, it seems to me that this formulation is essentially the conventional wisdom in sophisticated garb. Once the distinction between affirmative and negative duties is seen as an untenable means of defining constitutional protection, the important issue becomes simply what duties the Constitution mandates. If a governmental duty is mandated under the Constitution, judicial review of the exercise of that duty is appropriate. The fact that the same duty might be mandated under state tort law neither detracts from the existence of the constitutional duty nor renders judicial review of its discharge any less appropriate. The distinction between the scope of tort protection and that of constitutional protection, so often invoked to restrict constitutional duties, also works to ensure that they are not unduly limited by the scope of tort law. *See supra* text accompanying notes 259-76.

308. Davis, *supra* note 62, at 722; P. SCHUCK, *supra* note 65. Of course, government discretion can be controlled in numerous ways. Professor Davis suggests, in the context of police departments, that administrative or legislative controls are the solution of choice, and that the judiciary should step in only in the absence of action by the political branches. Davis, *supra* note 62, at 724.

309. I. BERLIN, *supra* note 174, at 131; C. MACPHERSON, *supra* note 183, at 105-16.

hold that due process requires the government to perform a statutorily mandated duty to protect a known individual from threatened harm, we will next be forcing cities to create police and fire departments and will ultimately be guaranteeing every person a living wage and enough to eat.[310] In the tort context, a duty of easy rescue is rejected because it would lead to forcing the wealthy to support the poor.[311] The discussion of the moral or legal advisability of narrowly phrased duties, such as the duty of a person on shore to throw a drowning child a life preserver, invariably turns to Macaulay's hypothetical question of whether the surgeon who refuses to go from Calcutta to Meerut to perform a necessary operation only he can perform should be obligated to do so.[312]

The question arises: why must we end up talking about doctors traveling through India? This ubiquitous hypothetical is emblematic of the slippery slope argument. The argument is that if we require only that each person be left to her own devices and not obligated to assist others, we need never venture into the moral thicket of motivations, morals and values. Once we say that people may sometimes have a duty to help others, even if the inconvenience is slight and the benefit is vast, we have intruded on personal autonomy. That is, we have enforced beneficence at the expense of individual determination, and thus introduced the principle which will lead to forced charity or dangerous rescue though it causes great personal hardship.[313]

Whether or not this is so, its connection to governmental duties is not immediately obvious. Government has no liberty or autonomy interests akin to those of individuals,[314] a distinction which the private law focus of much of negative rights theory tends to obscure.[315] Nevertheless, the slippery slope argument takes a similar form when the

310. See, for example, Estate of Gilmore v. Buckley, 787 F.2d 714 (1st Cir. 1986), which rejected a claim on behalf of a woman murdered after government officials ignored threats against her by a mentally ill inmate and released him without notifying her. The court spoke of the enormous economic consequences which would follow from the reading of the fourteenth amendment urged by the plaintiff, which would permit myriad errors by state officials to be found violative of the Constitution. 787 F.2d at 722-23; *see also* Douglas v. California, 372 U.S. 353, 362 (1963) (Harlan, J., dissenting) (result could lead to affirmative duties to lift handicaps flowing from differences in economic circumstances); Harris v. McRae, 448 U.S. 297, 317 (1980) (same); Robert Bork, *The Impossibility of Finding Welfare Rights in the Constitution,* 1979 WASH. U. L.Q. 695, 699 (if a claimant can demand broadening of a welfare program, he can demand it be started from scratch).

311. *See, e.g.,* R. EPSTEIN, *supra* note 43, at 61-68. *But see* Weinreb, *supra* note 41, at 272-73 (arguing that Epstein's analysis is flawed, and that a duty of easy rescue does not necessarily lead to a general duty of charity).

312. *See, e.g.,* Ames, *supra* note 101, at 112.

313. R. EPSTEIN, *supra* note 43, at 6-63.

314. Weinrib, *supra* note 41, at 278.

315. Singer, *supra* note 38, at 982.

government's duties are at issue. Berlin's argument against positive rights, which is concerned specifically with the role of government, is the seminal slippery slope argument in the philosophical context. The argument assumes that as long as government's only duty is to leave its citizens to their own devices, the moral thicket may be avoided. Once government begins helping people it must make value determinations about the kind of help they need, and must judge the validity of their motivations.[316] This introduces the principle which will lead to a totalitarian society which seeks to dictate a particular view of freedom to unwilling citizens.

The slippery slope argument as it appears in constitutional discourse is not well articulated, and yet it is presented as decisive.[317] The argument is that the duty of government is to avoid coercing citizens and to ensure that they do not coerce each other. Once it is held that government must provide a service competently, or ensure access to that service, it becomes a partner in coercion. In Judge Posner's words: "To adopt these proposals [to guarantee certain services] would change [the due process clause] from a protection against coercion . . . to a command that the state use its taxing power to coerce some of its citizens to provide services to others."[318] This is a classic slippery slope argument because it spends little time considering the actual governmental duty proposed. The proposed duty, as in *DeShaney,* is usually narrowly defined, and would obligate an existing public agency to perform a specific (and often, already promised or statutorily mandated) action on behalf of an identified individual or class. Yet the court resolves the issue by raising the specter of mandatory provision of goods and services.[319] The assumption is that as long as the Constitution has nothing to say about how or whether goods and services are provided, it has maintained a neutral stance on the difficult moral issue of their distribution.

In sum, the slippery slope argument is that by avoiding imposition of any affirmative duties, the judiciary can also avoid value judgments. The argument is thus fatally flawed because it fails to see the implicit

316. *See* Taylor, *supra* note 277, at 179-81.

317. As Professor Schauer puts it, "Where do you draw the line?" is regarded as a "knockdown argument." Schauer, *supra* note 292, at 380.

318. Jackson v. City of Joliet, 715 F.2d 1200, 1203-04 (7th Cir. 1983), *cert. denied,* 465 U.S. 1049 (1984). Similar arguments are made in the equal protection context. For example, Justice Harlan's famous dissents in the *Griffin-Douglas* cases speak of the danger of using the equal protection clause to "eliminate the evils of poverty." Douglas v. California, 372 U.S. 353, 362 (1963) (Harlan, J., dissenting).

319. *See, e.g.,* Archie v. City of Racine, 847 F.2d at 1221; Douglas v. California, 372 U.S. at 362 (Harlan, J., dissenting).

value choices on which it rests and the impossibility of avoiding the question of values.

The slippery slope argument assumes that the parade of horribles (legislated morality, forced redistribution of wealth, totalitarianism) can be held at bay by a purely mechanical conception of liberty as the right to be left alone by each other and by government. As Professor Charles Taylor described it, this conception "has no place for the notion of significance"; it presents itself as "purely quantitative."[320] It tries to avoid value judgments about which interests government will protect by positing government's role as completely passive. Yet this in itself is a value choice in favor of individual autonomy and the status quo as the highest values. In addition, it is unworkable even on its own terms. As discussed earlier, no liberty or autonomy is possible without some protection from coercion, and no society can function in which each person is completely free to define and practice his or her own version of liberty. Thus the courts must enforce value choices about which interests deserve protection and which must be sacrificed; they must give some content to the notion of protectable liberty.[321]

If the courts cannot stay off the slippery slope entirely, how can chaos be avoided? To consider this question, it is helpful to examine the slippery slope methodology. The classic argument is that a certain result in the case at hand would not be troublesome, but it should be rejected because it would inevitably lead to bad results in future cases. That is, there is no principled way to draw the line.[322] As Professor Schauer points out, the slippery slope argument contains an implicit concession that the result would be acceptable in the instant case, but blocks the result for fear of its application in the danger case.[323] Though the instant case might be easily resolved, the slippery slope methodology is to search for a universal rule which would also resolve every difficult case, naturally fail to find one, and therefore decline the acceptable solution to the instant case.

In the *DeShaney* case, for example, it would have been consistent with due process for the Court to construct a narrow holding that the state had abused its power by failing to provide statutorily required services to the plaintiff when it had promised to do so, had notice of his life threatening situation and had indeed contributed to that situation when it returned him to his violent home. The Court never really explained why this result was unacceptable; it simply refused to ven-

320. Taylor, *supra* note 277, at 183.

321. *See infra* text accompanying notes 366-91.

322. Schauer, *supra* note 292, at 368-70.

323. *Id.*

ture from the well-defined confines of its custody exception onto the slippery slope of requiring government services.[324] The result was to ratify a conception of liberty which did not include a minor's right to protection from anticipated physical injury. Likewise, in the abortion funding cases, the Court could have held that funding for a constitutionally protected medical procedure like abortion cannot be withdrawn in the context of a program which subsidizes all other medically necessary procedures. The Court's refusal to do so was based in large part on its fear of the danger case: forced funding of abortions in the absence of any other subsidized medical care.[325] The result was to exclude from the definition of liberty the right of access to constitutionally protected, medically necessary services.

In a sense the slippery slope is the mirror image of the Court's baseline methodology. When determining whether the government has caused a worsening in the plaintiff's position, the Court uses a complete lack of government services as its point of comparison. When determining whether it should remedy the plaintiff's harm, the Court posits a full complement of constitutionally required government services as the inevitable outcome. Neither a lack of services nor required subsistence accurately describes the current world.[326] Yet the Court moves immediately to the decontextualized abstraction to decide the actual case.

The alternative would be to decide the case before it by determining what particular justice the Constitution demands. The facility to do this, and to draw lines between the case before it and all the cases not before it, is the most important role of a court and an important way in which it differs from a legislature. The paradox is that by refusing to draw the line, the Court does so anyway. In *DeShaney,* it drew the line at physical custody, proving that it can be drawn, but failing to discuss whether it was drawn in the right place. More generally, in drawing the line at government inaction, the Court ensures that government will do nothing to redress entrenched barriers to ac-

324. *See infra* text accompanying notes 366-91.

325. *See, e.g., Harris,* 448 U.S. at 318.

326. However, a full complement of government services is a much more accurate description of current conditions in the United States than is a complete lack of such services. In truth, the courts' horror at the idea of required police and fire protection seems somewhat anachronistic. It has been argued that government protection from harm is an essential part of the social contract under which citizens give up their right to protect themselves. *See, e.g.,* Edelman, *supra* note 205, at 21. An argument could also be made that in the wake of the Civil War amendments, certain minimum expectations about government protection of safety and welfare have been shifted to the federal government and that access to such protection should not fluctuate based on locality. Increasingly since the 1930s, these expectations have been fulfilled. Whether or not the argument for required services could be made successfully, the threat that affirmative governmental duties would lead to forced police and fire protection does not seem particularly alarming.

cess but will instead continue to protect the injustices inherent in the current order.

In short, for fear of the wrong result later, the Court chooses the wrong result now, based on the mistaken belief that by preserving the status quo it has not acted; that by choosing a rough form of justice it has avoided the question of justice entirely. It freezes the law and prevents it from taking account of evolving moral, social, and political norms, assuming that by excluding these forces it has safeguarded its fixed certainty.[327] In truth, only half the goal is achieved. The law is fixed, but justice is too often sacrificed for want of an abstract rule.

3. *The Reciprocity and Administrative Implementation Arguments*

Proponents of the traditional view frequently argue that it would be impracticable to impose affirmative duties. They reason that when a negative duty is imposed, it is obvious when it has been breached, who caused the breach, who suffered from it, and what the remedy should be. If an affirmative duty were imposed, such as the duty to protect others from harm, it would not be obvious who owes the duty to whom, and thus it would be too difficult to enforce.[328]

There are several distinct strands to this argument which bear closer examination. First, it would be too difficult to determine who has *caused* a harm which consisted of the breach of an affirmative duty.[329] Second, it would be too difficult to determine who was *responsible* for discharging an affirmative duty. Finally, it would be too difficult to *enforce* an affirmative duty.

a. Causation. Turning first to the causation issue,[330] the argument is sometimes made that, as a semantic matter, one does not cause harm through an omission in the same way one causes harm through an act.[331] Alternatively, it is argued that although one might cause harm through an omission, the causal connection is more difficult to prove.[332]

327. *See* ROBERT SAMUEL SUMMERS, INSTRUMENTALISM AND AMERICAN LEGAL THEORY 182 (1982). Professor Summers argues that when judges believe they have no authority to "make law" they are unwilling to extend a doctrine to the full extent of its moral implications or change it in response to moral criticism. "They have viewed the law as something to be nailed down . . . rather than as something that could be in [the] process of evolution." *Id.*

328. *See, e.g.,* Epstein, *supra* note 186, at 208-17.

329. R. EPSTEIN, *supra* note 43, at 51-53.

330. It is beyond the scope and expertise of this article to attempt a full consideration of the complex issues of causation, on which Professor Epstein, among others, has written extensively. *See, e.g.,* R. EPSTEIN, *supra* note 43; Richard A. Epstein, *Intentional Harms,* 4 J. LEGAL STUD. 391 (1975).

331. R. EPSTEIN, *supra* note 43, at 51-53.

332. In the context of liability under 42 U.S.C. § 1983 (1982), for example, the Court has

Concededly, by pushing a nonswimmer into the water one causes a harm, in a descriptive sense, that one does not cause by failing to throw an already drowning person a rope. The former actor physically brought about the harm, while the latter made no physical movement which contributed to the harm. As Professor Fletcher describes, the early common law of homicide found the distinction significant, and "tainted" those who had physically caused death without regard to justification or excuse.[333] However, since at least the nineteenth century the common law has recognized that one may cause death without performing a physical act.[334] Modern criminal law may find a harm which the defendant physically caused to be excusable, and may find a harm caused by omission to be culpable. Although the notion of physical causation still has descriptive force, it is by itself a wholly inadequate basis for determining culpability.

In every area of law, causation is determined through a set of criteria which are designed to assess culpability. Intent, fault, proximate cause, and duty, all are legal constructs which seek to determine, from all the possible antecedent causes of an injury, which are legally significant.[335] The law is simply not coherent without some means of affixing blameworthiness, apart from notions of actual cause or but-for cause. Thus a concession that cause by action can be distinguished from cause by omission, or even that the former is easier to demonstrate than the latter, would not resolve the issue of whether omissions should be actionable. As to both acts and omissions, the law must make difficult policy determinations about which causes require the assessment of fault.[336] Difficulty of proof is simply one element in the calculus.

In addition, it would be incorrect to concede a significant distinction between causation by acts and omissions. First, the distinction

created more stringent requirements for proof of omissions than for proof of acts. For example, in *City of Canton v. Harris,* it held that to establish municipal liability for a policy of failure to train, the plaintiff must show a heightened state of mind: deliberate indifference, though no such requirement exists for proof of "direct" acts. The Court justifies the heightened requirement by reference to the difficulty of proving causation where an omission is alleged. 109 S. Ct. 1197, 1204-07 (1989); *see also* Michael Gerhardt, *The Monell Legacy: Balancing Federalism Concerns and Municipal Accountability Under Section 1983,* 62 S. CAL. L. REV. 539, 610 (1989) (defending heightened state of mind requirement); Barbara Kritchevsky, *"Or Causes to be Subjected": The Role of Causation in Section 1983 Municipal Liability Analysis,* 35 UCLA L. REV. 1187, 1225-26 (1988) (criticizing court for confusing proof of policy with causation).

333. G. FLETCHER, *supra* note 39, § 5.1.1-5.1.2, at 343-50.

334. *Id.* at § 8.2.2, at 594 (citing Regina v. Instan, 1 Q.B. 450 (1893), which upheld a manslaughter conviction against a woman for letting her aged aunt die).

335. *See* John C. Jeffries, Jr., *Compensation for Constitutional Torts: Reflections on the Significance of Fault,* 88 MICH. L. REV. 82, 93-96 (1989).

336. *See, e.g.,* Palsgraf v. Long Island R.R. Co., 248 N.Y. 339, 351-55, 162 N.E. 99, 103-05 (1928) (Andrews, J., dissenting).

will hinge on the way the activity in question is defined. In the tort context, failure to apply brakes in a moving vehicle, or to remove a sponge from a patient at the end of an operation, are considered negligent acts, not omissions. This is because they are part of an ongoing activity.[337] In the constitutional context, all wrongful acts of government must be evaluated in light of government's ongoing nature and ability to cause harm by its inaction.

Second, omissions cause harm when they give rise to the breach of a duty to act.[338] A court may find that a parent caused the death of a child by failing to feed him, but that thirty-eight onlookers did not cause the death of Kitty Genovese by failing to come to her aid.[339] The distinction lies in the scope of duty; which must be determined from the constitutional, statutory or common law provision which creates the duty.

In the constitutional context, it is meaningless to speak of causation without reference to the scope of particular rights. A violation of the sixth amendment is caused by the failure to provide trial counsel to an indigent defendant;[340] a violation of the fourteenth amendment is caused by a failure to provide an indigent defendant a free trial transcript at the appellate level.[341] Did the failure of DSS to act competently cause Joshua DeShaney's injuries? The question can be answered only by determining the scope of its duty under the due process clause. In a legal as opposed to a semantic context, the question of causation hinges on rights, relationships and duties: causation does not exist in a vacuum.

b. Responsibility. A closely related argument against liability for omissions is that it would be difficult to determine who was obligated to compensate for the harm. In this vein, Professor Epstein argues against affirmative duties because they would not be reciprocal. As he describes it, the clarity of a negative duty comes from its reciprocal nature. The reciprocal nature of negative duties is obvious: *A* refrains from harming *B* and *B* refrains from harming *A*. *A* knows the identity of the person to whom he owes a duty, and to whom he will be liable if he breaches it. However, when a duty is positive in nature, such as the duty to protect others from harm, the reciprocity is lost, since there is "no single obvious neighbor, who must satisfy any particular person's

337. G. Fletcher, *supra* note 39, § 8.2, at 586-88. *See* text accompanying notes 46-48.

338. G. Fletcher, *supra* note 39, § 8.2, at 586-88.

339. *Id.* at § 8.2.3, at 601; § 8.2.4, at 605.

340. Gideon v. Wainwright, 372 U.S. 335 (1963).

341. Griffin v. Illinois, 351 U.S. 12 (1956).

needs."[342]

One immediate response to this argument is that it assumes a choice between perfect reciprocity and duties owed to the world at large. It is possible to construct a duty which is owed to a discrete and identifiable group of people. The difficulties in determining who should be liable would be merely administrative, and no different from any situation in which there were several tortfeasors.[343]

The more significant objection, in the constitutional realm, is that the notion of reciprocity is irrelevant to the question of governmental duties.[344] First, the duties which flow from individuals to government cannot be the same as those which flow the other way. Second, government may be obligated to prevent harm it has not caused.

The government is an inanimate object; a bureaucracy; an institution with certain powers. The Constitution gives it enumerated powers over the citizenry and then forbids it to abuse them. It cannot kill its citizens, search them or force them to trial without certain safeguards. It makes no sense to speak of reciprocal obligations flowing from citizens to government. Citizens have certain obligations to government, such as the duty to pay taxes[345] or serve in the military.[346] They are reciprocal only in the sense that both government and citizens have some duties to each other, but the duties are not mirror images in Epstein's sense.

But if reciprocity means only that both government and its citizens possess *some* duties, then it says nothing about whether these duties must be negative or may be affirmative. In fact, many of the individual duties are classically affirmative in nature: paying taxes, risking life and limb in defense of country. As social contract theory suggests, arguably the government ought to owe some affirmative duties in return.[347] If the power to tax engenders a correlative right, it is sensible that this right is one to services, or at least to a voice in how tax money

342. Epstein, *supra* note 186, at 209-10.

343. Weinreb, *supra* note 41, at 259.

344. Epstein recognizes in passing that "[t]he shift from private lawsuit to government action obscures the linkage between rights and correlative duties" but argues that it does not eliminate it: "[s]omeone must still take from someone else, even if a third party mediates the transfer." Epstein, *supra* note 186, at 210. The short answer is that government is perpetually taking "something," specifically, money, from all of us and redistributing it; this is inherent in the power to tax and spend. The question is simply to whom it is distributed. Though Epstein would argue for constitutional restrictions on this redistribution, *see* Epstein, *supra* note 155, at 94, these would simply freeze the status quo, itself a product of government choices about distribution.

345. U.S. CONST. art. I, § 8, cl. 1.

346. U.S. CONST. art. I, § 8, cl. 12.

347. *See* J. LOCKE, THE SECOND TREATISE OF CIVIL GOVERNMENT AND A LETTER CONCERNING TOLERATION 62-64 (J. Gough ed. 1946); J. ROUSSEAU, THE SOCIAL CONTRACT AND DISCOURSES Bk. I, at 173-78 (G. Cole trans. rev. ed. 1973).

is spent. If citizens have a duty to refrain from private violence, there ought to be a correlative government duty to protect them.[348]

Ultimately, the nature of government's duties cannot hinge on the nature of individual duties. Instead, both hinge on what the Constitution provides. Individuals are guaranteed certain rights under the Constitution. Government has no correlative rights.[349] On the contrary, the rights granted by the Constitution are meant to protect individuals from excessive government power rather than to augment governmental power.[350] Furthermore, the duties owed by government are often owed collectively, rendering Epstein's idea of an "obvious neighbor" irrelevant when governmental obligations, like the duties to refrain from unreasonable searches and seizures[351] and from denying the equal protection of law,[352] are in issue.[353] As to these duties, no particular individual can be identified to reciprocate, nor is there any conceivable reciprocal duty, other than those inhering in the vague contours of the social contract.

At bottom, if reciprocity means only that both government and citizens possess some duties, it says nothing at all about the scope of those duties. This is a question which must be faced on its own terms, and which the search for neat pairings of rightholders and dutyholders can only obscure.

c. Redistribution and enforcement. There is another, more subtle, variation on the argument that affirmative duties would obscure the identity of the dutyholder. Its premise is that positive rights are often stated as "claims made against society in general" which "tend to collapse into amorphous, ideal statements about the way the world should be."[354] Or, as Professor Robert Cover put it, to speak of a right "is not even an intelligible principle unless we know to whom it

348. *See* Edelman, *supra* note 205, at 20-21; Black, *supra* note 205, at 1106.

349. *See* Bandes, *supra* note 260. Likewise the Lockean theory of natural rights assumes a compact in which the government is obligated to the people, not they to it, and therefore "[the] government may not properly insist upon any rights accruing to it from the people's compact." Doernberg, *"We the People": John Locke, Collective Constitutional Rights, and Standing to Challenge Government Action,* 73 CALIF. L. REV. 52, 61 (1985); Bandes, *supra* note 260, at 1023 n.24.

350. *See* R. DWORKIN, TAKING RIGHTS SERIOUSLY (1977); Gideon v. Wainright, 372 U.S. 335, 344 (1963); Duncan v. Louisiana, 391 U.S. 145, 155-56 (1968).

351. *See* Amsterdam, *supra* note 52, at 367-72; Doernberg, *"The Right of the People": Reconciling Collective and Individual Interests Under the Fourth Amendment,* 58 N.Y.U. L. REV. 259 (1983); Bandes, *supra* note 260, at 1048 (fourth amendment rights are collectively held).

352. *See* Tribe, *supra* note 9, at 333-34 (certain rights are not individual and alienable, but systemic; concerned with structuring power relationships).

353. Although the Court has often held that the collective nature of rights renders them unenforceable by individuals, *see* Allen v. Wright, 468 U.S. 737 (1984); Schlesinger v. Reservists Comm. to Stop the War, 418 U.S. 208 (1974), I have argued that such rights should be enforceable by all who are harmed by their violation. *See* Bandes, *supra* note 213, at 284-87.

354. Chase, Book Review, 60 N.Y.U. L. REV. 304, 321 (1985) (reviewing T. CAMPBELL,

is addressed."[355] A related premise is that even if the applicable dutyholder is identified, it may claim an inability to discharge the duty.[356]

These concerns seem particularly relevant to the broad claims for a guaranteed subsistence income or satisfying work which are traditionally the province of scholars or jurists warning about the slippery slope. When the Court refuses to find an "affirmative" duty in a *DeShaney* situation, involving a particular social service agency's duty to a known individual, or a *Webster* situation, involving the scope of an existing federal subsidy program, it is clear enough which governmental agency would shoulder the obligation. If instead we talk about the obligation to *create* a police department or social welfare agency, or even to ensure a subsistence income for everyone through unspecified means, identifying the dutyholder becomes a good deal more difficult. This particular discussion, however, is not about whether some agency somewhere ought to provide these things, but about the scope of constitutional protection and whether it ought to include affirmative duties. This does not solve the problem, but it does narrow it somewhat. In the constitutional context, a claim for protection or provision of services is made, not against society in general, but against the government.

Even so, the objection is made that identifying government as the dutyholder is problematic: government is too diffuse and affirmative duties are too difficult to implement. Several observations can be made about this objection. First, it is directed only to implementation of duties which appear redistributive, not to those which appear to enforce the status quo, although the latter may be equally difficult to implement. Second, it is simplistic, because it fails to recognize the numerous affirmative duties with which government routinely complies. Finally, it treats the issue of defining constitutional norms as contiguous with the issue of enforcing them.[357] If the issue is whether the Constitution does, or ought to, impose on the political branches a duty to reallocate resources, the manifold problems in enforcing that duty must be kept separate.

The argument might run that the police department has a duty not to harm citizens physically; the public schools have a duty not to per-

THE LEFT AND RIGHTS: A CONCEPTUAL ANALYSIS OF THE IDEA OF SOCIALIST RIGHTS (1983) and M. GIBSON, WORKERS' RIGHTS (1983)).

355. Robert M. Cover, *Obligation: A Jewish Jurisprudence of the Social Order,* 5 J.L. & RELIGION 65, 71 (1988).

356. Chase, *supra* note 354, at 321.

357. *See generally* Lawrence Gene Sager, *Fair Measure: The Legal Status of Underenforced Constitutional Norms,* 91 HARV. L. REV. 1212 (1978).

petuate segregation. This duty is merely a command to existing officials in existing agencies and therefore is easy to implement. However, a duty to provide adequate police protection or schooling for the poor and minorities would be a request for reallocation of funds, which would not be directed to specific agencies or individuals, and therefore would be too difficult to implement.

In this scheme, everything turns on whether government is asked to reallocate funds or continue to implement existing programs. The question is why this distinction ought to be of constitutional significance. The problem seems to be mainly one of enforcement. If a court were to determine that government could not discharge its duty to protect and provide for its citizens without establishing new police or school facilities, it could order that such facilities be built. It would then be faced with the undeniably difficult task of obtaining funding from the legislature to implement this duty and of obtaining executive enforcement of its order. This judicial action would be different (if at all) only in degree from the reallocations of government funds which courts have been ordering for years. In order to implement the guarantees of the eighth amendment, courts have had to order that government money be reallocated for expanded and improved prison facilities.[358] In order to ensure equal protection of the laws for minorities, courts have had to order substantial expenditures by school districts.[359] The Supreme Court this Term reviewed judicial efforts to enforce equal protection guarantees by ordering local governments to build new public housing and school facilities. At issue were not the underlying constitutional norms, but the courts' aggressive methods of enforcement.[360]

358. *See, e.g.,* Holt v. Sarver, 309 F. Supp. 362 (E.D. Ark. 1970), *affd.,* 442 F.2d 304 (8th Cir. 1971); Pugh v. Locke, 406 F. Supp. 318 (M.D. Ala. 1976), *affd. sub nom.* Newman v. State of Alabama, 559 F.2d 283 (5th Cir. 1977), *revd. in part sub nom.* Alabama v. Pugh, 438 U.S. 781, *cert. denied sub nom.* Newman v. Alabama, 438 U.S. 915 (1978).

359. *See, e.g.,* Milliken v. Bradley, 433 U.S 267 (1977). In *Milliken* the Court upheld an order which required state and local government to spend substantial sums of money for educational programs, including remedial reading, in order to implement a desegregation decree. The case illustrates the often fictional nature of the distinction between preservation of the status quo and reallocation. Since the state was a defendant, the eleventh amendment bar could be lifted only if the relief were prospective in nature, in light of the holding in *Ex parte* Young, 209 U.S. 123 (1908), that prospective injunctive relief, unlike retrospective damage relief, *see* Edelman v. Jordan, 415 U.S. 651 (1974), does not impact on the state treasury. The Court characterized the order to spend millions of state dollars as "part of a plan that operates *prospectively* to bring about the delayed benefits of a unitary school system." 433 U.S. at 290. That is, the state was not ordered to disturb the status quo by reallocating funds it had already committed, but only to ensure the availability of future funds. Hence Justice Rehnquist's often quoted understatement in Edelman that "the difference between [prospective and retrospective relief] . . . will not in many instances be that between day and night." 415 U.S. at 667.

360. In Spallone v. United States, 110 S. Ct. 625 (1990), the Court held that the district court had abused its discretion in levying contempt citations, fines and imprisonment against individual

It is crucial to separate the issue of identifying constitutional norms from the problems of enforcing them. Enforcement of constitutional guarantees often requires judicial oversight of government's allocational decisions. As the Court's conception of its role and its remedial powers has evolved, it has become more willing to enforce norms it once thought unenforceable.[361] That their enforcement sometimes requires creativity is not a constitutional objection to the underlying norms. The Court continues to express grave reservations about upholding relief it deems too intrusive on state and local prerogatives. When the Court expresses these reservations by questioning the lower courts' exercise of remedial discretion, its logic is difficult to attack even if one disagrees with its conclusions. However, when the Court blurs the distinction between remedial concerns and the definition of the underlying norms, its decisions lose force and clarity.[362] It may be that the Constitution contains some duties to provide basic necessities and ensure bodily survival which are not "perfectly enforceable in courts of law."[363] To deny the existence of these duties based on current judicial reluctance or inability to enforce them is to risk permanently sacrificing their implementation.[364]

IV. The Question of Values

I have argued that the conventional wisdom about affirmative rights is based on a series of anachronistic assumptions, easy slogans and either-or categories which impede understanding of constitutional duties. However, the fault with the conventional wisdom is not simply its reliance on questionable assumptions and distinctions. The crux of the problem is that the conventional wisdom masquerades as neutral reason, but in fact reflects extremely restrictive value choices about the role of government. Because these choices are masked by rhetoric,

city council members who refused to comply with a court order to enact legislation required by a consent decree to fund public housing. It upheld contempt citations and fines against the city itself. In Missouri v. Jenkins, 110 S. Ct. 1651 (1990), the Court struck down on comity grounds a district court order imposing an increase on the amount of property taxes levied by a school district to fund public school desegregation, but held that federal courts may require the school districts themselves to levy taxes in order to fund desegregation.

361. *Compare* Colgrove v. Green, 328 U.S. 549 (1946) (malapportionment nonjusticiable because beyond judicial competence) *with* Baker v. Carr, 369 U.S. 186 (1962) (courts can enforce voter franchise through injunctive remedies); *see also* Bandes, *supra* note 213, at 304 n.530.

362. See, for example, City of Los Angeles v. Lyons, 461 U.S. 95 (1983), in which the Court denied article III standing based on asserted lack of requisites for injunctive relief. For criticism of the decision as blurring the distinction between justiciability and remedial concerns, see Richard Fallon, *Of Justiciability, Remedies, and Public Law Litigation: Notes on the Jurisprudence of* Lyons, 59 N.Y.U. L. Rev. 1, 22-35 (1984).

363. L. Tribe, *supra* note 51, § 15-9, at 1337.

364. *See* Sager, *supra* note 357, at 1221.

they are never fully articulated. It is not the inevitable failure to attain neutral reason, but the pretense, that is dangerous. The slogans and categories encourage the complacent notion that the restrictive results they yield are inevitable.[365] In fact, the results reflect choices which must be judged on the merits.

The conventional approach to defining constitutional duties claims to avoid the need to give content to the abstract principles of liberty and equality by simply commanding government to do nothing at all. Yet through this command it gives content to these principles. Liberty is defined as governmental noninterference, and thus government becomes complicit in preserving the current distribution of goods, services, and entitlements. Equality is defined as the freedom to compete against others in the marketplace, even for those things the Constitution guarantees.

To the extent that these principles lead to injustice and inequality, the conventional wisdom is that these are the unfortunate but unavoidable result of private, individual forces. Yet the distinction between public and private limits, or internal and external constraints, is of little use in determining whether one's loss of liberty is attributable to the government. At best, it is a description of the status quo, and says nothing about the way things ought to be. The inability to afford medical care or infant formula or to obtain a basic education is attributable to private action or individual limitations only to the extent there is no governmental obligation to provide these things. The line between public and private spheres of influence is not immutable.[366] This is not to suggest that the scope of governmental obligation is without inherent limits. The limits are in the Constitution, but the Constitution cannot be interpreted without reference to values.

For example, in *DeShaney* and *Webster* the Court's conclusion that the plaintiffs' plight was private and individual — that the government did not act to worsen the position of the injured parties — assumed a baseline of a complete lack of government services. This

365. *See* Minow, *supra* note 37, at 35: "[T]hese patterns of legal analysis [which focus on categorization] imply that legal reasoning yields results of its own accord, beyond human control."

366. The *Webster* opinion illustrates this point with an ironic twist. It upheld a statute under which even private doctors who perform abortions on private patients paying for services with private funds will be affected if their admission privileges are at a medical facility which leases or rents equipment or land from governmental entities. *See* Mo. Rev. Stat. § 188.200(2) (1986); ACLU/Reproductive Freedom Project, *supra* note 176, at 7, 25. Thus it adopts an expansive definition of the public realm, not in order to impose expanded governmental duties, but to intrude on formerly private consensual relationships between individuals, private doctors and private hospitals.

baseline could not be justified as descriptive of the status quo.[367] Even if it had been, its use would have been a choice to use the status quo as a standard.[368] Ultimately, the baseline becomes normative: it adopts government inaction as the standard against which all its conduct is measured; the way things are as the way they should be.

The choice of baseline cannot be made value-free.[369] The unavoidable issue is what we *ought* to expect from government. If the answer is nothing at all, that we are lucky not to be living a nasty, brutish, and short life,[370] then anything government decides to give will be largess, and it can decide to give nothing for any reason at all. If the answer is minimal subsistence, or reasonably competent services, the government's burden is substantially greater.

How should the scope of constitutional duty be determined? Whether government has an affirmative duty will depend in large part on the requisites of the particular constitutional provision at issue. Whether or not those requisites will prove determinative, they must at least provide the initial focus of the inquiry.

The trial-related rights, for example, reflect a recognition that unless a trial is accompanied by certain affirmative guarantees, such as the right to counsel and compulsory process, the core sixth amendment promise of a fair (speedy, public, impartial) trial becomes a nullity.[371] The equal protection clause is concerned with the hazards of inequality and discriminatory treatment.[372] To avoid both these hazards and the imposition of unequal burdens on independently protected rights, it must sometimes impose an affirmative duty on government to provide access, for example to judicial services,[373] to public fora,[374] and to the voting franchise.[375] The due process guarantee of procedural regularity holds that in order to guard against the danger of arbitrary government action, government is charged with an affirm-

367. *See supra* text accompanying notes 88-94; 168-75.

368. *See* Kreimer, *supra* note 9, at 1359-63 (discussing use of history or status quo as a baseline).

369. *See* Sullivan, *supra* note 18, at 1450 n.150 (criticizing Kreimer's three suggested baselines as importing unstated normative theories).

370. *See* Kreimer, *supra* note 9, at 1357 (discussing use of Hobbesian state of nature as a baseline).

371. Duncan v. Louisiana, 391 U.S. 145, 155-56 (1968) (jury trial); Washington v. Texas, 388 U.S. 14 (1967) (compulsory process); Gideon v. Wainwright, 372 U.S. 335, 344 (1963) (counsel); *In re* Oliver, 333 U.S. 257 (1948) (public trial).

372. Michelman, *supra* note 20, at 9.

373. *See* Boddie v. Connecticut, 401 U.S. 371 (1971); Griffin v. Illinois, 351 U.S. 12 (1956).

374. *See* Police Dept. of Chicago v. Mosley, 408 U.S. 92 (1972).

375. *See* Harper v. Virginia State Bd. of Elections, 383 U.S. 663 (1966) (striking down poll tax).

ative obligation to provide a hearing before depriving individuals of life, liberty, or property.[376]

The conventional wisdom stubbornly explains all such examples as exceptions which prove the rule,[377] but, more accurately, the exceptions which riddle the rule of negative rights are evidence of its irrelevance. In its insistence on categorizing and then dismissing whole categories of government obligation,[378] the rule obscures the correct focus of constitutional discourse: the requisites of the Constitution. Certain constitutional commands cannot be met without an affirmative effort by the government.

However, identifying the Constitution as the correct focus of the inquiry is not the same as resolving the inquiry. The constitutional text is only a starting point. Particularly as to the open-textured provisions of the Bill of Rights and the fourteenth amendment, their scope cannot be determined without reference to substantive values.[379]

The sixth amendment's comparatively straightforward guarantee of the right to counsel, for example, leaves for interpretation the question of whether the government must *provide* such counsel free of charge.[380] The Court's winding path to its eventual conclusion in favor of appointed counsel evidences the necessity, and the difficulty, of giving content to the guarantees of counsel and a fair trial.

The spare language of the equal protection clause raises issues which have proved more intractable. It is necessary to identify the objectionable inequalities,[381] and how to correct them. If equal protection were merely a command to treat all persons the same, it would lead to a burdening of rights in many instances. In some contexts, equal protection involves treating differently placed people differently.[382] The ideal of equality is "empty" unless it is given substantive

376. Goldberg v. Kelly, 397 U.S. 254 (1970); Bell v. Burson, 402 U.S. 535 (1971).

377. Currie, *supra* note 28, at 873-74; *supra* text accompanying note 27.

378. *See* Chase, *supra* note 354 (distinction between positive and negative rights is used unnecessarily to subordinate the former to the latter).

379. *See supra* text accompanying notes 206-08.

380. The right to appointed counsel was first recognized in Powell v. Alabama, 287 U.S. 45 (1932), and then only under extremely narrow circumstances. In fact, *Powell* was a fourteenth amendment case premised on fundamental fairness guarantees. Johnson v. Zerbst, 304 U.S. 458 (1938), found a right to appointed counsel in the sixth amendment in federal cases. It was not extended to the states until 1963. *See* Gideon v. Wainwright, 372 U.S. 335 (1963) (overruling Betts v. Brady, 316 U.S. 455 (1942)).

381. *See* Michelman, *supra* note 20; Kreimer, *supra* note 9, at 1367.

382. Minow, *supra* note 37, at 22-25; Michelman, *supra* note 20; *see also* L. TRIBE, *supra* note 51, § 16-1, at 1437-38 (discussion of the difference between equal treatment (all persons have same access) and treatment as an equal (all persons treated with equal regard, though this means taking cognizance of their differences)). One of the most intractable equal protection questions is the treatment of poverty. For example, the *Griffin-Douglas* principle holds that to some extent government has an affirmative obligation to alleviate some of the obstacles posed by poverty. *See*

content.[383]

The due process guarantee has proved similarly opaque. The guarantee is directed at the arbitrary use of governmental power.[384] It is impossible to give meaning to the guarantee without a notion of the proper uses of that power. The Court has avoided the issue by reliance on a series of bright lines: only intentional,[385] direct,[386] and coercive[387] acts may cause deprivations. Application of these bright lines has led to unjust results because they are too coarse to capture the complex ways in which government can abuse power.[388] The Court never explained why the state's disastrous incompetence in *DeShaney* did not offend deeply held notions about governmental obligations toward defenseless children which ought to be imbedded in the Constitution.[389] Likewise it would have been consistent with due process notions to hold that the deliberately skewed subsidies in *Webster* impermissibly burdened privacy rights in contravention of *Roe v. Wade.*[390] The Court is discomfited by the amorphous quality of the due process clause, and reacts by treating it restrictively. This reaction does not succeed in freeing due process jurisprudence of value choices; it is a choice in itself. Because it is justified only by reliance on easy slogans, it is in danger of appearing as arbitrary as the very action the clause condemns.

Ultimately, the objections to affirmative rights are based on a vision of the Constitution as a negative document which prevents government and citizens alike from harming one another by force. A

Douglas v. California, 372 U.S. 353 (1963); Griffin v. Illinois, 351 U.S. 12 (1956). But later cases made clear that this obligation is, as Tribe said, not a guarantee of equal access to criminal justice, but of minimal access. L. TRIBE, *supra* note 51, § 16-52, at 1653; *see* Murray v. Giarratano, 109 S. Ct. 2765 (1989) (state not required to appoint counsel for indigent prisoners seeking collateral review); Pennsylvania v. Finley, 481 U.S. 551 (1987) (same in death penalty context); Ross v. Moffit, 417 U.S. 600 (1974) (state not required to appoint counsel for indigent prisoners seeking discretionary appellate review). The poverty cases illustrate the point that the equal protection guarantee is unavoidably interpreted in light of choices about which services and commodities must be protected from the workings of the free market. *See* Radin, *supra* note 181, at 1903.

383. *See* Erwin Chemerinsky, *In Defense of Equality: A Reply to Professor Westen,* 81 MICH. L. REV. 575 (1983); Peter Westen, *The Empty Idea of Equality,* 95 HARV. L. REV. 537 (1982).

384. *See* Daniels v. Williams, 474 U.S. 327, 331 (1986).

385. *See* Davidson v. Cannon, 474 U.S. 344 (1986); Daniels v. Williams, 474 U.S. 327 (1986).

386. *See* DeShaney v. Winnebago County Dept. of Social Servs., 109 S. Ct. 998, 1006-07 (1989).

387. *See* Webster v. Reproductive Health Servs., 109 S.Ct. 3040, 3052-53 (1989).

388. *See* Bandes, *supra* note 105, at 125-27; *see also* Burnham, *supra* note 215, 550-70, (advancing a definition of the abuse of power prohibited by the due process clause).

389. *See, e.g.,* Taylor v. Ledbetter, 818 F.2d 791, 797 (11th Cir. 1987); Estate of Bailey by Oare v. County of York, 768 F.2d 503 (3d Cir. 1985); Aristotle P. v. Johnson & Morgan, 721 F. Supp. 1002, 1009 (N.D. Ill. 1989).

390. *See* Perry, *supra* note 155; *Webster,* 109 S. Ct. at 3068 n.1 (Blackmun, J., dissenting).

more appealing vision would recognize that just as we are inextricably bound to each other, we are dependent on government to preserve our liberty by providing certain things we require and expect, and that these things must be singled out for constitutional protection. The identification of the things we require and expect, as a constitutional matter, is crucial. The Court has concerned itself with the elusive and ultimately irrelevant distinction between "freedom from and freedom to."[391] The question that should be asked instead is: what must we have in order to be free?

---

391. I. BERLIN, *supra* note 174; J. FEINBERG, *supra* note 190, at 27.

[19]

Taking Dependency Seriously: The Family and Medical Leave Act Considered in Light of the Social Organization of Dependency Work and Gender Equality

EVA FEDER KITTAY

Contemporary industrialized societies have been confronted with the fact and consequences of women's increased participation in paid employment. Whether this increase has resulted from women's desire for equality or from changing economic circumstances, women and men have been faced with a crisis in the organization of work that concerns dependents, that is, those unable to care for themselves. This is labor that has been largely unpaid, often unrecognized, and yet is indispensable to human society.

Dependents require care. They are unable either to survive or to thrive without attention to basic needs. Dependency needs range from the utter helplessness of a newborn infant to the incapacity of illness or frail old age. Dependency can be protracted (e.g., the extended dependency of early childhood) or brief (e.g., a temporary illness). An individual who is dependent may be able to function otherwise independently if only she is given needed assistance in limited areas, or she may be dependent in every aspect of her being, that is, utterly dependent. At some stage in the lives of each of us we face at least one period of utter dependency; and, with accident and disease forever a danger to the most independent of us, we are all, at least potentially, dependents. In our dependency, we not only require care, but require a sustaining relation with a care-giver who provides this care—for *who* does the caring is often as important as the care itself. These dependencies may be alleviated or aggravated by cultural practices and prejudices, but given the

Hypatia vol. 10, no. 1 (Winter 1995)

immutable facts of human development, disease, and decline, no culture that endures beyond one generation can secure itself against the claims of human dependency. While we are all dependent on some form of care or support, at least minimally, and although dependencies vary in degree, those that involve the survival or thriving of a person cut most deeply through the fiction of a social order presumably constituted by independent equal persons.

For the past two decades, feminists have argued that this fiction is parasitic on a tradition in which women attend to those dependencies. The labor has been seen as part of their familial obligations, obligations that trump all other obligations. Women who have been sufficiently wealthy or of sufficiently high status have sometimes had the option to confer the daily labor of dependency care to others—generally other women, mostly poor and ill-situated. Poor women who have had dependency responsibilities along with paid employment have often relied on female familial help. The gendered and privatized nature of dependency work has meant, first, that men have rarely shared these responsibilities—at least with the women of their own class—and, second, that the equitable distribution of dependency work, both among genders and among classes, has rarely been considered in the discussions of political and social justice which take as their starting point the public lives of men.

As women from many different classes increasingly participate in paid employment, adequate provisions for dependency care—child daycare, care for the elderly, time for family members to care for ill children, and so on—have surfaced as a major social concern. One response has been various kinds of social legislation that provide for leaves for parents with newborn children and for workers with family members who are ill or temporarily disabled. It is no secret that among industrialized nations, the United States, in spite of its early history of equal opportunity employment legislation, is especially primitive in its response to the concerns of dependency work. At long last, in 1993, a national piece of legislation, The Family and Medical Leave Act (FMLA) (Public Law 103-3, February 5, 1993, 107 Stat., 6-29) provides for some parental leave and some leave time to take care of ailing family members. The act is a rare piece of social policy insofar as it recognizes a public responsibility for dependency care.

The standard liberal tradition that policymakers appeal to, most especially in the United States, but to varying degrees in other Western democracies as well, does not acknowledge the claims of dependency. The liberal political philosophy that supplies the idealizations and the utopian visions of which contemporary society is an (albeit poor) approximation have as little to say about dependency as do the policymakers. The result is particularly detrimental to women's aspirations to empowerment and equality. And this despite the pretensions to a gender egalitarianism in the rhetoric of Western democracies and in the presumed gender-blindness of liberal political philosophy.

This neglect suggests that the ability to incorporate dependency concerns serves as a criterion of adequacy for any theory of a just social order that purports to advocate gender equality. John Rawls's egalitarianism will serve as the case study for the adequacy of liberal philosophy in recognizing dependency concerns. Elsewhere I discuss the adequacy of Rawlsian contractual liberalism to dependency concerns in detail (Kittay, N.d.). Here I focus on the notion of social cooperation as a keystone of that theory. The egalitarian ideal informing and informed by the idea of social cooperation leaves no space for dependency concerns because it requires the idea of mutual reciprocity by cooperating members. But such reciprocity cannot always pertain to persons in a relation of dependency, that is, between dependent and care-giver. In order to include the fact of dependency and its impact on those who do dependency work, we are compelled to enlarge the concept of social cooperation to consider a form of social interaction that, without being exploitative or neglectful of the concerns of any party, does not presume equality in power and situation of all parties. In the FMLA, we find elements of the expanded notion of social cooperation I advocate. But it falls short of what the crisis requires, and its limitations can be attributed to its fundamental adherence to the liberal model that is being criticized. The inadequacy of the FMLA reveals the failure of liberal theories to conceptualize social cooperation in such a way that provides women with the gender equality they purport to endorse.

THE DEPENDENCY CRITIQUE OF LIBERAL EGALITARIANISM

Contemporary liberal egalitarians tend to regard gender as a morally irrelevant category and endorse the ideal of sexual equality. Feminists, however, have asked not only what it will take for women to achieve equality but have interrogated liberal understandings of the ideal itself. Some feminists have evoked both women's difference from men and women's differences among themselves.[1] Their *difference critiques* of equality have pointed to the implicit use of men—*more specifically white middle-class men*—as *the* standard against which equality is assessed. These feminists have argued that this norm is unfit for incorporating all whose identity is marked by their gender, race, class, and other socially salient difference.[2] Other feminists, elaborating a *dominance critique*, have underscored the power difference between men and women. Men's entrenched dominance over women means that gender-neutral, equality-based policies either fail to address issues that specifically affect women or merely preserve the relations of dominance that are already in effect.[3] The considerations to which I have alluded in the introductory paragraphs of this essay form still another critique of dominant views of equality. This I call the *dependency* critique.[4] The dependency critique maintains that by construing society as an association of equals, conceived as individuals with equal powers, equally situated in the competition for the benefits of social cooperation, one disregards the inevitable dependencies of the human condition, thereby neglecting the condition both of dependents and those who care for dependents (see Kittay, N.d.).

The dependency critique looks beyond women's socially prescribed differences from and subordination to men by considering the difficulties in assimilating women to the liberal ideal of equality. Its focus is on the circumstances under which the ideal was conceived and, more specifically, on the presumption that inevitable human dependencies and the consequences of such dependency for social organization are outside the political sphere for which the ideal of equality was articulated. Traditional formulations of liberal equality which originated as a challenge to feudalism posited an ideal for male heads of household. The feudalistic dependencies inherent in political hierarchy were targets of liberal thinkers such as Locke and Rousseau. Yet by positing equality for the male heads of households the dependencies of human development and frailty can remain unaddressed, at least as long as the household can accommodate these needs—an accommodation made possible by the privatized labor of women. The dependencies that cannot be banished by fiat are sustained by a social organization that creates a secondary dependence in those who care for dependents. They remain outside the society of equals insofar as they cannot function as the independent and autonomous agents of liberal theory who are presumed to be equally empowered and equally situated to engage in a fair competition for the benefits of social cooperation. For the woman who cares for dependents, the *dependency worker*, is not so situated—not as long as her responsibilities lie with another who cannot survive or thrive without her ministrations. Her attention is directed to another's needs; even her understanding of her own needs are enmeshed with the needs of a vulnerable other whose fundamental well-being is entrusted to her. And yet, within a liberal doctrine of society as a contractual agreement between equals, she should be an autonomous and independent individual. Liberalism constructed an equality for heads of households (wherein dependencies exist within the household and are attended to by women), and then counted the head of household as an *individual* who is independent and who can act on his own behalf. The equality for individuals overlays the equality for household heads, creating the illusion that dependencies do not exist and that the extension of equality to all, not only heads of households, is easily accomplished.

The illusion sustains a fiction that society is composed only of independent individuals who come together to form associations of social cooperation[5] and that an egalitarian notion of justice is served by considering those individuals to be free and equal (that is, self-originating sources of claims) who are equally situated and equally empowered. But social cooperation is required not only by autonomous and independently functioning individuals for the purposes of mutually improving life chances, but first and foremost for the purpose of sustaining those who are not independently functioning, those who are not equally situated, and those who are unable to benefit from an equal empowerment. They are persons who are too young, too ill, too disabled, or too enfeebled by old age to care for themselves and to speak for themselves. These persons are our children, our parents, our siblings, our companions, and, at some points in life, ourselves. In states of dependency, we are unable to discharge the responsibilities and carry the burdens of the *equal* citizen; we have to rely on our caretaker to fulfill our basic needs; and we have no public or political voice except the voice of the dependency worker charged with articulating as well as meeting our needs. These dependencies are part of a network of interdependencies that form the central bonds of human social life. The care and attention to the vulnerabilities of dependent persons on the part of the dependency worker and the trust invested by the dependent in the dependency worker are among the most essential of social interactions.

When the fact of dependency and its social dimensions within the political conception of society is omitted, the secondary dependence of the dependency worker and the contribution of even the most dependent to the fabric of human relations is missed. The dependency worker acquires a dependence on others to supply the resources needed to sustain herself and the dependents who are in her charge. The dependency relation is a cooperative arrangement sustained by these resources, the labor of the dependency worker, and the responsiveness to care on the part of the cared-for.[6] The dependency worker may be unpaid, caring for familial dependents, or paid, caring for dependents in an institutional or home setting. Whether her work is done for pay or as a familial obligation,[7] the dependency worker attends to and voices the needs and desires of her charge in addition to, and sometimes at the expense of, her own; she assumes the same responsibilities other citizens have to each other and to themselves and assumes the added responsibility on behalf of one who cannot meet these responsibilities alone. In the distribution of burdens and benefits, most liberal egalitarian theories count each person as one. The incapacity of the dependent—to sustain her share of burdens and claim her share of benefits—and the obligation of the dependency worker—to assume the burdens of more than one and, at times, to put the benefits to her charge ahead of her own—ill-suits an economy of social cooperation presumed for an association of equals: that each will equally assume a share of the burdens and each will claim her own share of benefits. That women historically and customarily assume the role of dependency worker means that such an account of equality leaves out many women who retain their role and status as dependency workers. Because a redistribution of dependency work has too often exploited the situation of poor women, the dependency critique provides a framework for investigating theories and policies of equality across race and class as well as gender, and looks toward a more adequate understanding of gender equality.

PRESUPPOSITIONS OF RAWLSIAN EQUALITY

Rawls identifies society "as a fair system of social cooperation" and looks for "principles specifying the basic rights and liberties and the forms of equality most appropriate to those cooperating, once they are regarded as citizens, as free and equal persons" (Rawls 1993, 27).

Free and equal persons come together in the initial situation to choose principles of justice they can accept when they do not know their own status in life, their own conception of the good, their own particular dispositions and psychological propensities, and to what generation they belong. In *Political Liberalism* Rawls again characterizes the modeling of the equality of citizens: "To model this equality in the original position we say that the parties, as representatives of those who meet the condition, are symmetrically situated. This requirement is fair because in establishing fair terms of social cooperation (in the case of the basic structure) the only relevant feature of persons is their possessing the moral powers . . . and their having the normal capacities to be a cooperating member of society over the course of a lifetime" (Rawls 1993, 79). He speaks of the "representation for equality" as "an easy matter" of situating the parties to the original position symmetrically to one another and describing them identically. And yet in this easy and seemingly transparent move, so much is presumed.

First, *all* citizens are idealized as "fully cooperating members of society *over the course of a complete life*" (Rawls 1980, 546; emphasis mine). Rawls continues, "The idealization means that everyone has sufficient intellectual powers to play a *normal* part in society, and no one suffers from *unusual* needs that are *especially difficult* to fulfill, for example *unusual and costly medical requirements*" (1980, 546; emphasis mine).[8] The theory is constructed for the "normal" situation and only afterwards made to accommodate *unusual* circumstances. But if the normal situation is not that of a fully functioning person who is a cooperating member throughout his or her lifetime, if we are instead all potential dependents and the "unusual" needs are an inevitable feature of any human community, and if these needs demand dependency workers constrained in the degree of their full cooperation as *independent* citizens, then the idealization does not merely grease the wheels of the Rawlsian construction but renders it of questionable value in providing a theory that will deliver justice for dependents and dependency workers.

Second, the symmetry that Rawls posits for the representatives in original position is bound to a notion of persons as *free* and equal. For a person to be free means here, in part, to view oneself as a "self-originating" or "self-authenticating source of valid claims." But can the dependency worker be seen as "a self-originating source of valid claims"? She is as likely to put forward the claims of her charge as she is to put forward her own. Furthermore, there is often no clear separation between claims that she makes on her own behalf and those that originate with the charge—even though the conflict between these sets of claims can sometimes be palpable. If there is an important notion of freedom for the dependency worker, it is often one that recognizes the bond she shares with her dependent, even as it recognizes her own independent personhood.

Third, equality requires a measure. In Rawls's theory the comparative measure of interpersonal well-being is the index of primary goods, a list of goods that all persons require if they are to be able to realize their own conception of the good, given the moral powers that we have as free and equal persons. Rawls's moral powers do not include the responsiveness to vulnerability needed for care; nor do they include the good of being cared for when we become dependent or having the support we require to care for another if another becomes dependent on us. Consequently, the centrality of dependency in human life, and the concomitant value of human relationship and care in a relationship are absent from the list of primary goods.

Fourth, Rawls, building on Hume, identifies the "circumstances of justice." These are the circumstances under which the constitution of a society of free and equal persons who cooperate in the benefit and the burdens of social organization takes place. Missing from these is the circumstance of human development that incurs a period of dependency for each of us, a period during which we are unequally situated relative to those who are independent.[9]

Last, a sense of justice depends on an acceptance of a conception of social cooperation. Rawls writes of "the equally sufficient capacity (which I assume to be realized) to understand and to act from *the public conception of social cooperation*" (Rawls 1980, 546; emphasis mine). It is this notion of social cooperation that I explore here.

THE RAWLSIAN CONCEPTION OF SOCIAL COOPERATION

Social cooperation, writes Rawls, involves "fair terms of cooperation," not "simply . . . coordinated social activity efficiently organized and guided by publicly recognized rules to achieve some overall end" (1993, 300). That is, along with coordinated self-interested activity—what Rawls calls the *rational*—social cooperation demands a sense of what is fair—what Rawls calls the *reasonable*.

If they are both rational and reasonable, dependency concerns ought to be included within the features of a well-ordered society reflected in the public conception of social cooperation. To insist that it is reasonable to expect that the social order consider the care of dependents follows directly from the observation that any society into which we are born and expect to live out our lives contains those who are dependent and thus unable to realize any of their moral capacities—much less survive or thrive—independently. Only if a human society exists under especially hard conditions would we exempt its members from the moral responsibility to care for its dependents. Thus it is reasonable to expect that a well-ordered society is one that attends to the needs of dependents and whatever else that necessitates.

Furthermore, we can argue for the rationality of each individual—acting in their own self-interest—to choose principles that would include such concerns among the terms of social cooperation, for given the developmental nature and the fragility of human life, it is likely that dependency will touch each of our lives in some form. Whether we find ourselves dependent or needing to care for a dependent, it is rational to suppose that we would wish to be cared for or to be provided the resources by which we can provide care.

Although the inclusion of dependency concerns within a conception of social cooperation is both reasonable and rational, the mention of such are not to be found. The acknowledgment of "*normal* health care" (1993, 21; emphasis mine), covers some dependency concerns, but leaves out the daily care of infants and young children—which are not *health* care—and prolonged illness or states of diminished independence (e.g., a handicapping condition), which arguably are not conventionally understood as "normal" health care.

Rawls has many times acknowledged limits to his theory and expressed hopes that the theory could be extended, but the omission of dependency concerns is a result of the characterization of social cooperation—a characterization which it is the goal of this essay to identify and dispute. "Fair terms of cooperation," according to this view, articulates "an idea of reciprocity and mutuality: all who cooperate must benefit, or share in common burdens, in some appropriate fashion judged by a suitable benchmark of comparison" (Rawls 1993, 300). The point is made still sharper when Rawls writes, "Those who can take part in social cooperation over a complete life, and who are willing to honor the appropriate fair terms of agreement are regarded as equal citizens" (1993, 302).

But this understanding of social cooperation leaves out many persons. The second quotation cited in the preceding paragraph even suggests that Rawls does not extend *citizenship* to those who are permanently and so sufficiently incapacitated that they cannot be expected to restrict their freedoms in relevant ways[10] or to participate and so reciprocate in relevant ways. But why should the contingent fact that someone is born, let us say, sufficiently mentally disabled necessitate his or her exclusion from citizenship? There are some political activities the mentally disabled may not be able to engage in—for example, they may be incapable of enough political understanding to vote—but surely they need to receive the protections of political justice all the same.[11] The temporarily dependent can defer reciprocating until the individual regains full capability. But during our period of dependency we cannot reciprocate. Those who restrict their liberty, or use their labor, resources, or energy on our behalf cannot be repaid by us as long as we remain dependent. We may or may not be able to reciprocate at some future time, but the labor expended on our behalf cannot be so expended on the condition that we will reciprocate: a child may not reach maturity; an ill person may die; a now needy and elderly parent may not have been an adequate provider or nurturer. Who then is to reciprocate the efforts of the caretaker?[12] Unless the needs of their caretakers are to be met in some other form of reciprocity, the only available moral characterizations of the caretaker's function is as exploitation or supererogation. When we consider relations of dependency, we see that they are not characterized as social cooperation according to fair terms of cooperation, and those whose social relations are defined by the dependency relation then fall outside the bounds of social cooperation as understood by Rawls's characterization.

Relations of dependency may be excluded from the discussion either because (1) they are not appropriately characterized as pertaining to *political* justice or (2) they pertain to political justice but not to a theory that holds that justice is fairness.[13] Is it then appropriate to exclude the dependent and the dependency worker from a fully adequate conception of social cooperation? First, if political justice is to express the principles of a well-ordered society, then it seems that dependency concerns do fall within the scope of political justice. A society that does not care for its dependents or that cares for them only by unfairly exploiting the labor of some cannot be said to be well-ordered any more than a society that enslaves part of its population. I cannot see how any thoughtful reflection would yield an opposing insight. Second, if the "fair terms of cooperation" are identified as the reasonable and the rational, then I have already shown that it is both reasonable and rational to consider dependency matters in formulating principles of justice for a well-ordered society. Furthermore, if we reorient our political insights so that we see the centrality of human relationship to our happiness and well-being, and we recognize dependency relations as foundational human relations, then it becomes obvious that such concerns are among the basic motivations for creating a social order, and that a just social order must concern itself with what fairness requires for both dependents—who, even in their neediness, contribute to the ongoing nature of human relationships—and the one who cares for dependents—whose social contribution is invisible when dependency is thought to be outside the social order. If our reflective judgments confirm that those who are dependent (whether temporarily or permanently) ought to be appropriately cared for, and if those reflections focus on the importance of the central human bonds that form around dependency needs, then a society is well-ordered only if it offers adequate support to dependents and those who care for them in relations of dependency.[14]

SOCIAL COOPERATION AS *DOULIA*

If fairness obtains only for those who are themselves fully functioning, have normal capacities, and are in social interactions with others who are similarly endowed, then even if we insist that dependency concerns have a political dimension, justice as fairness will not pertain to dependency concerns. This idea of fairness and social cooperation is grounded on a notion of reciprocity alien to those in dependency relations. But if social cooperation can be seen to involve a second sort of interaction (similar to, but distinct from, the reciprocal interaction among those equally situated and equally empowered), then there is a way we can expand the conception of justice as fairness. Cooperation between persons where intergenerational needs are to be met will illustrate the point. When we consider the Family and Medical Leave Act, we see how it incorporates, to a limited degree, an expanded notion of reciprocity and social cooperation.

Families in modern industrial and urbanized societies are often not grounded in a community and often live far from other family members. Periods in which some family members are stressed by special dependency cares are particularly difficult. These are the stressful times that the FMLA is meant to alleviate. The situation of the postpartum mother who is caring for her newborn is especially interesting. Her need is most acute directly after childbirth when her infant is utterly dependent and her own body requires healing and rest—even for the production of her infant's food. Traditional societies sometimes mark this period as a time when the mother is entitled to special privileges and care. Contemporary mothers in the United States have had to make do with very inadequate provisions. At least until the enactment of FMLA (which as we will see only applies to some, not all, workers), the father (if present) has rarely been released from his employment, regardless of employment status; the mother is often pressured to return to paid employment as soon as possible, a situation alleviated but not fully remedied by FMLA; friends and relatives, whose assistance is not an option in FMLA, since it defines family narrowly, are rarely available to help and less so since so many women are now in the paid work force; and paid help, for those who can afford help, is the "baby nurse." Generally, however, it is not the baby who needs a nurse; the recuperating mother is normally capable of caring for the baby only if someone helps her take care of herself and her other duties. Adapting a strategy found in a number of traditional cultures, some have instituted a form of caretaking whereby the postpartum mother is assigned a postpartum care-giver, a *doula*, who assists the mother, and at times relieves her.[15] *Doula* originally meant slave or servant in Greek, but it is appropriated here to mean a person who renders a service to another who renders service to a dependent. A doula is not provided for in the FMLA, nor am I arguing here that it be provided. But I want to reflect on the principle embodied in the person of the doula and in the practice which we will call *doulia*.[16]

Let us extend the idea of a doula beyond one who provides a service to the postpartum mother, so that it describes those who attend to the needs of those who attend to another who is utterly dependent upon them (whether temporarily or permanently). In so doing we displace both the relation of servant and served and the traditional relation of reciprocity among equals as models of cooperative activity and put at the center a relation of *nested dependencies*. These nested dependencies link those who help and those who require help to give aid to ones who cannot help themselves. Extending the notion of the service performed by the doula, let us speak of "doulia" to indicate a concept by which service is rendered to those who become needy by virtue of attending to those in need, so that all can be well cared for.[17] The form of social cooperation that emerges from the relation between the doula, the mother, and the infant is captured by the colloquial phrase "What goes round comes round" when it is used to describe a form of cooperation often engaged in by members of poorer communities:[18] I, as a member of the community, help another who requires my help, with the expectation that someone in the community, not necessarily the individual whom I helped, will come to my aid if and when that is required.

This notion of social cooperation is not as far from the Rawlsian project as it may at first seem. Rawls understands that society is an association that persists through generations and that our efforts to pass the world on to the next generation without depleting its resources—a responsibility entailed by the "just savings principle"—is not reciprocated to us by those we benefit. The "chronological unfairness" to which Rawls refers resembles the cooperative idea embodied in doulia. And indeed, both the savings principle and doulia are consequences of the facts of human development and generation: as the benefit of the previous generation passes through us to the next and so on, the care a mother bestows on her child calls not only for reciprocation from the adult child but also for the grown children to care appropriately for a future generation.[19]

But how, one might ask, does this private interaction of mother, infant, and doula translate into a public conception of social cooperation? For this we need a public conception of doulia. To urge that the well-being of dependents *and* their caretakers *and* the relation itself between caretaker and dependent must be seen as requirements of public understanding of social cooperation, I invoke the fact that dependency is inherent to the human condition, that it often marks our most profound attachments, that care of a dependent morally obliges the dependency worker to give a certain priority to the welfare of her charge, and that the constitution of dependency relations is such that the parties are of necessity unequal. That is, it is the responsibility of the public order to ensure that a dependent has a caretaker, that the dependency relation is respected, and that the caretaker is adequately provided for so that her dependency work does not in turn deplete her. Without a broadened conception of reciprocity and a suitably modified sense of fairness, the dependency worker and dependent cannot be embraced within the bonds of social cooperation and accorded their full moral worth as equals in a well-ordered society.

In the next section, I argue that to the extent that the FMLA recognizes the dependency responsibilities of those engaged in paid employment and accepts a public responsibility to assure that those in a relation of dependency have adequate care and can give adequate care, it identifies social cooperation in the enlarged sense of doulia. Where it restricts leave time and opportunities, and where it limits resources allocated to those in relations of dependency, it reverts to the traditional liberal model.

Reading the Family and Medical Leave Act of 1993

The FMLA is, in many ways, emblematic of the sort of legislation and social policy that is required to meet dependency needs of paid workers. It permits up to twelve workweeks of unpaid leave within any twelve-month period for one or more of the following reasons:

> (A) Because of the birth of a son or daughter of the employee and in order to care for such son or daughter.
> (B) Because of the placement of a son or daughter with the employee for adoption or foster care.
> (C) In order to care for the spouse, or son, daughter, or parent of the employee, if such spouse, son, daughter, or parent has a serious health condition.
> (D) Because of a serious health condition that makes the employee unable to perform the functions of the position of such employee. (Public Law 103-3—Feb. 5, 1993, 107 Stat. 9)

This law expressly recognizes the dependency relations that I have argued are so grievously ignored in much political theory. And it recognizes the importance of acknowledging some of the demands of dependency not only of the employee herself, but those of the individuals who depend on her. Given that the United States has had no provisions set by law to address the needs of paid employees with such concerns, the Family and Medical Leave Act is an immensely important piece of legislation.

But the law is relatively limited in its scope and in the real benefits it provides, and so its contribution to fair equality for all is circumscribed. I suggest that the limitations are traceable to an ideology of reciprocity and equality that continues to push dependency concerns back into the domain of the private, that is, to a conception of dependency concerns which still fails to recognize the extent to which addressing these needs is a matter of the social cooperation required for a well-ordered and just society.

Among the limitations of the act are the following: leave is unpaid; employers with less than fifty employees are exempt from the FMLA; and the FMLA construes family in relatively traditional terms. Let us look at the "Findings and Purposes" of the FMLA, and then return to consider if these bear on the limitations of the act.

(a) FINDINGS.—Congress finds that—

> (1) the number of single-parent households and two-parent households in which the single parent or both parents work is increasing significantly;
> (2) it is important for the development of children and the family unit that fathers and mothers be able to participate in early childrearing and the care of family members who have serious health conditions;
> (3) the lack of employment policies to accommodate working parents can force individuals to choose between job security and parenting;
> (4) there is inadequate job security for employees who have serious health conditions that prevent them from working for temporary periods;
> (5) due to the nature of the roles of men and women in our society, the primary responsibility for family caretaking often falls on women, and such responsibility affects the working lives of women more than it affects the working lives of men; and
> (6) employment standards that apply to one gender only have serious potential for encouraging employers to discriminate against employees and applicants for employment who are that gender. (Public Law 103-3, 107 Stat. 6-7)

First among the findings is that the number of single-parent households and two-parent households in which the parent(s) all work has significantly increased. The fact that this counts as a finding for a bill such as the FMLA is indicative of the way in which the breakdown of the sexual division of labor on the male side of the divide—expanding the paid labor force to include more women—is putting pressure on de-genderizing the female side of the divide—the largely private and unpaid care for dependents. This is the first significant step in understanding that dependency concerns need to be a part of the public understanding of social cooperation: that decisions to undertake dependency care cannot remain matters of private decision making with only private consequences, but belong within the public arena.

The second finding serves to recognize the nonfungibility of many dependency relations—e. g., the need of a sick child to have a parent attending her—but also moves retrogressively in the direction of the privatization of dependency care by suggesting that the importance of early child rearing and care of family members who have serious health conditions is for "the development of children and the family unit" rather than for the general welfare of the nation and so a public feature of social cooperation.

The third finding points to the need for policies that avoid pitting job security against parenting demands. Both job security and parenting are regarded as matters that are important for the well-being of individuals. The law recognizes the importance of the state in assuring both goods to those individuals who may be torn between competing concerns, and so it establishes a responsibility of public institutions to assure that individuals can fulfill dependency responsibilities as well as job-related duties, and that the burden of dependency work must sit not solely on the shoulders of those who undertake these obligations.[20] But how far does it go? Not very far. The leave is unpaid and the exemption for employers of fewer than fifty persons is not insignificant. There is no acknowledgment of public responsibility to assure job security, given parental responsibility for children. Why should parenting responsibilities be privileged with respect to job security? The basis for securing such a privileged relation is tenuous indeed, as the law's limited scope indicates.

It is here that a public conception of doulia needs to be brought into play—the reciprocity of doulia. More than "accommodation" is required. Accommodation presumes the situation of employment as it is now; accommodation neither challenges concepts of what counts as part of the economy nor employment conditions that presume privatized dependency arrangements. To acknowledge the contribution of those engaged in dependency work to the larger society—the contribution to the continuity, stability, and resources of society—means that the larger society has an obligation to support dependency work. Supporting dependency work means relieving the dependency worker of some of the costs and burdens of responsibility for the care of dependents. The argument from a public conception of doulia is that *fairness* demands that business or government—whatever public institutions are appropriate—carry some of the costs of dependency work so that dependents within our society can be properly cared for without exploiting dependency workers.

The fourth finding, which addresses the inadequate job security for workers with serious or prolonged health conditions, is an acknowledgment of the vulnerability to dependency that is shared by all employees.

The fifth and sixth findings are of special interest, for they acknowledge the inequity that results from the gender-specific nature of much dependency work. That work has occupied the female side of the sexual division of labor. The fifth and sixth findings call our attention to the failure of efforts to bring about gender equality on the side of the sexual division of labor traditionally occupied by men when the labor on the other side of the divide—the side traditionally occupied by women (see Hadfield 1993) remains the sole, and unsupported, responsibility of women. The justification for the bill that can be garnered from findings five and six is an equality argument, an inference sustained by the fourth and fifth stated purposes of the bill (see below). But until we reconstrue equality and political conceptions such as justice and social cooperation, and until it becomes a public priority to refashion sensibilities accordingly, the FMLA cannot alter the gender-structured nature of dependency concerns nor can it move us sufficiently in the direction of understanding that dependency work cannot be privatized and genderized without violating justice and equality.

Now let us now look at the "Purposes" of the act. I reproduce these in full: (b) PURPOSES.—It is the purpose of this Act—

> (1) to balance the demands of the workplace with the needs of families, to promote the stability and economic security of families, and to promote national interests in preserving family integrity;
> (2) to entitle employees to take reasonable leave for medical reasons, for the birth or adoption of a child, and for the care of a child, spouse, or parent who has a serious health condition;
> (3) to accomplish the purposes described in paragraphs (1) and (2) in a manner that accommodates the legitimate interests of employers;
> (4) to accomplish the purposes described in paragraphs (1) and (2) in a manner that, consistent with the Equal Protection Clause of the Fourteenth Amendment, minimizes the potential for employment discrimination on the basis of sex by ensuring generally that leave is available for eligible medical reasons (including maternity-related disability) and for compelling family reasons, on a gender-neutral basis; and
> (5) to promote the goal of equal employment opportunity for women and men, pursuant to such clause. (Public Law 103-3, 107 Stat. 6-7)

The purposes of this act recognize "national interests in preserving family integrity." But the act does not identify what about family integrity is important for the national interest, and so it cannot count anything but a limited set of traditional structures as family. The purpose stated in (3) is to "accomplish the purposes described in (1) and (2) in a manner that accommodates the legitimate interests of employers." But if there are national interests in preserving family integrity, why should (1) and (2) not trump the interests of employers? And if they don't, what are the consequences?

In the light of the reading of the "Findings and Purposes," let us consider what I have listed as the limitations of the act. First, the leave is unpaid—all twelve weeks of permissible leave time are unpaid. To take off from work to attend a sick child then remains a luxury, or a factor moving one closer to impoverishment. Not only is the United States one of the last industrialized countries to have a family leave policy, it is also the only one in which the leave is entirely unpaid.[21] One of the purported findings to which the act is addressed is the increase in the number of single-parent households. But how many single-parent employees can afford to be without pay for three months of the year? How are they supposed to put food on the table of a sick and needy person? One need not argue that the full twelve weeks ought to be paid, but surely some of that time needs to be paid leave—by law, not merely by the goodwill of some employers who provide paid leave—if it is to have a substantial impact on the practices of single-parent households—which now constitute one-fourth of all households.[22]

Second, employers with fewer than fifty employees are exempt from the family leave policy. But employees in companies with fewer than fifty employees make up a very large portion of the American work force. In fact, they make up the *majority* of the work force.[23] That means that a majority of paid employees in this country are not covered under the FMLA! What is clear, again, is that heeding dependency concerns is not viewed as a general responsibility. These can be trumped by the employers' needs—benefits for whom are not only thought to be personal but also to be part of the economic well-being of the wider public—and nothing is put in place to meet the putatively *personal* demands of the employee, even when family integrity is identified as a "national interest." Dependency care is not counted as part of the economic structure; it does not figure into the Gross National Product.

Third, the FMLA construes family in relatively traditional terms. Although *parent* includes not only biological parents but also any individuals who have stood in *loco parentis*, and the term *son or daughter* is defined as "a biological, adopted, or foster child, a stepchild, a legal ward, or a child of a parent standing in loco parentis," the term "spouse" is restricted to husband or wife, leaving out nonmarried adults who are cohabitating, gay and lesbian families, extended families, and so forth. Contrast this with the "nurturance leave" proposed by feminist legal theorist Nadine Taub (1984, 85), which argues for nurturance leaves for any adult members of a household. If the stress in our policies is to support dependency relations because the fabric of social structure is founded on the maintenance of such relations, then the relations themselves and not the social institutions in which they have traditionally been lodged ought to become the focus of our concern.

The decisions or situations from which these dependency relations result may appear to be private decisions between the parties involved—decisions between parties which do not devolve obligations on third parties. But there are some social institutions which appear to be formed by private decisions between the parties involved and which nonetheless induce obligations in third parties.[24] Marriage is such an institution. The private decision another and I make to be a married couple means that socially and legally certain actions are binding on my employer, my landlord, hospitals, insurance agencies, the IRS, and so on. In an analogous fashion, the private decision to take on the work of dependency and to form a dependency relation with a charge ought to induce third party obligations to support the dependency worker in his or her care for the charge. In the case of marriage, the binding obligations are part of a larger societal interest in maintaining the institution of marriage. Recognition of its legal and social status means that the existence of a connection between two individuals is acknowledged.

A major reason, however, to recognize such institutions is that they are the loci of the care and sustenance of dependents. The relation of dependency is morally and socially still more salient and fundamental than marriage, and so forms the very ground of this feature of the marriage relation. But the social technology of traditional marriage and family makes the dependency worker and charge within the nuclear family vulnerable to the vicissitudes of the marriage arrangement and vulnerable in a relation of (to use Amartya Sen's term) "cooperative conflict."[25] The claim on third parties to support and help sustain the dependency relation, independent of a particular arrangement such as marriage, has morally the stronger claim. This claim is realized in the public obligation of social cooperation I have called *doulia.* The argument for such doulia transcends the institution of marriage as traditionally understood and family arrangements sanctioned by traditional marriage and biological relation. Its basis is the undertaking of care, and responsibility for care, and the dependency to which the caretaker then becomes vulnerable.

The FMLA is an example of the legislative and policy directions in which the dependency critique urges us, but it remains still all too firmly grounded in a conception of society primarily constituted by those who are healthy, autonomous adults, who, as Rawls would have it, are "fully functioning" and for whom justice requires the reciprocity of those equally situated. We need to shift our vision and see society as constituted by the nested dependencies that require a concept of justice between persons who are equal in their connectedness but unequal in their vulnerability and for whom a notion of doulia—of caring for those who care—is central.

The arguments in this essay have been directed at demonstrating that the Rawlsian and the liberal account of social cooperation is at best incomplete and at worst inadequate, and that legislation such as the FMLA falls short of meeting the needs of dependency demands as long as it remains within a framework which is represented in the Rawlsian account. The claim here is that a society cannot be well-ordered, that is, it cannot be one in which all its members are sustained and included within the ideal of equality, if it fails to be a society characterized by care. For a society to be characterized by care, we need something other than the affirmation of the importance of family integrity. We need structures that will assure that dependency work, whether done in families or other social institutions, can be carried out under non-exploitative conditions. What is required is that the public understanding of social cooperation include respect for the importance of caring for one another and the value of receiving care and giving care. It then becomes a matter of political justice for basic institutions to *make provisions for and facilitate satisfactory dependency relations*. The only assurance that both dependents and dependency workers are well cared for and can benefit from an egalitarian ideal is the inclusion of enabling conditions and resources for care through the social institutions that reflect the public understanding of social cooperation. For a well-ordered society, therefore, to instill in its citizens a sense of justice and a sense of what is right, it must also be sensitive to our vulnerability to dependency and to the vulnerability of those who attend to dependents.[26] Rawls speaks of the need to give priority to the basic liberties and points out that even when the political will does not yet exist to do what is required (as it does not in the society in which we live), "part of the political task is to help fashion it" (1993, 297). The possibilities of the FMLA and its shortcomings indicate that it is no less the case that since the political will to imbue citizens with such a sensitivity and sense of priority for care does not yet exist, "part of the political task is to help fashion it."

NOTES

I thank the editors of this special issue and the anonymous reviewers for their suggestions. I also thank Lisa Conradi for her comments at the Conference on Feminism and Social Policy, the audience at the session for their remarks, and members of the New York City Society for Women in Philosophy Research Group in Ethical, Social and Political Philosophy for their helpful discussion of an earlier draft.

1. The literature is extensive. I mention but a few discussions of difference feminists. See Allen (1987); hooks (1987); Kay (1985); Littleton (1987); Minow (1990); Scales-Trent (1989); West (1987); Williams (1982, 1985); Wolgast (1980).

2. bell hooks (1987) asks, "Since men are not equals in white supremacist, capitalist, patriarchical class structure, which men do women want to be equal to?" The point stressed by a number of feminists and captured by hooks is that the striving for equality on the part of the largely white and middle-class women's movement presumes an egalitarianism into which women can integrate themselves. In Kittay (N.d.), I call this the "heterogeneity critique." It speaks to a heterogeneity among women not acknowledged in demands for sexual equality. Because the heterogeneity critique is aimed less at any particular formulation of equality than at a prevailing formulation of sex equality which masks intragender inequalities, inequalities that result from race, class, sexual orientation, age, and disabilities, as well cross-gender inequalities, it is orthogonal to the other critiques. The force of the heterogeneity critiques emerges with special poignancy when one looks at the racial complexion of dependency workers in countries blighted by racial inequity.

3. Catharine MacKinnon is the main exponent of this view (1987, 1989).

4. Several feminist theorists have regarded the work of liberal political philosophers with an eye toward issues of dependency without articulating the dependency critique. Those who have done so have spoken of "the need for more than justice," as Baier (1987) entitles one work expounding this theme (see also Baier 1985, 1986). Others, such as

Patemen (1988) and Held (1987a, 1987b) have shed light on the unacknowledged gender considerations that undergird a social contract engaged in by men. The work of Okin (1979, 1989a, 1989b) brings the historical and contemporary neglect of women's involvement in dependency to the forefront of her political considerations. Okin has been the most articulate, yet sympathetic critic of the influential political theory of John Rawls on matters that concern familial dependency relations. Tronto's (1993) work bringing the notion of care into the arena of political theory may also be seen to be a contribution to the dependency critique.

5. See Young (N.d.) for an interesting discussion of a false ideal of independence in understanding citizenship.

6. Tronto (1993) points out that caring is an activity that requires several stages for its completion: caring about, caring for, response to care. We may note that the person cared for need be only potentially responsive in order for her to be a part of a dependency relation.

7. I thank John Baker for suggesting that I make explicit my view that the dependency critique is meant to hold for dependency workers whether they voluntarily take on that task or whether they are perforce burdened with it.

8. Rawls repeats a similar statement in *Political Liberalism*: "The normal range is specified as follows: since the fundamental problem of justice concerns the relations among those who are full and active participants in society, and directly or indirectly associated together over the course of a whole life, it is reasonable to *assume that everyone has physical needs and psychological capacities within some normal range*. *Thus the problem of special health care and how to treat mentally defective are set*. If we can work out a viable theory for the normal range, we can attempt to handle these other cases later" (Rawls 1993, 272 n. 10; emphasis is mine).

9. Each of the above points, as well as a discussion of social cooperation are elaborated in Kittay (unpublished).

10. In *A Theory of Justice*, Rawls writes: "The main idea is that when a number of persons engage in a mutually advantageous cooperative venture according to rules, and thus restrict their liberty in ways necessary to yield advantages for all, those who have submitted to the restrictions have a right to a similar acquiescence on the part of those who have benefitted from their submission" (Rawls 1971, 112).

11. I thank Susan Okin for valuable discussion on this point.

12. It needs to be pointed out that the paid dependency worker is often paid not by the dependent, but by someone who stands in a relation of guardianship or stewardship to the dependent.

13. "How deep a fault this is must wait until the case itself can be examined," says Rawls and reminds us that political justice needs to be complemented by additional virtues (1993, 21).

14. When we look back to *A Theory of Justice*, we see that for Rawls the problem appears to be how to have strangers cooperate. Friends and intimate associates, so the supposition goes, cooperate because they have ties of sentiment. But consider, when a mother acts toward a child through ties of sentiment, many of her own needs—often including the need to earn an income—go unattended unless she has intimate ties to someone who is willing to cooperate and attend her needs. That is, her ties of sentiment provide little in the way of societal cooperative efforts that suffice to sustain her and her children. (Furthermore, the assumption that the mother's cooperative behavior toward her children are motivated by parental ties of sentiment makes a puzzle of the apparent frequency with which men so often feel less obligated by ties of sentiment to provide for

their children when no longer involved with the mother—U.S. fathers currently owe mothers $24 billion in unpaid child support, according to the *Report of the Federal Office of Child Support Enforcement [1990]*). It is just such a precarious dependence on ties of sentiment on the part of those (women mostly) who do dependency work, especially when it is unpaid—that leave them (again, women for the most part) so vulnerable to exploitation, (male) domination, and poverty. It is such precariousness that makes her inclusion in the political sphere so tentative.

15. See Aronow (1993). One of the doulas "recalls arriving at home late morning to find mothers who haven't eaten or dressed. 'They are so concerned that the baby is O.K., they forget to take care of themselves' " (Aronow 1993, 8).

16. I wish to thank Elfie Raymond for helping me search for a term to capture the concept articulated here.

17. See Stacks (1974) for a discussion of this ethic in the African American community. What Stacks describes as "swapping" is more like a one-to-one reciprocal arrangement than what I am trying to characterize by *doulia*. However, it resembles *doulia* insofar as reciprocity is deferred and is geared to the meeting of needs as they arise rather than as payment qua tit-for-tat exchanges.

18. This is a phrase Rawls borrows from Alexander Herzen. See Rawls (1971, 291).

19. I do not mean to suggest that we have a duty to *have* children because we have been cared for, but that we owe to any children we may have a quality of care at least as high as the care we received. And furthermore that the care bestowed on us is, in fact *reciprocated*, through care to the next generation.

20. That burden can be measured, in part, in economic terms. Estimates of the costs to workers of not having a parental leave only are $607 million versus approximately $110 million as based on the more generous leave policies of earlier versions of the act (Spalter-Roth and Hartmann 1990, 42). The cost is greatest to those least able to bear these costs, namely workers with the lowest incomes, with African American men doing worse than white men, white women doing worse than white men, and African American women doing worse than white women (Spalter-Roth and Hartmann 1990, 2833). See Spalter-Roth and Hartmann (1990) for a detailed analysis. It is curious that in speaking of the cost of meeting dependency needs, the cost to businesses is a seen as a public concern, while the cost to the workers who bear the major burden is regarded a private concern.

21. Ellen Gilensky, Families and Work Institute, personal communication with author, New York City, 1 August 1994.

22. On the morning of the day I was to read this paper at the Feminist Theory and Social Policy Conference held at the University of Pittsburgh, the public radio station announced on its news program that in Pittsburgh the figure was one-third of all households.

23. Only 44 percent of women workers and 52 percent of men workers are covered by the current act which exempts employers with fewer than fifty employees (see Spalter-Roth and Hartmann 1990, 44).

24. This idea can be found in Kaplan (1993).

25. Sen (1990) has argued this point with respect to certain third world countries. Borrowing from the work of Okin (1989) and others, I extend Sen's argument to apply to traditional marriage within the industrialized world as well (Kittay N.d.).

26. See Goodin (1985) for a very useful discussion of our obligations to protect those who are vulnerable.

REFERENCES

Allen, Anita L. 1987. Taking liberties: Privacy, private choice, and social contract theory. *University of Cincinnati Law Review* 56(1-2).

Aronow, Ina. 1993. Doulas step in when mothers need a hand. *New York Times*, 1 August, 1, 8, Westchester Weekly.

Baier, Annette. 1985. Caring about caring. In *Postures of the mind: Essays on mind and morals*. Minneapolis: University of Minnesota Press.

———. 1986. Trust and antitrust. *Ethics* 96: 231-60.

———. 1987. The need for more than justice. In *Science, morality and feminist theory*, ed. Marsha Hanen and Kai Nielsen. Calgary: University of Calgary Press.

Daniels, Norman. 1990. Equality of what: Welfare, resources, or capabilities? *Philosophy and Phenomenological Research Supplement* 50: 273-96.

Goodin, Robert. 1985. *Protecting the vulnerable*. Chicago: University of Chicago Press.

Hadfield, Gillian K. 1993. Households at work: Beyond labor market policies to remedy the gender gap. *Georgetown Law Journal* 82: 89.

Held, Virginia. 1978. Men, women, and equal liberty. In *Equality and social policy*, ed. Walter Feinberg. Urbana: University of Illinois Press.

———. 1987a. Non-contractual society: A feminist view. *Canadian Journal of Philosophy* 13: 111-37.

———. 1987b. Feminism and moral theory. In *Women and moral theory*. See Kittay and Meyers 1987.

hooks, bell. 1987. Feminism: A movement to end sexist oppression. In *Equality and feminism*, ed. Anne Phillips. New York: New York University Press.

Jaggar, Alison M. 1985. Women: Different but equal? Douglass College, Rutgers University.

Kaplan, Morris. 1993. Intimacy and equality: The question of lesbian and gay marriage. Paper delivered at the Stony Brook Philosophy Colloquium Series, 4 March.

Kay, Herma Hill. 1985. Equality and difference: The case of pregnancy. *Berkeley Women's Law Journal* 1.

Kittay, Eva Feder. N.d. *Equality and the inclusion of women*. New York: Routledge. Forthcoming.

———. Unpublished. Equality, Rawls and the dependency critique.

Kittay, Eva F. and Diana T. Meyers. 1987. *Women and moral theory*. Totowa, NJ: Rowman and Littlefield.

Littleton, Christine A. 1987. Equality across difference: A place for rights discourse? *Wisconsin Women's Law Journal* 3: 189-212.

MacKinnon, Catharine A. 1987. *Feminism unmodified: Discourses on life and law*. Cambridge: Harvard University Press.

———. 1989. *Toward a feminist theory of the state*. Cambridge: Harvard University Press.

Minow, Martha. 1990. *Making all the difference: Inclusion, exclusion and the American law*. Ithaca: Cornell University Press.

Okin, Susan. 1979. *Women in western political thought*. Princeton: Princeton University Press.

———. 1989a. *Justice, gender, and the family*. New York: Basic Books.

———. 1989b. Humanist liberalism. In *Liberalism and the moral life*, ed. Nancy L. Rosenbaum. Cambridge: Harvard University Press.

Pateman, Carol. 1988. *The sexual contract*. Stanford: Stanford University Press.

Public Law 103-3, 5 February 1993, 107 Stat., pp. 6-29.

Rawls, John. 1971. *A theory of justice*. Cambridge: Harvard University Press.

———. 1980. Kantian constructivism in moral theory: The Dewey lectures. *The Journal of Philosophy* 77(9): 515-72.

———. 1993. *Political liberalism*. New York: Columbia University Press.

Scales-Trent, Judy. 1989. Black women and the constitution: finding our place, asserting our rights. *Harvard Civil Rights-Civil Liberties Law Review* 24: 9-44.

Sen, Amartya. 1990. Gender and cooperative conflict. In *Persistent inequalities*, ed. Irene Tinker. Oxford: Oxford University Press.

Spalter-Roth, Roberta M. and Heidi I. Hartmann. 1990. Unnecessary losses: Cost to Americans of the lack of a family and medical leave. Washington, DC: Institute for Women's Policy Research.

Stacks, Carol B. 1974. *All our kin: Strategies for survival in a black community*. New York: Harper and Row.

Taub, Nadine. 1984-85. From parental leaves to nurturing leaves. *Review of Law and Social Change*, 13.

Tronto, Joan C. 1993. *Moral boundaries: A political argument for an ethic of care*. New York: Routledge.

West, Robin L. 1987. The difference in women's hedonic lives: A pheno-meno-logical critique of feminist legal theory. *Wisconsin Women's Law Journal* 3: 81-145.

Williams, Wendy W. 1982. The equality crisis: Some reflections on culture, courts, and feminism. *Women's Rights Law Reporter* 7: 175-200.

———. 1985. Equality's riddle: Pregnancy and the equal treatment/special treatment debate. *New York University Review of Law and Social Change*, 13.

Wolgast, Elizabeth. 1980. *Equality and the rights of women*. Ithaca: Cornell University Press.

Young, Iris Marion. N.d. Mothers, citizenship and independence: A critique of pure family values. *Ethics*. Forthcoming.

[20]

THE RIGHTS OF STATISTICAL PEOPLE

*Lisa Heinzerling**

The use of cost-benefit analysis to evaluate the wisdom of life-saving regulatory programs presents a puzzle. Deciding to allow one person to harm, even to kill, another person on the basis of how much it costs the person doing the harm to refrain from doing it denies the person harmed a right against harm. It makes a person's freedom from harm, indeed her life, contingent upon the financial profile of the life-threatening activity.

The puzzle is that we do not allow this kind of cost-benefit balancing in all life-threatening contexts. We do not, for example, believe that so long as it is worth $10 million to one person to see another person dead, and so long as current estimates of the value of human life are lower than $10 million, it is acceptable for the first person to shoot and kill the second. Indeed, in this setting we refrain entirely from placing a monetary value on life. Yet when it comes to regulatory programs that prevent deaths—deaths also due to the actions of other people—it has become commonplace to argue that the people doing the harm should be allowed to act so long as it would cost more for them to stop doing the harm than the harm is worth in monetary terms. Why are these two situations coming to be viewed so differently?

In this Comment, I argue that the use of cost-benefit analysis to evaluate life-saving regulatory programs has, in a society that eschews reliance on cost-benefit analysis in other life-saving situations, been justified by the creation of a new kind of entity—the statistical person. A primary feature of the statistical person, as I will explain, is that she is unidentified; she is no one's sister, or daughter, or mother. Indeed, in one conception, the statistical person is not a person at all, but rather only a collection of risks. By distinguishing statistical lives from the lives of those we know, economic analysts have attempted to sidestep the uncomfortable fact that most of us profess ourselves quite incapable of identifying the monetary equivalent of the lives of our sisters, daughters, mothers, and friends.

The framing of life in statistical terms has generated, for statistical people, two disadvantages not suffered by those whose lives are not so framed. First, the people whose lives are framed in statistical terms are explicitly priced in advance of their deaths. Second, this pricing has come to vary depending on the age, health, disability status, and wealth of the people who might be harmed. Thus the most basic kind of right—the right to be protected from physical harm caused by other people, on

---

* Professor of Law, Georgetown University Law Center. For helpful discussion, I am grateful to Steven Goldberg, Richard Lazarus, David Luban, Mike Seidman, David Vladeck, Robin West, and participants in a faculty workshop at Georgetown.

he right to be protected from physical harm caused by other people, on equal terms with other people—is denied to those whose lives are framed in statistical terms.

Despite the increasing importance of the concept of statistical life in informing regulatory policy, regulatory scholars to date have not provided a standard definition of the statistical life. There are two possible conceptions of statistical life. According to the first conception, a statistical life is a life expected to be lost as a function of probabilities of death applied to a population of persons. On this understanding, the salient features of the statistical life are *unidentifiability* and *uncertainty*: the person who is expected to die is not identifiable before (or perhaps even after) death, and the probabilistic estimates are uncertain. The second conception of statistical life is that it is not a life at all, but only an aggregation of relatively small risks of harm to the individuals in a population. These risks can be summed, together with the size of the population, to estimate how many lives are likely to be lost as a result of the risk. But, under this conception, "statistical life" refers to the collective risk, not to life itself.

Neither of these two conceptions of the statistical life justifies the differential treatment that regulatory policy has begun to afford statistical and nonstatistical life. Identifiability does not explain our differing responses to situations that threaten the lives of others; our varying reactions likely have more to do with identifying *with* the victim of the threat. Moreover, any person in a situation of risk can be framed in statistical or nonstatistical terms. Making regulatory policy turn on this framing threatens to ratify the apathy or prejudice society may exhibit toward certain kinds of people or certain kinds of risks. As for uncertainty, the analytical devices that have sprung up around statistical lives—monetization according to willingness-to-pay and according to age, health, and disability—simply have nothing to do with the uncertainty of estimates of physical risk. Using monetary valuations, and discriminatory ones at that, to adjust for scientific uncertainty cloaks scientific uncertainty in the garb of moral choice. It is, among other things, a strange commentary on our times that it has proven easier to persuade regulatory agencies to abandon their longstanding commitment to the equal worth of human lives than it has proven to persuade them that their scientific analysis is unsound.

The idea that a statistical life is really not a life at all, but only an aggregation of relatively small risks of harm, also does not justify differential treatment of statistical and nonstatistical lives. Close examination of the manipulations analysts perform on the monetary valuation of statistical life—including discounting and adjusting for life-years saved—reveals that these analysts in fact treat statistical lives as lives, and not merely as collections of small risks. Since the statistical life, according to this second conception, turns out to be a life after all, and not simply an aggregation of risks, the ground for distinguishing it from nonstatistical lives evaporates.

I. Discriminatory Pricing

Much modern regulation aims to prevent people from being killed by the actions of other people. In discussing the benefits of this kind of regulation, regulators often refer to the lives of the people who would have died without the regulation as "statistical."[1] Below, this Comment will develop and explore several different possible meanings of statistical life. For now, I would like to establish how important the modifier "statistical" has become in influencing the discourse concerning life-saving measures. In particular, I will try to show how common it has become to strip statistical lives of rights against harm enjoyed by those whose lives are not described in statistical terms.

People whose lives are described in statistical terms suffer from two large disadvantages. First, the lives of statistical people are *explicitly priced in advance of their deaths*. We are told, for example, that the life of a statistical person is worth $5.8 million to the Environmental Protection Agency,[2] $2.5 million to the Department of Transportation,[3] and $5 million to the Consumer Product Safety Commission.[4] The analysts who have helped develop these monetary values readily explain that the values do not apply to "identified" lives, nor to the deaths of "named individuals," but only to "statistical" lives.[5] They deny having any special knowledge of the value of identified lives, and they appear to tolerate, if not embrace, the widely held assumption that we will do more to avoid the death of an identified person than to avoid the death of a statistical person.[6] As a result, identified lives remain unpriced while statistical lives wear price tags.

---

1. For a recent example, see Control of Air Pollution from New Motor Vehicles: Proposed Tier 2 Motor Vehicle Emissions Standards and Gasoline Sulfur Control Requirements, 64 Fed. Reg. 26,004, 26,079 (1999) (to be codified at 40 C.F.R. pts. 80, 85–86).

2. *See* Radon in Drinking Water Health Risk Reduction and Cost Analysis, 64 Fed. Reg. 9560, 9576 (1999).

3. *See* Memorandum from Walter B. McCormick, Jr., General Counsel, U.S. Dep't of Transp., & Jeffrey N. Shane, Assistant Secretary for Policy and Int'l Affairs, U.S. Dep't of Transp., to Assistant Secretaries and Modal Adm'rs, U.S. Dep't of Transp., Treatment of Value of Life and Injuries in Preparing Economic Evaluations 2 (Jan. 8, 1993) (on file with the *Harvard Environmental Law Review*) [hereinafter McCormick & Shane].

4. *See* U.S. Consumer Prod. Safety Comm'n, Estimating the Cost to Society of Consumer Product Injuries: The Revised Injury Cost Model 6–8 (Jan. 1998).

5. *See* W. Kip Viscusi, Fatal Tradeoffs: Public and Private Responsibilities for Risk 21 (1992) [hereinafter Viscusi, Fatal Tradeoffs]; Thomas C. Schelling, *The Life You Save May Be Your Own*, *in* Thomas C. Schelling, Choice and Consequences 113 (1984).

6. *See generally* Viscusi, Fatal Tradeoffs, *supra* note 5, at 21, 29.

It might be argued that, in fact, our legal system prices identified lives as well: the tort system has for many years effectively priced identified human lives by awarding compensation for wrongful deaths.[7] Because the tort system responds to harms that have already occurred, and because its remedy is money damages, the system faces a choice between not providing financial compensation for wrongful deaths, because lives are priceless, or providing compensation for them and risking damage to the belief that human lives are beyond price. Refusing to compensate at all for a death caused by wrongful action would seem a perverse way of giving force to a belief in the pricelessness of human life. Thus tort law, at least, can plausibly place a monetary value on human life for purposes of retrospective compensation, and at the same time hold to the belief that human lives should remain, in a fundamental sense, unpriced.

Resolving the contradiction between pricelessness and pricing when a monetary value is placed on human lives *in advance of death* presents a more difficult conundrum. In that case, the government in essence decides that it is not worth more than a certain finite sum of money to prevent someone from dying, even when death will come about through the actions of another person, and even when the person being killed has done nothing wrong. This proposition is equivalent to saying that a person can kill another person if it would cost too much to avoid killing her. This is a striking proposition, and so far one that has been applied only to lives described in statistical terms. Indeed, as mentioned above, the major writers in the literature on the pricing of human lives take pains to emphasize that they are discussing *only* statistical lives.[8] Government analysts have been equally fastidious about the distinction between the value of an identifiable life and the value of a statistical life.[9]

The second disadvantage to being a statistical person is that statistical lives are valued differently from each other on the basis of characteristics not used to distinguish among nonstatistical lives. Some analysts lately have become dissatisfied with the practice of placing an equal monetary value on all statistical lives. Lives are never *saved*, they ob-

---

7. *See* Guido Calabresi, Ideals, Beliefs, Attitudes, and the Law 89 (1985).

8. *See, e.g.*, Viscusi, Fatal Tradeoffs, *supra* note 5, at 19.

9. An internal memo of the Department of Transportation advises:

> Under limited circumstances, computational procedures in investment analyses may require insertion of an explicit value for fatalities averted. In such limited cases, the [willingness-to-pay] value can be used, but the accompanying text should avoid implying that the Department has set a dollar price on lives or injuries. *Rather than saying something like, "The Office of the Secretary has set the value of life at $2.5 million dollars . . ." the preferable language would be more like, "Economic research indicates that $2.5 million per statistical life saved is a reasonable estimate of people's willingness to pay for safety."*

McCormick & Shane, *supra* note 3, at 4 (emphasis added).

serve, but only *prolonged*, and thus, it only makes sense to ask ***by how much*** regulation prolongs the lives it protects.[10] Thus, we now see a parade of normally equality-minded writers extolling the virtues of evaluating regulatory action on the basis of the number of "quality-adjusted life-years" saved by it.[11] (Often the concept goes by the even more occlusive abbreviation "QALY.") This technical approach obscures its implications: that regulation saving the statistical lives of the elderly, the sick, and the disabled will be a lower priority than regulation saving the statistical lives of the young, the healthy, and the able-bodied. One's age, health, and disability status suddenly have become good grounds for distinguishing the value of one's life from another, for the explicit reason that the lives of those situated on the undesirable side of the statuses of age, health, and ability (the elderly, the sick, and the disabled) are worth less than the lives on the desirable side.[12] And, although few analysts will admit it, the upshot of the prevailing method for valuing statistical lives—which asks how much individuals are willing to pay to reduce risk in their own lives—also favors the statistical lives of the rich over the statistical lives of the poor.[13]

The disaggregation of statistical lives based on characteristics like age, health, disability status, and wealth deserves notice not only because of the inequality it facilitates, but also because it subtly alters the very concept of statistical life. Although the concept of statistical life has several possible meanings, all of these meanings contain one common feature: a statistical life is an unidentified life. We do not know the names of statistical people. Indeed, prior to the recent interest in disaggregating statistical people, one would have said that we know nothing about statistical people except that they are humans. But now, we are beginning to learn various facts about the statistical people whom regulation affects,

---

10. *See, e.g.*, Cass R. Sunstein, *Bad Deaths*, 14 J. RISK & UNCERTAINTY 259, 260 (1997).

11. *See, e.g.*, Richard H. Pildes & Cass R. Sunstein, *Reinventing the Regulatory State*, 62 U. CHI. L. REV. 1, 83–85 (1995).

12. The Food and Drug Administration recently described the benefits of a rule in terms of the "quality-adjusted life-*days*" affected by the rule. Preliminary Regulatory Impact Analysis and Initial Regulatory Flexibility Analysis of the Proposed Rule to Require Refrigeration of Shell Eggs at Retail and Safe Handling Labels, 64 Fed. Reg. 36,516, 36,522 (1999). The Environmental Protection Agency ("EPA") has been slower to embrace QALYs as the measure of the benefits of its rules. Compare Regulatory Impact Analysis for the Petroleum Refineries NESHAP, EPA Office of Air Quality Planning and Standards, EPA-452/R-004, at 174 (Aug. 1995) (suggesting that "[l]ife years saved may be a more relevant measure" of regulatory benefits than lives saved) with EPA, THE BENEFITS AND COSTS OF THE CLEAN AIR ACT: 1970 TO 1990, EPA Office of Air and Radiation, at ES-9 (1997) (noting problems associated with calculating life-saving benefits based on life-years saved).

13. *See* W. Kip Viscusi, *Equivalent Frames of Reference for Judging Risk Regulation Policies*, 3 N.Y.U. ENVTL. L.J. 431, 447 (1994) ("[T]he United States Department of Transportation should want to place a higher value of life on the well-being of the lives of airline passengers than those killed in motor-vehicle crashes because the airline passengers have a higher income.").

such as whether they are young or old, healthy or unhealthy. We should expect that, if this disaggregation continues, we will soon know whether the statistical lives relevant to a regulatory decision are men or women, white or black, infants or preschoolers.

The evaluation of life expectancy alone has the potential to introduce many such specific features of a person's identity into the regulatory equation. A large lurking question, neglected in the recent rush to embrace QALYs, is what baseline level of life expectancy to use in calculating the life-years lost due to a given hazard.[14] In keeping with the whole premise of the QALY movement—that only the portion of life *actually lost* due to regulation should concern regulators—there is good reason to expect that the baseline level will be the life expectancy of *the group to which the affected people belong*, insofar as group identity is an important determinant of life expectancy.[15] Thus, one can imagine race, ethnicity, socioeconomic status, gender, and other life expectancy–related characteristics all being fed, quite invisibly, into the equation that determines the worth of a person's life. In this way, the very identifiedness that, when it comes to nonstatistical people, helps justify their equal protection from harm, becomes, for statistical people, the very thing that leads to inequality among them.

Whether consciously or unconsciously, analysts have softened the discriminatory appearance of these analytic developments in two ways. First, rather than using as a baseline the life expectancy of the specific group to which the affected statistical people belong, analysts typically use the average life expectancy of the whole population. For example, in one influential analysis,[16] Robert Hahn of the American Enterprise Institute calculated life-years saved by comparing the average age of death from broad categories of hazards—such as "accident," "fire," "worker injury," and "cancer"—to estimates of the average life expectancy of the entire population of people of a given age.[17] The use of overall life expectancy as the baseline for comparison avoids the awkward fact that life expectancy is strongly associated with statuses like race, gender, disability, and socioeconomic status. While it may be that analysts like Hahn use overall life expectancy rather than the specific life expectancy of the group to which

---

14. *See* Lisa Heinzerling, *Environmental Law and the Present Future*, 87 GEO. L.J. 2025, 2062, 2075–76 (1999).

15. Professor Revesz has proposed that regulatory analysts consider the "age profiles" of the population targeted by regulation. *See* Richard L. Revesz, *Environmental Regulation, Cost-Benefit Analysis, and the Discounting of Human Lives*, 99 COLUM. L. REV. 941, 967 n.120 (1999).

16. The Office of Management and Budget relies heavily on Hahn's analysis in developing its own estimates of the costs and benefits of environmental regulation. *See* OFFICE OF INFO. AND REGULATORY AFFAIRS, OFFICE OF MANAGEMENT & BUDGET, REPORT TO CONGRESS ON THE COSTS AND BENEFITS OF FEDERAL REGULATIONS 16 (1998).

17. *See* Robert W. Hahn, *Regulatory Reform: What Do the Government's Numbers Tell Us?*, *in* RISKS, COSTS, AND LIVES SAVED 208, 247 n.40 (Robert W. Hahn ed., 1996).

the target population belongs as a means of avoiding inappropriate distinctions between classes of people, one must then wonder why the same concern for equality does not persuade them to abandon the entire QALY project.[18]

A second way analysts have attempted to soften the discriminatory thrust of currently popular methods of valuing human life is to avoid making these valuations, and thus, life-saving policies, turn on ability, rather than willingness, to pay. In other words, they have tried to dilute the effect of wealth on the valuation of life. Professor Kornhauser, for example, suggests that life be valued according to the preferences of a group that has an "acceptable" level of wealth, such as the median wealth of the overall population.[19] Similarly, Professor Revesz proposes valuing lives based on the preferences of a population having "representative characteristics of the population of the United States," and argues that valuations be adjusted upward where the subjects of willingness-to-pay studies "have relatively low incomes" compared to the group targeted by regulation.[20] Under both proposals, of course, wealth would still determine the willingness to pay for risk reduction and thus the value of statistical life, but the value of life would be nudged upwards by excluding the highly income-constrained preferences of the worst off among us.

Thus, analysts have obscured—but not eliminated—the unequal protection of life afforded by identifying the features of human lives that make them worth saving or not. Most important for present purposes, however, is the fact that analysts have often used the bare adjective "statistical" to justify their pricing of, and discriminations among, human lives.[21] What is it about statistical lives that supposedly makes them so expendable? Answering this question requires an exploration of the different possible meanings of statistical life.

II. Unidentifiability and Uncertainty

The literature on risk and its regulation contains two different conceptions of the statistical life. According to the first conception, the statistical life is a life expected to be lost as a function of probabilities of death applied to a population of persons. The person expected to die is not identifiable in advance of death, and the probabilistic estimates are

18. *See* Heinzerling, *Environmental Law and the Present Future*, *supra* note 14, at 2075–76.

19. *See* Lewis A. Kornhauser, *The Value of Life*, 38 Clev. St. L. Rev. 209, 221–22 (1990).

20. Revesz, *supra* note 15, at 967–68.

21. *See, e.g.*, Jeremy D. Fraiberg & Michael J. Trebilcock, *Risk Regulation: Technocratic and Democratic Tools for Regulatory Reform*, 43 McGill L.J. 835, 860 (1998); James F. Blumstein, *Rational Medical Resources: A Constitutional, Legal, and Policy Analysis*, 59 Tex. L. Rev. 1345, 1353–54 (1981).

uncertain.[22] However, neither unidentifiability nor uncertainty justifies differential protection against harm for statistical and nonstatistical people.

A. *Unidentifiability*

One of the features thought to set the statistical life apart from the nonstatistical life is unidentifiability. We will spend a fortune, it is regularly remarked, to rescue miners trapped in a mine, or a little girl trapped in a well, or a downed balloonist, but we will not spend an equivalent amount to protect these people from getting in harm's way in the first place.[23] Observers have asserted that the identifiedness of the miners, the little girl, and the balloonist makes us especially willing to help them.[24] As an empirical matter, this assertion is unproved and probably mistaken. As a normative matter, it seems clear that the rights of people not to be harmed should not depend on the identifiedness of the people who will be harmed.

There is good reason to believe that our willingness to spend money, time, and other resources to save someone from harm does not turn on the identifiedness of the person who will be harmed unless we intervene. When Tylenol capsules were contaminated with cyanide and placed on the market in the fall of 1982, no one knew which capsules contained the cyanide. Accordingly, no one knew who would be poisoned if no preventive measures were taken. This unidentifiedness did not soften the response that followed the first poisonings. Indeed, it arguably magnified it, as unidentifiedness is a close cousin of the awful randomness—associated with terrorists and criminal maniacs—that many people uniquely fear.[25]

Contrast our response to the Tylenol poisonings with an equally familiar response to an identified life. Many of us who live in large urban areas come face to face, weekly if not daily, with homeless people who look cold, hungry, desperate, and sick. Often these people explicitly ask for our help and we do not give it. Or we give a little—a dime, a quarter, a dollar or two—enough to assuage our consciences but not enough really to help. Yet it is hard to imagine a more clearly identified person in need.

---

22. Scholars who appear to embrace this conception of a statistical life include, among many others, Charles Fried and W. Kip Viscusi. *See* VISCUSI, *supra* note 5, at 21. *See generally* Charles Fried, *The Value of Life*, 82 HARV. L. REV. 1415 (1969).

23. *See, e.g.*, GUIDO CALABRESI & PHILIP BOBBITT, TRAGIC CHOICES 20–21 (1978); Fried, *supra* note 22, at 1415.

24. *See* Fried, *supra* note 22, at 1428–33 (labeling this the "personalist" argument).

25. *See Murder by Capsule*, N.Y. TIMES, Oct. 5, 1982, at A30.

The different responses to the Tylenol poisonings and to the homeless raise the possibility that the "identifiedness" that increases our willingness to save others from harm has little to do with our being able to identify the victim of harm. Rather, it probably has more to do with our being able to identify with her. Making individual—or, worse, public—responsibility to aid another person turn on the extent to which the person who needs help is like the people who might help her is a covert, but effective, way of making characteristics like race, class, gender, age, and personal habits determinative of our obligations to others. This approach is, needless to say, the antithesis of a regime of rights. In this way, the issue of identifiability also bears a strong resemblance to the unequal treatment of statistical people. People whose lives are framed in statistical terms thus suffer twice: first, when their lives are labeled statistical simply because the people doing the labeling do not identify with them, and second, when their lives are devalued precisely because they are statistical.

The possibility that the word "statistical" will be used as cover for an unconscious or invidious failure to identify with the person in danger is heightened by the fact that virtually any person in a situation of danger can be described in either statistical (unidentified) or nonstatistical (identified) terms. The classification of a threatened person as statistical or nonstatistical largely turns on one's definition of the harm the person faces and its cause. In the case of the homeless person, for example, one might say that the harms this person faces are acute hunger and exposure to the elements, and that the causes of these harms are inadequate food, clothing, and shelter. These are immediate harms, readily addressed by interventions any one of us might make. But if one says that the harm the homeless person suffers is poverty, and the causes are a lack of education, mental illness, and societal discrimination, then simple interventions seem inadequate indeed. Thus, if the obligation to help turns on whether the life of the person in need of help is framed in statistical or nonstatistical terms, we can give that obligation any shape and scope we want through our definition of harm and causation. And, oddly enough, the more chronic, intractable, and widespread the harm as we describe it—the more "statistical" the harm and its cause—the less will be the responsibility to intervene.

Returning, finally, to the paradigmatic cases of the identified victim—the trapped miner, the little girl in a well, the downed balloonist—it becomes obvious upon reflection that identifiedness—as in, what is the person's name? what does she look like?—probably has little to do with our willingness to help. Rescue workers traveled halfway across the world to try to locate survivors of the massive earthquake that hit Turkey in August 1999, yet most of those people found were not identifiable in advance of their rescues. They were known only by their cries for help. In that case, the important factor was that there was no doubt that the people buried in the rubble of the quake were in grave danger. The knowledge that might distinguish these victims from other people in need, therefore, is not knowledge of their personal identities, but knowledge of their need for help. Perhaps it is uncertainty, then, that distinguishes the statistical from the nonstatistical life.

B. Uncertainty

Suppose one million people are each exposed to a hazard estimated to pose a one-in-one-million risk of death. One life would be the expected loss to this population facing this probability of death. To say that this life is "statistical" might mean one of two things. Both relate to the uncertainty of the probabilistic estimate.

In one sense, the word "statistical" is a kind of pejorative; it often connotes an association that is contingent or random rather than intrinsic or causal. For example, suppose that ninety percent of all airplane crashes in the last two decades occurred on Tuesdays, yet only five percent of all airplane flights occurred on Tuesdays. Suppose further that regression analyses of the facts surrounding airplane crashes rule out, to a ninety-five percent certainty, the possibility that the association between flying on Tuesdays and airplane crashes is random. Yet assume that researchers lack any theory about why Tuesdays are especially dangerous for air travel. One might then regard estimates of the number of lives expected to be lost during Tuesday airplane flights as estimates of the loss of "statistical" life because the association between Tuesdays and crashes has been established only statistically.

This meaning of statistical life does not justify the monetization of, nor discrimination between, statistical lives. At most, the idea that statistical lives are different because the threat to them has been probabilistically identified, but not causally explained, suggests that we should proceed cautiously in our response to the hazard. If we believe that the probabilistic association we have identified is coincidental rather than causal, then we would be well advised to study the matter further before undertaking a major regulatory intervention. But if the statistical probabilities have been established over a large enough number of cases, in different settings, then the lack of a causal theory explaining the statistical association between the two events should not stop us from taking action. For example, it was not until 1996 that scientists identified the mechanistic link between cigarette smoking and lung cancer.[26] Prior to that time, the connection between smoking and cancer had been established only statistically, through decades of epidemiological and biological research.

26. *See* Mikhail F. Denissenko et al., *Preferential Formation of Benzo[a]pyrene Adducts at Lung Cancer Mutational Hotspots in P53*, 274 SCI. 430, 430 (1996).

Yet the absence of a causal theory did not prevent widespread acceptance of the idea that smoking causes lung cancer.[27]

More fundamentally, cautiousness in the face of uncertainty is not the same as a distinction based on value. If scientific uncertainty is the issue, then the solution is not to declare that statistical lives are less important, less valuable, more expendable, than nonstatistical lives, or that the age or health or wealth of the people who might be harmed should inform our willingness to help them. Monetization of human life and distinctions among humans based on age, health, disability, and wealth, have nothing to do with the meaning of statistical life that I am here considering. If the uncertainty of probabilistic estimates distinguishes statistical from nonstatistical life, then this uncertainty should be inserted in the regulatory equation as an adjustment to the probabilities themselves, and not as an adjustment to the value being measured. Doing otherwise allows scientific disagreement over the existence and magnitude of risk to masquerade as a value choice about who in our society is worth saving and at what cost.

Scientific uncertainty also may underlie another conception of statistical life. Even where there exists a causal theory as to why one event—say, exposure to asbestos—produces an adverse result, there may be disagreement over the conditions under which the adverse result will materialize. A statistical life might therefore be the life expected to be lost if each of a series of assumptions about the world holds true. But because the assumptions are uncertain, the loss of life is uncertain, too.

Modern risk assessment, which forms the basis of much health-related regulation, attempts to determine the probability of future harm to individuals exposed to particular hazards.[28] This analysis requires many assumptions about the potency of the hazard, the magnitude of exposures, and the susceptibility of the individuals to the harm in question. Often the assumptions must be made in the absence of conclusive proof. For example, many risk assessments attempt to determine the probability of cancer in a human population exposed to a particular substance by considering the effect of that substance on an animal population, such as rats or mice.[29] Extrapolating the results in animal studies to the human

---

27. *See* Denise Grady, *So, Smoking Causes Cancer: This Is News?*, N.Y. TIMES, Oct. 27, 1996, at D3. *See also* American Trucking Ass'n v. EPA, 175 F.3d 1027, 1055–56 (D.C. Cir. 1999) (rejecting the argument that the EPA could not regulate fine particulate pollution until it established the "biological mechanism through which particulate pollution causes adverse health effects").

28. The literature on quantitative risk assessment is enormous. For general discussion, see NATIONAL RESEARCH COUNCIL, SCIENCE AND JUDGMENT IN RISK ASSESSMENT (1994).

29. *See, e.g.*, Public Citizen Health Research Group v. Tyson, 796 F.2d 1479 (D.C. Cir. 1986) (upholding the Occupational Safety and Health Administration's rule limiting workplace exposure to ethylene oxide, based on animal studies); Synthetic Organic Chem. Mfrs. Ass'n v. Department of Health & Human Servs., 720 F. Supp. 1244, 1256 (W.D. La. 1989) (upholding Health and Human Service's classification of certain chemicals as known

population requires an assumption about the similarity between the relevant responses of animals and humans.[30] Risk assessments must also, to take another example, attempt to predict what level of exposure the relevant human population will experience with regard to the substance in question. Will the individuals in the population eat the substance, drink it, breathe it, or all of these and more? How often? For how many days or weeks or years? These are difficult questions to answer in advance. Risk assessors must therefore make assumptions about what the future exposures will be to estimate the risk the population faces.[31]

Often these assumptions lean in the direction of assumptions that will support findings of more rather than less risk. The Occupational Safety and Health Administration routinely assumes, for example, that worker populations exposed to a risky substance will be so exposed for their entire working lives; in other words, the workers will neither switch occupations nor quit working altogether nor limit their exposures in another way.[32] In fact, many workers do spend their working lives at one facility or at one type of facility, thus experiencing similar exposures throughout their years of work.[33] Yet this kind of assumption has led to several memorable depictions of the kinds of people risk assessment assumes to exist. Justice Breyer, for example, brought us the "dirt-eating children playing in . . . a swamp" by way of arguing that the government's decisions to clean up hazardous waste sites are often extravagant.[34] More recently, John Applegate has conjured the image of the "naked dirt-eating farmer," assumed in Environmental Protection Agency analyses of the risks from a nuclear weapons production facility in Ohio—a farmer who consumes the food, and some of the soil, from his own farm, and in the meantime covers his naked body with the farm's soil.[35]

Although no one has said so explicitly, I believe that the practice of using these kinds of assumptions in risk assessment may be what lies behind the demotion of "real" human lives to "statistical" lives. It may be

---

or suspected carcinogens based on results in animal studies).

30. For discussion of this assumption, see Proposed Guidelines for Carcinogen Risk Assessment, 61 Fed. Reg. 17,960, 17,966–68 (1996) (proposed Apr. 23, 1996).

31. *See, e.g.*, Leather Indus. of Am. v. EPA, 40 F.3d 392, 403–05 (D.C. Cir. 1994) (remanding an EPA rule for failure "to demonstrate a rational relationship between its highly conservative exposure assumptions and the actual usage regulated by those assumptions").

32. *See* STEPHEN BREYER, BREAKING THE VICIOUS CIRCLE: TOWARD EFFECTIVE RISK REGULATION 46 (1993).

33. *Cf.* Adam M. Finkel, *A Second Opinion on an Environmental Misdiagnosis: The Risky Prescriptions of* Breaking the Vicious Circle, 3 N.Y.U. ENVTL. L.J. 295, 351 (1995) (explaining why a similar assumption about residential exposures is not overly conservative).

34. *See* BREYER, *supra* note 32, at 12.

35. *See* John S. Applegate, *A Beginning and Not and End in Itself: The Role of Risk Assessment in Environmental Decision-Making*, 63 U. CIN. L. REV. 1643, 1654 (1995).

the reason why writers who normally would cringe at distinguishing among people based on characteristics like age and class find no difficulty embracing such distinctions when it comes to statistical people. The idea, I think, is this: statistical people do not exist. There are no dirt-eating children living in swamps and no naked dirt-eating Ohioan farmers. To be sure, there are children living near hazardous waste sites and near nuclear weapons facilities, but there are no children and no adults who do the things risk assessment imagines them to do. Thus, the statistical people of risk assessment exist only on paper; there is no person, no name, no face, no *body*, that could be matched to them even if one had perfect information. Consequently, to say that a statistical life is expected to be lost as a result of a particular hazard is to say that, in reality, *no one will die*.

If statistical people truly do not exist, if statistical deaths truly do not occur, a qualitative distinction between statistical and nonstatistical lives would indeed be justified. But the qualitative distinction would be the same as that between zero and any positive number. It would not be a distinction that would, for example, support attaching a monetary value to statistical but not nonstatistical lives. If nonstatistical lives truly do not exist, they are not worth $5 million, or $2.5 million, or in fact, anything at all; they have *no* value. The idea that statistical people do not exist also would not support distinctions among statistical people; it is incoherent, for example, to make age- or health-based distinctions between nonexistent people. Thus, once again, the meaning of statistical life that derives from scientific uncertainty does not justify the analytical practices that have accompanied the framing of life in statistical terms.

One might object that even if some statistical deaths do occur—even if quantitative risk assessment sometimes correctly predicts some loss of life—quantitative risk assessment vastly overstates the number of deaths likely to occur. But if the conservatism of quantitative risk assessment means only that fewer people may die than we expect—not *zero*, but *fewer*—then this uncertainty does not justify the *qualitative* difference in the treatment of statistical and nonstatistical lives that I have discussed. Only if the actual loss of life is zero—only if no one will die—can the situations of the statistical and nonstatistical lives be regarded as qualitatively distinct. And, as I have said, they would not be qualitatively distinct in the way analysts have imagined.

It would be difficult, however, to support the claim of zero risk. Many other assumptions commonly used in risk assessments are just as artificial as the ones I have described, but they are artificial in a way that likely understates rather than overstates actual risk. For example, one standard assumption in risk assessment is that the population targeted by regulation has the same susceptibility to the relevant harm as the population studied in the risk assessment.[36] Yet most of the epidemiological studies underlying the risk assessments used in developing regulation have involved only white male workers; women, children, the elderly, racial and ethnic minorities, and poor people may be more vulnerable to the risks in question than the relatively healthy white male workers assumed in most analyses.[37] The dueling assumptions of risk assessment—some conservative, some not—provide little support for the notion that statistical lives (and deaths) simply do not exist.

The necessity of maintaining the zero-risk scenario, which justifies a qualitative distinction between statistical and nonstatistical lives, may help to explain the incredible durability of scientific disagreement in environmental and health regulation. A quarter-century after the pesticide DDT was banned, there appears to be no universal agreement that the pesticide was, all things considered, harmful enough to be banned;[38] the same is true of the two-decade-old ban on PCBs.[39] Indeed, there is likely no industrial chemical or substance as to the harmfulness of which everyone of any influence would agree. Equally striking, even when claims of the direct harmfulness of a substance are quite undeniable, these claims are almost inevitably opposed by the claim that regulating the substance would at least indirectly harm the same health-related interests as much as, or more than, the substance itself. For example, in the handful of cases in which federal courts have struck down health regulations on the ground that the regulations took inadequate account of costs, the courts have coupled their economic conclusions with the suggestion that the regulations would not, in any event, have saved lives on balance, but more likely would have taken more lives than they saved.[40] This kind of reasoning is exactly the kind of "subterfuge" Calabresi and Bobbitt would predict to occur in this kind of situation;[41] it would, I think, be an unusual judge who could say explicitly and unqualifiedly that people will die because he struck down a regulation—and that this is fine, because the regulation cost too much money. The long latency period of many of

36. *See* Proposed Guidelines for Carcinogen Risk Assessment, 61 Fed. Reg. at 17,966.

37. *See, e.g., id.*; *see also* Robert R. Kuehn, *The Environmental Justice Implications of Quantitative Risk Assessment*, 1996 U. Ill. L. Rev. 103, 123.

38. *See* George M. Gray & John D. Graham, *Regulating Pesticides*, *in* Risk Versus Risk: Tradeoffs in Protecting Health and the Environment 173, 173–74, 179, 189 (John D. Graham & Jonathan Baert Wiener eds., 1995).

39. *See* Breyer, *supra* note 32, at 17, 92 n.72.

40. *See, e.g.*, Corrosion Proof Fittings v. EPA, 947 F.2d 1201 (5th Cir. 1991) (invalidating EPA's ban on asbestos on grounds that the rule may require spending an unreasonably large amount of money to save a human life and also may have created more risks than it avoided because nonasbestos brakes may not be as effective as asbestos brakes); American Trucking Ass'ns v. EPA, 175 F.3d 1027 (D.C. Cir. 1999) (invalidating EPA's national air quality standard for ozone on grounds that EPA failed to articulate an intelligible limiting principle for its standard and that ozone may be beneficial to human health because pollution may block cancer-causing ultraviolet radiation).

41. *See generally* Calabresi & Bobbitt, *supra* note 23.

the human diseases prevented by environmental and health regulation helps to preserve the subterfuge, as latency frustrates efforts to make a clear and crisp causal connection between exposure and harm. If the subterfuge were abandoned, if the zero-risk scenario were ever eliminated, it would become clear that human lives are being priced in advance of their deaths, based on explicit classifications the legal system normally would eschew.

Thus, preserving the zero-risk hypothesis by emphasizing and perhaps fomenting scientific disagreement maintains the qualitative distinction between statistical and nonstatistical lives. I repeat, however, that the qualitative distinction thus maintained—between real lives and nonexistent ones—does not justify the analytical devices that have been developed for statistical lives, namely monetization based on age, health, disability, and wealth.

In sum, neither identifiability nor scientific uncertainty justifies the differential treatment of statistical and nonstatistical lives. Perhaps another way of conceptualizing the statistical life would justify this treatment.

III. Risk

The second conception of the statistical life is that it is really not a life at all, but merely an aggregation of relatively small risks of harm to the individuals in a population. These risks can be summed, in combination with the size of the population, to determine how many lives are likely to be lost as a result of the risks. But, under this conception, "statistical life" refers to the collective risk, not to the life itself. According to this second understanding of the statistical life, a statistical life is indeed qualitatively different from a nonstatistical life because it is not a life at all but only a collection of risks.

This second approach is adopted, formally at least, by the analysts who advocate valuing life-saving measures according to individuals' willingness to pay.[42] These analysts note that while it is difficult to persuade people to think rationally and economically about the certain prospect of their own deaths, they can think rationally and economically about small increments of risk.[43] To put the idea in concrete terms: if each person in a population of 1000 faces a 1/1000 risk of death from a particular hazard, and each person is willing to pay $5 to eliminate this risk to herself, then the value of a "statistical life" in this population is $5,000. But, as analysts repeatedly remind us, it is the collection of 1000

---

42. *See* W. Kip Viscusi, Rational Risk Policy 45–46 (1998).
43. The seminal discussion is Schelling's. *See* Schelling, *supra* note 5, at 126–28.

risks of 1/1000, and not life itself, being valued here.[44] In practice, however, analysts treat the valuation achieved by consulting willingness-to-pay as a valuation of life itself. Since the statistical life, according to this second conception, thus turns out to be a life after all, and not just a collection of risks, the ground for distinguishing it from nonstatistical lives disappears.

One way in which analysts treat the valuation of risk as equivalent to a valuation of life is that they do not calculate the value of both statistical life and life itself.[45] They calculate only the value of statistical life. They do not go on to observe that their calculations drastically understate the value of their programs because they measure only the value of risk and not the value of life. The value of a discrete risk, however, remains the same regardless of whether anyone actually ends up dying as a result of that risk. Risk and death are two separate injuries.[46] If analysts behaved consistently with their claim that the monetary value of a statistical life reflects only risk and not life itself, they would either substantially upgrade their estimates of the benefits of life-saving programs by, for example, adding some measure of the loss of life itself (a rather outdated possibility would be the measure of lifetime earnings lost as a result of premature death),[47] or by acknowledging in every case that their estimates of the value of life-saving programs are dramatically understated because they reflect only risk and not life. Analysts do neither of these two things. It is hard, therefore, to escape the impression that, despite their protestations to the contrary, they do indeed believe they have found the measure of the value of life and not just risk.

Second, analysts commonly discount the monetary value of statistical life to reflect the temporal lag, if any, between the costs and benefits of regulation.[48] But rather than discounting from the moment when risk is imposed, they discount from the probable moment of death. In fact, the Office of Management and Budget recommends this practice.[49] If, how-

---

44. *See, e.g.*, VISCUSI, RATIONAL RISK POLICY, *supra* note 42, at 45; Richard Thaler & Sherwin Rosen, *The Value of Saving a Life: Evidence from the Labor Market*, *in* HOUSEHOLD PRODUCTION AND CONSUMPTION 265–66 (Nestor E. Terleckyj ed., 1976).

45. Indeed, if analysts did calculate the value of life itself according to the same compensation theory of value that underlies the valuation of risk, the benefits of regulatory programs that save human lives would be infinite, as "no finite amount of money could compensate a person for the loss of his life, simply because money is no good to him when he is dead." John Broome, *Trying to Value a Life*, 9 J. PUB. ECON. 91, 92 (1978).

46. *See generally* Heinzerling, *Environmental Law and the Present Future*, *supra* note 14, at 2029–46, 2061–63.

47. For discussion, see CLAYTON P. GILLETTE & THOMAS D. HOPKINS, ADMINISTRATIVE CONFERENCE OF THE UNITED STATES, FEDERAL AGENCY VALUATIONS OF HUMAN LIFE, REPORT FOR RECOMMENDATION 88-7 (1988).

48. For discussion, see Lisa Heinzerling, *Discounting Our Future*, 34 LAND & WATER L. REV. 39 (1999).

49. *See* OFFICE OF INFO. & REGULATORY AFFAIRS, INTERAGENCY GROUP CHAIRED BY A MEMBER OF THE COUNCIL OF ECONOMIC ADVISORS, ECONOMIC ANALYSIS OF FEDERAL REGULATIONS UNDER EXECUTIVE ORDER 12,866, at pt. III.B.5(a) (Jan. 11, 1996)

ever, monetary valuations of statistical life indeed represent only risk, and not life, then it is inappropriate to discount the value of statistical life from the probable date of death rather than from the date a risk is created.[50]

Third, the practice of disaggregating statistical lives into statistical life-years seems more consistent with the idea that a statistical life is a whole human life, than with the idea it is an aggregation of individual risks of death. Human lives are composed, in part, of years lived; risk is not. Although it might be argued that the value of a *risk* to individuals depends in part on how many years of life will be lost if one dies, the value of statistical life-years is not currently calculated in this manner. Instead, analysts estimate the value of a life-year by simply annualizing the value of a statistical life.[51] They rarely attempt to individualize the valuations of life-years to take into account the special characteristics of the risk in question. A jarring example of this insensitivity to context comes from the economic analysis of the Food and Drug Administration's rule on mammography quality standards. After noting that $5 million was "the implied value of society's willingness to pay to avoid the likelihood of an additional death," the agency stated:

> However, FDA recognizes that the studies upon which this estimate is based were conducted, for the most part, on male, blue-collar workers of approximately 30 years of age. At 30 years of age, the average male life expectancy is 44.2 years. Thus, the estimate implies that individuals are willing to pay $5 million for 44.2 years of life. Amortizing $5 million over 44.2 years using a 7 percent discount rate yields an unadjusted average annual value per life-year of $368,000. Adjusting the life expectancy of a 30-year-old male to account for future non-bed and bed disability . . . yields an expectation of 41.3 QALYs. Thus, FDA assumes that the average annual value of one QALY, using a 7 percent discount rate, equals $373,000.[52]

Thus, the agency estimated the value of life-saving mammography in women with breast cancer based on the amount thirty-year-old male workers are estimated to demand in higher wages given the possibility of workplace accidents. By disaggregating the value of a statistical life into statistical life-years without any consideration of the special qualities of

[hereinafter ECONOMIC ANALYSIS].

50. *See* Heinzerling, *Discounting Our Future*, *supra* note 48, at 71; Lisa Heinzerling, *Discounting Life*, 108 YALE L.J. 1911, 1913 (1999).

51. *See* ECONOMIC ANALYSIS, *supra* note 49, at pt. III.B.5(c).

52. Executive Summary, Economic Analysis of U.S. Food and Drug Administration's Final Rule Under the Mammography Quality Standards Act of 1992, at 5–26 (on file with the *Harvard Environmental Law Review*) (citations omitted).

the risk in question, the agency strongly suggested that it is striving toward a uniform, acontextual valuation of lives and life-years that is inconsistent with the premise that only risk—contingent, case-specific, fluidly perceived risk—is being valued.

In acknowledging the monetary value of reducing risk, economic analysts have contributed to our growing awareness that life-threatening risk itself—and not just the end result of such risk, death—is an injury. But they have erred in pretending that risk is all there is. The fundamental problem with the conception of statistical life as risk, not life, is the same as the problem with defining statistical life in terms of uncertainty: it implicitly assumes that statistical people do not die.[53] Because this is a question of science, not value, any attempt to resolve it through the monetization of, and differential valuation of, statistical lives, is to create a mismatch between the problem, if there is one, and its solution. In addition, because risk itself is an injury, it is wrong to allocate exposure to it based on characteristics like age, health, and wealth.

As I have explained, economic analysts do not act consistently with their assertions that they are valuing only risk and not life. In failing to develop an estimate for the value of life separate and apart from the value of risk, in discounting from the end of life rather than from the beginning of risk, and in treating life-years as components of life rather than risk, these analysts belie the truth of their assertions that their concern is with risk rather than life itself. Perhaps this is a way of trying to reconcile a very awkward tension in their methodology. By the analysts' own account, individuals are capable of rationally and economically valuing only risk, not life itself. An economic account of life-saving programs that excluded the value of life would be quite inadequate, however. By proclaiming that risk is their concern, but by in fact treating the valuations they derive as valuations of life itself, economic analysts have managed to have it both ways. They have retained the theoretical plausibility of the willingness-to-pay methodology, but have put it in the service of a system that appears, for all the world, to have arrived at the value of life itself. This strategy must fail. To the extent that the willingness-to-pay methodology can indeed value only risk and not life, it omits a large—probably the largest—benefit of life-saving regulation. Yet to the extent that it purports to value life, it is inconsistent with its own theoretical premises.

---

53. Throughout this Comment I have spoken only of the risk of death, and death that is associated with the hazards regulated by federal agencies. But of course many of the risks that can lead to death also cause other serious problems, including illnesses that are painful and debilitating. *See* Lisa Heinzerling, *Regulatory Costs of Mythic Proportions*, 107 YALE L.J. 1981, 2060–63 (1998). In focusing on death here, I do not mean to slight the other harms caused by modern hazards.

IV. Conclusion

Regulatory analysts have predicated their pricing of, and discriminations among, human lives on the idea that the lives protected by regulation are statistical. By this, they either mean that no lives will be lost or that only risk, not life itself, is at stake. In either case, the notion is that statistical people do not die. But this is true only if our scientific estimates of risk are so unreliable that they commonly predict deaths will occur where, in fact, none will. I believe this is an inaccurate, even hysterical, account of scientific uncertainty. In any event, if the problem were scientific uncertainty, the solution would not be to monetize the lives subject to an uncertain risk, nor to discriminate among them based on characteristics such as age, health, and wealth. The solution would be to develop better scientific estimates of risk.

In defending the monetization of, and discrimination among, human lives based on the statistical nature of those lives, economic analysts have dehumanized the suffering and death that scientific risk assessments tell us will occur due to particular hazards. It is hard to understand, much less empathize with, statistical pain and loss. It is easier to assume that statistical suffering and death are things that do not happen to us—real people—but only to others—statistical people—and then to assume that the other people—statistical people—do not exist. Describing pain and loss in statistical terms allows us to think coolly about them; it strips life-threatening risks of the moral and emotional texture they derive from their association with real humans with real bodies and real loved ones. Describing human lives in statistical terms thus creates the conditions under which human suffering and loss can be conceived of in economic terms, and under which this suffering and loss can be allowed to continue simply because the monetary value we have attached to them is lower than the costs of avoiding them. In inventing the statistical life, economic analysis has contrived the very entity it seeks to value.

Part IV
Rights Redux

[21]

THE CASE OF THE SPELUNCEAN EXPLORERS: REVISITED

Robin L. West and Alan M. Dershowitz

WEST, J.* Trapped in a cave, on the verge of starvation, with no credible hope of timely rescue, five speluncean explorers resolve that their only hope of survival is to eat one of their own. They determine to do so and to throw dice to identify who will be the sacrificial lamb. One member then denounces the plan and withdraws his participation. The group proceeds over his objection, with his dice being thrown for him by another. The dissenting member, by bad luck, loses the throw, is killed, and is eaten by his comrades. The group is soon rescued and hospitalized, but only after the accidental deaths of eight of the rescuers seeking to secure their release. The survivors are now charged with murder or, as defined by the relevant statute, with "willfully tak[ing] the life," N. C. S. A. (N. S.) § 12-A, of another human being, punishable in all cases by death.

Under our procedural rules, and acting within its discretion, the jury convened for this case requested that it be relegated only to the role of fact-finder, leaving this Court to determine the legal conclusions. The jury found the facts as briefly recounted above, and it is now our obligation to determine whether the defendants' conduct constitutes murder. If we decide that it does, then the mandatory punishment under the statute is death, unless commuted to a lesser penalty by the governor of the state.

---

* Professor of Law, Georgetown University Law Center.

I

The defendants present two novel arguments that require a response. First, they argue that they were operating beyond the jurisdiction of this or any other legal system, not for the usual territorial reason, but rather, for a jurisprudential one: they claim that their very survival in this peculiar situation demanded a course of action, the morality or legality of which is beyond the legitimate power of law to judge. The purpose of law, they urge, is to facilitate cooperative social living and to maximize the fruits of that cooperation. Law, then, is predicated upon the possibility that cooperation will not only increase chances of mutual survival, but will also yield additional benefits to all. Here, cooperation among all would only guarantee their mutual demise; thus, the logical predicate for law was absent. The purpose of law could not be to condemn these actions. Rather, it was both legal and moral for these trapped men to establish their own council and take whatever actions were necessary to assure the survival of the greatest number possible. This they did by agreeing to the procedures of the lottery.

Second, the defendants argue that even if our law applies, they are not guilty of the crime of murder because they acted in their own self-defense. A killing is in self-defense, the defendants argue, whenever the situation is such that one life must be taken in order to save one's own. Such killings are basically non-deterrable, the defendants explain: there is no threat of punishment that could change the rational decision to kill. The purpose of our criminal laws against homicide is deterrence, but these acts were non-deterrable; hence, they were not crimes. There is no point in applying the criminal sanction of the law, and therefore, the law does not apply.

Are these arguments meritorious? Of course, there is no authority for the proposition that the "purpose" of either the rule of law or the laws forbidding murder, whatever those purposes may be, should determine the limits of the law's reach. Nor is there authority for the narrow proposition that the self-defense justification should extend as far as the defendants contend. But that lack of authority is not fatal to the defendants' argument — at most, it implies that we are not compelled by precedent to follow the course the defendants urge. We still need to decide, as a matter of first impression, whether the arguments they have presented have merit. In my view they do not.

The defendants' first claim is powerful, well reasoned, and rests on seemingly incontrovertible premises. Much of our law — particularly contract and property law — is indeed based on the assumption that cooperation through legal mechanisms can increase the benefits of cooperative social living, and hence on the further, typically unstated, assumption that cooperative social living increases rather than decreases the chances of mutual survival. It is also true that a blanket acceptance of our laws by the defendants in their natural cage would have done nothing to increase their chances of survival or the benefits of cooperation. We might agree that in order to insure the survival of the majority of them, or for that matter even one of them, they would have had to break one or more of this jurisdiction's laws. If the purpose of law is to secure the gains of cooperation, with the most significant gain being mutual survival, and if law should not extend beyond the limits of its defining purpose, then it does seem to follow that the defendants were beyond the law's reach. There is also a good bit of sense in the defendants' claim that law, or a law, should not extend beyond the limits of its defining purpose. To do otherwise is capricious and irrational, rather than lawful, and, in the case of capital crimes, forces the state to engage in acts that are themselves unjustified killings. That degree of hypocrisy is intolerable.

The problem with the defendants' argument is not the lack of authority for their bold assertion that the law should not be pressed beyond its purpose, or with the logic of that assertion itself. The problem is that they have misidentified the law's driving purpose. The core purpose of law, or of the rule of law, is not contract, but rather, the protection of *rights*, the most important of which is the individual's right to equal respect, and accordingly, equal protection under the law. The point of law is to protect *all*, equally, against the wrongful private aggression of others. Indeed, it is only within the umbrella of such equal protection and the individual rights that guarantee it that contractual freedom and contract law yield any benefits at all.

The insistence on the right of each individual to the enjoyment of equal protection by the state from the private aggression of others — particularly homicidal aggression — is the essence of what distinguishes a society living under the rule of law from a society living under the whimsical dictates of a state of nature. In the state of nature, an individual or group may, for any number of reasons, decide that its own chances of survival would be well served by killing, enslaving, or oppressing another person or group, and such a decision would quickly become a political reality. The point of the rule of law is essentially to create and then protect the individual's right not to be so treated and to sanction the conduct of the group or individual who attempts to do so.

The defendants are surely right that contract, and the protection of social gain that it facilitates, is at the center of a great deal of our law. But that body of law is only intelligible once the more fundamental right of equal protection against private assault is secured. An individual may exploit his natural talents and strengths in whatever way imaginable in securing gains through contract. What he may not do is exploit his strength — whether the source of that strength be a natural inheritance, a cultivated talent, or the strength of numbers — in such a way as to violate the rights of others. The most central of those rights is, unquestionably, the right not to be killed, consumed, enslaved, or violently attacked for the benefit of his brothers. The individual has the right to expect the state to protect him against exactly this form of exploitation.

Much follows from this core purpose regarding the content of our law. For example, the common prescriptions against contracting oneself into slavery, contracting for the sale of a body part, or contracting for one's own death can be understood as stemming from our conviction that these rights to state protection against private aggression are so fundamental that they cannot even be voluntarily foresworn. Contract is predicated upon the provision of these core protections against private violence, and thus, these protections, in turn, define the limits of contractual freedom.

More important, if less obvious, than the limits on contract that are implied by the priority of the individual's right to protection against violence, are the limits this principle places on actions or inactions *of the state*. A state may not decide, for good reasons, bad reasons, or no reason, simply to withdraw its protective shield from the vulnerable lives of some individual or group, leaving that individual or group to the mercies of his or her stronger co-citizens. Nor may a state decide not to extend its protection. A state may not decide, for example, to proceed with the execution of a wrongly accused criminal defendant out of the belief that such an execution might prompt a serial killer to stop killing children. Even if such a belief is fully justified — even if the state knew that the true killer would in fact stop killing after the execution in order to reinforce the false societal belief that the correct killer had been identified — such an execution of an innocent person would nevertheless be an intolerable violation of the accused's right to equal protection of the law. Nor may a state decide not to protect a particular group — for example, poor people who live in dangerous neighborhoods — against private violence and aggression, even for the reason that to provide such protection threatens an exceedingly high number of policemen's lives. Nor, of course, may a state decide not to protect a subgroup — a racial or sexual minority, for example — against violence out of a habitual, unconscious, or calculated attempt to enable a favored group to secure the exploitative gains or benefits that might follow from a withdrawal of such protection. Such scapegoating is inimical to the system of rights that is at the heart of our rule of law. Indeed, it is no exaggeration to say that the core meaning of the rule of law is precisely that scapegoating — whether for noble or ignoble reasons and whether prompted by state or private calculations of benefit and loss — is paradigmatically illegal. As citizens of a society governed by the rule of law, we should not deny to any individual or group of individuals the state's protection against private violence in situations in which that violence is intended to secure benefits to —

or even the survival of — the favored. All individuals have the right to be protected against violence, including violence that is premised upon the moral calculation that the sacrifice will save more lives than it will take.

It is thus apparent that the defendants' actions in this case are not merely within the scope of the rule of law, as defined by its purpose, but rather, *are at the very heart of it*. There are indeed different degrees of moral culpability in the motives that prompt different murders. Some such motives are more or less reprehensible than others. But from the perspective of the virtues and values central to the ideal of the rule of *law*, the defendants' jurisprudential and jurisdictional challenge only raises differences in degrees of moral culpability that are ultimately inconsequential: the violation of the individual's right to equal respect and regard, and accordingly his right to equal protection of the law, is not lessened by the strength of the justification for the killing. That he cannot be so sacrificed is precisely what it means to have a right: a right, virtually by definition, cannot be outweighed by individual or group-based calculations of moral or economic gain, even when the gain is measurable in lives saved. The right to equal protection of the law against private violence is violated when the state allows, promotes, or acquiesces in such calculations, and does nothing to prevent or deter the violence to which it leads.

This conclusion, it may be necessary to add, is not undercut by the victim's ambivalence regarding his own participation in the scheme that eventually took his life. Even had the victim's participation been consistently voluntary and enthusiastic, the killing would nevertheless have been a murder for the reasons given above. Our well established prescriptions against assisted suicide, suicide pacts, and mutual contracts of self-destruction make clear that our fundamental right to the state's protection against the assaultive conduct of others takes priority over schemes that waive that protection, even with our full consent. The facts here, however, do not even present us with the admittedly more difficult question of whether the ban on assisted suicide can be reconciled with our strong traditions of individual autonomy. The victim in this case initially was supportive of the plan and did concede the fairness of the procedures governing the throwing of the dice. Nevertheless, the victim clearly withdrew his support from the overall plan. This is not, then, a question of assisted suicide. There was no suicide. This victim was killed against his will and without his consent.

The defendants' second argument is more modest, but if accepted, would also challenge some of our most defining legal ideals. The defendants argue that the recognized excuse of self-defense should be extended to include all killings in which the victim, if dead, could supply biological matter that could potentially save the defendant's life — rather than confine the defense, as we presently do, to those killings in which the victim himself aggresses against the perpetrator. But this we cannot do without inviting a lethal social chaos. Private violence, or even private ordering, cannot be given full sway whenever there are conditions of relative scarcity, rather than the conditions of abundance we have become accustomed to enjoying. To do so invites a slide to state-of-nature conditions, precisely when the need for law is greatest.

Contrary to the defendants' representations, we do not already accept such a limit on the criminal sanction, nor are the conditions or circumstances that might give rise to such a claim quite so rare or infrequent as the defendants suggest. For example, there are currently a sizable number of citizens in this country awaiting organ donations, bone marrow replacements, and blood transfusions. The profound scarcity of such organs, bone marrow, and non-contaminated rare blood types is the sad reality that all such patients (as well as those of us who may at any point become such a patient) are forced to endure. That scarcity prompts incomparable anguish among the needy donees, and tortured decisions by medical personnel. Clearly, some percentage of the total number of hopeful donees could conceivably identify potential donors whose organs, marrow, or blood might save their lives. If three, four, or five of those individuals could, in turn, identify the same potential donor — someone with the healthy liver, the matching bone marrow, or the requisite rare blood type — what is to prevent them, under the principle urged by the defendants here, from taking those organs by force, even at the cost of the donor's life? If we do not allow and should not allow such pillaging of another's organs in this not so fanciful scenario, why should we allow it here? The objective need for some body part is the same, whether the need is for the marrow within the bone or the flesh on the outside of it. The moral calculation is the same and comparably motivated: if one life is sacrificed, then a greater number will be saved. One could even imagine the killing in the medical transplant case being preceded by agreement, which was later withdrawn by the victim-donee, as was the case here. In both cases, nothing can excuse the subsequent murder. The broader principle, governing both the speluncean and the organ transfer cases, is simply this: that perpetrators require a part of a victim's body for the perpetrators' own survival does not make the killing that is so motivated one of "self-defense." No act of aggression is being defended. Rather, there is only a tragic dilemma of incompatible needs and scarce resources.

Nor is this action justified by the related doctrine of "moral necessity." The invasive, assaultive taking of the life or body parts of one individual is never "morally necessary," even if such body parts may be necessary to secure a greater number of lives of those in need. Even such an innocent creature as a full-term fetus, or, as some believe, an unborn child, is not permitted to pillage the bodily fluids and organs of the mother when the fetus's actions, although utterly involuntary, threaten the mother's life. The pregnant woman is not expected to sacrifice *her life* to promote the well-being of the fetus inside her who needs her body when that need is at the expense of her own life and the sacrifice is against her desires. Rather, it is in precisely these circumstances (and perhaps only in these circumstances) in the contested and difficult area of reproduction law that we have achieved a sort of societal consensus that the mother (not the fetus) has the right to defend herself against the needy and life-threatening fetus within her by expelling the fetus, even at the cost of the fetus's life.

This consensus is not surprising: surely if a born child — for example, an adult — who needed a parent's bone marrow, attempted to secure it from a non-consenting parent, the state would presumably help protect that parent against the child's aggression; the state would not grant the "moral necessity" of the child's action. Nothing here distinguishes the sacrificed speluncean from the pregnant woman whose life is threatened by the needs of the invasive fetus, or from the parent whose life is threatened by the child; indeed, the lack of a parent-child or mother-fetal relationship from which one might arguably infer a duty on the part of the parent or pregnant woman makes the speluncean's predicament a much *weaker* case. In all three cases, the sacrificial life is biologically necessary for the aggressor's survival, but in none of them does that fact make the killing (or the letting die, in the case of the pregnant woman) *morally* necessary. The defendants' actions in the cave, in short, were neither taken in self-defense against unwarranted aggression, nor were they morally necessary. The killing was not justified.

II

Having rejected the defendants' contentions, it is nevertheless clear to me that these men should not be executed and that to carry out the executions would constitute an injustice — indeed, a killing perhaps as unjustified, ultimately, as the one they committed. The action they took was criminal, and the crime was murder. But does it follow that the punishment must be death by hanging? These defendants have not been given a chance to show this Court — either the jury or the justices — that their actions, although not justified, might be partially or totally excused by the harshness of their circumstances, or alternatively, that the harshness of the penalty applied should be mitigated by a judicial recognition of the extraordinary conditions of hardship under which they struggled. Nor has this Court — again either jury or judge — been permitted to make such a determination. We have not heard the mitigating evidence — whether about the men themselves, their character, the conditions in the cave, the altered states of consciousness those conditions might have brought on, or the feel or the force of the natural imperative of survival to which they eventually acquiesced. This evidence might prompt the Court to recognize the unique horror that gripped these defendants and consequently impose a penalty that might be less severe than death for the all-too-human actions they took in response to that horror. But such an exploration — and possibly a recognition — seems to be precisely what this case requires for its just resolution. These men were in desperate circumstances and took desperate measures to survive. It is not obvious that any of us would have responded differently. Even though their action was a criminal homicide, it does not follow that the punishment of death is warranted.

These defendants are no threat to the survival of the state or the safety of the community. They have already suffered tremendously. Although not so unique as to remove them from the jurisdiction of our courts, their situation was surely peculiar — so much so that their execution would provide little in the way of general deterrence. Why kill them? Can it really be true that justice requires such a harsh conclusion, without even a hearing of facts or argument that might mitigate it?

Our criminal law, as presently constituted in 4300 A.D., seems to require as much. The judge and jury, according to theory, apply the law to the facts toward the end of *justice*; the Chief Executive, pursuing radically inapposite principles of mercy, can mitigate the punishment by reference to all that the Court, in its pursuit of justice, cannot hear: the stories of these defendants' lives, of their travails, of the pressures upon them, of their remorse, and of their fears and hopes for their future. But this bifurcation of justice and mercy, of "law" and mitigation, of the Court's province and the Chief Executive's office — so reminiscent of the antiquated split between law and equity, long ago abandoned in our civil jurisprudence — serves no one well. It forces defendants to make specious arguments. It forces the Court to make formalistic conclusions, and it tempts judges to make decisions for unstated reasons — an unstated hope, prayer, or expectation that the Chief Executive will or will not act in a certain way; an unsound argument accepted in defense of an action, when it is, in fact, a judge's imagined full accounting of the events in question that constitutes the real grounds of decision. The statute that seemingly requires this woodenness is classically and flagrantly overinclusive: it includes within its sweep acts and defendants whose differentiating circumstances are such that they ought to be treated differently. It also forces the ultimate decision of life or death upon an elected official who may or may not have the requisite popular support, and thereby the political power, to forego executions, even should he think it the morally right course of action. The statute puts the lives of these defendants at the dubious "mercy" of an elected official whose own political survival is beholden to the whims of majoritarian politics. In short, it makes our law unmerciful and the Executive's mercy lawless. The quality of our law and the quality of the Executive's mercy both suffer when we pretend that justice and mercy can be severed.

For these reasons, I hold that the provision of the murder statute that requires death by hanging as the punishment for the intentional taking of another human life, without any possibility for the *judicial* mitigation of the punishment, is an unconstitutional deprivation of the defendants' right not to have their lives taken from them without due process of law, and a deprivation of their right to a rational application of law. Just as the victim of criminal violence has a fundamental right to the protection of law, the charged defendant in a criminal case has a right to an individualized determination of an appropriate punishment that reflects the degree of his culpability. In a rights-based system of law such as ours, we can no more neglect a defendant's right to be individually judged than a victim's right to be included in the community and under the law's protection. The choices that the unconstitutional provision now presents us — a judicial finding of guilt, followed by execution; a judicial finding of guilt followed by an Executive's decision to decrease the punishment to six months; or an acquittal on dubious grounds — are too stark. The statute prevents the Court from pursuing merciful justice, and it deprives the defendants of precious constitutional rights. These defendants should be given the opportunity to present their own story in their own defense and in mitigation of the punishment for their criminal action, and this Court should be given the opportunity to so decide. We need to hold a hearing to determine the appropriate sentence. Accordingly, the provision of the statute that denies such an opportunity should be struck, to allow this case to proceed to a fully merciful — and hence more just — resolution.

DE BUNKER, J.*

I. OVERVIEW

This case raises disturbing questions about the continuing influence of such anachronistic concepts as "natural law," "inalienable rights," and other legal fictions of ages past. We have yet to reject these irrational residues of the past even in the present fifth millennium (a system of dating which itself is based on what we now recognize to be a religious myth).

As is well known from the history disks, shortly after the beginning of the third millennium, the world became engulfed in religious warfare among fundamentalist Christians, Muslims, Jews, and others. Apocalyptic religious extremists obtained access to weapons of mass

* Alan M. Dershowitz, Felix Frankfurter Professor of Law, Harvard University.

destruction. The result was the cataclysmic decimation of human life in the name of the various "gods" under whose symbols — crosses, crescents, and stars — the slaughters were implemented. The survivors of this apocalypse began to realize that the religious myths surrounding such deities as "the Holy Spirit," "Allah," and "Jehovah" were indistinguishable from those that had surrounded the gods of ancient Egypt, Greece, and Rome. Gradually, a new consensus emerged, at first questioning the existence of any supernatural god (the Agnostic Epoch or AGEP), and then, in the current age, disclaiming any such belief in deities (the Atheistic Epoch or ATEP).[1] Just as the Christian, Muslim, and Jewish primitives of the first and second millennia regarded the Greek and Roman myths of divinity, so too, our enlightened age regards the myths of the so-called monotheistic religions — myths such as the divine origin of the Bible, the divine paternity of Jesus, and the claim that Mohammed was a messenger of God.[2] We appreciate the poetry and occasional insights of the Bible and the often wonderful teachings of the so-called Hebrew prophets, Jesus, and Mohammed — much as the monotheists of the first and second millennia appreciated the religious art and literature of their polytheistic forebears — but we now know for certain that they are entirely of human origin.

We know, too, that the world has no "purpose," at least as imposed by some external superior force. Human beings are the product of es-

---

[1] It is to be regretted perhaps, though understood, that many atheists remained whetted to prior tribal groups. There were Jewish atheists, Catholic atheists, Protestant atheists, Muslim atheists, and other smaller groupings, arguing vigorously over which God *not* to believe in.

Even prior to the great apocalypse, many thoughtful people understood that their religious "beliefs" and practices were based on myths similar to those of their polytheistic predecessors. But they also saw that religion was important to the lives of many of their friends and that it produced much good — like a placebo taken by one who believes it to be a potent medicine. They were content to regard religion as a pious and harmless fraud. But the great apocalypse demonstrated how dangerous such myths had become, and most citizens began to demand that religion be treated like other irrational belief systems such as astrology, tarot cards, and voodoo. Soon it became as unfashionable to believe in the supernatural doctrines of formal religion as it was to believe that the earth was flat.

Even prior to the Great Fundamentalist Wars of the third millenium, some courageous intellectuals began to challenge monotheistic dogma, but they had considerable difficulties in persuading the masses. Part of the reason for their hardship was that certain evil totalitarian regimes had forced atheism on their citizens, thereby associating disbelief in God with tyranny. It became voguish for prudent intellectuals to argue that science (empirical truth) and faith (belief) must be kept separate and that matters of faith should not be judged by scientific criteria. This, too, however, was a myth because many of the claims of faith — for example, that Moses parted the Red Sea, that Jesus walked on water, and that Mohammed ascended to heaven on a horse — are empirical and historical: they either happened or they were made up. Following the wars, more people began to insist on proof of such claims and concluded that they were fictional.

[2] Contemporary historians still cannot solve the intellectual puzzle of why, for more than 2,000 years, so many people concluded that belief in one supernatural being (monotheism) was regarded as an "advance" over belief in many supernatural beings (polytheism).

sentially random processes, such as evolution, genetic mutations, or other largely non-purposive factors.

We have long understood these self-evident truths, and we apply them to most areas of our lives, such as science, education, and literature. But when it comes to law, we have stubbornly resisted the necessary process of rooting out of our current legal system the anachronistic remnants of the divine mythologies of our past. We persist in speaking about "natural law," as if the physical "laws" of nature carried with them any normative corollaries. We continue to invoke "inalienable rights," as if we believed that they derived from some preexisting, supernatural, non-human source.

Because this case raises questions that challenge the very basis of our laws, I see it as an appropriate vehicle for considering the meaning of such concepts as "natural law" and "inalienable rights" in a world free of superstitions about divine beings, supernatural forces, and purposive creation.

I am convinced that in such a world — in our world — there can be no such meaningful concepts as natural law or inalienable rights. Natural law presupposes a view of nature — of the nature of human beings and of the world — that is demonstrably false. The nature of human beings is so diverse — ranging from the most amoral and predatory to the most moral and self-sacrificing — that all or no normative conclusions can be drawn from its descriptive diversity.[3] Inalienable rights presuppose an externally imposed hierarchy that makes no sense in the absence of an external law-giver. We must now ac-

---

[3] To illustrate the point that principles of "natural law" can cut in different directions, consider the principle that every human life is of equal value. Justice West employs a variation on that principle to demand conviction in this case. Yet the American Law Institute cites precisely the same principle to justify the killing of one innocent person to save the lives of many: "The life of every individual must be taken in such a case to be of equal value and the numerical preponderance in the lives saved compared to those sacrificed surely should establish legal justification for the act." Model Penal Code § 3.02 commentary at 14–15 (1962).

As a gay woman of color, I am particularly skeptical of deriving moral laws from the nature of human beings because history has shown that most such laws have been derived from the purported nature of "man" — in the past, usually a white, heterosexual man of the dominant group. I am also skeptical of inalienable rights because, for centuries, such rights did not include those of women, gays, or racial minorities. Today, of course, whites are the racial minority in most nations, including our own. The principle, however, remains the same. Of course, positive laws — such as those enacted in Nazi Germany in the second millenium — have been used to subordinate (and worse) many human beings, but natural law has been likewise abused. These are all powerful arguments for why we should *prefer* laws that entrench certain basic rights, such as equality, freedom of conscience and expression, due process, and other protections against the tyranny of positive, natural, or other kinds of law and lawlessness.

I also prefer a system that assures both religious freedom for those few dissidents who continue to insist that there is a god — who gave Moses the Torah, is Jesus's father, and inspired Mohammed — and the freedom to believe in and practice other irrational superstitions, so long as such practices do not interfere with the rights of the vast majority of rational people to base our lives on principles of human reason. Efforts to impose atheism by law have failed, as have efforts to impose religion by law. The marketplace of ideas and beliefs has proved to be the better option.

knowledge that all law must be positive law and all rights must merely be strongly held preferences that we or our predecessors have agreed to elevate over other positive law. This elevated status of particular laws — such as the guarantee of free speech — can be the result of a constitution (written or oral), an entrenched tradition, or another form of super-positive law. It cannot come from any claim of supernatural or natural forces external to the human processes of lawmaking. Thus, the only basis for preferring one set of laws or rights over another is human persuasion and advocacy.

In this opinion, I will try to persuade others to accept my approach, not by reference to some natural or supernatural authority, but rather exclusively by reference to human reason and agreed-upon principles. These principles may take the form of preferred imperatives, such as those proposed by ancient philosophers including Immanuel Kant, or they may take the form of preferred situational rules, such as those proposed by Jeremy Bentham and others. But they are all merely *human preferences*, even if often articulated in the language of natural law and inalienable rights.[4]

II. Discussion

How then should a supreme court, unencumbered by concepts of natural law or inalienable rights, evaluate the actions that form the basis of this case? First, some preliminary observations are necessary: a civilized society could reasonably legislate either result advocated by my judicial colleagues. The legislature could have, if it had anticipated the current problem, written a clear, positive law explicitly prohibiting starving people from killing one of their number in order to save the rest. The arguments in favor of and in opposition to such a rule are fairly obvious and have been made over the ages.[5] Yet our legislature has never explicitly resolved this millennia-old debate by enacting legislation either prohibiting or permitting such life-saving killings. My preference in this situation is for the following rule of law: when a tragic choice is sufficiently recurring so that it can be anticipated, and when reasonable people over time have disagreed over whether a given choice should be permissible, the onus must be on the legislature to prohibit that choice by the enactment of positive law if it wishes to do so.

For those who argue that such a positive law would be ineffective because it is against the self-preservatory nature of human beings, there is a simple answer: legislate creative punishments that will be ef-

[4] I, too, believe that certain rights should be accepted *by agreement* as inalienable, or at least as not subject to abrogation by a simple majority. This is my preference, and I hope to persuade others to agree with it.

[5] As the ancient Talmud rhetorically asked: "[W]ho knows that your blood is redder?" Sanhedrin 74a *in The Babylonian Talmud* 503 (I. Epstein ed. & H. Freedman trans., 1935).

fective. Such punishments might include posthumous shame,[6] deprivation of inheritance rights for offspring, or enhanced painful punishments for survivors. The point is that this is largely an empirical, rather than a moral, objection to prohibiting the eating of one starving human to save others.[7]

A civilized society could also legislate a positive law permitting (even requiring) the sacrifice of one starving innocent person to save several others. The arguments in support of such a law are also obvious and long standing. As Oliver Wendall Holmes reportedly wrote, "[A]ll society has rested on the death of men and must rest on that or on the prevention of the lives of a good many." Objections, such as the slippery slope, are also commonplace.

The point is that neither approach is more "natural' than the other. Nor can the case be resolved by reference to any inalienable right, such as the "right to life." Both approaches claim to be natural and to further the right to life. Both also have considerable moral and empirical advantages and disadvantages, and no one in our society is inherently better suited to choose one over the other than anyone else.[8] Yet a choice must be made. Accordingly, we move the argument from the level of substance to the level of process: who shall be authorized to make such decisions, on what bases shall they be made, and if there are gaps in the primary decisionmaking, who shall be authorized to fill the gaps in particular cases? These issues must also be matters of preference and persuasion.

The problem presented by this case has existed since the beginning of recorded history. There are examples — at differing levels of abstraction — in numerous works of history, religion, and literature. Why then did the representative body that was authorized to enact general laws not specifically address this recurring issue? To be sure, the issue does not occur with the frequency of self-defense, but it is widely enough known to be capable of specific inclusion in any modern code governing homicide. Indeed, one of the most ancient of legal

---

6 In the old days, the prospect of punishment in the afterlife — eternity in hell — could be threatened. Today, of course, few believe in such irrational "ghost stories." Even in the past ages of religions it is doubtful whether many people actually believed in heaven and hell because so many sins were committed by "believers." The threat of eternal punishment and reward did not dispense with the need for earthly punishments to deter crimes that were also sins.

7 There may, of course, be moral objections if the penalties necessary to deter the conduct are too harsh or fall too heavily on innocent third parties. *See, e.g.*, *supra*, at 1897–99 (West, J.) (appearing to make such an argument in her rejection of the death penalty as a punishment for the defendants, although she does believe they are guilty under the statute).

8 It could be argued that elite philosophers or jurists are better suited because of their intellect and education to make such decisions. Many millennia ago, a Greek philosopher named Plato proposed such an elitist theory of decisionmaking. Most democracies have rejected it, concluding instead that representative decisionmaking is preferable. Choosing who should decide the law, too, is ultimately a matter of preference and persuasion. However, the advocates of representative decisionmaking have generally prevailed over time.

codes — the *Talmud* — did include specific discussions of this and related questions.[9] Philosophers and legal scholars have also considered these issues over the years. Yet few, if any, criminal codes explicitly tell starving cave explorers, sailors, or space travelers what they may, should, or must do if they find themselves in the unenviable position in which these defendants found themselves. It is to be noted that this case is not unlike one that occurred in the ninth century of the second millennium in a nation then known as Great Britain. *See Regina v. Dudley and Stephens*, 14 Q.B.D. 273 (1884). Yet even after the divided court in that case expressed considerable difficulty in arriving at a principled decision based upon those facts, the legislature did not enact a positive law to resolve the issue definitively. Nor can the legislature's silence in the face of the nominal affirmance of that conviction be deemed evidence of its intent to demand conviction in this case. The vast majority of comparable cases — both before and after that decision — resulted in acquittal or decisions not to prosecute, and the English case produced a pardon. The law is more than the isolated decisions of a small number of appellate courts.

What does this long history of legislative abdication of responsibility tell us about how *we*, a court, should resolve this case? It tells us that the people do not seem to want this issue resolved in the abstract by legislation. Our elected representatives apparently prefer not to legislate general approval or disapproval of the course of action undertaken by the defendants here. Our citizens cannot bring themselves to say that eating one's neighbor in the tragic situation presented here is morally just. Nor can they bring themselves to say it is unjust. They would prefer to leave the decision, as an initial matter, to the people in the cave (at least as long as they make it on some rational and fair basis). Then they would have a prosecutor decide whether to prosecute, a jury whether to convict, a court whether to affirm, and an executive whether to pardon or commute. That is the unwieldy process, composed of layers of decisionmakers, they seem to have chosen.

The question still remains: by what criteria should we, the Supreme Court, decide whether to affirm the jury's conviction (and recommendation for clemency)? The answer seems relatively obvious to me, and

[9] *See, e.g.*, David Daube, *Collaboration with Tyranny in Rabbinic Law* (1965); Marilyn Finkelman, *Self-defense and Defense of Others in Jewish Law: The* Rodef *Defense*, 33 Wayne L. Rev. 1257 (1987). Among the cases — some actual, others hypothetical — considered in the *Talmud* are the following: an enemy general surrounds a walled city and threatens to kill all of its inhabitants unless they turn over one individual for execution; two people are dying of thirst in the desert with enough water between them to save one but not both; a child, below the age of legal responsibility and thus deemed innocent, threatens the life of another innocent person and can be prevented from killing only by being killed (the filmmaker Alfred Hitchcock presented a variation on this theme in an episode from his television program); and a fetus endangers the life of a pregnant mother who can be saved only by killing the fetus (a variation is that during delivery, the baby endangers the life of the mother who can be saved only by killing the partially delivered baby).

I will try to persuade others to agree with the preferences on which it is based. I begin with my strong preference — a preference which I believe and hope is now widely shared — for a society in which any act that is not specifically prohibited is implicitly permitted, rather than for a society in which any act that is not specifically permitted is implicitly prohibited. As Johann Christoph Friedrich von Schiller similarly expressed, "Whatever is not forbidden is permitted."[10] The lessons of history have demonstrated why the former is to be preferred over the latter.

A general preference for freedom of action in the absence of specific prohibition does, however, raise some troubling problems. Innovative harm-doers often find ways to do mischief between the interstices of positive law, and old laws have difficulty keeping up with new technologies. Accordingly, this preference occasionally results in the failure to punish the initial group of creative criminals in any particular genre. Still, I would argue for a strong presumption in favor of freedom in the absence of a specific prohibition — even at the cost of letting some guilty go free.

In any event, the problem outlined above does not describe the situation we face. The actions committed by these defendants were not part of some technological innovation unknowable to the drafters of our positive law. Our drafters could easily have legislated against what the defendants did here. They did not. *Why* they did not — laziness, thoughtlessness, cowardice, superstition, or an unwillingness to resolve an intractable moral dilemma — is in the realm of speculation. *That* they did not is not fairly open to doubt. Some may argue, of course, that the general prohibition against willful killing is enough to cover the conduct at issue here because this killing was willful.[11] But I do not believe that it can be reasonably maintained that the absence of an explicit exception to the broad prohibition against killing contained in the positive law must be interpreted as an implicit prohibition against the kind of killing done here. That mode of reasoning would substantially compromise the principle that what is not specifically prohibited is implicitly permitted, especially in the context of a widely reported and debated historical genre of alleged crime such as the killing under consideration here.

Moreover, the law has long recognized justifications for taking actions expressly prohibited by the letter of the law when such actions are "necessary" to prevent a "greater harm." This principle has been

[10] Johann Christoph Friedrich von Schiller, *Wallenstein's Camp*, sc. 4 (1798), *quoted in Bartlett's Familiar Quotations* 365 (John Bartlett & Justin Kaplan eds., 16th ed. 1992).

[11] The killing was also premeditated, as are all judicial executions. The official death certificate in a famous death penalty case during the last century of the second millennium — the Sacco and Vanzetti case, *Commonwealth v. Sacco*, 151 N.E. 839 (Mass. 1926) — listed the cause of death of the defendants as "electric shock judicial homicide." Certificate of Death of Bartolomeo Vanzetti (1927) (on file with the Harvard Law School Library).

summarized by the quip, "Necessity knows no law."[12] It is a mischaracterization, however, because there is a well-developed, if imprecise, law of necessity that permits the choice of a lesser harm to prevent a greater harm.[13] Throughout history, philosophers and jurists have debated cases — both hypothetical and real — that tested this difficult principle. During the Nazi holocaust of the second millennium, a group of Jews who were hiding from Nazi killers smothered a crying baby in order to prevent the Nazis from discovering their hiding places and killing them all. When that terrible dilemma — which occurred in slightly differing contexts throughout the holocaust — was presented to distinguished religious leaders, the consensus was that the conduct could not be condemned. *See* Marilyn Finkelman, *Self-defense and Defense of Others in Jewish Law: The* Rodef *Defense*, 33 Wayne L. Rev. 1257, 1278–80 (1987). Nor do I believe that a secular court would have found these desperate people guilty of murder even if they willfully, deliberately, and with premeditation killed the innocent baby.[14]

Necessity as a general defense to crime "seems clearly to have standing as a common law defense."[15] Model Penal Code § 3.02 commentary at 10 (1962). Nearly all jurisdictions recognize the necessity

---

[12] One of my judicial colleagues, whom I will not name, is sometimes referred to as "Necessity," because he too "knows no law."

[13] *See* Sanford H. Kadish & Stephen J. Schulhofer, *Criminal Law and its Processes: Cases and Materials* 860–80 (6th ed. 1995). Surely the death of several people is a greater harm than the death of one person. *But see* Nezikin 5, *in The Babylonian Talmud* (I. Epstein ed. & H. Freedman trans., 1935) ("Whosoever preserves a single soul of Israel [it is] as though he had preserved a complete world.").

[14] Perhaps this decision would be influenced by the tragic reality that so many of those who created the dilemma — the Nazi murderers — got away with it.

[15] The necessity defense has been "anciently woven into the fabric of our culture." J. Hall, *General Principles of Criminal Law* 416 (2d ed. 1960), *cited in* Laura J. Schulkind, Note, *Applying the Necessity Defense to Civil Disobedience Cases*, 64 N.Y.U. L. Rev. 79, 83 n.20 (1989). It can be found in caselaw dating as far back as 1551 in *Reniger v. Fogossa*, 75 Eng. Rep. 1 (K.B. 1551). Arguing that a captain who docked his ship to avoid a storm would not have to forfeit his goods as the statute would have required, the Court concluded:

> [A] man may break the words of the law, and yet not break the law itself . . . . And therefore the words of the law . . . will yield and give way to some acts and things done against the words of the same laws, and that is, where the words of them are broken to avoid greater inconvenience, or through necessity . . . .

Id. at 29. The *Reniger* court reached even further back to the New Testament example in Matthew 12:3–4 of eating sacred bread or taking another's corn through necessity of hunger. *See id.* at 29–30; *see also* Edward B. Arnolds & Norman F. Garland, *The Defense of Necessity in Criminal Law: The Right to Choose the Lesser Evil*, 65 J. Crim. L. & Criminology 289, 291 n.27 (1974) (citing *Reniger*). Arnolds and Garland enumerate many other older, *see* Arnolds & Garland, *supra*, at 291 nn.29–34, and modern, *see id.* at 291–92 nn.35–37, English cases that "recognize the general principle of necessity," *id.* at 291, as well as both federal, *see id.* at 292 nn.38–44, and state, *see id.* at 292 nn.45–50, cases in the United States. The court system's recognition of the necessity defense is also acknowledged in casebooks. *See, e.g.*, Sanford H. Kadish & Stephen J. Schulhofer, *Criminal Law and Its Processes* 860–80 (6th ed. 1995).

defense for crimes that are short of killing.[16] Thus, if our defendants had found a locked food-storage box in the cave with a sign saying "private, personal property, do not open under any circumstances," and they had broken open the lock and eaten the food, no one would deny they were acting lawfully. I doubt that any of my colleagues would convict such defendants of theft even if the words of the theft statute provided for *no* exception. The general law of necessity provides the requisite exception in cases in which theft is a lesser evil than multiple deaths. However, some jurisdictions have explicitly refused to extend the necessity defense to the killing of an innocent person that is necessary to prevent the deaths of several innocent people.[17] Other jurisdictions have not limited the necessity defense to non-killings.[18] Academic opinion is divided, and the weight of the American Law Institute is on the side of not limiting the defense as long as the killing is necessary and results in the saving of more innocent lives than are taken. "[T]he principle of necessity is one of general validity .... It would be particularly unfortunate to exclude homicidal conduct from the scope of the defense."[19] Model Penal Code § 3.02 commentary at

[16] The necessity defense is part of the *Model Penal Code*, *see* Model Penal Code § 3.02, and has been incorporated into many state criminal codes, *see* Lawrence P. Tiffany & Carl A. Anderson, *Legislating the Necessity Defense in Criminal Law*, 52 Denv. L.J. 839 (1975) (examining how many states included the necessity defense when they recodified their criminal statutes).

[17] *See, e.g.*, Ky. Rev. Stat. Ann. § 503.030 (Michie 1985) (stating that "no justification can exist ... for an intentional homicide"); Mo. Rev. Stat. § 563.026 (1994) (stating that "conduct which would otherwise constitute any crime other than a class A felony or murder is justifiable and not criminal when it is necessary as an emergency measure to avoid an imminent public or private injury"); Wis. Stat. Ann. § 939.47 (West 1997–98) (stating that necessity "is a defense to a prosecution ... except that if the prosecution is for first-degree intentional homicide, the degree of the crime is reduced to 2nd-degree intentional homicide"); *Regina v. Pommell*, 2 Crim. App. 607, 608 (1995) (stating that the necessity defense does not apply to murder and attempted murder), *cited in* Alan Reed, *Duress and Provocation as Excuses to Murder: Salutary Lessons from Recent Anglo-American Jurisprudence*, 6 J. Transnat'l L. & Pol'y 51, 68 n.20 (1996).

Those jurisdictions that limit the necessity defense to crimes other than killing face the following conundrum: A person who was provoked into killing by seeing his wife in bed with another man can have the charges reduced from murder to manslaughter if he is deemed to have acted as a reasonable man would have acted under a similar provocation. But a man who kills one person to save multiple lives faces conviction for first-degree murder. Such cases and statutes also contradict the general principle found in the *Model Penal Code* commentaries that the defense is available [when] a person intentionally kills one person in order save two or more." 1 Wayne R. LaFave & Austin W. Scott, Jr., *Substantive Criminal Law* § 5.4, at 632 (1986).

[18] As Tiffany and Anderson conclude:

> The common law rejection [in *Dudley*] of the defense when the intentional killing of an innocent person was involved, appears now to be almost universally rejected itself. The most common statutory approach is to provide, merely, that if the other conditions of the defense are all satisfied, the actor's "conduct" is justified.

Tiffany & Anderson, *supra*, at 860 (footnotes omitted).

[19] The American Law Institute continued:

> For, recognizing that the sanctity of life has a supreme place in the hierarchy of values, it is nonetheless true that conduct that results in taking life may promote the very value sought to be protected by the law of homicide. Suppose, for example, that the actor makes a breach in a dike, knowing that this will inundate a farm, but taking the only course available to save a whole town. If he is charged with homicide of the inhabitants of the farm

14. The reason that judicial decisions about this issue are "rare," *see id.* at 10, is that prosecutors almost never bring charges against people who have chosen the lesser evil of taking one life to save many others.

Our jurisdiction has not resolved this debate or even confronted this issue. Our own common law of necessity is thus written in terms as general as our murder statute: "Anyone who commits an act that would otherwise be a crime under circumstances in which it is necessary to prevent a greater evil shall not be guilty." The issue before us, therefore, is whether the legislative silence should be interpreted as acceptance or rejection of the limitation adopted by some jurisdictions and rejected by others. Compounding the complexity of the problem is the fact that in the absence of legislative resolution, these defendants sought authoritative guidance from various sources before deciding what to do — the best they could do under the circumstances. They were denied any such guidance. To hold them criminally liable is to convict them of guessing wrongly regarding what the unpredictable vote of this Court would be. Moreover, to convict them under these circumstances — especially in the face of our legislature's refusal to resolve the debate over the limits of the necessity defense — would be to prefer a rule of judicial interpretation that resolves doubts in favor of expanding the criminal law rather than of resolving "ambiguity concerning the ambit of criminal statutes . . . in favor of lenity." *United States v. Bass*, 404 U.S. 336, 347 (1971) (quoting *Rewis v. United States*, 401 U.S. 808, 812 (1971)) (internal quotation marks omitted).[20] The same rule of lenity must apply, as well, in construing the common law of crime. *See Bouie v. City of Columbia*, 378 U.S. 347, 352–54 (1964). Where does our Supreme Court get the authority to narrow the law of necessity and thereby to make criminal what the legislature has declined explicitly to proscribe? My brothers and sisters do not answer this question.

> house, he can rightly point out that the object of the law of homicide is to save life, and that by his conduct he has effected a net saving of innocent lives. The life of every individual must be taken in such a case to be of equal value and the numerical preponderance in the lives saved compared to those sacrificed surely should establish legal justification for the act. So too, a mountaineer, roped to a companion who has fallen over a precipice, who holds on as long as possible but eventually cuts the rope, must certainly be granted the defense that he accelerated one death slightly but avoided the only alternative, the certain death of both. Although the view is not universally held that it is ethically preferable to take one innocent life than to have many lives lost, most persons probably think a net saving of lives is ethically warranted if the choice among lives to be saved is not unfair. Certainly the law should permit such a choice.

Kadish & Schulhofer, *supra*, at 877–78 (quoting Model Penal Code § 3.02 commentary at 14–15 (1985)).

[20] *See also United States v. Lanier*, 520 U.S. 259, 266 (1997) ("[T]he canon of strict construction of criminal statutes, or rule of lenity, ensures fair warning by so resolving ambiguity in a criminal statute as to apply it only to conduct clearly covered."); *Staples v. United States*, 511 U.S. 600, 619 (1994) (noting that under the rule of lenity, an "ambiguous criminal statute" should be "construed in favor of the accused").

Of course, if the legislature had explicitly considered the "choice of evils" presented by the case and expressly foreclosed the action taken, the necessity defense would not be available. But as I have shown, our legislature has not explicitly spoken to this specific problem, despite its prominent place in legal and philosophical discourse.[21] Accordingly, applying the salutary rule placing the onus on the legislature to prohibit questionable conduct by specific, targeted language, it follows that these defendants may not lawfully be punished.

III. The Views of My Colleagues

Several of my colleagues point to the plain language of the statute, while acknowledging that there must be exceptions, such as self-defense and executions, that are recognized from time to time at common law. But necessity also has been recognized from time to time, and there has been a great debate over the millennia regarding whether necessity can excuse a killing done to prevent greater harm, such as multiple deaths. Renowned authorities have come down on different sides of this debate, and our legislature has refused to resolve it explicitly. It is in this context that the words included in, and omitted from, the statute must be interpreted. That process can be undertaken in different ways.

---

[21] Indeed, it is fair to say that few lawyers get through law school without discussing this conundrum and its numerous variations. Most law students read *Dudley and Stephens* and *United States v. Holmes*, 26 F. Cas. 360 (C.C.E.D. Pa. 1842) (No. 15,383). Many also study the writings of the great twentieth-century philosopher Robert Nozick, who, in 1974, constructed the following prescient hypotheticals:

> If someone picks up a third party and throws him at you down at the bottom of a deep well, the third party is innocent and a threat; had he chosen to launch himself at you in that trajectory he would be an aggressor. Even though the falling person would survive his fall onto you, may you use your ray gun to disintegrate the falling body before it crushes and kills you? Libertarian prohibitions are usually formulated so as to forbid using violence on innocent persons. But innocent threats, I think, are another matter to which different principles must apply. Thus, a full theory in this area also must formulate the *different* constraints on response to innocent threats. Further complications concern *innocent shields of threats*, those innocent persons who themselves are nonthreats but who are so situated that they will be damaged by the only means available for stopping the threat. Innocent persons strapped onto the front of the tanks of aggressors so that the tanks cannot be hit without also hitting them are innocent shields of threats. (Some uses of force on people to get at an aggressor do not act upon innocent shields of threats; for example, an aggressor's innocent child who is tortured in order to get the aggressor to stop wasn't *shielding* the parent.) May one knowingly injure innocent shields? *If* one may attack an aggressor and injure an innocent shield, may the innocent shield fight back in self-defense (supposing that he cannot move against or fight the aggressor)? Do we get two persons battling each other in self-defense? Similarly, if you use force against an innocent threat to you, do you thereby become an innocent threat to him, so that he may now justifiably use additional force against you (supposing that he can do this, yet cannot prevent his original threateningness)?

Robert Nozick, *Anarchy, State, and Utopia* 34–35 (1974). Students have also debated the following hypothetical case: A doctor is experimenting with a deadly virus; the virus begins to spread (through no fault of the doctor); the only way to prevent the spread of the virus is to seal the room from which the doctor is trying to flee, thus dooming him.

One of my colleagues, Justice Kozinski, proposes an absolute rule of inclusion: unless there is an express exception, the literal words of the statute must apply, regardless of how absurd the result may appear to us. *See supra*, at 1876 (Kozinski, J.). Taken to its logical conclusion, this rule would punish the proper use of deadly force by policemen because the statute does not explicitly exclude such killings.

It is important to recognize that the legislation at issue here is an example of a "common law statute," prohibiting a general category of conduct — in this instance, willful killing — in the broadest of terms, while anticipating judicial narrowing. It cannot rationally be argued that the legislature intended the judiciary to recognize certain exceptions, such as self-defense, while precluding it from recognizing other defenses, such as necessity, that are accepted by numerous jurisdictions. Once it is agreed that this Court has the power to decide whether the defense of necessity is part of our law, it surely must follow that it has the power to define its parameters. It is plainly preferable to leave such decisions to the reasoned judgment of disinterested courts than to the unarticulated discretion of adversarial prosecutors.[22]

I am not suggesting that every possible category of crime be specifically mentioned in the statute, but rather that widely recognized defenses, such as necessity, cannot be deemed to have been abrogated by legislative silence, especially when the statute seems to invite inclusion of some recognized defenses that are not explicitly mentioned.

Another of my colleagues, Justice Sunstein, proposes an "absurdity exception" to the otherwise absolute rule of plain meaning. *See supra*, at 1883–84 (Sunstein, J.). This would permit prosecution in the following case: A train loses its brakes and heads in the direction of a fork. If the conductor does nothing, the train will hit a school bus full of children. If he takes the fork, it will hit a drunk sleeping on the track. There is no third alternative. He takes the fork, thus killing the drunk. Convicting him would be wrong because his beneficent *purpose* was to save lives, but it would not be "absurd" because he *intended* to kill the drunk.[23] Yet another of my colleagues tells us that all statutes must be interpreted by reference to a "right" whose source is nowhere identified, namely that "[a]ll individuals have the right to be protected against violence, including violence that is premised upon the moral calculation that the sacrifice will save more lives than it will take." *Supra*, at 1895 (West, J.). This rule would permit prosecution not only of the train conductor, but also of the hiding Jews who killed

---

[22] Justice Easterbrook premises his decision largely on the assumption that these defendants implicitly consented to the decision ultimately taken and the conclusion that "society should recognize th[at] agreement." *See infra*, at 1916 (Easterbrook, J.). The problem is that consent, even when explicit, has not always been accepted as a defense to willful killing, as evidenced by the ancient case of *People v. Kevorkian*, 527 N.W.2d 714 (Mich. 1994).

[23] Indeed, under governing case law, his homicide was even premeditated because premeditation can occur in an instant.

the baby in order to prevent their apprehension and murder by the Nazis. Would my colleagues really support their preferred rules in the face of these testing cases?

Justice West also poses a provocative hypothetical case, which should be troubling to any thoughtful judge or legislator. She asks whether a reversal of this conviction would require the conclusion that a group of people in need of organs to live may properly kill one person in order to harvest his organs so that all in the group might live. *See id.* at 1896. It is a good question. One must begin with the conclusion that any general rule of law that would routinely permit the killing of a human being for his organs is a rule of law that should not be accepted by a civilized society. That certainly would be my strong preference. Our case can be distinguished from this one on several grounds. First, there is a universal consensus that killing for organs should be deemed unacceptable. I am aware of no dissent to this proposition in all of jurisprudence, philosophy, or even ancient religion.[24] There is considerable disagreement, however, concerning the spelunean case and its sister case involving the crying baby during the Nazi Holocaust. This difference in the level of agreement alone may distinguish the speluncean case from the organ case, though the reasons underlying it may bolster the difference in outcome. A second distinction between the organ donor case and this case is that in this case the victim would have died within days even if the defendants had not killed him. In the organ donor case, the murdered organ donee could have lived out his life. Thus, the issue in the instant case is not *whether* the victim would have died, but only whether he was to die at the time he was killed so that others could live or whether he would die a few days later in which case no one would have lived. Quite a difference! Third, among the most powerful reasons why we universally reject killing to harvest organs is that organ shortages are a widespread and continuing problem, as Justice West acknowledges.[25] *See id.* Were we to approve the killing of a potential organ donor, no one would be safe. Everyone with a healthy life-saving organ would be placed at risk by such a rule. The situation is quite different with our explorers or the crying baby. Although these rare situations recur throughout history, they are unlikely to be experienced more than once

[24] There are, however, some who justify using organs of prisoners condemned to death, despite the reality that this might result in more executions for the sole purpose of using the prisoner's organs to save others' lives.

[25] As Justice West states:

> [T]here are currently a sizable number of citizens in this country awaiting organ donations, bone marrow replacements, and blood transfusions. The profound scarcity of such organs, bone marrow, and non-contaminated rare blood types is the sad reality that all such patients (as well as those of us who may at any point become such a patient) are forced to endure. That scarcity prompts incomparable anguish among the needy donees, and tortured decisions by medical personnel.

Supra, at 1896 (West, J.).

in a long period of time. Whatever we decide in *these* unusual cases will have little or no impact on the future actions of the infinitesimally tiny number of people who may find themselves in the unexpected situation faced by our explorers or the Jews hiding from the Nazis. These are sui generis cases, about which, in the absence of explicit legislative resolution, we can afford to provide pure retrospective justice, without fear of establishing a dangerous precedent. To be sure, every case contributes to the corpus of precedents, and if the legislature disapproves of our decision, it may announce a rule of law that forbids killing in these situations. The reason the legislature has not explicitly done so for organ-donor killing, is that no one has ever tried — or, likely, would ever try — to raise a defense of necessity in such circumstances. Such a result would be "absurd," to paraphrase another of my colleagues, and legislators need not explicitly reject every "absurd" defense, especially when no one has ever tried to use it. The defense raised in our case, however, is not absurd and it has been raised and even accepted. *See* Kadish & Schulhofer, *supra*, at 877–78. These are the differences. Does Judge West believe that smothering the crying baby and killing the person for his organs are really the same case? If not, is not the instant case closer to the former than to the latter?

IV. Conclusion

I believe that those who would punish the conduct at issue here have the burden of acting to prohibit it explicitly and provide for the appropriate punishment.[26] That burden has not been satisfied by the inaction here.

Accordingly, I conclude that the principles expressed above require the conclusion that the killing committed by the defendants in this case cannot be deemed unlawful. The people in the cave could not look to the law for guidance. The statute was not explicit. The precedents cut both ways. They made every reasonable effort to obtain advance guidance from authoritative sources. In the end they had to decide for themselves. They did the best they could under the circumstances, selecting a process which was rational and fair. The end result was a net saving of lives. I cannot find it in my heart — and, more important, I cannot find it in the law — to condemn what they did. If there is disagreement with the preferences stated herein or with the conclusions derived therefrom, let the debate begin. I have

---

[26] Another important indicium that our legislature did not intend to include the type of necessity killing under the general prohibition against murder is that it failed to specify an appropriate punishment for this kind of tragic-choice killing. Surely it would be wrong for a judge to be empowered to punish our defendants as severely as a defendant who killed for profit, thrill, or hatred.

an open mind, untrammeled by the "natural" and "supernatural" myths of the past.

Name Index